— Human Dynamics —

in Psychology and Education

—— Human Dynamics ——
in Psychology and Education

selected readings

Third Edition

Don E. Hamachek
Michigan State University

Allyn and Bacon, Inc.
boston london sydney toronto

Figures appearing on pages 114, 115, and 116 are reprinted with permission of Transcendental Meditation ®, TM ®, Science of Creative Intelligence, SCI, World Plan ®, service marks of World Plan Executive Council-United States, a nonprofit, tax-exempt, educational organization.

LIBRARY OF CONGRESS CATALOGING IN PUBLICATION DATA

Hamachek, Don E   comp.
  Human dynamics in psychology and education.

  Includes bibliographies and index.
    1.   Educational psychology—Addresses, essays, lectures.   I.   Title.
LB1051.H228   1977   370.15'08   76-25464

ISBN 0–205–05583–4

Contents

v

Preface

This is a book about the "human" dimensions involved in psychology and education. It focuses on ideas and controversies related to some of the personal, cognitive, and bio-chemical aspects of learning; the nature and nurture of motivation; expressions of intellectual functioning and creative output; considerations of classroom dynamics, teaching processes, and innovations in instruction; issues related to testing and grading; growth processes and developmental consequences; understanding maladaptive behavior and developing positive classroom management; and the importance of understanding oneself.

Although the emphasis on human dimensions remains the same as in the first and second editions, this is nonetheless a new and updated book. Of the fifty-four selections, forty-four are new to this edition. Frankly, it was difficult deciding which articles to retain from the second edition; they all seemed important to me. But time moves on, and so do ideas and points of view. And I wanted this collection to reflect as many new ideas as possible. Ten articles were retained because each said something so unique or novel or lasting that it just could not be better expressed in any other way—or so, at least, it seemed in my eyes.

As I organized this edition into its five major parts and fourteen chapters, I had in mind what you might call an "organizational philosophy," which I hoped would help the book to be consistent with itself and with me as a person. Primarily, I wanted the organizational plan to reflect the idea that there is much more to know and to think about in education and psychology than one book can offer. Hence, the deliberate emphasis in each of the five major parts on *toward* understanding, which, I trust, puts the emphasis where it properly should be, namely, on "we are moving toward," rather than on "we have arrived."

Second, I wanted to present a book that was able to talk to interested readers who might come from diverse backgrounds and have different interests and needs. Hence, the articles are drawn from a wide variety of sources; some are purely empirical or scientific, while others are purely speculative or interpretive. The fifty-four selections in this edition range over twenty-one different journals and magazines, fourteen books, one monograph, and three unpublished papers. All in all, forty-nine different authors are represented.

Third, I tried hard to include articles which seemed to be more than one psychologist or one educator talking to another. Some selections, to be sure, are more complex than others, but for the most part all are written in a language and style that most students in various fields of psychology and education should be able to comprehend.

Fourth, and consistent with the emphasis of the book, I deliberately endeavored to include articles that focus primarily on *human* behavior, *human* meanings, and *human* understandings that grow out of uniquely *human* experiences.

And fifth, I wanted this volume to reflect the idea that there is not necessarily any *one* best way to learn or teach or behave or understand oneself. Rather, there are many *different* ways of doing these things, and each has value, depending on the person, the time, and the circumstances. Hence, you will find many instances where two different authors are placed back-to-back, precisely because they present diametrically opposing viewpoints about a problem. If we begin by agreeing that at least one purpose of a total educational experience is to make us less similar to each other and more like ourselves, then there may be some merit in looking at different points of view as one way of finding out just what we believe in the first place.

All in all, if this volume can serve the ultimate end of being more expanding than constricting, more challenging than dulling, more personal than pedantic, then I will be very pleased indeed.

The ideas and toil of many people go into a volume of this sort and once again I say "thank you" to those authors whose efforts appear in this anthology. In particular, I want to thank professors Bob Caldwell, Southern Methodist University; William Gillooly, Rutgers University; Kathryn Linden, Purdue University; Richard A. Schmuck, University of Oregon; William Staffard, Lehigh University; Don Treffinger, University of Kansas; M. C. Wittrock, University of California at Los Angeles, for their critical reviews and very constructive suggestions for its improvement.

D.E.H.

— Human Dynamics —

in Psychology and Education

Part One · toward understanding learning and cognitive processes

He who has no inclination to learn more will be very apt to think that he knows enough.
        Sir John Powell (d. 1696)

The chapters and readings in this section are designed to introduce you to the complex and interrelated processes involved in cognition, learning, and motivation, and to some of the uniquely human aspects that are a part of any teaching–learning situation.

The first chapter begins with a look at the dominant laws of learning that have influenced teacher practices since the early 1900s. In reading 1, W. J. McKeachie wonders if perhaps these laws have considered the idea of motivation too lightly. This is an important reading, one that serves as a backdrop for the subsequent selections in Part I.

In reading 2, Abraham Maslow demonstrates the remarkable differences between learning for extrinsic and intrinsic reasons. After reading Maslow's article, you may quickly appreciate Frank Riessman's basic thesis in reading 3 that suggests that "there is more than one style for learning."

Chapter Two is specifically devoted to the "human" dimensions of learning. Whatever else learning involves, it surely does involve an interpersonal relationship between teacher and student, an idea that Arthur Combs sensitively develops in reading 4. In selection 5, Carl Rogers builds his case for learning by the *whole* person, which means, quite literally, allowing both feelings and ideas to merge in the learning process. Moral development particularly involves the human element, and in reading 6 Lawrence Kohlberg shares with us a cognitive-developmental approach to understanding and teaching moral education in our schools.

What is motivation? How does it influence learning? What can teachers do to enhance its energizing properties? Is it possible to reward good work too much? Is the use of praise a good way to motivate students? These and other questions are examined in Chapter Three. Maslow's "Theory of Motivation" in reading 7 is a classic in the psychological literature. He postulates that there are different levels of motivation and that different need states trigger different motivational levels. In reading 8, William Purkey presents strategies that teachers can use to influence motivation and self-concept in positive ways. You will be quite surprised, I think, to learn in reading 9 that extrinsic rewards can sometimes stifle motivation, rather than enhance it. According to the research findings of Mark Lepper and David Greene, tampering with intrinsic motivation may be the best way to kill it. Teachers, psychologists, and salesmen are schooled thoroughly in the power of praise as a motivational tool. It has positive functions, but it has some negative

1

ones, too. Reading 10 will give you some useful insights into the dynamics of praise.

Highly related to any discussion of learning and cognitive processes are the constructs of intelligence and creativity. Chapter Four exposes you to some points of view related to these constructs. It begins with Arthur Whimbey's assertion in reading 11 that intelligence may not be solely a genetic gift, as some think. There is on-going controversy about the origin of intelligence. Does it come primarily from the genes or the environment or from both? What is indisputable is that intelligence grows and declines. But the decline is not so startling as you may suppose, as John Horn points out in reading 12. We could not talk about intellectual growth without including a discussion of Piaget, who has taught us the most over the past 40 years. Jason Brunk (reading 13) gives a fine overview of Piaget's major contributions to our knowledge of cognitive and intellectual development.

What is creativity? How is it developed? What are some of the personal, social, and cultural forces associated with it? How can we enhance creative thinking in the classroom? These and many other intriguing questions are addressed by Natalie and Morris Haimowitz and E. Paul Torrance in readings 14 and 15.

Chapter Five explores the new frontiers of learning. It is difficult at this writing to know what ultimate impact (if any) these new frontiers will have on the teaching–learning process. Exciting new evidence indicates that there may be more biochemistry involved in learning than we may have thought. Maya Pines reports some provocative research findings related to this in reading 16. The new technology of biofeedback, which can give us autonomic nervous system information that could have vast implications for teaching and learning, is discussed by Thomas Mulholland in reading 17. Is it possible that even transcendental meditation has classroom learning applications? In reading 18 Paul Levine explains why he thinks it does and tells why.

Part I, then, exposes you to some basic issues and ideas associated with learning and cognitive processes. In the final analysis, I rather suspect that the subtle innuendos and complexities of the learning process will best be demonstrated by instructors and students engaging in discussions about the ideas presented in this section.

Chapter One · an overview of learning processes

1

The Decline and Fall of the Laws of Learning

W. J. McKeachie

EDITOR'S NOTE · *Some of our most basic alleged "laws of learning" can be traced back to the early 1900s and are still reflected in modern education in the theoretical formulations of B. F. Skinner and his followers. McKeachie's basic thesis is that the laws of learning have fallen from their lofty reaches. New research advances, among other things, strongly suggest that the idea of human motivation has been too lightly regarded. What are the "laws of learning"? Why has Skinnerian psychology been so popular? What are some alternative ways to view learning processes? This reading will introduce you to some interesting viewpoints and provide some informative answers.*

McKeachie, W. J., "The Decline and Fall of the Laws of Learning," *Educational Researcher*, March 1974, pp. 7–11. Copyright 1974, American Educational Research Association, Washington, D.C. Reprinted by permission.

This article first was presented as the Presidential Address to the Division of General Psychology, American Psychological Association, 1973.

Arthur Melton, John Atkinson, and David Birch read an earlier version of this paper and aided in my education. The remaining fault is in the learner rather than the teaching they gave me.

In his book, *Animal Intelligence* (1911), E. L. Thorndike wrote, "Two laws explain all learning." He then went on to document his case that all learning depends on the Law of Effect and the Law of Exercise. Thus appeared the "Laws of Learning," part of the basic tenets of psychological belief from that day on. In the decades following, the laws of learning were added to, restructured, and ornamented by new names, but the basic laws formulated by Thorndike remained at the center of both theoretical and applied formulations of learning. The major systematic attack upon them came from Tolman in his book *Purposive Behavior in Animals and Men* (1932). Hull and his students carried the major burden of the battle against Tolman so that the laws of learning recouched in Hullian terms continued to be part of the basic stuff in psychology. Even though Thorndike himself later made the Law of Exercise subordinate, the Law of Effect continued to be defended into the 1950's and 1960's and one would have been hard put to find the portents of decline in the outpouring of research articles on learning in the late 1940's and 1950's. One such portent surely was Spence's exasperated statement that Hullian theory was only a theory of rat learning, but the basic notion of the fundamental nature of the laws of Exercise and Effect persisted even after the great debates between Hull and Tolman, Spence and Krechevsky and their later followers began to decline in intensity.

Only one sturdy defender of faith in the laws of learning carried the gospel to the unenlightened with continuing zeal. B. F. Skinner, in "The Science of Learning and the Art of Teaching," said:

"Some promising advances have been made in the field of learning. The Law of Effect has been taken seriously; we have made sure that effects do occur and that they occur under conditions which are optimal for producing the changes called learning.... [In the teaching of arithmetic] when is a numerical operation reinforced as right? ... In the early stages the reinforcement of being right is usually accorded by the teacher. The contingencies she provides are far from optimal. . . . The lapse of only a few seconds between response and reinforcement destroys most of the effect . . . many seconds or minutes intervene between the child's response and the teacher's reinforcement. In many cases—for example when papers are taken home to be corrected—as much as 24 hours may intervene. It is surprising that this system has any effect whatsoever."

After this assertion of the importance of immediacy of reinforcement, a point made by Thorndike in his original statement, Skinner goes on to depict the dire state of modern education due to its failure to use the results of learning research and calls upon psychologists and others to change the schools. He says, "We can no longer allow the urgencies of a practical situation to suppress the tremendous improvements which are within reach. The practical situation must be changed."

Skinner then describes teaching machines incorporating the following principles of learning:

1. Practice of the correct responses (the Law of Exercise)
2. Knowledge of results and reinforcement of the right answer (the Law of Effect)
3. Minimum delay of reinforcement
4. Successive small steps with hints "so that the answers of the average child will almost always be right," an approach having some elements of Thorndike's Law of Associative Shifting, a law proposed by Thorndike somewhat later than Exercise and Effect.

Skinner asserted that teaching machines using these principles would be much more effective than teachers working without them and predicted that teaching machines would be commonplace in all instructional situations (Evans, 1968, p. 59). That prediction seemed well on the road to confirmation in the 1960's as both large corporations and individual entrepreneurs rushed in to capitalize on the Skinner-based technological revolution in education. But today teaching machines seem to have survived less well than hula hoops. Probably the most important thing Skinnerian teaching machines have taught us is that teaching machines are often not very effective teachers.

There are a number of reasons for this—and as psychologists anxious to defend the value of our

field, we are likely to be most critical of the technology of teaching machines—to feel that they simply were inconvenient and poorly designed. My thesis is that the weakness is more fundamental. It is not the teaching machine but the laws of learning themselves which were inadequate (at least when applied to human cognitive learning). The points I shall make are not new to learning theorists. They have been expressed and debated in one form or another for many years. But in our undergraduate teaching, in our advice to educators, in our attempts at application—the laws of learning have continued to be fundamental. My thesis today is that the laws of learning have *fallen* from preeminence in basic learning theory and that in educational learning and other applications, we must also depose them to a place in more complex structures.

The central law, of course, was the Law of Effect, later dubbed reinforcement. The nature and necessity of reinforcement has long been a major point of theoretical controversy. When I was a graduate student, we eagerly watched for new installments of the debate and for the research on latent learning and other attempts to demonstrate that learning could occur without reinforcement. More recently Walker (1969), Bindra (1969), Leeper (1970), Bolles (1972), Logan (1969), Atkinson & Wickens (1971), Estes (1971), and others [e.g., McKeachie (1957), McKeachie & Doyle (1966)] have not only challenged the idea that reinforcement automatically stamps in stimulus–response connections but in some instances have questioned the notion that any useful function is served by the concept of reinforcement.

I shall not review the research evidence at this point since Bolles' *Psychological Review* article does this well. I know that these experiments (e.g., Harlow's monkeys who were less effective in solving puzzles for a food reward than for no reward) can be interpreted in a reinforcement framework. Nevertheless it seems to me that when, as in some of the human studies I shall cite later, a child does less well in learning when materially rewarded, the Law of Effect can no longer be regarded as the first commandment for education.

Most of the alternatives for reinforcement suggested by other theorists emphasize the information value of reinforcement procedures and at least preserve the principle of knowledge of results. As you recall, one of Thorndike's (1931, p. 9) classic experiments was that in which a subject was asked to draw 4-inch lines with his eyes closed. After 3000 trials he was no better than on the earlier trials, demonstrating that practice without knowledge of results does not produce learning. Even those who denied reinforcement as a law of learning have generally accepted the principle that learning depends upon feedback or knowledge of results, and, as we have seen, this was one of the principles determining the design of teaching machines and programmed learning.

If we drop reinforcement, can we fall back to "knowledge of results" as the really fundamental law of learning in human education? Even here the research evidence is not very encouraging. For example, Olson (1972) found that giving college students knowledge of results on quiz items failed to produce generally better final performance than no knowledge of results and Oner (1972) also found no effect of feedback or praise in learning decimals in a programmed lesson. Similarly Pambookian (1972) and Centra (1972) found no overall improvement by teachers given feedback from student ratings of their teaching.

One immediately wonders about immediacy of feedback. Perhaps when knowledge of results was ineffective, it was because it did not occur promptly. Skinner has again and again called attention to the long delays in knowledge of results and reinforcement in most classroom situations and asserted that one of the strengths of programmed learning would be that reinforcement of correct responses would occur immediately. How important is immediate knowledge of results?

As early as 1935, Guthrie in *The Psychology of Learning* had cast doubts on the principle of immediacy of reinforcement by pointing out that a child spanked an hour after writing on the living room wall will usually learn not to write on the wall if he is told why he is being punished. Laboratory research on delay of reinforcement is also not consistent nor clear in supporting immediacy. (Atkinson & Wickens, 1971, Bourne, 1966). But here we are concerned about human educational learning. When we examine this arena, research evidence on prompt feedback in programmed learning similarly fails to support Skinner's position. Immediate knowledge of results has seemed in sev-

eral studies to make little difference in learning or even to be detrimental (e.g., Sturges, 1972, Kulhavy & Anderson, 1972). Programmed instruction proponents were understandably aghast to find that immediate knowledge of the correct response (expected to be a reinforcer) did not facilitate learning in programmed instruction. Anderson, Kulhavy, and Andre (1971) suspected that the reason prompt knowledge of results didn't work was that when knowledge of the correct result is immediately available, students become inattentive and careless in trying to answer the question. Thus Anderson *et al.* used a computer to give knowledge of correct response only after the student gave an answer. This helped. Moreover, on a test of immediate recall (but not on retention) a group who had been allowed during learning to peek at the correct response, whether or not they had given an answer, scored lower than students who had no feedback of the correct response.

One suspects that in a typical programmed learning situation in which most of the learner's responses are right, the cost of time required to get feedback seems to the learner to be too high for the value of information he receives. We might expect more positive effects of feedback in situations in which the task is more difficult and the information provided thus greater. But the Law of Effect and even the principle of knowledge of results can no longer stand as the major support of learning.

And what about the Law of Exercise? As I indicated earlier, this fell into decline even in Thorndike's own lifetime. His experiment on drawing 4-inch lines had convinced him that practice does *not* make perfect, and by 1931 he had relegated exercise to a secondary role. Extinction procedures also demonstrated that practice did not necessarily strengthen learning. Yet active practice done correctly with an attempt to minimize errors has remained as a general practical principle of education. In Skinnerian programmed learning, application of this principle involves constructed responses and small steps. This practice too seems to be of dubious value. Wright (1967) found that paragraphs were better than short frames and that reading the responses was superior to writing them. Such results are not uniformly found but are common enough to suggest that a constructed response and small steps are not uniformly facilitative of learning. The Keller plan (1968), now widely used in college courses, has departed widely from this aspect of programmed learning even though generally based upon Skinnerian concepts.

Thorndike's statement that his two laws would explain all learning is no longer tenable and Skinner's assertion that teaching machines would be vastly superior to teachers is even less supportable. The Laws of Learning have fallen from their central place in our psychological lexicon. Yet we cannot help feeling that they contain much truth. Even though the underlying principles may have been flawed, teaching machines were sometimes effective. Surely we should be able to recycle the cores of the laws of learning into something of use, and in the remainder of this paper I'd like to attempt this.

As I see it, there are two reasons for the failure of the Laws of Learning. Some of the problems in trying to apply the laws of learning to educational situations have been failures to take account of differences between humans and other animals— e.g., Man's greater ability to conceptualize, relate, and remember. Other problems have simply derived from failure to take account of important variables controlled in laboratory situations but interacting with independent variables in natural educational settings.

For example, let us look more closely at the Law of Effect. Skinner and his followers have usually taken a fairly pragmatic stance toward reinforcers—often analyzing with great acuity and indefatigability the reinforcers in a particular situation. In many cases they have succeeded, but as I noted earlier, some of the difficulties encountered in using reinforcement theory could be avoided by conceptualizing the usual "reinforcer" as combining two kinds of feedback—informational and affective. In simple human learning situations the reward tells the individual what the correct answer is and also tells him that getting the answer will have pleasant consequences. Even devoted Skinnerians ruefully admit that Skinnerian learning programs are usually boring—a problem deriving, I contend, from failure to take seriously the research literature on motivation, a construct Skinner would prefer to omit.

If one differentiates informational and affective feedback, some of the complex results of differing effects of reinforcers from elementary school learning seem reasonable. One hypothesis, for example, would be, as I stated earlier, that the value of feedback would depend upon the information it provided. Another hypothesis would be that informational feedback would be helpful for improvement in performance for a motivated student but Thorndike's "satisfiers" would be necessary for improvements in performance for those with little motivation for educational learning.

Studies of social class differences in educational achievement tend to support this hypothesis (if one assumes that low-achieving children are less motivated for conventional school learning). A number of studies show that informing a child of the correctness of his response increases achievement for middle-class normally achieving children, while other children may learn more effectively when given praise or tangible rewards (Terrell, Durkin & Wesley, 1959; Zigler & deLabry, 1962; Zigler & Kanzer, 1962). Similarly, Blair (1972) showed that normal achievers in the third grade learned more effectively for informational feedback or praise than for tangible rewards, and Cradler and Goodwin (1971) found that in groups of second and sixth graders, sixth grade middle-class subjects were more responsive to praise and symbolic feedback while second grade lower-class children were more responsive to candy.

Since teachers are likely to emphasize symbolic and social rewards, differences in educational achievement between social classes may be due in some part to lack of effective rewards for motivating underachieving children. It may well be that some Skinnerian techniques, such as fading or schedules of reinforcement, would be useful if applied to teaching motivation for learning activities rather than being directed solely to input-output relationships (where they are inadequate).

The effect of knowledge of results is also clarified if we introduce motivational constructs. Means and Means (1971), for example, found that low-grade-point-average students who were told that they had done *well* on an aptitude test did better on the mid-term in an adolescent psychology course. For high-grade-point-average students, being told that they had done *poorly* produced better performance. Such results remind one of Jack Atkinson's theory that achievement motivation is highest when probabilities of success are moderate.

If one hopes to use reward or knowledge of

results to affect human learning, he needs to know something about what expectancies of reward the learner brings to the situation, both in terms of the incentive value of the reward and the learner's estimate of the probability of achieving the reward. This helps explain why knowledge of results is often ineffective in programmed learning. A model Skinnerian program is written with very low probabilities of error. Thus the learner's probability of success on a given frame is often 90% or higher. Obviously knowledge of results provides little information here, and also, in terms of achievement motivation theory, this is a region of low motivation—thus one becomes bored. Consequently neither the informational nor the affective component of the feedback are potent in the typical Skinnerian program.

On the other hand, when the feedback is discrepant from expectancies (providing more information and perhaps more motivation), learning may occur. Thus Centra, who found no overall effect of feedback of student ratings on teacher improvement, found that teachers who initially rated themselves more favorably than their students did change in the direction suggested by the student ratings. Feedback of student ratings thus helped when it was discrepant from expectancy. And on the motivational side, Pambookian (1972) found that feedback to instructors did not help those who were rated as highly effective or as ineffective, but did help those rated as being moderately effective—again fitting the theory of achievement motivation, i.e., those rated poorly had such low probabilities of success that we would expect discouragement, withdrawal, or defensiveness; but those rated in the middle had a moderate probability of success as teachers and thus were at optimal motivation levels.

Pambookian's results fit nicely with those of Flook and Robinson (1972) who found that among students who were told their intelligence and anxiety test scores, those in the middle range of intelligence were the only group to show achievement during the freshman year superior to that of a control group not told their scores. Similarly Hammer (1972) showed that teachers' comments on undergraduate physics papers had a positive effect on later performance, especially when the comments were made with reference to the student's expected grade. These latter comments, from the examples given, seem likely to have moved probability of success to an intermediate level, thus increasing motivation and performance.

But motivation and information about what one has done wrong is not enough. It is fitting that I learned from E. L. Thorndike's grandson, Robert M. Thorndike, what I regard as the best generalization we can currently make. He suggests that knowledge of results eventuates in improved performance when the learner is motivated, when the knowledge of results is informative and when the learner knows or is told what to do to correct his errors.

When we turn to the principle of immediacy of reinforcement, we find once again that our basic law is reusable if we add some complications. Probably the chief reason that immediate reinforcement is often not important for human learning is that human beings can attend to and remember critical features of a learning situation better than many other experimental subjects. Thus Goldstein and Siegel (1972) found that immediate reinforcement in a task requiring discrimination learning of geometric figures was more effective than delayed reinforcement only when the subjects had no previous exposure to the figures and when they were not present during the delay. This suggests that delayed reinforcement should work as well as (or better than) immediate reinforcement if the relevant stimuli and responses are attended to and the subject can remember what he is being reinforced for. The laboratory research in this area is still not conclusive, but it is clear that what happens during the delay is important. Sturges (1972), for example, suggests that the advantages of delayed feedback found in his own and other studies may be due to the learner's exploration and organization of the material before feedback. Delayed feedback was also superior to immediate feedback in the experiment of Kulhavy and Anderson (1972) and their design provided support for the theory that the delay permits potentially interfering errors to be forgotten as well as contributing to greater attention to the feedback.

It probably appears that this lecture has been rather hard on one of the greatest figures of modern psychology, B. F. Skinner, and I confess that his confident assertions in *The Technology of Teach-*

ing provided the primary stimulus for my choice of this topic. The research evidence, I believe, demonstrates that each point enunciated by Skinner is untrue—at least in as general a sense as he believed. This does not mean that Skinner's attempts to influence education have been bad or that the principles are completely false; rather his attempt to make a systematic effort at application has revealed that what we psychologists once took to be the verities hold only under limited conditions. As a result, new vistas of needed research have been revealed.

If the laws of learning are inadequate, why has Skinnerian psychology been so popular? The answer, I think, lies in its simplicity. Education is ever seeking the philosopher's stone that will transmute stubborn, unmotivated students into learners. Skinner's pitch for his philosopher's stone is persuasive and powerful. Like any good salesman he shows how easy his psychology is to use. Those who buy his approach find that the basic ideas are simple to apply and work often enough to maintain their enthusiasm.

This is no small matter. Anyone who can take discouraged, dispirited teachers, mental health aides, or prison officials and revive their hope and vigor has done a great deal. Probably no one thing is more important in education than the teacher's enthusiasm and energy.

But once hope is revived and a start has been made, we need to take teachers beyond the level of the speeches I used to make to them about the principles of learning. Now I believe that these principles apply most clearly to the learning of animals in highly controlled artificial situations. It may well be that they also have application to other restricted situations, but meaningful educational learning is both more robust and more complex. This complexity, so frustrating to those who wish to prescribe education methods, is a reminder of the fascinating uniqueness of the learner. Fortunately most educational situations are interactive situations in which a developing, learning human being engages with a situation in ways designed to meet his learning needs. Part of that situation is another human being who has some resources for instruction and some capacity to adapt to the learner. It is this that makes education both endlessly challenging and deeply humane.

REFERENCES

Anderson, R. C., Kulhavy, R. W. & Andre, T. Feedback procedures in programmed instruction. *Journal of Educational Psychology*, 1971, 62, 148–156.

Atkinson, R. C. & Wickens, T. D. Human memory and the concept of reinforcement. *The nature of reinforcement*, (Ed.) R. Glaser, New York and London: Academic Press, 1971, pp. 66–67.

Bindra, D. The interrelated mechanisms of reinforcement and motivation, and the nature of their influence on response. *Nebraska Symposium on Motivation*, 1969, 17, 1–37.

Blair, J. R. The effects of differential reinforcement on the discrimination learning of normal and low-achieving middle-class boys. *Child Development*, 1972, 43, 251–255.

Bolles, R. C. Reinforcement, expectancy, and learning. *Psychological Review*, 1972, 79, 394–409.

Bourne, L. E. Information feedback: Comments on Professor I. McD. Bilodeau's paper. In E. A. Bilodeau (Ed.), *Acquisition of skill*, New York: Academic Press, 1966, 297–313.

Centra, J. A. The utility of student ratings for instructional improvement. Educational Testing Service, 1972, 74 pp.

Cradler, J. D. & Goodwin, D. L. Conditioning of verbal behavior as a function of age, social class, and type of reinforcement. *Journal of Educational Psychology*, 1971, 62, 279–285.

Estes, W. K. Reward in human learning: theoretical issues and strategic choice points. *The nature of reinforcement*, (Ed.) R. Glaser. New York: Academic Press, 1971, 16–44.

Evans, R. I. *B. F. Skinner: The man and his ideas.* New York: Dutton, 1968.

Flook, A. J. M., & Robinson, P. J. Academic performance with and without knowledge of scores on tests of intelligence, aptitude, and personality: A further study. *Journal of Educational Psychology*, 1972, 63, 123–129.

Goldstein, 　　& Siegel, 　　. 1972 (I've lost this one. If any reader recognizes it, I'd be grateful for the reference. W. McKeachie).

Guthrie, E. R. *The Psychology of learning.* New York: Harper, 1935.

Hammer, B. Grade expectations, differential teacher comments, and student performance. *Journal of Educational Psychology,* 1972, 63, 505–512.

Keller, F. S. "Good-bye, Teacher." *Journal of Applied Behavioral Analysis,* 1968, 1, 79–89.

Kulhavy, R. W. & Anderson, R. C. Delay-retention effect with multiple-choice tests. *Journal of Educational Psychology,* 1972, 63, 505–512.

Leeper, R. W. Cognitive learning theory. In M. H. Marx, (Ed.) *Learning theories.* New York: Macmillan, 1970.

Logan, F. A. *Fundamentals of learning and motivation.* Dubuque, Iowa: Brown, 1969.

McKeachie, W. J. Expectancy concepts in the first course. Paper delivered at the symposium "Key Concepts in Elementary Psychology," APA Meeting, 1957.

McKeachie, W. J. & Doyle, C. *Psychology* 1st Ed. Reading, Mass.: Addison-Wesley, 1966.

Means, R. S. & Means, G. H. Achievement as a function of the presence of prior information concerning aptitude. *Journal of Educational Psychology,* 1971, 62, 185–187.

Olson, G. H. A multivariate examination of the effects of behavioral objectives, knowledge of results, and the assignment of grades on the facilitation of classroom learning. Doctoral Thesis. *Dissertation Abstract International,* 1972, 32, 6214–6215.

Oner, N. P. Impact of teacher behavior and teaching technique on learning by anxious children. *Dissertation Abstract International,* 1972, 32, 6215.

Pambookian, H. S. The effect of feedback from students to college instructors on their teaching behavior. Unpublished Dissertation. University of Michigan, 1972.

Skinner, B. F. The Science of learning and the art of teaching. *Harvard Educational Review,* 1954, 24, 86–97.

Skinner, B. F. *The Technology of teaching.* New York: Appleton-Century-Crofts, 1968.

Sturges, P. T. Information delay and retention: effect of information in feedback and tests. *Journal of Educational Psychology,* 1972, 63, 32–43.

Terrell, G., Durkin, K. & Wesley, M. Social class and the nature of the incentive in discrimination learning. *Journal of Abnormal Social Psychology,* 1959, 59, 270–272.

Thorndike, E. L. Animal Intelligence. *Psychological Review.* Monograph Supplement No. 8, 1898.

Thorndike, E. L. *Animal intelligence.* New York: Hafner, 1911.

Thorndike, E. L. *Human learning.* New York: Century, 1931, p. 9.

Tolman, E. C. *Purposive behavior in animals and men.* New York: Appleton-Century-Crofts, 1932.

Walker, E. Reinforcement—the one ring. In J. L. Tapp (Ed.) *Reinforcement and behavior.* New York: Academic Press, 1969.

Wright, R. The use of questions in programmed learning. *Programmed Learning and Educational Technology,* 1967, 4, 103–7.

Zigler, E. & DeLabry, J. Concept switching in middle-class, lower-class and retarded children. *Journal of Abnormal & Social Psychology,* 1962, 60, 267–273.

Zigler, E. & Kanzer, P. The effectiveness of two classes of verbal reinforcers on the performance of middle- and lower-class children. *Journal of Personality & Social Psychology,* 1962, 30, 157–163.

2

Some Differences between Intrinsic and Extrinsic Learning

Abraham H. Maslow

EDITOR'S NOTE · The relative value and importance of extrinsic and intrinsic motivation is a controversy of long standing in education and psychology. Some psychologists say that people have to be motivated by forces outside themselves, and others say people are best motivated by their own inner feelings and subjective experiences. Dr. Maslow sensitively extracts some of the basic differences between extrinsic and intrinsic motivation in this article, which may give you pause as you consider the merits of each. Under which conditions are you best motivated? Under which conditions has your greatest learning occurred? This article may help you to better understand the answers to these questions.

We are now being confronted with a choice between two extremely different, almost mutually exclusive conceptions of learning.

From Abraham H. Maslow, "Some Educational Implications of the Humanistic Psychologies," *Harvard Educational Review* 38 (Fall 1968): 685–96. Copyright © 1968 by President and Fellows of Harvard College. Reprinted by permission of Bertha G. Maslow.

What we have in practically all the elementary and advanced textbooks of psychology, and in most of the brands of "learning theory" which all graduate students are required to learn, is what I want to call for the sake of contrast and confrontation, *extrinsic learning,* i.e., learning of the outside, learning of the impersonal, of arbitrary associations, of arbitrary conditioning, that is, of arbitrary (or at best, culturally determined) meanings and responses. In this kind of learning, most often it is not the person himself who decides, but rather a teacher or an experimenter who says, "I will use a buzzer," "I will use a bell," "I will use a red light," and most important, "I will reinforce this but not that." In this sense the learning is extrinsic to the learner, extrinsic to the personality, and is extrinsic also in the sense of *collecting* associations, conditionings, habits or modes of action. It is as if these were *possessions* which the learner accumulates in the same way that he accumulates keys or coins and puts them in his pocket. They have little or nothing to do with the actualization or growth of the peculiar, idiosyncratic kind of person he is.

I believe this is the model of education which we all have tucked away in the back of our heads and which we don't often make explicit. In this model the teacher is the active one who teaches a passive person who gets shaped and taught and who is *given* something which he then accumulates and which he may then lose or retain, depending upon the efficiency of the initial indoctrination process and of his own accumulation-of-fact process. I would maintain that a good 90 percent of "learning theory" deals with learnings that have nothing to do with the intrinsic self that I've been talking about, nothing to do with its specieshood and biological idiosyncrasy. This kind of learning too easily reflects the goals of the teacher and ignores the values and ends of the learner himself.

Now I'd like to contrast this with another kind of learning, which is actually going on, but is usually unconscious and unfortunately happens more outside the classroom than inside. It often comes in the great personal learning experiences of our lives.

For instance, if I were to list the most important learning experiences in my life, there comes to mind getting married, discovering my life work, having children, getting psychoanalyzed, the death of my best friend, confronting death myself, and the like. I think I would say that these were more important learning experiences for me than my Ph.D. or any 15 or 150 credits of any courses that I've ever had. I certainly learned more about *myself* from such experiences. I learned, if I may put it so, to throw aside many of my "learning," that is, to push aside the habits and traditions and reinforced associations which had been imposed upon me. Sometimes this was at a very trivial, and yet meaningful, level. I particularly remember when I learned that I really hated lettuce. My father was a "nature boy," and I had lettuce two meals a day for the whole of my early life. But one day in analysis after I had learned that I carried my father inside me, it dawned on me that it was my father, through *my* larynx, who was ordering salad with every meal. I can remember sitting there, realizing that *I* hated lettuce and then saying, "My God, take the damn stuff away!" I was emancipated, becoming in this small way me rather than my father. I didn't eat any more lettuce for months, until it finally settled back to what my body calls for. I have lettuce two or three times each week, which I now enjoy. *But not twice a day.*

Now observe, this experience which I mentioned occurred just once and I could give many other similar examples. It seems to me that we must call into question the generality of repetition, of learning by drilling. The experiences in which we uncover our intrinsic selves are apt to be unique moments, not slow accumulations of reinforced bits. (How do you repeat the death of your father?) These are the experiences in which we discover identity (3). These are the experiences in which we learn who we are, what we love, what we hate, what we value, what we are committed to, what makes us feel anxious, what makes us feel depressed, what makes us feel happy, what makes us feel great joy.

It must be obvious by now that you can generate consequences of this second picture of learning by the hundred. (And again I would stress that these hypotheses can be stated in testable, disconfirmable, confirmable form.) One such implication of the point of view is a change in the whole picture of the teacher. If you are willing to accept this conception of two kinds of learning, with the learning-to-be-a-person being more central and more basic than the impersonal learning of skills or the acquisition of habits; and if you are willing

to concede that even the more extrinsic learnings are far more useful, and far more effective if based upon a sound identity, that is, if done by a person who knows what he wants, knows what he is, and where he's going and what his ends are; then you *must* have a different picture of the good teacher and of his functions.

In the first place, unlike the current model of teacher as lecturer, conditioner, reinforcer, and boss, the Taoist helper or teacher is receptive rather than intrusive. I was told once that in the world of boxers, a youngster who feels himself to be good and who wants to be a boxer will go to a gym, look up one of the managers and say, "I'd like to be a pro, and I'd like to be in your stable. I'd like you to manage me." In this world, what is then done characteristically is to try him out. The good manager will select one of his professionals and say, "Take him on in the ring. Stretch him. Strain him. Let's see what he can do. Just let him show his very best. Draw him out." If it turns out that the boxer has promise, if he's a "natural," then what the good manager does is to take that boy and train him to be, if this is Joe Dokes, a *better Joe Dokes.* That is, he takes his style as given and builds upon that. He does not start all over again, and say, "Forget what kind of body you have," or "Forget what you are good for." He takes him and builds upon his *own* talents and builds him up into the very best Joe Dokes-type boxer that he possibly can.

It is my strong impression that this is the way in which most of the world of education could function. If we want to be helpers, counselors, teachers, guiders, or psychotherapists, what we must do is to accept the person and help learn what kind of person he is already. What is his style, what are his aptitudes, what is he good for, not good for, what can we build upon, what are his good raw materials, his good potentialities? We would be non-threatening and would supply an atmosphere of acceptance of the child's nature which reduces fear, anxiety and defense to the minimum possible. Above all, we would care for the child, that is, enjoy him and his growth and self-actualization. So far this sounds much like the Rogerian therapist, his "unconditional positive regard," his congruence, his openness and his caring. And indeed there is evidence by now that this "brings the child out," permits him to express and to act, to experiment, and even to make mistakes; to let himself be seen. Suitable feedback at this point, as in T-groups or basic encounter groups, or non-directive counseling, then helps the child to discover what and who he is.

In closing, I would like to discuss briefly the role that peak-experiences can play in the education of the child. We have no systematic data on peak-experiences in children but we certainly have enough anecdotes and introspections and memories to be quite confident that young children have them perhaps more frequently than adults do. However, they seem at least in the beginning to come more from sensory experiences, color, rhythm, or sounds, and perhaps are better characterized by the words wonder, awe, fascination, absorption, and the like.

In any case, I have discussed the role of these experiences in education in (2), and would refer the reader to that paper for more detail. Using peak-experiences or fascination or wonder experiences as an intrinsic reward or goal at *many* points in education is a very real possibility, and is congruent with the whole philosophy of the humanistic educator. At the very least, this new knowledge can help wean teachers away from their frequent uneasiness with and even disapproval and persecution of these experiences. If they learn to value them as great moments in the learning process, moments in which both cognitive and personal growth take place simultaneously, then this valuing, rather than to suppress his greatest moments of illumination, can validate and make worthwhile the more usual trudging and slogging and "working through" of education.

There is a very useful parallel here with the newer humanistic paradigm for science (1, 4) in which the more everyday cautious and patient work of checking, validating and replicating is seen, not as *all* there is to science but rather as follow-up work, *subsequent* to the great intuitions, intimations, and illuminations of the creative and daring, innovative, breakthrough scientist. Caution is then seen to *follow* upon boldness and proving comes *after* intuition. The creative scientist then looks more like a gambler than a banker, one who is willing to work hard for seven years because of a dazzling hunch, one who feels certain in the *absence* of evidence, *before* the evidence, and only *then* proceeds to the hard work of proving or disproving his precious revelation. First comes the emotion, the

fascination, the falling in love with a possibility, and *then* comes the hard work, the chores, the stubborn persistence in the face of disappointment and failure.

As a supplement to this conception in which a poetic illumination plays such an important role, we can add the harsh patience of the psychotherapist who has learned from many bitter disappointments that the breakthrough insight doesn't do the therapeutic job all by itself as Freud originally thought. It needs consolidation, repetition, rediscovery, application to one situation after another. It needs patience, time and hard work—what the psychoanalysts call "working through." Not only for science but also for psychotherapy may we say that the process *begins* with an emotional–cognitive flash but *does not end there!* It is this model of science and therapy that I believe we may now fairly consider for the process of education, if not as an exclusive model, at least as an additional one.

We must learn to treasure the "jags" of the child in school, his fascination, absorptions, his persistent wide-eyed wonderings, his Dionysian enthusiasms. At the very least, we can value his more diluted raptures, his "interests" and hobbies, etc. They can lead to much. Especially can they lead to hard work, persistent, absorbed, fruitful, educative.

REFERENCES

1. Maslow, A. *The psychology of science: a reconnaissance.* New York: Harper & Row, 1966.

2. Maslow, A. Music education and peak-experiences. *Music educators journal.* LIV (1968), 72–75, 163–171.

3. Maslow, A. *Toward a psychology of being* (Second edition). Princeton, N.J.: D. Van Nostrand, 1968.

4. Polanyi, M. *Personal knowledge.* Chicago: University of Chicago Press, 1958.

3

There Is More than One Style for Learning

Frank Reissman

EDITOR'S NOTE · I have a particular style for learning and assimilating information and so do you. We no doubt have certain approaches in common, but we retain preferences that are uniquely our own. Sometimes teachers forget that their students learn in different ways, and they make assignments and go about teaching as though every student were the same. Dr. Reissman gently reminds us that each of us has his or her own Achilles' heel.

I would like to discuss a concept which I think has been ignored a good deal in teaching and guidance. It is the concept of style—in particular, the style of learning. I believe a crucial element in the development of the individual's learning relates to a careful understanding of the idiosyncratic style elements in the learning process. Students of learning have focused a good deal on rather abstract, molecular concepts of learning derived from pigeons and rats via B. F. Skinner and Clark L. Hull. I am not suggesting that these concepts of learning are not useful, but I think that we have missed the possible value of a more wholistic (molar) or global dimension of learning,

Frank Reissman, "The Strategy of Style," *Teachers College Record* 65 (1964): 484–89. Reprinted by permission.

operative at the phenomenal level, which I am referring to as style.

AN ILLUSTRATIVE MODEL

One index of style relates to whether you learn things most easily through reading or through hearing or whether you learn through doing things physically, whether you learn things slowly or quickly, whether you learn things in a one-track way or whether you are very flexible in your learning. These examples are not to be conceived as separate from one another. There can be such combinations as a visual–physical learner who learns in a slow, one-track fashion. As a matter of fact, this last pattern is quite characteristic of the disadvantaged child. He learns more slowly; he learns through the physical (that is, by doing things, touching things); he learns visually, and he functions in a rather one-track way in that he doesn't shift easily and is not highly flexible in his learning. This is, of course, an ideal statement—a model.

Let me cite just a few other dimensions of style so that different aspects of it can be seen. For example, some people like to work under pressure; they like a deadline, and they like tests. (Low-income youngsters do not like such conditions.) Some people like to leave a lot of time for their work, enjoying a slow tempo. Some people like to think or even read while walking. Some people like to work in a cold room, some in a warm one. Some people like to work for long periods of time without a break; some people like to shift and take frequent breaks. Some people take a long time to warm up, whereas others get into their work very quickly. Some people like to have all of the facts in front of them before they can do any generalizing, and others prefer to have a few facts. Some people like "props," some people do not.

Typically, people do not know their own style nearly well enough. What I am really concerned about is how one can use this concept to improve one's manner of work—whether it be teaching or guidance, social work or psychiatry. Although I am mainly concerned with working with lower socioeconomic groups, I do not mean to imply that the concept of style must be limited to these social strata.

COGNITION VS. EMOTION

Guidance workers have focused far too much on the categories of emotion, motivation, and personality rather than on the cognitive categories of learning and thinking. There has been much too much emphasis on the emotional approach in attempting to understand why a child doesn't learn. Little careful analysis is given to how the child's learning might improve simply by concentrating on the way that he works and learns, rather than on his affective reasons for not learning. This thesis is almost directly counter to the current view. Today if a child doesn't learn (and if he has intellectual ability), it is quickly assumed that his difficulties must be due to some emotional block or conflict. I am trying to suggest a different way of looking at the problem. He may not be learning because his methods of learning are not suited to his style, and hence he cannot best utilize his power. I would be willing to argue that even where his troubles are, in part, emotional or due to conflict, it still may be possible to ignore this particular focus and concentrate profitably on the specific expression of the difficulty itself—his learning pattern. Even if one rejects my premise that the emotional causes have been overemphasized, one may still give a willing ear to the possibility of dealing with crucial problems of learning in nonemotional, nonpsychodynamic terms. Unfortunately, teachers too often have behaved like psychologists and social workers. It seems to me that they do not sufficiently stress learning processes and styles of learning, apparently preferring motivational categories. One way to build up appropriate prestige in the teaching profession is *not* simply to borrow from psychologists and sociologists, but to concentrate on the development of what education is most concerned with, learning and teaching. When one does borrow from psychology, it may be better to concentrate on learning and cognition rather than personality and motivation.

ANIMALS AND MEN

If we examine the outcomes of teacher-education courses in learning, educational psychology, and the like, we typically are forced to the suspicion that they amount to very little. Borrowing heavily from animal learning experiments (which by itself is not necessarily bad), such courses are victimized by the fact that the particular concepts and formulations developed in the animal literature have not been easily applicable to human learning problems—whether a child learns slowly, whether he is a physical learner, or whether it takes him a long time to warm up. Although these problems are nearer to our subjective experience, the psychological literature and animal experiments have not really helped us very much to deal effectively with them. When educational psychology courses have actually studied human learning, the focus has not been on the significant problems that I think are related to style. When they attempt, for example, to deal with study habits, they are entirely too general. There is a great deal more to study habits than meets the eye of the introductory psychology textbook. The typical suggestions in the chapter on study habits are based upon various experiments which seem to indicate that distributive learning is better, that one should survey material first, etc. But very little is directed toward the *idiosyncratic* factors that are involved.

For example, some people simply can't tolerate surveying a chapter first. They become so anxious, so disturbed, by being asked to look at the overall view of the chapter that they can't function. These people want very much to read a chapter atomistically. This is their style. It won't help simply to tell such a person that he is not proceeding in the right way and that he really ought to read the chapter as a whole first. The same is true in terms of the general recommendation that one should have a quiet place to study. Strangely enough, some people study quite well in a noisy place, or with certain kinds of noise, and completely quiet places are not best for them. Some people take a long time to warm up; consequently, a great deal of spacing (or distribution) of learning would not be useful for them. This is their style. But the textbook does not tell you this because, in general, over a large number of cases, spaced learning is best.

The same argument applies to examinations or tests. For some people, a test operates as just the right mild anxiety to stimulate the integration of a great deal of material that needs to be learned. On the other hand, there are large numbers of people for whom tests are terrible because they disorganize them, make them too anxious, and thus prevent them from working. Tests are not conducive to the style of these individuals. When it is argued that tests are educationally undesirable because they produce too much anxiety for learning, the arguments refer to such people. When others argue that tests are marvelous because they aid pupils by providing corrections and criticism, they are referring to persons with a different style. Undoubtedly, tests work happily for some pupils, but there are others who forget their wrong answers on tests because it disturbs them so much to remember them.

As a matter of fact, there is a great deal of controversy in the traditional literature on the very question of whether repression of wrong answers occurs or whether "punishment" for giving the wrong answers on tests helps to produce better recall. I am suggesting that two different kinds of styles are involved here. For some people, the information that they gave wrong answers is extremely useful and challenging. If this information is called to their attention in a definite and stimulating way, it makes the wrong answer the figure in the ground. It draws the incorrect responses productively to their attention. For other people, knowing that they have made a mistake is extremely disturbing, destructive of their morale, and leads to a repressing of this material. Therefore, depending upon one's style and one's way of dealing with these problems, tests may be useful or not useful.

STRATEGIES OF MODIFICATION

My main task is to try to formulate the possible ways in which the strengths of the individual's style can be utilized and its weaknesses reduced or controlled. At this stage in our discussion, I mean the more fundamental, underlying characteristics— for example, the physical style already discussed. This style is laid down early in life and is not subject to fundamental change, although it is possible to *bend* it and to *develop* it. Another aspect of style may be much more malleable and may be more related to habit or set; that is, it may be a derivative or secondary expression of style.

Let us take as an example, what I call the "games" focus of low-income youngsters. They like to learn things through games rather than through tests. To put something in the forms of games is an excellent transitional technique for winning their interest. But I do not know how basic a habit this is. It may be much more changeable than the underlying physical style. Such questions are obviously open to further investigation and research. I am simply trying to provide a general framework by means of which to deal with the issue. I am not sure which elements are more or less changeable, but I do believe that some are quite unchangeable and quite basic, whereas some are more susceptible to intervention. A person who likes to learn by listening and speaking (aural style) is unlikely to change completely and become, say, a reader. I am not suggesting that such a pupil will not learn to read and write fluently, but his best learning, the long-lasting, deep learning that gets into his muscles, is more likely to derive from speaking and hearing.

Now let me return to the problem I am essentially trying to deal with—the strategy of style, the strategy of producing basic changes in people through understanding and utilizing their styles. I want to develop the idiosyncratic strengths, find ways of employing the unorthodox, the specific, the unique, and in some ways limit the weaknesses in the person's style. Under certain conditions, one can overcome some of the weak elements of the style pattern through compensatory efforts and through special techniques. I think, however, that weaknesses in learning are more likely to be alleviated when they are at the level of sets and habits.

AWARENESS AND UTILIZATION

In approaching our problem, the first aim is to have the person become aware of the strengths and potentials in his style—because this is going to be the source of his power. Thus, if an individual has a physical style, he has to learn the special attributes of this style and how to use them. The guidance counselor or teacher will have to help him overcome the invidious interpretations of this style that are prevalent in our society.

Let us take an illustration of a different type. A youngster tells us that he sits down to work but cannot concentrate. It is extremely important at this point (and this is crucial in the diagnosis of style) to ascertain as precisely as possible exactly what takes place in this youngster's routine. For example, when does he study? What time does he come home from school? What does he do first when he comes into the house? He may say,

> "I come home, throw down my books, and then I start to remember that I have to do some work. So I get out my books. I try to work. I take out the book, but my mind wanders. I look at the book; I look away. I can't get into the work, and after a few minutes of trying this, I begin to feel discouraged; I begin to feel bad. I feel I can't work. I'm not interested, I'm no good. I get very worried, panic builds up, and then I run away from the work."

There are many possibilities operating in this pattern. One possibility is that this youngster has a slow period of warm up. He does not easily get into something new; he does not shift from whatever he's been doing before (whether he's been outside playing ball or inside listening to the radio). This may be due to a number of reasons. He may be a physical learner. If one is a physical learner, one generally must be involved physically in the work process. One has to get one's muscles into it, and this takes time. If this is our student's pattern, then he must come to understand that although he is slow to warm up, this is not necessarily a negative quality; it is simply a different way of approaching work.

As a matter of fact, it may very often be connected to perseverance, once he gets involved! Once he is immersed, he may go deeper and deeper and not be able to shift away from the work easily. The inability to shift doesn't then operate as a negative feature but as a positive element in his style. But the youngster I described here rarely gets to this point. It's not that he doesn't persevere somewhere, in baseball or somewhere else. But in his school work, he's never gotten past the point of the slow warm up. In order to use his pattern effectively, he has to schedule work accordingly. He cannot schedule his time so that he works for one hour. That's no good because it takes him a half hour to warm up. Even if he were to be successful and stick with it for the half hour as a result of a teacher's or guidance worker's support and stimulation, the problem would remain at the end of the half hour of only having a short time left to work. Conse-

quently, he has to plan a larger time period of work and recognize in advance that it will take him about a half hour to warm up. In other words, the person who would help him must give him a definition of his work pattern in order to realize the positive potentialities in it.

STRENGTH OVER WEAKNESS

When this new definition is provided, it is probable that a number of consequences will follow if I'm right about the diagnosis. Over a period of time, the warm-up period will shorten because part of the difficulty in the long warm up is the anxiety that emerges as he tries to get into the work and fails. Thus, by getting into the work, his anxiety decreases, and his interest has a chance, concomitantly, to increase.

Now let us take another example, one in which the person's strengths can be used to deal with his weaknesses. How do you teach a person how to read when reading is not his basic style? Everyone is going to need reading ability and writing ability regardless of his style. In order to teach reading to youngsters for whom it is stylistically uncongenial, one may want to use role-playing, which is more related to the physical style of the individual. He can read about something that he just role-played, or he can read about a trip he has recently taken. While teaching reading under these conditions, the teacher must remember that he is not developing a reading style; he is developing a skill, a *balance* in the pupil's style. He is developing minimal efficiency in an area which is not rooted in the learner's style. In a sense, the teacher is going after his Achilles' heel, his weakness, the reading difficulty, by developing it through his strength, whether it be visual, physical, or whatever. This is a basic tactic for defeating or limiting the weakness by connecting it and subjecting it to the strengths.

MINIMAL GOALS

There are some other things one can do in employing the strategy of style. Various transitional techniques can be used, for example, for overcoming some of a pupil's educational weaknesses. Illustratively, low-income youngsters come to the school situation ordinarily with a very poor auditory set. They're not accustomed to listening to people read stories to them. I suggest that this kind of pattern can be limited quite a bit and can be overcome up to a point. I don't think that the school can develop a basic aural style in such children, but effective teachers can teach them to learn through listening even though this isn't their *best* mode of learning. One of the techniques for doing this was developed by a man who worked with schizophrenic children. The technique was simply to make a game out of the auditory problem. He would say, for example, What is six and five? Everybody in the class would have to answer many different times. The pupil cannot fall asleep in such a class. Answering once doesn't leave him free because he may be asked the same question (or somewhat different ones) often. This is an excellent technique for waking up youngsters, and it has been effective with low-income students who are not used to listening. The objective is to bring them up to minimal listening ability, up to grade level. I want to bring low-income youngsters far beyond grade level in most areas, because I think they have considerable creative ability; but in their areas of weakness, I would be happy to bring them simply up to grade level. In areas of weakness, our primary aim should be functioning on a minimal level of adequacy so that weaknesses will not destroy strengths. Techniques of the kind described may be useful in reversing habits and sets which have grown out of the negative aspects of the person's style.

To sum up: In everybody's style, there are certain strengths, and each of us has his own Achilles' heel. The issue in developing a powerful change in a person is related to how one gets to the Achilles' heel and how one utilizes the strengths. This is the central problem of the strategy of style, especially in its application to the low-income pupils of our urban schools.

4

The Human Side of Learning

Arthur W. Combs

EDITOR'S NOTE · As Dr. Combs sees it, the trouble with education is not its lack of efficiency, but its lack of humanity. Combs's position is extreme, forceful, and deeply felt. He raises important questions about the use of behavioral objectives, performance-based criteria, and the alleged dangers of using competition as a motivational tool. All in all, Combs feels we are doing much to dehumanize the educational process. What is your opinion?

Anyone who doesn't know that education is in deep trouble must have been hiding somewhere for the last fifteen years. Somehow we have lost touch with the times, so we find young people opting out, copping out, and dropping out of the system. The processes of education have become concerned with nonhuman questions, and the system is dehumanizing to the people in it. Earl Kelley once said, "We've got this marvelous school system with beautiful buildings and a magnificent

Arthur W. Combs, "The Human Side of Learning," *The National Elementary Principal* (January 1973): 38–42. Copyright © 1973, National Association of Elementary School Principals. All rights reserved. Reprinted by permission.

curriculum and these great teachers and these marvelous administrators, and then, damn it all, the parents send us the wrong kids."

For a number of generations now, we have been dealing with learning from a false premise. Most of us are familiar with Pavlov's famous experiment conditioning a dog to respond to a bell. The principles he established then are the ones we still use to deal with the problems of learning in our schools today. But Pavlov's system depended on: 1) separating his dogs from all other dogs, which made the learning process an isolated event; 2) tying his dogs down so that they could only do precisely what he had in mind, a technique not very feasible for most elementary teachers; 3) completely removing the dogs from all other possible sources of stimuli, a hard thing to do in a classroom.

This point of view has taught us to deal with the problem of learning as a question of stimulus and response, to be understood in terms of input and output. Currently it finds its latest expression in behavioral objectives, performance-based criteria for learning that systematically demand that you: Establish your objectives in behavioral terms; set up the machinery to accomplish them; and then test whether or not you have achieved them. Such an approach seems straightforward, businesslike, and logical; and that's what is wrong with it. I quote from Earl Kelley again, who once said, "Logic is often only a systematic way of arriving at the wrong answers!"

I'm not opposed to behavioral objectives. Nobody can be against accountability. The difficulty with the concept is that its fundamental premise is only partly right. The fact is that behavioral objectives are useful devices for dealing with the simplest, most primitive aspects of education, the things we already do quite well. Unfortunately, they do not serve us so well when they are applied to other kinds of objectives, such as intelligent behavior requiring a creative approach to a problem.

Behavioral objectives do not deal with the problem of holistic goals. They do not help us in dealing with the things that make us truly human—the questions of human beliefs, attitudes, feelings, understandings, and concerns—the things we call "affective." Nor do they deal with the problems of self-actualization, citizenship, responsibility, caring, and many other such humanistic goals of educators.

Using this approach, we are evaluating schools and circumstances on the basis of what we know how to test. As a result, we are finding that our educational objectives are being established by default because the things we know how to test are the simplest, smallest units of cognitive procedures, which don't really matter much anyway.

We are spending millions and millions of dollars on this very small aspect of dealing with the educational problem, while the problems of self-concept, human attitudes, feelings, beliefs, meanings, and intelligence are going unexplored.

Although I do not oppose behavioral objectives, I do believe that those who are forcing accountability techniques on us need also to be held accountable for what they are doing to American education.

Performance-based criteria is the method of big business, a technique of management, and we are now in the process of applying these industrial techniques to education everywhere. We ought to know better. When industry developed the assembly line and other systematic techniques to increase efficiency, what happened? The workers felt dehumanized by the system and formed unions to fight it. And that is precisely what is happening with our young people today. They feel increasingly dehumanized by the system, so they are fighting it at every possible level. Applying industrial techniques to human problems just won't work. A systems approach, it should be understood, is only a method of making sure you accomplish your objectives. Applied to the wrong objectives, systems approaches only guarantee that your errors will be colossal.

The trouble with education today is not its lack of efficiency, but its lack of humanity. Learning is not a mechanical process, but a *human* process. The whole approach to learning through behavioral objectives concentrates our attention on the simplest, most primitive aspects of the educational endeavor, while it almost entirely overlooks the human values.

I believe we can get along better with a person who can't read than with a bigot. We are doing very little to prevent the production of bigots but a very great deal to prevent the production of poor readers.

Learning is a human problem always consisting of two parts. First, we have to provide people with some new information or some new experience, and we know how to do that very well. We are experts at it. With the aid of our new electronic gadgets, we can do it faster and more furiously than ever before in history. Second, the student must discover the meaning of the information provided him. The dropout is not a dropout because we didn't give him information. We told him, but he never discovered what that information meant.

I would like to give an alternate definition to the S–R theory most of us cut our teeth on: Information will affect a person's behavior only in the degree to which he has discovered its personal meaning for him. For example, I read in this morning's paper that there has been an increase in the number of cases of pulmonic stenosis in the state of Florida in the past two years. I don't know what pulmonic stenosis is, so this information has no meaning for me. Later in the day I hear a friend talking about pulmonic stenosis, so I look it up and find that it's a disorder that produces a closing up of the pulmonary artery. It's a dangerous disorder, and it produces blue babies. Now I know what it is, but it still doesn't affect my behavior very much. Later in the day I received a letter from a mother of one of my students who says, "Dear Teacher, we have taken Sally to the clinic, where we learned that she has got pulmonic stenosis, and she's going to have to be operated on when she reaches adolescence. In the meantime, we would appreciate it if you would keep an eye out for her."

This information has more meaning to me now because it's happening to one of my students, and my behavior reflects that meaning. I protect the girl, and I talk to other people on the faculty: "Did you hear about Sally? Isn't it a shame? She's got pulmonic stenosis. Poor child, she's going to have to be operated on."

Let's go one step further. Suppose I have just learned that my daughter has pulmonic stenosis. Now this information affects my behavior tremendously, in every aspect of my daily life.

This explains why so much of what we do in school has no effect on students. Sometimes we even discourage them from finding the personal meaning of a piece of information. We say, "Eddie, I'm not interested in what you think about that, what does the book say?" which is the same as telling him that school is a place where you learn about things that don't matter.

What do we need to do, then, if we're going to humanize the business of learning? We have to see the whole problem of learning differently. We have to give up our preoccupation with objectivity. In our research at the University of Florida, we find that objectivity correlates negatively with effectiveness in the helping professions we have so far explored.

Freud once said that no one ever does anything unless he would rather. In other words, no one ever does anything unless he thinks it is important. So the first thing we must do to humanize learning is to believe it is important.

Let me tell another story by way of illustration. In the suburbs of Atlanta there was a young woman teaching first grade who had beautiful long blonde hair which she wore in a pony tail down to the middle of her back. For the first three days of the school year she wore her hair that way. Then, on Thursday she decided to do it up in a bun on top of her head. One of the little boys in her class looked into the room and didn't recognize his teacher. He was lost. The bell rang, school started, and he didn't know where he belonged. He was out in the hall crying. The supervisor asked him, "What's the trouble?" and he said, "I can't find my teacher." She said, "Well, what's your teacher's name? What room are you in?" He didn't know. So she said, "Well, come on, let's see if we can find her." They started down the hall together, the supervisor and the little boy, hand-in-hand, opening one door after another without much luck until they came to the room where this young woman was teaching. As they stood there in the doorway, the teacher turned and saw them and she said, "Why, Joey, it's good to see you. We've been wondering where you were. Come on in. We've missed you." And the little boy pulled away from the supervisor and threw himself into the teacher's arms. She gave him a hug, patted him on the fanny, and he ran to his seat. She knew what was important. She thought little boys were important.

Suppose the teacher hadn't thought little boys were important. Suppose, for instance, she thought supervisors were important. Then she would have

said, "Why good morning, Miss Smith. We're so glad you've come to see us, aren't we boys and girls?" And the little boy would have been ignored. Or the teacher might have thought the lesson was important, in which case she would have said, "Joey, for heaven's sake, where have you been? You're already two pages behind. Come in here and get to work." Or she might have thought that discipline was important, and said, "Joey, you know very well when you're late you must go to the office and get a permit. Now run and get it." But she didn't. She thought little boys were important. And so it is with each of us. We have to believe humanizing learning is important.

To humanize learning we must also recognize that people don't behave according to the facts of a situation, they behave in terms of their beliefs. In the last presidential election, those who thought that the Democrats would save us and the Republicans would ruin us voted for the Democrats. And those who thought the Republicans would save us and the Democrats would ruin us voted for the Republicans. Each of us behaved not in terms of "the facts," but in terms of our beliefs. A fact is only what we believe is so. Sensitivity to the beliefs of the people we work with is basic to effective behavior. In our research on the helping professions, we found the outstanding characteristic of effective helpers was that the good ones are always concerned with how things look from the point of view of the people they are working with.

Let me give another illustration of what I mean by being aware of the other person's point of view. A supervisor and a teacher were talking about a little boy: "I don't know what to do with him," the teacher said. "I know that he can do it; I tell him, 'It's easy, Frank, you can do it'; but he won't even try." The supervisor said, "Don't ever tell a child something is easy. Look at it from the child's point of view. If you tell him it's easy and he can't do it, he can only conclude that he must be stupid, and if he can do it, you have robbed it of all its thrill! Tell him it's hard, that you know it's hard, but you're pretty sure he can do it. Then if he can't do it, he hasn't lost face, and if he can do it, what a glory that is for him."

So much of what we do in teaching is not concerned with people. It is concerned with rules, regulations, order, and neatness. I visited a school some years ago, and as I sat in the principal's office one of the bus drivers came in with a little boy in one hand and a broken arm from one of the seats of the bus in the other hand. How did this principal behave? He became very angry. It was as if the little boy had broken the principal's arm. And, in a sense, the boy had, I suppose.

In contrast to that, I am reminded of a visit I made to a school in Michigan. As I walked down the hall with the principal, a teacher and a group of children came out of one of the rooms of this very old building. We walked into the room and saw that it was in complete havoc. The principal said, "It's a mess, isn't it? And it can stay that way. The teacher has raised the reading level of her classes by two grades every year she's had them. If that's the way she wants to teach, it's all right with me!"

We walked along to the gymnasium and looked in. He said as we looked at the floor, "That's the third finish we've had on that floor this year. We use it in the evenings for family roller skating!" There is a man whose values are clear. He is more concerned with people than things.

There are hundreds of ways we dehumanize people in our schools, and we need to make a systematic attempt to get rid of them.

In *Crisis in the Classroom*, Charles Silberman says that he believes one of the major problems in American education is "mindlessness." We do so many things without having the slightest idea of why we're doing them. One dehumanizing element is the grading system. Grades motivate very few people, nor are they good as an evaluative device. Everyone knows that no two teachers evaluate people in exactly the same terms. Yet we piously regard grades as though they all mean the same thing, under the same circumstances, to all people at all times.

I remember my son coming home from college and asking, "Dad, how can you, as an educator, put up with the grading system? Grading on the curve makes it to my advantage to destroy my friends. Dad, that's a hell of a way to teach young people to live." I'd never thought of it that way before.

Another thing we need to understand is the serious limitation of competition as a motivational system. Psychologists know three things about motivation:

1. The only people who are motivated by compe-

tition are those who think they can win. And that's not very many. Everyone else sits back and watches them beat their brains out.

2. People who do not feel they have a chance of winning and are forced to compete are not motivated. They are discouraged and disillusioned by the process, and we cannot afford a discouraged and disillusioned populace.

3. When competition becomes too important, morality breaks down, and any means becomes justified to achieve the ends—the basketball team begins to use its elbows and students begin to cheat on exams.

Grade level and grouping is another mindless obstacle to humanizing. All the research we have on grouping tells us that no one method of grouping is superior to any other. And yet we go right on, in the same old ways, insisting that we must have grade levels. As a result, we might have an eleven-year-old child in the sixth grade reading at the third-grade level. Every day of his life we feed him a diet of failure because we can't find a way to give a success experience to such a child.

If we want to humanize the processes of learning, we must make a systematic search for the things that destroy effective learning and remove them from the scene. If we're going to humanize the processes of learning, we must take the student in as a partner. Education wouldn't be irrelevant if students had a voice in decision making. One of my friends once said that the problem of American education today is that "all of us are busy providing students with answers to problems they don't have yet." And that's true. We decide what people need to know and then we teach it to them whether they need it or not. As a result some students discover that school is a place where you study things that don't matter and so they drop out. It's intelligent to drop out. If it isn't getting you anywhere, if it doesn't have any meaning, if it doesn't do something for you, then it's intelligent to drop out. But we seldom think of it that way. Most of us regard the dropout as though there is something wrong with him.

Part of making education relevant to the student is allowing him to develop responsibility for his own learning. But responsibility can only be learned from having responsibility, never from having it withheld. The teacher who says, "You be good kids while I'm out of the room" is an example of what I'm talking about. When she comes back the room is bedlam. "I'll never leave you alone again," she says. By this pronouncement she has robbed the children of any opportunity to learn how to behave responsibly on their own.

Not long ago, I arrived at a school just after the election for student body president, and the teachers were upset because the student who was elected president had run on a platform of no school on Friday, free lunches, free admissions to the football games, and a whole string of other impossible things. The teachers thought it was "a travesty on democracy" and suggested that the student body have another election. I said, "If you do that, how are these kids ever going to discover the terrible price you have to pay for electing a jackass to office?"

We know that what a person believes about himself is crucial to his growth and development. We also know that a person learns this self-concept from the way he is treated by significant people in his life. The student takes his self-concept with him wherever he goes. He takes it to Latin class, to arithmetic class, to gym class, and he takes it home with him. Wherever he goes, his self-concept goes, too. Everything that happens to him has an effect on his self-concept.

Are we influencing that self-concept in positive or negative ways? We need to ask ourselves these kinds of questions. How can a person feel liked unless somebody likes him? How can a person feel wanted unless somebody wants him? How can a person feel acceptable unless somebody accepts him? How can a person feel he's a person with dignity and integrity unless somebody treats him so? And how can a person feel that he is capable unless he has some success? In the answers to those questions, we'll find the answers to the human side of learning.

5

Can Learning Encompass Both Ideas and Feelings?

Carl R. Rogers

EDITOR'S NOTE · The emphasis on learning that includes the whole person is not a particularly new idea, but it is an idea that is continually fighting the tides of various educational technologies stressing the purely cognitive aspects of education. Combs mentions some of these in the previous reading. Here, Rogers presents a strong case for the importance of both cognitive and affective dimensions of learning. He suggests that it is possible not only to know our facts, but to feel our knowledge as well. This is not so mystical as it may sound. Read on. See how you feel about it.

In classes and seminars I have tried to communicate ideas and intellectual concepts to others. In psychotherapy and in encounter groups I have facilitated personal learnings in the realm of feelings—the experiencing, often at a non-verbal gut level, of the important emotional events going on in the organism. But I cannot be satisfied with these two separate kinds of learning. There should be a place for learning by the *whole* person, with feelings and ideas merged. I have

Carl R. Rogers, "Can Learning Encompass Both Ideas and Feelings?" *Education* 95 (Winter 1974): 103–14. Reprinted by permission.

given much thought to this question of bringing together cognitive learning, which has always been needed, and affective-experiential learning, which is so underplayed in education today. Since I am using abstract terms, let me illustrate this merged kind of learning with a trivial personal example.

For four years I have been trying to grow two beautifully golden-leaved shrubs at either side of the entrance to our driveway. Recently they have, at long last, been really thriving. Then the other day I was in a hurry. I backed quickly down the driveway, swung the wheel, hit something, and stopped the car. To my horror the rear wheel had gone right over the center of one of the shrubs. My physiological reaction was extreme, as though my whole body tensed and shrunk at what I had done. As I surveyed the crushed shrub, calling myself names I can't repeat (certainly damaging to my self-concept), and feeling a regret possible only to a gardener, I found myself repeating over and over the sentence, "Don't turn your wheel until you're out in the street! Don't turn your wheel until you're out in the street!" Now that was *learning*. It had its cognitive element, which a five-year-old could have grasped. It certainly had its feeling components—several of them. And it had the gut-level quality of experiential learning. All of me had learned a lesson which I will not soon forget. That's the sort of thing I wish to talk about.

Of course, it does not need to be a negative learning. It can be the warm physical glow of discovering that someone you have just met has all sorts of congenial interests and you realize, in your mind and in your feelings, "I'm on the way to making a new friend!"

Let me try to give some additional dimensions of this kind of learning. It is obvious I'm not talking about a professor lecturing, where all the affective and experiential meanings exist outside of what is ostensibly going on. The professor, in addition to the ideas he is expounding, is anxiously asking himself, "Can I make this last for fifty minutes?" and his students, while partially grasping his thoughts, are experiencing equal anxiety. "Do you suppose he'll ask this junk on the final exam?" But all these affective-experiential aspects are completely divorced from the lecture itself.

And I don't mean a passionate intellectual argument between two professors. Here both the affective and the cognitive co-exist in the same ex-

perience, but they run in totally different directions. The mind of each is saying coolly, "My abstractions are more rational and logical than your abstractions," while the feelings are saying, "I'll beat you down, if it's the last thing I do!" The speakers, unfortunately, are aware only of their cognitive processes.

We get closer to what I'm speaking of in a human relations group, where a person may have a deeply moving experience of relating to another, and then attend a general session where the process of the encounter group is discussed. "Oh," he says to himself, ". . . that's what I've just been through." The affective-experiential and the cognitive have been brought close together in time, and each is well tied in with the other. I frequently receive letters from people who have read my books, saying essentially, "Now I understand what I've been going through in therapy (or in a group)." In other words, the cognitive and the affective-experiential have been brought together in awareness.

So if I were to attempt a crude definition of what it means to learn as a whole person, I would say that it involves learning of a *unified* sort, at the cognitive, feeling and gut level, with a clear *awareness* of the different aspects of this unified learning. I suspect that in its purest form, it occurs rarely, but perhaps learning experiences can be judged by their closeness or remoteness to this definition.

Let me give an example closer to the academic world. Roger Hudiburg, a teacher in a Colorado Junior High School, describes a number of the effects of his attempts to be open in his classroom. He says, "Openness scares the hell out of me—it also makes me feel good." In its effect on learning he speaks of the shared learning through inquiry and discovery. ". . . Excited girl peering through microscope at snow crystals: 'Wow, look at this, Teach!' Boy experimenting with electro-magnetism inadvertently produces copper carbonate: 'What's this weird blue stuff? Where'd it come from?' He follows this for weeks, happy and excited. Others are surprised when they put alcohol and salt in snow and frost forms on outside of container: someone says 'ice cream!'—they learn much more than this, for they fool around for days; in fact they turn the whole class on to their 'freezer.'

"Students do learn in an open environment. They learn about the excitement and importance of discovery, about their capabilities, their limits, self-discipline, and responsibility. They also learn facts. How many? Who knows? I just know that they learn some facts. They know this, too. I don't think I ever *really* knew this before, and I don't think that they did either. It makes me feel good to really know something and to know down deep that we are learning. Openness. . . . You've got to experience it, live it, do it!"*

To me that whole description sounds like learning by the whole person. It has plenty of cognitive elements—the intellect is working at top speed. It certainly has feeling elements—curiosity, excitement, passion. It has experiential elements—caution, self-discipline, self-confidence, the thrill of discovery. So it is another description of what I am endeavoring to speak about.

The Current Situation. I am deeply concerned with what is going on in American educational institutions. They have focused so intently on *ideas*, have limited themselves so completely to "education from the neck up" that the resulting narrowness is having serious social consequences. I think of a weekend attempt to close the communications gap at Columbia University—with trustees, administrators, students, and faculty participating. It made some progress, but not much. Toward the end one student, addressing himself particularly to the faculty, said: "I don't know if our two worlds can ever meet. Our world has feelings in it." This same opinion was voiced even more strongly by Greg Knox, another student at this same weekend. He tells how as a freshman he had heard a talk saying that the goal of the student at Columbia was to become a whole man, and this thought "blew" his mind. He continues:

> . . . I think I have succeeded, not just in becoming a whole man, but more importantly, in understanding what one is. What I discovered was that a whole man is comprised of mind, heart, soul, muscle, and balls. What I discovered about the faculty, for the most part, is that it is men comprised of mind. It was an unfortunate discovery, difficultly toler-

ated in an age in which so much understanding, strength and action are essential. . . . (Lyon, 1971, p. 26.)

Archibald MacLeish stated the problem very well years ago. "We do not feel our knowledge. Nothing could better illustrate the flaw at the heart of our civilization. . . . Knowledge without feeling is not knowledge and can lead only to public irresponsibility and indifference, and conceivably to ruin."* This "knowledge without feeling" has made it possible for our military men and for us as a people, to commit incredible atrocities without any particular sense of guilt. We should not forget some of the events of the war in Southeast Asia. One of our reconnaissance planes was shot down over North Vietnam. Two hundred bombers were ordered to engage in "a protective reaction strike," which received a scant paragraph in our papers. We simply did not let ourselves know, at any gut level, that this act of revenge meant that we were bombing and napalming both military posts and villages—killing and maiming men, women, and children—an unbelievably murderous action. For us it was simply an intellectual category—a "protective reaction strike."

This is not an isolated incident. In the bombings of North and South Vietnam, in the bombings of Cambodia, we were frequently engaged in a slaughter of the innocents. But thanks in part to our successfully compartmentalized cognitive education, we simply know the intellectual facts and do not *feel* our knowledge. Yet when we are forced to look at the bodies of men and women machine-gunned by our own boys, as at My Lai, then the gut level reaction breaks through, and we are horrified at what we have done. Only if we individually were to walk through the awful human aftermath of our bombing raids would the experiential horror be joined to the intellectual label, and we would *learn*, in a total way, the incredible things we have done.

But we have been schooled for years to stress only the cognitive, to avoid any feeling connected with learning. We have been denying a most important part of ourselves, and the awful split I have described is one result. Another result is that the

---

* Hudiburg, Roger. "Some Frank Comments on Openness." ES/ESTPP Newsletter No. 3, Burbank Junior High School, Boulder, Colorado.

* As quoted by James Reston, *New York Times*, 11-29-70.

excitement has in large measure gone out of education—even though no one can take the excitement out of real *learning*.

I have days when I think educational institutions at all levels are doomed, and perhaps we will be well advised to bid them farewell—state-required curricula, compulsory attendance, tenured professors, hours of lectures, grades, degrees, and all that—and let true learning begin to blossom outside the stifling hallowed walls. Suppose every educational institution, from kindergarten through the most prestigious Ph.D. program, were to close tomorrow. What a delightful situation that would be! Parents and children and adolescents and young people—even a few faculty members perhaps—would begin to devise situations in which they could *learn!* Can you imagine anything more uplifting to the spirit of all our people? It would be sad and it would be utterly marvelous at the same time. Millions of people would be asking the same question—"Is there anything I want to learn?" and finding that there were such things, and inventing means by which they could learn them.

It would forever kill the attitude best expressed by a student in a self-directed course at the University of Illinois facilitated by Robert Menges. "What is educational has been viewed by me as something to do before I can finally be left alone to do something I *want* to do. . . . When I came home from first grade my mother asked me, 'How did you like it?' She says I answered with a question, 'How long do I have to go?' *Until this course* I had never thought about *how* I learn, or *why*."*

THE CONDITIONS FOR INTELLECTUAL, AFFECTIVE, GUT LEVEL LEARNING

There are a few experiences in my professional life that I remember vividly. One is the beautiful, air-conditioned, plush-seated auditorium at the University of Michigan in 1956. Those elements only surprised me—it is not the reason I remember the occasion. I was talking to a highly sophisticated professional audience, and I was advancing a theoretical view—very new, very tentative, as to

what conditions were necessary and sufficient to produce change in individuals in one-to-one psychotherapy. And I was dimly aware—fortunately only dimly—that I was challenging almost all of the sacred cows in the therapeutic world. I was saying in effect, though not very openly, that it wasn't a question of whether the therapist had been psychoanalyzed, or had a knowledge of personality theory, or possessed expertise in diagnosis, or had a thorough acquaintance with therapeutic techniques. I was saying that his effectiveness in therapy depended on his *attitudes*. I even had the nerve to define what I thought those attitudes were (Rogers, 1957).

It wasn't a very popular talk. Perhaps because I was frightened by the possible reaction it is one of the most closely reasoned, carefully stated talks I have ever given. I am still proud of it. And, though not very popular, it has sparked more research than any talk I've ever given. First a number of studies showed that when these conditions existed in psychotherapy, the self-learning which went on did promote change.

Then I became bolder and postulated that these same attitudinal changes would promote any whole-person learning—that they would hold for the classroom as well as the therapist's office. This hypothesis has also sparked research. Before I comment briefly on some of these studies, let me describe these attitudinal conditions as they relate to education, and as I have come to see them over the years. They are attitudes, which in my judgment, characterize a facilitator of learning. I have described them before, but I am not willing to omit them, even though they may be familiar.

REALNESS IN THE FACILITATOR OF LEARNING

Perhaps the most basic of these essential attitudes is realness or genuineness. When the facilitator is a real person, being what he is, entering into a relationship with the learner without presenting a front or a facade, he is much more likely to be effective. This means that the feelings which he is experiencing are available to him, available to his awareness, that he is able to live these feelings, be them, and able to communicate them if appropriate. It means that he comes into a direct personal

---

* Unpublished paper.

encounter with the learner, meeting him on a person-to-person basis. It means that he is *being* himself, not denying himself. He is *present* to the student.

PRIZING, ACCEPTANCE, TRUST

There is another attitude which stands out in those who are successful in facilitating learning. I have observed this attitude. I have experienced it. Yet, it is hard to know what term to put to it so I shall use several. I think of it as prizing the learner, prizing his feelings, his opinions, his person. It is a caring for the learner, but a non-possessive caring. It is an acceptance of this other individual as a separate person, a respect for him as having worth in his own right. It is a basic trust—a belief that this other person is somehow fundamentally trustworthy. Whether we call it prizing, acceptance, trust, or by some other term, it shows up in a variety of observable ways. The facilitator who has a considerable degree of this attitude can be fully acceptant of the fear and hesitation of the student as he approaches a new problem as well as acceptant of the pupil's satisfaction in achievement. Such a teacher can accept the student's occasional apathy, his erratic desires to explore by-roads of knowledge, as well as his disciplined efforts to achieve major goals. He can accept personal feelings which both disturb and promote learning—rivalry with a sibling, hatred of authority, concern about personal adequacy. What we are describing is a prizing of the learner as an imperfect human being with many feelings, many potentialities. The facilitator's prizing or acceptance of the learner is an operational expression of his essential confidence and trust in the capacity of the human organism.

EMPATHIC UNDERSTANDING

A further element which establishes a climate for self-initiated experiential learning is empathic understanding. When the teacher has the ability to understand the student's reactions from the inside, has a sensitive awareness of the way the process of education and learning seems *to the student*, then again the likelihood of significant learning is increased.

This kind of understanding is sharply different from the usual evaluative understanding, which follows the pattern of, "I understand what is wrong with you." When there is a sensitive empathy, however, the reaction in the learner follows something of this pattern, "At last someone understands how it feels and seems to be *me* without wanting to analyze or judge me. Now I can blossom and grow and learn."

This attitude of standing in the student's shoes, of viewing the world through his eyes, is almost unheard of in the classroom. But when the teacher responds in a way which makes the student feel *understood*—not judged or evaluated, this has a tremendous impact.*

Perception of These Attitudes. There is still a further condition for learning by the whole person, which is especially important in education. It is that the student must to some extent perceive that these attitudinal elements exist in the teacher. Students are even more suspicious than clients in therapy. The student has been "conned" for so long that a teacher who is real with him is usually seen for a time as simply exhibiting a new brand of phoniness. To have a teacher prize him in a non-judgmental way arouses the deepest disbelief. To have a teacher truly and warmly understand his private world is so unbelievable that he is certain he must not have heard correctly. Yet it is this last, the empathic response, which is probably the first element to get through, the first reaction which begins to convince the student that this *is* a new experience.

WHAT ARE THE PERSONAL RESULTS?

What are the results? I would like first to give some living pictures of what happens when these attitudes exist, and then turn to the research findings.

Dr. "X" is a high school teacher whom I have come to know well. She teaches in a school which is a cross-section of an urban community. She seems to be without pretense or facade or defensiveness.

---

* These three descriptions are adapted from Rogers, *Freedom to Learn*, 1969, pp. 107, 109, 111–112.

You can't talk with her for five minutes without realizing that she thinks high school students are "the greatest." I have a suspicion that she likes the troublemakers best of all. And the way she can move sensitively and empathically (in her blunt direct manner) into the feelings and reactions of her students is uncanny.

Her courses have been titled Psychology, Human Relations, etc., but they would be better labeled Learning Experiences. The boys and girls discuss anything which concerns them—drugs, family problems, sex, pregnancy, contraception, abortion, dropping out, getting a job, the grading system—literally any topic. They have learned to trust her and each other, and the level of honesty and self-disclosure is amazing.

At this point some of you may be thinking, "O.K., O.K., perhaps they get help in their personal adjustment, but is there any *content?*" There is indeed. Miss "X" is a tremendous reader, and her enthusiasm for books is contagious. Her students are literally "turned on" by the chance to read the books they want on the subjects that interest them. And what books they choose! Some of the students are classed as slow learners, but they are reading Buber, Kierkegaard, Fromm, my books, Slater, Reich, Summerhill, John Holt—you name it, they have read it. People tell her these books are far too advanced for high school students, and she laughs and says they love to tackle difficult challenges. They also choose the films they want to see, and plan community trips. They are excited, personally involved, *learners.*

Miss "X" has received the oddest and most flattering compliment a teacher could receive. In her school, if a student is found to have any connection with drugs, he or she is suspended and not permitted to attend school. There are quite a number of these. But they have found that if they skirt the parking lot, go in a back door and take a circuitous route, they can reach Miss "X's" room without being observed. They know she won't throw them out, so they sneak into school to continue to attend her class. They are bootlegging their learning! And yet people say that high school students "just aren't motivated."

Let me give one more example. A university teacher tried to believe in the students' capacity to act responsibly in preparing themselves for the teaching positions they would soon be filling. He dropped all tests. He encouraged personally oriented book reviews and personal growth journals. He exemplified in himself, so far as he was able, the sort of attitudes I have been describing.

The results? The students read and reviewed an average of almost seven books apiece in a six weeks course. They kept personal journals. They tried a mini-school. They did a variety of innovative things. Here are three brief examples, the first from a personal journal.

"If anybody asks what the hell did you get out of that psych course? I'll say love. Love, man. Dig? I got a glimpse of the unity of all things. A moment of truth. How does it look on a transcript. Lovely. It's *empty.* I realized that which I have always tried to realize. I became motivated, and forever will allow the truth to soar through me."

Or if you wish less emotional examples, here is a reaction to the whole course. "I was honored to be given the responsibility for my own education, and in a more general sense, my own life."

Here is what one student—with the help of his pupils—learned from conducting a two week summer mini-school. "They taught me something. Children have a need to love people, and they readily give it away and all they need is someone to be receptive to this love. And this should be one of the functions of the teacher, that is, he should be able to receive love and give it back to them. They showed me that a teacher cannot stand aloof from his students but rather must participate and share with them.

"Never has a class helped me as much as this one. I really feel like I'm growing."*

Perhaps these examples indicate the way in which two educators have put together the cognitive and the affective-experiential to involve learning by the whole student. I could describe others—a teacher of poetry (Moon, 1966), a French teacher, a professor of higher mathematics, a teacher of "incorrigible non-readers" in the fifth grade, an English instructor (Carr, 1964)—but this would take too much space. Let us turn instead to the empirical studies which have been made, to see what they show us.

---

* Personal account of a class from Professor John E. Merryman.

WHAT ARE THE RESEARCH RESULTS?

It has been truly fascinating to see research evidence pile up over the years indicating that there is some validity to the hypotheses so tentatively presented eighteen years ago. I wish to dwell on the evidence from education, but first one small finding from the field of therapy.

Barrett-Lennard, in a study done in 1959 (Barrett-Lennard, 1962) of therapist-client relationships, found that those clients who eventually showed more therapeutic change perceived more of these conditions at the time of the fifth interview than did those who eventually showed less change. In other words, a prediction can be made very early in the game.* I feel certain this finding would hold in the classroom world as well. If we measured these attitudes in the classroom during the first five days of the school year—the attitudes as they exist in the teacher, and as they are perceived by the student—we could predict which classrooms would contain learners, and which would contain prisoners. To the degree that these attitudes were held and perceived, we could predict the classrooms in which learning would be by the whole person, with its accompanying involvement and excitement. We could also predict the classrooms which would be passive, restless or rebellious, with mostly rote learning going on.

The research which has endeavored to discover specific relationships between these attitudinal conditions and various elements of the learning process in school has come about largely through the efforts of Dr. David Aspy and his students and colleagues, though others have also contributed. I will not bore you with the details of the researchers, but simply describe very briefly some of the findings, making the more detailed references available. The research is continuing and expanding.

To give some samples. The levels of these interpersonal conditions can be measured with reasonable objectivity. It has been shown that they are significantly and positively related to a greater gain in reading achievement in third graders (Aspy, 1965). They are positively related to grade point average (Pierce, 1966); similarly to cognitive growth (Aspy, 1967; Aspy, 1969; Aspy and Hadlock, 1967); to an increase in creative interest and productivity (Moon, 1966); to levels of cognitive thinking; to the amount of student-initiated talk (Aspy and Roebuck, 1970). They are related to a diffusion of liking and trust in the classroom, which in turn is related to better utilization of his abilities by the student, and greater confidence in himself (Schmuck, 1966).

One exciting aspect is that Aspy (1971) has shown that it is possible, quite accurately, to select teaching personnel who possess those interpersonal qualities which have been shown to be specifically facilitative of whole-person learning. This has many implications.

Adding to his earlier research Aspy (1972) has not only presented in convincing form these and other investigations, but has shown that the attitudinal qualities we have discussed can be assessed by the teacher for himself, or by others. He also shows that a school can use such measures to increase the effectiveness of the learning climate in its classroom.

The conclusion to be drawn from these many studies is that it pays to be personal and human in the classroom. A humane atmosphere is not only more pleasant for all concerned. It promotes more —and more significant—learning. When attitudes of realness, respect for the individual, understanding of the student's private world are present, exciting things happen. The pay-off is not only in such things as grades and reading achievement, but also in more elusive qualities such as greater self-confidence, increased creativity, more liking for others. In short, such a classroom leads to a positive, unified learning by the whole person.

IMPLICATIONS FOR TEACHER TRAINING

If then we can choose to have learning which combines the cognitive and the affective-experiential— the intellectual and the gut-level—and if we know with a modest degree of accuracy the interpersonal conditions which produce that kind of learning, what is the next step? It seems to me it is obvious

---

* This has more recently been corroborated in a larger group of cases by Reinhard Tausch in Germany. Prediction, he found, could be made after the second interview.

that we need a change, amounting almost to a revolution, in the training of our teachers. Yet most teacher-training institutions are bastions of the traditional, and stress only cognitive learning and the methods by which it can be achieved. They are past masters at providing an atmosphere which says, "Don't do as I do. Do as I say." Is it possible to effect change in such institutions?

Let us first ask a prior question. Is it possible to help develop these interpersonal qualities in student-teachers or others preparing for the teaching field? I believe the answer is definitely yes on two counts. In the first place, as I have mentioned, it would be entirely possible now to select candidates who showed a high potentiality for realness, prizing, and empathetic understanding in their relationships. Thus we could select teacher candidates on different bases from those now used. Then there is increasingly ample evidence that such attitudes can be developed. I have seen them develop in counselors-in-training. Aspy has shown that teachers can improve through inservice training. I am sure we do not as yet know all the available means but some variant of the intensive group experience seems to be of great assistance, providing there is a follow-up of such a task-oriented or encounter group. Another avenue is to provide ample opportunity for independent study, which means that choice would become a part of his or her life for the student teacher, instead of passivity being the primary stance.

Let me give one example of how such changes can come about. This is a school principal in his thirties who, during the course of a seminar, had been exposed to much independent study and also to two encounter-group weekend experiences. For his final report he begins, "As I sit at my desk to begin this paper, I have a real feeling of inner excitement. This is an experience that I have never had. For as I write I have no format to follow and I will put my thoughts down as they occur. It's almost a feeling of floating for to me it doesn't seem to really matter how you, or anyone for that matter, will react to my thoughts. Nevertheless, at the same time I feel that you will accept them as mine regardless of the lack of style, format, or academic expression. . . . My real concern is to try to communicate with myself so that I might better understand myself.

"I guess what I am really saying is that I am

writing not for you, for a grade, nor for a class, but for *me*. And I feel especially good about that, for this is something that I wouldn't have *dared* to do or even *consider* in the past . . ." (Rogers, 1969, p. 84.)

I think it seems clear that he had learned a great deal at the affective and experiential level, for the first time in twenty years of education. He has grown as a person. However, one might well raise the question, would this change really make him a different kind of administrator or teacher? Here is another small portion of his report: ". . . My staff meeting Tuesday was truly significant as I was able to relate to the staff how I really felt. Many told me afterwards that they were very surprised and impressed and wanted to applaud, not because I had said anything so different, but it was the way I said it. I have had various teachers in my office daily who have wanted to relate to me and state they now find me more accepting than ever . . . I feel that life has so much more meaning." (Rogers, 1969, p. 89.)

This has been my experience—that when inner changes take place in the attitude and self-concept of the person, then changes begin to show up in his interpersonal behavior.

A PROGRAM OF CHANGE IN TEACHER TRAINING

I should like to turn now to the more difficult question of whether it would be possible to change the teacher-training institutions. I am bold and brash enough to say that if I were given a free hand and if I had the energy, and ample funding—say the equivalent of the cost of a half dozen B-52 bombers—I think that in one year I could introduce such a ferment into schools of education that it would initiate a revolution. Since I am sure that must sound like an arrogant statement, I would like to state as precisely as I can what I would do. Much of the plan would, of course, change as obstacles were encountered and as the participants desired to move in somewhat different directions.

First I would enlist the aid of a large number of skilled facilitators, who are familiar with small group process. This would be entirely feasible. Then, since it is necessary to begin somewhere, I would in each institution indicate that task-oriented groups would be formed around the topic, "How can this school help the whole person to learn?" Students and faculty would be invited to join, on a voluntary basis.

In a general meeting I would explain that the purpose of these groups would be not only to learn *about* the topics, but that the participants themselves would learn as whole persons. It would not be a purely cognitive experience. This would turn away a great many. People are fearful of getting personally and experientially involved in learning. Suppose only a very small percentage volunteered. That would not concern me.

I would aim to have three weeks of the intensive group experience with cognitive and experiential elements, probably during the summer; a follow-up session with each small group every week; and perhaps a weekend three months later for the same group to discuss the problems they have met, to evaluate the changes that have come about and the future steps that they want to take in the direction of change.

The choice of the facilitators would be extremely important, but again we have both objective measures and subjective guidelines for selecting facilitators who rank high in the qualities we have described. Aspy (1971) has shown the way for this, and unintentionally, I believe, shown how important such a choice is. He found that when the facilitator's rankings on these qualities were high, the teachers and supervisors in his group showed positive change in "interpersonal functioning, self-concept, and ability to obtain student-initiated behavior in their classrooms." But when the facilitator rated low, there were no significant changes in the group participants. In other words, to produce teachers who can provide the attitudinal conditions for whole-person learning, there must be facilitators who already possess those attitudes. Then the personal and behavioral changes which I have described in *Freedom to Learn* (1969) occur.

Many educators might be fearful that personal damage would result from these intensive group experiences. Yet, the research by Lieberman, Yalom, and Miles (1973) indicates that damage results primarily when the leader is confronting, challenging, attacking, intrusive. When the facilitator possesses the attitudes I have described, psychological damage is minimal. I have discussed this and many other problems related to the leadership

and process of the intensive group in my small book on this topic (1970).

One pre-condition, if this whole program were to be initiated in teacher-training institutions, would have to be absolutely clear. It could either be laid down by the dean or preferably by the funding agency. That is the condition that no one could be discharged because of dissent from the ongoing practices in the institution, or because of innovation in the classroom. There have been, in recent years, all too many well documented instances of teachers and teachers-in-training who have been dismissed from their institutions for non-conformity. The student teacher who believes pupils should have a voice in the curriculum; the instructor—elementary, high school, or college—who attempts to create a freer atmosphere in the classroom or to encourage independent thought or to experiment with a new approach to grading, is simply dismissed. (See Brownfield, 1973, for one instance.) Administrators are not happy with individuals who "rock the boat." Hence in our teacher-training experiment, protection from such arbitrary action must be provided.

CHANGE AND TURBULENCE

There is one institutional result which I would like to stress. I feel quite sure on the basis of experience that the process I have described would tend to polarize both the faculty and the students and create turbulence within the institution. I happen to believe that such turbulence would be constructive. Traditionalists would be angry at these new innovators and vice versa. Sacred cows would be questioned. Student teachers, and even their faculty, would tend to think and learn and grow.

One very probable outcome of this kind of ferment would take the form of a "free university" type of teacher-training institution in which the students would form their own curriculum, participate in the facilitation of learning, find other means of evaluation than grades. The person who emerged from such a training program could be channeled into one of a limited number of schools that would welcome him. And here again, some polarization is likely to occur in these schools.

What would such a new student-teacher *do* in

his classroom? Most importantly he would simply *be* the attitudes we have described, and new participatory methods would emerge. But if he felt somewhat at a loss, Harold Lyon's book *Learning to Feel—Feeling to Learn* (1971) is full of very practical means of implementing these attitudes. He would be developing a classroom so new in its approaches that there would be little or no resemblance to the old form.

THE FERMENT OF CONTINUING CHANGE

These then would be some of the steps in initiating changes in teacher training. Taken together, what is the essence of their meaning? By the end of the year there would be many people in the teacher-training institutions who would themselves have learned in a total way, and who would be enthusiastic and eager to have their students learn in the same fashion. This is like an infusion of yeast into a lump of dough. The numbers involved might be small but the pervasive effect would be enormous. You may well ask, "How can I be so sure of all this?" I feel assurance because I have with my own eyes seen it happen twice. The first was in the Immaculate Heart system in Los Angeles where self-directed change is going on apace years after our brief interventive efforts ceased. Then I have seen such a program with better financing and better planning introduce an incredible ferment into the inner-city school system of Louisville, Kentucky (Dickenson, et al., 1970; Dept. of Research and Evaluation, 1973). Can you imagine intensive communication workshops and human relations labs for 1600 school personnel in six months? And these included the Board of Education, central office staff, principals, and teachers. In both instances the polarization seemed most unfortunate for a time but out of it grew a new and confident sense of direction, with new and more vital individuals in charge of those new directions. The change in teacher-education at Immaculate Heart College was unbelievable.

A professor of education in the college wrote:

We are working on a self-initiated and self-directed program in teacher education. We had a fantastically exciting weekend workshop here recently. Students, faculty, and administration, 75 in all, brainstormed in a most creative and productive way. The outcome is that students will immerse themselves in schools all over the city observing classes, sitting in on faculty meetings, interviewing teachers, students and administrators. Our students will *then* describe what *they* need to know, to experience, to do, in order to teach. They will then gather faculty and other students around them to assist in accomplishing their own goals.

The lessons from this are several. The professor, who was just one faculty member at the beginning of the study, was very deeply affected by the encounter group experience, which led her to take further training in group leadership and group dynamics, and to facilitate groups on her own. She became not only much more open to her students, but a much more confident person, able to initiate and implement new ideas. She had learned as a whole person. She became so much more influential in the college that she was placed in charge of a teacher-training program. Now this letter gives evidence of the way in which she is encouraging these young teachers-to-be to incorporate both the cognitive and the affective-experiential into their learning. As usual, when given the chance to be self-directing, when trusted to learn, students work harder than anyone would have a right to demand of them. There can be little doubt that they in turn will provide a similar opportunity and conditions whereby *their* students can also learn to feel as well as to think. This is the exciting pervasive ferment occasioned when an individual has a chance to learn as a whole person.

CONCLUDING REMARK

I cannot help but conclude by saying that we have the theoretical knowledge, the practical methods, and the day-by-day skills with which to radically change our whole educational system. We know how to bring together, in one experience, the intellectual learning, the range of personal emotions, and the basic physiological impact, which constitute significant learning by the whole person. We know how to develop student teachers into agents for this sort of change. Do we have the will, the determination, to utilize that know-how to humanize our educational institutions? That is the question we all must answer.

REFERENCES

Aspy, D. N. A study of three facilitative conditions and their relationship to the achievement of third grade students. Unpublished doctoral dissertation, University of Kentucky, 1965.

————. Counseling and education. In R. R. Carkhuff (ed.), *The counselor's contribution to facilitative processes*. Urbana, Illinois: Parkinson, 1967. Chapter 12.

————. The effect of teacher-offered conditions of empathy, positive regard, and congruence upon student achievement. *Florida Journal of Educational Research*, 1969, 11 (1), 39–48.

————. Supervisors, your levels of humanness may make a difference. Unpublished.

————. *Toward a technology of humanizing education*. Champaign, Illinois: Research Press Co., 1974.

————, and Hadlock, W. The effect of empathy, warmth, and genuineness on elementary students' reading achievement. Reviewed in Truax, C. B., and Carkhuff, R. R. *Toward effective counseling and psychotherapy*. Chicago: Aldine Publishing Co., 1967.

————, and Roebuck, F. N. An investigation of the relationship between student levels of cognitive functioning and the teacher's classroom behavior. Study at the University of Florida, 1970.

————, and Roebuck, F. N. The necessity for facilitative interpersonal conditions in teaching. Gainesville, Florida: University of Florida, unpublished manuscript.

Barrett-Lennard, G. T. Dimensions of therapist response as causal factors in therapeutic change. *Psychological Monographs*, 1962. 76 (whole No. 562).

Brownfield, C. A. *Humanizing College Learning: A Taste of Hemlock*. New York: Exposition Press, 1973.

Carr, J. B. Project freedom. *The English Journal*, March, 1964, pp. 202–204.

Dept. of Research and Evaluation, Louisville Independent School District, 1972–73 Final Evaluation Report, Louisville, Kentucky, 1973 (mimeographed).

Dickenson, W. A., et al. A humanistic program for change in a large inner-city school system. *Journal of Humanistic Psychology*, 10 (2), Fall, 1970, 111–120.

Lieberman, M., Yalom, I., and Miles, M. *Encounter Groups: First Facts*. New York: Basic Books, Inc., 1973.

Lyon, H. C., Jr. *Learning to feel—feeling to learn*. Columbus, Ohio: Charles E. Merrill Publishing Company, 1971.

Moon, S. F. Teaching the self. *Improving College and University Teaching*. 14, Autumn, 1966, 213–229.

Pierce, R. An investigation of grade-point average and therapeutic process variables. Unpublished dissertation, University of Massachusetts, 1966. Reviewed in Carkhuff, R. R., and Berenson, B. G. *Beyond counseling and therapy*. New York: Holt, Rinehart and Winston, Inc., 1967.

Rogers, C. R. The necessary and sufficient conditions of therapeutic personality change. *Journal of Consulting Psychology*, 1957, 21, 95–103.

————. *Freedom to learn*. Columbus, Ohio: Charles E. Merrill Publishing Company, 1969.

————. *Carl Rogers on encounter groups*. New York: Harper & Row, 1970.

Schmuck, R. Some aspects of classroom social climate. *Psychology in the Schools*, 3, 1966, 59–65.

6

The Cognitive–Developmental Approach to Moral Education

Lawrence Kohlberg

EDITOR'S NOTE • For over 20 years, Dr. Kohlberg has been developing and refining his ideas and approaches to moral education in an effort to translate pure theory into practical application. Building upon the work of John Dewey and Jean Piaget, Kohlberg has defined six hierarchical stages of moral development. This reading clearly outlines what each of these stages involves and how each influences behavior. What stage of moral development does the U.S. Constitution reflect? The Ten Commandments? From what stage did Richard Nixon operate? From what stage do you make your moral judgments? Moral education is increasingly being considered an important human dimension of the learning process. This fine article may help you to better understand why it is pertinent.

In this article, I present an overview of the cognitive-developmental approach to moral education and its research foundations, compare it with other approaches, and report the experimental work my colleagues and I are doing to apply the approach.

Lawrence Kohlberg, "The Cognitive–Developmental Approach to Moral Education," *Phi Delta Kappan* (June 1975): 670–77. Reprinted by permission.

I. MORAL STAGES

The cognitive-developmental approach was fully stated for the first time by John Dewey. The approach is called *cognitive* because it recognizes that moral education, like intellectual education, has its basis in stimulating the *active thinking* of the child about moral issues and decisions. It is called developmental because it sees the aims of moral education as movement through moral stages. According to Dewey:

> The aim of education is growth or *development*, both intellectual and moral. Ethical and psychological principles can aid the school in the *greatest of all constructions—the building of a free and powerful character.* Only knowledge of the *order and connection of the stages in psychological development can insure this.* Education is the work of *supplying the conditions* which will enable the psychological functions to mature in the freest and fullest manner.[1]

Dewey postulated three levels of moral development: 1) the *pre-moral* or *preconventional* level "of behavior motivated by biological and social impulses with results for morals," 2) the *conventional* level of behavior "in which the individual accepts with little critical reflection the standards of his group," and 3) the *autonomous* level of behavior in which "conduct is guided by the individual thinking and judging for himself whether a purpose is good, and does not accept the standard of his group without reflection."*

Dewey's thinking about moral stages was theoretical. Building upon his prior studies of cognitive stages, Jean Piaget made the first effort to define stages of moral reasoning in children through actual interviews and through observations of children (in games with rules).[2] Using this interview material, Piaget defined the pre-moral, the conventional, and the autonomous levels as follows: 1) the *pre-moral stage*, where there was no sense of obligation to rules; 2) the *heteronomous stage*, where

---

* These levels correspond roughly to our three major levels: the preconventional, the conventional, and the principled. Similar levels were propounded by William McDougall, Leonard Hobhouse, and James Mark Baldwin.

the right was literal obedience to rules and an equation of obligation with submission to power and punishment (roughly ages 4–8); and 3) the *autonomous stage*, where the purpose and consequences of following rules are considered and obligation is based on reciprocity and exchange (roughly ages 8–12).**

In 1955 I started to redefine and validate (through longitudinal and cross-cultural study) the Dewey–Piaget levels and stages. The resulting stages are presented in Table 1.

We claim to have validated the stages defined in Table 1. The notion that stages can be *validated* by longitudinal study implies that stages have definite empirical characteristics.[3] The concept of stages (as used by Piaget and myself) implies the following characteristics:

1. Stages are "structured wholes," or organized systems of thought. Individuals are *consistent* in level of moral judgment.

2. Stages form an *invariant sequence*. Under all conditions except extreme trauma, movement is always forward, never backward. Individuals never skip stages; movement is always to the next stage up.

3. Stages are "hierarchical integrations." Thinking at a higher stage includes or comprehends within it lower-stage thinking. There is a tendency to function at or prefer the highest stage available.

Each of these characteristics has been demonstrated for moral stages. Stages are defined by responses to a set of verbal moral dilemmas classified according to an elaborate scoring scheme. Validating studies include:

1. A 20-year study of 50 Chicago-area boys, middle- and working-class. Initially interviewed at ages 10–16, they have been reinterviewed at three-year intervals thereafter.

2. A small, six-year longitudinal study of Turkish village and city boys of the same age.

3. A variety of other cross-sectional studies in Canada, Britain, Israel, Taiwan, Yucatan, Honduras, and India.

With regard to the structured whole or consistency criterion, we have found that more than 50% of an individual's thinking is always at one stage, with the remainder at the next adjacent stage (which he is leaving or which he is moving into).

With regard to invariant sequence, our longitudinal results have been presented in the *American Journal of Orthopsychiatry* (see footnote 8), and indicate that on every retest individuals were either at the same stage as three years earlier or had moved up. This was true in Turkey as well as in the United States.

With regard to the hierarchical integration criterion, it has been demonstrated that adolescents exposed to written statements at each of the six stages comprehend or correctly put in their own words all statements at or below their own stage but fail to comprehend any statements more than one stage above their own.[4] Some individuals comprehend the next stage above their own; some do not. Adolescents prefer (or rank as best) the highest stage they can comprehend.

To understand moral stages, it is important to clarify their relations to the stage of logic or intelligence, on the one hand, and to moral behavior on the other. Maturity of moral judgment is not highly correlated with IQ or verbal intelligence (correlations are only in the 30s, accounting for 10% of the variance). Cognitive development, in the stage sense, however, is more important for moral development than such correlations suggest. Piaget has found that after the child learns to speak there are three major stages of reasoning: the intuitive, the concrete operational, and the formal operational. At around age 7, the child enters the stage of concrete logical thought: He can make logical inferences, classify, and handle quantitative relations about concrete things. In adolescence individuals usually enter the stage of formal operations. At this stage they can reason abstractly, i.e., consider all possibilities, form hypotheses, deduce implications from hypotheses, and test them against reality.*

Since moral reasoning clearly is reasoning, ad-

** Piaget's stages correspond to our first three stages: Stage 0 (pre-moral), Stage 1 (heteronomous), and Stage 2 (instrumental reciprocity).

* Many adolescents and adults only partially attain the stage of formal operations. They do consider all the actual relations of one thing to another at the same time, but they do not consider all possibilities and form abstract hypotheses. A few do not advance this far, remaining "concrete operational."

TABLE 1. Definition of Moral Stages

I. PRECONVENTIONAL LEVEL

At this level, the child is responsive to cultural rules and labels of good and bad, right or wrong, but interprets these labels either in terms of the physical or the hedonistic consequences of action (punishment, reward, exchange of favors) or in terms of the physical power of those who enunciate the rules and labels. The level is divided into the following two stages:

Stage 1: The punishment-and-obedience orientation. The physical consequences of action determine its goodness or badness, regardless of the human meaning or value of these consequences. Avoidance of punishment and unquestioning deference to power are valued in their own right, not in terms of respect for an underlying moral order supported by punishment and authority (the latter being Stage 4).

Stage 2: The instrumental-relativist orientation. Right action consists of that which instrumentally satisfies one's own needs and occasionally the needs of others. Human relations are viewed in terms like those of the marketplace. Elements of fairness, of reciprocity, and of equal sharing are present, but they are always interpreted in a physical, pragmatic way. Reciprocity is a matter of "you scratch my back and I'll scratch yours," not of loyalty, gratitude, or justice.

II. CONVENTIONAL LEVEL

At this level, maintaining the expectations of the individual's family, group, or nation is perceived as valuable in its own right, regardless of immediate and obvious consequences. The attitude is not only one of *conformity* to personal expectations and social order, but of loyalty to it, of actively *maintaining*, supporting, and justifying the order, and of identifying with the persons or group involved in it. At this level, there are the following two stages:

Stage 3: The interpersonal concordance or "good boy—nice girl" orientation. Good behavior is that which pleases or helps others and is approved by them. There is much conformity to stereotypical images of what is majority or "natural" behavior. Behavior is frequently judged by intention—"he means well" becomes important for the first time. One earns approval by being "nice."

Stage 4: The "law and order" orientation. There is orientation toward authority, fixed rules, and the maintenance of the social order. Right behavior consists of doing one's duty, showing respect for authority, and maintaining the given social order for its own sake.

III. POSTCONVENTIONAL, AUTONOMOUS, OR PRINCIPLED LEVEL

At this level, there is a clear effort to define moral values and principles that have validity and application apart from the authority of the groups or persons holding these principles and apart from the individual's own identification with these groups. This level also has two stages:

Stage 5: The social-contract, legalistic orientation, generally with utilitarian overtones. Right action tends to be defined in terms of general individual rights and standards which have been critically examined and agreed upon by the whole society. There is a clear awareness of the relativism of personal values and opinions and a corresponding emphasis upon procedural rules for reaching consensus. Aside from what is constitutionally and democratically agreed upon, the right is a matter of personal "values" and "opinion." The result is an emphasis upon the "legal point of view," but with an emphasis upon the possibility of changing law in terms of rational considerations of social utility (rather than freezing it in terms of Stage 4 "law and order"). Outside the legal realm, free agreement and contract is the binding element of obligation. This is the "official" morality of the American government and constitution.

Stage 6: The universal-ethical-principle orientation. Right is defined by the decision of conscience in accord with self-chosen *ethical principles* appealing to logical comprehensiveness, universality, and consistency. These principles are abstract and ethical (the Golden Rule, the categorical imperative); they are not concrete moral rules like the Ten Commandments. At heart, these are universal principles of *justice*, of the *reciprocity* and *equality* of human *rights*, and of respect for the dignity of human beings as *individual persons* ("From Is to Ought," pp. 164, 165).

Reprinted from *The Journal of Philosophy*, October 25, 1973, by permission.

vanced moral reasoning depends upon advanced logical reasoning; a person's logical stage puts a certain ceiling on the moral stage he can attain. A person whose logical stage is only concrete operational is limited to the preconventional moral stages (Stages 1 and 2). A person whose logical stage is only partially formal operational is limited to the conventional moral stages (Stages 3 and 4). While logical development is necessary for moral development and sets limits to it, most individuals are higher in logical stage than they are in moral stage. As an example, over 50% of late adolescents and adults are capable of full formal reasoning, but only 10% of these adults (all formal operational) display principled (Stages 5 and 6) moral reasoning.

The moral stages are *structures of moral judgment* or *moral reasoning. Structures* of moral judgment must be distinguished from the *content* of moral judgment. As an example, we cite responses to a dilemma used in our various studies to identify moral stage. The dilemma raises the issue of stealing a drug to save a dying woman. The inventor of the drug is selling it for 10 times what it costs him to make it. The woman's husband cannot raise the money, and the seller refuses to lower the price or wait for payment. What should the husband do?

The choice endorsed by a subject (steal, don't steal) is called the *content* of his moral judgment in the situation. His reasoning about the choice defines the structure of his moral judgment. This reasoning centers on the following 10 universal moral values or issues of concern to persons in these moral dilemmas:

1. Punishment
2. Property
3. Roles and concerns of affection
4. Roles and concerns of authority
5. Law
6. Life
7. Liberty
8. Distributive justice
9. Truth
10. Sex

A moral choice involves choosing between two (or more) of these values as they *conflict* in concrete situations of choice.

The stage or structure of a person's moral judgment defines: 1) *what* he finds valuable in each of these moral issues (life, law), i.e., how he defines the value, and 2) *why* he finds it valuable, i.e., the reasons he gives for valuing it. As an example, at Stage 1 life is valued in terms of the power or possessions of the person involved; at Stage 2, for its usefulness in satisfying the needs of the individual in question or others; at Stage 3, in terms of the individual's relations with others and their valuation of him; at Stage 4, in terms of social or religious law. Only at Stages 5 and 6 is each life seen as inherently worthwhile, aside from other considerations.

MORAL JUDGMENT VS. MORAL ACTION

Having clarified the nature of stages of moral *judgment*, we must consider the relation of moral judgment to moral *action*. If logical reasoning is a necessary but not sufficient condition for mature moral judgment, mature moral judgment is a necessary but not sufficient condition for mature moral action. One cannot follow moral principles if one does not understand (or believe in) moral principles. However, one can reason in terms of principles and not live up to these principles. As an example, Richard Krebs and I found that only 15% of students showing some principled thinking cheated as compared to 55% of conventional subjects and 70% of preconventional subjects.[5] Nevertheless, 15% of the principled subjects did cheat, suggesting that factors additional to moral judgment are necessary for principled moral reasoning to be translated into "moral action." Partly, these factors include the situation and its pressures. Partly, what happens depends upon the individual's motives and emotions. Partly, what the individual does depends upon a general sense of will, purpose, or "ego strength." As an example of the role of will or ego strength in moral behavior, we may cite the study by Krebs: Slightly more than half of his conventional subjects cheated. These subjects were also divided by a measure of attention/will. Only 26% of the "strong-willed" conventional subjects cheated; however, 74% of the "weak-willed" subjects cheated.

If maturity of moral reasoning is only one factor in moral behavior, why does the cognitive–

developmental approach to moral education focus so heavily upon moral reasoning? For the following reasons:

1. Moral judgment, while only one factor in moral behavior, is the single most important or influential factor yet discovered in moral behavior.

2. While other factors influence moral behavior, moral judgment is the only distinctively *moral* factor in moral behavior. To illustrate, we noted that the Krebs study indicated that "strong-willed" conventional stage subjects resisted cheating more than "weak-willed" subjects. For those at a preconventional level of moral reasoning, however, "will" had an opposite effect. "Strong-willed" Stages 1 and 2 subjects cheated more, not less than "weak-willed" subjects, i.e., they had the "courage of their (amoral) convictions" that it was worthwhile to cheat. "Will," then, is an important factor in moral behavior, but it is not distinctively moral; it becomes moral only when informed by mature moral judgment.

3. Moral judgment change is long-range or irreversible; a higher stage is never lost. Moral behavior as such is largely situational and reversible or "loseable" in new situations.

II. AIMS OF MORAL AND CIVIC EDUCATION

Moral psychology describes what moral development is, as studied empirically. Moral education must also consider moral philosophy, which strives to tell us what moral development ideally *ought to be*. Psychology finds an invariant sequence of moral stages; moral philosophy must be invoked to answer whether a later stage is a better stage. The "stage" of senescence and death follows the "stage" of adulthood, but that does not mean that senescence and death are better. Our claim that the latest or principled stages of moral reasoning are morally better stages, then, must rest on considerations of moral philosophy.

The tradition of moral philosophy to which we appeal is the liberal or rational tradition, in particular the "formalistic" or "deontological" tradition running from Immanuel Kant to John Rawls.[6] Central to this tradition is the claim that an ade-

quate morality is *principled*, i.e., that it makes judgments in terms of *universal* principles applicable to all mankind. *Principles* are to be distinguished from *rules*. Conventional morality is grounded on rules, primarily "thou shalt nots" such as are represented by the Ten Commandments, prescriptions of kinds of actions. Principles are, rather, universal guides to making a moral decision. An example is Kant's "categorical imperative," formulated in two ways. The first is the maxim of respect for human personality, "Act always toward the other as an end, not as a means." The second is the maxim of universalization, "Choose only as you would be willing to have everyone choose in your situation." Principles like that of Kant's state the formal conditions of a moral choice or action. In the dilemma in which a woman is dying because a druggist refuses to release his drug for less than the stated price, the druggist is not acting morally, though he is not violating the ordinary moral rules (he is not actually stealing or murdering). But he is violating principles: He is treating the woman simply as a means to his ends of profit, and he is not choosing as he would wish anyone to choose (if the druggist were in the dying woman's place, he would not want a druggist to choose as he is choosing). Under most circumstances, choice in terms of conventional moral rules and choice in terms of principles coincide. Ordinarily, principles dictate not stealing (avoiding stealing is implied by acting in terms of a regard for others as ends and in terms of what one would want everyone to do). In a situation where stealing is the only means to save a life, however, principles contradict the ordinary rules and would dictate stealing. Unlike rules which are supported by social authority, principles are freely chosen by the individual because of their intrinsic moral validity.*

The conception that a moral choice is a choice made in terms of moral principles is related to the claim of liberal moral philosophy that moral principles are ultimately principles of justice. In essence, moral conflicts are conflicts between the claims of persons, and principles for resolving these claims are principles of justice, "for giving each his due." Central to justice are the demands of *liberty*,

---

* Not all freely chosen values or rules are principles, however. Hitler chose the "rule," "exterminate the enemies of the Aryan race," but such a rule is not a universalizable principle.

equality, and *reciprocity.* At every moral stage, there is a concern for justice. The most damning statement a school child can make about a teacher is that "he's not fair." At each higher stage, however, the conception of justice is reorganized. At Stage 1, justice is punishing the bad in terms of "an eye for an eye and a tooth for a tooth." At Stage 2, it is exchanging favors and goods in an equal manner. At Stages 3 and 4, it is treating people as they desire in terms of the conventional rules. At Stage 5, it is recognized that all rules and laws flow from justice, from a social contract between the governors and the governed designed to protect the equal rights of all. At Stage 6, personally chosen moral principles are also principles of justice, the principles any member of a society would choose for that society if he did not know what his position was to be in the society and in which he might be the least advantaged.[7] Principles chosen from this point of view are, first, the maximum liberty compatible with the like liberty of others and, second, no inequalities of goods and respect which are not to the benefit of all, including the least advantaged

As an example of stage progression in the orientation to justice, we may take judgments about capital punishment.[8] Capital punishment is only firmly rejected at the two principled stages, when the notion of justice as vengeance or retribution is abandoned. At the sixth stage, capital punishment is not condoned even if it may have some useful deterrent effect in promoting law and order. This is because it is not a punishment we would choose for a society if we assumed we had as much chance of being born into the position of a criminal or murderer as being born into the position of a law abider.

Why are decisions based on universal principles of justice better decisions? Because they are decisions on which all moral men could agree. When decisions are based on conventional moral rules, men will disagree, since they adhere to conflicting systems of rules dependent on culture and social position. Throughout history men have killed one another in the name of conflicting moral rules and values, most recently in Vietnam and the Middle East. Truly moral or just resolutions of conflicts require principles which are, or can be, universalizable.

ALTERNATIVE APPROACHES

We have given a philosophic rationale for stage advance as the aim of moral education. Given this rationale, the developmental approach to moral education can avoid the problems inherent in the other two major approaches to moral education. The first alternative approach is that of indoctrinative moral education, the preaching and imposition of the rules and values of the teacher and his culture on the child. In America, when this indoctrinative approach has been developed in a systematic manner, it has usually been termed "character education."

Moral values, in the character education approach, are preached or taught in terms of what may be called the "bag of virtues." In the classic studies of character by Hugh Hartshorne and Mark May, the virtues chosen were honesty, service, and self-control.[9] It is easy to get superficial consensus on such a bag of virtues—until one examines in detail the list of virtues involved and the details of their definition. Is the Hartshorne and May bag more adequate than the Boy Scout bag (a Scout should be honest, loyal, reverent, clean, brave, etc.)? When one turns to the details of defining each virtue, one finds equal uncertainty or difficulty in reaching consensus. Does honesty mean one should not steal to save a life? Does it mean that a student should not help another student with his homework?

Character education and other forms of indoctrinative moral education have aimed at teaching universal values (it is assumed that honesty or service are desirable traits for all men in all societies), but the detailed definitions used are relative; they are defined by the opinions of the teacher and the conventional culture and rest on the authority of the teacher for their justification. In this sense character education is close to the unreflective valuings by teachers which constitute the hidden curriculum of the school.* Because of the current unpopularity of indoctrinative approaches to moral

---

* As an example of the "hidden curriculum," we may cite a second-grade classroom. My son came home from this classroom one day saying he did not want to be "one of the bad boys." Asked "Who are the bad boys?" he replied, "The ones who don't put their books back and get yelled at."

education, a family of approaches called "values clarification" has become appealing to teachers. Values clarification takes the first step implied by a rational approach to moral education: the eliciting of the child's own judgment or opinion about issues or situations in which values conflict, rather than imposing the teacher's opinion on him. Values clarification, however, does not attempt to go further than eliciting awareness of values; it is assumed that becoming more self-aware about one's values is an end in itself. Fundamentally, the definition of the end of values education as self-awareness derives from a belief in ethical relativity held by many value-clarifiers. As stated by Peter Engel, "One must contrast value clarification and value inculcation. Value clarification implies the principle that in the consideration of values there is no single correct answer." Within these premises of "no correct answer," children are to discuss moral dilemmas in such a way as to reveal different values and discuss their value differences with each other. The teacher is to stress that "our values are different," not that one value is more adequate than others. If this program is systematically followed, students will themselves become relativists, believing there is no "right" moral answer. For instance, a student caught cheating might argue that he did nothing wrong, since his own hierarchy of values, which may be different from that of the teacher, made it right for him to cheat.

Like values clarification, the cognitive-developmental approach to moral education stresses open or Socratic peer discussion of value dilemmas. Such discussion, however, has an aim: stimulation of movement to the next stage of moral reasoning. Like values clarification, the developmental approach opposes indoctrination. Stimulation of movement to the next stage of reasoning is not indoctrinative, for the following reasons:

1. Change is in the way of reasoning rather than in the particular beliefs involved.

2. Students in a class are at different stages; the aim is to aid movement of each to the next stage, not convergence on a common pattern.

3. The teacher's own opinion is neither stressed nor invoked as authoritative. It enters in only as one of many opinions, hopefully one of those at a next higher stage.

4. The notion that some judgments are more adequate than others is communicated. Fundamentally, however, this means that the student is encouraged to articulate a position which seems most adequate to him and to judge the adequacy of the reasoning of others.

In addition to having more definite aims than values clarification, the moral development approach restricts value education to that which is moral or, more specifically, to justice. This is for two reasons. First, it is not clear that the whole realm of personal, political, and religious values is a realm which is nonrelative, i.e., in which there are universals and a direction of development. Second, it is not clear that the public school has a right or mandate to develop values in general.* In our view, value education in the public schools should be restricted to that which the school has the right and mandate to develop: an awareness of justice, or of the rights of others in our Constitutional system. While the Bill of Rights prohibits the teaching of religious beliefs, or of specific value systems, it does not prohibit the teaching of the awareness of rights and principles of justice fundamental to the Constitution itself.

When moral education is recognized as centered in justice and differentiated from value education or affective education, it becomes apparent that moral and civic education are much the same thing. This equation, taken for granted by the classic philosophers of education from Plato and Aristotle to Dewey, is basic to our claim that a concern for moral education is central to the educational objectives of social studies.

The term *civic education* is used to refer to social studies as more than the study of the facts and concepts of social science, history, and civics. It is education for the analytic understanding, value

---

* Restriction of deliberate value education to the moral may be clarified by our example of the second-grade teacher who made tidying up of books a matter of moral indoctrination. Tidiness is a value, but it is not a moral value. Cheating is a moral issue, intrinsically one of fairness. It involves issues of violation of trust and taking advantage. Failing to tidy the room may under certain conditions be an issue of fairness, when it puts an undue burden on others. If it is handled by the teacher as a matter of cooperation among the group in this sense, it is a legitimate focus of deliberate moral education. If it is not, it simply represents the arbitrary imposition of the teacher's values on the child.

principles, and motivation necessary for a citizen in a democracy if democracy is to be an effective process. It is political education. Civic or political education means the stimulation of development of more advanced patterns of reasoning about political and social decisions and their implementation in action. These patterns are patterns of moral reasoning. Our studies show that reasoning and decision making about political decisions are directly derivative of broader patterns of moral reasoning and decision making. We have interviewed high school and college students about concrete political situations involving laws to govern open housing, civil disobedience for peace in Vietnam, free press rights to publish what might disturb national order, and distribution of income through taxation. We find that reasoning on these political decisions can be classified according to moral stage and that an individual's stage on political dilemmas is at the same level as on nonpolitical moral dilemmas (euthanasia, violating authority to maintain trust in a family, stealing a drug to save one's dying wife). Turning from reasoning to action, similar findings are obtained. In 1963 a study was made of those who sat in at the University of California, Berkeley, administration building and those who did not in the Free Speech Movement crisis. Of those at Stage 6, 80% sat in, believing that principles of free speech were being compromised, and that all efforts to compromise and negotiate with the administration had failed. In contrast, only 15% of the conventional (Stage 3 or Stage 4) subjects sat in. (Stage 5 subjects were in between.)*

From a psychological side, then, political development is part of moral development. The same is true from the philosophic side. In the *Republic*, Plato sees political education as part of a broader education for moral justice and finds a rationale for such education in terms of universal philosophic principles rather than the demands of a particular society. More recently, Dewey claims the same.

In historical perspective, America was the first nation whose government was publicly founded on postconventional principles of justice, rather than upon the authority central to conventional moral reasoning. At the time of our founding, postconventional or principled moral and political reasoning was the possession of the minority, as it still is. Today, as in the time of our founding, the majority of our adults are at the conventional level, particularly the "law and order" (fourth) moral stage. (Every few years the Gallup Poll circulates the Bill of Rights unidentified, and every year it is turned down.) The Founding Fathers intuitively understood this without benefit of our elaborate social science research; they constructed a document designing a government which would maintain principles of justice and the rights of man even though principled men were not the men in power. The machinery included checks and balances, the independent judiciary, and freedom of the press. Most recently, this machinery found its use at Watergate. The tragedy of Richard Nixon, as Harry Truman said long ago, was that he never understood the Constitution (a Stage 5 document), but the Constitution understood Richard Nixon.*

Watergate, then, is not some sign of moral decay of the nation, but rather of the fact that understanding and action in support of justice principles are still the possession of a minority of our society. Insofar as there is moral decay, it represents the weakening of conventional morality in the face of social and value conflict today. This can lead the less fortunate adolescent to fixation at the preconventional level, the more fortunate to movement to principles. We find a larger proportion of youths at the principled level today than was the case in their fathers' day, but also a larger proportion at the preconventional level.

Given this state, moral and civic education in the schools becomes a more urgent task. In the high school today, one often hears both preconventional adolescents and those beginning to move beyond convention sounding the same note of disaffection for the school. While our political institutions are

---

* The differential action of the principled subjects was determined by two things. First, they were more likely to judge it right to violate authority by sitting in. But second, they were also in general more consistent in engaging in political action according to their judgment. Ninety percent of all Stage 6 subjects thought it right to sit in, and all 90% lived up to this belief. Among the Stage 4 subjects, 45% thought it right to sit in, but only 33% lived up to this belief by acting.

* No public or private word or deed of Nixon ever rose above Stage 4, the "law and order" stage. His last comments in the White House were of wonderment that the Republican Congress could turn on him after so many Stage 2 exchanges of favors in getting them elected.

in principle Stage 5 (i.e., vehicles for maintaining universal rights through the democratic process), our schools have traditionally been Stage 4 institutions of convention and authority. Today more than ever, democratic schools systematically engaged in civic education are required.

Our approach to moral and civic education relates the study of law and government to the actual creation of a democratic school in which moral dilemmas are discussed and resolved in a manner which will stimulate moral development.

PLANNED MORAL EDUCATION

For many years, moral development was held by psychologists to be primarily a result of family upbringing and family conditions. In particular, conditions of affection and authority in the home were believed to be critical, some balance of warmth and firmness being optimal for moral development. This view arises if morality is conceived as an internalization of the arbitrary rules of parents and culture, since such acceptance must be based on affection and respect for parents as authorities rather than on the rational nature of the rules involved.

Studies of family correlates of moral stage development do not support this internalization view of the conditions for moral development. Instead, they suggest that the conditions for moral development in homes and schools are similar and that the conditions are consistent with cognitive–developmental theory. In the cognitive-developmental view, morality is a natural product of a universal human tendency toward empathy or role taking, toward putting oneself in the shoes of other conscious beings. It is also a product of a universal human concern for justice, for reciprocity or equality in the relation of one person to another. As an example, when my son was 4, he became a morally principled vegetarian and refused to eat meat, resisting all parental persuasion to increase his protein intake. His reason was, "It's bad to kill animals." His moral commitment to vegetarianism was not taught or acquired from parental authority; it was the result of the universal tendency of the young self to project its consciousness and values into other living things, other selves. My son's vegetarianism also involved a sense of justice, re-

vealed when I read him a book about Eskimos in which a real hunting expedition was described. His response was to say, "Daddy, there is one kind of meat I would eat—Eskimo meat. It's all right to eat Eskimos because they eat animals." This natural sense of justice or reciprocity was Stage 1—an eye for an eye, a tooth for a tooth. My son's sense of the value of life was also Stage 1 and involved no differentiation between human personality and physical life. His morality, though Stage 1, was, however, natural and internal. Moral development past Stage 1, then, is not an internalization but the reconstruction of role taking and conceptions of justice toward greater adequacy. These reconstructions occur in order to achieve a better match between the child's own moral structures and the structures of the social and moral situations he confronts. We divide these conditions of match into two kinds: those dealing with moral discussions and communication and those dealing with the total moral environment or atmosphere in which the child lives.

In terms of moral discussion, the important conditions appear to be:

1. Exposure to the next higher stage of reasoning
2. Exposure to situations posing problems and contradictions for the child's current moral structure, leading to dissatisfaction with his current level
3. An atmosphere of interchange and dialogue combining the first two conditions, in which conflicting moral views are compared in an open manner

Studies of families in India and America suggest that morally advanced children have parents at higher stages. Parents expose children to the next higher stage, raising moral issues and engaging in open dialogue or interchange about such issues.[10]

Drawing on this notion of the discussion conditions stimulating advance, Moshe Blatt conducted classroom discussions of conflict-laden hypothetical moral dilemmas with four classes of junior high and high school students for a semester.[11] In each of these classes, students were to be found at three stages. Since the children were not all responding at the same stage, the arguments they used with each other were at different levels. In the course of these discussions among the students, the teacher first supported and clarified those arguments that were one stage above the lowest stage among the children; for example, the teacher supported Stage 3 rather than Stage 2. When it seemed that these arguments were understood by the students, the teacher then challenged that stage, using new situations, and clarified the arguments one stage above the previous one: Stage 4 rather than Stage 3. At the end of the semester, all the students were retested; they showed significant upward change when compared to the controls, and they maintained the change one year later. In the experimental classrooms, from one-fourth to one-half of the students moved up a stage, while there was essentially no change during the course of the experiment in the control group.

Given the Blatt studies showing that moral discussion could raise moral stage, we undertook the next step: to see if teachers could conduct moral discussions in the course of teaching high school social studies with the same results. This step we took in cooperation with Edwin Fenton, who introduced moral dilemmas in his ninth- and eleventh-grade social studies texts. Twenty-four teachers in the Boston and Pittsburgh areas were given some instruction in conducting moral discussions around the dilemmas in the text. About half of the teachers stimulated significant developmental change in their classrooms—upward stage movement of one-quarter to one-half a stage. In control classes using the text but no moral dilemma discussions, the same teachers failed to stimulate any moral change in the students. Moral discussion, then, can be a usable and effective part of the curriculum at any grade level. Working with filmstrip dilemmas produced in cooperation with Guidance Associates, second-grade teachers conducted moral discussions yielding a similar amount of moral stage movement.

Moral discussion and curriculum, however, constitute only one portion of the conditions stimulating moral growth. When we turn to analyzing the broader life environment, we turn to a consideration of the *moral atmosphere* of the home, the school, and the broader society. The first basic dimension of social atmosphere is the role-taking opportunities it provides, the extent to which it encourages the child to take the point of view of others. Role taking is related to the amount of social interaction and social communication in which the child engages, as well as to his sense of efficacy in

influencing attitudes of others. The second dimension of social atmosphere, more strictly moral, is the level of justice of the environment or institution. The justice structure of an institution refers to the perceived rules or principles for distributing rewards, punishments, responsibilities, and privileges among institutional members. This structure may exist or be perceived at any of our moral stages. As an example, a study of a traditional prison revealed that inmates perceived it as Stage 1, regardless of their own level.[12] Obedience to arbitrary command by power figures and punishment for disobedience were seen as the governing justice norms of the prison. A behavior-modification prison using point rewards for conformity was perceived as a Stage 2 system of instrumental exchange. Inmates at Stage 3 or 4 perceived this institution as more fair than the traditional prison, but not as fair in their own terms.

These and other studies suggest that a higher level of institutional justice is a condition for individual development of a higher sense of justice. Working on these premises, Joseph Hickey, Peter Scharf, and I worked with guards and inmates in a women's prison to create a more just community.[13] A social contract was set up in which guards and inmates each had a vote of one and in which rules were made and conflicts resolved through discussions of fairness and a democratic vote in a community meeting. The program has been operating four years and has stimulated moral stage advance in inmates, though it is still too early to draw conclusions as to its overall long-range effectiveness for rehabilitation.

One year ago, Fenton, Ralph Mosher, and I received a grant from the Danforth Foundation (with additional support from the Kennedy Foundation) to make moral education a living matter in two high schools in the Boston area (Cambridge and Brookline) and two in Pittsburgh. The plan had two components. The first was training counselors and social studies and English teachers in conducting moral discussions and making moral discussion an integral part of the curriculum. The second was establishing a just community school within a public high school.

We have stated the theory of the just community high school, postulating that discussing real-life moral situations and actions as issues of fairness and as matters for democratic decision would stimulate advance in both moral reasoning and moral action. A participatory democracy provides more extensive opportunities for role taking and a higher level of perceived institutional justice than does any other social arrangement. Most alternative schools strive to establish a democratic governance, but none we have observed has achieved a vital or viable participatory democracy. Our theory suggested reasons why we might succeed where others failed. First, we felt that democracy had to be a central commitment of a school, rather than a humanitarian frill. Democracy as moral education provides that commitment. Second, democracy in alternative schools often fails because it bores the students. Students prefer to let teachers make decisions about staff, courses, and schedules, rather than to attend lengthy, complicated meetings. Our theory said that the issues a democracy should focus on are issues of morality and fairness. Real issues concerning drugs, stealing, disruptions, and grading are never boring if handled as issues of fairness. Third, our theory told us that if large democratic community meetings were preceded by small-group moral discussion, higher-stage thinking by students would win out in later decisions, avoiding the disasters of mob rule.*

Currently, we can report that the school based on our theory makes democracy work or function where other schools have failed. It is too early to make any claims for its effectiveness in causing moral development, however.

Our Cambridge just community school within the public high school was started after a small summer planning session of volunteer teachers, students, and parents. At the time the school opened in the fall, only a commitment to democracy and a skeleton program of English and social studies had been decided on. The school started with six teachers from the regular school and 60 students, 20 from academic professional homes and 20 from working-class homes. The other 20 were dropouts and troublemakers or petty delinquents in terms of previous record. The usual mistakes and usual chaos of a beginning alternative school ensued. Within a few weeks, however, a successful democratic community process had been established. Rules were made around pressing issues: disturbances, drugs, hooking. A student discipline committee or jury was formed. The resulting rules and enforcement have been relatively effective and reasonable. We do not see reasonable rules as ends in themselves, however, but as vehicles for moral discussion and an emerging sense of community. This sense of community and a resulting morale are perhaps the most immediate signs of success. This sense of community seems to lead to behavior change of a positive sort. An example is a 15-year-old student who started as one of the greatest combinations of humor, aggression, light-fingeredness, and hyperactivity I have ever known. From being the principal disturber of all community meetings, he has become an excellent community meeting participant and occasional chairman. He is still more ready to enforce rules for others than to observe them himself, yet his commitment to the school has led to a steady decrease in exotic behavior. In addition, he has become more involved in classes and projects and has begun to listen and ask questions in order to pursue a line of interest.

We attribute such behavior change not only to peer pressure and moral discussion but to the sense of community which has emerged from the democratic process in which angry conflicts are resolved through fairness and community decision. This sense of community is reflected in statements of the students to us that there are no cliques—that the blacks and the whites, the professors' sons and the project students, are friends. These statements are supported by observation. Such a sense of community is needed where students in a given classroom range in reading level from fifth-grade to college.

Fenton, Mosher, the Cambridge and Brookline teachers, and I are now planning a four-year curriculum in English and social studies centering on moral discussion, on role taking and communication, and on relating the government, laws, and justice system of the school to that of the American society and other world societies. This will integrate an intellectual curriculum for a higher level of

---

* An example of the need for small-group discussion comes from an alternative school community meeting called because a pair of the students had stolen the school's video-recorder. The resulting majority decision was that the school should buy back the recorder from the culprits through a fence. The teachers could not accept this decision and returned to a more authoritative approach. I believe if the moral reasoning of students urging this solution had been confronted by students at a higher stage, a different decision would have emerged.

understanding of society with the experiential components of school democracy and moral decision.

There is very little new in this—or in anything else we are doing. Dewey wanted democratic experimental schools for moral and intellectual development 70 years ago. Perhaps Dewey's time has come.

REFERENCES

1. John Dewey, "What Psychology Can Do for the Teacher," in Reginald Archambault, ed., *John Dewey on Education: Selected Writings* (New York: Random House, 1964).

2. Jean Piaget, *The Moral Judgment of the Child*, 2nd ed. (Glencoe, Ill.: Free Press, 1948).

3. Lawrence Kohlberg, "Moral Stages and Moralization: The Cognitive–Developmental Approach," in Thomas Lickona, ed., *Man, Morality, and Society* (New York: Holt, Rinehart, and Winston, in press).

4. James Rest, Elliott Turiel, and Lawrence Kohlberg, "Relations Between Level of Moral Judgment and Preference and Comprehension of the Moral Judgment of Others," *Journal of Personality*, vol. 37, 1969, pp. 225–52, and James Rest, "Comprehension, Preference, and Spontaneous Usage in Moral Judgment," in Lawrence Kohlberg, ed., *Recent Research in Moral Development* (New York: Holt, Rinehart, and Winston, in preparation).

5. Richard Krebs and Lawrence Kohlberg, "Moral Judgment and Ego Controls as Determinants of Resistance to Cheating," in Lawrence Kohlberg, ed., *Recent Research*.

6. John Rawls, *A Theory of Justice* (Cambridge, Mass.: Harvard University Press, 1971).

7. John Rawls, ibid.

8. Lawrence Kohlberg and Donald Elfenbein, "Development of Moral Reasoning and Attitudes Toward Capital Punishment," *American Journal of Orthopsychiatry*, Summer, 1975.

9. Hugh Hartshorne and Mark May, *Studies in the Nature of Character: Studies in Deceit*, vol. 1; *Studies in Service and Self-Control*, vol. 2; *Studies in Organization of Character*, vol. 3 (New York: Macmillan, 1928–30).

10. Bindu Parilch, "A Cross-Cultural Study of Parent-Child Moral Judgment," unpublished doctoral dissertation, Harvard University, 1975.

11. Moshe Blatt and Lawrence Kohlberg, "Effects of Classroom Discussions upon Children's Level of Moral Judgment," in Lawrence Kohlberg, ed., *Recent Research*.

12. Lawrence Kohlberg, Peter Scharf, and Joseph Hickey, "The Justice Structure of the Prison: A Theory and an Intervention," *The Prison Journal*, Autumn–Winter, 1972.

13. Lawrence Kohlberg, Kelsey Kauffman, Peter Scharf, and Joseph Hickey, *The Just Community Approach to Corrections: A Manual, Part I* (Cambridge, Mass.: Education Research Foundation, 1973).

Chapter Three · the nature and nurture of motivation

7

A Theory of Human Motivation

Abraham H. Maslow

EDITOR'S NOTE · Human motivation is an enormously complex phenomenon. Maslow's theory of human motivation does not propose to answer all of the questions related to motivation, but it does show how the intensity and direction of behavior can be influenced by certain basic felt needs. The term "self-actualization" has great currency; at the conclusion of this reading, you may understand better why self-actualization—although it may be an individual's primary motivation—is difficult to attain. As you read, you might consider, "Where am I in the basic hierarchy of needs?"

This chapter is an attempt to formulate a positive theory of motivation that will conform to the known facts, clinical and observational as well as experimental. It derives most directly, however, from clinical experience. This theory is, I think, in the functionalist tradition of James and Dewey, and is fused with the holism of Wertheimer, Goldstein, and Gestalt psychology,

From pp. 35–47, 51–53 of "A Theory of Human Motivation" in *Motivation and Personality*, 2nd edition, by Abraham H. Maslow. Copyright © 1970 by Abraham H. Maslow. Reprinted by permission of Harper & Row, Publishers, Inc. and Bertha G. Maslow.

and with the dynamicism of Freud, Fromm, Horney, Reich, Jung, and Adler. This integration or synthesis may be called a holistic-dynamic theory.

THE BASIC NEEDS

THE PHYSIOLOGICAL NEEDS

The needs that are usually taken as the starting point for motivation theory are the so-called physiological drives. Two recent lines of research make it necessary to revise our customary notions about these needs: first, the development of the concept of homeostasis, and second, the finding that appetites (preferential choice among foods) are a fairly efficient indication of actual needs or lacks in the body.

Homeostasis refers to the body's automatic efforts to maintain a constant, normal state of the bloodstream. Cannon (1) has described this process for (1) the water content of the blood, (2) salt content, (3) sugar content, (4) protein content, (5) fat content, (6) calcium content, (7) oxygen content, (8) constant hydrogen-ion level (acid-base balance), and (9) constant temperature of the blood. Obviously this list could be extended to include other minerals, the hormones, vitamins, etc.

Young (2, 3) has summarized the work on appetite in its relation to body needs. If the body lacks some chemical, the individual will tend (in an imperfect way) to develop a specific appetite or partial hunger for that missing food element.

Thus it seems impossible as well as useless to make any list of fundamental physiological needs, for they can come to almost any number one might wish, depending on the degree of specificity of description. We cannot identify all physiological needs as homeostatic. That sexual desire, sleepiness, sheer activity and exercise, and maternal behavior in animals are homeostatic has not yet been demonstrated. Furthermore, this list would not include the various sensory pleasures (tastes, smells, tickling, stroking), which are probably physiological and which may become the goals of motivated behavior. Nor do we know what to make of the fact that the organism has simultaneously a tendency to inertia, laziness and least effort and *also* a need for activity, stimulation, and excitement.

These physiological drives or needs are to be considered unusual rather than typical because they are isolable, and because they are localizable somatically. That is to say, they are relatively independent of each other, of other motivations, and of the organism as a whole, and second, in many cases, it is possible to demonstrate a localized, underlying somatic base for the drive. This is true less generally than has been thought (exceptions are fatigue, sleepiness, maternal responses) but it is still true in the classic instances of hunger, sex, and thirst.

It should be pointed out again that any of the physiological needs and the consummatory behavior involved with them serve as channels for all sorts of other needs as well. That is to say, the person who thinks he is hungry may actually be seeking more for comfort, or dependence, than for vitamins or proteins. Conversely, it is possible to satisfy the hunger need in part by other activities such as drinking water or smoking cigarettes. In other words, relatively isolable as these physiological needs are, they are not completely so.

Undoubtedly these physiological needs are the most prepotent of all needs. What this means specifically is that in the human being who is missing everything in life in an extreme fashion, it is most likely that the major motivation would be the physiological needs rather than any others. A person who is lacking food, safety, love, and esteem would most probably hunger for food more strongly than for anything else.

If all the needs are unsatisfied, and the organism is then dominated by the physiological needs, all other needs may become simply nonexistent or be pushed into the background. It is then fair to characterize the whole organism by saying simply that it is hungry, for consciousness is almost completely preempted by hunger. All capacities are put into the service of hunger-satisfaction, and the organization of these capacities is almost entirely determined by the one purpose of satisfying hunger.

The receptors and effectors, the intelligence, memory, habits, all may now be defined simply as hunger-gratifying tools. Capacities that are not useful for this purpose lie dormant, or are pushed into the background. The urge to write poetry, the desire to acquire an automobile, the interest in American history, the desire for a new pair of shoes are, in the extreme case, forgotten or become of secondary importance. For the man who is extremely and dangerously hungry, no other interests exist but food. He dreams food, he remembers food, he thinks about food, he emotes only about food, he perceives only food, and he wants only food. The more subtle determinants that ordinarily fuse with the physiological drives in organizing even feeding, drinking, or sexual behavior, may now be so completely overwhelmed as to allow us to speak at this time (but *only* at this time) of pure hunger drive and behavior, with the one unqualified aim of relief.

Another peculiar characteristic of the human organism when it is dominated by a certain need is that the whole philosophy of the future tends also to change. For our chronically and extremely hungry man, Utopia can be defined simply as a place where there is plenty of food. He tends to think that, if only he is guaranteed food for the rest of his life, he will be perfectly happy and will never want anything more. Life itself tends to be defined in terms of eating. Anything else will be defined as unimportant. Freedom, love, community feeling, respect, philosophy, may all be waved aside as fripperies that are useless, since they fail to fill the stomach. Such a man may fairly be said to live by bread alone.

It cannot possibly be denied that such things are true, but their *generality* can be denied. Emergency conditions are, almost by definition, rare in the normally functioning peaceful society. That this truism can be forgotten is attributable mainly to two reasons. First, rats have few motivations other than physiological ones, and since so much of the research upon motivation has been made with these animals, it is easy to carry the rat picture over to the human being. Second, it is too often not realized that culture itself is an adaptive tool, one of whose main functions is to make the physiological emergencies come less and less often. In most of the known societies, chronic extreme hunger of the emergency type is rare, rather than common. In any case, this is still true in the United States. The average American citizen is experiencing appetite rather than hunger when he says, "I am hungry." He is apt to experience sheer life-and-death hunger only by accident and then only a few times through his entire life.

Obviously a good way to obscure the higher motivations, and to get a lopsided view of human capacities and human nature, is to make the organism extremely and chronically hungry or thirsty. Anyone who attempts to make an emergency picture into a typical one, and who will measure all of man's goals and desires by his behavior during extreme physiological deprivation is certainly being blind to many things. It is quite true that man lives by bread alone—when there is no bread. But what happens to man's desires when there *is* plenty of bread and when his belly is chronically filled?

At once other (and higher) needs emerge and these, rather than physiological hungers, dominate the organism. And when these in turn are satisfied, again new (and still higher) needs emerge, and so on. This is what we mean by saying that the basic human needs are organized into a hierarchy of relative prepotency.

One main implication of this phrasing is that gratification becomes as important a concept as deprivation in motivation theory, for it releases the organism from the domination of a relatively more physiological need, permitting thereby the emergence of other more social goals. The physiological needs, along with their partial goals, when chronically gratified cease to exist as active determinants or organizers of behavior. They now exist only in a potential fashion in the sense that they may emerge again to dominate the organism if they are thwarted. But a want that is satisfied is no longer a want. The organism is dominated and its behavior organized only by unsatisfied needs. If hunger is satisfied, it becomes unimportant in the current dynamics of the individual.

This statement is somewhat qualified by a hypothesis to be discussed more fully later, namely, that it is precisely those individuals in whom a certain need has always been satisfied who are best equipped to tolerate deprivation of that need in the future, and that furthermore, those who have been deprived in the past will react differently to current satisfactions than the one who has never been deprived.

THE SAFETY NEEDS

If the physiological needs are relatively well gratified, there then emerges a new set of needs, which we may categorize roughly as the safety needs (security; stability; dependency; protection; freedom from fear, from anxiety and chaos; need for structure, order, law, limits; strength in the protector; and so on). All that has been said to the physiological needs is equally true, although in less degree, of these desires. The organism may equally well be wholly dominated by them. They may serve as the almost exclusive organizers of behavior, recruiting all the capacities of the organism in their service, and we may then fairly describe the whole organism as a safety-seeking mechanism. Again we may say of the receptors, the effectors, of the intellect, and of the other capacities that they are primarily safety-seeking tools. Again, as in the hungry man, we find that the dominating goal is a strong determinant not only of his current world outlook and philosophy but also of his philosophy of the future and of values. Practically everything looks less important than safety and protection (even sometimes the physiological needs, which, being satisfied, are now underestimated). A man in this state, if it is extreme enough and chronic enough, may be characterized as living almost for safety alone.

Although in this chapter we are interested primarily in the needs of the adult, we can approach an understanding of his safety needs perhaps more efficiently by observation of infants and children, in whom these needs are much more simple and obvious. One reason for the clearer appearance of the threat or danger reaction in infants is that they do not inhibit this reaction at all, whereas adults in our society have been taught to inhibit it at all costs. Thus even when adults do feel their safety to be threatened, we may not be able to see this on the surface. Infants will react in a total fashion and as if they were endangered, if they are disturbed or dropped suddenly, startled by loud noises, flashing light, or other unusual sensory stimulation, by rough handling, by general loss of support in the mother's arms, or by inadequate support.*

In infants we can also see a much more direct reaction to bodily illnesses of various kinds. Sometimes these illnesses seem to be immediately and *per se* threatening, and seem to make the child feel unsafe. For instance, vomiting, colic, or other sharp pains seem to make the child look at the whole world in a different way. At such a moment of pain, it may be postulated that, for the child, the whole world suddenly changes from sunniness to darkness, so to speak, and become a place in which anything at all might happen, in which previously stable things have suddenly become unstable. Thus a child who because of some bad food is taken ill may for a day or two develop fear, nightmares, and a need for protection and reassurance never seen in him before his illness. The recent work on the psychological effects of surgery on children demonstrates this richly (4).

Another indication of the child's need for safety is his preference for some kind of undisrupted routine or rhythm. He seems to want a predictable, lawful, orderly world. For instance, injustice, unfairness, or inconsistency in the parents seems to make a child feel anxious and unsafe. This attitude may be not so much because of the injustice *per se* or any particular pains involved, but rather because this treatment threatens to make the world look unreliable, or unsafe, or unpredictable. Young children seem to thrive better under a system that has at least a skeletal outline of rigidity, in which there is a schedule of a kind, some sort of routine, something that can be counted upon, not only for the present but also far into the future. Child psychologists, teachers, and psychotherapists have found that permissiveness within limits, rather than unrestricted permissiveness is preferred as well as *needed* by children. Perhaps one could express this more accurately by saying that the child needs an organized and structured world rather than an unorganized or unstructured one.

The central role of the parents and the normal family setup are indisputable. Quarreling, physical assault, separation, divorce, or death within the family may be particularly terrifying. Also parental outbursts of rage or threats of punishment directed to the child, calling him names, speaking to him harshly, handling him roughly, or actual physical punishment sometimes elicit such total panic and terror that we must assume more is involved than the physical pain alone. While it is true that in some children this terror may represent also a fear of loss of parental love, it can also occur in completely rejected children, who seem to cling to the hating parents more for sheer safety and protection than because of hope of love.

Confronting the average child with new, unfamiliar, strange, unmanageable stimuli or situations will too frequently elicit the danger or terror reaction, as for example, getting lost or even being separated from the parents for a short time, being confronted with new faces, new situations, or new tasks, the sight of strange, unfamiliar, or uncontrollable objects, illness, or death. Particularly at such times, the child's frantic clinging to his parents is eloquent testimony to their role as protectors (quite apart from their roles as food givers and lover givers).*

From these and similar observations, we may generalize and say that the average child and, less obviously, the average adult in our society generally prefers a safe, orderly, predictable, lawful, organized world, which he can count on and in which unexpected, unmanageable, chaotic, or other dangerous things do not happen, and in which, in any case, he has powerful parents or protectors who shield him from harm.

That these reactions may so easily be observed in children is in a way proof that children in our society feel too unsafe (or, in a world, are badly brought up). Children who are reared in an un-

---

* As the child grows up, sheer knowledge and familiarity as well as better motor development make these dangers less and less dangerous and more and more manageable. Throughout life it may be said that one of the main conative functions of education is this neutralizing of apparent dangers through knowledge, e.g., I am not afraid of thunder because I know something about it.

* A test battery for safety might be confronting the child with a small exploding firecracker, a bewhiskered face, or a hypodermic injection, having the mother leave the room, putting him upon a high ladder, having a mouse crawl up to him, and so on. Of course I cannot seriously recommend the deliberate use of such tests, for they might very well harm the child being tested. But these and similar situations come up by the score in the child's ordinary day-to-day living and may be observed.

threatening, loving family do *not* ordinarily react as we have described. In such children the danger reactions are apt to come mostly to objects or situations that adults too would consider dangerous.

The healthy and fortunate adult in our culture is largely satisfied in his safety needs. The peaceful, smoothly running, stable, good society ordinarily makes its members feel safe enough from wild animals, extremes of temperature, criminal assault, murder, chaos, tyranny, and so on. Therefore, in a very real sense, he no longer has any safety needs as active motivators. Just as a sated man no longer feels hungry, a safe man no longer feels endangered. If we wish to see these needs directly and clearly we must turn to neurotic or near-neurotic individuals, and to the economic and social underdogs, or else to social chaos, revolution, or breakdown of authority. In between these extremes, we can perceive the expressions of safety needs only in such phenomena as, for instance, the common preference for a job with tenure and protection, the desire for a saving account, and for insurance of various kinds (medical, dental, unemployment, disability, old age).

Other broader aspects of the attempt to seek safety and stability in the world are seen in the very common preference for familiar rather than unfamiliar things (5), or for the known rather than the unknown. The tendency to have some religion or world philosophy that organizes the universe and the men in it into some sort of satisfactorily coherent, meaningful whole is also in part motivated by safety seeking. Here too we may list science and philosophy in general as partially motivated by the safety needs (we shall see later that there are also other motivations to scientific, philosophical, or religious endeavor).

Otherwise the need for safety is seen as an active and dominant mobilizer of the organism's resources only in real emergencies, e.g., war, disease, natural catastrophes, crime waves, societal disorganization, neurosis, brain injury, breakdown of authority, chronically bad situations.

Some neurotic adults in our society are, in many ways, like the unsafe child in their desire for safety, although in the former it takes on a somewhat special appearance. Their reaction is often to unknown, psychological dangers in a world that is perceived to be hostile, overwhelming, and threatening. Such a person behaves as if a great catastrophe were almost always impending, i.e., he is usually responding as if to an emergency. His safety needs often find specific expression in a search for a protector, or a stronger person on whom he may depend, perhaps a Fuehrer.

The neurotic individual may be described with great usefulness as a grown-up person who retains his childhood attitudes toward the world. That is to say, a neurotic adult may be said to behave as if he were actually afraid of a spanking, or of his mother's disapproval, or of being abandoned by his parents, or having his food taken away from him. It is as if his childish attitudes of fear and threat reaction to a dangerous world had gone underground, and untouched by the growing up and learning processes, were now ready to be called out by any stimulus that would make a child feel endangered and threatened.* Horney (6) especially has written well about "basic anxiety."

The neurosis in which the search for safety takes its clearest form is in the compulsive-obsessive neurosis. Compulsive-obsessives try frantically to order and stabilize the world so that no unmanageable, unexpected, or unfamiliar dangers will ever appear. They hedge themselves about with all sorts of ceremonials, rules, and formulas so that every possible contingency may be provided for and so that no new contingencies may appear. They are much like the brain-injured cases, described by Goldstein, who manage to maintain their equilibrium by avoiding everything unfamiliar and strange and by ordering their restricted world in such a neat, disciplined, orderly fashion that everything in the world can be counted on. They try to arrange the world so that anything unexpected (dangers) cannot possibly occur. If, through no fault of their own, something unexpected does occur, they go into a panic reaction as if this unexpected occurrence constituted a grave danger. What we can see only as a none-too-strong preference in the healthy person, e.g., preference for the familiar, becomes a life-and-death necessity in abnormal cases. The healthy taste for the novel and unknown is missing or at a minimum in the average neurotic.

---

* Not all neurotic individuals feel unsafe. Neurosis may have at its core a thwarting of the affection and esteem needs in a person who is generally safe.

The safety needs can become very urgent on the social scene whenever there are real threats to law, to order, to the authority of society. The threat of chaos or of nihilism can be expected in most human beings to produce a regression from any higher needs to the more prepotent safety needs. A common, almost an expectable reaction, is the easier acceptance of dictatorship or of military rule. This tends to be true for all human beings, including healthy ones, since they too will tend to respond to danger with realistic regression to the safety need level, and will prepare to defend themselves. But it seems to be most true of people who are living near the safety line. They are particularly disturbed by threats to authority, to legality, and to the representatives of the law.

THE BELONGINGNESS AND LOVE NEEDS

If both the physiological and the safety needs are fairly well gratified, there will emerge the love and affection and belongingness needs, and the whole cycle already described will repeat itself with this new center. Now the person will feel keenly, as never before, the absence of friends, or a sweetheart, or a wife, or children. He will hunger for affectionate relations with people in general, namely, for a place in his group or family, and he will strive with great intensity to achieve this goal. He will want to attain such a place more than anything else in the world and may even forget that once, when he was hungry, he sneered at love as unreal or unnecessary or unimportant. Now he will feel sharply the pangs of loneliness, of ostracism, of rejection, of friendlessness, of rootlessness.

We have very little scientific information about the belongingness need, although this is a common theme in novels, autobiographies, poems, and plays and also in the newer sociological literature. From these we know in a general way the destructive effects on children of moving too often; of disorientation; of the general over-mobility that is forced by industrialization; of being without roots, or of despising one's roots, one's origins, one's group; of being torn from one's home and family, and friends and neighbors; of being a transient or a newcomer rather than a native. We still underplay the deep importance of the neighborhood, of one's

territory, of one's clan, of one's own "kind," one's class, one's gang, one's familiar working colleagues. I will content myself with recommending a single book that says all this with great poignancy and conviction (7) and that helps us understand our deeply animal tendency to herd, to flock, to join, to belong. Perhaps also, Ardrey's *Territorial Imperative* (8) will help to make all of this conscious. Its very rashness was good for me because it stressed as crucial what I had been only casual about and forced me to think seriously about the matter. Perhaps it will do the same for the reader.

I believe that the tremendous and rapid increase in T-groups and other personal growth groups and intentional communities may in part be motivated by this unsatisfied hunger for contact, for intimacy, for belongingness and by the need to overcome the widespread feelings of alienation, aloneness, strangeness, and loneliness, which have been worsened by our mobility, by the breakdown of traditional groupings, the scattering of families, the generation gap, the steady urbanization and disappearance of village face-to-faceness, and the resulting shallowness of American friendship. My strong impression is also that *some* proportion of youth rebellion groups—I don't know how many or how much—is motivated by the profound hunger for groupiness, for contact, for real togetherness in the face of a common enemy, *any* enemy that can serve to form an amity group simply by posing an external threat. The same kind of thing was observed in groups of soldiers who were pushed into an unwonted brotherliness and intimacy by their common external danger, and who may stick together throughout a lifetime as a consequence. Any good society must satisfy this need, one way or another, if it is to survive and be healthy.

In our society the thwarting of these needs is the most commonly found core in cases of maladjustment and more severe pathology. Love and affection, as well as their possible expression in sexuality, are generally looked upon with ambivalence and are customarily hedged about with many restrictions and inhibitions. Practically all theorists of psychopathology have stressed thwarting of the love needs as basic in the picture of maladjustment. Many clinical studies have therefore been made of this need, and we know more about it perhaps than any of the other needs except the physiological ones. Suttie (9) has written an excellent analysis of our "taboo on tenderness."

One thing that must be stressed at this point is that love is not synonymous with sex. Sex may be studied as a purely physiological need. Ordinarily sexual behavior is multidetermined, that is to say, determined not only by sexual but also by other needs, chief among which are the love and affection needs. Also not to be overlooked is the fact that the love needs involve both giving *and* receiving love.

THE ESTEEM NEEDS

All people in our society (with a few pathological exceptions) have a need or desire for a stable, firmly based, usually high evaluation of themselves, for self-respect, or self-esteem, and for the esteem of others. These needs may therefore be classified into two subsidiary sets. These are, first, the desire for strength, for achievement, for adequacy, for mastery and competence, for confidence in the face of the world, and for independence and freedom.* Second, we have what we may call the desire for reputation or prestige (defining it as respect or esteem from other people), status, fame and glory, dominance, recognition, attention, importance, dignity, or appreciation. These needs have been relatively stressed by Alfred Adler and his followers, and have been relatively neglected by Freud. More and more today, however, there is appearing widespread appreciation of their central importance, among psychoanalysts as well as among clinical psychologists.

Satisfaction of the self-esteem need leads to feelings of self-confidence, worth, strength, capability, and adequacy, of being useful and necessary in the world. But thwarting of these needs produces feelings of inferiority, of weakness, and of helplessness. These feelings in turn give rise to either basic discouragement or else compensatory or neurotic trends. An appreciation of the necessity of basic self-confidence and an understanding of how helpless people are without it can be easily gained from a study of severe traumatic neurosis (10).**

From the theologians' discussion of pride and *hubris*, from the Frommian theories about the self-perception of untruth to one's own nature, from the Rogerian work with self, from essayists like Ayn Rand (16), and from other sources as well, we have been learning more and more of the dangers of basing self-esteem on the opinions of others rather than on real capacity, competence, and adequacy to the task. The most stable and therefore most healthy self-esteem is based on *deserved* respect from others rather than on external fame or celebrity and unwarranted adulation. Even here it is helpful to distinguish the actual competence and achievement that is based on sheer will power, determination and responsibility, from that which comes naturally and easily out of one's own true inner nature, one's constitution, one's biological fate or destiny, or as Horney puts it, out of one's Real Self rather than out of the idealized pseudo-self (17).

THE NEED FOR SELF-ACTUALIZATION

Even if all these needs are satisfied, we may still often (if not always) expect that a new discontent and restlessness will soon develop, unless the individual is doing what *he*, individually, is fitted for. A musician must make music, an artist must paint, a poet must write, if he is to be ultimately at peace with himself. What a man *can* be, he *must* be. He must be true to his own nature. This need we may call self-actualization.

This term, first coined by Kurt Goldstein (18), is being used in this book in a much more specific and limited fashion. It refers to man's desire for self-fulfillment, namely, to the tendency for him to

---

* Whether or not this particular desire is universal we do not know. The crucial question, especially important today, is, Will men who are enslaved and dominated inevitably feel dissatisfied and rebellious? We may assume on the basis of commonly known clinical data that a man who has known true freedom (not paid for by giving up safety and security but rather built on the basis of adequate safety and security) will not willingly or easily allow his freedom to be taken away from him. But we do not know for sure that this is true for the person born into slavery. See discussion of this problem in reference 11.

** For more extensive discussion of normal self-esteem, as well as for reports of various researches, see the bibliography on page 53. Also see the work of McClelland and his co-workers (12, 13, 14). Also (15).

become actualized in what he is potentially. This tendency might be phrased as the desire to become more and more what one idiosyncratically is, to become everything that one is capable of becoming.

The specific form that these needs will take will of course vary greatly from person to person. In one individual it may take the form of the desire to be an ideal mother, in another it may be expressed athletically, and in still another it may be expressed in painting pictures or in inventions.* At this level, individual differences are greatest. . . .

The clear emergence of these needs usually rests upon some prior satisfaction of the psychological, safety, love, and esteem needs.

THE AESTHETIC NEEDS

We know even less about these than about the others, and yet the testimony of history, of the humanities, and of aestheticians forbids us to bypass this uncomfortable (to the scientist) area. I have attempted to study this phenomenon on a clinical–personological basis with selected individuals, and have at least convinced myself that in *some* individuals there is a truly basic aesthetic need. They get sick (in special ways) from ugliness, and are cured by beautiful surroundings; they *crave* actively, and their cravings can be satisfied *only* by beauty (19). It is seen almost universally in healthy children. Some evidence of such an impulse is found in every culture and in every age as far back as the cavemen.

Much overlapping with conative and cognitive needs makes it impossible to separate them sharply. The needs for order, for symmetry, for closure, for completion of the act, for system, and

---

* Clearly creative behavior, like painting, is like any other behavior in having multiple determinants. It may be seen in innately creative people whether they are satisfied or not, happy or unhappy, hungry or sated. Also it is clear that creative activity may be compensatory, ameliorative, or purely economic. It is my impression (from informal experiments) that it is possible to distinguish the artistic and intellectual products of basically satisfied people from those of basically unsatisfied people by inspection alone. In any case, here too we must distinguish, in a dynamic fashion, the overt behavior itself from its various motivations or purposes.

for structure may be indiscriminately assigned to *either* cognitive, conative, or aesthetic, or even to neurotic needs. For myself I have thought of this area of study as a meeting ground for Gestalters and dynamic psychologists. What, for instance, does it mean when a man feels a strong conscious impulse to straighten the crookedly hung picture on the wall?

FURTHER CHARACTERISTICS OF THE BASIC NEEDS

THE DEGREE OF FIXITY OF THE HIERARCHY OF BASIC NEEDS

We have spoken so far as if this hierarchy were a fixed order, but actually it is not nearly so rigid as we may have implied. It is true that most of the people with whom we have worked have seemed to have these basic needs in about the order that has been indicated. However, there have been a number of exceptions.

1. There are some people in whom, for instance, self-esteem seems to be more important than love. This most common reversal in the hierarchy is usually due to the development of the notion that the person who is most likely to be loved is a strong or powerful person, one who inspires respect or fear, and who is self-confident or aggressive. Therefore such people who lack love and seek it may try hard to put on a front of aggressive, confident behavior. But essentially they seek high self-esteem and its behavior expressions more as a means to an end than for its own sake; they seek self-assertion for the sake of love rather than for self-esteem itself.

2. There are other apparently innately creative people in whom the drive to creativeness seems to be more important than any other counterdeterminant. Their creativeness might appear not as self-actualization released by basic satisfaction, but in spite of lack of basic satisfaction.

3. In certain people the level of aspiration may be permanently deadened or lowered. That is to say, the less prepotent goals may simply be lost, and may disappear forever, so that the person who has experienced life at a very low level, i.e., chronic unemployment, may continue to be satisfied for the rest of his life if only he can get enough food.

4. The so-called psychopathic personality is another example of permanent loss of the love needs. These are people who, according to the best data available, have been starved for love in the earliest months of their lives and have simply lost forever the desire and the ability to give and to receive affection (as animals lose sucking or pecking reflexes that are not exercised soon enough after birth).

5. Another cause of reversal of the hierarchy is that when a need has been satisfied for a long time, this need may be underevaluated. People who have never experienced chronic hunger are apt to underestimate its effects and to look upon food as a rather unimportant thing. If they are dominated by a higher need, this higher need will seem to be the most important of all. It then becomes possible, and indeed does actually happen, that they may, for the sake of this higher need, put themselves into the position of being deprived in a more basic need. We may expect that after a long-time deprivation of the more basic need there will be a tendency to reevaluate both needs so that the more prepotent need will actually become consciously prepotent for the individual who may have given it up lightly. Thus a man who has given up his job rather than lose his self-respect, and who then starves for six months or so, may be willing to take his job back even at the price of losing his self-respect.

6. Another partial explanation of *apparent* reversals is seen in the fact that we have been talking about the hierarchy of prepotency in terms of consciously felt wants or desires rather than of behavior. Looking at behavior itself may give us the wrong impression. What we have claimed is that the person will *want* the more basic of two needs when deprived in both. There is no necessary implication here that he will act upon his desires. Let us stress again that there are many determinants of behavior other than the needs and desires.

7. Perhaps more important than all these exceptions are the ones that involve ideals, high social standards, high values, and the like. With such values people become martyrs; they will give up everything for the sake of a particular ideal, or value. These people may be understood, at least in part, by reference to one basic concept (or hypothesis), which may be called increased frustration-tolerance through early gratification. People who have been satisfied in their basic needs throughout their lives, particularly in their earlier years, seem to develop exceptional power to withstand present or future thwarting of these needs simply because they have strong, healthy character structure as a result of basic satisfaction. They are the strong people who can easily weather disagreement or opposition, who can swim against the stream of public opinion, and who can stand up for the truth at great personal cost. It is just the ones who have loved and been well loved, and who have had many deep friendships who can hold out against hatred, rejection, or persecution.

I say all this in spite of the fact that a certain amount of sheer habituation is also involved in any full discussion of frustration tolerance. For instance, it is likely that those persons who have been accustomed to relative starvation for a long time are partially enabled thereby to withstand food deprivation. What sort of balance must be made between these two tendencies, of habituation on the one hand, and of past satisfaction breeding present frustration tolerance on the other hand, remains to be worked out by further research. Meanwhile we may assume that both are operative, side by side, since they do not contradict each other. In respect to this phenomenon of increased frustration tolerance, it seems probable that the most important gratifications come in the first few years of life. That is to say, people who have been made secure and strong in the earliest years, tend to remain secure and strong thereafter in the face of whatever threatens.

REFERENCES

1. Cannon, W. G., *Wisdom of the Body*, New York: Norton, 1932.

2. Young, P. T., "Appetite, palatability and feeding habit: a critical review," *Psychological Bulletin*, 1948, 45, 289–320.

3. Young, P. T., "The experimental analysis of appetite, *Psychological Bulletin*, 1941, 38, 129–164.

4. Levy, D. M., "Psychic trauma of operations in

children, *American Journal of Diseases in Children*, 1945, 69, 7–25.

5. Maslow, A. H., "The influence of familiarization on preference," *Journal of Experimental Psychology*, 1937, 21, 162–180.

6. Horney, K., *The Neurotic Personality of Our Time*, New York: Norton, 1937.

7. Hoggart, R., *The Uses of Literacy*, Boston: Beacon, 1961.

8. Ardrey, R., *The Territorial Imperative*, New York: Atheneum, 1966.

9. Suttie, I., *The Origins of Love and Hate*, New York: Julian Press, 1935.

10. Kardiner, A., *The Traumatic Neuroses of War*, N.Y., Hoeber, 1941.

11. Fromm, E., *Escape from Freedom*, New York: Farrar, Straus and Giroux, 1941.

12. McClelland, D., *The Achieving Society*, New York: Van Nostrand Reinhold, 1961.

13. McClelland, D., *The Roots of Consciousness*, New York: Van Nostrand Reinhold, 1964.

14. McClelland, D., and Winter, D. G., *Motivating Economic Achievement*, New York: Free Press, 1969.

15. White, R., "Motivation reconsidered: the concept of competence," *Psychological Review*, 1959, 66, 297–333.

16. Rand, A., *The Fountainhead*, Indianapolis: Bobbs-Merrill, 1943.

17. Horney, K., *Neurosis and Human Growth*, New York: Norton, 1950.

18. Goldstein, K., *The Organism*, New York: American Book, 1939.

19. Maslow, A. H., "A theory of metamotivation: the biological rooting of the value-life," *Journal of Humanistic Psychology*, 1967, 7, 93–127.

8

Teacher Beliefs and Behaviors That Have a Positive Impact on Student Motivation and Self-Concept

William W. Purkey

EDITOR'S NOTE • Increasing research evidence strongly suggests that what teachers believe about students and how they behave toward students can influence—for better or for worse—both a student's motivation and self-concept. This excellent reading discusses a variety of ways in which teachers can have an impact on motivation through the attitudes they convey and the atmosphere they create. In addition, you will see how a teacher's use of freedom and reflection of respect, control, and warmth contribute to a student's ultimate success and feelings of self-worth. The preceding article by Maslow talked about the nature of motivation; in this reading, you will find some ideas on how to nurture it.

The ways significant others evaluate the student directly affects the student's conception of his academic ability. This in turn

From William W. Purkey, *Self-Concept and School Achievement*, copyright © 1970, pp. 47–56. Reprinted by permission of Prentice-Hall, Inc., Englewood Cliffs, New Jersey.

establishes limits on his success in school. Teachers, in their capacity of significant others, need to view students in essentially positive ways and hold favorable expectations. This is particularly important at the elementary level, but is vital in all grades. Several studies bear directly on the importance of what the teacher believes about students.

Davidson and Lang (1960) found that the student's perceptions of the teacher's feelings toward him correlated positively with his self-perception. Further, the more positive the children's perceptions of their teacher's feelings, the better their academic achievement and the more desirable their classroom behavior as rated by the teacher. Clarke (1960) reported a positive relationship between a student's academic performance and his perception of the academic expectations of him by significant others.

One of the most comprehensive studies of the self concept of ability and school success was that of Brookover and his associates (1965, 1967). Brookover and his associates conducted a six-year study of the relation between the self concept of academic ability and school achievement among students in one school class while in the seventh through the twelfth grades. A major purpose of the study was to determine whether improved self concept results from the expectations and evaluations held by significant others as perceived by the students. As Brookover, Erickson, and Joiner conclude: "The hypothesis that students' perceptions of the evaluations of their academic ability by others (teachers, parents, and friends) are associated with self concepts of academic ability was confirmed" (1967, p. 110). The almost unavoidable conclusion is that the teacher's attitudes and opinions regarding his students have a significant influence on their success in school. In other words, when the teacher believes that his students can achieve, the students appear to be more successful; when the teacher believes that the students cannot achieve, then it influences their performance negatively. This self-fulfilling prophecy has been illuminated by the research of Rosenthal and Jacobson (1968).

The basic hypothesis of Rosenthal and Jacobson's research was that students, more often than not, do what is expected of them. To test this hypothesis, the two researchers conducted an experiment in a public elementary school of 650 students. The elementary-school teachers were told that, on the basis of ability tests administered the previous spring, approximately one-fifth of the students could be expected to evidence significant increases in mental ability during the year. The teachers were then given the names of the high-potential students. Although in fact the names had been *chosen at random* by the experimenters, when intelligence tests and other measures were administered some months later, those identified as potential spurters tended to score significantly higher than the children who had not been so identified. Also, Rosenthal and Jacobson found that these children were later described by their teachers as happier, more curious, more interesting, and as having a better chance of future success than other children. The conclusion drawn by Rosenthal and Jacobson is that the teacher, through his facial expressions, postures, and touch, through what, how, and when he spoke, subtly helped the child to learn. This may have been accomplished, according to the researchers, by modifying the child's self concept, his expectations of his own behavior, and his motivations, as well as his cognitive style. They summarized their study by stating that the evidence suggests strongly that "children who are expected by their teachers to gain intellectually in fact do show greater intellectual gains after one year than do children of whom such gains are not expected" (1968, p. 121). The full educational implications of the self-fulfilling prophecy remain to be explored, but it seems certain that the ways the teacher views the student have a significant influence on the student and his performance.

WHAT THE TEACHER DOES

As we have seen, the key to building positive and realistic self-images in students lies largely in what the teacher *believes* about himself and his students. These beliefs not only determine the teacher's behavior, but are transmitted to the students and influence their performance as well. Yet we cannot ignore what the teacher *does* in the classroom, for the behavior he displays and the experiences he provides, *as perceived by students*, have a strong impact in themselves. In this section we will consider two important aspects of the teacher's role: (1) *the attitudes he conveys;* and (2) *the atmosphere he develops.*

THE ATTITUDE THE
TEACHER CONVEYS

It is difficult to overestimate the need for the teacher to be sensitive to the attitudes he expresses toward students. Even though teachers may have the best intentions, they sometimes project distorted images of themselves. What a person believes can be hidden by negative habits picked up long ago. Therefore, teachers need to ask themselves:

Am I projecting an image that tells the student that I am here to build, rather than to destroy, him as a person? (Spaulding, 1963, reported that there is a significant relationship between a student's positive self concept as reported, and the degree to which teachers are calm, accepting, supportive, and facilitative, and a negative relationship between a student's self concept and teachers who are threatening, grim, and sarcastic.)

Do I let the student know that I am aware of and interested in him as a unique person? (Moustakas, 1966, maintains that every child wants to be known as a unique person, and that by holding the student in esteem, the teacher is establishing an environmental climate that facilitates growth.)

Do I convey my expectations and confidence that the student can accomplish work, can learn, and is competent? (Rosenthal and Jacobson, 1968, have shown that the teacher's expectations have a significant influence on the student's performance.)

Do I provide well-defined standards of values, demands for competence, and guidance toward solutions to problems? (Coopersmith, 1967, has provided evidence that self-reliance is fostered by an environment which is well-structured and reasonably demanding, rather than unlimitedly permissive.)

When working with parents, do I enhance the academic expectations and evaluations which they hold of their children's ability? (Brookover, et al., 1965, has illustrated that this method yields significant results in enhancing self concept and improving academic achievement.)

By my behavior, do I serve as a model of authenticity for the student? (Both Jourard, 1964, and Rogers, 1965, suggest that a most important factor in the helping relationship is the helper serving as a model of genuineness, without "front.")

Do I take every opportunity to establish a high degree of private or semi-private communication with my students? (Spaulding, 1963, found a high relationship between the pupil's self concept and the teacher's behavior when it involved personal and private talks with students.)

The above questions are samples of how the teacher may check himself to see if he is conveying his beliefs in an authentic and meaningful fashion. As Gill reported, teachers' attitudes toward students are vitally important in shaping the self concepts of their students. Gill summarized his study by saying that "teachers should consider self concept as a vital and important aspect of learning and development which the school, through its educational process, should seek to promote and foster in every child" (1969, p. 10).

THE ATMOSPHERE THE
TEACHER CREATES

Six factors seem particularly important in creating a classroom atmosphere conducive to developing favorable self-images in students. These are (1) challenge; (2) freedom; (3) respect; (4) warmth; (5) control; and (6) success. A brief discussion of each of these may be helpful.

Challenge. Because of the focus of this book, little has been said about high standards of academic accomplishment. This omission should not be taken to mean that achievement should be minimized. As we have seen, high academic expectations and a high degree of challenge on the part of teachers have a positive and beneficial effect on students. A good way to create challenge is to wait until the chances of success are good, and then say: "This is hard work, but I think that you can do it." The teacher chooses the right moment to put his trust on the line with students. Of course, an important part of challenge is relevance. If the required learning is relevant to the student's world of experience and has some personal meaning to him, then he is likely to work hard—*if* he feels free to try. This brings us to the question of freedom.

Freedom. It is difficult for self-esteem to grow in an environment where there is little or no freedom of choice. If the student is to grow and develop as an adequate human being, he needs the opportunity to make meaningful decisions for himself. This also means that he must have the freedom to make mistakes, and even to laugh at his inadequacies. Carlton and Moore (1966, 1968) have shown that the freedom of self-directed dramatization improved the reading ability and enhanced the self concept of elementary-school youngsters. This general emphasis on freedom has been highlighted by Moustakas, who wrote: "Self values are in jeopardy in any climate where freedom and choice are denied, in a situation where the individual rejects his own senses and substitutes for his own perceptions the standards and expectations of others" (1966, p. 4ff). When the student has a say in his own development and is given personal decisions to make, he develops faith in his own judgments and thoughts.

Closely related to the notion of freedom of choice is the idea of freedom from threat. Children seem to learn and develop best in an atmosphere characterized by much challenge and little threat. Kowitz has noted, for example, that if the child feels evaluation takes place with "vicious assault upon his self concept" (1967, p. 163), there can be little real freedom. In fact, some students fear failure so much that they avoid achievement whenever they can and, when they cannot, do not try to succeed. In this way, they can avoid the task of trying to achieve. A comprehensive study of the person who fears failure is provided by Birney, Burdick, and Teevan (1969).

What this means to the teacher is that students will learn, provided the material appears to be relevant to their lives and provided they have the freedom to explore and to discover its meaning for themselves. We know that exploration is curtailed in an atmosphere in which one must spend most of his time avoiding or reducing the experience of anxiety brought about by threat to the self. Sarason (1961) has reported that a poor performance by anxious subjects occurred only when the task was presented as a threat. When anxious subjects were told that failure was normal and expected, they actually outperformed subjects who were less anxious. The freedom to try without a tiger springing at you if you fail is essential to a healthy atmosphere in the classroom.

In considering the factors of freedom and challenge, the classroom teacher can ask himself:

> *Do I encourage students to try something new and to join in new activities?*
>
> *Do I allow students to have a voice in planning, and do I permit them to help make the rules they follow?*
>
> *Do I permit students to challenge my opinions?*
>
> *Do I teach in as exciting and interesting a manner as possible?*
>
> *Do I distinguish between students' classroom mistakes and their personal failure?*
>
> *Do I avoid unfair and ruthless competition in the classroom?*

Questions like these can help the teacher evaluate himself and the classroom climate he creates.

Respect. A basic feeling by the teacher for the worth and dignity of students is vital in building self concepts in them. No aspect of education is more important than the feeling on the part of the teacher that the individual student is important, valuable, and *can* learn in school. Sometimes teachers forget the importance of respect and run roughshod over the personal feelings of students. Using both official and unofficial school practices, teachers sometimes lower the feelings of worth of many young people. One of my students told me why he could never get along with his previous English teacher. It was because, although his name is Cribbidge, "She always called me cabbage whenever she called roll, and then laughed." The rule seems to be that whenever we treat a student with respect, we add to his self-respect, and whenever we embarrass or humiliate him, we are likely to build disrespect in him both for himself and for others.

If the teacher genuinely values and respects students, it will be reflected in everything he does. Davidson and Lang (1960) found that when students feel that teachers value and respect them, they are likely to value and respect themselves. Moustakas summed it up this way: "By cherishing and holding the child in absolute esteem, the teacher is establishing an environmental climate that facilitates growth and becoming" (1966, p. 13).

The need for respect is particularly important

in working with culturally disadvantaged students. These are the children whose behavior makes them most difficult to respect, but who probably need respect the most. Teachers must make an extra effort to communicate to these young people a feeling of trust, positive regard, and respect. Closely related to respect is the concept of warmth.

Warmth. There is considerable evidence to support the assumption that a psychologically safe and supportive learning situation encourages students to grow academically as well as in feelings of personal worth. Cogan (1958) reported that students with warm, considerate teachers produced unusual amounts of original poetry and art. Christensen (1960) found the warmth of teachers significantly related to their students' vocabulary and achievement in arithmetic. Reed (1962) concluded that teachers characterized as considerate, understanding, and friendly, and with a tolerance for some release of emotional feeling by students, had a favorable influence on their students' interest in science.

Relating more directly to the task of building favorable self concepts, Spaulding's research (1964) supported the findings of previous investigators regarding positive attitudes toward the self. He found significant correlations between the height of the self concept and the degree to which the teachers in his study were calm, accepting, supportive, and facilitative. It is interesting to note that significant negative correlations with the height of pupils' self concepts were found when teachers were dominating, threatening, and sarcastic.

An important part of warmth is commitment. Teaching has been described as a delicate relationship, almost like a marriage, where, in a sense, the teacher and student belong to each other. The student says "There is *my* teacher" and the teacher says "These are *my* students." The process of commitment is illustrated by the story of the chicken and pig who were walking down a country lane: The chicken excitedly told the portly pig of his latest business idea. "We'll prepare and franchise the best tasting ham n' eggs money can buy, and we'll make a fortune." The pig thought it over for a moment and replied: "It's easy for you to get enthused. For you it's an occupation, but for *me* it means *total* commitment!" Perhaps total commitment is asking too much of teachers, but certainly

they need to feel that their work with students is more than an occupation. A warm and supportive educational atmosphere is one in which each student is made to feel that he belongs in school and that teachers care about what happens to him. It is one in which praise is used in preference to punishment, courtesy in preference to sarcasm, and consultation in preference to dictation.

Some practical questions about respect and warmth which the teacher might ask himself are:

Do I learn the name of each student as soon as possible, and do I use that name often?

Do I share my feelings with my students?

Do I practice courtesy with my students?

Do I arrange some time when I can talk quietly alone with each student?

Do I spread my attention around and include each student, keeping special watch for the student who may need extra attention?

Do I notice and comment favorably on the things that are important to students?

Do I show students who return after being absent that I am happy to have them back in class, and that they were missed?

It is in ways such as these that we tell the student that he is important to us.

Control. Coopersmith (1967) has suggested that children who are brought up in a permissive environment tend to develop less self-esteem than those reared in a firmer and more demanding atmosphere. The assumption that clearly established and relatively firm guidance produces more self-esteem in children can also be applied to the classroom. It is important for the teacher to maintain discipline, for the type of control under which a child lives has considerable effect on his self-image. It is yet another way of telling the student that the teacher cares about him and what he does. Classroom control does not require ridicule and embarrassment. The secret seems to be in the leadership qualities of the teacher. When he is prepared for class, keeps on top of the work and avoids the appearance of confusion, explains why some things must be done, and strives for consistency, politeness, and firmness, then classroom control is likely to be maintained. When punishment is unavoidable (and often it *can* be avoided), then it is best to withdraw the student's privileges. Of course, this means that teachers must be sure that there *are* some privileges in school which can be withdrawn. Poor control procedures would include punishing the entire class for the transgressions of a few, using corporal punishment, or using school work as punishment.

In considering classroom control, teachers might ask themselves:

Do I remember to see small disciplinary problems as understandable, and not as personal insults?

Do I avoid having "favorites" and "victims"?

Do I have, and do my students have, a clear idea of what is and what is not acceptable in my class?

Within my limits, is there room for students to be active and natural?

Do I make sure that I am adequately prepared for class each day?

Do I usually make it through the day without punishing students?

Questions such as these help the teacher to estimate his ability to handle students in a way which maintains discipline and, at the same time, builds positive and realistic self concepts in students.

Some teachers believe that warmth and firmness are in opposition to each other, but this is not so. Warmth is more than the obvious display of affection; it is also expressed by firmness which says to the student, "You are important to me and I care about the ways in which you behave."

Success. Perhaps the single most important step that teachers can take in the classroom is to provide an educational atmosphere of success rather than failure. Reviewing over a dozen experiments, Wylie (1961) made the tentative statement that students are likely to change their self-evaluations after experimentally induced success or failure. This statement has been echoed in more recent studies. Costello (1964) found that over-all, regardless of the task or the ability of the students, praise produces more improvement in performance than blame. Ludwig and Maehr (1967) showed that the

approval of significant others caused an increase in self-ratings and an increased preference for activities connected with the criterion task, and that disapproval resulted in a lowered self-rating and a decreased preference for related activities. Moreover, the reaction to the evaluation was followed by a spread of effect, from the areas directly approved by the significant others to related areas of self-regard.

A number of writers have pointed out some of the steps involved in giving honest experiences of success. Page's (1958) research showed that pupils' performance improved significantly when teachers wrote encouraging comments on their written work. A control group, given conventional grades without comment, lost ground. Walsh (1956) explains that it is helpful to show students that they have mastered even the smallest step, rather than vaguely saying "That's nice" about everything.

The sensitive teacher points out areas of accomplishment, rather than focusing on mistakes. Continuing awareness of failure results in lowered expectations, not learning. According to Combs and Snygg (1959) a positive view is learned from the ways people treat the learner. People learn that they are able, not from failure but from success. Questions about success which the teacher might ask himself when he thinks about success experiences for students include:

Do I permit my students some opportunity to make mistakes without penalty?

Do I make generally positive comments on written work?

Do I give extra support and encouragement to slower students?

Do I recognize the successes of students in terms of what they did earlier?

Do I take special opportunities to praise students for their successes?

Do I manufacture honest experiences of success for my students?

Do I set tasks which are, and which appear to the student to be, within his abilities?

What all of this discussion hopes to say to teachers is that a backlog of challenge, freedom, respect, warmth, control, and success develops positive self-images in students and encourages academic achievement. The absence of these factors makes for the person who is crippled psychologically.

REFERENCES

Birney, R. C.; Burdick, H.; and Teevan, R. C. 1969. *Fear of Failure.* Princeton, N.J.: D. Van Nostrand Co., Inc.

Brookover, W. B., *et al.* 1965. *Self-concept of ability and school achievement. II: Improving academic achievement through students' self-concept enhancement.* U.S. Office of Education, Cooperative Research Project NO. 1636. East Lansing: Office of Research and Publications, Michigan State University.

Brookover, W. B.; Erickson, E. L.; and Joiner, L. M. 1967. *Self-concept of ability and school achievement. III: Relationship of self-concept to achievement in high school.* U.S. Office of Education, Cooperative Research Project NO. 2831. East Lansing: Office of Research and Publications, Michigan State University.

Carlton, L., and Moore, R. H. 1966. The effects of self-directive dramatization on reading achievement and self concept of culturally disadvantaged children. *Reading Teacher.* 20: 125–30.

————. 1968. *Reading, self-directive dramatization and self concept.* Columbus, Ohio: Charles E. Merrill Books, Inc.

Christensen, C. M. 1960. Relationships between pupil achievement, pupil affect-need, teacher warmth, and teacher permissiveness. *J. Educ. Psychol.* 51: 169–74.

Clarke, W. E. 1960. The relationship between college academic performance and expectancies. Ph.D. dissertation, Michigan State University.

Cogan, M. 1958. The behavior of teachers and the productive behavior of their pupils. *J. Exptl. Educ.* 27: 89–124.

Combs, A. W., and Syngg, D. 1959. *Individual behavior.* 2nd ed. New York: Harper & Row, Publishers.

Coopersmith, S. 1967. *The antecedents of self-esteem.* San Francisco: W. H. Freeman and Co., Publishers.

Costello, C. G. 1964. Ego involvement, success and failure: A review of the literature. *Experiments in motivation,* ed. H. J. Eysenck, pp. 161–208. New York: The Macmillan Company.

Davidson, H. H., and Lang, G. 1960. Children's perceptions of their teachers' feelings toward them related to self-perception, school achievement, and behavior. *J. Exptl. Educ.* 29: 107–18.

Gill, M. P. February 1969. Pattern of achievement as related to the perceived self. Paper read at the annual meeting of the American Educational Research Assoc. Convention, Los Angeles.

Jourard, S. M. 1964. *The transparent self: Self-disclosure and well-being.* Princeton, N.J.: D. Van Nostrand Co., Inc.

Kowitz, G. T. 1967. Test anxiety and self concept. *Childhd. Educ.* 44: 162–65.

Ludwig, D. J., and Maehr, M. L. 1967. Changes in self-concept and stated behavioral preferences. *Child Developmt.* 38: 453–67.

Moustakas, C. 1966. *The authentic teacher: Sensitivity and awareness in the classroom.* Cambridge, Mass.: Howard A. Doyle Publishing Company.

Page, E. B. 1958. Teacher comments and student performance: A seventy-four classroom experiment in school motivation. *J. Educatl. Psychol.* 49: 173–81.

Reed, H. B. 1962. Implications for science education of a teacher competence research. *Science Educ.* 46: 473–86.

Rogers, C. R. (1965). The therapeutic relationship: Recent theory and research. Reprinted in *The Shaping of Personality,* ed. G. Babladelis and S. Adams. Englewood Cliffs, N.J.: Prentice-Hall, Inc., 1967.

Rosenthal, R., and Jacobson, L. 1968. *Pygmalion in the classroom: Teacher expectation and pupils' intellectual development.* New York: Holt, Rinehart & Winston, Inc.

Sarason, I. G. 1961. The effects of anxiety and threat on the solution of a difficult task. *J. Abn. and Soc. Psychol.* 62: 165–68.

Spaulding, R. L. 1963. Achievement, creativity, and

self concept correlates of teacher-pupil transactions in elementary schools. U.S. Office of Education, Cooperative Research Report NO. 1352. Urbana: University of Illinois.

————. 1964. Achievement, creativity, and self concept correlates of teacher-pupil transactions in elementary schools. In *Readings in child behavior and development*, ed. C. B. Stendler, 2nd ed., pp. 313–18. New York: Harcourt, Brace & World, Inc.

Walsh, A. M. 1956. *Self concepts of bright boys with learning difficulties.* New York: Bureau of Publications, Teachers College, Columbia University.

Wylie, R. C. 1961. *The self-concept: A critical survey of pertinent research literature.* Lincoln: University of Nebraska Press.

9

When Two Rewards Are Worse than One: Effects of Extrinsic Rewards on Intrinsic Motivation

Mark R. Lepper
David Greene

EDITOR'S NOTE · *Common sense and research have taught us that motivation is improved and performance is enhanced when some*

Mark R. Lepper and David Greene, "When Two Rewards Are Worse Than One: Effects of Extrinsic Rewards on Intrinsic Motivation," *Phi Delta Kappan* (April 1975): 565–66. Reprinted by permission.

kind of payoff is offered for doing well. This is the usual way to increase extrinsic *motivation. But what do you suppose happens when students begin a task with high* intrinsic *motivation and are offered explicit extrinsic rewards to complete what they are already interested in? Is it possible that rewarding a student can stifle performance? Intrinsic motivation seems to influence how extrinsic motivators are received. This interesting reading will help you understand how and why this process works the way it does.*

The use of powerful systems of tangible extrinsic rewards to modify and control children's behavior in school settings has increased dramatically in the past decade. Such programs have proved effective in producing marked changes in children's behavior, but relatively little attention has been paid to the effects of these reward systems on children's *intrinsic motivation* in other situations in which the child is not expecting further external rewards. In a series of recent experiments, we studied the effects of offering a child a tangible reward to engage in an initially interesting task on his subsequent intrinsic motivation to engage in that task in the absence of any expectation of external rewards.

The results of these experiments, carried out in preschool and elementary school classrooms, suggest that the use of overly powerful extrinsic rewards can, under certain conditions, actually *undermine* intrinsic motivation. Daryl Bem's self-perception theory partially prompted our interest in this question.[1] If a person undertakes an activity in order to obtain an extrinsic reward, this theory suggests, he may come to view the activity and his engagement in it differently. What was once an end in itself may become merely a means to an end, of little inherent interest in the absence of that end. More formally, the "overjustification" hypothesis examined in these studies suggests that a person's initial intrinsic interest in an activity may be decreased if he is induced to engage in the activity as an explicit means to some extrinsic goal.

To test this hypothesis, we conducted an initial experiment at the Bing Nursery School, located on the Stanford campus.[2] In this study, preschool children were first observed unobtrusively during extended "free-play" periods in their regular classrooms; only children showing an initial intrinsic interest in our particular drawing activity during these baseline observations were selected as subjects. These children were then randomly exposed to one of three experimental treatments, in individual experimental sessions conducted in a room apart from the classroom. In the Expected Award condition, children agreed to engage in the drawing activity in order to obtain an extrinsic reward—a "Good Player Award" certificate adorned with a gold seal and red ribbon—which they received at the end of the session. In the Unexpected Award condition, children engaged in the same activity and received the same reward, but had no knowledge of the reward until after they had finished the activity. In the No Award condition, children neither expected nor received the reward, but otherwise duplicated the drawing experience of children in the other two conditions.

One to two weeks after these sessions, the drawing activity was again introduced during free-play periods in the classroom and measures of intrinsic interest were obtained unobtrusively by observation from behind a one-way mirror. As predicted, subsequent intrinsic interest in the target activity in the classroom—where extrinsic rewards were not expected—was significantly lower for children who had received an expected extrinsic reward than for children receiving the same reward unexpectedly or receiving no tangible reward. In addition, relative to preexperimental baseline measures of classroom interest, children in the Expected Award condition showed a significant decrease in interest while subsequent interest in the other conditions did not change from baseline. Contracting to engage in an initially interesting activity to obtain an external reward, it seemed, had turned "play" into "work." Children who had previously received an expected extrinsic reward were no longer as likely to engage in the target activity when the extrinsic reward was not available.

To assess the reliability and generality of these findings, we performed two additional experiments with other children in the same nursery school setting.[3,4] In these studies, however, we varied the nature of the particular activity, the particular reward, and the contingency employed. In both cases, the results replicated our earlier findings. In the

three studies combined, children receiving unexpected rewards or no rewards were nearly 50% more likely to play with the experimental activity in the classrooms later than children receiving an expected tangible reward for playing with the activity during the experimental sessions.

These three experiments convinced us that the "overjustification" effect we had observed was genuine and of potential practical significance. To determine whether similar effects would appear following more long-term programs in situations such as those in which systematic reward programs are commonly employed, however, required one further study.

In this fourth experiment, we examined the effects on intrinsic motivation of the introduction and subsequent withdrawal of a "token economy" program in ongoing elementary school classrooms.[5] During an initial baseline phase, children's choices among a variety of mathematical teaching materials were monitored. Then, during a three-week treatment phase, extrinsic rewards were introduced. In three experimental groups, children were selectively rewarded for engaging only in certain target activities; in the control group, children were reinforced non-differentially. At the end of this phase, the extrinsic rewards were withdrawn, but the various activities remained available. During this withdrawal phase, to allow the measurement of relative *intrinsic* motivation, no attempt was made to "replace" the withdrawn rewards with social approval or other extrinsic rewards.

The data from this study showed two basic effects. In the treatment phase, when extrinsic rewards were available, children's behavior was controlled by the rewards. All the experimental groups spent more time on their target activities than did the control subjects. By contrast, in the withdrawal phase, when extrinsic rewards were no longer available, two of the three experimental groups spent significantly less time with their target activities than the control subjects, while the third group did not differ from the control group. While the immediate effect of the reward system was positive, the subsequent effect of the reward system on intrinsic motivation was negative, at least for two of the three groups.

Together, these studies seem sufficient to establish that the use of overly powerful extrinsic rewards *can* undermine a child's intrinsic interest in the activities for which he was rewarded. These studies should *not* be seen, however, as suggesting that extrinsic rewards will always, or even usually, undermine intrinsic motivation.

It is important to keep in mind that these studies were specifically designed to allow the demonstration of an "overjustification" effect. In our studies, for example, children began with an intrinsic interest in our target activities. Obviously, when children are rewarded for activities of no initial interest to them, there will be no intrinsic motivation to be lost. Similarly, our studies examined the performance of responses learned previously by the child and did not deal with the learning or acquisition of new skills. When extrinsic rewards are used to promote engagement in activities resulting in the acquisition of new, generalizable skills by the child, however, we would expect the availability of such skills to enhance intrinsic motivation—particularly when some minimal level of competence is necessary to experience the intrinsic satisfactions of complex activities, such as reading or problem solving. Finally, in our studies, the rewards children received did not provide them with additional information concerning their ability at the experimental task. When rewards are used in a manner which provides a child with new information about his ability at a task, leading him to believe that he has been successful and is personally responsible for that success, we would expect his feelings of increased competence to enhance his intrinsic motivation to engage in that task.

The principal implication of our findings, therefore, is *not* that we should always, or even typically, avoid using extrinsic rewards to modify children's behavior. Our analysis does suggest the wisdom of avoiding unnecessarily powerful reward systems when less powerful rewards would be sufficient to bring the desired behavior under control.[6] Since overly powerful rewards are more likely than minimally sufficient rewards to be perceived as the end to which an activity is explicitly directed, we would expect needlessly powerful reward systems to be more likely to produce decrements in subsequent intrinsic interest.

However, the point which deserves greatest emphasis is that we simply cannot evaluate the effects of extrinsic rewards on intrinsic motivation unless we examine behavior in settings where rewards are not expected. To allow informed judgments concerning the relative merits of applied reinforcement programs, research presumed to evaluate these reinforcement programs should include measures capable of assessing intrinsic as well as extrinsic motivation.

REFERENCES

1. Daryl J. Bem, "Self-Perception Theory," in L. Berkowitz, ed., *Advances in Experimental Social Psychology*, vol. 6 (New York: Academic Press, 1972).

2. Mark R. Lepper, David Greene, and Richard E. Nisbett, "Undermining Children's Intrinsic Interest with Extrinsic Rewards: A Test of the 'Overjustification' Hypothesis," *Journal of Personality and Social Psychology*, October, 1973, pp. 129–37.

3. David Greene and Mark R. Lepper, "Effects of Extrinsic Rewards on Children's Subsequent Intrinsic Interest," *Child Development*, December, 1974, pp. 1141–45.

4. Mark R. Lepper and David Greene, "Turning Play into Work: Effects of Adult Surveillance and Extrinsic Rewards on Children's Intrinsic Motivation," *Journal of Personality and Social Psychology*, 1975, in press.

5. David Greene, Betty Sternberg, and Mark R. Lepper, "Overjustification in a Token Economy: Immediate and Subsequent Effects of Differential Rewards on Intrinsic Motivation," unpublished manuscript (Carnegie-Mellon University: Pittsburgh, 1975).

6. K. Daniel O'Leary, Ronald Drabman, and Ruth E. Kass, "Maintenance of Appropriate Behavior in a Token Program," *Journal of Abnormal Child Psychology*, April, 1973, pp. 127–38.

10

Praise as a Motivational Tool: Negative Aspects, Positive Functions, and Suggestions for Using It in Healthy Ways

Richard E. Farson

EDITOR'S NOTE • Praise is an enormously powerful and complex expression of external reinforcement or recognition. We use it and receive it frequently. How do people react when they receive praise? What is your usual reaction? Can you handle praise comfortably or do you respond with red-skinned embarrassment? Have you ever wondered why praise turns some on and others off? Consider the ideas here carefully. You may reconsider what you think praise does for people and perhaps use it a bit more selectively. And maybe accept it better, too.

I am beginning to question the cherished idea that people enjoy being praised. I realize that I am in unfriendly territory because praise is perhaps the most widely used and thoroughly endorsed of all human relations techniques. Parents, businessmen, psychologists, teach-

Richard E. Farson, "Praise Reappraised," *Harvard Business Review* (September–October 1963). Copyright © 1963 by the President and Fellows of Harvard College. All rights reserved. Reprinted by permission. This article originally appeared under the title, "Praise Reappraised."

ers—everyone seems to believe in its value as a motivational tool, a reward, a way to establish good relationships.

But I wonder if praise accomplishes just what we think it does. Not that it does not have valuable functions (of which we are largely unaware), but I will bet our beliefs about its *value* are erroneous.

With considerable trepidation let me tentatively suggest:

Praise is not only of limited and questionable value as a motivator, but may in fact be experienced as threatening.

Rather than functioning as a bridge between people, it may actually serve to establish distance between them.

Instead of reassuring a person as to his worth, praise may be an unconscious means of establishing the superiority of the praiser.

Praise may constrict creativity rather than free it.

Rather than opening the way to further contact, praise may be a means of terminating it.

Although we may be fooling ourselves as to what praise accomplishes, some of its functions—such as maintaining distance, terminating contacts, establishing status or superiority—are in fact quite necessary and socially useful, even though we may prefer not to acknowledge these hidden benefits.

DEFINITION

What is praise? We are all quick to distinguish praise from flattery, which has connotations of insincerity and expediency. For my purpose here, praise is any statement that makes a *positive* evaluation of an object, person, act, or event, and that contains very little supplementary information —for instance:

"Nice work, you've done a fine job."
"You're a good boy."
"That painting of yours is excellent."

These are examples of praise—positive evaluations with little additional meaning.

On the other hand, a positive evaluation *plus* other information is not essentially, or merely, praise. A statement such as "The reason I think you've done such a good job . . ." or "How did you get that beautiful effect with ink alone?" invites a response and extends the encounter. Obviously such statements are more than praise and have different qualities and perhaps different results.

A simple definition or a simple analysis of praise is, of course, not possible. One must take into account the situation in which praise occurs, the history of the relationship one has with the other person, the attitudes that underlie the act of praise, and the motivations for it. Also, specific acts and techniques can never overcome the effects of one's basic attitudes toward others. Good relationships are dependent on good fundamental attitudes. And a good relationship can withstand many difficulties—even such difficulties as are brought on by praise.

NEGATIVE ASPECTS

What are the problems with praise?

First of all, the findings of scientific experiments on praise do not clearly demonstrate its value. Most of the studies done on this subject have compared praise with reproof or blame as motivational techniques. The results of these studies are mixed: in some cases praise was slightly more effective than reproof; in others, reproof was more effective than praise. In essence, all that can really be concluded from most research is that *some* response motivates people better than no response at all.

It has been demonstrated in psychological laboratories that we can shape human behavior by the use of rewards—symbols such as lights and bells which indicate that the subject is making correct responses or is gaining the approval of judges. But in the extremely complex situations of real life does praise work the same way? Does praise reward? After considerable observation I have come to the conclusion that it usually does not.

Watch people responding to praise. Don't they usually seem to be reacting with discomfort, uneasiness, and defensiveness? I have noted that a very common response is a vague denial or derogation:

"I really can't take the credit for it."
"You're just saying that."
"Well, *we* like it."
"It was just luck."

"I like yours, too."
"Well, I do the best I can."

The only element these statements have in common is that they are all defensive reactions—efforts to cope with a difficult situation. Praise a house or garden and its owner hastens to point out its defects; praise an employee for a project and he is quick to play down his role in it. Under the stress of praise, some people often become uncomfortable, almost to the point of imitating the toe-digging reactions of small children. Apparently praise is something to be coped with, to be handled.

REASONS FOR DEFENSIVENESS

Why do people react to praise with defensiveness? Part of the reason may be that in praise there *is* threat—something one must defend against. After all, praise is an evaluation, and to be evaluated usually makes us uncomfortable. If we are weighed, we *may* be found wanting.

Most of us feel uncomfortable when we are negatively evaluated, so we tend to believe that positive evaluations should have the opposite effect, that they should be enhancing. Really, though, praise has many of the same basic problems and characteristics as do negative evaluations. Research indicates that *any* evaluation is likely to make people uncomfortable, defensive. Perhaps this is because, when you evaluate a person, you are often in some way trying to motivate him, to move him in a certain direction, to *change* him. Now while he himself may want to change, and while he may not like the person that he *is*, at the same time he is that person; his identity is very important, indeed essential, because it makes possible an answer to the question "Who am I?" Bad or good he must hold onto his identity. For this reason, the threat of change is one of the most fundamental and disquieting of psychological threats. So even though praise may only imply that one should change a bit in the direction one is already going, it *does* imply change, and therefore it may be almost as threatening as a negative evaluation.

Another reason why positive evaluation is discomforting lies in the fact that when a person praises us, it is clear that he is sitting in judgment. We become uneasy when we know someone is not only trying to change us but is continually judging us, grading us. In this situation, the absence of praise is especially threatening because we know that we are still being evaluated.

Often the change which praise asks one to make is not necessarily beneficial to the person being praised but will redound to the convenience, pleasure, or profit of the praiser. When we praise Tommy for making it to the bathroom in time, we are probably not so much delighted on Tommy's behalf as on our own; the change that complicated Tommy's life will make our own more convenient and pleasant. Much the same is true when we praise a salesman for neat call reports. Understandably, people feel threatened when they are being manipulated for another's benefit.

Our enthusiastic belief that praise is pleasing to people has resulted in its becoming a piece of psychological candy. We sugarcoat blame with praise, or use the "sandwich technique" whereby praise is followed by reproof, then again by praise. "I'm very pleased with your work, Fred," says the boss, "you're really getting the work out, *but...*" Fred then gets the unhappy part of the story, the reprimand. The boss finishes up with "Keep up the fine work," and Fred is shuttled out without quite knowing what hit him. This is also a favorite technique of parents and teachers. In fact, we have become so conditioned by its use from early childhood that when we are praised, we automatically get ready for the shock, the reproof.

Undoubtedly, the most threatening aspect of praise is the obligation it puts on us to be praiseworthy people. If we accept praise, if we really believe the best about ourselves, then we are under an obligation to behave accordingly. This is deeply frightening to us. For if we really believe it when we are told that we are competent, or intelligent, or beautiful, then we are continually on the spot to be competent, or intelligent, or beautiful, not only in the eyes of the person who praised us but, even worse, in our own eyes. The responsibility to be continually at our best, to live up to our talents and abilities, is perhaps our most difficult problem in living—and we naturally defend against it.

ISSUE OF CREDIBILITY

It may be that there simply is no effective response to praise given in a face-to-face situation. Even saying "thank you" is not entirely satisfactory—although it may be the least defensive way of coping with the behavioral impasse which praise uniformly produces. Perhaps this is one reason why written praise may be somewhat easier to accept. We can savor it without having to invent a modest response.

Of course, part of the problem hinges on the issue of credibility. Can we really believe what the praiser seems to want us to believe? Written praise may be more credible and therefore more rewarding to us. It most certainly is when we discover a praising remark about us written in a letter not intended for us to see. But part of credibility comes from within us. Are we psychologically prepared to accept the validity of comments which indicate our value? If you tell a person who strongly believes himself to be inadequate that he is in your opinion entirely adequate, then your statement is likely to be met with some resistance. The credibility of the praising remark has been determined by the person's internal needs to see himself in consistent ways.

POSITIVE FUNCTIONS

If praise is threatening to people for so many reasons, then why do we use it so often? Surely we do not want to retain in our repertoire responses that do not serve us in some functional way. What are the functions of praise? Why is it a conversational staple?

For one thing, people expect praise. We fish for compliments, subtly or openly. Why do we do this, if we don't really like praise? Probably because it is so important for each of us to feel valued by others. We hope that praise will make us feel that way. Sometimes it does. But because praise means so many things and exists in such complicated motivational contexts, its ability to reward us and indicate our value is questionable. Still, we invite it at the same time that we resist it. Perhaps in our other-directed society we have become so dependent on the approval of others that we must continually check just to make sure that we are not being devaluated.

For another thing, giving praise is easy to do. It makes conversation, and most of us have not enough energy, interest, or imagination to offer witty retorts, penetrating criticism, brilliant insights, or sensitive responses. We really do not want the burden of conversation to be that heavy anyway. Gross evaluations, like praise, are simpler and less demanding.

Then, too, praise, as we have seen, is a way of gaining status over another by establishing the fact that one is capable of sitting in judgment. Status is important to all of us, and though the person being evaluated may feel that the praise is threatening or diminishing, the praiser himself has increased his psychological size or, if he praises an inferior, has claimed or reinforced his status. It is interesting to note here that when the work of a high-status person is praised by a low-status person, this is often seen as presumptuous or even insulting. If a layman should tell Picasso, "You're a very good painter," he is not likely to be particularly well received. In order to be acceptable, he must give the praise in a way that respects the status difference.

Praise is also useful in maintaining the interpersonal distance. We talk a good deal about wanting to be close to people, but when you come right down to it, there really are very few people whom we want to be close to, or whom we admit to closeness with us. It is necessary to be able to maintain distance from people, to keep a little free space around ourselves—psychological elbowroom—especially in a society which fills our daily lives with so many contacts. In the search for techniques to establish distance between ourselves and others we find that praise is one of the most effective, simply because, when we evaluate people, we are not likely to gain emotional proximity to them. Compare the effects of praise with other behaviors—for instance, listening to another or revealing your feelings to another, and see for yourself if praise doesn't tend to hold off, to separate, while the other behaviors tend to include, to embrace.

CONTROL OF RELATIONSHIPS

Praise also helps to keep relatively stable patterns of relationship between people. If organizations are to function smoothly, it is probably quite important that certain hierarchies or structures be maintained.

How does praise work toward this end? Let's take as an example a problem-solving committee meeting that includes the executive vice president at one end of the hierarchy and a new junior assistant at the other.

If the assistant comes up with the brightest and most useful idea, some way must be found to accept it without lowering the status of the vice president in the eyes of the group, thereby disturbing the group's stability. Intuitively, the vice president may say to the young assistant, "That's a very good idea, young man." This not-so-simple act of praise has greased the whole situation. Status has been maintained (because as we remember, praise is a way of claiming status); the young man has been reminded of his place in the hierarchy; and the group is restored to comfortable equilibrium. Now the group can use the young man's idea without upsetting its psychological structure.

I am amazed to note how frequently we use praise as a sign that a conversation or interview is over. Listen and discover for yourself how many interpersonal transactions are ended with a positive evaluation. "It's good to talk with you" means "I've finished talking with you." And "You're doing fine; keep up the good work" communicates as well as any exit cue we have. For the busy parents to say to a child who has just offered her latest artistic creation, "Yes, Janie, that's a beautiful painting" may not better the relationship, but it will probably end the conversation. It is often tantamount to saying, "Go away; I'm busy right now." But of course we must have ways of doing just this, and praise is a very effective method.

So we see that by enabling us to terminate an encounter, by enabling us to keep a certain amount of psychological space between ourselves and others, by enabling us to maintain status—in short, to control our relationships—praise functions as one of the most important means by which we maintain consistent structure and equilibrium in any organization.

A HELPFUL ALTERNATIVE

It is when we want to develop initiative, creativity, judgment, and problem-solving ability in people that praise fails us most. To liberate these qualities in people we need to rely on internal motivation. We need to make people feel that they are free of our control. We *may* need to establish a more equalitarian atmosphere, and sometimes we need to create a closeness with superiors. But if praise produces status differences, not equality; if it creates distance, not closeness; if it is felt as a threat, not as a reassurance; then how do you establish a free, accepting, yet close relationship that will encourage independent judgment, effective decisions, and creative actions?

There is much that is unknown about this, but from a variety of settings including psychotherapy, education, and business we are learning that perhaps the most important aspects of a helpful relationship are a person's ability to be *honest* and to *listen*. This sounds simple enough, but these behaviors are very seldom displayed in our relations with others.

BEING HONEST

This does not mean being brutally frank; it means showing some of yourself to another person, transparently exhibiting some of your own feelings and attitudes. This is not easy because from early childhood we have learned to play roles which mask our feelings, as if being honest about them would only hurt others and destroy relationships. Actually, it is the other way around; we mask our feelings so that we will not have too many close—and possibly burdensome—relationships. The inevitable consequence of exposing and sharing feelings is emotional closeness. But closeness, as rewarding as it sometimes can be, is often uncomfortable, unpredictable. Masking our feelings may result in some alienation and anxiety but also in a lot of superficial psychological comfort.

Hiding our feelings and playing roles help to make situations predictable. We want to know what we and other people are going to do and say. We want behavior to be patterned and familiar, not continually spontaneous and varied. Maybe this is necessary in order to have a society at all. Perhaps there is a limit to the amount of spontaneity, emotionality, honesty, and variation that can be tolerated by any social system.

Curiously, we are no more honest about the positive, loving feelings we have than about our feelings of annoyance, mistrust, resentment, or boredom. As a matter of fact, negative feelings usually are less difficult to express honestly than are positive feelings. For some reason it is easier for most people to be honest about their feelings of anger than it is for them to be honest about their feelings of caring and love. In either case, the times when one can risk vulnerability are perhaps life's richest moments—but are not often psychologically comfortable moments.

EMPATHIC LISTENING

The other response which we find helpful in creating close relationships is to listen. This does not merely mean to wait for a person to finish talking, but to try to see how the world looks to this person and to communicate this understanding to him. This empathic non-evaluative listening responds to the person's feelings as well as to his words; that is, to the total meaning of what he is trying to say. It implies no evaluation, no judgment, no agreement (or disagreement). It simply conveys an understanding of what the person is feeling and attempting to communicate; and his feelings and ideas are accepted as being valid for him, if not for the listener.

One reason we do not listen more, of course, is because it is too difficult. To see how difficult it is, try establishing in any group discussion the ground rule that no one may present his own view until he has first satisfied the person who has just spoken that he fully comprehends what this person meant to communicate. That is, he must restate in his own words the total meaning of the message and obtain the person's agreement that this was indeed his message—that accurate listening did take place. In doing this we will find out that—

> It is extremely difficult to get one person to agree that he meant what another thought he meant;
>
> We usually fail in our attempts to understand;
>
> We typically spend our listening time preparing what we are going to say;
>
> When we do listen intently, we have a hard time remembering what it was that we were going to say, and when we do remember, we discover that it is a little off the subject;
>
> Most argument and emotionality goes out of such a discussion;
>
> After a few minutes of this sort of "complete communication" we become rather weary.

It is also difficult to listen because if we allow ourselves to see the world through another's eyes and to fully understand his point of view, then we run the risk of changing ourselves, our own point of view. And, as previously indicated, change is something we try to avoid.

But at times when we *do* want to develop creativity and self-confidence in others, when we *do* want to establish a close relationship in which the other person feels free "to be himself," then expressing our own feelings honestly and listening sensitively may be far more helpful than offering praise.

TRY AN EXPERIMENT

If you doubt the effects of praise outlined here, you might experiment a bit with it. Check for yourself. The next time you praise someone, see what sort of reaction you get:

Does he open up or does he become defensive, diffident, or uncomfortable?

Does he appear to want to continue talking or to terminate the talk?

Does he seem to be more motivated to work or does he seem less motivated?

Then check yourself, too:

How do *you* feel when you receive praise?

What do *you* do and say in response to it?

How do *you* feel when you give praise?

What are *you* trying to accomplish by it?

Another experiment, perhaps even more telling, is to accept the praise offered to you just as it seems to be intended. That is, the next time some praise comes your way indicating that the praiser wants you to believe that you are competent, or good, or smart, or attractive, show him that you accept this evaluation of you by saying something like, "I guess you think I'm very competent" or "You must think I'm a pretty good salesman." His reactions to this may indicate to you that his praise was intended to do much more than just convey that simple idea.

Let me sum up this way: It is questionable that praise is a fuel which motivates and stimulates people. On the other hand, praise is very useful indeed as a lubricant that keeps the wheels going around smoothly and predictably; we must have techniques like praise to keep our human relations in equilibrium.

Perhaps someday we will be able to look inward for evaluation rather than outward, to tolerate less order and equilibrium in our social organizations, and to enjoy increasing emotional closeness with greater numbers of people. But until that day praise will probably continue to serve us well in ways we seldom recognize.

Chapter Four · growth of intelligence and creative expression

11

Intelligence: A Genetic Gift or a Learned Skill?

Arthur Whimbey

EDITOR'S NOTE · The controversy about whether environment or heredity contributes most to intelligence rages on. Dr. Whimbey takes a look at both sides of this issue in an effort to put both sides in focus. Is intelligence largely a skill that can be learned through appropriate pedagogical methods? Or is it primarily determined by genetic makeup and beyond the scope of educational efforts? Do you feel that your intelligence is fixed and immutable, or can it be modified by experience? Is intelligence a genetic gift or a learned skill?

A radical redefinition of intelligence is emerging from a growing number of studies that regard the specific capabilities measured by IQ tests as an important, but trainable, pattern of intellectual skills. These studies lead to the conclusion that IQ tests do not measure innate intellectual capacity, but rather a group of learned skills that can be taught in the classroom or in the home. Specifically, they measure the learned ability to

Arthur Whimbey, "Something Better Than Binet?" *Saturday Review*, June 1, 1974, pp. 264–67. Copyright © 1974 by the Saturday Review. Reprinted by permission.

form relationships with verbal and symbolic concepts.

Five and a half years ago, Arthur R. Jensen rocked the educational world with his scholarly study of race and intelligence in the *Harvard Educational Review*, in which he concluded that blacks are intellectually inferior to whites and that the difference between the races is overwhelmingly due to genetic factors. Therefore, he asserted, compensatory educational programs are bound to fail, and minority children who have inherited low intelligence can never master the standard academic curriculum.

Jensen's study touched off a new round in a controversy that has simmered ever since modern intelligence testing began in 1904, when Alfred Binet, Parisian minister of education, was charged with the construction of a test to separate slow learners from other pupils so that they could be placed in special remedial classes. The debate over the relative importance of genetic and environmental factors in determining intelligence has been heated and sometimes acrimonious, but conclusive evidence has proved elusive. The new studies suggest, however, that while genetic factors may influence the development and expression of intelligence, the extent of this influence depends upon the environment in which a child is raised.

Nevertheless, it is important to recognize that children do come to school with varying IQs—that they do differ, as Jensen points out, in "the ability to learn the traditional scholastic subjects." Only by recognizing this can the new methods of training intelligence be further developed and incorporated into school programs so that all pupils will have a more nearly equal chance for academic success and later professional advancement.

The researchers who have developed programs for training intelligence typically have begun with an analysis of the errors and thinking difficulties of students with low academic aptitude. Two such descriptions are notably thorough and revealing. Carl Bereiter's and Siegfried Engelmann's book, *Teaching Disadvantaged Children in the Preschool*, analyzes the lack of scholastic readiness that slum youngsters bring to elementary school, which, in turn, is responsible for their spiraling deficiencies in reading and arithmetic as they advance through the grades. Benjamin Bloom's and Lois Broder's *The Problem-Solving Process of College Students* focuses on the inappropriate "mental habits" of low-aptitude college students. What is most interesting about the two studies is that although they treat opposite extremes on the educational continuum, they present almost identical pictures of the thinking patterns characterizing low-ability students.

With both pre-schoolers and young adults, poor comprehension and reasoning ability may be traced to three principal causes: (1) inadequate attention to the details of the problem to be solved, (2) inadequate utilization of prior knowledge that would help in solving the problem, and (3) absence of sequential, step-by-step analysis of the relationships among the ideas involved. These three thinking characteristics are, of course, interrelated, but it has proved useful to distinguish among them in understanding the nature of low academic aptitude and in guiding the improvement of low-aptitude students.

Both Bereiter/Engelmann and Bloom/Broder found a distinct set of personality differences between high- and low-aptitude students closely tied to these cognitive failings. Bloom and Broder note that low-aptitude students are "inclined to take the view that in solving problems, reasoning is of little value and that either one knows the answer to a problem at once or one does not." Similarly, Bereiter and Engelmann observe: "Faced with problems that could be dealt with by a 'one-shot' approach, these students were able to perform adequately, but when faced with complex problems that could not be solved except by a sequence of steps, such students would brood a while and then say, 'I don't know the answer to that one.' Answers either had to be grasped at once, or they were inaccessible."

The problem-solving approach of low-aptitude college students is illustrated by their responses to intelligence test items (see box). Consider the figural-reasoning item. In the case of one student of very low aptitude with whom I worked, the instruction to compare the first two figures was not sufficient; he had to be explicitly asked to count the lines before answering, "Two less lines." Then, when asked to compare the next two figures, he quickly replied, "Two less lines," although in this step only one line was deleted. Moreover, when he finished the last comparison, he didn't review the series carefully to form an encompassing rule—one that would have allowed him to select the correct answer. Instead, he jumped quickly to one of the wrong answers.

On the verbal-reasoning item, low-IQ students, being unskilled in sequential analysis, pick an answer that is not based on a sufficiently detailed consideration of the relationships involved. *Foot* might be chosen as an answer, on the "reasoning" that elbow and shoulder are parts of the arm, while knee and foot belong to the leg. Or the alternative *ankle* might be selected because it is a joint, in keeping with elbow, shoulder, and knee.

Several low-aptitude students whom I tested were unable to answer the "Grace Plumbuster" reading-comprehension question. The sentence basically requires that each point be clarified so that it can contribute to the interpretation of the ideas that follow. A high-aptitude student does this so automatically that he is hardly aware of his own mental activities. Only when he meets with an especially intricate or confusing series of ideas does his sequential sorting become "intentional" and conscious. However, to the low-aptitude student the pattern of gradual, sequential reconstruction of an author's meaning is foreign.

Several researchers have pointed out the basic difference between the approach of cognitive therapy and that of Project Head Start. Head Start is founded on the theory that broad perceptual enrichment—clay molding, painting, experience with a wide range of toys, friendly social exchanges, field trips—will compensate for the cultural disadvantages of underprivileged children and will stimulate their academic thinking ability. Cognitive therapy, on the other hand, sees certain types of parent–child verbal interactions as the crucial advantage provided by middle-class homes. To a much greater extent in middle-class, than in lower-class, homes, verbal exchanges explain causes of events, ask and answer questions, point to perceptual discriminations, classify objects by function or other significant characteristics—and, in general, form the basis of academic readiness when the child enters school. Lacking such home background, culturally disadvantaged pre-schoolers need direct training in thinking and in language skills more urgently than they need broad perceptual enrichment.

The Bereiter and Engelmann pre-school program illustrates the general characteristics of the direct-training approach to stimulating intelligence. The pre-school class consists of fifteen four-year-old children and three teachers, bringing the pupil-teacher ratio to a low five-to-one. Each teacher has a specialty area: language (with the emphasis on verbal reasoning rather than on expression), reading, or arithmetic. The class splits into three groups, which go into separate rooms for instruction in one of the three areas. The groups periodically change rooms so that each child receives instruction in all three areas every day. Teaching sessions are twenty minutes long and are distributed over two hours—with intervening periods for lunch, singing, reading, and story discussion.

Analytical reasoning and sequential deduction is taught with a variety of problem tasks. For example, a lesson in *if–then* reasoning begins by placing five squares on the blackboard—two big white ones, one small white one, and two small red ones. The children then learn to draw correct conclusions of the following type:

If a square is red, it is _____. (little)
If a square is big, it is _____. (white)
If a square is little, it is _____. (white or red)
If a square is *not* white, it is _____. (little)

Subsequently, *if–then*s in everyday situations are demonstrated.

Ideas such as these are presented gradually. The teacher continually asks questions to ensure that she has the children's attention and that they are learning. Occasionally a question is directed at one particular child; but for the most part the children answer in unison, thereby drawing them all into the lesson. In addition to teaching general thinking ability, the respective classes teach specific content material in arithmetic and reading.

A battery of standardized tests has evaluated the effectiveness of the program. Bereiter reports that in four recent replications of the project, IQ gains have averaged fifteen points. Moreover, on the wide-range achievement test, the children score

WHAT DO IQ TESTS MEASURE?

These IQ test questions illustrate three different expressions of the reasoning ability which is called academic intelligence:

Test Item 1. Figural Reasoning

Instructions: The first four figures below change in a systematic manner according to some rule. Your task is to discover the rule and choose from among the alternatives the figure that should occur next in the series.

I.   II.   III.   IV.

Alternatives

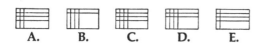

A.   B.   C.   D.   E.

Test Item 2. Verbal Reasoning

Elbow is to Shoulder as Knee is to _____.
(A) Foot   (B) Ankle   (C) Hip   (D) Wrist

Test Item 3. Reading Comprehension

If a serious literary critic were to write a favorable, full-length review of *How Could I Tell Mother She Frightened My Boyfriends Away*, Grace Plumbuster's new story, his startled readers would assume either that he had gone mad or that Grace Plumbuster was HIS editor's wife.
To whom does the capitalized "HIS" (third word from the end) refer?

approximately a year above their age norms in reading and arithmetic. Without pre-school training, such underprivileged children generally fall significantly below the national norms.

The Milwaukee Project, under the directorship of Rick Heber, is another noteworthy experiment in compensatory education. It has probably continued over a longer period of time than any other intelligence-training study ever undertaken, and, not surprisingly, it has produced the most dramatic gains in IQ.

The project began with a survey of the IQs of schoolchildren in a section of Milwaukee that had the lowest family income, poorest housing, and highest index of overcrowding. Maternal IQ was found to be a factor of primary importance—the lower a mother's IQ, the lower her child's IQ tended to be. Repeated home visits made by the researchers, however, convinced them that this maternal influence on IQ was not necessarily hereditary. Instead, they observed that low-IQ mothers create a distinct verbal-social environment that appears to be responsible for the perpetuation of low intelligence.

In 1966 the Infant Education Center was established so that it could be seen whether this slum-related form of low mental ability could be prevented. Forty mothers whose IQs were less than 75, and who were, for the most part, illiterate, participated on a voluntary basis. The newborn infants of one-half of the mothers were selected for the experimental group, while the remainder served as a control group. Teachers visited the infants of the experimental group for several hours a day shortly after they had been brought home from the hospital, until they were about three months old. After that, the mothers took their children to the center. Each child received a wide variety of stimulation (designed to develop perceptual, motor, and language abilities) from an adult on a one-to-one basis, until he was two years old. The mother, in turn, was invited into a program of instruction in homemaking and baby-care skills, and vocational training.

At two years of age, the child was placed in a class with five other youngsters and three teachers; by age four the class size was increased to eight; and at age five the class size rose to eleven. The program ran from 9:00 A.M. to 4:00 P.M., Monday through Friday. Basically, the training was similar to that used by Bereiter and Engelmann. However,

the smaller student–teacher ratio and the greater amount of teacher time (in terms of both hours per day and duration of the program) allowed for more personal attention, a broader range of thinking exercises and academic topics, and more freedom in instructional format.

The children were tested regularly so that the effects of the training could be evaluated. On various measures of academic and cognitive abilities, the experimental group greatly outscored the control group, which has been left to mature in the slum environment. Specifically in the most recent testing, at the age of five and a half years, the mean IQ of the experimentals was 124, whereas the control group's mean was thirty points lower. In fact, some of the experimental children registered IQs as high as 135; this is especially remarkable when contrasted with their mothers' IQs of less than 75.

Heber is reserved in commenting on just how successful the compensatory program has been in affecting long-term behavior. The Wisconsin group will continue to collect test data on the children for a number of years. However, Heber does point out that it is hard to imagine these children ever backsliding to the academic deficiency typically found among children raised by low-IQ mothers in low-income homes.

The procedure directed at improving the academic-thinking skills of older students, developed by Bloom and Broder, illustrates the three primary features of cognitive therapy: (1) demonstrate to the student the mental processes of analytical thinking, (2) require extensive response from the student during problem solving so that his thinking can be monitored, and (3) provide feedback and correction of the student's thinking.

Bloom and Broder began by asking high-aptitude students to think aloud while solving academic-reasoning problems. These introspective reports were designated "model solutions" and were employed in the training program. The actual training was conducted on an individual basis with under-achieving university students who volunteered for the remedial program.

The trainee was told that problem solving is a skill much like playing tennis or golf and that the remedial program was designed to teach this skill. Training began with the trainee's being required to think aloud while attempting to solve a reasoning problem. His solution to the problem was reviewed and discussed, and then the pattern of a model's solution to the problem was read. Subsequently, the trainee was asked to make a list of the differences between his solution and that of the model. The instructor emphasized that the trainee should look for differences that occurred regularly, rather than those that were unique to individual problems. In a short time the student was able to compile a list of the differences between his solution and the model's solution to a problem.

In the sessions that followed, the time was divided between practice in acquiring the approach used by the model and comparison and analysis of solutions. During practice the student thought aloud as he solved problems, he frequently referred to the list he had made of differences between his solution and the model's, and he tried to apply general principles derived from the list. The instructor continually reminded him to evaluate his approach and to consider the steps he thought the model would take with the problem at hand.

No standardized tests of academic aptitude or IQ were used in evaluating the effects of the training. Bloom's and Broder's primary interest was raising academic achievement through the improvement of thinking skills, and so scholastic grades were taken as the criterion of success. Comparison with various control groups indicated that grades on comprehensive examinations did increase to a statistically significant degree, and students, who were originally failing and on probation, were able to continue in college. In a slightly modified replication of the experiment, improvement was found to be directly related to time spent in training. Those students who attended many training sessions made the greatest gains in academic grades; those who attended only a few sessions, little or none.

Intelligence tests have been widely and profitably used for some seventy years; nevertheless, the precise definition of intelligence remains stubbornly elusive. The recent intelligence-training studies have focused on the mental patterns that distinguish high-IQ pupils from low-IQ pupils and have given educators new insights regarding the nature of intelligence. Moreover, the picture of intelligence obtained from these studies agrees well with the definition of intelligence suggested by Binet, who saw intelligence as composed of perception and the active mental reconstruction of events and relationships in the external world.

The intelligence-training studies have taught students to perceive all elements of a problem accurately and then take the necessary steps to effect an analysis and mental reconstruction of the relationships among the elements. This view of intelligence as an information-processing skill is undoubtedly only one dimension of a complete theory of intelligence. Quite likely there are neurological correlates of skilled thinking, and analyses of intelligence that focus on such neurological mechanisms will contribute additional perspectives to our understanding. (It is noteworthy that training can affect such neurological functions as the Alpha pattern.) Nevertheless, this conception summarizes the common core of mental activities that the cognitive therapy studies have focused on —the mental activities that distinguish the successful reasoning of persons of high IQ from what Bereiter and Engelmann call the one-shot thinking of persons of low IQ.

Viewing intelligence as a skill does not preclude the possibility that genetic factors may influence its development and expression. However, the question of whether genetic factors produce IQ differences— either within a race or between races—is really of only secondary interest to educators. The primary question is what can be accomplished through education. If pedagogical methods can be found that allow all people to assume a productive role in our literate-technical culture, then genetic differences become largely irrelevant.

Jensen focuses on this primary question when he contends that programs of compensatory education are doomed to failure because they cannot counteract the overwhelming influence that genetics has on intelligence. However, the evidence appears not to bear him out. The intelligence-training studies—only a small sample of which have been cited here—stand as a strong counter-argument. Many children must be taught by the schools *how* to comprehend, analyze, and integrate academic and technical materials. Appropriate learning-to-learn instructional methods are being developed and tested in a number of experimental programs. When perfected for incorporation into the entire educational system, these methods may give all children an equal chance for academic and professional success, irrespective of social-class and home background.

12

Intelligence: Why It Grows, Why It Declines

John L. Horn

EDITOR'S NOTE • Intelligence is made up of different kinds of primary mental abilities. Research shows that there are also different types of intelligence associated with these primary abilities. In this interesting and informative article, you will find examples of types of intelligence and their relationship to learning and to age. Does intelligence stop developing beyond a certain age? Does learning become more difficult as one grows older? How true is the old myth that says you can't teach an old dog new tricks? This article will help you answer these questions.

One of the oldest and most thoroughly studied concepts in psychology is the concept of intelligence. Yet the term "intelligence" still escapes precise definition. There are so many different kinds of behavior that are indicative of intelligence that identifying the essence of them all has seemed virtually impossible. However, some recent research indicates that much of the diversity seen in expressions of intelligence can be understood in terms of a relatively small number of concepts.

Published by permission of Transaction, Inc., from *Transaction*, Volume 5, #1. Copyright © 1967 by Transaction, Inc.

What's more, this research has also given us insight into understanding where intelligence originates; how it develops; and why and when it increases or decreases.

Studies of the interrelationships among human abilities indicate that there are two basic types of intelligence: *fluid* intelligence and *crystallized* intelligence. Fluid intelligence is rather formless; it is relatively independent of education and experience; and it can "flow into" a wide variety of intellectual activities. Crystallized intelligence, on the other hand, is a precipitate out of experience. It results when fluid intelligence is "mixed" with what can be called "the intelligence of the culture." Crystallized intelligence increases with a person's experience, and with the education that provides new methods and perspectives for dealing with that experience.

These two major kinds of intelligence are composed of more elementary abilities, called "primary" mental abilities. The number of these primaries is small. Only about 30 can be accepted as really well-established. But with just these 30 primaries, we can explain much of the person-to-person variation commonly observed in reasoning, thinking, problem-solving, inventing, and understanding. Since several thousand tests have been devised to measure various aspects of intelligence, this system of primaries represents a very considerable achievement in parsimony. In much the same way that the chemical elements are organized according to the Periodic Law, these primary mental abilities fall into the patterns labeled fluid and crystallized intelligence.

FLUID INTELLIGENCE

What follows are some examples of the kinds of abilities that define fluid intelligence—and some of the tests that measure this kind of intelligence.

Induction is the ability to discover a general rule from several particular incidents and then apply this rule to cover a new incident.

For example, if a person observes the characteristics of a number of people who are members of a particular club or lodge, he might discover the rule by which membership is determined (even when this rule is highly secret information). He might then apply this rule to obtain an invitation to membership!

Among the tests that measure induction ability is the letter series. Given some letters in a series like

ACFJO

the task is to provide the next letter. Of course, the test can be used only with people who know the alphabet, and this rules out illiterates and most children. We can't eliminate the influence of accumulated learning from even the purest examples of fluid intelligence.

Figural Relations refers to the ability to notice changes or differences in shapes and use this awareness to identify or produce one element missing from a pattern [*see* Figure 1].

An everyday example of intelligence in figural relations is the ability to navigate cloverleaf and expressway turnoff patterns—an ability that may mean as much for adequate adjustment today as skill in finding one's way through a virgin forest had in the days of Daniel Boone. This ability also has ready application in interior decorating and in jobs where maps (or aerial views) must be compared a good deal—as by cartographers, navigators, pilots, meteorologists, and tourists.

Span of Apprehension is the ability to recognize and retain awareness of the immediate environment. A simple test is memory span: Several digits or other symbols are presented briefly, and the task is to reproduce them later, perhaps in reverse order. Without this ability, remembering a telephone number long enough to dial it would be impossible.

Other primary abilities that help define fluid intelligence include:

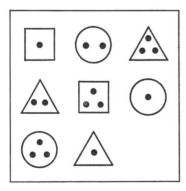

FIGURE 1. What figure fits into the lower right? (Answer: A square with two dots.)

General Reasoning (example: estimating how long it would take to do several errands around town);

Semantic Relations (example: enjoying a pun on common words);

Deductive Reasoning, or the ability to reason from the general to the particular (example: noting that the wood of fallen trees rots and concluding that one should cover—for example, paint—wooden fence posts before inserting them into the ground);

Associative Memory, or the ability to aid memory by observing the relationships between separate items (example: remembering the way to grandmother's house by associating various landmarks en route, or remembering the traits of different people by association with their faces).

CRYSTALLIZED INTELLIGENCE

Most of what we call intelligence—for example, the ability to make good use of language or to solve complex technical problems—is actually crystallized intelligence. Here are some of the primary abilities that demonstrate the nature of this kind of intelligence:

Verbal Comprehension could also be called general information, since it represents a broad slice of knowledge. Vocabulary tests, current-events tests, and reading-comprehension tests all measure verbal comprehension, as do other tests that require a person to recall information about his culture. The ability is rather fully exercised when one quickly reads an article like this one and grasps the essential ideas. Verbal comprehension is also called for when a person reads news items about foreign affairs, understands their implications, and relates them to one another and to their historical backgrounds.

Experiential Evaluation is often called "common sense" or "social intelligence." Experiential evaluation includes the ability to project oneself into situations, to feel as other people feel and thereby better understand interactions among people. Everyday examples include figuring out why a conscientious foreman is not getting good results from those under him, and why people disobey traffic laws more at some intersections than at others.

One test that measures experiential evaluation in married men is the following:

> Your wife has just invested time, effort, and money in a new hairdo. But it doesn't help her appearance at all. She wants your opinion. You should:
>
> 1. try to pretend that the hairdo is great;
> 2. state your opinion bluntly;
> 3. compliment her on her hairdo, but add minor qualifications; or,
> 4. refuse to comment.

Answer 3 is considered correct—on the grounds that husbands can't get away with answers 1 and 4, and answer 2 is likely to provoke undue strife.

Formal Reasoning is reasoning in ways that have become more or less formalized in Western cultures. An example is the syllogism, like this one:

> No Gox box when in purple socks.
>
> Jocks is a Gox wearing purple socks.
>
> Therefore: Jocks does not now box.

The task is to determine whether or not the conclusion is warranted. (It is.)

An everyday example of formal reasoning might be to produce a well-reasoned analysis of the pros and cons of an issue presented to the United Nations. Formal reasoning, to a much greater extent than experiential evaluation or verbal comprehension, depends upon dealing with abstractions and symbols in highly structured ways.

Number Facility, the primary ability to do numerical calculations, also helps define crystallized intelligence, since to a considerable extent it reflects the quality of a person's education. In a somewhat less direct way, this quality is also represented in the primary abilities called mechanical knowledge, judgment, and associational fluency.

Semantic Relations and General Reasoning, listed as primary aspects of fluid intelligence, are also—when carrying a burden of learning and culture—aspects of crystallized intelligence. This points up the fact that, although fluid and crystallized intelligence represent distinct patterns of abilities, there is some overlap. This is what is known as *alternative mechanisms* in intellectual performance. In other words, a given kind of problem can sometimes be solved by exercise of different abilities.

Consider the general-reasoning primary, for example. In this, typical problems have a slightly mathematical flavor:

> There are 100 patients in a hospital. Some (an even number) are one-legged, but wearing shoes. One-half of the remainder are bare-footed. How many shoes are being worn?

We may solve this by using a formal algebraic equation. Set x equal to the number of one-legged patients, with 100–x then being the number of two-legged patients, and $x + \frac{1}{2}(100-x)2$ being the number of shoes worn. We don't have to invent the algebraic techniques used here. They have been passed down to us over centuries. As Keith Hayes very nicely puts it, "The culture relieves us of much of the burden of creativity by giving us access to the products of creative acts scattered thinly through the history of the species." The use of such products is an important part of crystallized intelligence.

But this problem can also be solved by a young boy who has never heard of algebra! He may reason that, if half the two-legged people are without shoes, and all the rest (an even number) are one-legged, then the shoes must average one per person, and the answer must be 100. This response, too, represents learning—but it is not so much a product of education, or of the accumulated wisdom passed from one generation to the next, as is the typical product of crystallized intelligence. Fluid intelligence is composed of such relatively untutored skills.

Thus the same problem can be solved by exercise of *either* fluid intelligence *or* crystallized intelligence. We can also see the operation of such alternative mechanisms in these two problems.

ZEUS—JUPITER:		:ARTEMIS—?		
	Answer:	Phidias	Coria	*Diana*
HERE—NOW:		:THERE—?		
	Answer:	Thus	Sometimes	*Then*

The first problem is no harder to solve than the second, *provided* you have acquired a rather sophisticated knowledge of mythology. The second problem requires learning too, but no more than simply learning the language—a fact that puts native-born whites and Negroes on a relatively equal footing in dealing with problems of this sort, but places Spanish-speaking Puerto Ricans or Mexican-Americans at a disadvantage. As measures of fluid intelligence, both items are about equally good. But the first involves, to a much greater extent, crystallized intelligence gleaned from formal education or leisure reading.

Because the use of alternative mechanisms is natural in the play of human intelligence, most intelligence tests provide mixed rather than pure measures of fluid or crystallized abilities. This only reflects the way in which we usually go about solving problems—by a combination of natural wit and acquired strategies. But tests can be devised in which one type of intelligence predominates. For example, efforts to devise "culture fair" intelligence tests that won't discriminate against people from deprived educational or cultural backgrounds usually focus on holding constant the effect of crystallized capabilities—so that fluid capabilities can be more fully represented.

Now that we have roughly defined what fluid and crystallized intelligence are, let us investigate how each of them develops over time.

The infant, whose reasoning powers extend little beyond the observation that a determined howl brings food, attention, or a dry diaper, becomes the man who can solve legal problems all day, execute complicated detours to avoid the five o'clock traffic on his way home, and deliver a rousing speech to his political club in the evening. But how? To understand the intertwined development of the fluid and crystallized abilities that such activities require, we need to consider three processes essential to the development of intelligence: *anlage function*, the *acquisition of aids*, and *concept formation*.

Anlage function, which includes the complex workings of the brain and other nervous tissue, provides the physical base for all of the infant's future mental growth. ("Anlage" is a German word meaning "rudiment.") The second two factors—the aids and concepts the child acquires as he grows up—represent the building blocks that, placed on the anlage base, form the structure of adult intelligence.

The anlage function depends crucially and directly upon physiology. Physiology, in turn, depends partly on heredity, but it can also be influenced by injury, disease, poisons, drugs, and severe shock. Such influences can occur very early in life—often even in the womb. Hence it is quite possible that an individual's anlage functioning may have only a remote relationship to his hereditary potential. All we can say for sure is that the anlage process *is* closely tied to a physiological base.

A good everyday measure of a person's anlage functioning is his memory span (provided we can rule out the effects of anxiety, fatigue, or mental disturbance). Given a series of letters or numbers, most adults can immediately reproduce only about six or seven of them in reverse order. Some people may be able to remember 11, others as few as four, but in no case is the capacity unlimited or even very great. Memory span increases through childhood—probably on account of the increasing size and complexity of the brain—but it is not much affected by learning. This is generally true of other examples of anlage functioning.

SHORT-CUTS TO LEARNING

Aids are techniques that enable us to go beyond the limitations imposed by anlage functioning. An aid can, for example, extend our memory span. For example, we break up a telephone or social-security number with dashes, transforming long numbers into short, more easily recalled sets, and this takes the strain off immediate memory.

Some aids, like the rules of algebra, are taught in school. But several psychologists (notably Jean Piaget) have demonstrated that infants and children also invent their own aids in their untutored explorations of the world. In development, this process probably continues for several years.

Concepts are categories we impose on the phenomena we experience. In forming concepts, we find that otherwise dissimilar things can be regarded as "the same" in some sense because they have common properties. For instance, children learn to distinguish the features associated with "bike"—two wheels, pedaling, riding outside, etc.—from those associated with "car." Very early in a child's development, these categories may be known and represented only in terms of his own internal symbols. In time, however, the child learns to associate his personal symbols with conventional signs—that is, he learns to use language to represent what he "knows" from direct experience. Also, increased proficiency in the use of language affords opportunities to see new relations and acquire *new* concepts.

The concepts we possess at any time are a residue of previous intellectual functioning. Tests that indicate the extent of this residue may, therefore, predict the level of a person's future intellectual development. A large vocabulary indicates a large storehouse of previously acquired concepts, so verbal ability itself is often taken as a good indication of ability to conceptualize. Many well-known tests of intelligence, especially of crystallized intelligence, are based on this rationale.

However, language is really only an indirect measure of concept awareness. Thus verbally oriented tests can be misleading. What about the child raised in an environment where language is seldom used, but which is otherwise rich in opportunity to perceive relationships and acquire concepts (the backwoods of Illinois, or by a pond in Massachusetts)? At the extreme, what about a person who never hears the spoken word or sees the written word? He does not necessarily lack the awareness that we so glibly represent in language. Nor does he necessarily lack intelligence. A child who doesn't know the spoken or written word "key" surely understands the concept if he can distinguish a key from other small objects and use it to open a lock.

What is true of conventional language is also true of conventional aids. Lack of facility or familiarity with aids does not mean that a child has failed to develop intellectually, even though it may make him *appear* mentally slow on standard intelligence tests. Just as verbally oriented tests penalize the child who has not had the formal schooling or proper environment to develop a large vocabulary, many tests of so-called mathematical aptitude rely heavily on the use of conventional aids taught in school—on algebraic formulas, for example. Someone who has learned few of these conventional aids will generally do poorly on such tests, but this does not mean that he lacks intelligence.

We cannot overlook the fact that an intelligent woodsman may be just as intelligent, in one sense of this term, as an intelligent college professor. The particular combination of primary abilities needed to perform well may differ in the two cases, but the basic wherewithal of intellectual competence can be the same—adequate anlage functioning, plus an awareness of the concepts and a facility with the aids relevant to dealing with the environment at hand. Daniel Boone surely needed as much intelligence to chart the unexplored forests of the frontier as today's professor needs to thread his way through the groves of academe.

EDUCATION AND INTELLIGENCE

It is obvious, then, that formal education is not essential to the development of important aspects of intelligence. Barring disruption of anlage functioning by accident or illness, the child will form concepts and devise aids to progressively expand his mental grasp as he grows up, and this will occur whether he goes to school or not.

Where formal instruction *is* significant is in making such development easier—and in passing along the concepts and aids that many people have deposited into the intelligence of a culture. The schools give children awareness of concepts that they may not have had the opportunity to gain from first-hand experience—the ability to recognize an Australian platypus, for example, without ever having seen one, or a knowledge of how the caste system works in India. Aids, too, are taught in school. A child well-armed with an array of mathematical formulas will likely be able to solve a problem faster and more accurately than one who must work it out completely on his own. Indeed, some problems simply cannot be solved without mathematical aids. Since the acquisition of both concepts and aids is cumulative, several years of formal education can put one child well ahead of another one, unschooled, who has roughly the same intellectual potential.

Education can thus play a powerful role in developing intelligence. Too often, however, it doesn't. Even in school, some children in perfectly good health and physical condition fail to develop, or develop slowly. Some even seem to be mentally stunted by their school experience. Why? What sorts of experiences can foster—or retard—the developmental processes of concept-formation and aid-formation in the school environment?

Even though we are only beginning to find answers in this area, it is already clear that learning can be speeded up, slowed down, or brought almost to a dead halt by a variety of school experiences. On the favorable side, abilities improve by *positive transfer*. Learning one skill makes it easier to learn a related one. A student who already knows Spanish, for example, will find it easier to learn Portuguese. And positive transfer also works in less obvious ways. There is even evidence to suggest that new learning is facilitated simply by having learned before—by a sort of learning how to learn.

But other factors too can affect the course of learning, and these factors are particulary prominent in the context of our formal educational system. For example, merely having the *opportunity* to learn may depend on both previous learning and previous opportunity to learn. Thus, even if his native potential and level of self-education are good, the person who has not had the opportunity to finish high school has a poor chance of going on to college.

Labeling operates in a similar way. If a person is labeled as lacking in ability, he may receive no further chance to develop. Kenneth B. Clark states this very well:

> If a child scores low on an intelligence test because he cannot read and then is not taught to read because he has a low score, then such a child is being imprisoned in an *iron circle* and becomes the victim of an educational self-fulfilling prophecy.

Avoidance-learning is similar. This is learning not to learn. Punishment in a learning situation—being humiliated in school, for example—may make a child "turn off." Problem-solving may become such a threat that he will avoid all suggestion of it. Since an active, inquiring curiosity is at the root of mental growth, avoidance-learning can very seriously retard intellectual development. Moreover, since a child typically expresses avoidance by aggression, lack of attention, sullenness, and other behavior unacceptable to educators and parents, they—being human—may react by shutting the child out of further learning situations, and thus create another kind of iron circle.

Labeling, lack of opportunity, and avoidance-learning affect the development of both fluid and crystallized intelligence. Both depend upon acculturational influences—the various factors that provide, or block, chances for learning. And both depend upon anlage function and thus open physiological influences as well. However, fluid intelligence depends more on physiological factors, and crystallized intelligence more on acculturational ones. It is the interplay of these factors throughout a child's development that produces the fact that fluid and crystallized intelligence can be separated in adult intellectual performances. But how does this separation arise?

A CLIMATE FOR GROWTH

In many respects, the opportunities to maintain good physiological health are the same for all in our society. The climate, air pollution, water, the chances of injury, and other hazards in the physical environment do not vary greatly. Even the social environments are similar in many ways. We acquire similar language skills, go to schools that have similar curricula, have a similar choice of television programs, and so on. In this sense, the most advantaged and the most disadvantaged child have some of the same opportunities to develop anlage functioning, and to acquire concepts and aids.

Moreover, we should be careful about how we use the term "disadvantaged." We do not yet know what is superior in all respects, at every age level, for the development of all the abilities that go into intelligence. At one stage, what seems a "bad" home may give intelligence a greater impetus than an apparently "good" home. It may be, for instance, that in early childhood "lax" parents allow more scope for development. In later development, "stimulating" and "responsible" (but restrictive?) parents might be better. Some of the intellectual leaders of every period of history and of every culture have developed in environments that, according to many definitions, would have had to be classified as "disadvantaged."

It is clear, however, that favorable conditions for the development of intelligence are not the same for all. To avoid the iron circle, to gain opportunities to go on, children have to display the right abilities at the right times. To some extent, this depends on early and basic endowment. Intelligent parents may provide good heredity, good environmental conditions for learning, and good stimulation and encouragement. But the opportunities a child gets, and what he meets them with, can also be quite independent of his own characteristics. His opportunities depend on such haphazard factors as the neighborhood in which he lives, the kind of schooling available, his mother's interests and his father's income, the personality qualities of the teachers he happens to get, and the attitudes and actions of his playmates.

Thus, through a child's years of growth and education, societal influences can produce an effect that is largely independent of those produced by physiological influences. In an infant, cultural influences could not have accumulated independently of the physiological. But as children pass through preschool and school, their awareness of concepts and use of aids becomes more evident, and the influence of acculturation is felt and exhibited. The probable shape of future learning and opportunity becomes more clear. The child who has already moved ahead tends to be ready to move farther ahead, and to be accepted for such promotion. Crystallized intelligence feeds the growth of crystallized intelligence. By contrast, the child who has not moved ahead, for whatever reasons, tends to be less ready and to be viewed as such. His acquisition of the lore of the culture proceeds at a decelerating rate. This is how two children with roughly the same hereditary potential can grow apart in their acquisition of crystallized intelligence. Among adults, then, we should expect to find great variation in the crystallized pattern of abilities—and we do!

The cultural influences that can produce this kind of inequality operate almost independently of physiological factors, however. Thus, the child who fails to progress rapidly in learning the ever-more-abstruse concepts and aids of crystallized intelligence may still acquire many concepts and aids of a more common type. And if he is lucky in avoiding accidents and maintaining good health, this kind of development can be quite impressive. His intellectual growth may even surpass that of a seemingly more favored child who is slowed down by illness or injury. Thus, two children with about the same hereditary makeup can grow apart in fluid intelligence, too. The result is a wide range of variation in adult fluid intelligence—a range even wider than we would expect to be produced by differences in heredity alone.

THE DECLINING YEARS

Both fluid and crystallized intelligence, as we have just seen, develop with age. But intelligence also declines with age. This is especially true of the fluid kind. Looked at in terms of averages, fluid intelligence begins to decline before a person is out of his 20s. Crystallized intelligence fares better, however, and generally continues to increase throughout life. Because crystallized intelligence usually increases in this fashion, the decline in fluid abilities may not seriously undermine intellectual competence in people as they mature into middle age and even beyond. But let us look at these matters more analytically.

Figure 2 represents results from several studies, each involving several hundred people. Notice, first, that the curves representing fluid intelligence (FI) and crystallized intelligence (CI) are at first indistinguishable, but become separate as development proceeds. This represents the fact that both are products of development. It also illustrates the fact that it is easier to distinguish between fluid intelligence and crystallized intelligence in adults than in children.

The maturation curve (M) summarizes evidence that the physical structures and processes that support intellect (the brain, for instance) grow and increase in complexity until the late teens or the early 20s. Development is rapid but decelerating. Since both fluid and crystallized intelligence depend on maturation, their curves more or less follow it.

But maturation accounts for only part of the change in the physical structures that support intelligence. They are also affected by injuries, such as birth complications, blows to the head, carbon-monoxide poisoning, intoxication, and high fever. Such injuries are irreversible and thus cumulative. In the short run, they are difficult to discern, and their effects are masked during childhood by the rising curves of learning and maturation. In the long run, however, injuries resulting from the exposures of living take their toll. The older the person, the greater the exposure. Thus, part of the physiological base for intellectual functioning will, on an average, decrease with age (curve PB).

The sum of the influences represented by M and PB form the physiological base for intellectual processes at any particular time. In the early years, the effects of one compensate for the effects of the

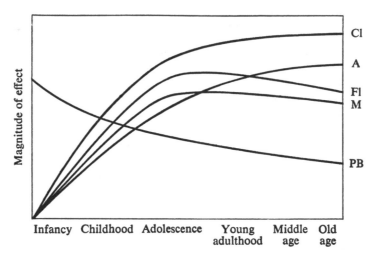

FIGURE 2. Development of Fluid Intelligence (FI) and Crystallized Intelligence (CI) in relation to effects produced by Maturation (M), Acculturation (A), and loss of Physiological Base (PB) due to injury.

other. But as the M curve levels off in young adulthood and the PB curve continues downward, the total physiological base drops. Those intellectual abilities that depend very directly upon physiology must then decline.

The effects of brain-tissue loss are variable, however. At the physiological level, an ability is a complex network of neurons that "fire" together to produce observable patterns of behavior. Such networks are over-determined—not all of the neurons in the network need to "fire" to produce the behavior. And some networks are much more over-determined than others. This means that when a loss of brain tissue (that is, a loss of neurons) occurs, some networks, and hence some abilities, will be only minimally affected. Networks that are not highly overdetermined, though, will become completely inoperative when a critical number of neurons cease to fire.

The crystallized abilities apparently correspond to highly over-determined neural networks. Such abilities will not be greatly affected by moderate loss of neurons. The fluid abilities, on the other hand, depend much more significantly upon anlage functions, which are represented by very elementary neural networks. These abilities will thus "fall off" with a loss of neurons.

Curve A in Figure 2 shows how, potentially at least, the effects of acculturation and positive trans-

fer may accumulate throughout a lifetime. On this basis alone, were it not for neural damage, we might expect intelligence to increase, not decline, in adulthood.

Whether intellectual decline occurs or not will depend upon the extent of neuron loss, and upon whether learning new aids and concepts can compensate for losing old skills. For example, the anlage capacity to keep six digits in immediate awareness may decline with loss of neurons. But the individual, sensing this loss, may develop new techniques to help him keep a number in mind. Thus the overall effect may be no loss of ability. What the evidence does indicate, however, is that, with increasing age beyond the teens, there is a steady, if gentle, decline in fluid intelligence. This suggests that learning new aids and concepts of the fluid kind does not quite compensate for the loss of anlage function and the loss of previously learned aids and concepts.

On a happier note, and by way of contrast, the evidence also shows that crystallized intelligence *increases* throughout most of adulthood. Here alternative mechanisms come into play. Compensating for the loss of one ability with the surplus of another, the older person uses crystallized intelligence in place of fluid intelligence. He substitutes accumulated wisdom for brilliance, while the younger person does the opposite.

A word of caution about these results. They

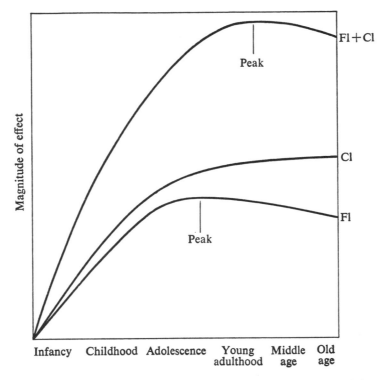

FIGURE 3. **Fluid intelligence, crystallized intelligence, and the effect of the two added together.**

represent averages, and averages can be affected by a relatively few extreme cases. For example, if only a relatively few individuals experience brain damage, but the effect is rather pronounced in each case, this will show up in the averages. If such damage occurs more frequently with older people than with younger people, a corresponding decline of abilities with age will show up—even though such decline may not be an inevitable aspect of aging for everyone. But even though these cautions must be kept in mind, we should not lose track of the fact that the FI curve parallels the PB in adulthood.

Intelligence tests that measure mixtures of fluid and crystallized intelligence (and most popular ones do) show varying relationships between aging and intelligence in adulthood. If fluid tests predominate, decline is indicated. If crystallized intelligence is well represented, then there is no apparent decline.

Intellectual performance in important jobs in life will depend on both kinds of intelligence, and may be represented by a composite curve (FI and CI in Figure 3).

Notice that the peak of this curve occurs later than the peak of the FI curve below it. If fluid intelligence reaches its peak in the early 20s, intelligence in overall performance, influenced by the cultural accretion, may peak in the 30s. The evidence indicates that the greatest intellectual *productivity* tends to occur in the 30s or early 40s, although the most *creative* work often is accomplished earlier. For example, half of the 52 greatest discoveries in chemistry (as judged by chemists) were made before the innovator had reached age 29, and 62 percent were made before he was 40. It would seem that creativity and productivity represent somewhat different combinations of fluid and crystallized intelligence, with productivity being relatively more affected by cultural factors.

The age at which the combined FI and CI function peaks varies from one person to another, depending on the development of new concepts and aids, the amount of brain damage, and other factors such as diet and general health.

Perhaps the most interesting result of all this recent work is the questions it provokes. What are the factors producing the apparent decline in fluid intelligence? Are they intrinsic to aging, or do they merely reflect the hazards of living? Are they associated with the hazards of different occupations? Do auto mechanics, for example, who are repeatedly exposed to carbon monoxide, show more decline in fluid intelligence than cement finishers, who work in the open air?

Most important of all, what experiences in infancy and childhood have favorable or unfavorable effects on the future growth of fluid intelligence? Of crystallized intelligence? Of both? Do experiences that affect fluid intelligence always affect crystallized intelligence, too? We are still far from finding firm and comprehensive answers to these questions, but they very clearly hold massive implications for our child-rearing practices, for our educational system, and for the whole complex of fields that bear on the development and management of human potential.

13

Piaget's Theory of Cognitive and Intellectual Development

Jason W. Brunk

EDITOR'S NOTE · No contemporary discussion about the nature and growth of intelligence would be complete without including the monumental discoveries Jean Piaget has made over the past 50 years. Piaget, a Swiss psychologist, has mapped an elaborate series of periods and subperiods of intellectual growth into five interrelated stages, which begin at birth and progress through adolescence. Dr. Brunk gives an overview of the basic concepts related to Piaget's stage theory, adds a critique of Piaget's work, and discusses the implications Piaget's theories have for teaching practices.

Piaget has become perhaps the foremost child psychologist of the century. During the past fifty years he and his collaborators have produced a volume of research and theory in child psychology unsurpassed by any other individual or group of investigators.

His theoretical formulations are based on an enormous set of empirical data amassed through years of observing, interviewing, and testing children of all ages. He has highlighted problems that had previously gone unrecognized or had been ignored. Perhaps most significantly, his theories

Jason W. Brunk, "The Cognitive Theory of Jean Piaget," *Strategies for Teaching, A Monograph*, Research and Practice Series, Ohio Education Association, 1973. Reprinted by permission.

have been imaginative and comprehensive, and they have fundamentally altered current conceptions of child development.

Piaget's early interests were not with children but rather with certain theoretical problems in epistemology: what is knowledge; how is it acquired; can one come to an objective comprehension of reality? These are philosophical problems, and Piaget's training was in biology. He became intrigued with the possibility of using the scientific framework of biology to investigate his interests in epistemology.

While there were a number of important influences in Piaget's early life, his experience in the Binet Laboratory in Paris was almost surely a pivotal one. He was asked to develop a standardized French version of certain English reasoning tests. Understandably, the imaginative young Piaget was less than enthusiastic about such a mechanical task. But it was in this work that Piaget made an important discovery. Although intelligence tests are oriented toward correct responses, Piaget became fascinated with the incorrect responses of children. For one thing, the same wrong answers were given frequently by children of about the same age. Then he found that children of different ages were giving a different set of common wrong answers.

Piaget pondered these mistakes. Perhaps it is not that older children just know more than younger ones, he hypothesized, but that the thought processes of the two groups are qualitatively different. This was a fundamental break with the accepted notion that intelligence is quantitative—that it can be measured by the number of correct responses. A new conception of intelligence was forming in Piaget's thinking.

Piaget turned his attention to the evolution of knowledge in and the methods of thinking used by children of various ages. For a research strategy he adopted a modified form of clinical observation and turned to logic and mathematics for a formal language of sufficient precision to describe his ideas.

INTELLIGENCE IN PIAGET'S SYSTEM

In Piagetian theory, mature intelligence is the ability to think objectively and critically and to handle abstractions and hypothetical logic.

For Piaget, intelligence involves *adaptation*, *equilibrium*, and *mental operations*. The concept of *adaptation* reflects Piaget's biological orientation. It refers to the process whereby the individual interacts with and thereby comes to "know" his environment. It is a two-way process, however, in that adjustments are necessary for both the individual and his environment. *Equilibrium* is the name Piaget gives to this adjustment. *Mental operations* refers to the cognitive functioning of the individual in his interaction with the environment. Knowledge does not come passively; reality must be constructed through the activity of the individual, that is, as the young child interacts with his environment he accumulates experiences that are "stored" in his nervous system. But it is not "dead" storage like phone numbers waiting to be recalled if needed. Rather, the experiences become an operational part of his cognitive functioning, so that each experience changes the child, and the cumulative changes lead to higher levels of functioning.

THE GENETIC BASIS OF INTELLIGENCE

Piaget believes that every organism inherits certain *physical structures* that, according to their natures, permit certain kinds of performance and prohibit others. A wing is a physical structure permitting flight; a tooth is a physical structure permitting chewing. In like manner, the physical structure of the nervous system permits certain cognitive processes.

In addition to the physical structures, the organism inherits certain automatic behavioral reactions, the best example of which is the reflex. During the first days of the newborn's existence his reflexive actions are modified by his experiences, resulting in a new mechanism—the *psychological structure*. Such structures form the basis of all future intellectual activity. Briefly, then, the inherited physical structure sets the limits of intellectual performance, and the inherited behavioral reactions, modified by experience, result in psychological structure.

In addition, the organism inherits two basic tendencies which Piaget calls *invariant functions*. They are *adaptation* and *organization*. Adaptation involves two complementary processes: (1) *accommodation*, whereby the individual tends to change his existing cognitive structures in response to environmental demands, and (2) *assimilation*, whereby the individual tends to process current environmental experiences according to his existing cognitive structures. *Organization* refers to the tendency of the individual to integrate his psychological structures into coherent systems. Just as the individual continues to gain experiences, he must continue to reorganize his developing psychological structures in order to achieve equilibrium. More than that, however, there is a kind of inherited tendency to seek equilibrium. Equilibrium, therefore, may be viewed (1) as an internal consistency and (2) as a form of motivation.

Put differently, Piaget seems to be saying that the developing child seeks active involvement with his environment. As he grows to maturity, many of his experiences will be at odds with his previous learning (i.e., in Piagetian terms, with one or more of his existing psychological structures). Now either he must adjust these existing structures to the new experience as he perceives it (that is, he must accommodate himself to it), or he must adjust the new perception to fit his existing structures (that is, he must distort it in order to assimilate it), or he must do both. To the extent that he is successful in achieving an adjustment through cognitive reorganization, he attains the sought-for equilibrium and is ready for another step in his cognitive development.

STAGES IN DEVELOPMENT

Piaget believes that as the individual grows to maturity the invariant functions of adaptation and organization will remain the same in principle, hence the term invariant. But the structures that are developed through the process of adaptation and organization as the individual interacts with his environment change both quantitatively and qualitatively. These qualitative changes are the basis of Piaget's stage theory of cognitive development. Piaget defines four periods through which all children must advance successfully and in unvarying sequential order if they are to achieve their potential cognitive abilities.

THE SENSORY–MOTOR PERIOD

The sensory-motor period extends from birth to the acquisition of language. During this period—

roughly 18 months—the infant moves from a reflex level of response to a level of organized sensory-motor interactions with the environment. It is a time of basic adjustment between the infant and his world—a coming to terms with the most rudimentary aspects of reality through sensory-motor exploration. The infant learns, for example, that objects exist even though he cannot see them and that he and such objects are differentiated realities. His achievements during this period are the foundation for all his future cognitive development and activity.

PREOPERATIONAL PERIOD

Whereas the sensory-motor period is characterized by preverbal, non-representational knowledge, the preoperational period (approximate ages 2–7) is ushered in by the first crude attempts at symbolization. It is the time of accelerated language development, and though his limited experience and maturation restrict his thinking, the preoperational child is freed from the restraint of simple motoric functioning. In addition to language development, it is a time of increasing social development.

Yet, notwithstanding the notable achievements of the child during this period, his thinking is still restricted in many ways. For example, he is unable to attend simultaneously to several aspects of an event. He is likely to believe that a row of five beads spread out contains more beads than a row of five beads spaced closely together. If they are rearranged, while he observes, so that the beads are spaced equally in each row and the two rows are the same length, he will say that the two rows now contain the same number of beads. Also, his thinking is said to be egocentric. He is able to deal only with his own viewpoint and in fact appears to assume that there are no other viewpoints.

PERIOD OF CONCRETE OPERATIONS

In the period of concrete operations (approximate ages 7–11), the child becomes capable of logical thought processes that can be applied to *concrete problems*. He is able to handle problems of transformation in which he coordinates and understands the relationship among the successive steps in a logical sequence. He is also capable of reversible thought and can follow a line of reasoning back to its beginning point. He is able to conserve matter in his thinking. That is, he is able to recognize that the quantity of matter remains constant regardless of changes in its shape or position. He is able to deal with concepts of time, space, causality, classification, and seriation (arranging objects in serial order according to some characteristic such as size).

But the child during this period can use logic to solve problems involving real objects or events only; he is not yet ready to apply logic to hypothetical or purely verbal problems. When we remember that this period roughly parallels the elementary school years, we can see the tremendous significance of this proposition.

THE PERIOD OF FORMAL OPERATIONS

By the end of this period (approximate ages 11–15), the adolescent has achieved the final stages in the development of his cognitive structures. He is now capable of mature thought processes and is potentially able to handle all classes of problems. He can deal with hypothetical problems and propositional logic, and he can detect logical incongruities in hypothetical contexts. While he will, of course, continue to learn, there are no further fundamental qualitative changes in cognitive function to be achieved.

The foregoing sketch can do no more than provide a feeling for the style and direction of Piaget's thinking. It is hopelessly inadequate to the task of explaining or even of summarizing Piagetian theory. A serious study of Piaget's contributions seems indicated for any educator who would consider himself a knowledgeable professional.

CRITIQUE

Piaget's research with young children is frequently hailed as bold and imaginative. Certainly his work has been highly productive. But Piaget has been criticized on several counts. Some criticisms on a theoretical level have been lodged against perceived internal contradictions of Piaget's system. On a practicing level, Piaget seems to have been criticized more for what he has not done than for what he has. For example, he is criticized for having paid too little attention to individual differences and to the early perceptual training of very young children. Much of the criticism of Piaget, however, seems to be a semantic debate between his followers and his critics. Criticism is generally healthy, and surely Piaget's system is not without its faults. But there can be no doubt that Piaget has made and is making a solid contribution to education.

Knowledgeable teachers are familiar with the proposition that children are not miniature adults but that there are qualitative differences between the thought processes of the two. Piaget's theory not only provides support for this proposition but is helpful in specifying where and how it applies.

First, the young child's ability to understand physical phenomena is different from that of the adult. The young child sees no problem, for example, in the conclusion that a liquid poured from a short, wide glass into a tall, narrow one gains in quantity. Or again, he may be able to work simple arithmetic problems without any comprehension of the fundamental concepts involved.

Piaget has identified several reasons to account for these observations. For one thing, the child's thinking is egocentric; he fails to consider points of view other than his own, which he believes to be correct. For another thing, he tends to concentrate on only one aspect of an object or event. For example, he may consider length but ignore width. Also, the child tends to focus on the product rather than on the sequence of events that led to the product. As Piaget might say, the child attends to states rather than to transformations.

Second, the uses of language by the child and adult are different. Children's language pivots on the concrete, sensory aspects of reality. Adults' language can and often does deal with abstractions. For children Santa Claus is a person, but for adults he represents an idea.

But even the meanings that words have for children as compared with adults may be different. Piaget has demonstrated that we cannot assume that because a child knows the word for an object or event he understands the underlying concept. The "meanings" he has depend, first, on the experiences he has had with the objects and events and, second, on his cognitive ability to deal with those experiences.

The fact that the language and thought of children are qualitatively different from those of adults has clear implications for teaching. It suggests that lecturing and other forms of verbal communication such as "telling" or explaining are inefficient and perhaps useless teaching techniques, particularly for elementary school children. It suggests that workbooks and textbooks may have much less usefulness than formerly believed. And it suggests that an idea that is easily grasped by an adult may make no sense at all to a child. Who of us has not had the deflating experience of having "explained" an idea to a class in an unusually lucid and articulate manner only to be greeted by thirty or forty blank faces?

According to Piaget, children's cognitive development proceeds through a series of stages. At each stage the child's thinking is qualitatively different from that at every other stage. It is clearly defeating to expect children at some intermediary stage to work at tasks requiring a level of cognitive activity that they have not yet attained. Therefore, the characteristic modes of thinking at each level provide a basis for deciding what to teach when.

For example, children in the preoperational period (approximate ages 2–7) would not normally be expected to solve problems involving formal logic. On the other hand, we might expect them to make rapid advances in the use of language both in facilitating thought and in social communication.

The concept of readiness—involved so frequently in connection with beginning reading instruction—is seen to have application at all levels and to other areas of learning, particularly problem solving. The stage theory, again, provides a basis for (1) diagnosing readiness levels and (2) prescribing appropriate learning activities.

As the child grows, social interaction becomes increasingly important, not only because of the part it plays in affective development but also for its value in cognitive development. Children need many opportunities to interact with other children, to become aware of other persons' viewpoints and perceptions. This would seem to be especially important for children in the preoperational period, when their thinking is characteristically egocentric. Suitable activities would include role playing, games, and discussions with their peers.

There is evidence that a teacher's attitudes and expectations influence for better or worse the achievements of the children he teaches. His attitudes in turn are influenced by his own beliefs and conceptualizations.

If, for example, a teacher believes that intelligence is fixed at birth, his attitudes and behavior toward children will presumably be different from his attitudes and behavior if he believed that intelligence is amenable to environmental influences.

Conversely, if a teacher believes that a child is capable of thought processes that in actuality are beyond his developmental level, the teacher's attitudes and behavior may very well reflect unrealistic expectations, unnecessary and useless pressures, and perhaps disapproval or even rejection. Even though Piaget's formulations are not complete and will surely be revised with continued research, they offer teachers a scientifically based theoretical foundation out of which can be deduced objective beliefs and attitudes about children's learning. These are certainly to be preferred to the haphazard, unfounded, or illogical positions held by many educators.

If there is a single most important conclusion to be drawn from Piaget's work, it is that children learn best when they are actively involved in concrete learning experiences. For much of the time for very young children, it may be the only way they learn. The implication is unmistakable: school must become a place of activity. Children must be given opportunities to manipulate objects, explore situations, role play, and enter discussions with both teacher and peers.

The teaching function is not necessarily less active, but it is less directive and limiting. There should be a reduction in teacher dominated activity, in verbal teaching, and in the kind of control that requires children to sit quietly and passively. There should be an increase in (1) teachers' sensitivity to children and their requirements, (2) teachers' observation of children, and (3) teachers' diagnosis of children's progress.

There should be teaching materials that children can see, touch, listen to, taste, and smell—materials they can manipulate, explore, dismantle, reshape, reconstruct, or even destroy. It is one thing to tell a child that a triangle is a closed geometric figure with three sides and three angles. It would be an improvement to show him a picture of a triangle while telling him it is a triangle. But it is a completely different matter to let him see triangles, make triangles from sticks, crawl through triangular openings, handle triangular objects, and make triangular pancakes or cookies. If homework is thought desirable, young children might bring in a picture of something (or an object) with a triangular shape. Older children might make a list of the ways triangles are used around their homes or invent a game using triangles.

Finally, teaching can move out of the school building—as indeed learning already has. Field trips take on added significance, particularly for children whose life-space has been confined to the small area around their homes.

REFERENCES

Athey, Irene J., and Duane O. Rubadeau. *Educational Implications of Piaget's Theory.* Waltham, Mass.: Ginn-Blaisdell, 1970.

Beard, Ruth M. *An Outline of Piaget's Developmental Psychology for Students and Teachers.* New York: Basic Books, Inc., 1969.

Bernard, Harold W. *Human Development in Western Culture.* 3rd ed. Boston: Allyn & Bacon, Inc., 1970.

Chittenden, Edward A. "Piaget and Elementary Science." *Science and Children,* 8 (December 1970), 9–15.

Evans, Ellis D. *Contemporary Influences in Early Childhood Education.* New York: Holt, Rinehart and Winston, Inc., 1971.

Flavell, John H. *The Developmental Psychology of Jean Piaget.* Princeton, N.J.: D. Van Nostrand Co., Inc., 1963.

Frost, Joe L. *Early Childhood Education Rediscovered.* New York: Holt, Rinehart and Winston, Inc., 1968. Chapter 12.

Furth, Hans G. *Piaget for Teachers.* Englewood Cliffs, N.J.: Prentice-Hall, 1970.

Ginsburg, Herbert, and Sylvia Opper. *Piaget's Theory of Intellectual Development: An Introduction.* Englewood Cliffs, N.J.: Prentice-Hall, 1969.

Inskeep, James E., Jr. "Building a Case For the Application of Piaget's Theory and Research in the Classroom." *Arithmetic Teacher,* 19 (April 1972), 255–260.

Karplus, Robert, and Herbert D. Thier. *A New Look at Elementary School Science.* New Trends in Curriculum and Instruction Series. Chicago: Rand McNally & Co., 1967.

Piaget, Jean. "Cognitive Development in Children: Development and Learning." *A New Look at Elementary School Science.* By Robert Karplus and Herbert D. Thier. Chicago: Rand McNally & Co., 1967.

Rowland, T., and C. McGuire. "Development of Intelligent Behavior I: Jean Piaget." *Early Childhood Education Revisited.* By J. L. Frost. New York: Holt, Rinehart and Winston, Inc., 1968.

Wadsworth, Barry J. *Piaget's Theory of Cognitive Development.* New York: David McKay, Inc., 1971.

Weaver, J. Fred. "Some Concerns About the Application of Piaget's Theory and Research to Mathematical Learning and Instruction." *Arithmetic Teacher,* 19 (April 1972), 263–270.

14

Personal, Social, and Cultural Factors that Encourage Creativity

Natalie R. Haimowitz
Morris L. Haimowitz

EDITOR'S NOTE · Creativity is an elusive concept. It can be as complex as a Bach symphony or as simple as Aunt Sarah's strawberry-cherry pie. Why do some people so easily think of novel ideas? Why do some people so freely experiment with different ways of doing things? Why are some innovators, while others are fearful of change? This article offers some fascinating speculations about the growth, development, and necessary conditions for creative expression, which may shed some light on your understanding of your own creative urges.

Today the world is seeking creative men and women to invent better solutions to problems and to help us live together more peacefully in a rapidly changing and increasingly complex world.

Creativity, often regarded as a magical, inborn quality, sometimes equated with intelligence and talent, is neither of these. Many people, though

Reprinted from Natalie R. Haimowitz and Morris L. Haimowitz (eds.), *Human Development*, 2nd ed., New York: Thomas Y. Crowell Company, Inc., 1966, pp. 34–43, by permission. Copyright © 1973 by Thomas Y. Crowell Company, Inc.

possessed of high intelligence and able to grasp and use established methods, cannot innovate or invent. Similarly, many are born with a congenital "facility" known as talent, a physiological predisposition for certain skills and abilities, but are nevertheless unable to create or invent, even in the areas in which they demonstrate talent.

Creativity has been defined as the capacity to innovate, to invent, to place elements in a way in which they have never before been placed, such that their value or beauty is enhanced. Contrasted with conformity, it is the capacity to transcend the usual ways of dealing with problems or objects with new, more useful, and more effective patterns. MacKinnon has defined creativity as "a process, extended in time and characterized by originality, adaptiveness and realization." "It may be brief," he observes, "as in a musical improvisation, or it may involve a considerable span of years, as was required for Darwin's creation of the theory of evolution." It will be the proposition of this paper that this ability is not inborn, but is a product of experience, that certain geographical, social, and cultural milieus favor or hamper creativity. We will explore some of the psychological and sociological phenomena that appear to be related to the emergence of creative adults.

WHAT IS CREATIVITY?

In problem solving, we may observe two different methods of approach, both of which have value in a complex culture. On the one hand there is "convergent" thinking, which integrates what is already known, unifying or harmonizing existing facts in a logical, well-organized, orderly manner; it is thinking which conforms to existing knowledge and exacting methods. "Divergent" thinking, on the other hand, reaches into the unknown. Its essence is not its orderliness but its originality. Guilford (8), having elaborated on these qualitatively dissimilar kinds of thinking, demonstrates that existing intelligence tests rest heavily on skills which are convergent, reflecting cultural values which reward and esteem existing knowledge more highly than they reward innovation and invention.

Obviously, both convergent and divergent thinking are important in the development of a science. A report of the Foundation for Research on Human Behavior at Ann Arbor, Michigan (5), which defines creativity as "looking at things in a new and different way," points out that this kind of thinking occurs at the discovery phase, the insight phase, the intuitive phase of problem solving, and concludes that it is to be contrasted with the kind of restrained thinking concerned with validation of insights and testing of hypotheses. It is the former kinds of abilities, however, that are creative.

As in the world of physical objects and physical forces, creativity is often demonstrated in the interpersonal sphere by finding new ways to resolve interpersonal problems, by discovering new and more satisfying ways to interact with others. Foote and Cottrell in their book *Identity and Interpersonal Competence* (4) see creativity as "the actor's capacity to free himself from established routines of perception and action, and to redefine situations and act in the new roles called for by the situations." Anyone who has observed sensitive and insightful handling of an interpersonal problem can testify that there is such a thing as inventiveness in social relationships. In marked contrast are formal, traditional relationships, in which everyone's behavior is prearranged, where everyone knows what is to be done and who will do it.

COMPONENTS OF CREATIVITY

The following components of creativity have been suggested in the literature: basic security, intelligence, flexibility, spontaneity, humor, originality, ability to perceive a variety of essential features of an object or situation, playfulness, radicalness, eccentricity; we would add freedom, marginality, and secularity to this list. Conversely, characteristics which would hypothetically correlate negatively with creativity would be neatness, rigidity, control, thoroughness, reason, logic, respect for tradition and authority, and a tendency to routinize and organize tasks.

DISCOVERING CREATIVE PERSONS

One type of test wherein creative people function differently from equally "intelligent" but less creative persons is the word association test; the more creative person associates a larger number of categories with each word. Another is a hidden-shapes test which requires that the subject find a given geometrical form in a complex pattern in which it is "hidden." Another presents the beginning of a story and asks the subjects to compose first a funny, then a sad, and finally a moralistic ending.

An interesting, simple test asks the subject to draw two parallel lines and to use these lines in making a design. If he makes a design inside the lines, he is restricting himself more than if his design goes outside the two lines:

Less creative stays in bounds

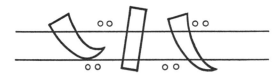

More creative transcends bounds but holds close

Still more creative adds lines, invents a melody

Another test gives the subject a problem. "You are newly married. About a month after the wedding your parents come to visit you for Sunday dinner. Your mother starts cleaning your house. You are angry about this. Let's act it out for 3 or 4 minutes. Now let's act it out again, you taking the part of your mother." The creative person finds new solutions to this stress situation.

Another test asks for a written story: "Here is a picture. Write a story about it." The creative person writes stories or endings to half-completed stories that few others imagine.

Still another test says: "Here is a newspaper. How many uses can you find for it?" The more creative can think of more and better uses than the less creative.

The Rorschach Test uses standardized ink blots. The subject is asked, "Tell me what you see." The creative person perceives objects, forms, and relationships others don't see.

In all these tests, it is assumed that the person who offers creative solutions in the test situation will be more creative in solving real life problems. This is a bold assumption, since many creative persons, being nonconformists, may not be willing to invest motivation and energy in the rather arbitrary test situation; they may not care at all about what a newspaper can be used for, nor will they necessarily find pleasure or even interest in making up stories about pictures or ink blots.

CREATIVITY AND OBSESSION

For some persons the act of creating is analogous to pains of labor for those women who can relax and enjoy it as a most exhilarating experience, the grandest, most exciting event of their lives. Others seem to be driven obsessively, without rest or diversion, until completing the task they had set for themselves. Einstein spoke of being driven by an obsession; the Curies worked without reward for many years before they discovered radium. Edison, the Wright brothers, and Louis Daguerre, who worked for six years to discover a way to make photographs—all seemed to have a clear purpose in mind. Andrew Carnegie said the key to success was first a clear, concise mental picture of the thing one seeks, "A Definite Major Purpose grown or forced into the proportions of an obsession.... I knew I wanted to go into the making of steel. I whipped up that desire until it became a driving obsession with me ... my desire drove me day and night." His second step was the development of "a Mastermind principle," which meant that he involved others in the obsession, others who possessed the qualities he lacked and needed. Carnegie said, "Jesus understood the principle of the Mastermind

and made effective use of it in His alliance with His Disciples. That is where I got my first clue...."

Some of these highly creative persons could hardly be called well rounded. Mozart, for example, was busy writing music at a younger age than boys today can join the Boy Scouts, or even the Cub Scouts. Carnegie felt very strongly that anyone could accomplish just about anything he really tried to accomplish. His biographer Napoleon Hill said to him, "I take it that most of the men who work for you have no Definite Major Purpose in life, for if they had, they, too, would be as rich as you. Is this correct?" To this, Carnegie replied, "You will find that the highest aim of a majority of the men working for me is to hold the jobs they have. They are where they are and they are drawing the wages they receive solely because of the limitations they have set up in their own minds. Nothing I can do will change it. Only the men themselves can change it...." He felt that the major requirement of persons in the Mastermind group was that they must have a single definite purpose, to work together in harmony, to feel and act positively toward others, and, most important of all, to WORK.

When Carnegie developed an idea, he used it conscientiously in all areas of his life. Thus, in his home his wife became the partner to the Mastermind: "There are but few marriages which do not need a new and improved plan of relationship at frequent intervals.... The time would be well spent if married people set aside a regular hour for a confidential Mastermind meeting at least once every week during which they would come to an understanding concerning every vital factor in their relationship.... Keep the fire of romance burning. Let it become a part of the Mastermind ceremony and your marital relationship will yield priceless returns. ... The force that is born of a combination of love and sex is the very elixir of life through which nature expresses all creative effort...." (9)

CREATIVITY AND BASIC SECURITY

There are two conflicting views concerning the relationship between inner security and creativity. The reluctance of some talented people to seek psychological help for their emotional problems is supported by the belief that if the individual becomes more comfortable, he may become less creative. We hear this view also from individuals who are associated with minority political or religious movements. The belief is held that with increased security one becomes more satisfied, more conforming, and one loses his need for and interest in unpopular, deviant opinions and activities. According to this view, creativity emerges from dissatisfaction and neurosis.

The other view regards creativity as emerging only when the organism has solved its basic problems of biological and social survival. Maslow, for instance, holds that only when the individual has achieved some sense of basic security—being fed, clothed, safe from harm, achieving sexual satisfaction, being loved by others, esteeming himself— can he spare the energy for the more whimsical, relaxed capacity to innovate and improvise. Similarly Erikson, with his concepts of "autonomy" and "initiative," suggests that only when the individual has solved his more primitive, elemental problems in relating to his world, only when he feels secure enough to initiate, and realistic enough to build a stable sense of personal identity, do "higher" kinds of human activity emerge. In this view, frustration blocks creativity. Both theorists postulate that while the individual is experiencing insecurity in the gratification of the "lower level" of needs, he cannot really be creative.

Carefully conducted, longitudinal studies of creative and not-so-creative individuals and societies might help to clarify the conflicting evidence. Scattered evidence from biographies of famous creative individuals in the arts and sciences (evidence obtained and presented by students of literature rather than by social scientists) fails to support the notion that creativity can only emerge under conditions wherein the individual's basic needs have been satisfied and his life prospects are for continued satisfaction. The childhood of such eminent innovators as Darwin, Schubert, Sarah Bernhardt, Brahms, Van Gogh, the Brontës, Gauguin do not stand out as models of security, love, and the satisfaction of basic needs. Darwin was shy, afraid of his successful father. Schubert lived in unbelievable poverty, loving music which his father denied him. Sarah Bernhardt was an illegitimate daughter of a milliner-courtesan with no home and no person to call her own. Alfred

Nobel was a hunchback and Schiller reportedly an epileptic.

Of course, doting biographers often play up the Horatio Alger struggles of the impoverished, crippled child who by hard work and courage overcomes impossible obstacles and achieves greatness and immortality. When we attempt, as social scientists, to recreate the lives of those who are no longer living from biography, we must wonder whether what we read is factual or partly the inventiveness of the biographer.

When we study highly creative persons, we often find poverty or physical defects for which the individual must certainly have been striving to compensate. We find broken homes suggesting that the individuals must certainly have experienced loss of parental love through death, rejection, or desertion, and we often notice minority group status in political, religious, or racial groups such that the individual must have experienced some sense of insecurity in his "belongingness" to the larger society. If biography is enough rooted in fact, then we know that factors other than basic security are equally crucial. Some of these worthy of explanation are intelligence, freedom, marginality, and secular values.

CREATIVITY AND INTELLIGENCE

The observation has been made that the more creative are not necessarily the more intelligent. Creativity appears to be in some way associated with intelligence, but the two do not refer to the same dimensions of behavior. Just as creativity is measured operationally, that is, is defined as being what the creativity test measures, so is intelligence measured operationally, as what the intelligence test measures. We assume that the person who shows intelligence in an intelligence test will also show intelligence in other aspects of his life. Yet the intelligence test may fail to tap the devices used by a general planning campaign, or those of a young lady seeking a husband, or the behavior of an architect planning a new school. The kinds of intelligence valued on intelligence tests are verbal, memory, or convergent—organizing, logical *skills* —rather than divergent, original kinds of *talents*. Creative talents may be penalized or missed in typical intelligence tests. While those who seem to innovate successfully are apparently those also with high intelligence, it is quite possible to discover highly intelligent persons who do not innovate and discover, and to find highly creative persons who do not show superiority on intelligence tests.

Getzels and Jackson (6) did just that. They gave both intelligence tests and tests of creativity to 449 adolescents. As might be expected, many scored high in both intelligence and creativity tests, others low in both kinds of tests. From the 449 subjects, two special groups were selected out: one of 24 individuals who scored in the highest 20 percent in intelligence, but not highest in creativity; and the second group of 28 who scored in the top 20 percent in creativity but did not excel in intelligence.

Comparing these two groups showed that "despite striking differences in mean IQ the creative and intelligent groups were equally superior to the total population in school performance as measured by the standardized achievement tests." Yet, from teachers' ratings, they found that teachers preferred the intelligent group rather than the creative. They also found that the need for achievement was no different in either group from the total population. Most striking differences were found when comparing the fantasy materials of the two groups. Judges, working blindly, could with high accuracy place authors of fantasy productions in the correct group—either "high intelligence" or "highly creative." The creative subjects consistently used more stimulus-free, humorous, and playful themes. Intelligent subjects' fantasy productions were orderly, logical, but "bound."

Other studies indicate that original people prefer certain types of intellectual tasks, prefer the complex to the simple problem or solution—they delay coming to conclusions until most of the pieces can be fitted together—and that creative people have more energy and are more impulsive and responsive to emotion, even when solving problems.

In *The Creative Process*, a study of 38 geniuses, including the introspective reports of such men as Einstein, Henry James, D. H. Lawrence, and Van Gogh, Ghiselin (7) suggests that those who are creative have passion and skill for their work and, when concerned with major problems which they cannot solve, appear to "forget" the problem for a time. But they would suddenly, while asleep, taking a walk, reading a book, or talking about something else, be struck with the solution as by lightning. The idea would appear to be coming from their own unconscious, which had been working on the problem all the time. Ghiselin's study suggests that in addition to intelligence there is a freedom of thought such that unconscious forces may be available in creative individuals for productive, constructive activity, assisting the more conscious intellectual processes.

CREATIVITY AND FREEDOM

Indeed, the creative person must be able to remain free from certain restraints. The very act of creating something new and different involves the courage to go beyond cultural limits. When we study the childhood biographies of creative artists, scientists, inventors, such as the Brontës, Fermi, Thomas Jefferson, Shaw, Whitney, Edison, Robert Burns, we are impressed with the apparent freedom they experienced in their early lives, even though it may have been associated with parental neglect, death, or desertion. They seemed to live in the midst of broad areas in which to roam, with freedom to explore, with privacy to contemplate. In many biographies, we find the absence of the parent of the same sex. Perhaps the trauma of the loss had its compensations in freedom, absence of parental coercion, and less oedipal competition, and an absence of "a mold into which to fit oneself and with which to identify."

Such hypotheses arise as we recognize the fact that so many renowned persons have come from broken homes: Washington, Jefferson, Lincoln, Herbert Hoover, Bach, Beethoven, Schubert, Schumann, Stalin, Hitler, Stonewall Jackson, the Brontës, Robert Burns, Robert Fulton, Sibelius, Debussy, Andrew Johnson, Tchaikowsky, Gauguin, Leonardo da Vinci, James Garfield, Joseph Conrad, Andrew Jackson, and hundreds of others.

No statistical study has been made to determine whether such a hypothesis as this would be true: the fathers of eminent men died before the child reached puberty in greater proportions than the fathers of the noneminent. If this hypothesis is valid, precisely what in the experience of parental loss liberates creativity in some, imposes constraint in others?

Certainly the death of a parent in the child's infancy may so shatter basic security as to make creativity impossible. However, losing a parent in middle or late childhood may give the child more freedom and more responsibility. A number of studies by Watson, Baldwin, Lafore, Hattwick, Symonds, and Carpenter indicate that children from permissive homes, homes where considerable personal freedom is permitted, are much more likely to be creative than children from restrictive homes.

Imagine the courage it takes to tackle the proposition that the world is composed of atoms and that these atoms are made up of neutrons and electrons. One cannot see an atom, or an electron or neutron; one cannot even demonstrate them easily, as one can the invisible forces of gravity or electricity. The same is true for concepts in psychology. One cannot see motivation or the superego, and they are very difficult to demonstrate. If it takes courage to try to understand these concepts, think how much more courage would be required to imagine the concept, to create it. When developing new concepts, one is leaving the culture, leaving the traditional, taking off for a new world, in the manner of Columbus, and as with Columbus this requires courage, the courage to be different, not as a small religious sect is different, because here at least the members are all similar, but to be different from everyone else in the world, and the courage to test out one's ideas in the midst of disbelief, disapproval, and often ridicule.

Creativity thus appears to be associated with freedom in the self which arises from freedom in the family, in the committee, the club, the social gathering, or any small group. By "freedom" here is meant the absence of a domineering group member or leader and the absence of felt status differences. In our experiments with small groups we have noted more willingness of members to explore, to suggest wild ideas, to joke about the purposes or methods of the group when the designated leader is quietly receptive to such behavior. Very often a leader may superficially try to encourage group participation, but his domineering ways block participation and creativity. For example, he may ask the group to make suggestions but, instead of waiting patiently for them, would go ahead and make

his own. Later he may report, "I tried to get them to open up, but they wouldn't. They just don't have ideas." The leader who tries to impose standards against the wishes of the group will evoke more apathy or rebellion than creativity.

Jack Gibbs' experiments show that more creative suggestions come from groups when the leader speaks, acts, and dresses informally than when his manner is formal. Studies in the classroom show similar results. We are not suggesting absence of leadership; we are suggesting absence of smothering leaders. The famous study of Lewin, Lippitt, and White (10) points out some differences between a no-leader (laissez-faire) situation and a democratic leadership situation.

Studies in group dynamics suggest leadership is essential for a creative atmosphere. Leadership may be defined as any act of any member which helps the progress of the group. Thus, if two members are blocking each other's actions and dividing the group into two anxious and opposing camps, progress may be blocked. An act of leadership might be to point this situation out to the group, or it might be a suggestion for a five-minute break, or a suggestion that the collection of some data would settle the differences, or a joke about how much we all hate each other. Every classroom needs creative ideas for the optimum advancement of the class. Thus, the best teacher is not only one skilled in the content of the subject matter, but also one skilled in group leadership.

Thelan in his exciting research tells us that some children learn better working alone; others work better in pairs or in small groups; still others do best in large groups. Some children are aware of their peculiar needs in this respect, but others are not. In our own classes we have often asked for volunteers for a committee job. When the job calls for six persons on one committee, different people will respond than when the task calls for three committees of two each. When we ask the students about this, some say, "I like to work with only one other person," or "I like to work in a larger group." Recognition, acceptance, and use of individual differences in such matters greatly benefits the teacher as well as the students; and leadership in the home, school, church, camp, or factory is a major factor in creativity. Leland Bradford and Gordon Lippitt of the National Training Laboratory are in the forefront of those developing creativity in group leadership.

CREATIVITY AND MARGINALITY

Some students of civilization, such as Hume, Teggart, Bucher, William James, and Robert Park, have described a catastrophic theory of progress. Park (13) in his book *Race and Culture* points out that races are the product of isolation and inbreeding, while civilization is a consequence of contact and communication. The decisive events in man's history have been those which brought men together through the catastrophes of mass migration. The collisions, conflicts, and fusions of peoples and cultures incidental to these migrations cause both tragedy and creativity. Bucher writes that every advance in culture commences with a new period of wandering.

Somewhere in his own wanderings over the earth, Robert Park invented the term "marginal man" to indicate what Simmel had called "the stranger." The stranger is one who stays but is a potential wanderer; he is thus not bound, as others are, by the local properties and customs. He is the freer man. He is less involved with others, and he can be more objective in his judgment since he is not confined by one set of customs, pieties, or precedents. The stranger is the man of the cities, where division of labor and increased production have emancipated him from the age-old struggle against starvation and have given him freedom from ancient customs as well as leisure to create.

The marginal man is a man who is part of a culture but not of it. In his autobiography *Up Stream*, Ludwig Lewisohn (11) wavers between the warm security of the ghetto which he has left and the cold freedom of the outer world where he is a stranger. Heine had the same problem, struggling to be a German and also a Jew. He was both, and being both he was not fully either. He was a marginal man, and he was creative.

The marginal man is the Okie in California, the Puerto Rican in New York, the southern white migrant in Chicago, the European in America and the American in Europe, the mulatto who mingles with whites, the white man in Africa, the Irishman in England, the Catholic in Asia or in the Protestant South.

The point is that marginality, while personally costly, also sets a man free, makes it possible for him to be creative, to see aspects of a culture in a new light because he comes from another culture. When we study the highly esteemed creative men of our culture, it seems that marginality is far more the rule than the exception.

George Bernard Shaw, for example, was born a Protestant in Catholic Ireland. Economically and socially on the fringes of the middle class, his social position was continually threatened by the economic embarrassment and alcoholism of his father. He was personally neglected by parents who found neither time for him nor interest in him. Shaw departed from the home of his childhood to live and work as an Irishman in London, clearly an outgroup position. His circumstances can be easily said to have led to his cynicism. And his cynicism about his father, his religion, his economic and social order, and most of the institutions of his day is the essence of his creativity.

In similar fashion, we note that Freud was a Jew in a non-Jewish society, as was Karl Marx; that Joseph Conrad was the orphaned child of Polish nationals exiled in Russia, that Sarah Bernhardt was the child of unmarried parents of different religions. Mme. Curie was Polish, living in France; Gershwin was the son of immigrants. Stalin was a Georgian; Hitler an Austrian; Napoleon a Corsican; and Churchill, half-American. Their marginality may lead to creativity or to other intense effort—the pursuit of political power. It may be that the outcast position of marginality enables the individual to get diverse, multidimensional views of values and customs that those thoroughly "in" any society or class fail to achieve or do not need. It may be this very multidimensionality, and perhaps the insecurity and defensiveness that goes with marginality, which prevents the individual from "swallowing" wholeheartedly the traditional values, practices, and beliefs of the dominant society. This very lack of acceptance of one set standard and one set tradition appears to free the individual to innovate. The marginal man can innovate partly because he does not accept the cultures as he sees them (his isolation creates resistance) and partly because he sees two or more divergent possibilities where "belongers" see only one way, the way to which they are accustomed.

The group most responsible for emotionalized

attitudes is the primary group. If the individual is fairly secure in his early family relationships and if the values of the family place great emphasis on the family traditions, we would expect the individual to carry on the family traditions. If, however, he is marginal in his family (feels "left-out" emotionally, physically, or psychologically), we expect originality to emerge. It may also emerge when a person is thoroughly entrenched in a family which honors innovation and change as important values.

Although marginality may be a precondition of creativity, it is not always so. It may produce the reverse. No one can be so uncreative, so rigid as the marginal man. The new convert, for example, is typically the most conforming. The 100 percent American is often a European who just got here, or one of his children. The *nouveau riche* are the most careful about their clothes, carpets, and coiffures. What makes the creative marginal man different from the marginal man who is an extreme conformist? We suggest that one major difference is the former's sense of humor, which involves an acceptance of one's own playful, childish, spontaneous, loving, hating, stingy, and generous impulses. (Aristotle, St. Augustine, Newton, Galileo, and Freud are striking exceptions.) Watson suggests that a permissive home atmosphere is most important in the development of creativity, while MacKinnon finds that an openness to one's experience, a freedom to be aware of one's feelings, a preference for the complex and asymmetrical are essential qualities.

SACRED AND SECULAR VALUES

In a sacred or folk society, creativity is discouraged. The late Robert Redfield (14) defined a folk society as a relatively stable, small, homogeneous, isolated community, where unchanging traditions guide behavior. This kind of society does not seek change and tends to reject innovations. Most traditions have religious meaning. To alter them is sacrilegious.

Redfield contrasted the folk society with the secular society, which is rapidly changing, large, heterogeneous, in communication with distant lands; its values favor the new, the different, where nothing is more worthless than yesterday's newspaper or last season's styles, and nothing so valuable as a new cloth for men's shirts or a new spray for mosquitoes. A child reared in such a society, assimilating his culture, learns to value the novel, to adopt new fads, with pleasurable expectations, and perhaps he begins to look forward to setting the pace himself. If his innovations or inventions should strike the popular fancy, he is a great man, for a moment at least.

Thus, if the group has a favorable attitude toward change, a milieu is created in which creativity is favored. In interviews with 200 scientists and artists, we asked "Were you ever seriously encouraged by a teacher?" Nearly all said, "Yes."

In an analysis of the childhood of 1,400 great men and women, we repeatedly found the overwhelming importance of an outstanding teacher. We believe the single most crucial step in increasing creativity in our society would be to recruit and hold the best teachers.

SUMMARY

In exploring some of the environmental and experiential factors in creativity, the following have been considered: enough feeling of security to risk venturing beyond social norms; intelligence involving divergent rather than convergent thinking, which seems to be related to a highly developed sense of humor; freedom to explore, to think, to feel, to roam; enough pressure from marginality to push the person outside his family or social group; and a secular social climate which favors innovation. Such a social climate is fostered by good teachers, informality, freedom for all to participate, skilled but not domineering leadership, opportunity to rotate roles, and a feeling of trust and equality among group members.

REFERENCES

1. Barron, F., "Originality in Relation to Personality and Intellect," *Journal of Psychology*, 25 (1957), 730–742.

2. Beck, S. J., *Rorschach's Test* (New York: Grune and Stratton, 1946), Vols. I and II.

3. Cartwright, D., and A. Zander, *Group Dynamics: Research and Theory* (Evanston, Ill.: Row Peterson and Company, 1953).

4. Foote, Nelson N., and L. S. Cottrell, *Identity and Interpersonal Competence: A New Direction in Family Research* (Chicago: The University of Chicago Press, 1955).

5. Foundation for Research on Human Behavior, "Creativity and Conformity" (Ann Arbor, Mich.: The Foundation, 1958). (Includes an excellent short bibliography.)

6. Getzels, J. W., and P. W. Jackson. "The Highly Creative and the Highly Intelligent Adolescent: An Attempt at Differentiation." A paper presented at the American Psychological Association Convention, Washington, D.C., August, 1958.

7. Ghiselin, Brewster, *The Creative Process* (Berkeley: University of California Press, 1952).

8. Guilford, J. P., *et al.*, "A Factor-Analytic Study of Creative Thinking," report from Psychological Laboratory, University of Southern California, 1951–1952.

9. Hill, Napoleon, *How to Raise Your Salary* (Chicago: Combined Registry Co.).

10. Lewin, K., R. Lippitt, and R. White, "An Experimental Study of Leadership in Group Life." Selection 40 in the present volume.

11. Lewisohn, L., *Upstream* (New York: Boni & Liveright, 1922).

12. Maier, N. R. F., and A. R. Solem, "The Contributions of a Discussion Leader to the Quality of Group Thinking: the Effective Use of Minority Opinions," *Human Relations*, 5 (1952), 277–288.

13. Park, R. E., *Race and Culture* (Glencoe, Ill.: The Free Press, 1950).

14. Redfield, Robert, *The Folk Culture of Yucatan* (Chicago: University of Chicago Press, 1941).

15. Simmel, Georg, *Soziologie* (Leipzig: Duncker und Humblot, 1908).

16. Stanton, H. R., and E. Litwak, "Toward the Development of a Short Form Test of Interpersonal Competence," *American Sociological Review*, 20, No. 6 (December, 1955), 668–674.

15

Ways to Enhance Creative Thinking

E. Paul Torrance

EDITOR'S NOTE • *Although some people seem naturally more creative than others, the fact is, that creative expression can still be taught and encouraged in persons who may not be as gifted. Dr. Torrance is an eminent authority on the subject of creativity, and in this enlightening article he offers a variety of novel and—of all things, creative—ways to increase creative expression.*

Creativity is an infinite phenomenon. A person can be creative in an endless number of ways. The outcomes of creative behavior are inexhaustible.

The coming of the space age and knowledge explosions in every field of human inquiry are making it increasingly necessary for people to learn to be comfortable with infinity. There was a time when we thought we knew the limits to space, to man's potential, to knowledge. A person could

E. Paul Torrance, "Creativity and Infinity," *Journal of Research and Development in Education* 4 (1971): 35–41. Reprinted by permission.

learn some good things in school, college, or an apprenticeship and these learnings would last him for the rest of his life. This day is no more. Men of the future will have to behave creatively.

As computers do more and more of the routine or repetitive work we become freer to behave creatively and there is no limit to what we might do and become. A person may produce a few original or creative ideas by chance but sustained creativity requires an ability to continue to get glimpses of infinity. Unfortunately, we have done little about teaching children to be comfortable with infinity. Usually, infinity astonishes, wearies, confounds, and frightens us. The ancient Greeks had a favorable attitude toward infinity and attributed it to the boundless environment of our cosmos. The Romans, however, regarded infinity unfavorably and negatively. To them, it meant "obscure, variable, unfinished, bad, irrational, flowing or formless, and indefinite."* Theologians have emphasized God's infinity and man's finiteness.

Quite interestingly, young children seem to grasp the concept of infinity intuitively. For example, when you show them Bruno Munari's *Zoo* (1963) with the drawing of birds captioned, "An infinity of birds," they understand. They will say, "Oh, yes, there are so many birds you can't count them." Provided open-ended experiences with opportunities to use their individuality and their creativeness, young children will get glimpses into infinity.

Like the concept of infinity, open-ended kinds of education programs and methods of instruction give the learner the opportunity to respond in terms of his or her experiences and abilities whatever these may be. Some teachers regard such methods and programs as dangerous. When a child responds in terms of his experiences and abilities, this takes the teacher outside his own experiences and abilities. Open-ended programs and methods of instruction cannot be pre-inspected and certified for safety. One never knows for sure where the open ends will lead.

Open-endedness does not imply a lack of structure. For effective learning, there must be some structure, some guides to behavior. One must never lose sight, however, of the self-acting nature

of the human mind. This recognition is especially important in the education of creatively gifted children. It is almost as if their creativity has plugged them into infinity. No matter how much structure is provided the highly creative child, he or she will want to know about things beyond this structure. Such children will produce ideas that go beyond the wildest predictions of the teacher or curriculum maker. This requires of the teacher the most alert and sensitive kind of guidance possible.

The author's recent work with language arts activities has offered excellent opportunities that illustrate the characteristics of educational experiences that make children comfortable with the limitlessness of infinity. Any other aspect of the curriculum can provide equally good examples.

OPEN-ENDEDNESS AND INCOMPLETENESS

One of the simplest ways of giving children glimpses into infinity is through books and stories that have open ends with limitless possibilities. An example of such a book is Fenn Lasell's *Fly Away Goose* (1965). This beautiful story is of a little girl who is hesitating over collecting the goose's egg and letting it become a part of the omelet that night. She thinks of many of the consequences that might result if she leaves the egg and it hatches into a little gosling—both the joyful consequences as well as the sorrowful ones like having to take the mature goose to market, or the goose's being shot by hunters. At the end, the little girl concluded, "I think I'll leave it for mother goose and see if it will hatch. Who knows?" Thus, this deep-moving, emotion-arousing story is left open for the children to produce a limitless number of exciting possibilities. The child is not limited to the single, most probable response. Since no one really knows, each child is free to guess, to speculate.

The following kinds of activities are effective in creating open-endedness in all curricular areas:

1. Playing with ambiguities and uncertainties
2. Freeing children from inhibiting sets or expectations—helping them find the "tops in their cages"
3. Producing awareness of incompleteness of the information presented

---

* *Encyclopedia Britannica*, Vol. 12, pp. 235–8.

4. Making divergent thinking legitimate
5. Examining fantasies for solutions to everyday problems
6. Encouraging multiple hypotheses
7. Letting one thing lead to another
8. Encouraging transformation of information

5. Requiring reorganization of information, objects, etc.
6. Synthesizing unorganized objects, ideas, etc. into meaningful arrangements.

COMBINING APPARENTLY IRRELEVANT ELEMENTS

When two or more somewhat unrelated elements must be synthesized into a single response, the mental leap that occurs is likely to result in something original. This can be done as in a "make-up-your-own stories" exercise such as is found in the reader, *How It Is Nowadays* (Clymer and Ness, 1969). In one of these, the reader is asked to make up a story about a wicked king named Bong; a beloved Princess, Rose; and an errand boy, Wug.

Exercises such as these produce an endless variety of stories which, when read to a class, can give a little glimpse into infinity. Using a design similar to *Tell a Tall Tale* (Salisbury, 1966), the idea can be extended. This intriguing book contains six stories, each with two characters, two places, and three actions. These elements can be combined in such a way as to produce 279,936 stories. It is easy to show children that if 30 of them make up six such simple stories, a total of 8,398,080 stories results immediately. Then, when all 180 of their stories (instead of 6) are combined, an astronomical number of possibilities results. If this can result so effortlessly, think what would happen if we really tried.

The following ways of encouraging the combination of apparently irrelevant elements may be applied in almost any curriculum area:

1. Searching for elegant solutions (i.e., simplest solutions taking into account largest number of variables)
2. Playing with analogies as a basis for searching for solutions to problems
3. Experimenting and manipulating objects, ideas, etc.
4. Encouraging children to use knowledge in one field to solve problems in another.

PRODUCING ELEMENTS AND COMBINING

Open-endedness can be increased still further by having children themselves produce the elements to be combined into a story, a drama, a picture, a dance, or some other communication.

An effective procedure found in the author's research has been termed *Magic Net* technique. This procedure can be used endlessly to produce exciting stories and dramas. To produce an atmosphere of magic, pieces of colored nylon net, music, and at times lights are used. Usually, about six actors take part. Each actor selects a piece of the colored net which turns him into whatever character he wants to play. To "warm up" the actors, they are encouraged to stand, walk, and dance as their character would. Then a member of the audience is given the magic story teller's net and asked to start a story involving the six characters. When the story teller finishes the first episode, the actors enact it. A second story teller resumes the story which is then acted by the cast wearing the magic nets. This involves a continuous problem solving process in which each subsequent story teller must get the characters out of the predicament created by the previous story teller and create another predicament. Each character must translate the action of the story into bodily movement in his own way, adding still other dimensions to the production.

The following kinds of activities are useful in implementing the strategy of producing elements and then combining them:

1. Examining a problem, piece of information, or object from several points of view and then combining the insights engendered
2. Searching for all the facts in a mystery and then solving it
3. Making a series of predictions on the basis of accumulating information

4. Learning the component skills for a complex task and then combining them in the performance of the task

5. Producing multiple analogies and then combining the insights gained from their use

BRAINSTORMING WITHIN A GIVEN STRUCTURE

The brainstorming technique (Osborn, 1963; Parnes, 1967) can be used to generate an endless variety of ideas for the open-ended stories, combinations of unrelated elements, the production of elements to be combined, or any other given structure. This would be likely to increase the imaginativeness of whatever is produced and at the same time give a quicker and deeper glimpse into infinity. The usual rules of brainstorming are applicable such as:

1. Evaluation is suspended.
2. Free-wheeling and wild ideas are welcomed.
3. Quantity is wanted.
4. Combination and improvement are sought.
5. Discussion and argument are unwelcome.

The technique can be applied to the production of cinquains, for example. We could follow one of the usual structures such as the following:

First line—one word (title)
Second line—two words describing the title
Third line—three words expressing action
Fourth line—four words expressing feeling
Fifth line—another for the title

Let us say we wanted to make up a cinquain about the color "blue." We would brainstorm words to describe "blue" and then select the two that do the best job. Then we would brainstorm words telling what "blue" does and select the three words that tell best what "blue" does. Next we would brainstorm words to describe how "blue" feels or makes us feel and select the four most appropriate words. Finally, we would brainstorm words that synthesize all of these things and select the one that best distills the essence of "blue."

WARM-UP EXPERIENCES

Well designed and executed *warm-up* experiences can be quite useful in helping children free their imagination and plug them into infinity. The experience may be a field trip, a musical recording, a socio-drama, a poem, creative movement, or about any other experience having high arousal value.

The Cunnington and Torrance (1965) *Sounds and Images* materials provide one model for designing warm-up experiences. The *Sounds and Images* recordings provide a series of four sounds, ranging from a familiar, coherent sound effect to a strange one consisting of six rather unrelated sound elements. As each sound is played, the listener is asked to think of an image and express it in a word picture. The sounds are presented a second time and the listener is asked to let his imagination swing wider. Finally, they are presented a third time with the listener being asked to let his imagination "go the limits." These materials can be then used for stories, drawings, and the like. This can be done by having the listener select the most interesting of the storehouse images that he produced or some combination of them.

The following kinds of warm up activities may be applied in almost any subject in the curriculum:

1. Heightening anticipation and expectation
2. Heightening concern about a problem
3. Building onto existing information or skills
4. Stimulating curiosity and wanting to know
5. Making purpose of activity clear and meaningful
6. Giving minimal clues and direction

ENVIRONMENTAL WARM-UP

Classroom environments frequently inhibit the *warm-up* necessary for creative language arts activity and make it difficult to help children catch glimpses of infinity. Some classrooms can be modified easily to create a mood or arouse affect.

To facilitate the creation of such moods, Gerard Pottebaum (1970) and his associates have created what they call *The Tree House Learning Environment*. These environments give the intimacy, excitement, and delight of a tree house and consist of panels or flexible dividers that make possible an endless variety of environments within a given classroom. One set of panels might create a jungle environment free from the distractions of the frozen Arctic environment of another group. These settings make it easier for children to transcend the commonplace and obvious and make those mental leaps that result in original productions, if not in glimpses of infinity.

IDENTIFYING GAPS IN KNOWLEDGE

Infinity is incompatible with completeness, but as children learn to read and progress in school, they tend to accept what they read or see as complete. To break this up and make them more comfortable with infinity, teachers can show children that an endless number of questions remain and employ exercises to develop question-asking skills based upon pictures, objects, or stories.

For this purpose, puzzling or ambiguous pictures are desirable. An example of this is one of a dog driving an unusual-looking automobile on a busy city street in *The Dog Next Door* (Clymer and Martin, 1969). The best stories for this purpose are those which are emotionally involving. A favorite for this purpose with preschool and primary grade children is Aileen Fisher's (1964) *Listen, Rabbit*. Throughout this beautifully written story, a little boy wants to make friends with a rabbit. He wonders what the rabbit is doing, whether it be on a moonlight night or when it is snowing. Finally, in the spring he finds the rabbit's nest with five little cotton tails. After reading this very moving story, the children are asked to pretend that the teacher is the rabbit and that they can ask any question they like about the life of the rabbit in the story. To facilitate this, the author makes use of a puppet rabbit similar to the one in the story. Whether the children get glimpses into infinity is not known. In his role of the rabbit, however, the author knows that the story teller does.

PLAYING WITH IMPROBABILITIES

Another kind of experience that gives children glimpses of infinity is playing with improbabilities. This may take any of several formats. One is the "what-could-happen-if" technique Myers and Torrance (1965) used in *Can You Imagine?* Examples are:

> What could happen if it always rained on Saturday?
> What could happen if it were against the law to sing?

Another is the "just-suppose" techniques used in tests of creative thinking (Torrance, 1966) and in preprimary programs in recent years. Examples of these are:

> Just suppose you could make the kind of weather you want by dancing certain ways?
> Just suppose you could visit the prehistoric section of the museum and the animals could come alive?
> Just suppose you could enter into the life of a pond and become whatever you wanted to become?

These "just-supposes" can be brain-stormed and enacted. For example, each child might be asked to decide what he wants to be and do in the pond. We can then enact life in the pond or enact each child's version of life in the pond. After such experiences as these, children find it easy to make up interesting stories, songs, and poems about life in the pond.

MULTI-MODAL EXPRESSION

Frequently, we involve children in an experience and they find it almost impossible to find words to express their reactions to it. They might be able to express their reactions by creative movement, sounds, or even drawings, but we insist that they express their reactions in words. They may produce something but it is likely to lack depth and may even be irrelevant to the experience. If they could first express their reactions in the mode that seems natural, they might then be able to write or talk with deep and imaginative insight about the experience. Creative movement, producing sounds, or making drawings may provide the break-through that challenges the ability to express insights in words.

PROVOCATIVE QUESTIONS

The *provocative question* is one that causes people to think about something in ways that they have never thought of before. Myers and Torrance (1970) and Torrance (1970) have written rather extensively about asking provocative questions. The following types of questions are usually provocative:

1. Questions that confront the pupil with ambiguities and uncertainties
2. Questions that make the familiar strange or the strange familiar
3. Questions that cause the pupil to look at the same thing from several different physical, psychological, sociological, or emotional points of view
4. Questions that require speculation and predictions based on limited information
5. Questions that juxtapose apparently irrelevant or unrelated elements
6. Questions that call for the exploration of mysteries or puzzling phenomena
7. Questions that stimulate the explanation of fantasies to facilitate the understanding of realistic problems.

CONCLUSION

The author has made a first, halting attempt to identify and illustrate the kinds of educational experiences that will give children glimpses into infinity and make them more comfortable with infinity through the use of their creative powers. There are surely others or elaboration and modification of the ones suggested in this article.

REFERENCES

Clymer, T. and Martin, P. M. *The Dog Next Door.* Boston: Ginn and Company, 1969.

Clymer, T. and Ness, P. H. *How It Is Nowadays.* Boston: Ginn and Company, 1969.

Cunnington, B. G. and Torrance, E. P. *Sounds and Images.* Boston: Ginn and Company, 1965.

Fisher, A. *Listen, Rabbit.* New York: Thomas Y. Crowell, 1964.

Lasell, F. H. *Fly Away Goose.* Boston: Houghton Mifflin, 1965.

Munari, B. *Zoo.* Cleveland: World Publishing Company, 1963.

Osborn, A. F. *Creative Imagination.* (3rd Ed.) New York: Charles Scribner's Sons, 1963.

Parnes, S. J. *Creative Behavior Guidebook.* New York: Charles Scribner's Sons, 1967.

Pottebaum, G. A. *The Tree House Learning Environment.* Kettering, Ohio: The Tree House, 1970.

Salisbury, K. *Tell a Tall Tale.* New York: Western Publishing, 1966.

Torrance, E. P. *Torrance Tests of Creative Thinking: Norms-Technical Manual (Research Edition).* Princeton, N.J.: Personnel Press, 1966.

Torrance, E. P. *Encouraging Creativity in the Classroom.* Dubuque, Iowa: Wm. C. Brown Company, 1970.

Torrance, E. P. and Meyers, R. E. *Creative Learning and Teaching.* New York: Dodd, Mead and Company, 1970.

Chapter Five · new frontiers in the understanding of learning and behavior

16

The Biochemistry of Memory and Forgetfulness

Maya Pines

EDITOR'S NOTE · In this intriguing article, Maya Pines introduces you to some of the basic biochemical processes involved in remembering and forgetting. Since the brain can absorb as many as one quadrillion (1,000,000,000,000,000) separate bits of information in a lifetime, it is remarkable that we can remember anything in a systematic way. But we do remember, sometimes in spite of our best efforts not to. We have not yet reached the age of memory pills and other biochemical memory stimulants, but we may not be far away from the time when such science fiction-like possibilities become realities. What are some of the basic biochemical components of memory and forgetfulness? Read on.

Every day, the 49-year-old man reads the same copy of the *Reader's Digest*, which seems eternally new to him. If you meet him, he

Maya Pines, "Speak, Memory: The Riddle of Recall and Forgetfulness," *Saturday Review*, August 8, 1975, pp. 16–20. Copyright © 1972 by the Saturday Review. Reprinted by permission.

appears quite normal—but if you leave the room for 15 minutes and then return, he thinks he has never seen you before. He cannot recognize his next-door neighbors. His family moved to his present house 22 years ago, shortly after he had a brain operation to relieve him of severe epilepsy. As a result of this operation (which was experimental and has never been performed on anyone else in the same way, now that its effects on memory are known), he cannot form new memories. Unlike some victims of amnesia, he remembers his early past very clearly, but every new thing he does, says, sees, or feels disappears from his mind so quickly that his own life since 1953 remains a total blank.

Thousands of old people suffer from mild forms of such impairment, simply as a result of their age. "My mind is like a sieve," complains an 85-year-old woman. "I don't remember anything I read in the newspaper—don't know why I read it. But I remember very clearly what happened long ago. . . ." Many other persons have transient, but frightening, lapses of memory after receiving shock treatment for depression.

Memory sometimes fails, but it can also preserve events with extraordinary precision and detail for nearly a century after they have occurred. We still know very little about this precious quality. Nevertheless, we are beginning to control it. Scientists can already improve or destroy the memory of animals with surprising ease. And now, amid much excitement, a new crop of drugs that might help the aged to retain their memories is about to be tested. However, scientists, such as Dr. James McGaugh of the University of California, Irvine, warn that it will take at least a decade before such drugs—if they work—go past the experimental stage.

The past two years have been especially rewarding for memory researchers, whose subject has always been the most difficult and exasperating of all areas in the brain sciences. For a long time progress was slow because it was thought that memory depended entirely on electrical activity—on electrical circuits in various parts of the brain which laid down lasting patterns, or "engrams." Harvard's famed neuropsychologist Karl Lashley spent a lifetime looking for such engrams. Convinced that they must be located somewhere in the cortex, he trained thousands of rats to run mazes and learn other skills, then systematically cut out piece after piece of their cortex, expecting that at some point this would also wipe out the memory of their training. But no matter where he cut, the memory survived. Even when the brain injury was severe enough to make the animal limp or stagger, even when 90 percent of its visual cortex had been removed, the rat still found its way across the maze. Finally, after decades of struggling with the problem of how information is encoded in the brain and how people learn, Lashley came to the tongue-in-cheek conclusion that "learning is just not possible at all."

About a decade ago researchers began to emphasize the chemical aspect of memory. Whatever memory consisted of, it clearly had to have some chemical component; otherwise, long-term memories would not survive deep-freeze hibernation, electroconvulsive shock, coma, anesthesia, or other conditions that radically disrupt the electrical activity of the brain. A chemical trace would also explain why memories are so widespread—why the engram eluded all who tried to find its specific location in the brain.

The chemical approach led to a series of intriguing experiments in the United States and abroad. At the University of Michigan's Mental Health Research Institute, for example, Dr. Bernard Agranoff, a biochemist, began to inflict memory losses on goldfish. After his treatments, the fish had much in common with the old woman who complained that she could not remember what she had just read in the morning paper. Dr. Agranoff did not cut anything out of the goldfish's brains, nor did he do any permanent damage to them. He merely injected some puromycin, an antibiotic that blocks the formation of protein, into their skulls immediately after they had learned a new skill, and the skill vanished.

It vanished because, according to current theories, there are several stages of memory—short-term memory, long-term memory, and perhaps some others in between—and moving from one stage to the next requires a chemical step. Unless a new impression is fixed by some chemical process in the brain, it will fade away. The puromycin apparently interfered with this step.

Normally, goldfish that have learned to cross an underwater barrier in their tank whenever a light is flashed (in order to avoid a mild electric shock) will remember this skill for at least one month. In order to make the goldfish forget it, Agranoff had to inject his puromycin immediately after the training session. If he waited as long as one hour, it was too late—the memory had been fixed. He could also administer the injections *before* the training began; in that case, the fish would learn to avoid shocks just as rapidly as any other fish and would even remember it for a short time, but three days later all memory of the training had disappeared. This finding showed that the chemical had no effect on the acquisition of memory but acted on its consolidation, which occurred during the hour immediately following the event.

Entranced by the possibility of wiping out specific memories of something just learned—of a murder, perhaps, or the location of military secrets—in this fashion, a reporter once asked Dr. Agranoff, only half in jest, whether the CIA had been in touch with him about his work. Agranoff smiled and replied, "I forget." His own experiments have been limited to animals, however, and he is quick to point out that puromycin could have lethal effects on man. Almost defensively, he emphasizes that his real goal is to learn how memory deficits occur in the aged and in people with degenerative neurological disease, so as to prevent this loss. "The only way we have to study the fixation process is to disrupt it," he declared.

If the consolidation of memory could be disrupted, could it also be improved? At Irvine, Dr. McGaugh decided to give it a try. Years earlier, he remembered, Karl Lashley had shown that animals would learn new skills more rapidly if they were given stimulants such as strychnine before the training. These experiments were difficult to interpret, however. The drug might simply have made the animals more alert or more eager for the food reward; it did not necessarily affect their memory. To clarify the situation, McGaugh left a group of rats alone during their training and *then* injected the strychnine. He saw at once that the more strychnine he gave them, up to a point, the better they learned. Instead of going to the wrong arm of a maze about 25 times before grasping that they had to choose the white alley at every turn, the mice that had received the largest dose of the drug learned after only five or six errors.

These dramatic results were soon duplicated with metrozol, a convulsant drug, and with amphetamine, although these two chemicals had to be injected within 15 minutes after the training session, while the strychnine could be given as much as an hour later. After trying several different drugs, in graduated doses, at varying times, and with different kinds of learning tasks, McGaugh concluded that he had made his case. "The robust nature of the effect is beyond question," he declared. "The effects are as long-lasting as those of ordinary memory. What we produce is either a quicker or a stronger consolidation of memory, so that whatever is learned is learned better."

The drugs could even bring back memories that appeared to have been suppressed by electroconvulsive shocks. "We can now block and unblock," said McGaugh, a psychobiologist who is currently vice-chancellor of Irvine. "If we produce retrograde amnesia by electroshock, we can undo it with drugs. But all this is time-dependent."

From the point of view of the aged, the most interesting aspect of such experiments was the discovery (by other researchers) that old mice and rats responded to the memory drugs much better than did young animals: their memory improved even when the amphetamine was injected two hours after a training session, for instance, while young rats had to have it within 15 minutes of their training. Evidently, their memory-fixing process had slowed down. It might then be speeded up and sharpened with drugs.

This finding led to the hope that effective memory drugs might soon be developed to help old people whose memory had begun to fail. But there remained a major hurdle: all the drugs that seemed effective were either addictive (amphetamine) or poisonous (strychnine), or they led to convulsions.

Enter the hero of this story: a Dutch pharmacologist, Dr. David DeWied of the University of Utrecht, who works with substances that the body produces naturally and are thus much safer. His most recent experiments on animals have led to a tremendous feeling of excitement among researchers.

The new substances are natural hormones, such as ACTH, which the body produces in response to stress. Until a few years ago, scientists believed that ACTH acted only as a messenger, going from the pituitary gland at the base of the brain to the adrenal glands atop the kidneys and ordering them to release their steroid hormones. ACTH was not supposed to act directly on the brain. But it now turns out that ACTH has two different functions, and that one of its components —which does not affect the adrenals at all—is clearly related to the fixation of memory. Dr. DeWied narrowed this down to a small chain of four amino acids, $ACTH^{4-7}$, although most researchers are working with a slightly larger component called $ACTH^{4-10}$. Judging from the results of a recent flurry of research, this chain of chemicals alerts the memory machine to the importance of an event and orders the brain to "print"—to fix the short-term memory so that it can go into permanent storage.

Treating animals or people with this natural chemical would be much like revving up their normal memory mechanisms. It might prevent them from forgetting certain events or skills—a mixed blessing, depending on how it was used.

Doctors who believe that electroconvulsive therapy is the best treatment for severe depression have long wished for some way to reduce the amnesia that follows the shocks. It is not surprising, therefore, that one of the first experimental uses of the new substance in human beings has been with patients undergoing such treatment. Previous work in the Netherlands had shown that $ACTH^{4-10}$ would prevent a loss of memory in rats that had been given electroconvulsive shocks. Tests are now under way in Indiana to see whether the same will prove true in human beings.

The next step is to try out these chemicals on the aged. This will be done, starting this summer, in two New York hospitals, according to Dr. Max Fink, a professor of psychiatry at the State University of New York at Stony Brook, who is monitoring American studies of the effects of $ACTH^{4-10}$ on human beings. At present, the hospitals (New York Medical College and NYU College of Medicine) are working only with younger, normal volunteers.

Dr. Fink adds that chemists in the Netherlands

have succeeded in making synthetic $ACTH^{4-10}$ that is 1,000 times more potent than the original—a great advantage, since a chemical of this strength could be taken by mouth, in pill form, rather than through injections.

As if this were not enough, last March Dr. DeWied announced that yet another hormone, vasopressin (which is produced by the hypothalamus and stored in the posterior pituitary), has even more dramatic effects on the memory of animals. While $ACTH^{4-10}$ will prevent rats from forgetting a new skill for some time, vasopressin appears to engrave it in their memories forever. It has not yet been tried out on human beings.

Eventually doctors may learn to measure the hormone level of people who have lost their memory and then to correct it, if necessary, with pills. What causes senile forgetfulness remains a mystery, but it may well involve the brain's inability to synthesize certain hormones. Even though the amino acids from which the hormones are made can be found in common foodstuffs, an active pituitary or hypothalamus is required to make them—unless they are made available as drugs. Possibly some kinds of mental retardation that involve poor memory might also be relieved to some extent through such drugs. The memory researchers emphasize, however, that these are only speculations at the moment. They have been burned before: a decade ago, for instance, some scientists had high hopes that memory defects could be treated with RNA, but nothing came of their expectations. They do not want to have to write hundreds of letters to distraught relatives explaining that, at present, there is nothing they can do to help the senile or the retarded.

Meanwhile, McGaugh and his associate, Dr. Paul E. Gold, are trying to put various pieces of the puzzle together. They have been wondering how their experiments with strychnine and other stimulants which improved the fixation of memory in rats fit in with present experiments showing that some hormones do just the same thing. Perhaps the stimulants acted by releasing the hormones, they speculate. Or, perhaps neither of these chemicals is actually involved in the process of information storage. The researchers may have stumbled, instead, on the mechanism by which people evaluate whether a recent experience was trivial enough to

forget or important enough to store in the memory files. If so, it is a considerable achievement, potentially of enormous importance for the aged. But, on the other hand, it leaves the underlying mystery of memory untouched.

The basic questions are: how does information of any sort get coded in the brain? What does short-term memory actually consist of? How does a memory become permanently fixed? How do memories change with time, as they often do? How do people retrieve any specific memory, out of the welter of a lifetime's experiences? And how do they forget? Neither the scientists who study behavior nor those who work with microscopic particles of brain tissue or chemicals have any answers. Yet these questions are at the heart of everything that makes us human.

In some cases it may be dangerous to remember too well. The Russian psychologist A. R. Luria poignantly described such dangers in his book *The Mind of a Mnemonist*. The man whom he studied, S., never forgot anything. He had no difficulty reproducing any lengthy series of words whatever, wrote Luria, "even 15 or 16 years after the session in which he had originally recalled the words." He did not have to "memorize" data, but simply "registered an impression," which he could "read" at a much later date. Luria soon gave up trying to find the limits of his memory—there were none. On first acquaintance, however:

> S. struck one as a disorganized and rather dull-witted person, an impression that was even more marked whenever he had to deal with a story that had been read to him. If the story was read at a fairly rapid pace, S.'s face would register confusion and finally utter bewilderment. "No," he would say. "This is too much. Each word calls up images; they collide with one another, and the result is chaos."

Finally, Luria discovered the terrible flaw that went along with S.'s perfect memory: because he remembered every specific image, he was never able to single out the key points in a situation. Thus, while he could recite long texts, his grasp of their total meaning was not good. After S. began working as a mnemonist, a further problem came to plague him: he could not forget images that he no longer needed. He sometimes gave several performances a night in the same hall, where the long charts of numbers that he had to recall were written on a single blackboard and then erased before the next performance. But in his mind's eye, he still *saw* them in the same place. "When the next performance starts and I walk over to that blackboard, the numbers I have erased are liable to turn up again," S. complained. He even thought of writing things down so he would forget them, but it did not work. There seemed to be some failure in the metabolism of his short-term memories: whereas old people have difficulty converting any of these into permanent memories, S. was forced to convert them all. Conceivably, he suffered from an excess of the hormones DeWied has been studying.

In the future, we may be able to select either one of these alternatives at various times: we may decide to take amnesic drugs before events so horrible that we want no permanent record of them, or we may seek a heightening of experience through drugs that sharpen our memory for special occasions.

There is also a built-in danger of abuse. Memory drugs, like tranquilizers and behavior-modification therapies, may easily be forced on unwilling subjects. Children with learning problems (caused by poor teaching, perhaps), patients in institutions, soldiers, and other captive populations might be given such drugs indiscriminately. The drugs might even be combined with behavior-modification techniques, to make these "stick" better—to turn some "aversive" experience into a warning that cannot be forgotten. In other cases, people might be forced to take drugs that prevent the consolidation of memory.

As with all the new discoveries about the brain, we are being offered high-powered tools that have direct access to our identity. What we make of them depends on how effectively we plan ahead, what guidelines we set for their use, and whether we keep a close watch on what the brain researchers are doing today.

17

Biofeedback Technology: Implications for Teaching and Learning

Thomas B. Mulholland

EDITOR'S NOTE • *Biofeedback machines are designed to give us feedback about various bodily processes. They pick up the imperceptible bioelectric signals emitted by the body and record them in amplified forms that we can see and hear. Once we are aware of these signals, to some extent we can control the bodily processes the signals reflect; i.e., we can learn to relax our muscles, slow our brain waves, and lower our blood pressure. Like the preceding article, this is reading about a "new frontier." It reflects not so much where we are as it does where we might direct our efforts with this new technology in classroom settings. For instance, how would you like to learn how to control your alpha brainwaves in order to increase your attention span? Or, better yet, to learn how to stay awake during a dull lecture?*

Biofeedback technology has arrived. Physiological processes can now be connected, with proper electronics, to light or sound displays that give a person new information about physiological happenings in his own body or brain.

Thomas B. Mulholland, "It's Time to Try Hardware in the Classroom," *Psychology Today Magazine* (December 1973): 103–04. Copyright © 1973 Ziff-Davis Publishing Company. Reprinted by permission of *Psychology Today Magazine*.

Though there have been some excessive enthusiasms for biofeedback, it is unquestionably an important and impressive new way to expand self-awareness, extend self-exploration, and improve self-control. Biofeedback training can serve as an adjunct to meditation, as a complement to drug experience, as a method of treatment for some stress- or anxiety-related disorders, and as a technique for producing relaxation of mind and body.

Among professionals in the field of education who should be involved in promoting self-awareness, self-exploration and self-control, the techniques of biofeedback remain relatively unknown. Perhaps biofeedback researchers have not given enough consideration to this problem, or perhaps educators are suspicious of strangers, and resistant to new ideas. Whatever the cause, a communication gap clearly exists between biofeedback and education.

The Uses of Biofeedback. Educators can use biofeedback in three ways: as a vehicle to allow them to participate in the new interest in self-awareness, self-exploration, and self-control; as a general method for accentuating processes conducive to learning, and diminishing those that impede learning; and as a way to strengthen specific skills, such as relaxing certain muscles, or increasing certain brain rhythms.

A trip into inner space "turns on" modern youth. They recognize the uniqueness and untapped potential of their own mental processes. Introspection and contemplation are still relevant, but powerful new techniques such as drugs and meditative practices have become popular methods for expanding awareness and exploring the mind. Any educator who fails to recognize this cultural change will necessarily lose some touch with youth. Educators need such contact, yet most will not use drugs, and meditation has become "something to know about" rather than a part of educational practice. Neither mind-expanding chemicals nor Eastern meditative practice fits the contemporary American educational model—pragmatic, information oriented, and technologically biased.

Biofeedback may be an acceptable solution. Many young people share its goals of self-awareness, self-exploration, and self-control. At the same time, biofeedback uses sophisticated electronic and display devices that give a tangible and objective connection to the real world, or at least the kind of real world with which most of the older generation can feel comfortable.

Right now, at this early stage of its development, biofeedback provides a way of reaching goals shared by students and educators. Not too far ahead, one can see other direct applications of biofeedback technology in the learning process. Educators could use the procedure to encourage body and brain states that facilitate learning, memory and retrieval, and to diminish those body and brain states that impede them. Most of these applications exist today in the heads of various researchers. But then, that's where all good ideas start. The speculative applications of biofeedback I propose here obviously require further research. I do not offer them as miracle methods, for by its very nature biofeedback training demands long hours of practice to yield enduring control. It requires a well-motivated learner, patient instruction, and skillful use of sophisticated electronic instruments. As in all learning, some people learn readily; others are much less adept.

Learning to Pay Attention. One of the obvious potential uses of biofeedback technology is *attention*, the basic requirement for learning. All educators want and try to get attention from their students, for without it they waste their efforts to communicate. One of the first commands the student gets in school is "Pay attention!" whether to visual stimuli, as in reading, or to aural stimuli, as in listening to a lecture. If attention declines to the point of insufficient arousal, unselective scrutiny, or undifferentiated reception of stimuli, the student's perception becomes less accurate and his comprehension declines.

We know surprisingly little about the optimum combination of attentional processes that enable a student to learn most efficiently. We don't know the proper degree of arousal for learning a list of words. We don't know whether relaxed muscles permit better learning than a high level of muscular tension. Whatever the best conditions for learning, there is clearly some critical level of attention, arousal or alertness below which learning becomes impaired.

Turning Off Alpha. Biofeedback researchers are currently very interested in changes in certain brain-wave rhythms that accompany increases and decreases of visual attention. When we are keenly attentive to visual stimuli, alpha rhythms, which originate in the posterior cortex of the brain, and which are measured by electroencephalograph (EEG), become irregular, and less frequent, with reduced amplitude. With biofeedback techniques, we can train students to decrease the amount of alpha produced by their brains. By getting feedback tones or lights which report when alpha waves occur, a person can learn to "turn his alpha off." By learning to regulate feedback the student also acquires skill at regulating his own attention level, at least in the presence of the feedback display.

When the feedback display itself is included in the educational process, the possibilities for feedback training multiply. For example, instead of a tone or light signaling the absence or presence of alpha waves, an information display can provide material for the students to learn at the same time it gives feedback about his alpha production. Prototype systems already exist in our laboratory with which children can view television, filmstrips, or light shows, regulated by their control of their own alpha rhythms, or visual attention.

These complex, multipurpose displays introduce new opportunities for reinforcements into the feedback system. For instance, a display could remain on, giving the student the information he wants, only as long as his EEG shows a low level of alpha. If too much alpha occurred, then the display could become scrambled, or an unpleasant noise might sound. This signal would prompt the student's return to a state of diminished alpha or increased attentiveness.

Repeated exposure to any visual display usually causes a drop in one's EEG reaction to it, an effect called "habituation." Complex displays stand up better than simple displays, in terms of slowing the process of habituation, but even with complex displays one's attention declines after repeated exposure. A technician can chart this decline with a mathematical curve. A computer can use these "impact" and "fade-out" functions to control further the feedback displays. When attention lags, the display would change. For example, if the attentional reaction dropped off after repetitive sampling of one class of verbal stimuli, say, names of state capitals, the display could then shift to an arithmetic lesson, or an art appreciation lesson.

Such use of biofeedback technology could lead to a new category of teaching machines, controlled by physiological processes associated with attention. The technology now exists for the new man–machine interactions, and the time has arrived for examining the potential of this technology for teaching.

• The emotional state of the student has perhaps as much effect as attention on the learning process. Unpleasant emotions such as anxiety, fear, or anger can impede learning, as can too much or too little emotional arousal. By using biofeedback techniques we could train a person to maintain the physiological states associated with moderately pleasant feelings while he learned. This accomplishment would facilitate learning, remembering and retrieval.

• Overactive or "hyperactive" children could also benefit from the use of biofeedback technology in education. Many teachers must now contend with children who fidget, or who waste energy by unproductive movement or by maintaining too much tension in their muscles. We already know that biofeedback training can help bring muscle relaxation under voluntary control. Educators should explore the ways that muscle-relaxation and muscle-tension training can help the overactive, jittery or restless child whose motor activity impedes his learning. Today, educators must rely on tranquilizers to do the same job. Biofeedback training offers a non-chemical alternative to this misuse of tranquilizers.

• Drowsiness is another common student problem that biofeedback training might help eliminate. While drowsiness actually may be a sign of fatigue, it is often a result of classroom monotony, or high temperature or humidity. One way to avoid drowsiness is to learn physiological responses incompatible with it. By using biofeedback techniques, students can learn to increase their alertness to a level compatible with the requirements for learning. This would enable them to take notes at a monotonous lecture without drifting off into a state of drowsiness.

• In addition to its potential for solving such general problems as attention, biofeedback training can also counteract specific processes that hinder learning. For example, students sometimes subvocalize when they read, an activity which, though not resulting in audible speech, does slow down their reading rate, and may act as a fatiguing interference.

Two biofeedback experiments on this problem have been reported by Curtis Hardyck and Lewis Petrinovich in 1969. They first worked with a sample of 50 college students at UC, Berkeley. The experimental subjects learned to eliminate subvocal activity within the first hour of treatment. The control group, which received no feedback, showed no change over three recording sessions. After the experiment, the control group received the feedback treatment, and learned to inhibit their subvocal activity also. Only two out of the 50 subjects failed to respond to the biofeedback conditioning.

Hardyck and Petrinovich achieved similar results with a group of 30 high-school students, although they did take longer to learn. They needed as many as three sessions before they eliminated subvocal activity. When the researchers correlated IQ with the number of sessions required for learning, they found that average and above-average high-school students learned as quickly as college students. Subjects with below average IQ scores required many more sessions to eliminate subvocal activity, and follow-up studies conducted the following year showed that they had reverted to subvocalization. The students with average and above-average IQ scores continued to read without subvocalization.

Hardyck and Petrinovich concluded that the treatment of subvocal speech might help high-school and college populations improve their reading skills. If educators used the technique together with established reading improvement methods, these students might learn to read faster and still retain their comprehension. On the other hand, perhaps we should encourage students who have difficulty comprehending even relatively low-level material, to subvocalize. Teachers could reverse the treatment sequence to insure that they learn how to subvocalize, and to insure maximum possible comprehension. Of course, further research is necessary before we understand all aspects of the relationship between subvocal speech and reading speed.
• Biofeedback could be creatively used to teach human psychology, and the physiology of the higher nervous functions. The student could be his own laboratory material, and do experiments on himself. One would surely want to avoid gimmickry, but a balanced approach could make fruitful use of biofeedback technology as an adjunct to classroom discussion and reading.

It should be recognized by now that, despite gigantic expenditures for mass education in recent years, there is still a great deal we don't know about the learning process. Many biofeedback researchers have already demonstrated the potential value and uses of their technology for education. It's now time for educators to take advantage of these opportunities. By intelligent and creative application of the new biofeedback technology, the educational community may achieve major advances in the processes of communicating, teaching and training.

18

Transcendental Meditation as a Way to Expand Creative Intelligence

Paul H. Levine

EDITOR'S NOTE • According to Maharishi's TM headquarters in Los Angeles, over 300,000 Americans have learned to meditate and another 15,000 start TM every month. In many ways, Maharishi's teachings and method of transcendental meditation appeal to our identity-confused and electronic society in the way Emerson's transcendentalism appealed to the changing society of his era. What is transcendental meditation? How is it related to "creative intelligence"? What are the implications of this approach for education? These and other questions are addressed in this interesting reading.

The search for definition of basic goals which is so prominent a concern of the educational community echoes a similar quest for purpose within my own field of science and, indeed, within society at large. While educators are asking, "What are schools for?"[1] scientists are asking, "What is the significance of science?"[2] and political leaders still seek to define our "national purpose."

Paul H. Levine, "Transcendental Meditation and the Science of Creative Intelligence," *Phi Delta Kappan* (December 1972): 231–35. Reprinted by permission.

The soul-searching is widespread, yet within each profession or field of activity the search is carried out within the boundaries of that field, solutions are sought in the framework of the problem perceived, and more fundamental aspects of the situation are consequently overlooked.

It seems clear that what is really being asked is, What should be the objectives of human activity? with specific reference in each of the examples cited to the activities of teaching, doing science, or running a nation. If we adopt the common-sense position that the principal objective of *any* activity is to promote the fulfillment of the individuals engaged in and influenced by that activity, then the real goal of education is seen to encompass nothing less than the *fulfillment* of the student.

In the sense we are using it here, fulfillment implies the actualization of the full potentialities for growth latent in the individual. Therefore, the measure of any educational system is first the breadth of its implicit *vision* of the range of these potentialities and second its *effectiveness* in providing every student with a practical means for achieving such full development. If a crisis is felt to exist in education, then it may logically be asked whether the fault lies in too narrow a vision of the possibilities and, in consequence, too restricted an armamentarium for achievement.

This article discusses a particular conception of the range of potential human development which, if further validated by a growing body of anecdotal and scientific evidence, must necessarily change our ideas about individual fulfillment and with this our views on the structure and responsibility of education. The conception is that of Maharishi Mahesh Yogi; it is being taught as part of a new discipline called the Science of Creative Intelligence.

CREATIVE INTELLIGENCE

The concept of creative intelligence arises from an examination of the structure of purposeful change in nature. No matter where we look, new forms and relationships are continually being created from lesser developed states. This evolution appears to be orderly, i.e., governed by intelligible laws. The intelligence displayed by nature in this process may be called creative intelligence. When we observe creation in action, whether it be in astronomy or biology—or even the growth of a rose—we encounter striking parallels in the structure of the creative process as it unfolds in each case. Through such interdisciplinary analyses, it comes to be appreciated that a fundamental significance can be accorded to creativity (and to the intelligence shaping its expression), a significance which transcends the particular sphere of activity in which the creativity is being manifested. Creative intelligence thus becomes a valid object of intellectual inquiry in its own right.

The relevance of such inquiry to education, and to practical life in general, stems from the circumstance that the creative impulse in man, as expressed in his progressive thoughts and actions, is found upon close examination to be structured along precisely the same lines as creative processes in the purely physical domain. This circumstance (not as remarkable as it may seem at first glance, since we are, after all, part of nature) immediately suggests a transcendental aspect to human creativity which necessarily casts consideration of the human condition into broader evolutionary contexts.

Fulfillment, for example, comes to mean full expression in an individual's life of the creative intelligence inherent in his nature. Lack of fulfillment (which we may call suffering) in this view is ascribed to some restriction of the flow of creative intelligence from its source at the core of one's being to the level of conscious awareness from which one perceives and acts. A practical consequence of this approach is the intriguing possibility that human problems can be attacked at a common fundamental level—without specific regard to the nature of the problem—much in the same way that a gardener simultaneously attends to deficiencies in the development of the many separate leaves of a plant by simply watering the root.

TRANSCENDENTAL MEDITATION

The existence of a simple natural technique called transcendental meditation lends substance to the above considerations, removing them from the realm of purely philosophical speculation. TM, as it is frequently abbreviated, is a systematic procedure of "turning the attention inwards towards the subtler levels of a thought until the mind transcends

the experience of the subtlest state of the thought and arrives at the source of the thought. This expands the conscious mind and at the same time brings it in contact with the creative intelligence that gives rise to every thought."[3]

This technique for the direct *experience* of the field of creative intelligence at the root of one's being is apparently a universal human faculty not requiring any particular intellectual or cognitive facility other than the ordinary ability to think. It is easily learned by anyone in about six hours of instruction (spread out over four consecutive days) from a Maharishi-trained teacher.[4] Once learned, it can be continued without the necessity for additional instruction. It is primarily on the basis of this systematic and apparently universally applicable procedure for the empirical[5] verification of theoretical constructs involving creative intelligence that one may validly speak in terms of a *science* of creative intelligence, or SCI.

The rapidly expanding interest in SCI, both in and out of academia, and—surprisingly—both within the establishment and the youth subculture, presently derives not so much from an appreciation of its inherent scope as from a desire for a fuller understanding of the immediate practical benefits of TM.[6] Notwithstanding the simplicity of the practice, meditators unanimously report improvements in the energy and enthusiasm with which they approach their activities and in their clarity of mind, mental and physical health, and ability to interact harmoniously with their environment.[7] Marked reductions in tension and moodiness are frequently cited, even by those in particularly stressful occupations or family situations. The list goes on to include increased creativity, perceptiveness, self-confidence, productivity, reading speed, psychomotor facility, and learning ability. As one might expect, meditators report concurrent reductions in their use of tranquilizers, stimulants, and other prescribed drugs—and, most significantly, of non-prescription drugs as well.[8] The combined effect is succinctly expressed by a Yale biology instructor: "There's been a quantum increase in the quality of my life since I started meditating."

Experiences during meditation vary from individual to individual and from one meditation to the next. A common experiential denominator, observed even in the first meditation, is a unique blend of deep physical relaxation and expanded

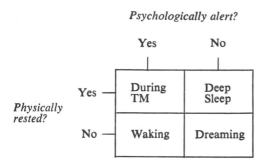

Psychologically alert?

FIGURE 1. Relationship of TM to Other States of Consciousness

mental awareness. The relationship of this state of mind and body to the more familiar states of waking, dreaming, and deep sleep may be schematized as in the matrix shown in Figure 1.

Viewed in this context, TM can perhaps be accepted as just another natural albeit very useful style of functioning of the nervous system, to be alternated with the others on a regular daily basis. Since the dynamism of daily activity in large measure depends on the thoroughness of the psychophysiological rest achieved during the deep sleep and dreaming states, the additional profound rest claimed to occur during TM would account for the enlivened functioning in the waking state reported by meditators.

SCIENTIFIC RESEARCH

The anecdotal claims for TM, even when they are echoed by people of unquestioned objectivity and stature, must nevertheless be verified by the tools of science before they can be accepted by a society grappling with the very ills TM is purported to relieve so effortlessly. A unique aspect of TM vis-à-vis other techniques for mental or physical development is the depth of scientific investigation of its effects currently in progress throughout the world. Major research projects on TM are being carried out at over 40 universities and institutes, including the Harvard Medical School, Stanford Research Institute, and the Universities of Cambridge, Cologne, Rome, and Capetown. In great measure, this widespread research activity is made possible by the availability of large numbers of cooperative meditators at virtually every major uni-

versity, as well as by the effortlessness of the technique itself, which permits experimentation to be performed without disturbing the meditation.

Much of the meditation research is still in its early phases, particularly the long-term clinical studies of TM's *possible* value for hypertensives (Harvard Medical School) and in the relief of mental illness (Hartford's Institute of Living). The research that has reached publication stage, however, is already sufficient to establish that the psychophysiological effects both during and after TM are real and unique in their degree of integration.

In the *American Journal of Physiology*, a team of Harvard and University of California researchers has reported on these integrated characteristics of mind and body during TM, calling it a "wakeful hypometabolic physiologic state," i.e., a state of restful alertness (see Figure 2).[9] They found that the degree of metabolic rest after 5–10 *minutes* of TM was characterized by an average decrease in oxygen consumption of 17%, deeper than that achieved after 6–7 *hours* of sleep. They found a reduction in heart rate of three beats per minute, which, when correlated with an earlier study reporting a drop in cardiac output of 25% during TM,[10] indicates a significant reduction in the workload of the heart. EEG (i.e., "brain wave") measurements showed a predominance of slow alpha wave activity in the central and frontal areas of the brain, thereby clearly distinguishing TM from the waking, dreaming, and sleeping states.[11]

Most significant were the observations of an approximately threefold increase in skin resistance during TM, indicating relaxation and a reduction of anxiety. Biochemical studies of the meditators' blood showed a remarkable reduction in lactate concentration both during and after meditation. Anxiety symptoms are believed to be correlated with high blood lactate levels. Thus, as reported in a recent *Scientific American* article, Robert K. Wallace and Herbert Benson are led to view TM as an integrated response or reflex which is opposite in its characteristics to the "fight or flight" response believed to be primarily responsible for the high incidence of hypertension and related diseases in today's fast-paced society.[12]

Psychological studies of personality changes attributable to TM have also begun to appear in the literature. In the *Journal of Counseling Psychol-*

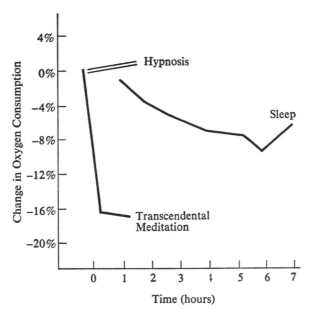

FIGURE 2. Levels of Rest: Change in Metabolic Rate. During transcendental meditation, oxygen consumption and metabolic rate markedly decrease, indicating a deep state of rest (*Scientific American*, February 1972). (Figure 2 is adapted from *Scientific Research on Transcendental Meditation*, a publication of the Maharishi International University Administration Center, 1015 Gayley Ave., Los Angeles, Calif. 90024.)

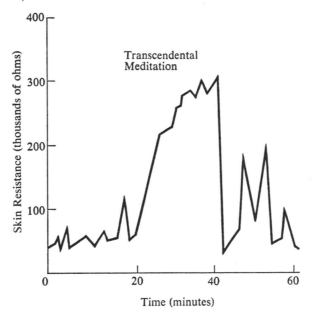

FIGURE 3. State of Relaxation: Change in Skin Resistance. During stress or anxiety, skin resistance decreases. During transcendental meditation, skin resistance increases significantly, indicating deep relaxation and reduction of anxiety and emotional disturbances. (Figure 3 is adapted from *Scientific Research on Transcendental Meditation*, a publication of the Maharishi International University Administration Center.)

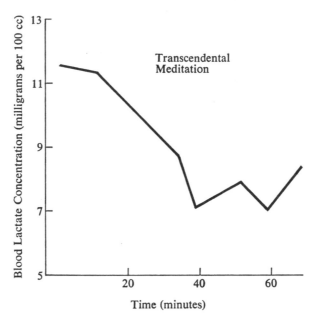

FIGURE 4. Biochemical Changes. High concentration of lactate in the blood has been associated with anxiety neurosis, anxiety attacks, and high blood pressure. During transcendental meditation, the concentration of blood lactate markedly decreases (*Scientific American*, February 1972). (Figure 4 is adapted from *Scientific Research on Transcendental Meditation*, a publication of the Maharishi International University Administration Center.)

ogy, a University of Cincinnati team concluded that "the practice of meditation for a 2-month period would appear to have a salutary influence on a subject's psychological state as measured by the Personal Orientation Inventory."[13] Changes in the direction of increased "self-actualization" were found to occur for meditating subjects.

Another study, reported in the *Journal of Psychosomatic Medicine*, gives insight into a possible explanation for the wide variety of beneficial results apparently following from the simple practice of TM.[14] It was found that meditators habituated more rapidly to a stressful environment than nonmeditators and, furthermore, that meditators' nervous systems displayed greater autonomic stability. This evidence, together with the lactate observations cited earlier, tends to substantiate the view (presented in SCI) that TM acts to reduce one's store of psychophysiological stress while simultaneously reducing the likelihood of further stress accumulation. When one considers the manifold deleterious effects of stress, it becomes apparent that any technique which can reduce stress

—e.g., the twice-daily experience of a hypometabolic wakeful state—has the potential for simultaneous improvement of one's life on all those levels previously stress afflicted. A "quantum jump in the quality of life" suddenly becomes credible.

IMPLICATIONS FOR EDUCATION

In the broader vision of SCI, stresses are viewed as impediments to the spontaneous flow of creative intelligence from the inner being to the level of conscious awareness from which one perceives and acts. An integral component of fulfillment, therefore, becomes the progressive physiological refinement of the nervous system in the direction of a reduced accumulation of stress. Indeed, SCI associates such refinement with a "growth in consciousness" and delineates the remarkable potentialities of a fully stress-free, fully normalized nervous system. The attainment of higher states of consciousness, long thought to be incompatible with an active life, now is said to be within the reach of anyone through TM, and experiential evidence of this possibility seems to be one of the common cumulative effects of the practice.

The implications of all of this for education are quite exciting. At the most superficial level, the level of the problems, reduction of drug abuse among students and of social tension in the classroom is a likely concomitant of a widespread introduction of TM into the schools. The improved attitudes and behavior which generally are among the more immediate of TM's effects offer a chance for achieving affective goals without sacrificing performance goals. Indeed, preliminary reports of increased learning ability and reading speed with TM would seem to indicate that affective dispositions and cognitive resources grow hand in hand. Students at ease inside can be expected to respond more spontaneously and creatively to a learning environment.

On the other side of the desk, a meditating teacher (or administrator), being more at ease, energetic, healthy, clear-minded, creative, and perceptive, should naturally become more effective. Already there is concrete evidence that these are all valid expectations if the implementation of a TM/SCI-based program is approached with proper planning.

On a deeper level, if further research continues to substantiate "growth in consciousness" as a pragmatically meaningful concept, can this dimension of human development be overlooked by an educational system whose goal is the actualization of the full potentialities for growth latent in the student? One of the most ancient expressions of man's wisdom, the Vedas (to which SCI traces its ancestry), hold that "knowledge is structured in consciousness," the implication being that the higher the level of consciousness the more profound the level of knowledge which can be owned.

This leads finally to the most fundamental possibility for educational fulfillment of all those opened through SCI. The holistic ideal of education is to provide a common basis for all branches of learning. Certainly, *knowingness,* that very intimate relationship between the knower and the object of knowledge, is this common basis. The science of creative intelligence is principally the study of this relationship, both through intellectual analysis and through the direct experience of the field from which all knowledge springs. The whole

tree is captured by capturing the seed. In the fullest sense, therefore, creative intelligence may be said to be both the goal and the source of education.

A WORLD PLAN

Concrete programs are already under way for the widest diffusion of SCI and TM. Since its inauguration as an accredited course at Stanford in the 1970 winter quarter, SCI has achieved recognition from a rapidly growing number of universities and colleges around the world. The SCI course at Yale this past year, for example, explicitly demonstrated its integrative and interdisciplinary nature by bringing together psychologists, philosophers, political scientists, and artists in a common exploration of the potentialities of consciousness.

SCI is being taught at other educational levels, including junior and senior high schools and adult education, in industry, and even in the military. Indeed, the commandant of the U.S. Army War College, Major General Franklin M. Davis, speaking at the First International Symposium on the Science of Creative Intelligence,[15] said, "In military education, creative intelligence appears to have a definite potential, because it carries with it so much in the way of innovation, creative thinking, and what we in the military call 'challenging the assumption'!" To which Maharishi added, "When the military rises in creative intelligence, world peace will be a reality."

Educators at MIU (Maharishi International University), the institution founded in 1971 to formalize the training of SCI teachers, are now completing the preparation of syllabuses and teaching aids—including color video cassettes—for the teaching of SCI at all educational levels. MIU is currently embarked on an ambitious world plan to open 3,600 centers for the training of SCI teachers —one center per million population—throughout the world. Each center has as its goal the training of 1,000 teachers by means of a 33-lecture video-based course prepared specially for this purpose by Maharishi. The stated objectives of the world plan include the development of the full potential of the individual and the "realization of the highest ideal of education."

A utopian vision? Perhaps. But who would

have imagined that a scant 14 years after a lone monk walked out of the Himalayas armed only with knowledge and his dedication to a long tradition of educators, the Illinois House of Representatives would formally resolve:

> That all educational institutions, especially those under State of Illinois jurisdiction, be strongly encouraged to study the feasibility of courses in Transcendental Meditation and the Science of Creative Intelligence on their campuses and in their facilities; and be it further . . . resolved that a copy of this resolution be sent to: the Superintendent of Public Instruction, the deans of all state universities, the Department of Mental Health, State of Illinois, to inform them of the great promise of the program herein mentioned. . . .[16]

REFERENCES

1. Robert L. Ebel, "What Are Schools For?" *Phi Delta Kappan*, September, 1972, p. 3.

2. Victor F. Weisskopf, "The Significance of Science," *Science*, April 14, 1972, p. 138.

3. Maharishi Mahesh Yogi, *Maharishi Mahesh Yogi on the Bhagavad-Gita: A New Translation and Commentary* (Baltimore: Penguin Books, 1969), p. 470.

4. A number of nonprofit tax-exempt organizations coordinate the activities of TM teachers. The educational community is served by the Students' International Meditation Society (SIMS), whose national headquarters is located at 1015 Gayley Avenue, Los Angeles, California 90024. Inquiries may be directed to the attention of the Science and Education Communications Coordinator.

5. The customary view that subjective experience is ipso facto beyond the purview of science is undergoing change. See, for example, "States of Consciousness and State-Specific Sciences," by Charles T. Tart, in *Science*, June 16, 1972, p. 1,203.

6. The rate of instruction in TM has doubled each year since 1968. By the fall of 1972 over 150,000 Americans had learned TM. The broad base of this appeal can be gauged from the range of publications featuring articles on TM and SCI during the past year: *Time* (October 25, 1971), *Yale Alumni Magazine* (February, 1972), *Soldiers Magazine* (February, 1972), *Kentucky Law Journal* (1971–72, Vol. 60, No. 2), *Seventeen* (July, 1972), *Wall Street Journal* (August 31, 1972), *Today's Health* (April, 1972), *Science Digest* (February, 1972), and *Psychology Today* (March, 1972).

7. TM is a purely mental technique practiced individually every morning and evening for 15 to 20 minutes at a sitting. It requires no alteration of life-style, diet, etc., and being a technique of direct experience (rather than a religion or philosophy), it does not require belief in the efficacy of the practice nor an understanding of the underlying theory.

8. The widely publicized efficacy of TM in promoting the voluntary reduction of drug abuse as documented, for example, in the retrospective study of 1,862 subjects by Drs. R. K. Wallace and H. G. Benson of the Harvard Medical School (see "Narcotics Research, Rehabilitation, and Treatment" in "Hearings Before the Select Committee on Crime, House of Representatives," Serial No. 92-1, Part 2, p. 682—U.S. Government Printing Office, 1971) tends to overshadow public understanding of the broader effects of the practice and particularly its utility for the non-drug abuser.

9. Robert Keith Wallace, Herbert Benson, and Archie F. Wilson, "A Wakeful Hypometabolic Physiologic State," *American Journal of Physiology*, September, 1971, pp. 795–99.

10. Robert Keith Wallace, "The Physiological Effects of Transcendental Meditation: A Proposed Fourth Major State of Consciousness," Ph.D. Dissertation, University of California, Los Angeles, 1970; see also *Science*, March 27, 1970, p. 1,751.

11. The physiological measurements also show that TM is radically different from hypnotic states and other so-called "altered states of consciousness."

12. Robert Keith Wallace and Herbert Benson, "The Physiology of Meditation," *Scientific American*, February, 1972, p. 84.

13. William Seeman, Sanford Nidich, and Thomas Banta, "Influence of Transcendental Meditation on a Measure of Self-Actualization," *Journal of Counseling Psychology*, May, 1972, pp. 184–87.

14. David W. Orme-Johnson, "Autonomic Stability and Transcendental Meditation," *Journal of Psychosomatic Medicine*, in press.

15. Held at the University of Massachusetts, Amherst, July 18 through August 1, 1971. International symposia on SCI are now held regularly each year at a number of universities throughout the world. Participants in 1971 included Buckminster Fuller, Harvey Brooks (dean of engineering and applied physics, Harvard University, and president, American Academy of Arts and Sciences), Melvin Calvin (Nobel Laureate in chemistry), and Willis Harman (director, Educational Policy Research, Stanford Research Institute). Symposia in 1972 featured Donald Glaser (Nobel Laureate in physics), Hans Selye, Marshall McLuhan, astronaut Rusty Schweickart, and the State Department China expert Alfred Jenkins.

16. House Resolution No. 677, adopted May 24, 1972.

Part Two • toward understanding the nature of instruction

The method of teaching which approaches most nearly
to the method of investigation, is incomparably the best;
since, not content with serving up a few barren and lifeless
truths, it lends to the stock on which they grew.

Edmund Burke (1729–1797)

I have known some persons who thought teaching was the easiest job in the world—until they did it themselves. Teaching involves a complex relationship between instructor and students that either enhances or interferes with the quality and quantity of learning. The chapters and readings in Part II acquaint you with some of the basic classroom dynamics involved in the teaching process, with some innovative and some controversial approaches to instruction, and with some of the major issues related to testing and grading.

The readings in Chapter Six are a sampling of the broad spectrum of research and ideas related to the strategies and purposes of instruction. N. L. Gage is a nationally prominent educational psychologist whose eminent research on teacher effectiveness qualifies him to answer the question, "Can Science Contribute to the Art of Teaching?" You may be surprised to learn which teacher characteristics are associated with effective instruction.

And then, of course, there is always the question about what is worth teaching and knowing about in the first place. In reading 20, Neil Postman and Charles Weingartner think that most of what we teach seems outdated and irrelevant to contemporary youth. They say we are in our "intellectual infancy." Well, maybe. See what you think. Robert Ebel argues in reading 21 that instructional activities should be aimed primarily toward the goal of giving students more "cognitive competence." From his point of view, teaching is an active, purposeful activity. Carl Rogers' view (reading 22) differs radically from Ebel's; he says that "anything that can be taught to another person is relatively inconsequential." Ebel, in effect, says you *can* teach. Rogers says, well, you can, but it doesn't really matter. In reading 23, Robert Rosenthal discusses what happens to students when they begin to sense a teacher's expectations for them. According to Rosenthal's research, when you expect more, you are apt to get more. This article will help you to see how the expectancy phenomenon works.

Chapter Seven exposes you to some of the recent innovations and issues in instruction. Maurice Gibbons' "walkabout" idea in reading 24 is one of the most creative sojourns away from traditional thinking that I, for one, have seen in a long time. Imagine our high schools modeling their graduation ceremonies on the activities of Australian aboriginal youth! That will stretch your thinking. Readings 25 and 26 are back-to-back presentations by Jonathan Kozol and Gene Maeroff, which promote two very different instructional concepts—the free school and the traditional school, both a part of the contemporary scene. Each type of school has distinct ideas about the purpose and place of instruction. A continuing topic of heated dispute is the use of behavioral objectives. In reading 27, Robert Gagné says they are absolutely necessary for good instruction. And with equal vigor in reading 28, George Kneller says they are *not* necessary for good instruction. The debate goes on, and these two readings may help you see why. You may also come closer to your own feelings about the issue.

The problems and issues tackled in Chapter Eight are as old as education itself. Sooner or later, every teacher, whether in kindergarten or graduate school, must test, assess, weigh, or in some way measure school achievement. Robert Feldmesser begins in reading 29 by asserting that grades are useful and serve a positive function. Sidney Simon is equally convinced that grading students is nonsense (reading 30). Henry Dyer provides us with an objective analysis of how to use tests correctly in the final selection of this chapter. Are grades teachers give valid? Is testing a menace to education? Should grades be abolished altogether? These are not easy questions to answer, but they are questions that every concerned person must come to grips with sooner or later. Hopefully, this chapter will stimulate you to probe deeper into your private philosophy of testing and grading.

19

Can Science Contribute to the Art of Teaching?

N. L. Gage

EDITOR'S NOTE · This seemed to me a very appropriate article with which to begin this chapter, dealing as it does with classroom dynamics and teaching processes. This reading presents an overview of the qualities and characteristics associated with effective and ineffective teaching by examining a broad sample of research. Do we have reason to be optimistic about the state of the teaching art? How important are teacher variables, such as warmth, indirectness, cognitive organization, and enthusiasm, in determining a teacher's success or lack of it? As you read, you might think about those qualities in your own personal makeup. How about it—will you be an effective teacher?

Can science contribute to the art of teaching? To successful teacher behavior? It would be nice if the answer could be a resounding "Yes," based on a long parade of conclusive evi-

From Gage, N. L., *Teacher Effectiveness and Teacher Education: The Search for a Scientific Basis.* Palo Alto, Calif.: Pacific Books, Publishers, 1972, pp. 27–39. Reprinted by permission.

dence and examples of richly useful findings. Unfortunately, that happy paper cannot yet be written in any honest way. Instead, the question must receive a rather more complex response.

First, I shall define the term "successful teacher behavior" and delimit the setting of the kind of teaching to be considered. Second, I shall outline reasons for pessimism as to whether research on teaching has any real likelihood of yielding scientific findings that can be used to improve teaching. Then I shall sketch the nature of the findings that would alleviate the pessimism.

DEFINITION AND DELIMITATION

My definition of "successful teacher behavior" is one based on research on teaching. The findings of such research may or may not accord with common sense. They may or may not accord with the virtues of personality and character, or desirable behaviors, described in writings on ethics, the Boy Scout Handbook, or a Dale Carnegie course. Also, a research-based characterization of successful teacher behavior may not be extremely original, or completely non-obvious. Neither must such a description of behavior be highly systematic, since research findings at any given moment do not necessarily form a coherent scheme. As for validity, it is not inconceivable that in the long run, some non-scientific insight or artistic hunch may turn out to be superior to what can now be cited on the basis of research evidence. The truths propounded in the past by novelists, essayists, or skilled supervisors of teachers may eventually prove more valid than the results of research now available.

Despite these possible limitations, I shall consider here only what the research literature has to offer. This literature takes the form of reports on empirical studies of one kind or another. In these studies, various kinds of teacher behavior have been related to other variables on which some sort of educational valuation can be placed. So, by the present definition, "successful" teacher behaviors or characteristics are those that have been found through empirical research to be related to something desirable about teachers. The "something desirable" may be improved achievement by students of any of the various cognitive, affective, or psychomotor objectives of education. Or, the "something desirable" may be a favorable evaluation of the teacher by students, a supervisor, a principal, or someone else whose judgment is important. . . .

Now let us specify the kind of setting in which the teacher behavior to be considered takes place. Various innovations now being considered by educators may more frequently in the future make the setting of teaching something other than the conventional classroom. The setting may change in accordance with the needs of the students and the kinds of learning in which they are engaged. For some kinds of learning, students may be taught in large-group settings, such as motion picture theaters and lecture halls. For other kinds, the setting may be the small-group seminar, or a booth for programmed instruction, "individually prescribed instruction," or independent study. In the future, these settings will, it is said, supplement and perhaps supplant today's conventional classroom.

But these different kinds of settings still lie in the future, for the most part. And my definition of successful teaching requires empirical research demonstrating a relationship between the behaviors of teachers and other desirable things. Most of that research, by far, has been done in classrooms. So this discussion will be restricted to the behavior of teachers in the conventional classroom.

REASONS FOR PESSIMISM

Let us now consider reasons for pessimism on the question, Can science contribute to the art of teaching? To begin, it should be noted that making positive statements about the results of research on successful teacher behavior is not fashionable among educational research workers. Many reviewers of research on teaching have concluded that it has yielded little of value.

This disparaging style in appraising research

results has had a great vogue. In 1953, a Committee on the Criteria of Teacher Effectiveness rendered the verdict that "the present condition of research on teacher effectiveness holds little promise of yielding results commensurate with the needs of American education" (American Educational Research Association, 1953, p. 657). In 1958, Orville Brim (1958, p. 32) concluded from his examination of reviews of the literature that there were no consistent relations between teacher characteristics and effectiveness in teaching. In 1963, in the *Handbook of Research on Teaching*, the authors of the chapter on teaching methods reported an impression that "teaching methods do not seem to make much difference" and that "there is hardly any evidence to favor one method over another" (Wallen and Travers, 1963, p. 484). The authors of the chapter on teacher personality and characteristics concluded that ". . . very little is known for certain . . . about the relation between teacher personality and teacher effectiveness" (Getzels and Jackson, 1963, p. 574). And the authors of the chapter on social interaction in the classroom concluded that "until very recently, the approach to the analysis of teacher-pupil and pupil-pupil interaction . . . has tended to be unrewarding and sterile" (Withall and Lewis, 1963, p. 708). It would not be hard to find other summary statements to the effect that empirical research on teaching has not yielded much enlightenment about successful teaching.

After a thorough review, Dubin and Taveggia (1968) concluded that college teaching methods make no difference in student achievement as measured by final examinations on course content. Their review was unique in that they examined the data, rather than merely the conclusions, of nearly 100 studies made over a 40-year period. Of 88 independent comparisons of the lecture and discussion methods, reported in 36 experimental studies, 51 percent favored the lecture method and 49 percent favored the discussion method! . . .

Some writers hold that all research on school variables, not merely research on teacher behavior, has yielded negative results for the most part. The view that educational research yields negative findings has even been assimilated into a whole theory of the origins and process of schooling. Stephens (1967), after looking at the research reports and summaries, concluded that practically nothing seems to make any difference in the effectiveness of instruction. He considered this "flood of negative results" to be understandable in the light of his theory of spontaneous schooling. This theory postulates spontaneous, automatic forces in the background of the student—his maturational tendencies, various out-of-school agencies such as the home and the general community, and the reputation of the school as a place concerned about academic matters. The theory also refers to various spontaneous tendencies on the part of humans in the role of the teacher—tendencies to manipulate and communicate. These two kinds of force, the background forces and the automatic teaching forces, account for most of the learning that takes place. Furthermore, these spontaneous and powerful forces operate early in the growth process, when influences on learning have greater effects. Hence, the changes introduced by research variables, administrative factors, and pedagogical refinements of one kind or another are inadequate to produce any major difference.

Stephens documented his position with references to summaries of studies of a host of educational variables, procedures, practices, and orientations—namely, school attendance, instructional television, independent study and correspondence courses, size of class, individual consultation and tutoring, counseling, concentration on specific students, the student's involvement, the amount of time spent in study, distraction by jobs and extracurricular activities, size of school, the qualities of teachers that can be rated by principals and supervisors, non-graded schools, team teaching, ability grouping, progressivism vs. traditionalism, discussion vs. lecture, group-centered vs. teacher-centered approaches, the use of frequent quizzes, and programmed instruction. Studies of all these have failed to show that they make a consistent and significant difference. . . .

Apparent support for this view of the effects of educational variables on scholastic achievement can be found in the massive report on *Equality of Educational Opportunity* (Coleman et al., 1966). According to that report, when the social background and attitudes of individual students and their schoolmates are held constant, achievement is only slightly related to school characteristics, such as per-pupil expenditures, books in the library, and a number of other facilities and curricular measures. Conversely, the report found that family back-

ground accounted for a relatively high proportion of the variance in student achievement. Stephens seems to be vindicated by these findings.

QUESTIONING THE PESSIMISM

So far we have considered reasons for pessimism about the promise of empirical research on teaching. Now let us raise some questions about these lugubrious views.

In the first place, these dismal generalizations may not do complete justice to the research domains for which they have been made. Here and there, in research on teaching methods, on teacher personality and characteristics, and on social interaction in the classroom, it may be possible to come up with more sanguine judgments about the meaning of the research findings. . . . If so, future conclusions about research on teaching may be less melancholy. Later in this chapter, some preliminary examples of such sifting will be offered.

What about the report on *Equality of Educational Opportunity*? Here also there are reasons to question the pessimism. According to Bowles and Levin (1968a), the research design of that study "was overwhelmingly biased in a direction that would dampen the importance of school characteristics." For example, expenditure-per-pupil was measured in terms of the average expenditure within an entire school district rather than within the given school in which the pupils were located. Hence, the expenditure-per-pupil was overstated for schools attended by lower-class students and understated for schools attended by students of higher social status. . . .

Despite these biases, the report found that measures of teacher quality were significantly related to achievement, probably because teacher characteristics were measured individually and averaged for each school. Indeed, the report stated that teacher characteristics accounted for a ". . . higher proportion of variation in student achievement than did all other aspects of the school combined, excluding the student body characteristics" (Coleman *et al.*, 1966, p. 316). These teacher characteristics were family educational level, years' experience, localism (living in the area most of their lives), teachers' own educational level, score on a vocabulary test, preference for middle-class students, and proportion of teachers in the school who were white. And such factors make a bigger difference, according to the report, for Negro than for white students, perhaps because their out-of-school environment contributes less of the spontaneous educative forces to which Stephens referred.

Accordingly, the characteristics of teachers who work with culturally disadvantaged pupils become all the more important. In subsequent re-analyses of some of the data of the report, Bowles and Levin (1968b) found that teacher characteristics were very significantly related to the verbal achievement of twelfth-grade Negro students, even when social background factors were held constant....

SOME POSITIVE STATEMENTS

Having emphasized the difficulties of making positive research-based statements about successful teaching behaviors, I wish nonetheless to attempt such statements. My purpose is merely to illustrate the nature of the conclusions that might be drawn from more adequate examination of better research. My procedure will be to present a series of operational definitions of teacher behaviors that seem, more or less, to belong on the same dimension. These definitions will be drawn from various research procedures and measuring instruments. Then I shall cite some of the evidence on which it is possible to base the inference that these behaviors or characteristics are desirable.

Warmth. One example of this dimension can be seen in the responses of teachers to the Minnesota Teacher Attitude Inventory (MTAI) (Cook, Leeds, and Callis, 1951). Here, the teacher responds on a five-point agree-disagree scale to such statements as "Most children are obedient," "Minor disciplinary situations should sometimes be turned into jokes," "Most pupils lack productive imagination," and "Most pupils are resourceful when left on their own."

As a second example, consider teachers' responses to the California F scale (McGee, 1955), which has been found to correlate substantially... with the MTAI (Gage, Leavitt, and Stone, 1957; Sheldon, Coale, and Copple, 1959). Among the F scale's items are "Obedience and respect for authority are the most important virtues children should

learn," "People can be divided into two distinct classes: the weak and the strong," and "Most of our social problems would be solved if we could somehow get rid of the immoral, crooked, and feeble-minded people."

A final example can be drawn from the work of Ryans (1960), who developed a Teacher Characteristic Schedule that included such items as the following: "Pupils can behave themselves without constant supervision," "Most pupils are considerate of the teacher's wishes," and "Most teachers are willing to assume their share of the unpleasant tasks associated with teaching."

Now what is the basis for the proposition that certain patterns of responses to attitude statements of this kind are "desirable"? The answer is that these kinds of attitudes and behaviors tend to be correlated positively with favorable assessments of the teachers by students and trained observers, and with students' scores on achievement tests. The Minnesota Teacher Attitude Inventory has fairly consistently been found to correlate positively with favorable mean ratings of the teachers by their pupils (Yee, 1967). The items of Ryans' inventory correlated positively with observers' ratings of elementary school teachers on all three of his teacher behavior patterns—warm, understanding, friendly vs. aloof, egocentric, and restricted; responsible, businesslike, systematic vs. evading, unplanned, and slipshod; and stimulating, imaginative vs. dull, routine (Ryans, 1960). McGee (1955) found that teachers' scores on the California F Scale correlated highly with previous ratings of the teachers by trained observers on dimensions like aloof vs. approachable; unresponsive vs. responsive, dominative vs. integrative, and harsh vs. kindly. Cogan (1958) found that descriptions of teachers by their students on similar items correlated positively with the amount of required and also voluntary school work done by the students.

In short, a substantial body of evidence supports two conclusions: (a) Teachers differ reliably from one another on a series of measuring instruments that seem to have a great deal in common. (b) These reliable individual differences among teachers are fairly consistently related to various desirable things about teachers.

What term can be applied to the desirable end of this dimension of behaviors and attitudes? Teachers at this desirable end tend to behave approvingly, acceptantly, and supportively; they tend to speak well of their own students, students in general, and people in general. They tend to like and trust rather than fear other people of all kinds. How they get that way is not our concern at the moment. The point is that it is not impossible to find extremely plausible similarities among the teacher behaviors measured and found desirable by a number of independent investigators working with different methods, instruments, and concepts. Although any single term is inadequate, it seems safe to use the term "warmth." Warmth, operationally defined as indicated above, seems—on the basis of varied research evidence—to be quite defensible as a desirable characteristic of teacher behavior.

Indirectness. To identify a second dimension of teacher behavior, we begin with two of Flanders's categories. His Category 3 is "Accepts or uses ideas of student: clarifying, building, or developing ideas suggested by a student," and Category 4 is "Ask questions: asking a question about content or procedure with the intent that a student answer." In the classrooms of teachers that behave in these ways relatively often, one also finds more instances of Category 8: "Student talk-response: talk by students in response to teacher. Teacher initiates the contact or solicits student statement," and Category 9: "Student talk-initiation: talk by students which they initiate. If 'calling on' student is only to indicate who may talk next, observer must decide whether student wanted to talk. If he did, use this category."

A second example of this dimension of teacher behavior may be seen in the research on what is called "learning by discovery." This research deals with the question, "How much and what kind of guidance should the teacher provide? . . . the degree of guidance by the teacher varies from time to time along a continuum, with almost complete direction of what the pupil must do at one extreme to practically no direction at the other" (Shulman and Keisler, 1966, pp. 182, 183). This dimension consists of the degree to which the teacher permits pupils to discover underlying concepts and generalizations for themselves, giving them less rather than more direct guidance. The teacher at the higher level of this dimension realizes that it is not always desirable merely to tell the pupil what you want him to know and understand. Rather, it is some-

times better to ask questions, encourage the pupil to become active, seek for himself, use his own ideas, and engage in some trial and error. This kind of teaching represents a willingness to forbear giving the pupil everything he needs to know; it does not mean abandoning the pupil entirely to his own devices.

Now what is the evidence that this dimension of teacher behavior—exemplified in Flanders's categories, and teaching-by-discovery—has a significant relationship to something educationally desirable? Flanders and Simon (1969) concluded from their examination of a dozen studies that "*the percentage of teacher statements that make use of ideas and opinions previously expressed by pupils is directly related to average class scores on attitude scales of teacher attractiveness, liking the class, etc., as well as to average achievement scores adjusted for initial ability*" (p. 1426, italics in original). Ausubel (1963, p. 171) reviewed the experiments on learning by discovery and concluded that the furnishing of completely explicit rules is relatively less effective than some degree of arranging for pupils to discover rules for themselves.

It seems safe to say that some use of the guided discovery method, and "indirectness," in teaching is desirable. Teachers not sensitized to its desirability typically exhibit too little indirectness. As Flanders (1965, p. 114) put it, "our theory suggests an indirect approach; most teachers use a direct approach."

Cognitive Organization. The third dimension of teacher behavior is more difficult to define operationally. And its connection with desirable outcomes is, despite great plausibility, not as well established empirically. This is the kind of behavior that reflects the teacher's intellectual grasp, or "cognitive organization" of what he is trying to teach.

In one investigation, teachers were tested as to whether they understood the processes and concepts of arithmetic, such as the reason for moving each sub-product one digit to the left when the multiplier has more than one digit (Orleans, 1952). Other studies have dealt with the degree to which the teacher's verbal behavior reflects an understanding of the logical properties of a good definition, explanation, or conditional inference (Meux and Smith, 1961). Others have studied the degree to which the teacher, or his instructional material, provides a set of subject-matter "organizers" that embody "relevant ideational scaffolding," discriminate new material from previously learned material, and integrate it "at a level of abstraction, generality, and inclusiveness which is much higher than that of the learning material itself" (Ausubel, 1963, p. 214). Similar ideas have been put in such terms as "cognitive structure" (Bruner, 1966), "learning structure" (Gagné, 1965), and "logic tree" (Hickey and Newton, 1964).

Although the general conception of this aspect of teaching behavior can be identified, operational definitions are hard to come by. Perhaps the best operational definitions of such variables must be inferred from the procedures of those who develop programmed instructional materials. These procedures call for behavioral definitions of objectives and detailed "learning structures" (Gagné, 1965) that analyze the steps involved in achieving a "terminal behavior" into hierarchies of subtasks. Gagné (1965) illustrated such learning structures in mathematics and science; Glaser and Reynolds (1964) worked out a detailed example in the form of the sequence of sub-behaviors involved in programmed instructional materials for teaching children to tell time from a clock.

In some ways, the lessons derived from this kind of technical work on teaching and learning have implications for curriculum development rather than for teaching as such. But the curriculum is inevitably shaped through the teacher's behavior in the classroom as well as by the materials that his pupils read. The implications of such instructional research for the behavior of the live teacher in the classroom seem clear: if curricular material should exhibit a valid cognitive organization, so should the behavior of the teacher.

Enthusiasm. Our last example of a sifting of the literature to identify a desirable kind of teacher behavior is one recently provided by Rosenshine (1970). He reviewed the evidence from a variety of sources on the degree to which the teacher's "enthusiasm" was desirable. Some of the studies reviewed were experiments in which "enthusiasm" was manipulated. In other, correlational, studies, enthusiasm as it occurred "naturally" was rated, counted, or measured with an inventory. In some of the studies, the dependent variable was measured achievement; in others, evaluative ratings of

the teacher by his students or other independent observers. The varied evidence seemed remarkably consistent in supporting the desirability of teacher enthusiasm. Positive differences between means and positive correlation coefficients appeared far more often than did those indicating a negative relationship between teacher enthusiasm and something desirable about the teacher.

Two examples of experiments will illustrate these findings. Coats and Smidchens (1966) had two 10-minute lessons presented by two teachers in a static, or unenthusiastic fashion (read from a manuscript, with no gestures, eye contact, or inflections), and also in a dynamic, or enthusiastic fashion (delivered from memory, with much inflection, eye contact, gesturing, and animation). Tests immediately after the lesson indicated much greater learning from the dynamic lecture. Similarly, Mastin (1963) had 20 teachers lecture on two different topics a week apart—presenting one topic in an "indifferent" manner and the other "enthusiastically." In 19 of the 20 classes, the student's mean achievement was higher for the lesson taught enthusiastically.

These four variables—warmth, indirectness, cognitive organization, and enthusiasm—merely illustrate the kinds of contributions that research on teaching, in its present early stages, can support. In themselves, these findings are far from startling. Any clever student, teacher, or novelist could have told us decades ago about these characteristics of good teaching. But what is important about these tentative conclusions is their basis in empirical research. The ease with which others have told us such truths in the past is matched by their untrustworthiness. Glib insights based on uncontrolled experience can lead us astray. Research on teaching—the effort to apply scientific method to the description and improvement of teaching—is much more laborious and usually makes much less interesting reading than the essay of the shrewd, compassionate, and imaginative observer. The same tortoise-hare comparison would have applied in past centuries to research on psychiatry and the writings of phrenologists, to research on chemistry and the writings of alchemists, and so on. In the long run, as humanity has learned, it is safer in matters of this kind to rely on the scientific method. Applying that method to the phenomena and problems of teaching is our concern.

REFERENCES

American Educational Research Association, Committee on the Criteria of Teacher Effectiveness. (1953) Second report, *Journal of Educational Research*, 46, 641–658.

Ausubel, D. P. (1963) *The Psychology of Meaningful Verbal Learning: An Introduction to School Learning*. New York: Grune & Stratton.

Bowles, S., and Levin, Henry M. (1968a) "The Determinants of Scholastic Achievement—An Appraisal of Some Recent Evidence." *Journal of Human Resources*, 3, 3–24.

———— (1968b) "More on Multicollinearity and the Effectiveness of Schools." *Journal of Human Resources*, 3, 393–400.

Brim, O. G., Jr. (1958) *Sociology and the Field of Education*. New York: Russell Sage Foundation.

Bruner, J. S. (1966a) *Toward a Theory of Instruction*. Cambridge: Harvard University Press.

Coats, W. D., and Smidchens, U. (1966) "Audience Recall as a Function of Speaker Dynamism." *Journal of Educational Psychology*, 57, 189–191.

Cogan, M. I. (1958) "The Behavior of Teachers and the Productive Behavior of Their Pupils: I. 'Perception' Analysis. II. 'Trait' Analysis." *Journal of Experimental Education*, 27, 89–105, 107–124.

Coleman, J. S., et al. (1966) *Equality of Educational Opportunity*. Washington, D.C.: U.S. Government Printing Office.

Cook, W. W., Leeds, C. H., and Callis, R. (1951) *The Minnesota Teacher Attitude Inventory*. New York: Psychological Corp.

Dubin, R., and Taveggia, T. C. (1968) *The Teaching-Learning Paradox: A Comparative Analysis of College Teaching Methods*. Eugene, Ore.: Center for the Advanced Study of Educational Administration, University of Oregon.

Flanders, N. A. (1965) *Teacher Influence, Pupil Attitudes, and Achievement*. U.S. Department of Health, Education, and Welfare. Office of Education, Cooperative Research Monograph no. 12 (OE–25040). Washington, D.C.: U.S. Government Printing Office.

Flanders, N. A., and Simon, A. (1969) "Teacher Effectiveness." In R. L. Ebel (Ed.), *Encyclopedia of Educational Research*, (4th ed.) New York: Macmillan, pp. 1423–1436.

Gage, N. L., Leavitt, G. S., and Stone, G. C. (1957) "The Psychological Meaning of Acquiescence Set for Authoritarianism." *Journal of Abnormal and Social Psychology*, 55, 98–103.

Gagné, R. M. (1965) *The Conditions of Learning*. New York: Holt, Rinehart and Winston.

Getzels, J. W., and Jackson, P. W. (1963) "The Teacher's Personality and Characteristics." In N. L. Gage (ed.), *Handbook of Research on Teaching*. Chicago: Rand McNally, pp. 506–582.

Glaser, R., and Reynolds, H. H. (1964) "Instructional Objectives and Programmed Instruction: A Case Study." In C. M. Lindvall (ed.), *Defining Educational Objectives*. Pittsburgh: University of Pittsburgh Press, pp. 47–76.

Hickey, A. E., and Newton, J. M. (1964) "The Logical Basis of Teaching: I. The Effect of Sub-concept Sequence on Learning." Final Report to Office of Naval Research. Personnel and Training Branch, Contract Nonr-4215(00).

Mastin, V. E. (1963) "Teacher Enthusiasm." *Journal of Educational Research*, 56, 385–386.

McGee, H. M. (1955) "Measurement of Authoritarianism and Its Relation to Teachers' Classroom Behavior." *Genetic Psychology Monographs*, 52, 89–146.

Meux, M. O., and Smith, B. O. (1961) "Logical Dimensions of Teaching Behavior." Urbana: University of Illinois, Bureau of Educational Research. (Mimeographed.)

Orleans, J. S. (1952) *The Understanding of Arithmetic Processes and Concepts Possessed by Teachers of Arithmetic*. New York: Board of Education of the City of New York, Division of Teacher Education, Office of Research and Evaluation.

Rosenshine, B. (1970) "Enthusiastic Teaching:

A Research Review." *School Review*, 78, 499–514.

Ryans, D. G. (1960) *Characteristics of Teachers*. Washington, D.C.: American Council on Education.

Sheldon, M. S., Coale, J. M., and Copple, R. (1959) "Concurrent Validity of the 'Warm Teacher Scales,'" *Journal of Educational Psychology* 50, 37–40.

Shulman, L., and Keislar, E. (eds.) (1966) *Learning by Discovery: A Critical Appraisal*. Chicago: Rand McNally.

Stephens, J. M. (1967) *The Process of Schooling*. New York: Holt, Rinehart and Winston.

Wallen, N. E., and Travers, R. M. W. (1963) "Analysis and Investigation of Teaching Methods." In N. L. Gage (ed.), *Handbook of Research on Teaching*. Chicago: Rand McNally, pp. 448–505.

Withall, J., and Lewis, W. W. (1963) "Social Interaction in the Classroom." In N. L. Gage (ed)., *Handbook of Research on Teaching*. Chicago: Rand McNally, pp. 683–714.

Yee, A. H. (1968) "Is the Minnesota Teacher Attitude Inventory Valid and Homogeneous?" *Journal of Educational Measurement*, 4, 151–161.

20

What's Worth Teaching and Knowing About?

Neil Postman
Charles Weingartner

EDITOR'S NOTE · *Not only do Drs. Postman and Weingartner wonder what's worth teaching and knowing about, but they also wonder what might be worth forgetting, in order to proceed to more important things. This article presents a point of view that raises important questions about academic and personal survival in a rapidly changing technological society. Change seems to be occurring all the time all around us. What can we do to ensure an ongoing relevancy in our educational system? What kind of person do we want to encourage as a product of our educational efforts? What do you think is worth knowing about?*

The basic function of all education, even in the most traditional sense, is to increase the survival prospects of the group. If this function is fulfilled, the group survives. If not, it doesn't. There have been times when this function was not fulfilled, and groups (some of them we even call "civilizations") disappeared. Generally, this resulted from changes in the kinds of threats the group faced. The threats changed, but the education did not, and so the group, in a way, "disappeared itself" (to use a phrase from *Catch-22*). The tendency seems to be for most "educational" systems, from patterns of training in "primitive" tribal societies to school systems in technological societies, to fall imperceptibly into a role devoted exclusively to the conservation of old ideas, concepts, attitudes, skills, and perceptions. This happens largely because of the unconsciously held belief that these old ways of thinking and doing are necessary to the survival of the group. And that is largely true, IF the group inhabits an environment in which change occurs very, very slowly, or not at all. Survival in a stable environment depends almost entirely on remembering the strategies for survival that have been developed in the past, and so the conservation and transmission of these becomes the primary mission of education. But, a paradoxical situation develops when change becomes the primary characteristic of the environment. Then the task turns inside out—survival in a rapidly changing environment depends almost entirely upon being able to identify which of the old concepts are relevant to the demands imposed by the new threats to survival, and which are not. Then a new educational task becomes critical: getting the group to unlearn (to "forget") the irrelevant concepts as a prior condition to learning. What we are saying is that "selective forgetting" is necessary to survival.

We suggest that this is the stage we have now reached environmentally, and so we must now work to reach this stage educationally. The only thing that is at stake is our survival.

It is not possible to overstate the fact that technologically wrought changes in the environment render virtually all of our traditional concepts (survival strategies)—and the institutions developed to conserve and transmit them—irrelevant, but not merely irrelevant. If we fail to detect the fact that they are irrelevant, these concepts themselves become threats to our survival.

This idea is not, of course, original with us, even though it is new. It is new because up until just recently changes in the environment did not require it. As might be expected, the idea was first articulated by those most familiar with and concerned about technologically produced change—scientists. Not all scientists to be sure, since not all scientists themselves have been able to unlearn irrelevant old concepts. After all, science is itself so new that 95 percent of all the scientists who ever lived are alive right now! . . .

To date, a great deal of human energy has been spent on the search for the "holy grail" of the illusion of certainty. As a group, we are still in our intellectual infancy, depending much more upon magic and superstition than upon reason to allay our anxieties about the universe in which we are trying to live. After all, we haven't had much practice at figuring things out scientifically. So far, the use of scientific method is still largely confined to producing things normally intended to increase physical comfort. Up until just recently, technological "progress" has been confined almost solely to extending and shifting the function of human physical strength and energy to machines with which we cannot now compete. And while we have yet to figure out solutions to the problems this elementary kind of "progress" has produced, we are just beginning to confront the problems emerging as a consequence of the assumption by electronic machines of human intellectual functions. Electronic machines just happen to perform—already—a range of intellectual tasks better than human beings can. Our space-probing program, for example, would simply not be possible without electronic extensions of human information-handling and decision-making functions. The environmental changes electronic machines will produce in the near future —if not in the immediate present—is the subject of serious concern and discussion right now. One such discussion, accessible to a large public audience via television, occurred on the NBC *Open Mind* program. The participants were Paul Armer, associate head of the Rand Corporation's Computer Science Department, Theodore Kheel, Secretary-Treasurer of the American Foundation on Automation and Employment, Charles De Carlo, Director of Automation Research at I.B.M., and Robert Theobald, consulting economist and author of *The Challenge of Abundance*.

Threaded throughout the expert estimates of actual and imminent changes were references to the educational tasks to be fulfilled if these changes are not to disrupt the society in which they are occurring and will increasingly occur.

Robert Theobald, focusing on education, re-stated the sense of the discussion by saying that incredible changes are going to take place within 35 years and that no human group has ever before faced the problem of coping with changes of such magnitude. Noting that cultures have failed because they were incapable of changing their old concepts and ways of thinking, he suggested that we have to help the young people in our culture learn a new set of beliefs, a new set of institutions, and a new set of values, which will allow them to live in a totally different world. The issue, he said, lies here: how do you change the thinking of a culture with enormous speed?

Our response is that you do it through the school system—which is the only social institution that exists to fulfill this function—and by explicitly helping students to internalize concepts relevant to new environmental demands. Theobald, empha-sizing that this is not a hypothetical problem and synthesizing the sense of the remarks of other par-ticipants, made the point that as a culture we have yet to see and understand the changes that have already taken place much less those that are about to. He noted also that the term "future shock" is coming into currency.

Clearly, there is no more important function for education to fulfill than that of helping us to recognize the world we actually live in and, simultaneously, of helping us to master concepts that will increase our ability to cope with it. This is the essential criterion for judging the relevance of all education. . . .

A decade earlier, Lynn White, Jr. (*Frontiers of Knowledge*, New York: Harper and Bros., 1956) summed up the probable meaning of the newest knowledge of that time under the title "Changing Canons of Culture." Possibly illustrating the rate at which change is occurring, White's views now seem much more sanguine than the state of our schools would seem to permit. . . .

If, as he wrote, White had thoughtfully looked at the schools, he would have found that they were deeply devoted to the job of "inculcating" the old canons he said had changed. Anyone who looks at the schools today will find them still "inculcating" the old canons. The schools stare fixedly into the past as we hurtle pell-mell into the future.

Not only are the archaic canons—or concepts—White hopefully suggested had changed still being "taught," but so are a series of other equally out-of-joint concepts, some deriving from those he noted. Among the more obvious of these are the following:

1. The concept of absolute, fixed, unchanging "truth," particularly from a polarizing good-bad perspective.

2. The concept of certainty. There is always one and only one "right" answer, and it is abso-lutely "right."

3. The concept of isolated identity, that "A is A" period, simply, once and for all.

4. The concept of fixed states and "things," with the implicit concept that if you know the name you understand the "thing."

5. The concept of simple, single, mechanical cau-sality; the idea that every effect is the result of a single, easily identifiable cause.

6. The concept that differences exist *only* in parallel and opposing forms: good-bad, right-wrong, yes-no, short-long, up-down, etc.

7. The concept that knowledge is "given," that it emanates from a higher authority, and that it is to be accepted without question.

This list is not exhaustive, but, alas, it is rep-resentative. What difference does it make—now and in the future—whether students internalize these concepts? What kind of people are they as a result? Here we move to what might be called the "non-intellectual" level of attitudes rather than concepts.

Most criticism of the old education, and the old concepts it conserves and transmits, from Paul Goodman to John Gardner, makes the point that the students who endure it come out as passive, acquiescent, dogmatic, intolerant, authoritarian, in-flexible, conservative personalities who desperately need to resist change in an effort to keep their il-lusion of certainty intact.

It would be difficult to imagine any kind of education less liable to help students to be able to meet a drastically changing future than one which fosters the development of concepts and attitudes such as those noted above.

The concepts that we must all learn—that are now the *raison d'être* of education—are those which both shape technological change and derive from it: they are characteristics of the spirit, mood, lan-guage, and process of science. They are operative wherever evidence of social change—including theological versions—can be found.

Some of them you may recognize, and perhaps even accept, at least in certain domains. Others may seem odd or obscure, indicating their, to date, "fugitive" status.

Intellectual strategies for nuclear-space-age survival—in all dimensions of human activity—include such concepts as relativity, probability, contingency, uncertainty, function, structure as process, multiple causality (or noncausality), nonsymmetrical relationships, degrees of difference, and incongruity (or simultaneously appropriate difference).

Concepts such as these, as well as others both implicit in and contingent upon them, comprise the ingredients for changing ourselves in ways that complement the environmental demands that we all must face. The learning of such concepts will produce the kinds of people we will need to deal effectively with a future full of drastic change.

The new education has as its purpose the development of a new kind of person, one who—as a result of internalizing a different series of concepts—is an actively inquiring, flexible, creative, innovative, tolerant, liberal personality who can face uncertainty and ambiguity without disorientation, who can formulate viable new meanings to meet changes in the environment which threaten individual and mutual survival.

The new education, in sum, is new because it consists of having students use the concepts most appropriate to the world in which we all must live. All of these concepts constitute the dynamics of the questing-questioning, meaning-making process that can be called "learning how to learn." This comprises a posture of stability from which to deal fruitfully with change. The purpose is to help all students develop built-in, shockproof crap detectors as basic equipment in their survival kits.

21

A Case for Cognitive Competence as a Major Purpose of Education

Robert L. Ebel

EDITOR'S NOTE • This is a provocative article. Dr. Ebel, a former president of the American Educational Research Association, takes a strong, firm stance about what he feels the major purpose of schools should be. I think you will find it difficult not to have an opinion about the implications of Ebel's ideas for teaching and learning. Dr. Ebel asserts that schools are not adjustment centers responsible for helping youth come to terms with life; that they are not recreational facilities designed to entertain and amuse; and that they should not be responsible for the success of each student's learning. A school's primary objective should be to teach cognitive competence, that is, a command of useful knowledge. The stress on cognitive education is one side of the coin. Immediately following this reading, Carl Rogers offers a dramatically different point of view.

When the history of our times is written, it may designate the two decades following World War II as the golden age of American education. Never before was education more highly

Robert L. Ebel, "What Are Schools For?" *Phi Delta Kappan*, 54 (September 1972): 3–7. Reprinted by permission.

valued. Never before was so much of it so readily available to so many. Never before had it been supported so generously. Never before was so much expected of it.

But in this eighth decade of the twentieth century public education in this country appears to be in trouble. Taxpayers are revolting against the skyrocketing costs of education. Schools are being denied the funds they say they need for quality education. Teachers are uniting to press demands for higher pay and easier working conditions.

College and high school students have rebelled against what they call "the Establishment," resisting and overturning regulations, demanding pupil-directed rather than teacher-directed education, and turning in some cases to drink, drugs, and delinquency. Minorities are demanding equal treatment, which is surely their right. But when integration makes social differences more visible, and when equality of opportunity is not followed quickly by equality of achievement, frustration turns to anger which sometimes leads to violence.

Surely these problems are serious enough. But I believe there is one yet more serious, because it lies closer to the heart of our whole educational enterprise. We seem to have lost sight of, or become confused about, our main function as educators, our principal goal, our reason for existence. We have no good answer that we are sure of and can agree on to the question, What are schools for?

It may seem presumptuous of me to suggest that I know the answer to this question. Yet the answer I will give is the answer that an overwhelming majority of our fellow citizens would also give. It is the answer that would have been given by most educators of the past who established and operated schools. Indeed, the only reason the question needs to be asked and answered at this time is that some influential educators have been conned into accepting wrong answers to the question. Let me mention a few of these wrong answers:

Schools are not custodial institutions responsible for coping with emotionally disturbed or incorrigible young people, for keeping nonstudents off the streets or out of the job market.

Schools are not adjustment centers, responsible for helping young people develop favorable self-concepts, solve personal problems, and come to terms with life.

Schools are not recreational facilities designed to entertain and amuse, to cultivate the enjoyment of freedom, to help young people find strength through joy.

Schools are not social research agencies, to which a society can properly delegate responsibility for the discovery of solutions to the problems that are currently troubling the society.

I do not deny that society needs to be concerned about some of the things just mentioned. What I do deny is that schools were built and are maintained primarily to solve such problems. I deny that schools are good places in which to seek solutions, or that they have demonstrated much success in finding them. Schools have a very important special mission. If they accept responsibility for solving many of the other problems that trouble some young people, they are likely to fail in their primary mission, without having much success in solving the rest of our social problems.

Then what is the right answer to the question, What are schools for? I believe it is that schools are for learning, and that what ought to be learned mainly is useful knowledge.

Not all educators agree. Some of them discount the value of knowledge in the modern world. They say we ought to strive for the cultivation of intellectual skills. Others claim that schools have concentrated too much on knowledge, to the neglect of values, attitudes, and such affective dispositions. Still others argue that the purpose of education is to change behavior. They would assess its effectiveness by examining the pupil's behavior or performance. Let us consider these three alternatives in reverse order.

If the schools are to be accountable for the performance of their pupils, the question that immediately arises is, What performance? A direct answer to this question is, The performance you've been trying to teach. But that answer is not as simple or as obviously correct as it seems at first glance. Many schools have not been primarily concerned with teaching pupils to perform. They have been trying to develop their pupils' knowledge, understanding, attitudes, interests, and ideals; their cognitive capabilities and affective dispositions rather than their performances. Those who manage such schools would agree that capabilities and dispositions can only be assessed by observing performances, but they would insist that the performances themselves are not the goals of achievement, only the indicators of it. A teacher who is concerned with the pupil's cognitive capabilities and affective dispositions will teach quite differently, they point out, than one whose attention is focused solely on the pupil's performances. And, if performances are not goals but only indicators, we should choose the ones to use in assessment on the basis of their effectiveness as indicators. Clearly we cannot choose them in terms of the amount of effort we made to develop them.

But, if we reject performance goals, another question arises: What should be the relative emphasis placed on affective dispositions as opposed to cognitive capabilities? Here is another issue that divides professional educators. To some, how the pupil feels—his happiness, his interest, his self-concept, his yearnings—are what should most concern teachers. To others the pupil's cognitive resources and capabilities are the main concern. Both would agree that cognition and affect interact, and that no school ought to concentrate solely on one and ignore the other. But they disagree on which should receive primary emphasis.

In trying to resolve this issue it may be helpful to begin by observing that the instructional programs of almost all schools are aimed directly at the cultivation of cognitive competence. Pupils are taught how to read and to use mathematics, how to write and to express perceptions, feelings, ideas, and desires in writing, to be acquainted with history and to understand science. The pupil's affective dispositions, his feelings, attitudes, interests, etc., constitute conditions that facilitate or inhibit cognitive achievement. They may be enhanced by success or impaired by failure. But they are by-products, not the main products, of the instructional effort. It is almost impossible to find any school that has planned and successfully operated an instructional program aimed primarily at the attainment of affective goals.

That this situation exists does not prove that it ought to exist. But it does suggest that there may be reasons. And we need not look too far to discover what they probably are.

Feelings are essentially unteachable. They cannot be passed along from teacher to learner in the way that information is transmitted. Nor can the learner acquire them by pursuing them directly as he might acquire understanding by study. Feelings are almost always the consequence of something—of success or failure, of duty done or duty ignored, of danger encountered or danger escaped. Further, good feelings (and bad feelings also, fortunately) are seldom if ever permanent possessions. They tend to be highly ephemeral. The surest prediction that one can make when he feels particularly good, strong, wise, or happy is that sooner or later he is going to feel bad, weak, foolish, or sad. In these circumstances it is hardly surprising that feelings are difficult to teach.

Nor do they need to be taught. A new-born infant has, or quickly develops a full complement of them—pain, rage, satiety, drowsiness, vitality, joy, love, and all the rest. Experience may attach these feelings to new objects. It may teach the wisdom of curbing the expression of certain feelings at inappropriate times or in inappropriate ways. And while such attachments and curbings may be desirable, and may be seen as part of the task of the school, they hardly qualify as one of its major missions.

The school has in fact a much more important educational mission than affective education, one which in the current cultural climate and educational fashion is being badly neglected. I refer to moral education—the inculcation in the young of the accumulated moral wisdom of the race. Some of our young people have been allowed to grow up as virtual moral illiterates. And as Joseph Junell points out elsewhere . . . we are paying a heavy price for this neglect as the youth of our society become alienated, turn to revolt, and threaten the destruction of our social fabric.

This change in our perception of the function of the school is reflected in our statements of educational objectives. A century ago Horace Mann, Herbert Spencer, and most others agreed that there were three main aspects of education: intellectual, moral, and physical. Today the main aspects identified by our taxonomies of objectives are cognitive, affective, and psychomotor. The first and third elements in these two triads are essentially identical. The second elements are quite different. The change reflects a shift in emphasis away from the pupil's duties and toward his feelings.

Why has this come about? Perhaps because of the current emphasis in our society on individual liberty rather than on personal responsibility. Perhaps because we have felt it necessary to be more concerned with civil rights than with civic duties.

Perhaps because innovation and change look better to us than tradition and stability. Perhaps because we have come to trust and honor the vigor of youth more than the wisdom of age.

In all these things we may have been misled. As we view the contemporary culture in this country it is hard to see how the changes that have taken place in our moral values during the last half century have brought any visible improvement in the quality of our lives. It may be time for the pendulum to start swinging back toward an emphasis on responsibility, on stability, on wisdom. Older people are not always wiser people, but wisdom does grow with experience, and experience does accumulate with age.

Schools have much to contribute to moral education if they choose to do so, and if the courts and the public will let them. The rules of conduct and discipline adopted and enforced in the school, the models of excellence and humanity provided by the teachers, can be powerful influences in moral education. The study of history can teach pupils a decent respect for the lessons in morality that long experience has gradually taught the human race. Schools in the Soviet Union today appear to be doing a much more effective job of moral education than we have done in recent years. This fact alone may be enough to discredit moral education in some eyes. But concern for moral education has also been expressed by educational leaders in the democracies.

Alfred North Whitehead put the matter this way at the end of his essay on the aims of education:

> The essence of education is that it be religious. Pray, what is religious education?
>
> A religious education is an education which inculcates duty and reverence. Duty arises from our potential control over the course of events. Where attainable knowledge could have changed the issue, ignorance has the guilt of vice. And the foundation of reverence is this perception, that the present holds within itself the complete sum of existence, backwards and forwards, that whole amplitude of time which is eternity.[1]

---

[1] Alfred North Whitehead, *The Aims of Education* (New York: Macmillan, 1929).

If these views are correct, moral education deserves a much higher priority among the tasks of the school than does affective education. But it does not deserve the highest priority. That spot must be reserved for the cultivation of cognitive competence. Human beings need strong moral foundations, as part of their cultural heritage. They also need a structure of knowledge as part of their intellectual heritage. What schools were primarily built to do, and what they are most capable of doing well, is to help the student develop cognitive competence.

What is cognitive competence? Two distinctly different answers have been given. One is that it requires acquisition of knowledge. The other is that it requires development of intellectual skills. Here is another issue on which educational specialists are divided.

To avoid confusion or superficiality on this issue it is necessary to be quite clear on the meanings attached to the terms *knowledge* and *intellectual skills*. Knowledge, as the term is used here, is not synonymous with information. Knowledge is built out of information by thinking. It is an integrated structure of relationships among concepts and propositions. A teacher can give his students information. He cannot give them knowledge. A student must earn the right to say "I know" by his own thoughtful efforts to understand.

Whatever a person experiences directly in living or vicariously by reading or listening can become part of his knowledge. It will become part of his knowledge if he succeeds in integrating that experience into the structure of his knowledge, so that it makes sense, is likely to be remembered, and will be available for use when needed. Knowledge is essentially a private possession. Information can be made public. Knowledge cannot. Hence it would be more appropriate to speak of a modern-day information explosion than of a knowledge explosion.

The term *intellectual skills* has also been used with a variety of meanings. Further, those who use it often do not say, precisely and clearly, what they mean by it. Most of them seem not to mean skill in specific operations, such as spelling a word, adding two fractions, diagraming a sentence, or balancing a chemical equation. They are likely to conceive of intellectual skills in much broader terms, such as observing, classifying, measuring, communicating, predicting, inferring, experimenting, formulating hypotheses, and interpreting data.

It seems clear that these broader intellectual skills cannot be developed or used very effectively apart from substantial bodies of relevant knowledge. To be skillful in formulating hypotheses about the cause of a patient's persistent headaches, one needs to know a considerable amount of neurology, anatomy, and physiology, as much as possible about the known disorders that cause headaches, and a great deal about the history and habits of the person who is suffering them. That is, to show a particular intellectual skill a person must possess the relevant knowledge. (Note well at this point that a person cannot look up the knowledge he needs, for knowledge, in the sense of the term as we use it, cannot be looked up. Only information can be looked up. Knowledge has to be built by the knower himself.) And, if he does possess the relevant knowledge, what else does he need in order to show the desired skill?

Intellectual skill that goes beyond knowledge can be developed in specific operations like spelling a word or adding fractions. But the more general (and variable from instance to instance) the operation becomes, the less likely it is that a person's intellectual skills will go far beyond his knowledge.

Those who advocate the development of intellectual skills as the principal cognitive aim of education often express the belief (or hope) that these skills will be broadly transferrable from one area of subject matter to another. But if the subjects are quite different, the transfer is likely to be quite limited. Who would hire a man well trained in the measurement of personal characteristics for the job of measuring stellar distances and compositions?

Those who advocate the cultivation of knowledge as the central focus of our educational efforts are sometimes asked, "What about wisdom? Isn't that more important than knowledge?"

To provide a satisfactory answer to this question we need to say clearly what we mean when we speak of wisdom. In some situations wisdom is simply an alias for good fortune. He who calls the plays in a football game, who designs a new automobile, or who plays the stock market is likely to be well acquainted with this kind of wisdom—and with its constant companion, folly. If an action that might turn out badly in fact turns out well, we call it an act of wisdom. If it turns out badly, it was clearly an act of folly.

But there is more than this to the relation of knowledge to wisdom. C. I. Lewis of Harvard has expressed that relation in this way:

> Where ability to make correct judgments of value is concerned, we more typically speak of wisdom, perhaps, than of knowledge. And "wisdom" connotes one character which is not knowledge at all, though it is quality inculcated by experience; the temper, namely, which avoids perversity in intentions, and the insufficiently considered in actions. But for the rest, wisdom and knowledge are distinct merely because there is so much of knowledge which, for any given individual or under the circumstances which obtain, is relatively inessential to judgment of values and to success in action. Thus a man may be pop-eyed with correct information and still lack wisdom, because his information has little bearing on those judgments of relative value which he is called upon to make, or because he lacks capacity to discriminate the practically important from the unimportant, or to apply his information to concrete problems of action. And men of humble attainments so far as breadth of information goes may still be wise by their correct apprehension of such values as lie open to them and of the roads to these. But surely wisdom is a type of knowledge; that type which is oriented on the important and the valuable. The wise man is he who knows where good lies and how to act so that it may be attained.[2]

I take Professor Lewis to mean that, apart from the rectitude in purposes and the deliberateness in action that experience must teach, wisdom in action is dependent on relevant knowledge. If that is so, the best the schools can do to foster wisdom is to help students cultivate knowledge.

Our conclusion at this point is that schools should continue to emphasize cognitive achievements as the vast majority of them have been doing. Some of you may not be willing to accept this conclusion. You may believe some other goal deserves higher priority in the work of the school, perhaps something like general ability to think (apart from any particular body of knowledge), or perhaps having

[2] C. I. Lewis, *An Analysis of Knowledge and Valuation* (LaSalle, Ill.: Open Court, 1946).

the proper affective dispositions, or stable personal adjustment, or simply love of learning.

If you do, you ought to be prepared to explain how different degrees of attainment of the goal you would support can be determined. For if you can not do this, if you claim your favored goal is intangible and hence unmeasurable, there is room for strong suspicion that it may not really be very important (since it has no clearly observable concomitants or consequences to render it tangible and measurable). Or perhaps the problem is that you don't have a very concrete idea of what it is you propose as a goal.

Let us return to the question of what schools are for, and in particular, for what they should be accountable. It follows from what has been said about the purposes of schooling, and about the cooperation required from the student if those purposes are to be achieved, that the school should not accept responsibility for the learning achievement of every individual pupil. The essential condition for learning is the purposeful activity, the willingness to work hard to learn, of the individual learner. Learning is not a gift any school can give. It is a prize the learner himself must pursue. If a pupil is unwilling or unable to make the effort required, he will learn little in even the best school.

Does this mean that a school should give the student maximum freedom to learn, that it should abandon prescribed curricula and course content in favor of independent study on projects selected by the pupils themselves? I do not think so. Surely all learning must be done by the learner himself, but a good teacher can motivate, direct, and assist the learning process to great advantage. For a school to model its instructional program after the kind of free learning pupils do on their own out of school is to abandon most of its special value as a school, most of its very reason for existence.

Harry Broudy and John Palmer, discussing the demise of the kind of progressive education advocated by Dewey's disciple William H. Kilpatrick, had this to say about the predecessors of our contemporary free schools and open classrooms:

> A technically sophisticated society simply does not dare leave the acquisition of systematized knowledge to concomitant learning, the by-products of projects that are themselves wholesome slices of juvenile life. Intelligence without systematized knowledge will do only for the most ordinary, everyday problems. International amity, survival in our atomic age, automation, racial integration, are not common everyday problems to which common-sense knowledge and a sense of decency are adequate.[3]

Like Broudy and Palmer, I believe that command of useful knowledge is likely to be achieved most rapidly and most surely when the individual pupil's effort to learn is motivated, guided, and assisted by expert instruction. Such instruction is most likely to occur, and to be most efficient and effective, when given in classes, not to individuals singly.

If the school is not held to account for the success of each of its pupils in learning, for what should it be accountable? I would say that it should accept responsibility for providing a favorable learning environment. Such an environment, in my view, is one in which the student's efforts to learn are:

1. guided and assisted by a capable, enthusiastic teacher;
2. facilitated by an abundance of books, films, apparatus, equipment, and other instructional materials;
3. stimulated and rewarded by both formal and informal recognition of achievement; and
4. reinforced by the example and the help of other interested, hard-working students....

Let me now recapitulate what I have tried to say about what schools are for.

1. Public education in America today is in trouble.
2. Though many conditions contribute to our present difficulties, the fundamental cause is our own confusions concerning the central purpose of our activities.
3. Schools have been far too willing to accept responsibility for solving all of the problems of young people, for meeting all of their immediate needs. That schools have failed to discharge these obligations successfully is clearly evident.

---

[3] H. S. Broudy and J. Palmer, *Exemplars of Teaching Method* (Chicago: Rand McNally, 1965).

4. Schools are for learning. They should bend most of their efforts to the facilitation of learning.

5. The kind of learning on which schools should concentrate most of their efforts is cognitive competence, the command of useful knowledge.

6. Knowledge is a structure of relationships among concepts. It must be built by the learner himself as he seeks understanding of the information he has received.

7. Affective dispositions are important by-products of all human experience, but they seldom are or should be the principal targets of our educational efforts. We should be more concerned with moral education than with affective education.

8. Intellectual skills are more often praised as educational goals than defined clearly enough to be taught effectively. Broadly general intellectual skills are mainly hypothetical constructs which are hard to demonstrate in real life. Highly specific intellectual skills are simply aspects of knowledge.

9. Wisdom depends primarily on knowledge, secondarily on experience.

10. Schools should not accept responsibility for the success of every pupil in learning, since that success depends so much on the pupil's own efforts.

11. Learning is a personal activity which each student must carry on for himself.

12. Individual learning is greatly facilitated by group instruction.

13. Schools should be held accountable for providing a good learning environment, which consists of (a) capable, enthusiastic teachers, (b) abundant and appropriate instructional materials, (c) formal recognition and reward of achievement, and (d) a class of willing learners.

14. Since learning cannot be made compulsory, school attendance ought not to be compulsory either.

Schools ought to be held accountable. One way or another, they surely will be held accountable. If they persist in trying to do too many things, things they were not designed and are not equipped to do well, things that in some cases can not be done at all, they will show up badly when called to account. But there is one very important thing they were designed and equipped to do well, and that many schools have done very well in the past. That is to cultivate cognitive competence, to foster the learning of useful knowledge. If they keep this as their primary aim, and do not allow unwilling learners to sabotage the learning process, they are likely to give an excellent accounting of their effectiveness and worth.

22

Personal Thoughts on Teaching and Learning

Carl R. Rogers

EDITOR'S NOTE • The preceding readings in this chapter in one way or another have suggested that teaching is important. None have said that teaching does not or cannot continue, which is in striking contrast to what you are about to read. Dr. Rogers is an eminent psychologist who has been a major influence on psychological theory and practice for over forty years. From his personal experience and research, he has fathered a widely accepted theory of counseling called "client–centered counseling." Even if you disagree intensely with his ideas, you will probably find it difficult to shrug them aside. Is it true that "anything that can be taught to another person is largely inconsequential. . . .?"

I wish to present some very brief remarks, in the hope that if they bring forth any reaction from you, I may get some new light on my own ideas.

I find it a very troubling thing to *think,* par-

From Carl R. Rogers, *On Becoming a Person* (Houghton Mifflin Company, 1961), pp. 164–78. Reprinted by permission of Houghton Mifflin Company and Constable & Co., Ltd.

ticularly when I think about my own experiences and try to extract from those experiences the meaning that seems genuinely inherent in them. At first such thinking is very satisfying, because it seems to discover sense and pattern in a whole host of discrete events. But then it very often becomes dismaying, because I realize how ridiculous these thoughts, which have much value to me, would seem to most people. My impression is that if I try to find the meaning of my own experience it leads me, nearly always, in directions regarded as absurd.

So in the next three or four minutes, I will try to digest some of the meanings which have come to me from my classroom experience and the experience I have had in individual and group therapy. They are in no way intended as conclusions for some one else, or a guide to what others should do or be. They are the very tentative meanings, as of April 1952, which my experience has had for me, and some of the bothersome questions which their absurdity raises. I will put each idea or meaning in a separate lettered paragraph, not because they are in any particular logical order, but because each meaning is separately important to me.

1. I may as well start with this one in view of the purposes of this conference. *My experience has been that I cannot teach another person how to teach.* To attempt it is for me, in the long run, futile.

2. *It seems to me that anything that can be taught to another is relatively inconsequential, and has little or no significant influence on behavior.* That sounds so ridiculous I can't help but question it at the same time that I present it.

3. *I realize increasingly that I am only interested in learnings which significantly influence behavior.* Quite possibly this is simply a personal idiosyncrasy.

4. *I have come to feel that the only learning which significantly influences behavior is self-discovered, self-appropriated learning.*

5. *Such self-discovered learning, truth that has been personally appropriated and assimilated in experience, cannot be directly communicated to another.* As soon as an individual tries to communicate such experience directly, often with a quite natural enthusiasm, it becomes teaching, and its results are inconsequential. It was some relief recently to discover that

Søren Kierkegaard, the Danish philosopher, had found this too, in his own experience, and stated it very clearly a century ago. It made it seem less absurd.

6. As a consequence of the above, *I realize that I have lost interest in being a teacher.*

7. When I try to teach, as I do sometimes, I am appalled by the results, which seem a little more than inconsequential, because sometimes the teaching appears to succeed. When this happens I find that the results are damaging. It seems to cause the individual to distrust his own experience, and to stifle significant learning. *Hence I have come to feel that the outcomes of teaching are either unimportant or hurtful.*

8. When I look back at the results of my past teaching, the real results seem the same— either damage was done, or nothing significant occurred. This is frankly troubling.

9. As a consequence, *I realize that I am only interested in being a learner, preferably learning things that matter, that have some significant influence on my own behavior.*

10. *I find it very rewarding to learn,* in groups, in relationships with one person as in therapy, or by myself.

11. *I find that one of the best, but most difficult ways for me to learn is to drop my own defensiveness, at least temporarily, and to try to understand the way in which his experience seems and feels to the other person.*

12. *I find that another way of learning for me is to state my own uncertainties, to try to clarify my puzzlements, and thus get closer to the meaning that my experience actually seems to have.*

13. This whole train of experiencing, and the meanings that I have thus far discovered in it, seem to have launched me on a process which is both fascinating and at times a little frightening. *It seems to mean letting my experience carry me on, in a direction which appears to be forward, toward goals that I can but dimly define, as I try to understand at least the current meaning of that experience.* The sensation is that of floating with a complex stream of experience, with the fascinating possibility of trying to comprehend its ever changing complexity.

I am almost afraid I may seem to have gotten away from any discussion of learning, as well as teach-ing. Let me again introduce a practical note by saying that by themselves these interpretations of my own experience may sound queer and aberrant, but not particularly shocking. It is when I realize the *implications* that I shudder a bit at the distance I have come from the commonsense world that everyone knows is right. I can best illustrate that by saying that if the experiences of others had been the same as mine, and if they had discovered similar meanings in it, many consequences would be implied.

1. Such experience would imply that we would do away with teaching. People would get together if they wished to learn.

2. We would do away with examinations. They measure only the inconsequential type of learning.

3. The implication would be that we would do away with grades and credits for the same reason.

4. We would do away with degrees as a measure of competence partly for the same reason. Another reason is that a degree marks an end or a conclusion of something, and a learner is only interested in the continuing process of learning.

5. It would imply doing away with the exposition of conclusions, for we would realize that no one learns significantly from conclusions.

I think I had better stop there. I do not want to become too fantastic. I want to know primarily whether anything in my inward thinking as I have tried to describe it, speaks to anything in your experience of the classroom as you have lived it, and if so, what the meanings are that exist for you in *your* experience.

23

When You Expect More, You Are Apt to Get More

Robert Rosenthal

EDITOR'S NOTE • In 1968, Dr. Rosenthal, along with Dr. Lenore Jacobson, created quite a stir in educational and psychological circles with their book, Pygmalion in the Classroom, *which advanced the idea that when teachers expect more of their students, they receive more. Although there have been criticisms in the professional literature about Rosenthal's research design and data analysis, research related to teacher expectations has continued. Not all of the research has supported the idea that teacher expectancies influence student performance, but much of it has. This reading will expose you to some of the major findings of expectancy research. You will also learn about Rosenthal's four–factor "theory," by which he proposes to explain how teacher expectancies work in the first place. Fascinating reading.*

Pygmalion created Galatea out of ivory and desire. In Ovid's account, Pygmalion fell in love with his own sculpture of the perfect woman, and Venus, who spent a lot of time granting requests in those days, gave life to Galatea. In George Bernard Shaw's version 19 centuries later, Henry Higgins turns a Cockney flower girl into an elegant lady, relying on language rather than love.

Most of us do not have Pygmalion's power to manufacture the ideal mate, nor do we all share Higgins' fondness for phonetics. But we may have an extraordinary influence, of which we are often oblivious, on others. Psychologists have not yet learned how to produce Galatea or her male equivalent in the laboratory, but they have demonstrated that the power of expectation alone can influence the behavior of others. The phenomenon has come to be called self-fulfilling prophecy: people sometimes become what we prophesy for them.

This point has long been argued on an intuitive basis. It is obvious, for example, that ghetto children, whose academic performance worsens the longer they remain in school, tend to have teachers who are convinced that the children cannot learn. However, one could argue that teachers expected little because the students behaved poorly, rather than the other way around. To see which comes first, the expectation or the performance, we turned to the laboratory.

In the first study of this problem, over a decade ago, Kermit Fode and I asked 10 students to be "experimenters." We gave each experimenter, in turn, about 20 subjects. The experimenter showed each of his subjects a series of faces, which the subject rated on "degree of success or failure" from +10 to −10. We had previously selected photos that most people consider quite neutral.

We gave our experimenters identical instructions on how to administer the test, with one exception. We told half of them that the "well-established" finding was that the subjects would rate the photos positively; we told the rest that subjects would probably rate the photos negatively.

Expectant Voices. In spite of the fact that all experimenters read the *same* instructions to their subjects, we found that they still managed to convey their expectations. Experimenters who anticipated positive photo ratings got them, while those who expected negative ratings got them too. How did the experimenters silently let their subjects know what they wanted? John Adair and Joyce Epstein repeated this experiment and tape-recorded the experimenters reading the instructions.

Robert Rosenthal, "The Pygmalion Effect Lives," *Psychology Today Magazine* (September 1973): 56–60. Copyright © Ziff-Davis Publishing Co. Reprinted by permission of *Psychology Today Magazine*.

They got the same results we did, and then repeated their experiment, this time using only the tape recordings of their experimenters to instruct their new sample of subjects. They found that subjects exposed only to these tape recordings were just as much influenced by their experimenter's expectations as were those subjects who had experienced "live" experimenters. Apparently, tone of voice alone did the trick.

Such results generated a spate of studies. Larry Larrabee and L. Dennis Kleinsasser found that experimenters could raise the IQ scores of children, especially on the verbal and information subtests, merely by expecting them to do well. Samuel Marwit found that patients will interpret Rorschach inkblots as animals or human beings, depending on what the examiner has been led to expect. And Ronald Johnson, in an ingenious and carefully controlled study, found that experimenters could improve their subjects' performance on a task requiring subjects to drop as many marbles as possible through one of several holes in the table top by expecting them to do well.

Self-fulfilling prophecies even work for animals. Bertrand Russell, who had something to say about nearly everything, noticed that rats display the "national characteristics of the observer. Animals studied by Americans rush about frantically, with an incredible display of hustle and pep, and at last achieve the desired result by chance. Animals observed by Germans sit still and think, and at last evolve the solution out of their inner consciousness."

Fondling Smart Rats. Russell was not far off. Fode and I told a class of 12 students that one could produce a strain of intelligent rats by inbreeding them to increase their ability to run mazes quickly. To demonstrate, we gave each student five rats, which had to learn to run to the darker of two arms of a T-maze. We told half of our student-experimenters that they had the "maze-bright," intelligent rats; we told the rest that they had the stupid rats. Naturally, there was no real difference among any of the animals.

But they certainly differed in their performance. The rats believed to be bright improved daily in running the maze—they ran faster and more accurately—while the supposedly dull animals did poorly. The "dumb" rats refused to budge from the starting point 29 percent of the time, while the "smart" rats were recalcitrant only 11 percent of the time.

Then we asked our students to rate the rats and to describe their own attitudes toward them. Those who believed they were working with intelligent animals *liked* them better and found them more pleasant. Such students said that they felt more relaxed with the animals; they treated them more gently and were more enthusiastic about the experiment than students who thought they had dull rats to work with. Curiously, the students with "bright" rats said that they handled them more but talked to them less. One wonders what students with "dull" rats were saying to those poor creatures.

If rats act smarter because their experimenters think they are smarter, we reasoned, perhaps the same phenomenon was at work in the classroom. So in the mid-1960s Lenore Jacobson and I launched what was to become a most controversial study.

Intellectual Bloomers. We selected an elementary school in a lower-class neighborhood and gave all the children a nonverbal IQ test at the beginning of the school year. We disguised the test as one that would predict "intellectual blooming." There were 18 classrooms in the school, three at each of the six grade levels. The three rooms for each grade consisted of children with above-average ability, average ability, and below-average ability.

After the test, we randomly chose 20 percent of the children in each room, and labeled them "intellectual bloomers." We then gave each teacher the names of these children, who, we explained, could be expected to show remarkable gains during the coming year on the basis of their test scores. In fact, the difference between these experimental children and the control group was solely in the teacher's mind.

Our IQ measure required no speaking, reading, or writing. One part of it, a picture vocabulary, did require a greater comprehension of English, so we call it the verbal subtest. The second part required less ability to understand language but more ability to reason abstractly, so we call it the reasoning subtest.

We retested all the children eight months later. For the school as a whole, we found that the experimental children, those whose teachers had been led to expect "blooming," showed an excess in overall IQ gain of four points over the IQ gain of the control children. Their excess in gain was smaller in verbal ability, two points only, but substantially greater in reasoning, where they gained seven points more than the controls. Moreover, it made no difference whether the child was in a high-ability or low-ability classroom. The teachers' expectations benefited children at all levels. The supposed bloomers blossomed, at least modestly.

This experiment, and the book we wrote based on it, met with vigorous criticism. Professor Arthur Jensen of UC, Berkeley, for example, offered three basic arguments.

First, said Jensen, we should have compared classrooms rather than individual children, and this would have produced only negligible IQ changes. But Jensen ignored the fact that we had done that analysis, and that it led to even larger effects than the per-child comparisons.

Second, Jensen objected to the fact that we used the same IQ test twice. The children were familiar with the test when they took it again, he said, so their scores might have improved for that reason. However, Jensen must then explain why the experimental children showed more of these "practice effects" than the control children, who also took the test twice.

Finally, Jensen did not think that the teachers themselves should have given the tests. However, we had already accounted for this problem by having people who knew nothing of the experiment retest the children. The effects of the teachers' expectations actually increased.

R. L. Thorndike added another objection, namely that our IQ test was an unreliable measure, especially for the youngest children, and that any inference based on such a test would be invalid. I do not think that our test was as worthless as Thorndike implies, but even if it was seriously unreliable we are still left with the basic question. Why did the experimental children improve significantly? An unreliable measure would make it *harder* to find differences between the two groups, not easier.

The most ambitious critique of our Pygmalion in the classroom work was a book by Janet Elashoff and Richard Snow, who completely reanalyzed our original data. They could not disprove the fact that the experimental children did gain more IQ points than control children, even though they trans-

formed our original IQ measure into eight different forms, some of which were biased statistically to minimize any effects of teachers' expectations.

The debate continued, and so did the research. Others sought to discover the Pygmalion effect, and not everyone was successful, which contributed to the controversy. By now 242 studies have been done, with all sorts of subjects and situations. Of these, 84 found that prophecies, i.e. the experimenters' or teachers' expectations, made a significant difference.

But we must not reject the theory because "only" 84 studies support it; on the contrary. According to the rules of statistical significance, we could expect five percent of those 242 studies (about 12) to have come out as predicted just by chance. The fact that we have 84, seven times more than chance would dictate, means that the Pygmalion effect does exist in certain circumstances. Moreover, it is not limited to young children and rats; adolescents and adults are affected too.

Outside the Lab. And the Pygmalion effect is as likely to occur in the real world as in the experimenter's tower. Of the 242 studies that have been done to date, 57 took place outside the laboratory —in a classroom, a factory, an office, and the like. The proportion of significant results is about the same for experiments conducted in the field as in the laboratory, some 37 percent for the field and 34 percent for the laboratory.

For example, Randy Burnham and Donald Hartsough found Pygmalion in the swimming pool. Their subjects were boys and girls, ages seven to 14, who were learning to swim at a summer camp. Half of the instructors were led to think that they were dealing with a "high-potential" group, and their students became better swimmers, by the end of their two-week camping period, than the regular group. And another team of researchers found that it took only two weeks for teen-age girls, who were institutionalized for various offenses, to show a marked improvement in their classroom behavior when they had been labeled "potential bloomers."

Even the United States Air Force Academy Preparatory School succumbed. W. R. Schrank randomly assigned 100 enlisted airmen to one of five math classes, and he told the teachers that each class contained students selected for different levels of ability. The boys in the supposed high-ability classes improved their math scores substantially.

J. Michael Palardy tested the popular assumption that boys have a tougher time learning to read than girls. First-grade teachers are well aware of this folk belief, and thus have clear expectations when they give reading lessons. Palardy surveyed 63 teachers and found five who believed that boys could learn to read as well as girls in the first grade. He matched these five on a number of factors—background, teaching methods, etc.—with five who believed in the stereotype. Indeed, teachers who expected to discover sex differences in reading ability found them. But the boys did just as well as the girls when their teachers thought they would. (As a footnote to this study, the "well-known" sex difference in learning to read also tends to disappear when the children learn from teaching machines rather than from teachers.)

Albert King moved the Pygmalion paradigm into the work world with an ingenious set of five experiments. King was interested in the effects of supervisor expectations on the job performance of disadvantaged workers (unemployed or underemployed, mostly black and members of other minorities). In three of his studies the workers were women in training to become nurses' aides, presser-machine operators, or assemblers of electronic equipment. In the other two studies, the workers were men who were learning to become auto mechanics or welders.

In each experiment, King randomly picked the names of some of the trainees, and told the supervisors that these workers showed a special potential for their particular job. King collected several measures of the workers' performances: objective tests, peer ratings, absences and so on. (King ignored the supervisors' ratings of trainees, since these might reflect only their perception and not actual changes in their performance.) The Pygmalion effect worked in four of the five experiments —for every group of trainees but the nurses' aides. Trainees whose supervisors had expected high job performance of them did much better than the control groups. However, the effect was especially marked among male workers, the welders and mechanics, and less so among female workers, the pressers and assemblers. Perhaps the supervisors found it harder to accept the idea that women could have "special potential" for their work.

Average Performance Ranks (Lower Ranks Indicate Superior Performance)

STUDY	GROUP CONTROL	EXPERIMENTAL GROUP
1 welders	9.9	3.6
2 mechanics	10.7	4.3
3 pressers	9.2	5.3
4 assemblers	11.3	7.8
5 nurses' aides	9.2	8.3

All of this research supported our feeling that self-fulfilling prophecy is a real phenomenon, that it occurs both in and out of the classroom and the laboratory. The next step was to figure out what subtle forces are going on in the exchange between teacher and learner. What makes average kids increase their IQ, neophytes swim better, and trainees learn faster? How does A *communicate* his or her expectations to B, especially when both A and B probably are unaware of the process?

Explaining the Pygmalion Effect. The current evidence leads me to propose a four-factor "theory" of the influences that produce the Pygmalion effect. People who have been led to expect good things from their students, children, clients, or what-have-you appear to:

> —create a warmer social-emotional mood around their "special" students (*climate*);
> —give more feedback to these students about their performance (*feedback*);
> —teach more material and more difficult material to their special students (*input*); and
> —give their special students more opportunities to respond and question (*output*).

There is nothing magical or definitive about the choice of these four, and in fact, none of them is independent of the others. My criterion for including each as a factor is that there be at least five studies that support it and that no more than 20 percent of the studies bearing on each factor contradict it.

The Climate Factor. "Climate" apparently has to do with warmth, attention, and emotional support. Fourteen studies have investigated this factor, 12 of which came out as predicted. Not all of them dealt with the teacher-student relationship; some took place in industrial and clinical contexts as well.

For example, Geri Alpert told a group of psychiatrists that some of their patients had been specially selected for them on the basis of "therapeutic compatibility." She gave them no expectations about the rest of their patients. Later Alpert asked the patients to describe their therapists and their sessions together. From a patient's-eye view, psychiatrists behave more warmly toward people with whom they expect to be compatible and who are likely to get well.

Alan Chaikin, Edward Sigler, and Valerian Derlega asked male and female college undergraduates to teach a short unit on home and family safety to a 12-year-old boy. One third of the "teachers" thought that the boy had an IQ of 130 and did very well in school; one third thought that the child had an IQ of 85 and did poorly in school; and the last third had no information about the boy's IQ. Then the experimenters videotaped the exchange between teachers and student to see what nonverbal cues were going on.

Teachers who thought they were dealing with a bright student were more likely to smile at the boy, nod their heads approvingly, lean toward the boy, and look him in the eye for longer periods. A variety of analogous studies have found that "special-potential" subjects report their teachers or counselors as being more positive, accepting, perceptive, friendly, fond of them, and supportive.

The Feedback Factor. The difference between this factor and the previous one (for both involve warmth and attention) is that feedback depends on a response from the student. A teacher can be generally warm, but still react critically or indifferently to a child's answers or comments. Feedback refers specifically to how much active teaching occurs: often the teacher rewards a desired response, corrects a wrong answer, asks for the student's further thoughts, and so on. Ten studies explored this factor, of which eight supported it.

Jere Brophy and Tom Good asked first-grade teachers to name their high and low achievers. The researchers then watched the teachers work with the children. The teachers ignored only three percent of the high achievers' answers but they ignored 15 percent of the low achievers' answers. The good

students, then, get more feedback, whether their responses are right or wrong.

Teachers give more feedback to apt undergraduates as well as to apt first-graders. John Lanzetta and T. E. Hannah offered college students the chance to play teacher, and gave them the choice of five kinds of feedback for use in teaching a concept task: a strong electric shock, a mild shock, a neutral light, a small amount of money, and a larger amount of money. The "learner," who was a confederate of the experimenters, gave 36 correct and 84 incorrect answers in all cases.

When the student teachers thought the learner had a "high potential," they rewarded him with the larger sum of money when he was right, and shocked him more severely when he was wrong. When they thought that the learner had a "low learning potential," however, they gave him the lesser reward or punishment. In other words, teachers send clearer, stronger evaluations to students for whom they have greater expectations.

But another experiment found that children believed to be bright got more praise, but not more criticism; criticism was reserved for children believed to be dull. Yet a third study found that supposedly "gifted" children get more praise from their teachers, but found no difference between "gifted" and "regular" children in the criticism they got. The matter is complicated. Perhaps criticism for a wrong answer needs to be accompanied by enough praise and support on other occasions; otherwise the student may see the teacher as overly critical and cold. We can say with modest certainty that praise is a factor in achieving the Pygmalion effect, but the role of criticism is less clear.

The Input Factor. There are only five studies that directly deal with this factor, but all five find that teachers literally teach more to children of whom they expect more.

The most dramatic case in point is W. Victor Beez's work with 60 preschoolers and 60 teachers in a Headstart program. Beez told half of the teachers that they could expect poor performance from their supposedly "below-average" children; the rest expected exceptional performance from their "bright" children. Observers, who had not been told what the teachers' expectations were, noted the exchanges between teacher and child.

The teachers worked much harder when they believed they had a bright child. In a unit on word learning for example, 87 percent of the teachers of "bright" children taught eight or more words; but only 13 percent of the teachers of the "dull" children tried to teach them that many. Not surprisingly, 77 percent of the "bright" children learned five or more words, but only 13 percent of the "dull" children learned that many.

NUMBER OF WORDS TAUGHT	TEACHERS EXPECTATION: DULL CHILDREN	BRIGHT CHILDREN
11 or more	0	14
9 or 10	1	10
7 or 8	7	3
5 or 6	15	1
4 or less	7	2
	30	30

Such results tell us that a teacher's expectations about a student's performance are not simply transmitted in subtle voice nuances and a casual facial expression. The expectations may be translated into explicit, overt alterations in teaching style and substance.

The Output Factor. Eleven studies out of 12 done support this factor, indicating that teachers encourage greater responsiveness from students of whom they expect more. They call on such students more often, ask them harder questions, give them more time to answer, and prompt them toward the correct answer. Output is therefore closely related to feedback.

Mary Budd Rowe gives us a good example. She was interested in how long teachers wait for an answer to their question before going on to the next child. She found that many experienced teachers wait only one *second* before they ask the question again, often of someone else. However, Rowe found that teachers wait longer for the students whom they believe to be bright. When Rowe pointed this out to the teachers involved, they reacted with surprise and insight. "I guess we don't expect an answer [of the poor students]," said one, "so we go on to someone else." When these same teachers then deliberately increased their waiting

time for their "slower" students, they got increased responsiveness.

Jeffrey Hersh's work illustrates another facet of the output factor. He asked graduate students to administer the Stanford-Binet IQ Test to children in a Headstart program. Examiners who had been told the children had high intellectual ability immediately began with more difficult questions. They demanded more of the children, and got more.

An Unexpected Galatea. We knew from our original Pygmalion experiment in the classroom that favorable expectations could have a beneficial effect. At the end of the year the teachers had all sorts of good things to say about the "intellectual bloomers": they had a better chance of being successful in the future, said the teachers; they were more appealing, better adjusted, more affectionate and autonomous. So the teachers perceived them, in any case.

We thought that perhaps it was because the experimental children gained more in IQ that the teachers rated their behavior and aptitudes more highly. So we looked at the control-group children who had also gained in IQ that year, to see whether the teachers liked them as much as the bloomers. Such was not the case. To our astonishment, the more the control students increased in IQ, the *less* well adjusted, interesting and affectionate the teachers thought them.

It seems, then, that when a child who is not expected to do well does so, his teacher looks upon his behavior and personality as undesirable. This was especially true, we discovered, for children in low-ability classrooms. Teachers may have a difficult time thinking that a child who has a low-ability label can show an intellectual spurt. They may interpret this change as "maladjustment" or "trouble-making." Perhaps the child doesn't know his place. Several subsequent experiments confirmed this finding, so the hazards of unpredicted success are likely to be real rather than a freak of one study. Alfred Shore, for example, asked teachers to predict their students' intellectual achievement and to describe their students' classroom behavior. A month later, Shore gave the teachers the students' real IQ scores and asked for a reappraisal. Again, teachers downgraded those students in personality and adjustment who had done "too well"—i.e., contrary to their expectations.

Eleanor Leacock studied four schools in four neighborhoods, two poor and two middle-income. Within each income level one school was essentially all black and the other essentially white. Leacock interviewed the fifth-grade teachers about their feelings for the children, and scored their comments for positive, neutral, or negative feelings and attitudes.

Double Handicap.   Leacock found that the teachers were much less favorable to the lower-class children than they were to the middle-class children; 40 percent of their comments about the poorer children were negative, compared to 20 percent of their comments about the middle-class children. And the teachers were even more likely to talk negatively about black children than white children, 43 percent to 17 percent.

Leacock then went on to relate the children's IQ scores to the teachers' feelings toward them. IQ scores of the middle-income children, both black and white, were clearly related to the positive attitudes of their teachers. This relationship did *not* hold for the low-income children; in fact, it was reversed. That is, lower-income children who had *higher* IQs tended to have teachers who viewed them *negatively* and this was especially true for lower-income children who were black. The children who surpassed their teachers' expectations got resentment and complaints for their pains.

Thus children who are both black and lower-income have a double handicap. And this result cannot be attributed to white teachers' bias; both of the teachers of the black children were themselves black. The prejudice of stunted expectations knows no race barrier.

We still do not know exactly how the Pygmalion effect works. But we know that often it does work, and that it has powers that can hinder as well as help the development of others. Field and experimental studies are beginning to isolate the factors that will give some insight into the process. Such awareness may help some to create their Galateas, but it will also give the Galateas a chance to fight back.

24

Walkabout: Searching for the Right Passage from Childhood and School

Maurice Gibbons

EDITOR'S NOTE · *Complaining about the lack of relevancy between school-related activities and real life is easy, but are there positive, constructive suggestions for correcting this situation? This reading provides some constructive suggestions, which are as innovative as I, for one, have seen in a long, long time. Dr. Gibbons quite correctly observes that typical North American students spend most of their time writing about what they know and spend little time acting on what they know. The Australian aboriginal youth must survive the challenge of a "walkabout" before he can graduate to adult status. Using this experience as a model, Gibbons sketches the outline of a similar "graduation," modified for non-aboriginal youth. It's a new and different idea, but Dr. Gibbons informs me that it is already being tried in several American high schools. Would you support a "walkabout" idea?*

Maurice Gibbons, "Walkabout: Searching for the Right Passage from Childhood and School," *Education Digest* (October 1974): 596–602. Reprinted by permission of the author.

A year ago I saw an Australian film called *Walkabout* which was so provocative I am still rerunning scenes from it in my mind. In the movie, two children escape into the desert-like wilderness of the outback when their father, driven mad by failure in business, tries to kill them. Inappropriately dressed in private school uniforms, unable to find food or protection from the blazing heat, and with no hope of finding their way back, they seem certain to die. At the last moment they are found and cared for by a young aborigine, a native Australian boy on his walkabout, a six-month-long endurance test during which he must survive alone in the wilderness and return to his tribe as an adult, or die in the attempt. In contrast to the city children, he moves through the forbidding wilderness as if it were part of his village. He survives not only with skill but with grace and pride as well. When they arrive at the edge of civilization, the aborigine offers to share his life with the white girl and boy he has befriended, but they leave him and return home. The closing scenes show them immersed again in the conventions of suburban life, but dreaming of their adventure.

The movie is a haunting comment on education. What I find most provocative is the stark contrast between the aborigine's walkabout experience and the test of an adolescent's readiness for adulthood in our own society. The young native faces a severe but extremely appropriate trial, one in which he must demonstrate the knowledge and skills necessary to make him a contributor to the tribe rather than a drain on its meager resources. By contrast, the young North American is faced with written examinations that test skills very far removed from the actual experience he will have in real life. He writes; he does not act.

The isolation involved in the walkabout is also a sharp contrast. In an extended period of solitude at a crucial stage of development, the aborigine is confronted with a challenge not only to his competence, but also to his inner, or spiritual, resources. For his Western counterpart, however, school is always a crowd experience. He has little opportunity to confront his anxieties, explore his inner resources, and come to terms with the world and his future in it.

When the aborigine returns, his readiness and worth have been clearly demonstrated to him and his tribe. They need him. He is their hope for the future. It is a moment worth celebrating. The young native can clearly see that his life will depend on the skills he is learning and that after the walkabout his survival and place in the community will depend on them, too. What meaning and relevance to give to learning!

His Western counterpart spends years with abstractions and tests sucked dry of experience, in the end having little that is critical or even significant to his adult future. His high school graduation celebrates an escape from schooling. What values does it promote?

In my opinion, the walkabout could be a very useful model to guide us in redesigning our own rites of passage. It provides a powerful focus during training, a challenging demonstration of necessary competence, a profound maturing experience, and an enrichment of community life. I am not concluding that our students should be sent into the desert, the wilderness, or the Arctic for six months. What is appropriate for a primitive subsistence society is not likely appropriate for one as complex and technically sophisticated as ours. But the walkabout is a useful analogy, a way of making the familiar strange so we can examine our practices with fresh eyes. And it raises the question I find fascinating: *What would an appropriate and challenging walkabout for students in our society be like?*

CRITERIONS

The walkabout model suggests that our solution must measure up to a number of criterions. First, it should be experiential and the experience should be real rather than simulated. Second, it should be a challenge which extends the capacities of the student as fully as possible, urging him to consider every limitation he perceives in himself as a barrier to be broken through. Third, it should be a challenge the student chooses for himself. In primitive societies there are few choices; in technological societies like ours there is a bewildering array of alternatives in life-style, work, politics, possessions, etc. Success in our lives depends on the ability to make appropriate choices. Yet, in most schools, students make few decisions of any importance and receive no training in decision-making or in the implementation and reassessment cycle which constitutes the basic growth pattern.

In addition, the trial should be an important learning experience in itself. It should involve not only the demonstration of the student's knowledge, skill, and achievement, but also a significant confrontation with himself: his awareness, his adaptability to situations, his competence, and his nature as a person. Finally, the trial and graduation ceremony should be appropriate, not as a test of the schooling which has gone before, but a transition from school learning to the life which will follow afterward.

FIVE BASIC CHALLENGES

Keeping these features of the walkabout in mind, let us now ask what might a high-school walkabout experience include? I see five basic challenges:

1. *Adventure:* a challenge to the student's daring, endurance, and skill in an unfamiliar environment. These might include such things as a two-week solo on a high river living off the land, mapping underground caves, or some forms of self-explanatory, meditative, or spiritual adventures.

2. *Creativity:* a challenge to explore, cultivate, and express his own imagination in some esthetically pleasing form. Such esthetic works might include fashion shows of the student's creations, sculpture, painting, anthologies of poetry, gourmet foods, a car-body design and paint job, a stand-up comics art, or tapes of natural-sound music.

3. *Service:* a challenge to identify a human need for assistance and provide it; to express a caring without expectation of reward. In this category, students might include volunteer work with the old, ill, infirm, and retarded, surveys of community needs and opinions, or cleaning-up eyesore lots.

4. *Practical Skill:* a challenge to explore a utilitarian activity, to learn the knowledge and skills necessary to work in that field, and to produce something of use. In this realm there might be demonstrations of finely honed secretarial skills, ocean-floor plant studies, or inventions and designs of many kinds.

5. *Logical Inquiry:* a challenge to explore one's curiosity, to formulate a question or problem of personal importance, and to pursue an answer or solution systematically and, whenever appropriate, by investigation. These might include inquiries into such questions as: How does a starfish bring about the regeneration of a lost arm? How do you navigate in space? What are the 10 most important questions man asks but can't answer? What is insanity and where is the line that separates it from sanity?

The purpose here is not just to stimulate an impressive array of accomplishments, but to enable students to find out who they are by finding out what they can do, and to confirm the importance of that most essential human work.

It isn't far-fetched to think of schools adopting a program to accomplish these ends. The concept is flexible. Any school or community may adapt this proposal to its own circumstances. The basic principles—personal challenge, individual and group decision-making, self-direction in the pursuit of goals, real-world significance in activity, and community involvement at all stages of preparation and conclusion—can be accomplished in a variety of ways.

PREPARATION

Preparation for the walkabout challenge can be provided in various degrees of intensity, depending on how committed the school staff is to creating a curriculum which focuses on personal development.

1. It can be an extracurricular activity in which all planning and work is done during out-of-school time.

2. It can be one element of the curriculum which is included in the schedule like a course, giving students time for planning, consultation, and training.

3. It can be the core of the grade 12 program, one

in which all teaching and activity is devoted to preparing for trial.

4. It can be the goal around which a whole new curriculum is designed for the school, or for a school-within-the-school staffed by interested teachers for interested students.

If the school is junior secondary, students and parents should be notified of the graduation trial on entry in grade 8. Trial committees should be organized for meetings, likely as early as grade 9, to guide the student's explorations of possible challenges, so that serious planning and the preparation of formal proposals can begin in grade 10. The committee should involve students in a series of "Experience Weeks" during which they would be out of school pursuing activities, first of the school's design and later of their own design, as trial runs. During these early years the student could also benefit from association with "big brothers" in the school, older students in more advanced stages of preparation who can help their younger colleagues. The committee would also be responsible for helping the student make his own choices and find the resources and training necessary to accomplish them; and by their interest, they would also help the student to develop confidence in his decisions and commitment to his own goals.

If students were required to write a two-page report on each challenge, a collection of these reports could provide an accumulating resource for younger candidates as well as a permanent "hall of accomplishment" for graduates. In such ways the walkabout challenge could also become a real focus for training in such basic skills as speaking, writing, and use of the media. These are only a few of the ways this proposal can be implemented and integrated with other aspects of school life.

POTENTIAL PROBLEMS

But colleagues and parents with whom I have discussed the idea raise a number of problems potential in the walkabout challenge. What about the inequality that exists between students who have great resources for such walkabout activities at home and students who have few resources at their disposal? What about the risks involved for students on their own in the city and wilderness?

What if competition among students to outdo each other drives them to traumatic extremes or failure? How can we distinguish the apparently modest accomplishment that is a severe challenge for one student from the apparently grand accomplishment which is actually a modest challenge for another?

Such questions point to basic issues: motivation, risk control, support, and assessment. In each case resolution depends on close cooperation and communication between students, parents, teachers, and community members. Students will be motivated by personal challenge, but it will be essential for adults to confirm the importance of these challenges. Counseling by the parent/teacher committees will be essential to help students clarify their personal goals. Risk and liability must clearly be the student's, accepted as such by him and his family. But the adults should help the student to eliminate all unnecessary dangers and learn the skills which will help him master the dangerous situation. The adult committee can also help students to arrange for necessary resources. Competition is already a driving force in schooling. The difference in the proposed walkabout experience is that each student chooses goals and activities which are important to him.

I believe the trial proposed here provides a framework for nurturing the development of personal autonomy, initiative, and industry. The individual can clarify his own values and goals. He can make decisions about his own directions and efforts. He can explore his personal resources by testing them in action. Most important, the student will not only have begun to clarify his life goals through these challenges, he will have experienced the cycle by which life goals are pursued.

The school also seems likely to reap a number of benefits from the walkabout challenge program: a boost to school spirit; an opportunity to establish a better staff–student relationship; a new focus for parent and community cooperation; a constant source of information about what is important to students and parents; a means of motivating and focusing learning for everyone; a constant reminder of the relationship between education and living; and a device for transforming the nature of schooling to combine freedom and responsibility, independence, and clearly directed effort. And most important, it will enable us to communicate to our younger generation how important their growth and accomplishment is to us. In fact, the success of this concept depends on that communication.

25

Free Schools: A Time for Candor

Jonathan Kozol

EDITOR'S NOTE • The concept of free schools has been with us in one form or another since the early 1960s. Different free school advocates have different ideas about what a free school is or what it should be, but the essential idea is that students and teachers should be more or less free from the usual curriculum boundaries and bureaucratic red tape associated with traditional schools. The free school is one of education's very real innovations of the past fifteen years or so. Like any innovative movement, it has had and is having its trials and tribulations. Like any other kind of school, free schools may start with a sound idea, but they succeed or fail ultimately because of the people behind the ideas. Dr. Kozol has been a major force behind the free school movement, but, as he says, it is a time for candor.

For the past six years free schools have almost been pets of the media. Too little of this coverage, however, has focused on the deep and

Jonathan Kozol, "Free Schools: A Time for Candor," *Saturday Review*, March 4, 1972. Copyright © 1972 by the Saturday Review. Reprinted by permission.

often overwhelming problems that confront some of these schools: the terrible anguish about power and the paralyzing inhibition about the functions of the teacher.

The difficulties begin with a number of foolish, inaccurate, and dangerous cliches borrowed without much criticism or restraint from fashionable books by fashionable authors who do not know very much about either life within the cities or responsibilities that confront a free school for poor children in a time of torment and in a situation of great urgency and fear. It is almost axiomatic that the free schools that survive are those that start under the stimulus of a neighborhood in pain and that remain within the power of that neighborhood. Those that fail are, time and again, those that are begun on somebody's intellectual high or someone's infatuation with a couple of phrases from the latest book and then collapse after six months or a year of misery among the cuisenaire rods.

It is time for us to come right out and make some straightforward statements on the misleading and deceptive character of certain slogans that are now unthinkingly received as gospel. It is just not true that the best teacher is the one who most successfully pretends that he knows nothing. Nor is it true that the best answers to the blustering windbag of the old-time public school is the free-school teacher who attempts to turn himself into a human inductive fan.

Free schools that exist under the siege conditions of New York, Boston, or one of the other Northern cities should not be ashamed to offer classroom experience in which the teacher does not hesitate to take a clear position as a knowledgeable adult. Neither should these free schools be intimidated in the face of those who come in from their college courses with old and tattered copies of *How Children Fail* and *Summerhill*. Many of these people, fans of John Holt or A. S. Neill though they may be, are surprisingly dogmatic in their imposition of modish slogans on the réal world they enter. Many, moreover, have only the most vague and shadowy notion of what the free school represents.

Free schools at the present moment cover the full range of beliefs from the Third World Institute of all black kids and all black teachers, operated by a group of revolutionary leaders wearing military jackets, boots, and black berets, to a segregated Summerhill out in the woods of western Massa-chusetts offering "freedom" of a rather different kind and charging something like $2,000 or $3,000 yearly for it. The free schools that I care most about stand somewhere in between, though surely closer to the first than to the second. The trouble, however, is that the intellectual imprecision of the school-reform movement as a whole, and the very special imprecision of the free schools in particular, allow *both* kinds of free schools to advertise themselves with the same slogans and to describe themselves with the same phrases.

The challenge, then, is to define ourselves with absolutely implacable precision—and to do so even in the face of economic danger, even in the certain knowledge of the loss of possible allies. "This is what we are like, and this is the kind of place that we are going to create. This is the kind of thing we mean by freedom, and this is the sort of thing we have in mind by words like 'teach' and 'learn.' This is the sort of thing we mean by competence, effectiveness, survival. If you like it, join us. If you don't, go someplace else and start a good school of your own."

Such precision and directness are often the rarest commodities within free schools. Too many of us are frightened by the accusation of being headstrong, tough, authoritarian, and, resultingly, we have tried too hard to be all things to all potential friends. It is especially difficult to resist the offered assistance when we are most acutely conscious of the loneliness and isolation of an oppressive social structure.

The issue comes into focus in the choice of teachers and in the substance of curriculum. In an effort to avoid the standard brand of classroom tyranny that is identified so often with the domineering figure of the professional in the public system, innovative free-school teachers often make the grave mistake of reducing themselves to ethical and pedagogical neuters. The teacher too often takes the role of one who has *no* power.

The myth of this familiar pretense is that the teacher, by concealing his own views, can avoid making his influence felt in the classroom. This is not the case. No teacher, no matter what he does or does not say, can ever manage *not* to advertise his biases to the children.

A teacher "teaches" not only or even primarily by what he *says*. At least in part, he teaches by what he *is*, by what he *does*, by what he seems to *wish to be*. André Gide said, "Style is character."

In the free school, life-style is at the heart of education. The teacher who talks of "redistribution of the wealth" yet dresses in expensive clothes among the poor and spends the Christmas holidays in San Juan gets across a certain message, with or without words, about his stake in some of the nice things privilege can offer. A black woman with a conspicuous Afro and a certain definite quality of suppressed intensity in her manner and voice gets across a whole world of feelings and biases concerning race and rage and revolution. A white woman who dresses in old sandals, blue work shirt, Mexican skirt, whose long hair is frequently uncombed, who wears love beads or a molded-steel medallion on her breast, who calls things "neat," "right on," "downers," and "together" presents a living advertisement for a whole body of implied ideas, political tendencies, and ideological directions.

In certain respects, the things a teacher does not even *wish* to say may well provide a deeper and more abiding lesson than the content of the textbooks or the conscious message of the posters on the wall. When war is raging and when millions of people in our land are going through a private and communal hell, no teacher—no matter what he does or does not do—can fail to influence his pupils. The secret curriculum is in the teacher's own lived values and convictions, in the lineaments of his face, and in the biography of passion (or self-exile) that is written in his eyes. The young teacher who appears to children to be vague or indirect in the face of human pain, infant death, or malnutrition may not teach children anything at all about pain, death, or hunger, but he will be teaching a great deal about the capability of an acceptable adult to abdicate the consequences of his own perception and, as it were, to vacate his own soul. By denying his convictions during class discussion, he does not teach objectivity. He gives, at the very least, a precedent for nonconviction.

It is particularly disabling when a strong and serious free school begun by parents of poor children in an urban situation finds itself bombarded by young teachers who adhere without restraint or self-examination to these values. Not only does such behavior advertise gutlessness and weakness to the children, it also represents a good deal of deception and direct bamboozlement. The willingness of the highly skilled white teacher to blur and disguise his own effectiveness and to behave as if he were less competent and effective than he really is provides the basis for a false democracy between himself and the young poor children he works with. The children, in all honesty, *can't do nothing.* The young man from Princeton only *acts* as if he can't. The consequence of this is a spurious level of egalitarian experience from which one party is always able to escape, but from which the other has no realistic exit.

I believe, for these reasons, in the kind of free school in which adults do not try to seem less vigorous or effective than they are. I believe in a school in which real power, leverage, and at least a certain degree of undisguised adult direction are not viewed with automatic condescension or disdain. I believe in a school in which the teacher does not strive to simulate the status or condition of either an accidental "resource-person," wandering mystic, or movable reading lab, but comes right out, in full view of the children, with all of the richness, humor, desperation, rage, self-contradiction, strength, and pathos that he would reveal to other grownups. Nevertheless, some of the free schools that describe and advertise their high-priced, all-white, innovative education in the pages of *New Schools Exchange* seem literally to build the core of their life-style around the simulation of essential impotence, with competence admitted only in those areas of basic handiwork and back-to-nature skills where no serious competition from the outside world exists. "Wow!" I hear some of these free-school people say. "We made an Iroquois canoe out of a log!" Nobody, however, *needs* an Iroquois canoe. Even the Iroquois do not. The Iroquois can buy aluminum canoes if they should really need them. They don't, however. What they need are doctors, lawyers, teachers, organizers, labor leaders. The obvious simulation character of the construction of an Iroquois canoe by a group of well-set North American children and adults in 1972 is only one vivid example of the total exercise of false removal from the scene of struggle that now typifies the counterculture. There may be some pedagogic value or therapeutic function in this form of simulation for the heartsick or disoriented son or grandson of a rich man. It does not, however, correspond to my idea of struggle and survival in the streets and cities I know.

In the face of many intelligent and respected statements on the subject of "spontaneous" and "ecstatic" education, the simple truth is that you do not learn calculus, biochemistry, physics, Latin grammar, mathematical logic, Constitutional law, brain surgery, or hydraulic engineering in the same organic fashion that you learn to walk and talk and breathe and make love. Months and years of long, involved, and—let us be quite honest—sometimes nonutopian labor in the acquisition of a single unit of complex and intricate knowledge go into the expertise that makes for power in this nation. The poor and black cannot survive the technological nightmare of the next ten years if they do not have this expertise.

There is no more terrifying evidence of the gulf of race and class that now separates oppressor and oppressed within this nation than that so many of those people who are rich and strong should toil with all their heart to simulate the hesitation, stammer, and awkward indirection of impotence, while blacks in Roxbury, in Harlem, and in East St. Louis must labor with all their soul to win one-tenth of the *real effectiveness* that those white people conspire to deny. If there is a need for some men and women to continue in that manner of existence and that frame of mind, and if it is a need that cannot be transcended, then let there be two very different kinds of free schools and two very different kinds of human transformation and human struggle. But, at least within the urban free schools that we build and labor to sustain, let us be willing to say who we are and what we think and where we stand, and let us also say what things *we do not want.*

Those who fear power in themselves fear it still more in those whom they select to lead them. Several free schools that I know firsthand have gone through nightmarish periods in which they all but pick apart the man or woman they have chosen to be their headmaster or headmistress. The process is dangerous and debilitating not only because it does so much direct damage in terms of simple pain and hurt to many decent and courageous men and women but also because it wastes our time in minor skirmishes and diverts us from the serious struggle for the well-being and real survival of our children.

More importantly, however, fear of power places a premium on mediocrity, nonvital leadership, insipid character, and unremarkable life-style. An organization, of whatever kind, that identifies real excellence, effectiveness, or compelling life-style with the terrifying risk of despotism and authoritarian manipulation will, little by little, drive away all interesting, brilliant, and exhilarating people and will establish in their stead norms of communal mediocrity. The label reserved for those who do not learn to respect these norms is "ego-tripper." Without question, there is a need for realistic caution, but not every straightforward, unequivocal statement of position can be construed as an instance of ego-tripping. The perfect way to avoid an ego trip, of course, is to create a community of utterly alienated, dull, and boring people. There is no risk of ego-tripping if there is no ego. But there isn't any life or strength or truth or passion either.

Free schools, if they wish to stay alive and vital, must learn to separate the fear of domination from the fear of excellence. If a free school were ever able to discover or train a leader with the power and vision of a Jesse Jackson or, in a different sense, a George Dennison or a Truman Nelson, I hope it would have brains enough not to attempt to dull his edge or obscure his brilliant provocations with communal indecision. "Participation" and "the will of the full group," inherently eloquent and important aspects of a democratic and exciting free school, can easily turn into the code words for a stylized paralysis of operation and for a new tyranny of will and function.

It may well be that certain free schools, within a rural, safe, and insulated situation, will find it possible to function and survive without formal structure, leadership, or power apparatus. It is their choice if they should wish to do it in that way; but those who look for leaders, place them in power, and invest them with the trust and confidence of numbers ought then to stand beside them and help to make them stronger and less frightened in the face of the dangers they confront. Angry parents who never before had power in their hands and young white people who have forever hated anyone who wielded it, can together paralyze the operations of a free school and can gradually destroy the finest qualities in anyone that they select to lead them.

Statements of this kind run counter to a large part of the jargon that the media tend to associate with the free schools. Jargon, however, does not often correspond to the realities of struggle and survival. In every free school that has lasted longer than two years there is—*there always is*—some deep down and abiding power center. Free schools do not hang photographs of unremarkable individuals. They put up photographs of Malcolm X, of César Chavez, of Martin Luther King, of Tolstoy, of José Martí. What is true in history and on the poster-photographs is also true in our own numbers: Some women and some men *are* more powerful and more interesting than others. Behind every free school that survives are the special dedication, passion, and vocation of one woman, one man, or one small and trusted group of men and women. It is by now almost a rule of thumb that the less the free-school bylaws speak of "power" the more one person or one group turns out to hold it. It may be only by a look, a shrug, or a sense of peace within the quiet center of the pedagogic storm. Is A. S. Neill the "ego-tripper" or the "power center" or the "ethical fire" in the heart of his own school? Ask anyone who has ever been to Summerhill.

Still another dangerous tendency included in the syndrome of pretended impotence and threatening the survival of urban free schools is what Bernice Miller speaks of as an inclination toward The Insufficient—or what I think of sometimes as The Cult of Incompletion. It is the kind of hang-loose state of mind that views with scorn the need for strong, consistent, and uninterrupted processes of work and aspiration and, instead, makes a virtue of the interrupted venture, the unsuccessful campaign. I have in mind an almost classic picture of a group of rural free-school people I know, sitting on the lawn of someone's country farm or "radical estate" in an almost too comfortable mood of "resting on our elbows at a place of satisfying retrospect on our own failure" or at a kind of "interesting plateau of our half-success."

I think that it is time for us to face head on this problem of our own inherent fear of strength and effectiveness. We must be prepared to strive with all our hearts to be strong teachers, efficacious adults, unintimidated leaders, and straightforward and strong-minded provocators in the lives of children. We must work with all our hearts to overcome the verbal style of debilitation and subjunctive supposition—the interposition, for example, of the preposition or conjunction of arm's-length invalidation ("like") before all statements of intense commitment or denunciation. I know some free-school leaders and writers who now begin to justify and defend the will-to-failure by making a virtue of

the capability to start and stop things in response to sudden impulse. It is a curious revolution that builds its ideology and its morale upon the cheerful prospect of surrender. Men who walk the city streets with minds uncluttered by their own internal need for self-defeat, aware of the pain around them, could not make barbarous recommendations of this kind.

The free-school press and writers speak more often of Bill Ayers's free school in Ann Arbor, Michigan, which did not work out, than they do of Edward Carpenter's remarkable and long-sustained success at Harlem Prep. I have a good deal of respect and admiration for Bill Ayers. Still, it cannot be ignored that, insofar as the free schools are concerned, Bill Ayers's experience is perhaps the prototype of the eloquent exercise in self-defeat. I believe we ought to honor people like Bill Ayers in the same way many of us revere the name of Che Guevara. There is also Fidel, however, who was not afraid to sit in the victor's chair, and there are also strong and stable people like Ed Carpenter. It would not hurt to have upon the walls or in the stairways of our little schools photographs not only of those who do not fear to die for their beliefs but also of those who do not fear to win. I think that the children of the black and poor ought to be able to know and believe, right from the first, that the struggle for liberation does not need to end with sickness in the mountains or with steel helmets in Chicago or with a T-group in Manhattan. It can also end with personal strength, political passion, psychological leverage, and the deepest kind of moral and pragmatic power.

I do not intend to mock young people, or myself, or my own friends, who really try and honestly do fail; but I am thinking also of the anguish in success and in "too much effectiveness" of those who look upon effectiveness itself as bearing the copyright of evil men. There is no need for us to choose between a contaminated sense of competence and a benign sense of ineptitude. The opposite of the cold and avaricious doctor earning his $250,000 yearly in the kingdom of lighted pools and begonia hedges in Lexington, Massachusetts, does not need to be the spaced-out flautist in the shepherd's jacket on a mountaintop in Colorado or the mystical builder of the Pakistani mud hut in New Hampshire; it can also be the radical, bold, and inexhaustible young doctor working his heart out in the store-front clinics of Chicago. The opposite of the sleek corporation lawyer spooning up the cool lime sherbet from a silver dish in the air-conditioned confines of the Harvard Club in Boston does not need to be the barefoot kid in blue jeans in New Hampshire; it can also be the strong and passionate young woman who nails down her law degree while working nights to tutor kids within the nightmare of the Pruitt-Igoe projects in St. Louis —and then comes back to be their representative before the law. The preference for the unsuccessful, for the interrupted enterprise, for hesitation and low-key aspiration is not surprising or inexplicable in a hard and driving nation such as our own.

One final point: Free schools often prove to be almost irresistibly attractive to some of the most unhappy and essentially aggressive people on the face of the wide earth. In many instances, the very same people who have been "evicted" from someone else's free school precisely for the pain and hurt they cause will shop around until they come to us. There is, as many people in the free schools find, a rather familiar kind of man or woman who does not, in fact, care a great deal about children but who enjoys a power struggle. There is a kind of "energy devastation" in such people that can be helpful when it is directed at external obstacles but that can be incredibly destructive when it turns in on our own small numbers.

I have seen one of the kindest black people I know pause, and look gently, almost with sadness, into the eyes of someone of this sort and say quietly: "Well, you don't seem to be somebody that I want to work with. There has been too much unhappiness among us since you came. You do not seem to think we are sufficiently enlightened. You do not seem to think that we have read the right books. You may be right. We have not read many books in the past year. We have been too busy trying to build up our school and trying to keep off people who bring sadness and unhappiness into our ranks. We think that you are just that kind of person. We would rather have the courage of our errors than the kind of devastation forced upon us by your intellectual wisdom."

I do not like to end with a passage of this kind. It shows too much of the bitterness and the deep pain that have been part of the free schools I know. I am trying, however, to be as realistic and as candid as I can. There is a time when we must sit down and compose rhapsodic stories to raise money for the free schools; there is another time when we have to be as honest as we can. . . . It is the time for candor.

26

The Traditional School: Keep It Among the Alternatives

Gene Maeroff

EDITOR'S NOTE • This is an account of one high school, which, like many traditional high schools, does not welcome change for the sake of change. Traditional schools are typically associated with more rules, regulations, structure, and pre-established curricula than the free schools discussed in the preceding reading. Some teachers and students think that emphasis on rules and structure is a poor way to run a school system, while others view it as necessary and productive. As one twelfth-grader in this reading says, "I find it necessary to have a traditional atmosphere and marks to spur me on." What do you think? Should we keep the traditional school among the alternatives?

Bayside High School, in New York City's second-largest borough, Queens, contains no minischools. Its academic calendar is based not on modules but on standard semesters. Desks

Gene Maeroff, "The Traditional School: Keep It Among the Alternatives," *Phi Delta Kappan* (March 1973): 473–75. Reprinted by permission.

are bolted to the floors and the closest the school comes to having an open classroom is the informality of an art or home economics course. There is a dearth of independent study and individualization is unusual. Students are more or less outside the decision-making process and they are monitored at assemblies by faculty members who tell them where to sit, when to be quiet, how to salute the flag, and what to do when the assembly ends. All in all, in the opinion of the school's social studies chairman, the 3,800-student school is a place that does not welcome "change for the sake of change."

Bayside also sends some 80% of its graduates to post-high school education and produces championship football teams. It is safe and secure by comparison with most of New York City's 94 high schools and attendance figures rank among the highest. It has one of the city's finest honors programs and its advanced placement program has been one of the most successful. The emphasis in music is on Bach, Beethoven, and Mozart, and study can be pursued in eight foreign languages. There is sufficient ability in the student body to warrant the offering of such courses as nuclear chemistry, calculus, and microbiology.

Not counting such special institutions as the Bronx High School of Science, Bayside is perhaps one of the city's best examples of a traditional high school. Even the appearance of Bayside's sprawling, 3-story brick and stone building with its long, narrow windows invokes the classic image. Inside, the picture is reinforced by clean, quiet corridors in which art can be hung on the walls without being consumed by the graffiti that seem endemic to many New York City high schools. An air of venerability is lent by the fact that the school has had no renovation and little new equipment since its opening almost 40 years ago.

Across the street from a shady park, in a solid middle-class neighborhood, the school is more than 15 miles from trouble-plagued Manhattan. It serves predominantly the children of parents who still think that teachers are right and kids are wrong. Bayside, which once even imposed a ban on *Catcher in the Rye*, fits the no-nonsense concept of what its community thinks a high school is supposed to be. And a succession of nose-to-the-grindstone principals has endeavored to keep it that way.

"I was there for six years and inherited a good traditional school from my predecessor," says Abraham Margolies, who retired as principal last spring. "We kept the skeleton and added new courses without changing the basic structure. In a pure sense, the word 'traditional' is great. We make a great mistake to go in for a completely innovative school without reference to the past. It is gimmickry without substance. My great complaint with all those who have contempt for traditional education is that they think the word 'traditional' is something to be sneered at."

Lester Speiser, a tall, broad-shouldered former English teacher who enjoys writing poetry in his spare time, has taken on Margolies's mantle. "Tradition has become a dirty word in certain circles," says the mustachioed Speiser, himself a product of the New York City public schools. "It's very important not to run a popularity contest in education and pick up the latest fads. You have to examine and use what's good for your particular youngsters. Alternative education means different ways of approaching the understood goals of education. And we have to recognize that youngsters have different needs than they did 20 or 30 years ago. But educational experiments are not something to be accepted naturally, the way you would accept polio vaccine. The greatest creativity is not through mechanical structures and various alternatives but through a creative teacher. And we have many of them at Bayside. I don't believe the teacher should be made into a master of ceremonies. I'm not ashamed to say to kids that I think we know more than they do. I don't want an automaton, but I do want a student who will meet us halfway. I believe the teacher-pupil relationship is a great tradition."

Teachers count at Bayside. The faculty of 175 is an essentially experienced one and good teaching is valued. Excellent younger teachers—dedicated and enthusiastic—such as Alan Brodsky have joined and blended into the faculty, maintaining the accent on quality teaching. In a typical meeting recently of one of Brodsky's beginning chemistry classes, the students eagerly waved their hands, straining for recognition and a chance to join a discussion on the properties of metals. The youthful-looking Brodsky, wearing a white laboratory jacket and standing front and center in a small, tiered lecture hall that could just as easily have been in one of New England's leading prep schools, deftly ran through a series of experiments for the attentive students, questioning them carefully each step of the way, drawing into the conversation those few who were not bursting to participate. There was learning, as well as teaching, taking place that morning in Bayside High School.

Most Bayside teachers can expect to have many bright, responsive, well-prepared, highly motivated students. It is almost as if the majority of the students would succeed regardless of who was standing in front of the classroom and, if necessary, despite the teaching. As indeed they probably would. To its teachers, certainly to the veterans, Bayside is proof that the traditional approach deserves to be represented in the educational spectrum. "When you talk about alternative education," says Mark Yohalem, the school's science chairman, "one of the alternatives should be traditional education." But Bayside is by no means idyllic. It has its disquieting side.

Of the approximately 20% of the school's seniors who do not go beyond high school, woefully few are prepared to enter the job market with salable skills. Moreover, some Bayside graduates who become college dropouts may have belonged in postsecondary technical school, not in college, and they might have known it had they gone to some other kind of high school than Bayside. The school's vocational and technical education offerings are sorely limited. Its cooperative work-study program includes only about 70 youngsters. Some students at Bayside are clearly ill-served.

"There is an element here that we are not equipped to handle and that we don't know how to handle," says Larry Ganeless, Bayside's English chairman. "There is no use sweeping it under the rug. We just don't know how to handle them. Some of us say that maybe they can't be handled."

A substantial portion of "they" are black. More than 700 black youngsters from the impoverished South Jamaica section of Queens attend Bayside under the city's school integration program. The Bayside neighborhood itself has only a handful of blacks. A large number of the South Jamaica students, as well as some white youngsters, bring to the school educational deficiencies that cause them serious problems. "When we get them and they are reading below a fifth-grade level, our type of education doesn't work for them," says Yohalem. A remedial reading teacher claims that when he asked a class of incoming blacks to write the alphabet, one-half were unable to do it.

Pronounced disparities in background often separate the school's white students from the blacks and, sometimes, those with public school training from those with parochial school training. Also, the school has a sizeable contingent of "hitters"—no one can say where the name comes from—white youngsters who in dress and mannerisms try to emulate the "greasers" of the fifties and display an uncommon fondness for souped-up cars. Such divergencies seem to tear at the very fabric of traditional Bayside, which has been dependent on a degree of homogeneity in its student body.

Illustrative of the differences, an elementary school that feeds some of the white public school youngsters into Bayside, P.S. 184, led the city's 632 elementary schools in reading attainment this year and was second each of the last two years. A staff member at P.S. 184, which is itself operated along traditional lines, describes the pupils as "bright, willing, obedient, and neatly dressed"—attributes that should stand them in good stead at Bayside. By comparison, a test given to Bayside's ninth-graders, almost all of whom are black, showed 24% reading two or more years below grade level. Because of the integration plan and the zoning setup, most blacks enter Bayside as ninth-graders (along with a scattering of white parochial school transfers) and most white public school graduates begin as tenth-graders.

Having an overwhelmingly middle-class student body allows Bayside to benefit from almost none of the programs for the disadvantaged. Only four remedial reading classes at the school are paid for through federal funds. At the expense of the regular program, in a school that is already overcrowded and on double sessions, the faculty has on its own added three other remedial sections of reading and 10 of math.

Bayside's difficulties have not escaped Principal Speiser's attention. "This is part of the problem that a school like Bayside with an academic tradition has," he says. "Our obligation is to try to reach those youngsters who are in various states of miseducation. One of our problems is that we get increasingly more youngsters like this every year and we do not receive the money for the special services that should accompany them. It is like

'Catch-22.' The reasoning is that Bayside is a good school and doesn't need Title I money, so therefore it's all right to have 20% Title I kids without the money." Personnel services of all kinds are limited at Bayside, for neighborhood students as well as those who are bused in, by a budget that permits the hiring of only three guidance counselors for the entire school. "We have to constantly resort to outside agencies for services that should be available within the school," says one teacher. There is a widespread belief among faculty and administrators that "because Bayside is stable and not on the verge of exploding it is ignored by the board of education and inadequately financed in all respects."

If one listens carefully at Bayside he may also detect some discord among the students themselves. There are youngsters such as Ira Peppercorn, an eleventh-grader, who complains: "Things are still going on here the way they were 30 or 40 years ago. It is very, very structured. There is a system and you can't move out of that system."

Or, there are the comments of Debbie Lewis, an eleventh-grader, and other girls in Mrs. Hazel Kidd's sewing class, who wonder why the marvelously open environment they experience in that course cannot be duplicated in the mainline subjects. "There is more freedom and less pressure in here," says Debbie. "It is possible other subjects could be this way. I was in an ecology class in junior high that operated like this. We sat in small groups and talked. People were interested and they got good marks. In here we are free to sit where we want—with our friends—instead of in assigned seats like in other classes. We can talk and there isn't homework unless we want it. Kids would like it more and it would be better if all classes were like this."

Nonetheless, Bayside is not likely to undergo any sort of radical alterations in spirit in response to such observations. Counterbalancing such opinions as Debbie's are those of a student such as Howard Speicher, who thinks that "what a student gets out of Bayside depends on his goals." Howard's are academic, and for him the school has been "successful."

"There is an excellent faculty here," says Howard, who is a twelfth-grader with a 92 average and editorship of the student newspaper. "There is nothing like marks as a stimulus. I find it necessary to have a traditional atmosphere and marks spur me on. I experienced independent study in junior high school and it was nice to goof off and get good marks, but it just didn't work."

While the pace of change at Bayside is not expected to be rapid, there is a feeling shared by the principal and others that carefully charted steps in new directions would not compromise the commitment to traditional education. "My definition of tradition," says Ganeless, the English chairman, "includes a place for innovation. My experience at Bayside has been that the so-called traditional curriculum in the hands of a good, resourceful teacher has meant exploiting every avenue at hand in terms of content and method."

The school already has a standing committee investigating possible curricular innovations. An expanded effort in vocational and technical education is being planned. A consultative council with the potential of bringing students and the community in on policy making has been formed. If money can be found, there are hopes of strengthening the remediation efforts. If such steps lead to more of the students and faculty sharing Speiser's sense of what education should mean, it could be a good thing. "I'm one of those," says the baldish, graying, 46-year-old principal, "who is lucky enough on Sunday night to look forward to Monday morning." One almost couldn't ask any more of education than that.

27

Behavioral Objectives Are Necessary for Good Instruction

Robert M. Gagné

EDITOR'S NOTE · As you will see in the contrasting views reflected in this reading and the one immediately following, there is heated debate about the use of behavioral objectives in education. Dr. Gagné is firm in his belief that good instruction must be preceded by specific instructional objectives; that is, only when the outcomes of learning are specified beforehand will teaching be effective. Some agree. Some do not. For the position of those who do not think behavioral objectives are useful, see reading 28.

Few people who are professionally concerned with education in the United States are unacquainted with "behavioral objectives." Knowledge of this term and its meaning has become widespread. It is therefore timely to pose a question which inquires about the need for behavioral objectives, the possible uses they may have, and the

Robert M. Gagné, "Behavioral Objectives? Yes!" *Educational Leadership* 29 (February 1972): 394–96. Reprinted with permission of the Association for Supervision and Curriculum Development and Robert M. Gagné. Copyright © 1972 by the Association for Supervision and Curriculum Development.

educational functions that may be conceived for them.

NATURE OF INSTRUCTIONAL OBJECTIVES

The statement of a behavioral objective is intended to communicate (to a specified recipient or group of recipients) the outcome of some unit of instruction. One assumes that the general purpose of instruction is learning on the part of the student. It is natural enough, therefore, that one should attempt to identify the outcome of learning as something the student is able to do following instruction which he was unable to do before instruction. When one is able to express the effects of instruction in this way, by describing observable performances of the learner, the clarity of objective statements is at a maximum. As a consequence, the reliability of communication of instructional objectives also reaches its highest level.

To some teachers and educational scholars, it appears at least equally natural to try to identify the outcomes of learning in terms of what capability the learner has gained as a result of instruction, rather than in terms of the performance he is able to do. We therefore frequently encounter such terms as "knowledge," "understanding," "appreciation," and others of this sort which seem to have the purpose of identifying learned capabilities or dispositions. Mager (1962) and a number of other writers have pointed out the ambiguity of these terms, and the unreliability of communications in which they are used.

Actually, I am inclined to argue that a complete statement of an instructional objective, designed to serve all of its communicative purposes, needs to contain an identification of *both* the type of capability acquired as a result of learning, and also the specific performance by means of which this capability can be confirmed (cf. Gagné, 1971a). Examples can readily be given to show that perfectly good "behavioral" verbs (such as "types," as in "types a letter") are also subject to more than one interpretation. For example, has the individual learned to "copy" a letter, or to "compose" a letter? The fact that no one would disagree that these two activities are somehow different, even though both are describable by the behavior of "typing," clearly indicates the need for descriptions of what has been learned which include more than observable human actions. Complete instructional objectives need to identify the capability learned, as well as the performance which such a capability makes possible.

The implications of this view are not trivial. If in fact such terms as "knowledge" and "understanding" are ambiguous, then we must either redefine them, or propose some new terms to describe learned capabilities which can be more precisely defined. My suggestion has been to take the latter course, and I have proposed that the five major categories representing "what is learned" are motor skills, verbal information, intellectual skills, cognitive strategies, and attitudes (Gagné, 1971b). Completing the example used previously, the statement of the objective would be "Given a set of handwritten notes, *generates* (implies the intellectual skill which is to be learned) a letter *by typing* (identifies the specific action used)."

The alternatives to such "behavioral" statements have many defects, as Mager (1962) and other writers have emphasized. However they may be expanded or embellished, statements describing the *content* of instructional presentations invariably fail to provide the needed communications. The fact that a textbook, or a film, or a talk by a teacher, presents "the concept of the family" is an inadequate communication of the intended learning outcome, and cannot be made adequate simply by adding more detail. The critical missing elements in any such descriptions of instruction are the related ideas of (a) what the student will have learned from instruction, and (b) what class of performances he will then be able to exhibit.

USES OF BEHAVIORAL OBJECTIVES BY SCHOOLS

Statements describing instructional objectives have the primary purpose of *communicating*. Assuming that education has the form of an organized system, communication of its intended and actual outcomes is necessary, among and between the designers of instructional materials, the planners of courses and programs, the teachers, the students, and the parents. In order for the process of education to serve the purpose of learning, communications of these

various sorts must take place. When any of them is omitted, education becomes to a diminished degree a systematic enterprise having the purpose of accomplishing certain societal goals pertaining to "the educated adult." There may be those who would argue that education should not serve such goals. Obviously, I disagree, but cannot here devote space to my reasons.

Some of the most important ways in which the various communications about objectives may be used by schools are indicated by the following brief outlines.

1. The Instructional Designer to the Course Planner. This set of communications enables the person who is planning a course with predetermined goals to select materials which can accomplish the desired outcomes. For example, if a course in junior high science has the goal of "teaching students to think scientifically," the planner will be seeking a set of materials which emphasize the learning of intellectual skills and cognitive strategies, having objectives such as "generates and tests hypotheses relating plant growth to environmental variables."

In contrast, if the goals of such a course are "to convey a scientific view of the earth's ecology," the curriculum planner will likely seek materials devoted to the learning of organized information, exhibited by such objectives as "describes how the content of carbon dioxide in the air affects the supply of underground water."

2. The Designer or Planner to the Teacher. Communications of objectives to the teacher enable the latter to choose appropriate ways of delivering instruction, and also ways of assessing its effectiveness. As an example, a teacher of foreign language who adopts the objective, "pronounces French words containing the uvular 'r,' " is able (or should be able) to select a form of instruction providing practice in pronunciation of French words containing "r," and to reject as inappropriate for this objective a lecture on "the use of the uvular 'r' in French words."

Additionally, this communication of an objective makes apparent to the teacher how the outcome of instruction must be assessed. In this case, the choice would need to be the observation of oral pronunciation of French words by the student, and could not be, for instance, a multiple-choice test containing questions such as "which of the following French words has a uvular 'r'?"

3. The Teacher to the Student. There are many instructional situations in which the learning outcome expected is quite apparent to the student, because of his experience with similar instruction. For example, if the course is mathematics, and the topic changes from the addition of fractions to the multiplication of fractions, it is highly likely that the naming of the topic will itself be sufficient to imply the objective.

However, there are also many situations in which the objective may not be at all apparent. A topic on "Ohm's Law," for example, may not make apparent by its title whether the student is expected to recognize Ohm's Law, to state it, to substitute values in it, or to apply it to some electric circuits. It is reasonable to suppose that a student who knows what the objective is will be able to approach the task of learning with an advantage over one who does not.

4. The Teacher or Principal to the Parent. It is indeed somewhat surprising that parents have stood still for "grades" for such a long period of time, considering the deplorably small amount of information they convey. If the trend toward "accountability" continues, grades will have to go. Teachers cannot be held accountable for A's, B's, and C's—in fact, grades are inimical to any system of accountability. It seems likely, therefore, that the basis for accountability will be the instructional objective. Since this must express a learning outcome, it must presumably be expressed in behavioral terms. Several different forms of accountability systems appear to be feasible; objectives would seem to be necessary for any or all of them.

These appear to be the major communication functions which schools need to carry out if they are engaged in systematically promoting learning. Each of these instances of communication requires accurate and reliable statements of the *outcomes of learning,* if it is to be effective. Such outcomes may be described, accurately and reliably, by means of statements which identify a) the capability to be learned, and b) the class of performances by means of which the capability is exhibited. There appears to me to be no alternative to the use of "behavioral

objectives," defined as in the previous sentence, to perform these essential functions of communication.

REFERENCES

R. M. Gagné. "Defining Objectives for Six Varieties of Learning." Washington, D.C.: American Educational Research Association, 1971a. (Cassette tape.)

R. M. Gagné. "Instruction Based on Research in Learning." *Engineering Education* 61: 519–23; 1971b.

R. F. Mager. *Preparing Instructional Objectives.* Belmont, California: Fearon Publishers, Inc., 1962.

28

Behavioral Objectives Are Not Necessary for Good Instruction

George F. Kneller

EDITOR'S NOTE • Dr. Kneller's position on behavioral objectives is quite different than the one presented in the preceding article. Although Kneller would not throw the entire concept of behavioral objectives out the window, he would redefine it and use the concept in what he sees as a more flexible way. Someday you may be asked to specify the objectives of your teaching in behavioral terms. How would you feel about this? After considering the arguments presented in readings 27 and 28, how would you vote: Behavioral objectives, yes? Or behavioral objectives, no?

The use of behavioral objectives in instruction is characteristic of a culture which sets a high value on efficiency and productivity. Such a culture seeks to measure accomplishment in standard units. Theoretical justification for be-

havioral objectives comes from behavioral psychology (Kendler, 1959, p. 179). This type of psychology defines learning as behavior that is changed in conformity with predicted, measurable outcomes and with little or no measurable "waste."

Teacher education institutions that advocate the use of behavioral objectives transmit methods of instruction that are standardized, empirically tested, and aim at measurable results. Such methods work best in school systems that are highly sensitive to the economic and behavioral determinants of educational practice.

ANALYSIS

This approach to instruction rests on assumptions about human behavior that are reductionist, deterministic, and physicalist. It is opposed to the view that learning is self-directed, unstructured, and in large part unpredictable.

Advocates of the behavioral approach deny these two points (Popham, 1968; Block, 1971). Behavior, they say, covers a wide range of experience, including creativity, imagination, even serendipity. Nor need objectives be fixed; they can be modified, adjusted to individuals, even abandoned in favor of others (Baker, 1968; Block, 1971, p. 291). But if so, if the terms "behavior" and "objectives" can be made to mean many different things, what things could they not mean? If a term is to have a clear-cut meaning, we must at least be able to define its contradictory.[1]

Many advocates now speak of "instructional" rather than "behavioral" objectives (Mager, 1962). Nevertheless, one's notion of instruction depends on assumptions about the nature of the mind and of the persons involved in the instructional process (Noddings, 1971, p. 40). The new term may imply a more modest approach to instruction and force us

---

[1] The meaning of "behavior" becomes more complicated still when, in relation to learning, it is stratified according to dispositions. Learning defined as changed behavior then includes changes in *dispositions* to behave. See: James E. McClellan. "B. F. Skinner's Philosophy of Human Nature." *Studies in Philosophy and Education* 4: 307–32; 1966; and L. B. Daniels. "Behavior Strata and Learning." *Educational Theory* 20 (4): 377–86; Fall 1970. A satisfactory theory of human behavior has yet to be proposed.

to concentrate on matters more central to education. Yet learning still is conceived as a series of measurable responses to carefully prearranged stimuli (Steg, 1971). The sameness of individuals is judged to matter more than their differences; schooling is systems-oriented; adjustment to the curriculum is presupposed; replication is prized; and computer-assisted instruction is cordially welcomed (Broudy, 1970, p. 49; Dreyfus, 1967, pp. 13–33).

It is claimed that, using behavioral objectives, a teacher can teach an entire class and cater to individual differences as well (Block, 1971). He can do so, it is said, either by adapting predetermined objectives to individuals or by composing a special set of objectives for each member of the class. However, this proud claim entails that the teacher must (a) handle a staggering number of objectives,[2] (b) accept a scientific theory of human behavior which tends to exclude individualized (idiosyncratic) learning, and (c) act on the false assumption that learning, knowing, and behaving are the same process.

As regards (c), not only are there many kinds of learning, pacing being only one of them, there are also many kinds of knowing and behaving. These processes, psychologically speaking, are separate and distinct. The subject is too complex to be argued here, but this much may be said: Learning leads to no particular behavior. It is impossible to coordinate learning or knowing with behaving, because there is no theory which interrelates these phenomena, and consequently there is no way of understanding how their putative instances might be brought into relation in actual

practice (Deese, 1969, pp. 516–17). To use behavioral objectives in individualized instruction is to overlook the essential differences between individual learning, knowing, and behaving.

Behavioral objectivists are apt to be scornful of teachers who refuse to adopt clearly specified goals. This refusal, we are told, is partly responsible for the "present failure" of American education (Popham, 1968). I do not see how this could be shown to be the case. I am still less impressed by the claim that if we adopted behavioral objectives, we would solve most of our instructional problems.

All depends on what one considers good teaching and learning to be. Teachers might be held more "strictly" accountable, learning might be evaluated more "reliably," and parents might perceive their children's achievements more "accurately"—but only if teaching and learning are drastically circumscribed. Here is the heart of the matter. Undoubtedly, the process of education can be more tightly controlled, most simply by giving everyone less freedom of choice. This suits the behavioral objectivist, because his philosophy is one of control, but it does not suit educators of other persuasions.

SPECULATION

Under what circumstances may schools be said to "need" behavioral objectives? For one thing, such objectives can be used to define and measure accomplishments in those basic intellectual abilities that all students need if they are to pass successfully from one learning experience to another. Failure by a student to acquire a basic skill may, if uncorrected, hinder all his future learning and so his whole attitude toward education. The young man who desires to be a master mechanic must first acquire the skills of an apprentice, and then of a journeyman. He cannot acquire them unless he can read, write, and compute. A long history of painful, unsuccessful learning experiences can severely damage a student's self-concept, his personality development, and his entire life style (Block, 1971, pp. 297–98).

That many of our youth are damaged in this way, especially in the elementary school, is distressingly obvious. The school has a clear responsibility to ensure that *all* students succeed in

---

[2] Behavioral objectivists maintain that the number of objectives for a single course could run as high as two thousand, if the teacher sought to cover everything. If there were 30 students in a class, the number of individual objectives would amount to as many as sixty thousand. The high school teacher of 150 students would be handling millions of objectives—conceivably. Given the behaviorists' claim that behavior includes everything that can occur in a learning situation, these figures are plausible enough. Block (1971, p. 292) correctly observes that the computer has a tremendous capacity to tailor-make programs. Item banks could be constructed and stored. Yet this of course would require that the teacher specify goals in appropriate computer terms.

learning basic skills. In order to meet this responsibility, the school must possess a schedule of clearly specified objectives for all students to achieve, together with adequate instruments for measuring what is achieved. Every student must know concretely and specifically what he is accomplishing relative to (a) what may reasonably be expected of him, and (b) what his peers are achieving.

"SPECIFIED" OBJECTIVES

The objectives I suggest are "specified" rather than "behavioral." They are chosen, or specified, by the school according to its own philosophy of education, and they are specified only for certain subject matter which the school considers basic.[3] Certain specific content (or skills) could be required of all students at certain levels, and the students could be tested on how well they had acquired it. It would be the sort of content on which it is fairly easy to test in accordance with minimum standards of achievement.

Yet at another level, a level at which standardization is difficult, impossible, or undesirable, the individual teacher should specify objectives, to be achieved by either the individual student or groups of students, in accordance with (a) a theory of knowledge and value adopted by the teacher himself, and (b) the talents and choices of the student. Take two subjects where rigorous evaluation is quite impossible, art and music. The teacher might perhaps stipulate that a certain number and kind of songs be learned, that at least one song be composed, and that a symphony be analyzed. He might also stipulate that a number of drawings be made, and that one essay be written on a painting and another on an art movement such as dadaism or impressionism. In teaching these and other subjects, the teacher should be guided by a defensible philosophy and psychology of learning and instruction.[4]

Ultimately, however, it is not the schools but the teachers who must decide what objectives should be specified, and they must do so as individuals, taking their students into consideration. They must therefore acquire the knowledge and skills that are needed to specify educational objectives and evaluate the results obtained. Behavioral objectivists can help by providing models to spur investigation. Yet if these models are adopted uncritically by the rank and file of teachers, education will decline into an inauthentic and spiritless conditioning.

For, properly conceived, education is a dialogue between persons in the community of the school, a dialogue in which the teacher encourages the student to enter into acts of learning that fulfill him personally. This is education at its finest, and the program of the behavioral objectivist has very little place in it.

REFERENCES

Eva Baker. *Defining Content for Objectives*. Los Angeles: Vincet Associates, 1968.

James H. Block. "Criterion-Referenced Measurements: Potential." *School Review* 79 (2): 289–98; February 1971.

Harry S. Broudy. "Can Research Escape the Dogma of Behavioral Objectives?" *School Review* 79 (1): 43–56; November 1970.

L. B. Daniels. "Behavior Strata and Learning." *Educational Theory* 20 (4): 377–85; Fall 1970.

---

[3] I agree with Maccia (1962) and Steg (1971) that although some learning goals can be specified, we should give wide play to the discovery impulse in learning. Much knowledge may be set out for the student to acquire. Yet the teacher must also open the gates for students both to acquire knowledge that interests them personally and to inquire beyond the knowledge we now have.

[4] On learning goals and knowledge considerations, see Maccia (1962) and Steg (1971). Maccia shows that knowledge is an open system, and Steg warns against using objectives as anything more than a means for focusing purposes: "They must never become the overriding concern of education." Although both writers deal primarily with teaching machines, they are concerned with means by which students can create knowledge (and values, for that matter) instead of simply absorbing it. Learning, says Steg, is "the possibility of *going outside* a frame of activity" (p. 49). "We must consider logical goodness," says Maccia, "in relation to [new] knowing as well as in relation to knowledge" (p. 238).

James Deese. "Behavior and Fact." *American Psychologist* 24 (5): 515–22; May 1969.

H. I. Dreyfus. "Why Computers Must Have Bodies To Be Intelligent." *Review of Metaphysics* 21 (1): 13–33; September 1967.

Robert L. Ebel. "Behavioral Objectives: A Close Look." *Phi Delta Kappan* 52 (3): 171–73; November 1970.

E. W. Eisner. "Educational Objectives: Help or Hindrance?" *School Review* 75 (3): 250–66; Autumn 1967.

E. W. Eisner. *Instructional and Expressive Objectives: Their Formulation and Use in Curriculum.* AERA Monograph Series. Chicago: Rand McNally & Company, 1969.

Howard H. Kendler. "Teaching Machines and Psychological Theory." In: Eugene Gallanter, editor. *Automated Teaching.* New York: John Wiley & Sons, Inc., 1959.

Elizabeth S. Maccia. "Epistemological Considerations in Relation to the Use of Teaching Machines." *Educational Theory* 12 (4): 234ff.; October 1962.

Robert F. Mager. *Preparing Instructional Objectives.* Belmont, California: Fearon Publishers, Inc., 1962.

Nellie L. Noddings. "Beyond Behavioral Objectives: Seeing the Whole Picture." *Focus on Learning* 1 (1): 35–41; Spring 1971.

David Nyberg. *Tough and Tender Learning.* Palo Alto, California: National Press Books, 1971. p. 68.

W. James Popham. "Probing the Validity of Arguments Against Behavioral Goals." Symposium presentation, AERA meeting, Chicago, February 1968.

D. R. Steg. "The Limitations of Learning Machines and Some Aspects of Learning." *Focus on Learning* 1 (1): 43–51; Spring 1971.

Chapter Eight · issues and concerns about testing and grading

29

The Positive Function of Grades

Robert A. Feldmesser

EDITOR'S NOTE · In one form or other, grading systems have always been used to evaluate student achievement. There are intense pros and cons about the use and functions of grades, to which the next two readings will introduce you. Dr. Feldmesser is very much in favor of grades, and in this reading he builds a substantial case for the idea that grades serve an important evaluative function that cannot be done as well by other means. Although he discusses the function of grades at the college level, the same arguments can be applied to grading at lower levels. How do you feel about grading? If you are a teacher or if you plan to teach, you must eventually decide this very basic issue for yourself.

The custom of giving grades in college courses, recording them in permanent form, and calculating a grade point average is clearly under attack. A survey conducted by the American Council on Education in fall 1970 found that 44 percent of entering freshmen favored abolishing grades.[1] Many faculty members find merit in the objections of students, and many institutions are, indeed, modifying their grading practices.

Yet there is general agreement that it is educationally beneficial for a college student to receive some evaluation of his work, that is, some judgment about the quality of his academic performance which he can use to guide his future academic behavior. A grade is essentially one form of evaluation: specifically, a form so highly condensed or abstracted that it can be expressed as a number, or as a letter that can be converted into a number, and entered on a permanent record. Admittedly, all forms of evaluation may not be equally beneficial, and some may not be beneficial at all. The controversy about grades, therefore, resolves into the issue of the worth of this particular kind of evaluation.

Do grades serve any evaluative function that cannot be served, or served better, by some other form of evaluation? It is the contention here that they do. Grades have the first-order function of providing unique and useful information to the student, and second-order functions of generating other kinds of evaluation and enhancing their effectiveness. Grades *can* be justified on the basis of their contributions to student learning, apart from their putative usefulness to administrators, graduate schools, employers, or society in general. To support the benefits of grades *for the student* is to meet the opponents of grades on their most defensible ground.

Grades here mean the familiar A–F or 4–0 systems and their variants, as distinguished from both total abolition of grades and pass-fail and similar arrangements that allow no differentiations among students who meet minimum course requirements and which are advocated as a way to relieve the pressure of conventional grades. Although a

Robert A. Feldmesser, "The Positive Function of Grades," *Educational Record* (Winter 1972): 66–72. Reprinted by permission.

position supporting grades bucks a strong tide, one may hope that, in the long run, rationality can be made to prevail over the whims of fashion.

The kind of evaluation most widely favored is one highly detailed and specific, giving the student a maximum of information about his performance along each of the relevant dimensions of a course. This sort of feedback, it is said, helps him identify his strengths and weaknesses so he can most wisely allocate his time and energy in his future academic work. There is no quarrel here with the argument that this type of evaluation is indeed useful.

SUPPLEMENTARY ROLE

There is, nevertheless, an important role to be played by the summative evaluation called a grade. This role does not preclude a multidimensional evaluation but supplements it. A grade should be considered an effort to put back together, to synthesize, the separate judgments about a student's work. It gives the student some sense of the quality of his performance *on the whole*. To a student in a biology course, for example, it is not enough to know that his lab work was weak while his grasp of abstract concepts was strong, and that he was high on understanding of cell structure but low on understanding of ecological relationships and middling on understanding of reproductive systems. He will also want to know what it all adds up to: whether, all things considered, he did well or poorly or something in between. The grade thus satisfies a natural curiosity, but, while that seems like a virtue in itself,[2] the grade does more. It helps a student decide whether, taking one thing with another, biology is a field in which further inputs of his resources are likely to be productive for him, or whether he should switch to another field. In other words, if it is useful to him to have judgments about one aspect of his course work as distinguished from other aspects, it is also useful to him to have judgments about one course, holistically considered, as distinguished from other courses.

This same logic can and should be applied to the infamous grade point average. It helps a student to know how well he is doing in higher education generally, all *courses* considered, so that he can make a more informed decision about whether further study is the right thing for him and, if it is,

what sorts of institutions would be most suitable. In the absence of this information, he may waste his time by pursuing his studies or waste his talents by not pursuing his studies. Calculation of a grade point average obviously requires grades, as they have been defined above. . . .

SECOND-ORDER FUNCTIONS

The second-order functions of grades derive from another need: the need to report evaluations to a central agency of authority within the educational institution. If a central agency is to receive evaluations of all students in all courses during the entire time they are in college, the evaluations must be highly condensed—preferably to a single symbol —so the central agency does not have to devote an inordinate amount of resources to record keeping —which is to say that if evaluations are to be reported, they must take the form of grades. Thus, to establish the functional necessity of reporting is to establish by implication the need for grades.

Why, then, is reporting a functional necessity? In particular, why is it important to the student's learning, since that is the criterion here? There are two basic arguments. . . .

REPORTING REQUIREMENT

The reporting requirement exercises a coercive force on the instructor in behalf of his students. At the very least, it compels him to make some minimal evaluation—the minimal represented by the grade itself.

But in most cases, the reporting requirement probably prods the instructor to make more than a minimal evaluation. If he has to submit a grade, he will probably feel an obligation to develop some reasonable basis for it, if only so he can defend it if questioned. Hence, he will set up more or less detailed evaluative procedures; and if he is going to do that anyway, it takes little extra effort to inform his students of the results as his course progresses. This step also helps avoid a situation in which students could claim that their grade was unfair because it took them by surprise or that they could have taken corrective action if they had been informed earlier. Moreover, the reporting requirement has a quality-control function, analagous to that of the requirement for public trials: it restrains the instructor from making evaluations that merely reflect his ideological or punitive inclinations, lest he be called upon to justify his grade. In the absence of this requirement, some instructors would probably be quite ruthless about "maintaining academic standards."[3]

BASIS FOR DECISIONS

... [M]any students—and their number is, if anything, increasing—deliberately decide, on what seem to them sufficient grounds, that the content of a particular course, or particular parts of a course, is irrelevant to their needs and, therefore, should *not* be learned. It can be said that that is their business; if they choose not to learn, they will and should bear the consequences of their decision. But this attitude amounts to a shirking of the faculty's educational duty, if not to a denial of its educational pretensions.

The student, after all, is young, and his very presence in a course indicates that he knows relatively little about the field. Consequently, he does not necessarily know what parts of a course will be relevant to his needs over the long run. His teachers claim more foresight in such matters; if they are unwilling to make that claim, they should not be his teachers. Thus, instructors are entitled—and obliged—to exert some pressure on the student to induce him to learn material whose importance he is not yet in a position to perceive. One effective and appropriate way to apply this pressure is to make it in the student's immediate interest to take his instructors' evaluations seriously. This step can be accomplished, in turn, by using those evaluations as the basis for important short-run decisions about the student, for example, decisions about further study or employment. Finally, if evaluations are to be the basis for such decisions, the evaluations must be reported to some central agency with the authority to make those decisions or to transmit the information to others who can. The knowledge that important decisions will be based on a student's grade is another force compelling instructors, too, to take more care with grades than they otherwise might.

REINFORCING EFFECT

Something more is involved here than the familiar motivational function of grades (though it may be noted that students do have difficulty generating their own motivation in the absence of grades).[4] Students, like other people, interpret the significance of communications in part by the significance attributed to them by others. If no one else cared what evaluations had been made of his work, why should the student care? If no one else based any important decisions on those evaluations, wouldn't the message to the student be that the evaluations were, in fact, not important? Why, then, should he allow them to influence his academic behavior? It is apparent, then, that grades reinforce the feedback function of other evaluations. . . .

Whatever the merits of the preceding arguments, a great many criticisms of grades continue to be made.[5] It may be a plausible hypothesis that the dysfunctional outweigh the functional consequences of grades. However, some criticisms of grades are totally unwarranted, suffering from defects in logic. Others are more properly directed at the *misuse* of grades rather than at grades per se, or at evaluation generally rather than at grades specifically. A few do refer to the technical deficiencies of grades themselves. Most valid criticism can be met by institutional changes.

REWARDS FOR LEARNING

One common objection to grades is that they are extrinsic rather than intrinsic rewards. In the minds of many people, a moral stigma is attached to the pursuit of learning for the sake of external rewards. But, why is it so heinous to learn as a means toward an end? How well would college faculty fare on this test of academic purity: how much of a faculty member's time is spent acquiring new knowledge for the sheer delight of it, and how much to be a better teacher, or to contribute to the solution of a social or technological problem, or to dazzle students, or to have something to publish? This is not simply an ad hominem thrust; the model offered by the faculty is probably more powerful than the grading system in influencing attitudes toward learning. . . .

GRADES VS. SUCCESS

It is also said that there must be something wrong with grades because they are not good predictors of "success" in later life. But, as Donald P. Hoyt has suggested, that is not necessarily a condemnation. Grades should measure learnings; success is in large part a result of what has been done with the learning.[6] Moreover, it is not completely clear that knowledge and understanding are ingredients necessary to success in society. . . .

PROMOTING COMPETITION

A third unwarranted criticism is that grades foster competitive attitudes. This criticism applies to grades only insofar as it applies to evaluations of human performance generally, because a comparison with the performance of other humans is usually the most meaningful frame of reference, if not the only one, for such evaluations.

Furthermore, a certain kind of competitive perspective is actually quite desirable. In considering his future, a student should take into account his comparative advantages vis-à-vis others in his field so he can better determine where he can make his most satisfying contribution. Thus, he might want to choose a field in which other people would work less effectively than he. At the very least, a student deserves the information about which fields those are, and grades provide a convenient way to tell him. This aspect of grades has nothing to do with inducing men to cut each other's throats, or even with preparing them to live in a competitive world—the implications and justifications of grades which students are increasingly resisting. In the perspective suggested here, grades foster a competitive attitude only by spurring students to realize that their own talents and energies compete with each other in the sense that resources put to one use cannot be put to another.

Another unwarranted criticism is that a low grade discourages a student from further study of a subject. Isn't that exactly what a low grade should do? If, despite efforts to learn, a student is performing poorly in, say, math, he *should* be discouraged from taking further math courses; this action is an aid to his education, not a detriment, for he might learn more in art history or economic theory. Letting a student know that he is performing poorly is preferable to permitting him to entertain an illusion about himself.

A student can be given a negative evaluation in a course, however, without having it broadcast to the world, that is, without having it entered on his transcript and incorporated into his GPA. This permanent record, it is complained, does the damage. Since the GPA is important to students, even a slight decline is said to arouse inordinate anxiety, and students will go to great lengths to avoid it, for example, confining themselves to courses in which they are confident they can earn high grades.[7] That undesirable by-product implies a misuse of grades. . . .

FUNCTION OF ANXIETY

The anxiety aroused by fear of a low grade is but the obverse side of the motivational coin. If a grade is to motivate, then a high grade must be a never-guaranteed but ever-possible outcome; a low grade, therefore, must be an avoidable but also ever-possible outcome. If the possibility of a low grade creates anxiety in the student, he should be able to reduce that feeling by studying to avoid the low grade. That is one way in which the motivational function is served, and evidence indicates that it works, when the anxiety is *moderate*.[8]

Anxiety interferes with learning only when it becomes excessive, and—neurotic personalities aside—that happens when too much importance is attributed to a single grade. There are several ways to prevent excessive anxiety.

DIMINISHING PRESSURES

First, a student should be allowed to weight his grades differentially, so he can give low weight to grades in those courses that arouse the most anxiety in him. Second, he should be helped to understand that a grade is not a judgment of his moral worth, but merely an information statement, and a tentative and fallible one at that. Third, there should be strict limitations on the use of a student's grade record. While it must be available to college authorities, for reasons stated above, these officials should adopt explicit restrictions on its use. It should not be a basis for determining financial aid or participating in extracurricular activities. Certainly it should never have been given to draft boards without the student's permission. Indeed, beyond its use by the college itself, in admitting students to honor sections or in dismissing them for unsatisfactory academic work, the grade record should be regarded as the property of the student alone, so he can prevent its use as a threat. This rule would not defeat the reporting function. If graduate schools or employers wanted to see a student's grade record, they should be required to obtain it through the student, and he should have the right of refusal. He would be quite aware of the significance that would be attached to his exercise of that right. If he gave permission for his record to be sent outside the institution, the "authority" of the college would become simply the capacity to certify that the grade record was accurate. . . .

ACCURATE EVALUATION

In the end, it is their lack of validity that emerges as the most legitimate criticism of grades. Whatever valuable functions they could perform in the abstract will not be performed if grades are not valid measures of learning; and all too often, they are not. . . .

This, however, is a remediable defect. Valid educational evaluations are difficult but not impossible to arrive at; certainly they can be far more closely approached than at present. If they are rare in the experience of most college students, the main reason is that the overwhelming majority of college faculty have had no training whatsoever in making them. . . . As McGeorge Bundy said years ago:

> The ordinary college teacher, giving out grades in the ordinary way on the basis of a few special papers or tests and a single final examination, is a fountain of error, and everyone knows it except the man himself.[9]

Ultimately, training in evaluation should be the responsibility of the graduate schools that produce college teachers. Meanwhile, each college could well undertake to fill the gap itself. It could, for one thing, publish a clear statement about grading policies and practices;[10] faculty and students should naturally participate in drawing it up—an instructive experience in itself. For another thing, a college could conduct a seminar on evaluation at the opening of each academic year, with all faculty members expected to attend in their first year and perhaps every third or fourth year thereafter to keep up to date on theories and technologies. It would be highly desirable for students to attend this seminar, too. Exposure to the mundane procedures involved in evaluation would help students appreciate the fallibility of evaluative instruments, would tend to divest grades of their moral overtones, and might thereby lead to a more relaxed attitude. Furthermore, knowledge on the part of faculty that their students were moderately sophisticated in the matter of grades would be an efficacious way to enforce good practices. These steps would help overcome the evil that grades can do, allowing everyone to take full advantage of their positive functions.

REFERENCES

1. Staff of the Office of Research, *National Norms for Entering College Freshmen—Fall 1970* (Washington: American Council on Education, 1970), p. 43.

2. Melvin M. Tumin, "Evaluation of the Effectiveness of Education: Some Problems and Prospects," *Interchange*, 1 (1970): 96–109.

3. Burton R. Clark, *The Distinctive College: Antioch, Reed, Swarthmore* (Chicago: Aldine, 1970), p. 131.

4. William R. Torbert and J. Richard Hackman, "Taking the Fun Out of Outfoxing the System," in *The Changing College Classroom*, eds. Philip Runkel, Roger Harrison, and Margaret Runkel (San Francisco: Jossey-Bass, 1969), pp. 167–76; Robert A. Feldmesser, *The Option: Analysis of an Educational Innovation* (Hanover, N.H.: Dartmouth College, 1969), pp. 70–87.

5. Jonathan R. Warren, *College Grading Practices: An Overview* (Washington: ERIC Clearinghouse on Higher Education, George Washington University, 1971); Sidney B. Simon, "Grades

Must Go," *School Review*, May 1970, pp. 397–402.

6. "The Relationship Between College Grades and Adult Achievement, A Review of the Literature," *ACT Research Reports* (Iowa City, Iowa: American College Testing Program, 1965), p. 46.

7. Howard S. Becker, Blanche Geer, and Everett C. Hughes, *Making the Grade: The Academic Side of College Life* (New York: John Wiley, 1968).

8. Norman E. Wallen and Robert M. W. Travers, "Analysis and Investigation of Teaching Methods," in *Handbook of Research in Teaching*, ed. N. L. Gage (Chicago: Rand McNally, 1963), p. 496.

9. "An Atmosphere to Breathe: Woodrow Wilson and the Life of the American University College" (New York: Woodrow Wilson Foundation, 1959), p. 19. See also Becker, Geer, and Hughes, *Making the Grade*, p. 140.

10. George R. Bramer, "Grading and Academic Justice," *Improving College and University Teaching*, Winter 1970, pp. 63–65.

30

Grades Must Go!

Sidney B. Simon

EDITOR'S NOTE · *This article needs little introduction. Dr. Simon makes no bones about how he feels about the grading system, a feeling which, as you will readily see, contrasts sharply with the stance taken in the preceding article. Although the remarks here refer to grading systems as they exist at the college level, I think you will see that Simon's argument can be applied to high schools and elementary schools as well. Dr. Feldmesser and Dr. Simon present two sides of an emotionally charged issue: Where do you stand?*

In Shirley Jackson's eerie short story, "The Lottery," a village holds a drawing each year to decide whom they will stone to death. In our colleges and universities, we do it twice a year.

One character in Miss Jackson's story raises a question about why the villagers continue to perform this inhuman ritual, but an elder quiets them with, "We have always had a lottery."

So it is with grades, and midterms, and true and false questions, and multiple choices, and essay questions (choose three out of four), and bell-shaped curves, and deans' lists, and No-Doz, and

Reprinted from "Grades Must Go!" *School Review* 78 (May 1970): 397–402 by Sidney B. Simon by permission of the University of Chicago Press. Copyright © 1970 by the University of Chicago Press.

blue books, and crib sheets, and proctors, and the rest.

We have indeed always had them, although there is literally not a shred of research evidence which supports the present grading system. They are about as accurate as the gas mileage statements out of Detroit and about as objective as an old maid telling you her age. That we have tolerated grades for so long makes me seriously question whether we have even fewer brains than we do intellectuals on our college campuses.

Grades must go. Their only genuine function is to serve certain administrative conveniences. They *do* allow the registrar and members of the deanery to decide who is on probation, and who can take an honors course, and who sits on the dais at Phi Bet banquets, and so forth, but they are too destructive to be allowed to continue to debase what a university could be.

FIVE REASONS WHY

1. Grades separate students and professors into two warring camps, both armed with dangerous weapons, none of which has anything to do with a notion of a community of scholars. The grades keep student from teacher and teacher from student as effectively as if each wore the sweaty jerseys of two archrivals fighting for a bid to a bowl game.

A student cannot praise a professor's teaching within earshot of other students, or he would be slashed to ribbons for "brownnosing." However, in the comfortable privacy of a professor's office, the slippery students keep their appointments, and get in the "brownie points" which, they have well learned, is one practical way to raise their grade-point averages. Sadly, this same awareness keeps many students with integrity away from the professor's office.

If praise cannot be given, open criticism of a professor to his face is even rarer. It simply would not be politic. Even if you had some hint about how to make his course better, the implied disapproval would surely earn retaliation. So it passes that students and faculty—the two groups on a campus which most need to find each other—are separated by a wall as impenetrable as barbed wire, known as a transcript.

2. Grades overreward the wrong people and often punish students who need to be punished the least. There is something basically immoral about a system which passes out its highest institutional appreciation to a meritocracy based on memorization, clever use of mnemonic devices, test wisdom, and various symptoms of anal compulsiveness.

The dean's list is made up of just too many such people—grade grubbers who seem to lack that certain spark of creativity, sensitivity, or even humanity. The finely-sifted ones who make the honorary societies are often not necessarily dishonorable, but their unmitigated self-advancement tends to make you wonder why the university makes so much fuss over such people at graduation. The world is dying from selfishness, and yet the academic world gives asterisks for it on commencement programs.

At the other end of the continuum, grades have been used systematically to screen out black students, to decide who to ship out to Vietnam, and to firmly remind those who will not conform that they are failures. It becomes increasingly clear that those who knuckle under to the grading system and learn what reality is all about ("Look, the guy likes Buber, so I give him Buberisms all semester") are the ones who reap the rewards. Those who question the system or resist it often get flunked out, neatly and sometimes finally.

3. Grades tend to destroy what learning should be all about. Students sign up for snap and crap courses they neither need nor want but which give a sure "B" without requiring many papers, or much reading, and so on. Students avoid courses which they might be curious about but in which they cannot afford a low grade because it would mess up their "cum."

Craftier students soon learn to balance their 15–18 semester hours with a mixture of hard markers and easy markers, and like good consumers, they budget their time each night and study a little of this and a little of that. Passionately wanting to go and learn something in real depth is somehow looked upon as slightly uncouth. After all, those "meaty" courses with a midterm, a term paper or two, a final, and three snap quizzes scattered here and there (so we can divide by five and get a good, objective average in order to give you a good, objective grade) have to be spread out carefully if one is to "keep up."

Only the wastrel reads novels or plays which are not assigned, and no one except a fool spends more time in the library than he must to pad out, with the right number of footnotes, a paper which the student guesses the professor will like (whether the student cares deeply about it doesn't matter).

Pragmatism, then, requires students to begin approaching the selection of courses like the directors of a conservative mutual fund picking out a portfolio of safe investments—everything in moderation. It is little wonder that so many graduates later join the Book-of-the-Month Club to be told what to read.

4. Grades reinforce an archaic notion of "competition" which may well turn out to be deadly in the 1970s. Sure, life is competitive, at least if you are in the business of selling storm windows or aluminum siding. Yes, Ford, Chevy, and Plymouth would like to slice each other's throats for a bigger chunk of the market, and all three of them would like to rub Volkswagen off the map. Nevertheless, the skills of cooperation actually dominate a sane man's life much more than do the skills of competition.

God save the marriage where the man is in constant competition with his wife. Pray for the family where the siblings are turned against each other's jugular veins. Most of our efforts to make our neighborhoods and communities healthier and happier depend on some complex forms of cooperation. And almost everything the college graduate does today to make a living demands co-operation. Almost everything gets done through committees, and the really valuable co-worker knows the intricate skills of group process, and has the humanity necessary to control his ego and his competitive instincts. The point is, we don't have to teach competition; the beast in us is instinctively competitive. But we had better do more thinking about how to help ourselves become more civil so that we develop some range of responses beyond "What's in it for me?"

Competition for grades has made today's campuses lonely places. There are entirely too many students working for their own slightly sullied advancement into the above $20,000 brackets. Altruism and a sense of community just don't exist at most colleges and universities. Too many pages are slit from library books, making it impossible for the next person to get the assignment, and in one

of those classes where the prof proudly tells you he will give as many F's as A's, just don't be absent, because you won't find many people who will give you their notes.

Four years and more of this kind of competitive treadmill might prepare a college graduate for ruthless dashes down the expressway at rush hour, but I surely would not want to be the first Negro to move into his block.

5. Of all the destructive things grades do, probably the ugliest is that they contribute to debasing a student's estimation of his own worth. The emphasis and extreme focus upon grades, term after term, seem to squeeze a student's identity and self-image within the narrow confines of his transcript.

Students everywhere are in a quandary. They have too little else upon which to test themselves. They are saddles with an extended adolescence. They have no real opportunities to be either independent or courageous or to test under duress their love of their fellow-man. As a consequence, students often stake their identity, almost their total sense of self, upon that grade-point average.

We do not know how many of them, in the lonely hours of the night, sit and divide their grade-point averages out to the tenth decimal point. However, we do know that a large percentage of the suicides at our universities stem, in part, from those decimals—at least, from misguided interpretations of their significance.

How could we have allowed those numbers to spew widespread feelings of inadequacy, inferiority, and lack of power among perfectly useful and decent people? Have you heard of students who have given up careers because they thought they just didn't "have it" when they received a low grade in a basic course in their major? The worshipping at the shrine of numbers is a kind of madness which we accept almost without reflection and which has about as much validity as treating a cancer with a spray deodorant.

The pursuit of grades has dried up the average student's sense that he can shape and change the world around him. With his eye on the carrot at the end of the semester, he does not really believe that he can make a course better. He doesn't really believe that students can and should have some stake in evaluating their education. It is almost heresy for him to believe that he has some valid insights into the hiring and firing of professors. Not wanting to antagonize the grade givers, he does not complain about large classes, irrelevant lectures, inappropriate assignments, unnecessary prerequisites, or even an unreadable textbook.

How many of our students simply do not know who they are because for so many years they have been jumping hurdles put up by other people? Finally, on their own, they do not seem to have the resources for making meaningful choices or building values to live by. Otherwise, would so many of them end up like the characters in John Cheever's Shady Hill suburb? Those urbane, handsome, ivy-league types going off to high-paying jobs that they hate (made tolerable by martinis at lunch), marrying attractive-but-shallow girls, raising children who greet them with, "What did you buy me?" and tolerating terrible abuse from their bosses so as not to get fired and thereby jeopardize the country club membership, the $40,000 development house, the vinyl hardtop, and their credit with the orthodontist: Is that what a college education is supposed to produce?

Over and over I hear the phrase, "Well, that's reality." However, I think we are long overdue in examining a greater reality behind the grading system. It may be called "reality" to say, "All colleges have grades," but all colleges do *not* have them. It may be reality to say, "Grades are the only thing that graduate schools are concerned about," but the best of the graduate schools are becoming less and less concerned about them. When people say, "Well, that's the system," I want to shout, "Systems have been changed."

I believe we ignore at great peril the greater reality of a learning environment in which students and professors become increasingly alienated from each other, where cheating and the con man are daily operative, and where what a student gets out of a course can be boiled down to a single, crude letter of the alphabet.

I am convinced that a real onslaught upon the grading system could have dramatic and immediate positive impact upon our universities. If nothing else, many of the most flagrant academic abuses might be flushed out into the open.

Professors who can't teach will be forced to face the truth if we take away the production of their dangling A's and F's. Professors who can teach but who get more of the institutional rewards from doing research or playing grantsmanship may get back to teaching. Busy-work assignments will be challenged and so will those fraudulent reading assignments (2,000 pages a weekend?). Students will shape and change many assignments they now merely accept. Assignments will be more individualized and the curriculum will take on a new relevancy. It is no wonder that the old guard, including those Uncle Tom students who say, "Why, I don't see what's wrong with the grading system. Mister Charlie, he treats me real good, especially at transcript time," will resist doing away with the present grading system.

Change is coming, however. The danger is that we may merely be satisfied with a little tinkering here and a bit of adjusting there. A limited pass-fail system will not be sufficient to remove that insane cry from our colleges: "Wadjaget?"

What we really need is a sweeping awareness among students that they are being shortchanged at that supermarket they call alma mater. They need to realize that they are the customers, and, as such, they have every right to demand that they get a real education. They must learn to see through our ruses. They must not allow themselves to be bought off with green stamps which they glue into their transcripts and turn in at the redemption center at graduation time for credentials. Grades must go.

31

Common Misconceptions about Tests and Test Results

Henry L. Dyer

EDITOR'S NOTE · As you probably sensed from the previous two articles, testing and grading are not topics that most people can discuss without emotion. Indeed, our very emotional involvement may stand in the way of a more objective analysis of tests and test results. In this reading, Dr. Dyer points out the major misconceptions that may interfere with a better understanding of and more appropriate use of tests of intelligence, personality, achievement, and aptitude. I think you will find this a helpful and informative selection.

In his recent book called *The Schools*, Martin Mayer speaks of testing as a "necessary evil." I disagree. It is not *necessarily* evil. Tests *could* be a blessing to education if only teachers and counselors and educational administrators would divest themselves of a number of misconceptions about what tests can and cannot do and would learn to use test results more cautiously and creatively in the educational process.

There are nine principal misconceptions that

Henry L. Dyer, "Is Testing a Menace to Education?" *New York State Education* 49 (October 1961): 16–19. Reprinted and abridged by permission of the New York State Teacher Association.

seem to stand in the way of the appropriate use of tests.

The *first* misconception is the notion that aptitude or intelligence tests measure something called "native ability," something fixed and immutable within the person that determines his level of expectation for all time. I am not prepared to say such an inherent entity does not exist. The chances are it does. Studies in genetics certainly support the idea, and so do many psychological studies. But intelligence or aptitude tests do not *measure* such an entity—at least not directly, and certainly not in any interpretable manner.

What intelligence tests do measure is the individual's performance on certain types of mental tasks . . . a long time after the child has first entered the world. The kinds of mental tasks that appear in any intelligence or aptitude test are clearly the kinds that a student *learns* to perform from his experiences in the world around him. The amount of learning based on such experiences may depend on many things that can vary enormously from one child to another—the number and quality of books available in his home, the kind of talk he hears, the richness and variety of his surroundings, the vividness and emotional quality of the thousands of happenings in his life from day to day. It is absurd to suppose that a child's score on an intelligence test by-passes all these factors, to suppose that such a score gets directly at the brains he was born with.

I prefer to think of an intelligence test as essentially indistinguishable from an achievement test—that is, as a measure of how well, at a given point of time, a student can perform certain well-defined tasks. The main difference between the tasks in a so-called achievement test and those in a so-called intelligence test is, generally speaking, that the tasks in an achievement test are usually learned over a relatively short time and those in an intelligence test are learned over a relatively long time.

The consequences of thinking of an aptitude test as measuring some immutable determiner of student performance can be pretty serious. First, such thinking encourages the dangerous idea that one can, from an aptitude score, decide once and for all at a fairly early age what kind and level of educational or vocational activity a student is fitted for. It nurtures that hardy perennial, for instance, that if a student has an IQ of 115 or better he ought to prepare for college, and if his IQ is below 115 he ought to make other plans—this, despite all the studies which have shown that an IQ may be highly variable for a given student, that colleges vary enormously in the quality of students they enroll, and that some low scorers succeed in college while some high scorers fail. I have often wondered how many educational crimes are annually committed on the strength of the theory that intelligence tests measure something they cannot possibly measure.

A second consequence, almost as serious, is the conception that a student with a high aptitude score and low achievement scores (or low grades in school) is an "under-achiever"—another hardy perennial. It was exploded 30 years ago, but it is back and can lead to some rather distressing treatment of individual pupils. The diagnosis goes that a student with a high aptitude score and low achievement scores is "unmotivated" or "lazy" or suffering from some sort of emotional disturbance. Granted there may be some grounds for such diagnoses, nevertheless they are scarcely inferable from the discrepancy in scores alone. And some new and possibly more useful insights about such students might be forthcoming if one frankly regarded the discrepancies simply as differences in performance on one kind of achievement test as compared to another.

Finally, the idea that aptitude tests are supposed to measure native ability leads to the persistent and embarrassing demand that they should be "culture free"; that if they are, as they must be, affected by the student's background of experience in school and at home, then *ipso facto*, they are "unfair" to the underprivileged. I wish we could get it *out* of people's heads that tests are unfair to the underprivileged and get it *into* their heads that it is the hard facts of social circumstance and inadequate education that are unfair to them. If educational opportunities are unequal, the test results will also be unequal.

A *second* misconception about tests is the notion that a prediction made from a test score, or from a series of test scores, or from test scores plus other quantifiable data, are, or should be, perfectly accurate, and that if they are not, the tests must be regarded as no good. This fallacy arises from a confused conception of what constitutes prediction. There are some people—maybe most people—who

think of prediction as simply an all-or-none, right-or-wrong business. If a test score predicts that Johnny will get B in American history, the score is right if he actually gets a B; it is wrong if he gets a B— or a C. I suppose this is a legitimate way of thinking about prediction in certain circumstances, but it is scarcely fair to the test and it may well be unfair to Johnny. A more meaningful and useful way of thinking about a prediction is to regard it as a statement of the odds: A given test score might predict that Johnny has 8 chances in 10 of getting a grade of B or better in American history, and 3 chances in a hundred of flunking. This approach recognizes that in forecasting future events, especially human events, we never have sufficient information to be sure of being right every time, but we do have information, in the form of test scores and other data, which, if appropriately organized, can help us make better decisions than would be possible without them.

The *third* misconception is that standardized test scores are infallible or perfectly reliable. Reliability, I remind you, has to do with the degree to which the score of an individual stands still on successive testings. It rarely occurs to the uninitiated that a test can never be more than a *sample* of a student's performance and that, in consequence, the score on any test is afflicted with sampling error. To the man-in-the-street, to many teachers, school administrators and parents, who have never reflected on the problem, a score is a score is a score, and they are shocked to find that when a student takes one test today and an alternate form of the same test tomorrow, his score can change. Anyone who deals with a test score must always be conscious that such a score, like any sort of measurement whatever, is clouded with uncertainty, that it is never more than an estimate of the truth.

A *fourth* misconception is the assumption that an achievement test measures all there is to measure in any given subject matter area—that an achievement test in history, for example, measures everything a high school student should know about the facts of history and how to deal with them. It never seems to occur to some people that the content of a standardized achievement test in any particular subject matter area may be only partially related to what a specific course of study in that area may call for.

If people will only take the trouble to look critically at the insides of achievement tests and not just at their covers, they will almost certainly find that even the test best suited to their purposes still fails to sample *all* the types of learning that are sought in a given subject, or even all the most important types of learning. And it may also often include matters that the student is not expected to know. The consequence is, of course, that on a particular standardized achievement test a student may look considerably better or considerably worse than he really is, and decisions based on his score may miss the boat by a considerable margin.

A *fifth* misconception is that an achievement test can measure only a pupil's memory for facts. This used to be true. But a good modern achievement test gets at far more than a command of facts alone; it usually measures in addition the pupil's skill in reasoning with the facts he remembers and also his skill in reasoning with facts newly presented to him. It is this introduction into achievement tests of the requirement to reason, to cope with problems, to think clearly, critically and even creatively that helps to blur the distinction between aptitude and achievement tests. The modern achievement test recognizes that as students come up through the grades they are, or ought to be, learning to think as well as to know. It recognizes also that there may be many different kinds of thinking to measure, depending upon the subject matter in which the thinking is required. The result is that a well-conceived battery of achievement tests gives the same sort of information one would get from a general intelligence test plus a good deal more.

A *sixth* misconception has to do with profiles of achievement or aptitude scores, that a profile of scores summarizes clearly and efficiently a considerable amount of reliable information about the relative strengths and weaknesses of an individual. Test technicians have inveighed repeatedly against the use of profile charts on the grounds that they are often grossly misleading, that the differences they depict—even when they appear large—may be, and usually are, unreliable differences, that the score scales used for the several tests in the profile may not be comparable, that the several measures which show on the profile may have the appearance of being highly independent measures when, in fact, many of them may be highly correlated—in short,

that the apparent clarity and efficiency of a test score profile is really an illusion covering up all sorts of traps and pitfalls in score interpretation which even the most wary can scarcely avoid. Yet the profile chart is still in much demand and in wide use, primarily, I suppose, because it is extraordinarily convenient. Mere administrative convenience is hardly sufficient justification for hiding confusion under a false coat of simplicity. Good test interpretation takes mental effort, a bit of imagination and some willingness to cope with complexity.

A *seventh* misconception is that interest inventories measure some kind of basic orientation of a student irrespective of the kinds of experiences to which he has been or will be exposed. Let me cite just one example. A presumably well-trained guidance counselor in a high school where the large majority of students go on to college was confronted by a girl with top-notch scholastic standing in all of the college preparatory subjects. Her parents were college-trained people, had always expected their daughter would go to a liberal arts college; the daughter had always enthusiastically entertained the same idea. The counselor, however, was apparently bewitched by one of the girl's scores on an interest inventory which indicated her major interest was in clerical work. Disregarding all the other evidence, the counselor insisted that the girl was unfitted for the work of a liberal arts college and would be happy only in a secretarial school. Tears on the part of the child, anger on the part of the parents and hell-to-pay all around. Certainly interest test scores are useful in promoting thought and self-analysis, but certainly also the tests are scarcely capable of probing deeply enough into an individual's past and future to warrant anything approaching the dogmatism which characterized this counselor.

The *eighth* misconception is that on a personality test an individual reveals deep and permanent temperamental characteristics of which he himself may be unaware. I suppose there is nothing about the whole testing business that frightens me more than this. Anyone close to the research in personality testing who has any critical sense at all knows that we have still barely scratched the surface of a field whose dimensions are still far from defined. To put it perhaps a little too strongly, personality tests—the inventories, the projective tests, all of them—are scarcely beyond the tea-leaf-reading stage. To be sure, there is some interesting—even exciting—research going on in the area, but none of it yet adds up to tests that can be trusted as evidence leading to important decisions about children.

There are four major weaknesses in personality tests. First, they purport to measure traits such as introversion-extroversion, neurotic tendency, gregariousness, tolerance for ambiguity, and the like —all of which are highly fuzzy concepts, to say the least, and for none of which there are any agreed-upon definitions. There is not even any general agreement on what we mean by the word "personality" itself. How can you describe or classify a person meaningfully with a test whose scores do not themselves have any clear or rigorous meaning?

Secondly, it is characteristic of current personality tests that the behavior they sample is essentially superficial nonsignificant behavior. By this I mean when a subject answers such a question as "Do you often daydream?" his response of "Yes" or "No" may well be nothing more than a purely random phenomenon quite unconnected with any of his habitual behavior tendencies. The whole essence of the measurement problem is to secure reliable samples of human behavior under standardized conditions which will have strong correlates with the universe of behavior an individual habitually exhibits in his waking life. The personality tests currently available have yet to demonstrate that they can provide such samples.

Thirdly, even if we were able to establish some meaningful personality traits, we still know little or nothing about their stability. We still don't know whether an introvert at age 15 may not turn into an extrovert by the time he is 22.

Finally, of course, practically all personality tests can be faked. I proved to my own satisfaction how fakable such tests are when I gave one to a class I was once teaching. I asked the students to take a personality inventory twice—once to prove that they were thoroughly well adjusted people and once to prove that they were ready for a mental institution. The first set of scores showed that the whole class was a bunch of apple-cheeked extroverts; the second set showed that they were all nuts.

Please do not misunderstand me. I take a very dim view of current personality tests, and I think the general public is being much too frequently taken in by the mumbo-jumbo that goes with them. On the other hand, I am very much in favor of as much solid research as we can possibly get into the fundamental dynamics of human behavior, for we shall never be in full command of the educational process until we have far more understanding than we now have of what makes children tick. There are glimmerings of hope, but we are not out of the woods yet, and who can tell when we will be? In the meantime, let's not kid ourselves by putting our trust in gimmicks.

The *ninth* and final misconception is this: that a battery of tests can tell all one needs to know in making a judgment about a student's competence, present and potential, and about his effectiveness as a human being. The fact is that no test or series of tests now available is capable of giving the total picture of any child. Tests can illuminate many areas of his development, suggest something about his strengths and weaknesses, show in certain respects how he stands among his peers. But there are still many important aspects of learning and human development where we must still rely upon the observation and judgment of teachers if we are to get something that approaches a complete description of the child as a functioning individual. There are subtle but supremely important human elements in the teaching-learning situation that no combination of tests yet devised is able to capture. Such elements are elusive, but if ever we lose sight of them, the educational process in all its ramifications will become something less than the exciting human enterprise it should always be.

These are the nine misconceptions which I think most frequently lead to wide misuse of tests and test results. Some of our brasher critics have argued that, since tests are so widely misused, they do constitute a menace to sound education and therefore should be abolished. This argument is specious. It is the same as saying that automobiles should be abolished because they are a menace to human life when reckless drivers are at the wheel. Or it is the same as saying that teachers should be abolished because too many of them make psychometric hash out of marks and test scores.

In any case, I think it is highly unlikely that tests will be abolished any more than that textbooks will be abolished. Too many schools have discovered that, menace or not, they cannot operate effectively without them. The problem is not one of doing away with tests and testing but of getting people to use tests intelligently. When this happens testing will cease to be a mere administrative convenience or, worse still, a burden on the souls of teachers and pupils; it will become an effective instrument for vitalizing the total educational process and for helping to insure that in these days of skyrocketing enrollments the individual pupil will not be lost in the shuffle.

Part Three · toward understanding forces that influence growth and development

Just as the twig is bent, the tree is inclined.
    Alexander Pope (1688–1744)

Growth processes are both universal and individual. At the moment of birth, you and your friend were as much alike as you would ever be. From birth onward, you have grown increasingly *unlike* each other. Although you and your friend may share certain physical, emotional, or intellectual similarities, you have developed a particular combination of characteristics that makes you quite unlike any other person in the entire world.

The readings in Chapters Nine and Ten were selected to give you an idea of the range of internal and external forces that contribute to different growth processes and of their consequences.

The first selection in Chapter Nine will give you a good idea of why the first four years of growth exert such an influence on subsequent growth. Reading 33 discusses research on basic growth phenomena related to childhood and adolescence. Included is an interesting discussion about obesity, which can sometimes be predicted when a child is very young. Growing up to be a man or a woman, each with its own clearly defined sex-role boundaries is no longer a simple process of fitting into stereotypic molds. In reading 34, Carlfred Broderick shares some interesting insights about the changing definitions of masculinity and femininity. This reading also will help you to see what aspects of masculinity and femininity are *not* changing. What does research say about how sex relates to human development? Corinne Hutt's fine overview of research in reading 35 takes us from the level of personal speculation to the level of research-verified information about these differences. You will see that some of these differences are not simply psychological, but biologically determined as well.

The family and child-rearing practices serve as our focal points for Chapter Ten. What is happening to the American family? In what direction is it headed? Selection 36 speculates about this. What happens to children who are raised in authoritarian families, as opposed to those raised in authoritative families? Do child-rearing styles really make a difference? In reading 37, Diana Baumrind, an eminent developmental psychologist, explains how and why various child-rearing styles do indeed make a difference. For a glimpse at what a healthy family looks like, acts like, and feels like, see Joyce Maynard's sensitive portrayal of her own family in reading 38. She relates her appreciation of her family, a refreshing story in this age of increasing family alienation.

In the continuing exchange between what you already know and what you are learning, the selections in Part III show the impact of the family environment and the influence of child-rearing practices on a child's total growth and development.

Chapter Nine · growth processes and developmental consequences

32

Why the First 45 Months of Life Are So Important

Barbara Wyden

EDITOR'S NOTE · Research strongly indicates that what children experience from the moment of conception until three years of age may affect them—for better or for worse—for the rest of their lives. This is a fascinating, informative article about research findings related to early brain development and about relationships between nutrition and physical maturation. A great many changes occur within the first three years of a child's life. For example, by five years of age, the typical child is usually twice as tall as he was at two and weighs about five times more than he did at birth. This reading explains why the early years of life are so crucial to later development.

We tend to think of human physical growth as a leisurely 16- to 18-year process. Implicit is the notion that if a child falls behind in his development because of illness, deprivation or any other cause, he'll have a second, third or even fourth chance to catch up.

Barbara Wyden, "Growth: 45 Crucial Months," *Life Magazine*, December 17, 1971. Copyright © 1971 by Time, Inc. Reprinted with permission.

But he won't. Recent research breakthroughs have confirmed and reconfirmed that the first 45 months—from the moment of conception until 3 years of age—determine whether or not a child will be able to live up to his genetic potential. And the factor which can most influence a child's development during the 45 months is nutrition. A series of landmark studies, conducted in this country, Great Britain, Latin America and Africa, has pointed to the nutritional status of not only the child but also the pregnant mother as the key to that development. Some researchers are even beginning to speculate that the baby's temperament, degree of energy and many other characteristics may be affected by the dinner the mother ate the night she conceived.

A child's growth begins at the very moment of conception, when the male and female gametes come together and form the DNA (deoxyribonucleic acid)—the genetic endowment that determines a person's physical and mental characteristics. To some degree, growth is a lifelong process, but the sheer velocity of this first period is never again matched. The brain and skull, along with the eyes and ears, develop first. Then the rest of the body—the heart and lungs, the digestive organs, the kidneys, the arteries, the blood, the skeleton itself—forms and develops at an only slightly slower pace than the head.

For most of the body, these first months are crucial. The only important exception seems to be growth in height. Scientists have recently discovered that children who have not reached their full height because of illness or undernourishment or other trauma can gain their genetically indicated height if they are treated with growth hormone.

After birth, the infant continues to grow and starts to develop skills. He gains control of his body so he can roll over, sit, creep and eventually walk. He learns how to manipulate, to hold on to his father's finger, to grasp a rattle, to tear things. He coordinates his hands and eyes in such skills as piling blocks on top of each other or scribbling on paper with a crayon. He makes noises and then forms words, phrases and finally whole thoughts. And he develops the ability to relate to people—to smile, to be aware of others (sometimes to be afraid of them), to imitate, to be a social being. Whether or not the individual child reaches his full capacity in all these areas depends in large part on how his brain developed between the time of conception and 18 or 24 months of age.

The brain develops in four successive stages. Early growth—intrauterine growth—comes from the division of cells. The brain grows bigger as the cells divide and divide again. After birth, there's a transition period when the cells divide less rapidly and existing cells start growing in size. Then, somewhere around the end of the first year, the cells stop dividing altogether. All growth now comes from an increase in cell size, not number. The fourth and final stage is the forming of connections between the nerve cells. Each normal cell has some 10,000 of these connections and it may be that the number of connections between nerve cells is even more crucial than the number of cells.

AFTER EARLY INFANCY THE BRAIN NEVER GETS ANOTHER CHANCE

Nutrition, or more precisely malnutrition, has a direct effect on the way the brain grows: if a fetus does not receive enough nourishment, the rate of brain cell division slows down. A seriously deprived fetus may have 20% fewer brain cells than normal. If a newborn is seriously undernourished during the six months after birth, cell division is also slowed down—again by as much as 20%. If an infant should have been malnourished both in utero *and* after birth, the arithmetic is tragic. The brain may be 60% smaller.

"The brain never gets another chance," says Dr. Myron Winick, director of growth and development at New York Hospital-Cornell Medical College, one of the leaders in brain-growth research. "We found that cell division stops at approximately the same age in both undernourished and well-nourished children."

A report Dr. Winick made last year on starving Chilean babies under 6 months of age demonstrates the no-second-chance aspect of growth. These infants were brought to a hospital when they were so close to death that it was impossible to tell which babies would die and which would survive. Despite the most attentive medical care, nearly half died. The survivors then came under intense scrutiny. They were fed balanced diets, checked weekly by social workers, nutritionists and pediatricians, and tested by psychologists.

Preliminary findings showed that help had come too late for most. Ninety percent of the survivors had been irreparably damaged and were limited in their ability to "cope with their environment," the researchers reported: 51% were educable, but needed special teaching; 36% were only "trainable" to do simple tasks; 3% required custodial care. When these youngsters were compared with similar children who had not suffered from malnutrition, it was discovered that even if the survivors caught up to normal weight for their age and body build, their head circumference (one way of measuring brain size) was less than that of the youngsters who had been well nourished from birth. They were also retarded in motor skills.

Scientists are not willing to say that small brain size indicates lessened intelligence. They hesitate because it is not known how much of the brain we actually use, nor is it known exactly how and to what degree malnutrition slows down cell division in different areas of the brain. But all the evidence points inevitably to the conclusion that children with underdeveloped brains cannot function to their full genetic potential.

The rest of the body—heart, lungs, muscles, kidneys, etc.—develops the same way as the brain. The timing differs but the pattern is roughly similar. Studies have been made of rats who were undernourished in utero. Examined just before birth, these rats had lungs which were only 62% of normal weight, and hearts 84% of normal.

While poor sanitation, lack of education and substandard housing can also affect a child's growth, most researchers agree that nutrition is probably the crucial component, the one factor in the growth formula where dramatic improvements would yield dramatic results. Statistics show that prosperous mothers as well as low-income mothers suffer from protein deprivation. Women who snack on empty calories (soft drinks, salty tidbits, sweets), who get a significant proportion of their daily calories from alcohol, fats and carbohydrates rather than proteins, vegetables and fruits, or—at the other extreme—women who diet to neurotic excess do not provide the healthiest environment for a naturally greedy fetus.

"I can't emphasize how important it is for the mother not to just trust that her body will somehow have the reserves that are needed for her infant," says Dr. Merrill S. Read, director of the Growth and Development Program of the National Institute of Child Health and Human Development. And a mother's nutritional reserves, he says, cannot be suddenly accumulated during pregnancy. These assets are the cumulative result of a lifetime, Dr. Read says. "Getting ready to be a mother during a woman's adolescence is almost as important as the actual time when she's a mature woman and pregnant. It is particularly important before and during pregnancy to balance a diet with a variety of foods from the four basic food groups: meats, milk and dairy products, fruits and vegetables, breads and cereals." Dr. Read feels that special attention should be given to foods rich in iron— liver, eggs, dark-green leafy vegetables. A woman should control her caloric intake, he says, by limiting fats and carbohydrates and make everything she eats count nutritionally. "Vegetarians who exclude cheese, milk and eggs from their diets will have problems satisfying their protein needs during pregnancy when the fetus needs high-quality proteins," he said. "A mixture of cereal grains, beans, nuts, etc. may provide the essential amino acids, but it requires very careful food selection."

Dr. Michael Alderman, acting director of the Division of Community Medicine, Cornell Medical Center, feels that animal protein is essential to balanced nutrition. "The body is not capable of making nine essential amino acids, and the only way to get them is to ingest them. Meats are the major source of those proteins. Other proteins, from peanuts, beans and other vegetables, do not serve the same purpose. If a prospective mother relies solely on them she will be more likely to produce a baby with a low birth weight, increasing the risk of not surviving the first 28 days of life." A macrobiotic diet, whose main ingredient is brown rice, may be so lacking in protein that a pregnant mother might have difficulty in carrying her baby to term.

One immediate result of the new findings is that doctors are changing long-held ideas about optimal weight gain during pregnancy. The National Research Council recently alerted obste-

tricians that the current medical practice of limiting women to a gain of only ten to 14 pounds may be contributing to the high infant mortality in the United States. Restricting the pregnant woman's diet can be harmful both to the developing fetus and to the mother, and while no one is positive exactly what the optimal weight gain should be, there are new general guidelines. "We should probably be thinking in terms of 24 to 25 pounds," says Dr. Howard N. Jacobson of Harvard Medical School, a specialist in intrauterine development and a member of the National Research Council.

After the baby is born, overfeeding him can be almost as devastating as underfeeding. Overfeeding encourages a speedup in fat cell production, just as underfeeding produces a slow-down in brain cell production. Encouraging a baby to gobble up his formula to produce an impressive growth chart is dangerously old-fashioned. A recent study by Dr. Jerome Knittle of New York's Mt. Sinai School of Medicine and Dr. Jules Hirsch of the Rockefeller University has proved that infancy-formed fat cells stay in a person's body for life, although the amount of fat a cell is storing varies from month to month. Their experiments with newborn rats showed that rats who became fat on mother's milk remained fatter than normal-weight rats when both groups were allowed to eat whatever they wanted. Even when the fat rats were starved down to skin and bones, they still had a gross excess of fat cells —storage units of fat.

Applying the principle to humans, Dr. Knittle then turned to 200 children who had been obese since infancy and found 2-year-olds with twice the number of fat cells as a normal-weight child of that age, and 5-year-olds with twice the number of fat cells as a normal adult. The doctor's findings suggest that, for the rest of his life, someone who is overweight at age one is going to have a more difficult time than most other people when he tries to stay trim.

Although some specific recommendations for infant feeding do exist, most experts simply advise the mother to use her common sense and "don't stuff the baby." Doctors will confirm that it simply doesn't matter nutritionally or emotionally whether a baby is breast-fed or bottle-fed as long as mother and baby are pleased with the system they've adopted. Many pediatricians also feel that children should be fed only "modest" amounts of animal fats and eggs after 2 years of age. Animal studies on many species have proved that substituting poly-unsaturated vegetable oils for butter fat makes a real difference in the amount of blood cholesterol in the young—just as it does in the human adult. And there is circumstantial evidence that the same is true of human infants. But doctors are not yet sure what to do about this. They do recommend that most children be switched from whole milk to skim milk at the age of 2 (although not before).

The traditional three-meal-a-day pattern for children is also coming in for criticism. Dr. Samuel J. Fomon of the University of Iowa Medical School says, "Too many parents feel their kids are really growing up when they get them to adapt to our current three-widely-spaced-meals-a-day routine. Children really prefer snacking and it seems better for them—as long as the snacks are nutritious."

A sliver of white chicken meat, a dab of peanut butter on an apple slice, a carrot stick are nutritious snacks. Lollipops and cakes don't have the same nutritional values. Home-baked oatmeal cookies with raisins and nuts are fine within limits; chocolate cookies made with white sugar, fats and flour are not. Most American parents don't follow such guidelines and most American children are getting a lot of food, but of distressingly poor quality. A 15-state study of 3,444 preschoolers—ranging from lower- to upper-class economic backgrounds—showed that a significant number in all groups lacked proteins, vitamins and minerals in their diets. Another huge survey showed that nearly half of these preschoolers suffered from iron deficiencies. Although both studies were fact-finding efforts and the researchers did not attempt to analyze the effects of the dietary deficiencies, the children were noticeably susceptible to fatigue. They tended to tire in their play and it was expected they would probably tire in later years in their schoolrooms.

THE CALENDAR IS A POOR MEASUREMENT OF A CHILD'S PROGRESS

Given the solid foundation of good nutrition, each child will follow his own course of physical development. The patterns of physical growth of healthy children have such a wide range of variability that the calendar is a poor measurement of a child's progress. As every pediatrician has long been preaching, whether a baby starts walking "early" or "late," by age 3 there's no significant difference between his ability and that of another youngster. So there is absolutely no point to the perennial mothers' competition over whose baby walks first or talks first or is toilet-trained first. This needless race is prompted by our obsession for "firsts." Jean Piaget, the Swiss psychiatrist and educator, calls it "the American question": how can we make things happen faster? Piaget's answer is, "What's the advantage?" When children are ready to walk, they will walk. Or talk. Or use the toilet.

Youngsters who turn up at either end of the normal range are often given a rough time. For instance: the big 3-year-old who could be taken for a 5-year-old—and is expected to act as if he were 5; the small 5-year-old who could be considered 3—and often is, to his intense frustration. Precocious physical development often misleads parents in their expectations; precocious language development leads them to expect muscular coordination to match. The fact is that a child with the physical development usually attributed to age 3—he's toilet-trained, can feed himself completely (well, usually) with a spoon, can put on his shoes, can run and dance and jump—may have an emotional maturity of age 2 and a language ability of age 5. That's nothing to worry about if parents are conscientious about taking the child for regularly scheduled shots and check-ups and calling to the pediatrician's attention any concerns they have about their child's development, so that the doctor can determine if these problems indicate any serious retardation.

After age 3 the various aspects of a child's development will be more coordinated. By then a child is set on his biological track for life. Barring serious disease or accident, he is proceeding inexorably along the growth channels that are now set, and how well he does, how far he goes toward reaching his inborn potential, depends to a large extent on how he has been fed during the first 45 months of his life.

33

What Research Is Teaching Us about Human Growth and Development

Department of Health, Education, and Welfare

EDITOR'S NOTE • This article is a compilation of important research findings accumulated over the past 50 years that are related to how humans grow and develop over time. You will find important basic information about some of the fundamental growth processes associated with childhood and adolescence. Since so many persons in our contemporary society engage in an ongoing battle of the bulge, you may be interested in some of the intriguing research findings related to obesity in adults and children. You may recall your own adolescent years as you read about the impact of early and late puberty on overall development.

The mature human body is the end result of a remarkable growth process that requires almost two decades for completion. During this 20-year period, the individual who initially was the product of two germ cells, becomes an adult made up of 100,000 billion cells. Yet, contrary to popular belief, size increase is perhaps the least significant of the many components of human growth.

The human being at any age is very complex: he represents a marvel of specialized tissues and complementary functions—all coordinated to allow continuing integrity of his body as a whole. Fundamental to the growth process is the fact that all body systems must continue to work in concert at every stage of growth. Changes must be timed with exquisite precision, not only to culminate in a unified adult, but also to insure the integration of body activities which is essential at each intermediate point in growth. For this highly complicated process to evolve normally, physiologic systems must come into being in nicely ordered sequence, and they must be synchronized with others already in existence or yet to come. This is why the study of growth at its most basic levels may be viewed as an approach to better understanding of the nature of life itself.

Research in any branch of medicine is usually first conducted at the basic science level using laboratory animals. For growth research, rats are most commonly used since even after maturation they can be induced to grow almost at will. Growth research advances are next tested in primates (apes and monkeys) because their physiologic systems most closely parallel those of man. Finally, growth is studied in human volunteers, whose normal or disordered growth processes ultimately are not duplicated in any other living creature....

Medical scientists study periods of intense growth with unusual interest. In addition to providing ideal conditions for the basic study of growth and its derangements, these periods also represent a natural laboratory where solutions may be sought to many of the serious, nongrowth-related disorders that plague people throughout life.

For example, cells multiply at their greatest rate between the time of conception and the beginning of puberty. This period—the fetal and childhood years—is perfectly suited for research into the control of human cell multiplication. Through such research, physicians may in time learn why, in many people, abnormal cell division produces cells that, unfortunately, are not carbon copies of the orig-

"Clinical Research Advances in Human Growth and Development," Department of Health, Education and Welfare Publication No. (NIH) 73–166, General Clinical Research Centers Branch, Division of Research Resources, National Institute of Health (June 1972): 8–9; 19–21; 47–56.

inals, and why cellular growth in some people becomes completely uncontrolled or cancerous.

As the difference in growth between boys and girls becomes more fully documented, General Clinical Research Center investigators may also define those influences—both genetic and environmental—responsible for the greater longevity enjoyed by women in all developed nations of the world.

Also, growth studies will undoubtedly result in significant discoveries about the disabilities of old age, particularly those due to unstable cellular changes and to the diminishing ability of the body to repair itself. In time, physicians may even be able to circumvent many of these infirmities....

THE CHILDHOOD YEARS

Scientists are discovering that children throughout the world tend to show remarkably similar capacities for growth. Nursing infants in developing nations follow much the same pattern of growth as that considered normal for infants in the United States. The likelihood is that while each child proceeds to adulthood at his own pace, normal growth before puberty is dependent more on the life a child leads than upon the genes with which he is endowed.

The average, full-term male infant weighs 8 pounds and measures 20 inches. Some weight loss follows birth. Growth then becomes so rapid that he will probably weigh 14 pounds and measure 25 inches by the age of 4 months.

After the 4th month, growth starts to slow down. Height now becomes more important than weight in evaluating the health of the growing child. When he celebrates his first birthday, the average boy should have grown to a height of 30 inches.

By the time he is 2, a child's growth begins to reflect some genetic influence. The average healthy boy then measures about 35 inches and will have reached approximately half his adult height. On his third birthday, he is close to 38 inches. His growth rate then starts to level off, and for the next 9 years, he will grow at the relatively constant rate of only 2½ inches a year.

In marked contrast to the dramatic and rapid changes that occur during the pre- and early postnatal periods, growth during the later childhood years is slowly progressive, and derangements may be subtle. Probably one of the simplest gauges of a child's health status is whether he is adding inches and pounds according to accepted timetables of normal growth. The first indication that something is amiss with a child's health may be the fall of his growth curve below the third percentile for normal children. This youngster is probably suffering a period of depressed growth that should be investigated and its cause corrected.

Increase in height is due to progressive growth of bone. As noted earlier, development of the skeleton is quite incomplete at birth, and it continues to undergo many changes throughout childhood. Most primary centers of ossification, for example, develop after birth; some do not make their appearance until adolescence. Epiphyses normally are not completely closed until the end of adolescence.

Many investigators discuss human growth in terms of two ages: *chronological* age, timed from the date of birth, and *biological* age, a measure of the degree of physical maturity of the individual, determined by equating his degree of maturity with the average age at which that degree of maturity normally becomes manifest. X-rays of the bones are most often used to determine the biological age of children. The greater the number of centers of ossification present on X-ray, and the greater the degree of epiphyseal closure, the greater is the biological age of the child—regardless of his actual chronological age. Biological age, as measured by reference to X-ray of bones, is often referred to as *bone* age.

Bone X-rays have helped establish, for example, that skeletal maturation in a girl on the day of birth is one month ahead of that of her twin brother. The female, therefore, comes into life a biologically older, more highly developed organism. It will take the male close to 20 years to catch up.

Measures of height, weight, and bone age have served as the traditional bases of growth studies. Scientists now, however, are seeking increasingly specialized techniques by which human growth may be analyzed. Enlargement of the human organism is basically the result of a myriad of chemical reactions, some of which can be measured in a short period of time by new biochemical techniques. Researchers at General Clinical Research Centers and other facilities, therefore, are now investigating individual components of growth at the tissue, cellular, and even molecular levels.

At some General Clinical Research Centers, everything the research subjects eat, drink, or eliminate is carefully measured for weight, chemical composition, and caloric value. In fact, the child who enters the bathroom without telling the nurse is interrupted by an alarm system; this prevents the loss of waste materials which must be carefully analyzed as part of precise metabolic studies.

For almost three-quarters of a century, scientists believed that growth after birth was due solely to an increase in the *size* of body cells. Now General Clinical Research Centers investigators, in a new application of older knowledge, have shown that specialized cells also increase in *number* for many years after birth. For example, scientists have known for two decades that DNA is present in precisely equal quantities in the nuclei of all body cells and that the amount in each cell is constant throughout life. Therefore, from the total amount of DNA contained in a weighed muscle biopsy specimen, the number of cells constituting the specimen can be determined. Since the total weight of the specimen is known; the weight and size of each constituent cell is easily calculated. Serial repeats of such biopsies over a number of years, coupled with repeated measurement of total body muscle mass, allow investigators to calculate whether changes in muscle cell number or size have occurred.

An early conclusion drawn from such cellular analyses is that while bone maturation is an index of biological age, the number of muscle cells in the body correlates more closely with chronological age —and is related to the sex of the child. Boys and girls are probably born with the same number and size of muscle cells. By 3 weeks of age, however, the male child already has more, and larger, muscle cells than the female.

When she is 10, the girl will have undergone a fivefold increase in the number of her muscle cells; from this age, little further increase occurs in either her muscle cell size or number. In contrast, a boy's muscle cells continue to multiply until, at 18 years of age, he has 14 times as many muscle cells as he did at birth. (A tall 18-year-old boy may

have 20 times more muscle cells.) While muscle cell replication ceases at this age, some evidence exists that the muscle cells of the boy will contiue to enlarge in size for another 5 years.

Once muscle cells stop growing, gross enlargement of muscle is due to an increase in the diameter of the fibrils contained inside the muscle cells. This is often brought about by conscious exercise, such as that designed to enlarge the biceps, or by the unconscious but physiological effort of a muscle to sustain a greater body function. This latter phenomenon can occur in the heart of an athlete; the fibrils of his heart may grow in size to help handle an increased workload.

Scientists have also discovered that, right from the beginning, a girl will have a greater percentage of fatty tissue, increasing in greater proportional amounts as she grows, than the boy of equal age and size. Because she has these fatty tissue reserves, a girl's external requirements for maintaining her weight are less than her brother's, and her caloric needs throughout life will be, pound for pound, less than his.

In almost every respect, the physical development of the female is more stable than that of the male. Not only is she biologically more mature, as measured by bone X-rays, but when sister and brother are exposed to the same growth-retarding condition, the girl tends to show less damage. The growth-retarded boy, on the other hand, reacts more favorably to an improvement in the condition causing his growth lag, possibly because he has more catch-up growth to accomplish.

Each successive generation in most of the industrialized world has been growing taller than the generation preceding it. On an average, young adults of today measure 1 inch more than parents and 2 inches more than their grandparents. Males, moreover, are increasing in adult height more rapidly than females. Many researchers believe these height gains can be attributed to better medical care and nutrition . . . and that the more rapid rate of increase in the male indicates how quickly his growth can respond to better times.

Will people keep growing taller and taller? No one knows. But scientists do suspect that the increase is leveling off and that, once they complete growth, today's healthy and well-nourished boys and girls will have reached the maximum height allowed by the human genetic potential.

ADOLESCENCE

Puberty begins when the pituitary gland starts to secrete the gonadotrophins and the gonads, under their influence, begin to release sex hormones. No one knows what triggers the pituitary to begin this secretion or how the time of onset is synchronized with other body processes.

Each individual child, however, appears genetically programed for maturation. Indeed, puberty has now been shown to be the first time in the life of the normal child when heredity overshadows environment in determining how he will grow. Even among abnormally short children, the "least short" are usually the offspring of the tallest parents. Thus, although environmental factors are causing children of the United States today to enter puberty 3 years earlier than they did a century ago, heredity remains the primary reason tall parents beget tall adults, and short parents short adults.

Until the age of 10, boys and girls grow at almost identical rates. Children sharing the same chronological age vary only slightly in size. However, regardless of chronological age, the more advanced the biological age of any child, the closer he is to sexual maturation and the less growth potential he retains. Thus, just as the female comes into life with a more advanced biological age (as measured by bone age), so she enters puberty earlier and emerges from it an adult shorter than her male counterpart.

Puberty usually begins only after at least 85 percent of eventual height has been achieved. Its onset is marked typically by the beginning of breast development in the female and by genital changes in the male. And, although the initial manifestations may be subtle, the growth, the sexual development, and the emotional changes which subsequently characterize puberty can be sufficiently dramatic to make it as difficult a time as any the human must endure.

In both sexes, adrenal androgen appears to be instrumental in initiating the pubescent growth spurt. During the growth spurt, feet and hands first increase in size. The calves and forearms, the hips and chest, and the shoulders then follow, in that order. Because the last to increase is the size of the trunk and chest, the young teenager must almost invariably pass through a transitional stage where his hands and feet are large and ungainly relative to the rest of his body. However, the rate of growth of the trunk in time exceeds that of the lower limbs, and the overall increase in height which occurs during adolescence eventually is derived more from increase in length of the trunk than from growth of the legs.

Although there may be a variation of 3 years between the beginning of the growth spurt in one normal child and another, the typical girl in the United States now begins puberty at the age of 10½. For the next 2½ years, she grows at an average annual rate of 3 inches per year. With the onset of the menstrual cycle, about age 13, the adolescent girl then experiences a rapid decline in growth rate but will continue to grow, at a reduced pace, for another 3 years. By the age of 16, her epiphyses are usually closed, and further increase in height is impossible.

The average adolescent boy, on the other hand, is only beginning his growth spurt at age 13. It will usually be more marked, more intense, and of longer duration than that of the girl. For example, during the next 2½ years, when his height is increasing most rapidly, the adolescent boy usually grows at least 4 inches a year. This is close to the dramatic rate of growth experienced by 2-year-olds. By the time he is 15, he will be eating seven times more protein and 50 percent more calories than he consumed at age 9. Between the ages of 12 and 16, he will almost double in weight.

Although the teenage boy will experience ultimately a decrease in growth rate (and appetite), his decrease is not so precipitous as that of the girl. The epiphyses of his long bones usually do not close, and his increase in height is not over, until he reaches his late teens.

Perhaps as dramatic as the increase in body size which occurs during puberty is the concomitant development of male and female sexual characteristics. The pubescent girl develops rounded contours by accumulating fat on the breasts, hips, and thighs. The boy, on the other hand, becomes during puberty more lean than he will ever be again. The pelvis of the girl enlarges more than do her shoulders; in this way, she is prepared for childbearing. The shoulders and chest of the boy increase more in size than does his pelvis, and his total muscle mass makes tremendous competitive gains.

Bone age is a measure of degree of closure of the epiphyses. Since an adolescent may continue to amass new cells for some time after his epiphyses have closed and his height has stabilized, bone age cannot be used to determine when puberty is complete and adulthood achieved. After full adulthood is reached, however, net increase in total number of body cells does not usually occur; reproduction of cells does continue throughout adult life, but its rate is usually synchronized with cell destruction so that new cells just replace those which are lost. Adulthood, and the end of puberty, therefore, may be defined scientifically as the time a steady state of cell population is finally attained.

OBESITY

Fat infants and plump children may appear delightful to their parents; however, the chances are four out of five that the overweight child will become an overweight teenager, who, in turn, will carry his problem throughout adulthood. An estimated one-tenth to one-fourth of the adolescents in this country are overweight.

Adolescent girls negatively relate increasing weight with obesity, while boys tend to view increasing weight positively as a manifestation of growing strength. One recent study of close to 600 high school students showed this disparate, yet mutual, dissatisfaction with weight. Four-fifths of the girls wanted to weigh less; almost all of the boys wanted to weigh more. Only the obviously obese among the boys wanted to lose weight.

The young girl emerging into womanhood is frequently torn between social pressures that place a premium on being slender and a maturing metabolism that inexorably deposits fat on her growing body. From a medical standpoint, these fat deposits may fall within the range of healthy female growth. So great are the pressures, however, that previously thin girls may imagine themselves doomed to obesity unless they diet rigorously. These girls constitute a large portion of the American youngsters who, despite access to proper food, exist in a borderline state of nutrition because of ill-advised attempts at weight reduction. Ironically, the diets of overweight girls, whose caloric intake may even be excessive, are also frequently inadequate nutritionally.

To growth researchers, the high correlation between teenage obesity and the incidence of such disorders of the later years as hypertension, heart ailments, diabetes, and respiratory ills makes excess body fat more a medical than an aesthetic concern. For example, in 85 percent of all adult diabetics, obesity preceded the onset of the disease. One theory is that excess body fat in some way produces resistance to the activity of insulin, which in turn causes blood sugar levels to increase. A compensatory increase in secretion of insulin by the pancreas occurs and continues until the capacity of the pancreas to produce the hormone is exhausted. Then, insulin production falls, and clinical diabetes results. Studies of obese individuals who have lost weight indicate, on the other hand, that once normal weight is regained, elevated insulin levels will often return to normal.

Other studies have indicated that atherosclerosis (the most common form of hardening of the arteries) may begin in the pubescent male. Autopsy studies of boys in the late teen years demonstrate consistently that the fatty arterial plaques which are the constituent beginnings of atherosclerosis can begin during adolescence. As atherosclerosis is the fundamental cause of coronary artery disease, research into its causation and prevention during the adolescent years, and its relation to teenage obesity, may in time have significant influence in reducing the high mortality of American men from heart disease.

Unfortunately, physicians have discovered that for the medically obese boy or girl, puberty may be the most difficult time in life to shed excess pounds. The entire physiology of the adolescent is geared to promote growth, and any attempt to reverse any of its growth parameters may be met with insuperable resistance.

Only temporary decreases in weight have been experienced by obese adolescents in outpatient weight reduction programs. After 1 to 2 years, these teenagers have all reverted to their initial obese status. Greater success has frequently been achieved by teenagers enrolled as inpatients in either hospital or summer camp-based programs. Yet, even for these young people, long-term maintenance of relatively reduced weight has yet to be conclusively demonstrated.

For obese teenagers, therefore, an ounce of prevention is literally worth a pound of cure. The evidence is overwhelming that obesity is best averted, evaluated, or treated as early in life as possible.

The most common, and the simplest, procedure for determining whether an individual is too heavy is to compare his weight with the weight considered normal for one of his height, body frame, age, and sex. However, since total body mass is composed not only of fat but also of bone, muscle, and water, a person may be overweight "by the chart" without being obese. For example, a number of football players were rejected for military duty during World War II because of excess weight. Subsequent analysis revealed that they had little excess fat but were heavier than the normal weight the tables allowed due to their great muscle and bone development.

In recent years, more refined research techniques have been developed to assess with precision the amount of fat in overweight people. They have arisen from the increased interest of physicians in detecting and modifying actual fatness—the one component of overweight that can, and should, be reduced.

One technique relies on the principle of Archimedes. The patient is totally submerged under water, and the volume of water he displaces—which is equal to his body volume—is measured. Total body weight divided by measured body volume equals total body density. Since the densities of fat, bone, muscle, and water are all different, this calculation of body density enables investigators to determine the proportion of fat in the patient's total weight.

Procedures such as this, however, are too detailed for other than research use. Because half of all pubescent fat is located immediately beneath the skin, researchers have found that the thickness of a fold of skin on the back of the upper arm correlates reasonably well with the amount of body fat present. For example, a 15-year-old girl whose skin fold measures more than an inch is considered obese. Similarly, a 12-year-old boy with a skin fold thickness of at least three-quarters of an inch is also judged obese.

Careful measures of obesity, conducted in a large population of people, coupled with studies of families, documentation of differences in fat accumulation between the sexes, comparisons among racial and ethnic groups, and investigations of identical twins reared together and apart, are yielding impressive evidence that genetic factors may be very important in predisposing certain people to obesity. Too, heredity may also underlie why some underweight individuals do not gain weight despite an obviously excessive caloric intake.

Still unknown, however, is how a genetic predisposition to obesity can be reinforced or overcome by such environmental variables as nutrition, occupation, geography, climate, and emotion. One hypothesis, as noted earlier, is that overnutrition in infancy may stimulate into being a pathologic excess of fat cells which then persist throughout life and tend always to become laden with fat. Another hypothesis, being investigated at a General Clinical Research Center, is that overnutrition may trigger excess production of insulin and HGH in genetically susceptible newborns, which would also encourage excess fat storage. If any such hypothesis can be documented unequivocally, then a significant proportion of adolescent obesity may in time be ascribed more to hormonal or genetic influences than to simple overeating.

Some studies of obese teenage girls have in fact shown their daily caloric intake to be lower than that of lean controls. A possibility, which has not yet been proven, is that these obese girls have hormonal imbalances which in some fashion result in depressed estrogen activity. This, in turn, could allow adrenal androgen, present in normal but limited amount, to exert unopposed its masculinizing effects, with resultant weight gain.

However, neither hormonal dysfunction nor excess caloric intake seems to be the single determinant of obesity. For example, right from birth, obese children are decidedly less active than the non-obese. Movies taken during physical education classes at a swimming pool showed that the fatter teenagers spent 72 percent of their time standing around, whereas their normal weight peers spent 75 percent of their time vigorously engaged in water sports.

The causal relationship between obesity and inactivity is not known. Inactivity may contribute to obesity through reducing the number of food calories which are utilized for energy; alternately, the obese child may be inactive as a result of the heavier weight he must move about. Yet, one fact is certain—every calorie that is spent through increased physical activity is one less calorie that can be stored as fat.

In a recent test, 100 obese adolescent girls were enrolled in a public school physical education program which by design kept them in virtually constant motion for 45 minutes each school day. Also included in the program were nutrition education, psychological support, and encouragement to continue vigorous physical exercise during days off from school.

After 5 months, the girls were compared with a control group of about 70 nonprogram girls. The study group had decreased skin fold thickness an average of 50.5 percent, compared with a decrease of 31.9 percent in the control group. Average body weight decreased 27.7 percent, as against 11.6 percent in nonprogram girls.

As a result of this study, a number of schools are instituting physical education classes specifically designed to help the obese child, who in the past has emerged physiologically untouched (but often scathed psychologically) from traditional physical ed programs that have served only to enhance the skills of the athletically endowed.

EARLY AND LATE PUBERTY

Heredity, not environment, paces the changes of puberty. Since each individual advances from childhood to adulthood at his own genetically determined rate, a teenager cannot validly compare himself with others of the same age. Heredity can either delay biological age and, therefore, growth in the short teenager, or it can usher a tall teenager into puberty at an early age.

Recently developed clinical procedures, including the radioimmunoassay tests, usually reveal that all body systems, in both tall and short teenagers, are working harmoniously. X-rays of wrist epiphyses provide a measure of how far all epiphyses are from closure and, therefore, how much linear growth may yet be achieved.

These procedures reinforce more traditional observations that tall adolescents usually complete growth early, whereas short adolescents continue to grow for long periods. The tall girl will usually grow only a little taller; the height of the short boy can in time exceed that of his tallest friends. Such information can be of great help in reassuring and allaying the fears of the short boy who is afraid he is not growing enough or the tall girl who thinks she will be a giant.

A girl will usually have achieved most of her adult height by the time regular menstrual periods begin. The female hormones, estrogen and progesterone, are responsible for inducing the menarche. Under their influence, growth quickly slows down for the adolescent girl and usually terminates in 2 to 3 years. This influence is the basis for administering these hormones to induce growth retardation in pre-menstrual girls whose apprehension of excessive adult height has been scientifically confirmed.

Twenty years ago, administration of estrogen was found inadequate to slow down the girl who was growing too tall. In addition, considerable "breakthrough" vaginal bleeding occurred when it alone was given as therapy. In more recent years, however, a research treatment using estrogen in much larger doses and in combination with progesterone has proven very effective, and few adverse effects have been noted.

One General Clinical Research Center confines this research treatment to healthy girls who have inherited the propensity to be over 5 feet 10 inches and in whom the wrist epiphyses are still wide open.

Each day, the patient takes estrogen by mouth. The hormone induces proliferation of the uterine lining, causing it to become progressively soft and thick—just as if the girl were normally ovulating and the uterus were preparing for implantation of a fertilized ovum. To preclude this buildup reaching a point where excessive bleeding might occur, the uterine lining is caused to slough off by injection of a progesterone-like compound the first 5 or 6 days of each month. This duplicates as nearly as possible the cyclic bleeding brought on by the large quantities of progesterone produced physiologically in normally menstruating girls.

In one group of 11 girls, treatment required 8 to 24 months. A decrease in the rate of linear growth was observed in all. Some girls achieved complete growth arrest; others dropped from a growth rate of 4 inches to four-tenths of an inch per year. For patients whose biological age was under 13 when treatment was begun, therapy prevented 2 to 4 inches of predicted growth. Girls whose biological age was over 13 had predicted growth reduced by 1½ to 2½ inches.

Treatment was discontinued when wrist X-rays indicated that growth either had halted or had been reduced to a rate acceptable to the patient.

After therapy, menstrual periods resumed a normal pattern. No patient experienced impaired pituitary-ovarian function or blood clots in leg veins—both of which are known, infrequent, but potentially serious complications of this cyclic hormone therapy.

In another similar study, each potentially tall girl received estrogen via a capsule surgically implanted beneath the skin of the abdomen. Each capsule gradually released its hormone into the blood stream and had to be replaced every 6 months. A menstrual-like period was induced by having the patient take a progesterone pill for 5 days each month.

In this study, responsiveness to treatment varied. In about 90 percent of the girls, linear growth halted after 1 to 3 additional inches of growth had occurred. In the remaining 10 percent, less dramatic but still significant growth retardation resulted.

A number of girls from both studies have gone on to get married, enjoy healthy pregnancies, and produce normal babies.

Unlike the girls, adolescent boys are primarily concerned that they may not grow tall enough. Since most boys who are short in the early teenage years will eventually, if slowly, reach normal adult height, growth experts are less likely to intervene in their growth than in the case of girls who are growing too tall. However, if the boy is severely disturbed by his temporary short stature, some physicians will prescribe male hormones (androgens) to hasten his sexual maturation and, thereby, his growth spurt.

The time at which androgens are utilized to promote growth is important, however, because at the same time that they promote growth, they also begin to stimulate epiphyseal closure. There is a race against time. If sexual maturation proceeds too rapidly, epiphyseal closure may occur prematurely, and the patient may be deprived of the ultimate height he would have reached had his intrinsic chronology of growth been realized without intervention.

In an attempt to avert this danger, some researchers in recent years have begun administering androgens in low doses and on a discontinuous schedule. Usually the patient receives the hormone daily for 1 month and is then taken off all therapy the succeeding month. Bone maturation is evaluated frequently, and the medication is discontinued permanently as soon as the patient's biological age is observed to catch up with his chronological age.

In one study of 67 boys who underwent this intermittent therapy, growth proceeded at the rate of about 3 inches a year so long as all epiphyses remained open. In most cases, ultimate height attained was no more than that predicted; however, most of the boys achieved this height earlier, and a few even grew taller than expected.

The periodic interruption of the medication was felt to lessen the tendency to too-rapid epiphyseal closure. However, the studies are too recent to allow conclusion either that this therapy averts all danger of premature closure or, alternately, that it promotes growth to a height greater than the patient's genetic potential. In fact, one theory as to the efficacy of the treatment is that the small amounts of androgen administered have no direct effect on sexual maturation but that they promote growth only indirectly through stimulation of appetite.

Precocious puberty is the extreme opposite of delayed sexual maturation. In this condition, a girl may develop secondary sexual characteristics before the age of 8, or a boy before he is 10. This clearly can produce severe psychological problems for the affected child.

Of equal importance is the fact that precocious puberty stimulates the adolescent growth spurt to begin prematurely. In normal children, childhood growth is usually complete before the adolescent growth spurt is superimposed; in children with precocious puberty, the growth spurt begins long before the childhood phase of growth is complete. Since sexual maturation tends to promote closure of the epiphyses, this results in epiphyses closed before true potential height is realized and growth of the children into adults noticeably shorter than their contemporaries.

Precocious puberty is rare. Sometimes, it is the first symptom of a cyst or a tumor in the adrenal glands, the sex glands, or the brain. In certain instances, it occurs in families whose members have an inherited tendency to excrete at an early age excessive amounts of adrenal androgen. Many cases have no known origin and may be viewed only as normal puberty occurring at an abnormally early age.

In these latter cases, the continuing development of secondary sexual characteristics can usually be slowed down by the administration of a progesterone-like hormone. Within the past year, researchers have begun to report that this treatment may also slow the accelerated rate of epiphyseal closure. Although these findings remain preliminary, they do indicate that appropriate hormone therapy may eventually allow growth to continue sufficiently long in children with precocious puberty to allow them to attain normal adult height.

Through such studies, scientists are learning how to circumvent the whims of nature that too often impose heavy burdens on young people— particularly during those final years of growth when a young person's perception of himself can be permanently enhanced or flawed. Also, from the information derived, physicians are able to reassure the majority of young people concerned about their growth that, in time, all variations will be spontaneously resolved.

34

Observations about the Changing Definitions of Masculinity and Femininity

Carlfred B. Broderick

EDITOR'S NOTE • Growing up to be a man or a woman is not as simple as it used to be. The boundaries of the definition of what is "masculine" or "feminine" are not as fixed as they once were. Although this has the clear advantage of offering men and women more latitude in their behavioral expressions and vocational choices, there are some who say that it will make it more difficult for a growing boy and girl to clearly identify with one sex or the other. Mr. Broderick argues that although our cultural definitions of masculinity and femininity may change, our basic sexual differences will always make a difference. Maybe. What do you think? Be sure to read the next selection for a more research-oriented slant to this question.

Being a girl isn't what it used to be and probably isn't what it's going to be, but then and now it's different from being a boy. In these days of unisex, women's lib, and gay militance I am sometimes asked whether sexual differences

Carlfred B. Broderick, "The Importance of Being Earnest—or Evelyn," *J C Penny Forum* (Spring/Summer 1973): 16–17. Reprinted with permission.

are becoming meaningless. My answer is that sex will always matter so long as women bear children and men father them. Some retort that it may become technically possible to bring children into the world some other way (with frozen sperm and eggs and artificial wombs). Maybe. But I personally doubt it. And so long as men and women play complementary roles in producing babies it will be important for each to be able to identify potential partners readily. It doesn't matter much what the apparent differences are—whether hair style or clothing or mannerisms or voice inflection; always there will be adequate cues.

It is fascinating to study the ways our society operates to perpetrate sex differences. From the very beginning children are named differently, handled differently, dressed differently according to their sex. Girl infants have bows scotchtaped to their hairless scalps and boys are dressed in pants long before their mobility would make it an advantage. It is true that many children wear play clothes that are identical for the sexes but rarely are "dress-up" clothes sexually ambiguous. One proof that we do an effective job in training very young children to think and act differently according to their sex comes from a special clinic at Johns Hopkins University where they work with children who, for various physical reasons, need to have their sex assignment changed. If the change can be made before age two, no serious problems are liable to arise but from two to three it gets increasingly difficult for the child and for the adults around him to adjust to the new assignment. After three the task gets so difficult that the advisability of trying must be very carefully evaluated. Somehow, by that tender age we have so indoctrinated a child that *he* is a boy or *she* is a girl that their identity as a separate individual is thoroughly tangled with his/her sexual identity.

Of course, teaching a child which of the two halves of the human race he or she belongs to is only the beginning. It is one thing to be clearly labelled "boy" in your own and everyone else's mind but it is another to learn to behave in the way that boys are supposed to behave. What constitutes "masculine" or "feminine" behavior is socially determined and varies from culture to culture and from time to time in our own culture.

One famous personality inventory which has been used to collect data on large samples of men and women over the last 30 years shows that in our culture the concept of masculinity has changed more over that time period than the concept of femininity. (This may surprise some who feel that women's liberation is pioneering the way for men's liberation.)

Thirty years ago it was more masculine to be interested in mechanics than in music, in mathematics than in literature and in things than in people. Ideas were more masculine than emotions and technical skills more than social skills. Independence was more masculine than either emotional dependence or nurturance. Only one out of six males had as "feminine" a score in the early 1940's as the average college male in the early 1970's. It is not, I think, useful to say that today's young men are more effeminate than formerly. Rather, the standard for what is masculine has changed. Business and industry and many of the professions put a higher value on emotional openness and warmth than on tough-minded competitiveness. There is more demand for interpersonal sensitivity than for unemotional rationalism. Cultural polish is more richly rewarded than mechanical adeptness.

Women, on their part, show only a slight shift toward the more independent and competitive end of the scale, although current studies are attempting to assess the impact of the burgeoning women's movement in the last two or three years. It is interesting to me to note that women's libers are not attempting to imitate men stylistically (except, perhaps, in adopting the male vernacular). They are not anxious to have women become indistinguishable from men by masking or denying their physical differences. Rather they want women, while retaining their unique qualities as women, to have equal access to economic reward and decision-making power and personal fulfillment. They have recognized what other sinned-against groups have recognized, that blind imitation of more powerful groups is a denial of one's own worth.

Despite these shifts and convergences it is still important in our society for a man to act masculinely within the limits of contemporary definition. A man who walks or talks or gestures "like a woman" is no more admired today than formerly. A girl who comes across as over-direct or too angular or who walks flat-footed is still unappreciated.

The concepts of masculinity are not only in

the society, but in ourselves. This is a foundation for one of the most troublesome aspects of the highly advertised "generation gap." The parents' concepts of what is genuinely masculine or feminine were learned in another era and many are uncomfortable with their children's response to the different definitions of their own day.

But however the personal and sartorial style may have changed in the last 30 years it remains as important for a boy or girl to learn his/her sex role as ever. There are two unchanging bases for this. First, since in most cases a child's sense of self is fundamentally intertwined with its sense of being a boy or girl, great damage can be done by attacking either component. For example, in my marriage counseling practice I fairly often come across women who were clearly taught that one or the other of their parents wanted a boy. The sense of rejection this engendered lingered on into adulthood to interfere with the woman's basic feeling of worth. Similarly, there are men who as adults still live with the resentment they learned as children from their mothers who thought boys were "not nice" and "too much trouble" compared to girls. These experiences inevitably have an impact upon one's whole self-concept as an acceptable person and not just upon his sex role.

A second reason that every child continues to need and deserve strong support in his sex role is that we live in the most thoroughly heterosexual society in the Western world. There is perhaps nothing that is voluntary that more Americans do than get married. Ninety-five percent of us get married at least once by the age of 40. That is more than watch television. Since surveys show that almost 10 percent of adult males are preferential homosexuals, this suggests that even half of our homosexuals get married heterosexually, so great is the pressure. Despite all of the talk about marriage being passé the national marriage rate is higher in this decade than it was in the 1950's and 1960's.

Clearly in a culture that places this kind of emphasis on heterosexual pairing it is vastly important to gain skills in playing the approved role vis-à-vis the opposite sex. By 5 years of age over half of the girls are sure that they want to get married eventually and by 12 over ninety percent have accepted this as their eventual goal. Boys are a bit slower to become oriented to marriage but marriage is not the only form of heterosexual pairing and the evidence

is that boys are no less committed to heterosexuality than girls, albeit with a slightly different emphasis. From early grade-school onwards children have romantic fantasies and often real crushes on opposite sex classmates or adults. Success in these romantic endeavors becomes one of the chief cornerstones of self-image and peer evaluation. Indeed, much of adult fantasy and literature reveals the continuing preoccupation with these matters throughout life.

Some have been concerned that the new flexibility in role assignments between the sexes in courtship and marriage may either reflect or presage a loss of sex role identity. If men are more warmly involved with their wives and children than formerly, more open emotionally, more sensitive to others and more home-centered, does this mean [a man] has lost his sense of identity as a *man*? Similarly, does the woman who is more independent and assertive lose some essential essence of femininity? The issue will continue to be debated, but I would conclude from clinical experience that very often excessive rigidity grows out of anxiety, while flexibility in role definitions is more likely to occur among those secure in their sense of sex identity.

Differences between what is masculine and what is feminine need not be blatant to be of great importance. The point is illustrated by the tempest a few years ago when one of the Minneapolis papers ran a photograph of a pair of beautiful breasts with the caption, "Can you identify this famous movie star?" For three days they printed letters from outraged citizens who felt that the forces of rampant free sex had taken over a formerly responsible "family" newspaper. Then on the fourth day they showed the entire head and torso and it turned out to be the bust of Johnny Weissmuller of Tarzan fame (and a first class swimmer, hence the over-developed pectoral muscles). Then everyone laughed at the joke. But it was funny precisely because it *matters* whether the breasts belonged to a male or a female. If they belonged to a female they had powerful erotic significance for males, if to a male, none.

For all of these reasons I believe that sexual differences will always make a difference. No current social movement including women's lib or gay militancy is calculated to change that. In fact, both movements depend as heavily on categorizing the sexes as do traditional courtship, marriage and parenthood.

Times change and cultural definitions of what is masculine and what is feminine change. What does not change is the need in each individual to feel secure in his own identity and that includes his sexual identity. However the symbols may evolve which reassure me and others that I am a man and my mate is a woman, there will be such symbols and they will matter.

35

Sex Differences in Human Development

Corinne Hutt

EDITOR'S NOTE · *Do men and women really develop differently in how they think and function? If there are differences between them —aside from the obvious biological ones—are they attributable primarily to environmental influences? Or are there endocrinologic and neural bases that may explain them? Dr. Hutt presents us with an exhaustive review of research literature on these and related questions, which, regardless of your gender, I think you will find fascinating reading. There seems little question that there are differences in behavior between the sexes. This selection will help you to comprehend why these differences exist.*

During the past two decades there has been a regrettable silence on the subject of sex differences in human development in the psychological literature. What reports there were,

Corinne Hutt, "Sex Differences in Human Development," *Human Development* 15: 153–70. (Basel: Karger, 1972). Reprinted with permission.

clearly influenced by the "psychosexual-neutrality-at-birth" theory (Diamond, 1965), dealt mainly with questions of sex-role identification, sex-role adoption, learning of appropriate sex-role behaviours, and so on.

Two timely rebukes were administered recently by Garai and Scheinfeld (1968) and Carlson and Carlson (1960). Each pair of authors was lamenting the lack of attention paid to sex differences in their own field—the former in developmental psychology and the latter in social psychology. They noted that in each area a large number of studies failed to look for sex differences; others used single-sex samples, and some were even unaware of the sex of their subjects. Since these two areas account for a substantial proportion of psychological research undertaken, the neglect of sex differences seems to have been particularly regrettable.

A turning-point in this trend was the publication in 1966 of the book *The development of sex differences* edited by Eleanor Maccoby. Although still reflecting a predominantly "psychosexual-neutrality-at-birth" orientation, it nevertheless brought to light a large amount of incriminating evidence. Then followed the third edition of *The psychology of human differences* (Tyler, 1965) which contained a cogent review of cognitive sex differences, and more recently, the impressive monograph of Garai and Scheinfeld (1968). Since then, and given an ironic fillip by the Women's Liberation Movement no doubt, many reports acknowledging the presence of sex differences have once again appeared in the literature. It is notable that, since its inception two years ago, the journal *Developmental Psychology* has contained one or more reports on sex differences in nearly every issue.

In many ways, however, psychological sex differences are the tip of the iceberg. By the time differences in behaviour and performance manifest themselves, so much differentiation has already taken place. As contributors to the symposium on *The biological bases of psychological sex differences* made only too clear, many of these differences are determined from the moment an ovum is fertilised by a sperm carrying an X or a Y chromosome. Possession of a Y chromosome, for example, confers a particular flavour on the development of the male zygote and embryo—an effect more pervasive than would result from simply the determination of masculinity (Ounsted and Taylor, 1972). Subsequently, the gonadal hormones exert their organisational influence on reproductive structures and, more significantly, on the central nervous system (Harris, 1964, 1970; Levine, 1966; Whalen, 1968; Hutt, 1972a; Michael, 1971).

In this paper, therefore, I would like to discuss some empirical results of behavioural and intellectual sex differences in early human development in the context of what is known about the biological determination of such differences.

EMBRYOLOGICAL DEVELOPMENT

As Garai and Scheinfeld (1968) point out, from the moment of conception males and females exhibit radically different patterns of development. The neuroendocrinological processes and their influence on early development are essentially the same in all placental mammals and these have been adequately described elsewhere (Harris, 1964, 1970; Gorski and Wagner, 1965; Whalen, 1968; Hutt, 1972a).

The most notable feature of mammalian development is that there is no *neuter* sex. In the presence of a Y chromosome, the male gonad differentiates and then produces the androgenic evocator substance which exerts its action upon hypothalamic centres to produce the acyclic pattern of gonadotrophic hormone release characteristic of the male. In the absence of a Y chromosome, or more specifically, early androgenic influence, the natural propensity of mammalian creatures is to differentiate as *females*. This is so even in the case of a genetic male in whom, due to early castration or some disorder, the testicular hormone is absent or ineffective. Such an instance occurs in humans in the syndrome of testicular feminisation, where, due to a recessive disorder, the testes of the genetic male often develop in an inguinal hernia and the gonadal hormone, if produced at all, is without effect (Federman, 1967). This individual differentiates as a female. Conversely, in the presence of androgens during the critical period, even the genetic female will differentiate as a male, as happens in the case of the adrenogenital syndrome (Wilkins, 1962; Bongiovanni and Root, 1963; Federman, 1967). Curiously, in the absence of *any* gonadal hormone, the development might be described as excessively "feminine": this happens in

the case of Turner's syndrome, where one sex chromosome is lacking, the karyotype being XO, and there is gonadal dysgenesis. The comparison of behavioural and psychological features in androgenised females and in cases of Turner's syndrome made by Money and Ehrhardt (1968) is most instructive.

The particular interest of the processes and determinants of sexual differentiation to psychologists lies in the fact that it is not merely the reproductive structures which are organised in a typically male or female pattern, but higher neural centres as well. Characteristic differences appear, therefore, in patterns of sexual behaviour as well as in non-sexual behaviour. The behavioural differences are particularly striking in the higher mammals, namely, the primates (see Hamburg and Lunde, 1966; Goy, 1966, 1968, for informative reviews).

PHYSICAL GROWTH, MATURATION, AND SUSCEPTIBILITY

From very early in uterine life males show their characteristic vulnerability: an average of 120 males are conceived for every 100 females and by term this ratio has decreased to 110 : 100 (Glenister, 1956). The majority of spontaneous abortions (miscarriages), therefore, are of male foetuses (Stevenson and McClarin, 1957). In terms of live births the ratio is only 106 : 100, which indicates a greater male susceptibility to perinatal complications such as anoxia (Stevenson, 1966; Stevenson and Bobrow, 1967). Throughout life males remain more vulnerable to a variety of disorders, e.g., cerebral palsy, viral infections, ulcers, coronary thrombosis and some forms of mental illness (Taylor and Ounsted, 1972; Garai, 1970). In fact the male's longevity is so curtailed that by the 6th and 7th decades of life the sex ratio is reversed in favour of the females. The sex-linked recessive disorders like hemophilia and colour-blindness predominantly affect the males; the recessive genes being carried on the X chromosome, males manifest the disorder even in the heterozygotic condition, whereas females are protected, other than in the homozygous condition, by the normal allele on the other X chromosome. The adage of the male being the stronger sex requires a very literal interpretation indeed.

At birth, males are heavier and longer than females (Ounsted, 1972). From infancy on boys have a consistently higher basal metabolism and greater vital capacity, develop proportionately larger hearts and lungs, and have a higher concentration of hemoglobin, notably after puberty (Hutt, 1972). Moreover, the male hormone facilitates protein synthesis whereas the female hormones have no such direct action. All these features characterise the male for a more active and strenuous life.

In sharp contrast to his physical advantages, however, is the male's developmental retardation: growth velocity lags nearly 2 years behind the female's (Tanner, 1970), bone ossification is completed much later (see Hutt, 1972b) and puberty is attained about 2½ years after the girl (Nicholson and Hanley, 1953). The onset of walking and talking, as well as aspects of dentition occur earlier in girls than in boys. In terms of maturity the newborn girl is equivalent to a 4- to 6-week-old boy (Garai and Scheinfeld, 1968).

BEHAVIOUR DIFFERENCES IN INFANCY

MOTOR ACTIVITY AND SENSORY CAPACITIES

In general, male newborn infants exhibit more spontaneous motor activity and this consists predominantly of gross movements, whereas the activity of the female infants consists typically of finer movements, largely of the facial area, e.g., mouthing, smiling or sucking (Korner, 1969). Female neonates have lower tactual and pain thresholds (Lipsitt and Levy, 1959), and this sex difference very probably obtains throughout the lifespan since Galton observed it in adults and specifically commented upon it as early as 1894. Female infants also react more irritably to tactual stimulation (Bell and Costello, 1964).

There is now substantial evidence that the visual acuity of males is superior to that of females, at least from adolescence on (Burg and Hulbert, 1961), whereas females have better auditory discrimination and localisation (Corso, 1959; Schaie et al., 1964). The results obtained by Lewis suggest that such sensory proficiency and preferences may be evident even in early infancy: he found that

male infants showed greater interest in visual patterns generally, while female infants attended more to auditory sequences (Kagan and Lewis, 1965); of visual patterns female infants found *facial* configurations most interesting and at 3, 6 and 9 months of age they were able to differentiate between such patterns more effectively than the males (Lewis, 1969).

On the basis of results obtained from 3-month-old infants, Moss and Robson (1970) concluded that, whereas social experience and learning appeared to have a strong influence upon the visual behaviour of females, that of the males was more a function of endogenous attributes like state. These several results illustrate not merely the sex-dependent sensory capacities but also the differences in those influences to which they are amenable. Such differences, however, are not peculiar to the human species—very similar behaviour is shown by monkeys (Mitchell and Brandt, 1970).

The early dependence on particular sensory modalities has the consequence that auditory and visual stimuli have different reinforcing properties, depending on the sex of the subject. For instance, Watson (1969) found that visual fixation on a target could be operantly conditioned in 14-week-old infants, the effective reinforcers being visual for males and auditory for females. Moreover, the boys failed to learn under conditions of auditory reinforcement. This reliance of males and females on visual and auditory channels, respectively, is observable throughout childhood and adolescence (Stevenson et al., 1963) and persists in adulthood (Miller, 1963; Pishkin and Shurley, 1965).

MOTHER–INFANT INTERACTION

The earliest social behaviour displayed by the human infant is in the context of the mother–infant interaction. Many studies reporting differences in the way mothers handle their male and female infants, or for that matter, any sex differences in human behaviour, tend to account for such differences in terms of the mothers' expectations of a son or a daughter, of her greater affinity for the same-sex infant, or else in terms of the reinforcement of sex-appropriate behaviours. A study by Moss (1967) is notable, therefore, for the demonstration that considerable differences in the behaviour of male and female infants exist at the age of 3 weeks. The differential reactions of the mother are very probably contingent upon these behaviours and not contrariwise, as commonly supposed. Two of Moss' findings seem particularly significant, especially since they were also apparent at the age of 3 months: mothers stimulated their infant sons more, and imitated the vocalisations of their daughters more. The first of these raises the interesting possibility that we may have here the human analogue of the "early-handled" animals described by Levine (1960), Denenberg (1964) and others. If such findings are replicated, we may seriously have to inquire whether the early experience of male infants in any way contributes to their subsequent lower emotionality (Gray, 1971a; Gray and Buffery, 1971; Buffery and Gray, 1972). Secondly, the fact that mothers imitated, and thereby very probably reinforced, their daughters' vocalisations is surprising, since the actual amounts of vocalisation by boys and by girls were almost identical. Since a similar finding was also reported by Goldberg and Lewis (1969), it immediately raises the question as to what parameters of infants' vocal behaviour the mothers were responding. May this fact also explain, in part, the earlier acquisition of speech in girls?

Goldberg and Lewis (1969) were able to demonstrate striking sex differences in infants of 13 months, both in their behaviour towards their mothers as well as in the character of their play. Girls were more reluctant than boys to leave their mothers, tended to stay near them when playing and sought physical reassurance more frequently.

FEAR

Analysing data from the Berkeley Growth Study, Bronson (1969) found sex differences in the onset of the fear-of-stranger reaction: fear at 10–15 months was positively correlated with fear and shyness at a later age in *boys* but not in girls. This was chiefly due to a sub-group of boys who showed a precocious onset of fear (4–6 months) and remained so throughout childhood. Thus, an early onset of fear-of-novelty in male infants was predictive of fearfulness during the entire preschool period.

BEHAVIOURAL DIFFERENCES IN CHILDHOOD

SOCIAL INTERACTIONS

In an investigation of the types of activity boys and girls generally engaged in (Brindley et al., 1972), it was found that girls engaged in social interactions much more frequently than boys—a dramatic illustration of the early differentiation of masculine and feminine interests, boys being interested in objects or "things" and girls in people (Little, 1968). Honzik (1951) and Hattwick (1937) observed very similar differences in older children, as did Farrell (1957).

More specifically, *aggression* is an aspect of social behavior that has interested many students of child behavior and a number of studies have shown boys to be more aggressive than girls (Green, 1933; Dawe, 1934; Jersild and Markey, 1935; Hattwick, 1937; Walters et al., 1957; Jegard and Walters, 1960; Bandura et al., 1963; Digman, 1963; Pederson and Belling, 1970). Many of these results, however, were interpreted in terms of sex-role expectations and conventions, with no reference made to the fact that the males of most mammalian species are more aggressive than the females, nor was surprise expressed at the apparent universality of male aggression—despite differences in culture-patterns, conventions and social norms. In our own study of nursery school children (Brindley et al., 1972), we found that two thirds of all aggressive acts were initiated by boys. Moreover, not only did boys *display* more aggression, but they also *elicited* aggression. Many of such disputes arose over the possession of toys, equipment or territory. Girls, whose aggression generally found verbal expression, were equally aggressive to other girls, boys, teachers or objects. Boys retaliated more and hence prolonged such encounters whereas the girls usually submitted or else employed more devious strategies to secure their objectives (McCandless et al., 1961). These sex-dependent features of aggression are observable in older children as well as in adults. In experiments which allowed subjects to mete out punishment to a mock opponent, adult males gave bigger shocks when they thought their opponent was a male than when they thought it was a female (Buss, 1963; Taylor and Epstein,

1967). In a similar experiment, 10- and 11-year-olds, using noise as punishment, behaved exactly as the adults had done (Shortell and Biller, 1970).

Male monkeys engage in threat displays while the females show fear grimaces, and in a male monkey group the dominance hierarchy is established by the aggressive behaviour and threat displays of the ascendant male while in female groups the hierarchy is established and maintained by the submissive behaviours of the non-dominant females (Angermeier et al., 1968). Thus, when the human results are considered in the general context of primate social behaviour, any purely cultural or environmental sex-role theory of sexual differentiation becomes difficult to countenance. Elsewhere (Hutt, 1972a, b), I have also presented the experimental evidence regarding aggressive behaviour as primarily a function of the early sexual differentiation of the brain, and secondarily as an effect of circulating hormone levels.

Another aspect of early social behaviour that we studied was cooperative or mutual behaviour (Brindley et al., 1972), where children joined each other, either spontaneously or at the request of one of them, to engage in some mutual activity. Girls initiated such acts much more than boys, and directed their attention in this respect predominantly towards *younger* children (chiefly girls), thus manifesting their proclivities for fulfilling a nurturant and protective role (Mischel, 1970). This is evident in many ways: readiness to help younger ones carry things, to button pinafores or tie aprons, and to comfort a hurt or distressed child. The boys appear to show a remarkable indifference to a peer's discomfort or distress. McGrew (1972) has also described the characteristic tendency of the girls to shepherd and care for a new entrant to the nursery group, whereas boys manifest their customary indifference to such a newcomer. The boys in our study tended to direct their cooperative acts primarily towards other *older* boys, usually attempting to join a game or excursion already in progress. Similar sex-typical behaviours have been described in many infra-human primate groups too (DeVore and Jay, 1963; Harlow, 1962; Goodall, 1968).

In general, there is a marked tendency in humans—children and adults alike (Hutt, 1972; Tiger, 1969)—to interact with others of their own sex. The men's club, the officers' mess, the women's in-stitute, all clearly have their ontogenetic origins in the kindergartens and their phylogenetic origins in diverse primate groups. . . .

CONCLUDING DISCUSSION

The foregoing discussion of the process of sexual differentiation and the phenomena of sex differences has been an attempt to reiterate the many biological and psychological differences that characteristically differentiate males and females in our species. These particular properties have clearly been selected in accordance with, on the one hand, certain morphological features, and on the other, with the particular roles human males and females fulfill. That these morphological and functional requirements are not unique to a particular society, nor even to the human species is evident in the fact that very similar differences are demonstrable in infra-human primate species. This fact alone makes an exclusively environmental theory of sex differences difficult to countenance. Moreover, as Buffery and Gray (1972) point out, such similarities behoove us to seek a more appropriately biological explanation for the phenomena. Gray himself has discussed the endocrinological, neural and adaptive bases for sex differences in mammals generally (Gray, 1971a, b; Gray and Buffery, 1971; Buffery and Gray, 1972). The evidence reviewed by both Gray and myself (Hutt, 1972) shows that not only is behaviour affected by circulating hormones, but that these hormones have an important formative and organisational influence on brain function and structure.

It is a common, but nonetheless fallacious, assumption that the recognition of individual differences, be they sex- or personality-dependent, is to commit oneself to a psychological or behavioural determinism. On the contrary, the recognition of such differences and their possible determinants enables individuals to modify and/or exploit environmental circumstances to profitable advantage.

The conformity and consistency of the female's behaviour in fulfilling a predominantly nurturant role makes her a stable and reliable support for the dependent infant. Even her distractability (Garai and Scheinfeld, 1968) appears to be adaptive. In her intellectual faculties too the human female seems to have exploited those facets that ensure the optimal execution of her primary role—the maternal role. For more effective communication increasing reliance is placed on linguistic skills, and it is noteworthy that in verbal functions as in non-verbal ones, it is in *execution* that the female excels. The male on the other hand, and necessarily, excels in spatial and numerical abilities, is divergent in thought and action, and is generally superior in *conceptualisation*. The fact that such functional dimorphism exists may be unacceptable to many, but it is a dimorphism that has been uniquely successful.

REFERENCES

Angermeier, W. F.; Phelps, J. B.; Murray, S. and Howanstine, J.: Dominance in monkeys: sex differences. Psychon. Sci. 12: 344 (1968).

Bandura, A.; Ross, D. and Ross, S. A.: Transmission of aggression through imitation of aggressive models. J. abnorm. soc. Psychol. 63: 575–582 (1961).

Bayley, N.: Developmental problems of the mentally retarded child; in Philips: Prevention and treatment of mental retardation (Basic Books, New York 1966).

Bayley, N. and Schaefer, E. S.: Correlations of maternal and child behaviours with the development of mental abilities: data from the Berkeley Growth Study. Monogr. Soc. Res. Child Develop. 29: 1–80 (1964).

Bell, R. Q. and Costello, N. S.: Three tests for sex differences in tactile sensitivity in the newborn. Biol. Neonat. 7: 335–347 (1964).

Bennett, G. K.; Seashore, H. G. and Wesman, A. G.: Differential aptitude tests. Manual, 3rd ed. (Psychological Corporation, New York 1959).

Bhavnani, R. and Hutt, C.: Divergent thinking in boys and girls. J. child Psychol. Psychiat. (1972, in press).

Bongiovanni, A. M. and Root, A. W.: The adrenogenital syndrome. New Engl. J. Med. 268: 1283 (1963).

Brindley, C.; Clarke, P.; Hutt, C.; Robinson, I. and

Wethli, E.: Sex differences in the activities and social interactions of nursery school children; in Michael and Crook: Comparative ecology and behaviour of primates (Academic Press, London 1972, in press).

Bronson, G. W.: Fear of visual novelty: developmental patterns in males and females. Develop. Psychol. 1: 33–40 (1969).

Buffery, A. W. H.: Sex differences in cognitive skills. Paper Ann. Conf. Brit. Psychol. Soc., Exeter; in Symp. on Biological bases of psychological sex differences (1971).

Buffery, A. W. H. and Gray, J. A.: Sex differences in the development of perceptual and linguistic skills; in Ounsted and Taylor: Gender differences—their ontogeny and significance (Churchill, London 1972).

Burg, A. and Hulbert, S.: Dynamic visual acuity as related to age, sex and static acuity. J. appl. Psychol. 45: 111–116 (1961).

Buss, A. H.: Physical aggression in relation to different frustrations. J. abnorm. soc. Psychol. 67: 1–7 (1963).

Carlson, E. R. and Carlson, R.: Male and female subjects in personality research. J. abnorm. soc. Psychol. 61: 482–483 (1960).

Clark, A. H.; Wyon, S. M. and Richards, M. P.: Free-play in nursery school children. J. child Psychol. Psychiat. 10: 205–216 (1969).

Corso, J. F.: Age and sex differences in pure-tone thresholds. J. acoust. Soc. Amer. 31: 489–507 (1959).

Dawe, H. C.: An analysis of 200 quarrels of pre-school children. Child Develop. 5: 139–156 (1934).

Denenberg, V. H.: Animal studies on developmental determinants of behavioural adaptability; in Harvey: Experience, structure and adaptability, pp. 123–147 (Springer, New York 1966).

De Vore, I. and Jay, P.: Mother-infant relations in baboons and langurs; in Rheingold: Maternal behaviour in mammals (Wiley & Sons, 1963).

Diamond, M.: A critical evaluation of the ontogeny of human sexual behaviour. Quart. Rev. Biol. 40: 147–175 (1965).

Digman, J. M.: Principal dimensions of child personality as inferred from teachers' judgments. Child Develop. 34: 43–60 (1963).

Farrell, M.: Sex differences in block play in early childhood education. J. educ. Res. 51: 279–284 (1957).

Federman, M. D.: Abnormal sexual development (Saunders, Philadelphia 1967).

Galton, F.: The relative sensitivity of men and women at the nape of the neck by Webster's test. Nature, Lond. 50: 40–42 (1894).

Garai, J. E.: Sex differences in mental health. Genet. Psychol. Monogr. 81: 123–142 (1970).

Garai, J. E. and Scheinfeld, A.: Sex differences in mental and behavioural traits. Genet. Psychol. Monogr. 77: 169–299 (1968).

Glenister, T. W.: Determination of sex in early human embryos. Nature, Lond. 177: 1135 (1956).

Goldberg, S. and Lewis, M.: Play behaviour in the year-old infant: early sex differences. Child Develop. 40: 21–31 (1969).

Goodall, J. L. van: The behaviour of free-living chimpanzees in the Gombi Stream Reserve. Anim. Behav. Monogr. 1: 161–311 (1968).

Gorski, R. A. and Wagner, J. W.: Gonadal activity and sexual differentiation of the hypothalamus. Endocrinology 76: 226–239 (1965).

Goy, R. W.: Role of androgens in the establishment and regulation of behavioural sex differences in mammals. J. anim. Sci. 25: suppl., pp. 21–35 (1966).

Goy, R. W.: Organising effects of androgen on the behaviour of rhesus monkeys; in Michael: Endocrinology and human behaviour (Oxford University Press, London 1968).

Gray, J. A.: Sex differences in emotional behaviour in mammals including man: endocrine bases. Acta psychol., Amst. 35: 29–46 (1971a).

Gray, J. A.: The psychology of fear and stress (Weidenfeld and Nicolson, London, 1971b).

Gray, J. A. and Buffery, A. W. H.: Sex differences in emotional and cognitive behaviour in mammals including man: adaptive and neural bases. Acta psychol., Amst. 35: 89–111 (1971).

Green, E. H.: Friendships and quarrels among pre-school children. Child Develop. 4: 236–252 (1933).

Hamburg, D. A. and Lunde, D. T.: Sex hormones in the development of sex differences in human behaviour; in Maccoby: The development of sex differences (Tavistock, London 1966).

Harlow, H. F.: Development of affection in primates; in Bliss: Roots of behaviour (Harper, New York 1962).

Harris, G. W.: Sex hormones, brain development and brain function. Endocrinology 75: 627–648 (1964).

Harris, G. W.: Hormonal differentiation of the developing central nervous system with respect to patterns of endocrine function. Philos. Trans. B 259: 165–177 (1970).

Hattwick, L. A.: Sex differences in behavior of nursery school children. Child Develop. 8: 343–355 (1937).

Heilman, J. D.: Sex differences in intellectual abilities. J. educ. Psychol. 24: 47–62 (1933).

Hobson, J. R.: Sex differences in primary mental abilities. J. educ. Res. 41: 126–132 (1947).

Honzik, M. P.: Sex differences in the occurrence of materials in the play constructions of pre-adolescents. Child Develop. 22: 15–35 (1951).

Hudson, L.: Contrary imaginations (Methuen, London 1966).

Hudson, L.: Frames of mind (Methuen, London 1968).

Hutt, C.: Specific and diversive exploration; in Reese and Lipsitt: Advances in child development and behaviour, vol. 5 (Academic Press, London 1970a).

Hutt, C.: Curiosity in young children. Sci. J. 6: 68–72 (1970b).

Hutt, C.: Neuroendocrinological, behavioural and intellectual aspects of sexual differentiation in human development; in Ounsted and Taylor: Gender differences—their ontogeny and significance (Churchill, London 1972a).

Hutt, C.: Males and females (Penguin Books, 1972b, in press).

Jegard, S. and Walters, R. H.: A study of some determinants of aggression in young children. Child Develop. 31: 739–747 (1960).

Jersild, A. T. and Markey, F. V.: Conflicts between preschool children. Child Develop. Monogr. 21 (1935).

Kagan, J. and Lewis, M.: Studies of attention in the human infant. Behav. Develop. 11: 95–127 (1965).

Klein, V.: The demand for professional Woman I power. Brit. J. Sociol. 17: 183 (1966).

Korner, A. F.: Neonatal startles, smiles, erections, and reflex sucks as related to state, sex and individuality. Child Develop. 40: 1039–1053 (1969).

Levine, S.: Stimulation in infancy. Sci. Amer. 202: 80–86 (1960).

Levine, S.: Sex differences in the brain. Sci. Amer. 214: 84–90 (1966).

Lewis, M.: Infants' responses to facial stimuli during the first year of life. Dev. Psychol. 1: 75–86 (1969).

Lipsitt, L. P. and Levy, N.: Electrotactual threshold in the neonate. Child Develop. 30: 547–554 (1959).

Little, B.: Psychospecialisation: functions of differential interest in persons and things. Bull. Brit. psychol. Soc. 21: 113A (1968).

Maccoby, E. E. (ed.): The development of sex differences (Tavistock, London 1966).

McCandless, B. R.; Bilous, B. and Bennett, H. L.: Peer popularity and dependence on adults in preschool age socialisation. Child Develop. 32: 511–518 (1961).

McGrew, W. C.: Aspects of social development in nursery school children with emphasis on introduction to the group; in Blurton-Jones: Ethological studies of child behaviour (Cambridge University Press, London 1972).

Michael, R. P.: The endocrinological bases of sex differences. Paper Ann. Conf. Brit. Psychol. Soc., Exeter, in Symp. on Biological bases of psychological sex differences (1971).

Miller, A.: Sex differences related to the effect of auditory stimulation on the stability of visually fixed forms. Percept. Mot. Skills 16: 589–594 (1963).

Mischel, W.: Sex-typing and socialisation; in Mussen: Carmichael's manual of child psychology, vol. 2 (Wiley, London 1970).

Mitchell, G. and Brandt, E. M.: Behavioural differences related to experience of mother and sex of infant in the rhesus monkey. Develop. Psychol. 3: 149 (1970).

Money, J. and Ehrhardt, A. A.: Prenatal hormonal exposure: possible effects on behaviour in man; in Michael: Endocrinology and human behaviour (Oxford University Press, London 1968).

Moore, T.: Language and intelligence: a longitudinal study of the first 8 years I. Patterns of development in boys and girls. Human Develop. 10: 88–106 (1967).

Moss, H.: Sex, age and state as determinants of mother infant interaction. Merrill-Palmer Quart. 13: 19–36 (1967).

Moss, H. A. and Robson, K. S.: The relation between the amount of time infants spend at various states and the development of visual behaviour. Child Develop. 41: 509–517 (1970).

Nicolson, A. B. and Hanley, C.: Indices of physiological maturity: derivation and interrelationships. Child Develop. 24: 3–38 (1953).

Ounsted, C. and Taylor, D. C.: The Y chromosome message: a point of view; in Ounsted and Taylor: Gender differences—their ontogeny and significance (Churchill, London 1972).

Ounsted, M.: Sex differences in intrauterine growth; in Ounsted and Taylor: Gender differences—their ontogeny and significance (Churchill, London 1972).

Pedersen, F. A. and Bell, R. Q.: Sex differences in preschool children without histories of complications of pregnancy and delinquency. Develop. Psychol. 3: 10–15 (1970).

Pishkin, V. and Shurley, J. T.: Auditory dimensions and irrelevant information in concept identification of males and females. Percept. Mot. Skills 20: 673–683 (1965).

Schaie, K. W.; Baltes, P. and Strother, C. R.: A study of auditory sensitivity in advanced age. J. Geront. 19: 453–457 (1964).

Shortell, J. R. and Biller, H. B.: Aggression in children as a function of sex of subject and sex of opponent. Develop. Psychol. 3: 143–144 (1970).

Shouksmith, G.: Intelligence, creativity and cognitive style (Batsford, London 1970).

Stevenson, A. C.: Sex chromatin and the sex ratio in man; in Moore: The sex chromatin (Saunders, Philadelphia 1966).

Stevenson, A. C. and Bobrow, M.: Determinants of sex proportions in man, with consideration of the evidence concerning a contribution from x-linked mutations to intrauterine death. J. med. Genet. 4: 190–221 (1967).

Stevenson, A. C. and McClarin, R. H.: Determination of the sex of human abortions by nuclear sexing the cells of the chorionic. Nature, Lond. 180: 198 (1957).

Stevenson, H. W.; Keen, R. and Knights, R. W.: Parents and strangers as reinforcing agents for children's performance. J. abnorm. soc. Psychol. 67: 183–186 (1963).

Tanner, J. M.: Physical growth; in Mussen: Carmichael's manual of child psychology, 3rd ed. (Wiley, New York 1970).

Taylor, D. C.: Differential rates of cerebral maturation between sexes and between hemispheres. Lancet iii: 140–142 (1969).

Taylor, D. C. and Ounsted, C.: The nature of gender differences explored through ontogenetic analyses of sex ratios in disease; in Ounsted and Taylor: Gender differences—their ontogeny and significance (Churchill, London, 1972).

Taylor, S. P. and Epstein, S.: Aggression as a function of the interaction of the sex of the aggressor and sex of the victim. J. Personality 35: 474–486 (1967).

Tiger, L.: Men in groups (Nelson, London 1969).

Tyler, L.: The psychology of human differences, 3rd ed. (Appleton-Century-Crofts, New York 1965).

Wallach, M. A. and Kogan, N.: Modes of thinking in young children (Holt, Rinehart & Winston, New York 1965).

Walters, J.; Pearce, D. and Dahms, L.: Affectional and aggressive behaviour of preschool children. Child Develop. 28: 15–26 (1957).

Watson, T. S.: Operant conditioning of visual fixation in infants under visual and auditory reinforcement. Develop. Psychol. 1: 508–516 (1969).

Wechsler, D.: The measurement of adult intelligence (Williams & Wilkins, Baltimore 1941).

Wechsler, D.: The measurement and appraisal of adult intelligence, 4th ed. (Williams & Wilkins, Baltimore 1958).

Werner, E. E.: Sex differences in correlations between children's IQ and measures of parental ability, and environmental ratings. Develop. Psychol. 1: 280–285 (1969).

Whalen, R. E.: Differentiation of the neural mechanisms which control gonadotropin secretion and sexual behaviour; in Diamond: Reproduction and sexual behaviour (Indiana University Press, Bloomington 1968).

Wilkins, L.: Adrenal disorders. II. Congenital virilizing adrenal hyperplasia. Arch. Dis. Childh. 37: 231 (1962).

Chapter Ten · family influences and child-rearing outcomes

36

The American Family: Future Uncertain

Time magazine

EDITOR'S NOTE · The American family seems to be undergoing change, although it is difficult at this point to know the direction that the change is taking. For every three couples who marry, another couple are granted a divorce. Although the divorce rate is rising, the rate of remarriage among divorced people is also rising. Marriage does not seem to be the issue; evidence suggests that as many people as ever marry. The issue is the traditional idea of the family, which used to be a natural and hoped for consequence of marriage. Why is the concept of the family changing? What impact has the women's liberation movement had on the family? How has the family been influenced by increased mobility? Has the "pill" exerted an influence? These and other questions are addressed in this interesting article. How important is the concept of the family to you?

"The American Family: Future Uncertain," *Time*, December 28, 1970. Reprinted by permission from *Time*, The Weekly Newsmagazine; Copyright © Time Inc.

America's families are in trouble —"trouble so deep and pervasive as to threaten the future of our nation," declared a major report to last week's White House Conference on Children. "Can the family survive?" asks anthropologist Margaret Mead rhetorically. "Students in rebellion, the young people living in communes, unmarried couples living together call into question the very meaning and structure of the stable family unit as our society has known it." The family, says California psychologist Richard Farson, "is now often without function. It is no longer necessarily the basic unit in our society."

The data of doom—many familiar, some still startling—consistently seem to support this concern. One in every four U.S. marriages eventually ends in divorce. The rate is rising dramatically for marriages made in the past several years, and in some densely populated West Coast communities is running as high as 70%. The birth rate has declined from 30.1 births per thousand in 1910 to 17.7 in 1969, and while this is a healthy development in many respects, it implies considerable change in family life and values. Each year, an estimated half-million teen-agers run away from home.

ENORMOUS CRISES

The crisis in the family has implications that extend far beyond the walls of the home. "No society has ever survived after its family life deteriorated," warns Dr. Paul Popenoe, founder of the American Institute of Family Relations. Harvard Professor Emeritus Carle Zimmerman has stated the most pessimistic view: "The extinction of faith in the familistic system is identical with the movements in Greece during the century following the Peloponnesian Wars, and in Rome from about A.D. 150. In each case the change in the faith and belief in family systems was associated with rapid adoption of negative reproduction rates and with enormous crises in the very civilizations themselves."

It is not necessary to share this apocalyptic decline-and-fall theory to recognize many interrelated dangers to both society and family. Each of the nation's forces of change and conflict meet within the family. The "counterculture" of the young, the effects of the war, economic stresses and the decay of the cities—all crowd in on the narrow and embattled institution. The question, of course, is not whether the family will "survive," for that is like asking whether man or biology or society will survive. The question is whether it can survive successfully in its present form. All the evidence shows that in order to do so, it needs help.

Precisely that was uppermost in the minds of 4,000 delegates from across the nation who met in Washington last week for the once-in-a-decade Conference on Children. Among the proposals they urged on President Nixon were the establishment of a National Institute for the Family; universal day-care, health and early learning services in which parents would play a major role; the creation of a Cabinet-level Department of Family and Children; and an independent Office of Child Advocacy. There was also a lavish list of demands—though more modest than the one ten years ago—covering everything from prevention of child injuries to reforming the judiciary system.

WEAKENED SUPPORTS

Yet if the demands made on the Government on behalf of the family were too vast, this was in a sense only an understandable reaction against the fact that too many vast demands are made on the family these days. Throughout most of Western history, until the 20th century, society as a whole strongly supported the family institution. It was the family's duty to instruct children in moral values, but it derived those values from church, from philosophers, from social traditions. Now most of these supports are weakened, or gone. Yet politicians and other prophets often blame the family for decline in morals and morale—as if the family could be separated from society. The forces that are weakening the U.S. family structure are at the very heart of the changes that are taking place in American civilization. Some of the most significant:

Mobility. The mass exodus from rural to metropolitan areas, the increasingly common and frequent corporate transfer, the convenience of the automobile and the highway system built to accommodate it—all have contributed to a basic change in the character of the family. In the less complicated, less urbanized days, the average U.S. family was an "extended" or "kinship" family. This meant simply that the parents and their children were surrounded by relatives: in-laws, brothers, sisters, aunts, uncles, grandparents, cousins. If the relatives did not live within the same household, they were next door or down the block or on the next farm. But as Americans became more mobile, the kinfolk have been gradually left behind. As a result, the typical family has evolved into an isolated "nuclear" family. It consists simply of a father, a mother and their children, and is usually located miles away from the home of the nearest relative.

Says Dr. John Platt, associate director of the University of Michigan's Mental Health Research Institute: "All sorts of roles now have to be played by the husband and wife, whereas in the older, extended family they had all sorts of help—psychological support, financial advice, and so on. The pressures of these multiple roles are partially responsible for the high rates of divorce, alcoholism, tranquilizers, etc."

Women's Changing Role. "Put very simply," says Cornell Political Sociologist Andrew Hacker, "the major change in the family in recent years, and the problems of the future, are both summed up in one word: women. In the past and until very recently, wives were simply supplementary to their husbands, and not expected to be full human beings. Today, women are involved in much greater expectations and frustrations. For one thing, 40% of U.S. women are now employed. When a woman is working, she tends to have a new perception of herself. I see this most egregiously in those women who go to liberal arts colleges, because there the professor takes them seriously, and this gives them big ideas. The unhappiest wives are the liberal arts graduates. The trouble comes from the fact that the institution we call marriage can't hold two full human beings—it was only designed for one and a half."

It is not only woman's aspirations that have changed, Hacker adds, but society's support of her as a wife. "In the past, the role of wife and mother was reinforced by the church and community. The whole complex descended on women and said, 'This is what you are; this is what you will be.' Now marriage has to be on its own, because the reinforcements are no longer there. So women are listening to all the subversive messages."

One Women's Lib theoretician, Margaret Benston, has made an economic analysis that places the blame for the "exploitation" of women directly on the family. Since women's work in the home is not paid for, she reasons, it is considered valueless by society. Moreover, at present, equal opportunity of employment simply means that a woman has two jobs: one at work and one at home. All work must therefore be taken out of the home and paid for like any other product; only such innovations as communal kitchens and universal child-care centers will "set women free," she says.

Apotheosis of Childhood. In the Middle Ages, children were considered miniature adults, according to French Sociologist Philippe Aries. At about the age of seven, they were sent to other homes to serve as apprentices and often as servants. Thus they grew up in huge households, with no dependence on their parents. In contrast, the child of today, as the center of the tiny nuclear family, has become its *raison d'être* and is therefore kept psychologically, financially and emotionally bound to it.

Without realizing it, many American mothers, under the aegis of benevolent permissiveness and the pressure of civic obligations, actually neglect their children. Others, imbued by Dr. Spock with the notion that every child has a unique potential and that it is her mission to create a near-perfect being, become the child's shadow, with equally damaging results, according to Brandeis Sociologist Philip Slater. The child soon recognizes that he is the center of an extraordinary effort and that his happiness is a matter of great stakes. He will seldom turn out exactly as planned, and when family dissension ensues, the mother will resent her "sacrifices." Moreover, though she may have brought up her child to be "more cultured, less money-grubbing, more spontaneous and creative" than she

herself was brought up to be, she is nevertheless upset when he then refuses to remain on the same treadmill as his parents.

That refusal takes place in adolescence, which like childhood is a modern development. Thus the family has had no long historical experience in dealing with the new rebelliousness. Unlike youths of the pre-industrial age, who simply entered some form of apprenticeship for the adult world at the age of puberty, millions of teen-agers now remain outside the labor force to go to college. It is this fact that has made possible the existence of today's separate youth culture, by which parents feel surrounded and threatened in their sense of authority. "A stage of life that barely existed a century ago is now universally accepted as an inherent part of the human condition," says Yale Psychiatrist Kenneth Keniston. Keniston, in fact, now postulates still another new stage of life, that between adolescence and adulthood: he calls it "youth." The youth of the technetronic or post-industrial age often remain out of the work force until their late 20s. "They are still questioning family tradition, family destiny, family fate, family culture and family curse." Naturally, their very existence unsettles the families from which they sprang, and delays the development of the new life-styles that they will eventually adopt.

Limited Usefulness. According to Sociologist Reuben Hill, among others, the family has traditionally performed seven functions: reproduction, protection and care of children, economic production of family goods and services, socialization of children, education of children, recreation, and affection giving. But during the past century, he says, the economic, educational, recreational and socializing functions have been lost in varying degrees to industry, schools and government.

In three areas of traditional family life there has been little erosion: reproduction, child care, affection. As a matter of fact, many experts believe that the affectional function is the only one left that justifies the continued support of the family as a social institution. As "community contacts" become more "formal and segmental," says Hill, people turn increasingly to the family "as the source of affectional security that we all crave."

But the insistent demand for affection without the traditional supporting structure has dangers of its own. The pioneering sociologist Edward Westermarck observed that "marriage rests in the family and not the family in marriage." The corollary used to be that the family existed for many practical purposes beyond love. To base it so heavily on love —including the variable pleasures of sexual love— is to weaken its stability.

MOTHER'S KISS

A related danger is to romanticize and sentimentalize the family. From the Greek tragedians to the modern psychoanalysts, men have known that the family, along with being a source of immense comfort, is also a place of savage battles, rivalries, and psychological if not physical mayhem. Psychoanalyst R. D. Laing says that the "initial act of brutality against the average child is the mother's first kiss." He finds it hurtful that a child is completely at the mercy of his parents, even to having to accept affection. Laing's colleague, David Cooper, calls the nuclear family the "ultimately perfected form of non-meeting" and, in a new book called *The Death of the Family*, demands its abolition. These are extreme views, but it may be better to face the fierce aspects of family life than to expect only bliss. There is something of the disillusioned lover in many people who today are trying to live outside the conventional family.

Dissatisfied with the traditional family setup, or simply unable to cope with it, Americans by the thousands are seeking alternatives. One that has most captured the imagination of youth and that has an almost religious appeal to members of the counterculture is a family structure that is as old as antiquity: the commune. Utopians from Plato onward have visualized children as not being raised in traditional families but in various communal organizations; the instinct that pulls man toward a tightly knit "nuclear" family has often been counterbalanced by the dream of escaping from it.

Only five years ago, there were perhaps a hundred "intentional communities" in the U.S., founded mostly by religious fundamentalists, utopian socialists or conscientious objectors. Today, as an outgrowth of the hippie movement, there are about 3,000, a third of which are in rural settings. "There are farms everywhere now, and we might go in any direction on compass to find warm bread

and salt," writes Raymond Mungo in *Total Loss Farm*. Although Vermont, Oregon, California and New Mexico are still the favored states, some new commune clusters are cropping up in what Mungo calls "the relatively inferior terrain and vibration of Massachusetts and points south and west, and the huge strain of friendless middle America."

Most of the new communards are fleeing what they regard as the constriction, loneliness, materialism and the hypocrisy in straight society and the family life on which it is based. Yet some of the same old problems reappear—for example, the tug of war between individualism and submission to the group. One contributor to the *Whole Earth Catalog* summed up his own experience. "If the intentional community hopes to survive, it must be authoritarian, and if it is authoritarian, it offers no more freedom than conventional society. Those communes based on freedom inevitably fail, usually within a year."

But when they fail, their members often go on to join other tribes, now that there is a network of communes available to them. Benjamin Zablocki, a Berkeley sociologist who has visited more than 100 communes in the past six years, insists: "The children are incredibly fine. It's natural for children to be raised in extended families, where there are many adults." Yet in spite of the talk of extended families, the extension in the new communes does not reach to a third generation. Indeed, the "families" have a narrow age span, and it is possible that the children have never seen an adult over 30.

DEFORMED MONSTROSITY

Writes Brandeis' Sociologist Philip Slater, in *The Pursuit of Loneliness*: "It is ironic that young people who try to form communes almost always create the same narrow, age-graded, class-homogeneous society in which they were formed. A community that does not have old people and children, white-collar and blue-collar, eccentric and conventional, and so on, is not a community at all, but the same kind of truncated and deformed monstrosity that most people inhabit today."

Some communes actually form compromises with the nuclear family. Nowhere is this point better made than at Lama, a contemporary commune 18 miles north of Taos, N. Mex., which was re-revisited last week by Correspondent David De-Voss after an absence of 19 months.

"We work together—we collectively grow and distribute the crops, but we go back to our individual nests at night," explains Satya De La Manitov, 28, who has now moved from a tepee into a still unfinished A-frame house that took him $1,500 and twelve months to build. Most couples are in their upper 20s, are married, have children, own their own homes, have a deep respect for property rights and believe in the value of honest toil. Although the concept of complete sexual freedom retains its followers, it plays only a minor role in Lama society today. Indeed, reports DeVoss, "were it not for their long hair, predilection for grass and rejection of the American political system, Lama residents could pass for solid, middle-class citizens."

Most of today's communes are in the cities, and they indeed do have appeal for many middle-class citizens. To Ethel Herring, 30, married to a Los Angeles lawyer and active in Women's Lib, a city commune seemed the answer to growing frustrations, which culminated when she realized that she was spending $60 to $70 a week for baby sitters; the Herrings had no live-in grandparents or nearby relatives to care for their three children while Ethel was attending her frequent feminist meetings. In effect, she says, "we were suffering from the nuclear family setup."

With six other sympathetic couples in similar circumstances, the Herrings scouted around and finally found a U-shaped, six-unit apartment building in southern Los Angeles. They purchased it last September, and converted it into a successful, middle-class (most of the men are lawyers) city commune. Knocking out walls and doors, they built interjoining apartments and a communal nursery, TV room and library. "The apartments open up so that the kids' rooms can run into each other," Ethel explains, "and yet there is still plenty of privacy for adults."

The families share their services, following a schedule that calls for each couple to do all of the cooking and housework for one week. "That's KP once every six weeks per couple, which keeps everybody happy," says Ethel. Her husband, for instance, has curtailed his practice so that he can spend one day a week at home on child-care and cooking duty. Says Ethel, "The truth is that most men are deprived of a close relationship with their children, and our men are finding out what they've been missing. It's groovy."

Disillusionment with the traditional family has led to other alternative lifestyles. In Boston, David, 36, a divorced architect, and Sarah, 29, a researcher for a consulting firm, have an "arrangement"; like an increasing number of other American couples, they live together in David's Cambridge walkup apartment in a "marriage" that has endured solidly for two years without benefit of legal sanction. They sometimes join David's ex-wife and his son, Jonathan, 5, for dinner. Bubbly, attractive Sarah still maintains her own apartment and sometimes spends a few days there.

Both Sarah and David are convinced that their relationship is superior to a conventional marriage. It is the legal tie, they believe, that is the subtle influence in making a marriage go sour. "On the small scale," says David, "there's no difference, except that you know you could call it off when you want to. That makes you more careful and considerate. You don't say subconsciously, 'Oh, she's always going to be there.' So you make that little extra effort." Only under one circumstance would Sarah and David consider a legal marriage: if they decided to have children.

Doubts about conventional family life have also led to the growth of another phenomenon: the "single-parent family." No longer fearful about complete ostracism from society, many single girls who become pregnant now choose to carry rather than abort their babies and to support them after birth without rushing pell-mell into what might be a disastrous marriage.

POPULATION EXPLOSION

Judy Montgomery, 21, is a major in political science at the University of Cincinnati. She lives in the exclusive suburban area of Indian Hill with her parents and her son Nicky, 16 months. She became pregnant at 19 but did not want to get married. "I think having a mother and a father are important for a child, but Nicky can be raised so he isn't scarred. There are now substitutes in society that will allow him to grow up fatherless. I have no feeling of guilt. My own real hassle is with guys I meet who are interested in me, and I say, 'Oh, I have to go home and take care of my kid.' "

Liberalized adoption laws are also making it possible for single and divorced women to have children and to set up housekeeping without the necessity of a father. Ruth Taylor, a secretary at a hospital in suburban Warrensville township, near Cleveland, was divorced shortly after her daughter, Kelley, was born three years ago. Because she did not want the girl to grow up as an only child, she adopted a little boy who was listed as a "slow learner" by the agency (there was a three-year waiting list for normal Caucasian children). But in the year that she has had Corey, 2, the boy's personality and intelligence have blossomed. To Ruth, adopting a child is the answer for both single and married people who have decided to forego children because of their concern about the population explosion. "Form a family with what has already been provided," she suggests. "That way you will be helping to solve the problem."

The re-examination of the traditional family and the desire to try other forms have also produced some bizarre experiments. In La Jolla, Calif., Michael, an oceanographer, and his artist wife, Karen, both 27, had been married for four years when Michael met Janis, who was studying at the Scripps Institute of Oceanography. Janis often came to study at Michael and Karen's apartment, and a strong attachment developed. When Michael took off on a field trip to Antarctica, the two women became good friends and decided that because they both liked Michael, all three ought to live together. Last May the trio formalized it all with an improvised wedding ceremony attended, incidentally, by other trios.

As the three were leaving for a summer session at the University of Oregon, they were delighted to learn that Karen was pregnant. "We'll all take turns caring for it," says Janis, "just as we share all the household chores. That way each of us has time for things we like to do best."

There are other far-out experiments. One group, living at Sandstone, a handsome complex of houses near Los Angeles, has varied in size from three to twelve adults, and currently consists of only five: three men and two women. Says Barbara Williamson, a member of what she calls the "intentional" family: "It's a smorgasbord. It's so much more exciting to have nine different dishes than just one." The group has had no children yet because it wants to stabilize its "marriage" first.

Such eccentric arrangements obviously have no meaning for the vast majority of people, except perhaps as symptoms of an underlying malaise. Thus, while some sociologists and anthropologists make their plans for the reordering of the social structure, most are more immediately concerned with removing—or at least alleviating—the stresses of the nuclear family.

EMANCIPATED WOMEN

Psychologist Richard Farson, for one, believes that the increased emphasis on the role of the family "as an agent for human development and personal growth" will again make the family important in the field of education. "Parents will not necessarily teach the children," he says. "That is probably quite unlikely." But the family itself may become a learning unit, stimulated by new programs and new processes (like cartridge TV) that are even now being introduced into the home by industry. This, he feels, will help strengthen the nuclear family "by involving people in all kinds of interesting mutual experiences of learning."

While some fear that Women's Lib is a threat to the family, many experts believe that its more sensible goals could strengthen it. As women become increasingly emancipated—by child-care centers and equal-employment practices—they could have more time for intellectual and emotional fulfillment. Thus although their housekeeping role may diminish, they could become less frustrated and better wives. Though the idea is still shocking to many, some experts feel that certain women are better mothers if they are not with their children all day.

The Pill and abortion are obviously part of a loosening of morals that undermines the family in some ways; but these developments, too, can have their positive effects by reducing the number of pregnancies that lead to hasty and ill-considered marriages, and by allowing couples to put off having children until they are older and have had time to enjoy themselves, to travel and to grow up themselves. The reduction in unwanted pregnancies will also lessen the number of children who are rejected even before they are born and the financial hardships brought on by unplanned large families.

Adds Psychoanalyst Rollo May: "Even the growing frequency of divorce, no matter how sobering the problems it raises, has the positive psychological effect of making it harder for couples to rationalize a bad marriage by the dogma that they are 'stuck' with each other. The possibility of finding a new lover makes it more necessary for us to accept the responsibility of choosing the one we do have if we stay with him or her."

If the experts have their way, the nuclear family can be further strengthened in the future. Margaret Mead, for example, believes that many bad starts can be avoided if marriages can be postponed. She proposes a kind of universal national service that will take adolescents out of the nuclear home (where they apparently do not fit in), train them and keep them occupied until they are more mature. "We need something to allow those people who don't go to college to grow up without committing themselves to a marriage."

Instead of traditional marriages, Mead would also encourage a "two-step marriage" for young people. During the first phase, which would, in effect, be a trial marriage, the young couple would be required to agree not to have children. If a stable relationship developed and the couple decided to have children, a second license would be obtained and another ceremony performed.

Business, too, has a responsibility to relieve some of the stress on the contemporary family, according to Psychologist Urie Bronfenbrenner. In a report to last week's White House Conference on Children, he urged business to create flexible work schedules, cut back on travel, on transfers and on social obligations that keep parents away from their children. Bronfenbrenner also feels that large corporations should concern themselves with "where and how their families live," and with more part-time positions, better maternity leave, daycare centers and family recreation plans.

Another suggestion of the report, which urges that businesses "adopt" groups of young people to give them the opportunity to see adults at work, has already been tried by a few firms. At the White House conference, delegates saw a film about a highly successful program set up by Bronfenbrenner's colleague, David Goslin, of the Russell Sage Foundation. It showed children from the Detroit public-school system spending three days at the Detroit *Free Press*, learning to relate to the newspapermen and what they were doing, and saying things like "You know, in school you learn a subject, but here you meet people."

In Bronfenbrenner's view, meeting people—especially people of different ages—is all-important to the preservation of the family. Parents now spend their time with other parents, he suggests, children with children, the young with the young and the old with the old. To end this segregation, which is particularly acute in suburban living, Bronfenbrenner and others recommend planning by architects for community clusters where children, their parents and the elderly can intermingle, each group bringing its experience, knowledge and support to the other. University of Michigan's John Platt visualizes clusters he calls "child-care communities" which resemble communes: in addition to enlarged recreational and shopping facilities, they would include centralized schoolrooms, dining rooms (for both adults and children) and kitchens.

GYPSY CARAVAN

For all of the family's ills, the U.S. is still probably the most marriage-and-home oriented nation in the modern world. In the 1960s the number of U.S. families grew at a greater rate than the population; 87% of Americans live in families that include both parents. While the divorce rate is rising, so is the rate of remarriage among divorced people. Thus, the nuclear model will undoubtedly remain the basic family structure in the U.S. But that does not mean that it will function as a healthy institution unless ways are found to strengthen its concept and spirit.

A man's family used to be his fate; he could scarcely change it. In the modern U.S., people think easily of changing their family, like their occupation or their home. The result is psychologically unsettling and yet this changeability has obviously become a part of American life and the family will have to adjust to it. Theologian Sam Keen (*Apology for Wonder*) suggests that one should boldly take the notion of the family as a center for mobility: "It should be thought of like a gypsy caravan. You have that point of stability in the caravan, but it is continually moving and each member of it goes out to forage for food and then catches up with it."

That vision will probably never replace the image—and the dream—of the snug, permanent hearth, even suitably expanded by "clusters." But it may be closer to the reality of American life.

37

What Research is Teaching Us about the Differences between Authoritative and Authoritarian Child-Rearing Styles

Diana Baumrind

EDITOR'S NOTE · *What a child becomes depends to a large extent on how he or she is raised and treated by his or her parents. Peers also have an impact, as do teachers, relatives, and other secondary adults, but the primary figures in a child's life are his parents or parent-figures. This reading will help you to see how the way in which a child is reared shapes his or her personality. Is there a best way to raise children? What is the difference between authoritative and authoritarian child rearing? What kind of discipline is best for encouraging healthy*

Diana Baumrind, "Some Thoughts on Childrearing." The research discussed in this paper was supported by research grant HD-02228 from the National Institute of Child Health and Human Development, U.S. Public Health Service, and presented as a talk to the Children's Community Center in Berkeley, California, May 14, 1969. Used by permission.

growth? What are the consequences of being raised in a permissive home? What implications does this selection provide for how teachers might best relate to their students? This reading is packed with practical information that can be used in your role as teacher, psychological health care worker, or parent.

I want to speak with you today about my research findings relating patterns of parental authority to dimensions of competence in young children, and to share with you the conclusions I draw from those findings.

There are a few points I want to make before I discuss the findings themselves....

1. First, there is no such thing as a *best* way to raise children. Each individual family's total life situation is unique. A generalization which makes sense on a probability basis must be tailored to fit an individual family's situation, if indeed it fits at all. It is each parent's responsibility to become an expert on his own children, using information in books or parent effectiveness encounter groups or, best of all, by careful observation and intimate communication with the child.

2. Secondly, the generalizations which I make have a reasonable probability of being true for a particular sample, but the extent to which that sample is representative of a population, say eight years later, remains in question. Moreover, the extent to which any individual family is similar to the families in the sample affects how relevant the findings are for that family. In addition, the relationships found are not strong enough to predict for the individual family.

3. Third, to have any social meaning at all, research findings must be *interpreted* and integrated. Yet the interpretations I make of my findings may well be disputed by other equally expert investigators. I will speak *strongly* for my interpretations because I am that sort of person. But each of you must evaluate the relevance to your own family of what I say, and you must do so in the light of your personal value system and experience.

I should tell you that my *subjective* assurance about what I say rests as much upon my personal experience as a parent, as on my research findings. I have three daughters whose ages are 11, 13 and 15. My theories and my practice coincide rather well (I think), and I am subjectively satisfied with the effectiveness of what I call "authoritative parental control" in achieving my *personal* aim. I will generalize to say it is possible, if parents wish to —IF parents wish to—to control the behavior of children, even of adolescents, and to do so without suppressing the individuality and willfulness of the child or adolescent. What gets in the way of most parents who *do* wish to control the behavior of their children more effectively is lack of *expertness* as parents, *indecisiveness* about the application of power, *anxiety* about possible harm resulting from demands and restrictions, and *fear* that if they act in a certain way they will lose their children's love. Nowadays I think more parents are concerned about maintaining the approval of their children than vice versa, and, indeed, many parents become paralyzed with indecision when their authority is disputed, or their children are angered by discipline.

Now I will tell you something about my research.

RESEARCH VARIABLES

For the past eight years my staff and myself have been gathering data on the behavior of preschool children in nursery schools and in structured laboratory situations. Each child studied has been observed for at least three months. These data were related to information obtained about the parent-child interaction, and about the parents' beliefs and values. We made two home visits to each family between the difficult hours of five to eight in the evening, then subsequently interviewed the mother and father separately. So far more than 300 families have participated in the study, most of them middle class, well educated families.

A. CHILD VARIABLES

I think it is important to tell you what kinds of behavior we were looking for so that you will know what I mean by such general terms as "competence" when speaking of the child, or "authoritative parental control" when speaking of the parent.

In all correlational studies of children's social behavior, at least two dimensions are revealed. One dimension may be called *Responsible vs. Socially Disruptive Behavior*. The other dimension may be called *Active vs. Passive Behavior*. These two dimensions are independent of each other—that is, a socially responsible child can run the gamut from very active and self-assertive to very quiet and socially passive. Or, a socially disruptive child may be an active terrorist or he may be sullen, passive and detached from other children.

When we call a child *socially responsible*, we mean that relative to other children his age the child takes into account the ongoing activities of other children enough not to disrupt them—he will facilitate the routine of the group; he does not actively disobey or undermine the rules of the school; he can share possessions with other children; he is sympathetic when another child needs help; he does not try to get another child into trouble, and so on.

When we speak of a child as *active*, we are referring to the independent, self-motivated, goal-oriented, outgoing behavior of the child. When we call a child highly active, he is relative to other children his age likely to go after what he wants forcefully, to show physical courage, to be a leader, to feel free to question the teacher, to persevere when he encounters frustration, to show originality in his thinking, and so on.

Seventy-two very explicitly defined items were used by the raters to describe each child in relation to these two dimensions.

When I report my findings to you later on and I speak of the most *competent* group of children, I am speaking about children who were rated by the observers as being very active and very responsible. I am comparing these children to other children who are less competent in the sense that raters judged them to be lacking in self-assertiveness and self-control, or to be socially disruptive.

Clearly, any definition of competence makes certain tacit assumptions about the proper relationship of the individual to society. The child is *competent* to fulfill himself and succeed in a given society. The same qualities might not be as effective in a differently organized society. To the extent that an investigator believes that successful accommodation to the ongoing institutions of a society defines competence, he will stress the *social responsibility* dimension of competence. If an investigator believes in revolutionary change, he may reject social responsibility as a criterion of competence. To the extent that an investigator values thrust, potency, dominance, and creative push, he will stress *activity* as a dimension of competence. If, by contrast, he believes in an Eastern ideal—such as Zen Buddhism—an investigator may reject dominance and push as criteria of competence, emphasizing instead receptivity, openness, egolessness, and unwilled activity. My definition of *competence* assumes the importance both of accommodation to social institutions, and of self-assertive and individualistic action in relation to these institutions. In the preschool years, I regard the development of *social responsibility* and of *individuality* as equally important for both sexes, although I suppose that our society, at least in the past, has placed the emphasis in adulthood on activity and individuality for boys, and on responsibility and conformity for girls.

B. PARENT VARIABLES

Now I would like to tell you about what we were looking for when we observed parents with their children. Our focus has been upon facets of parental authority which might conceivably predict dimensions related to competence in young children. More specifically, we measured dimensions such as the following:

1. *Directive vs. nondirective behavior*—that is, the extent to which the child's life is governed by clear regulations and the parent in charge sets forth clearly the daily regimen for the child.
2. *Firm vs. lax enforcement policy*—the extent to which the parent enforces directives, resists coercive demands of the child, requires the child to pay attention to her when she speaks, and is willing to use punishment if necessary to enforce her demands.
3. *Expects vs. does not expect participation in household chores*—we measured the extent to which parents require the child to help with household tasks, to dress himself, to put his toys away, and to behave cooperatively with other family members.

4. *Promotes respect for established authority vs. seeks to develop an equalitarian, harmonious relationship with child*—here we sought to measure what is generally thought of as authoritarian control and its opposite, i.e. the extent to which the parent assumes a stance of personal infallibility on the basis of her role as parent rather than on the basis of her specific competencies and responsibilities, and requires of the child that he defer to her without question.

We also measured such variables as:

1. The extent to which the parent encourages self-assertion and independent experimentation.
2. The extent to which the parent uses reason and explanation when directing the child.
3. The extent to which the parent values individuality in behavior and appearance by contrast or in addition to social acceptability.

METHODS USED TO STUDY PARENT ATTITUDES AND BEHAVIOR

In studying parental attitudes and practices we used a variety of methods. As I have already indicated, we visited the home on two occasions between the hours of five and eight, and took complete notes on the interactions which transpired. We then interviewed the mother and the father separately, discussing with each the possible ways in which the presence of the observer might have affected the behavior witnessed during the home visit. We talked with parents about their general position on child rearing, their attitudes towards permissiveness, directiveness, and the use of reason, what their ideals were for the child, and so on.

Some parents have asked how we thought the presence of the observer in the home affected the interactions we witnessed. Our general conclusion is that while most families censored some behavior (such as intense emotional shows of love or anger), the interactions we observed and rated with regard to the variables we were measuring predict pretty well how parents interact with their children. We may think about the information we obtain from home visits somewhat as we do about on-the-job tests for a prospective employee. An employer can predict the typing efficiency of a prospective employee from a five-minute typing test on standardized material. While the typist will not handle all kinds of typing tasks in the same way that she does the typing test copy, her handling of the test copy will predict pretty accurately her general speed, her knowledge of format, and her ability to spell. Under the kind of pressure that preschoolers produce during the hours of five and eight, parents generally become sufficiently involved with their customary tasks so that they fall back upon their most practiced responses, modifying these perhaps in accord with their ideals. Very few parents sought consciously to disguise this customary behavior. Since our focus is upon conscious child rearing practices and values, the observational situation is reasonably successful in providing relevant information about parental practices and values. If we were concerned primarily with incidents of highly charged emotional events, direct observation in the home would probably not have provided us with the needed information. Most studies of the effects of child rearing practices in the past have used less valid data than home visits. They have relied upon psychological tests, or self-report, or experimental observation in the laboratory setting. With all its drawbacks, then, we found that the combination of direct observation in the home setting, with interview and self-report, gave us relatively valid information of the kind we were seeking.

CONCLUSIONS FROM THE STUDY

These are the general conclusions which we drew from our data about the child rearing antecedents of *responsible vs. irresponsible behavior* and *active vs. passive behavior.*

In the middle class group we studied, parental practices which were intellectually stimulating and to some extent tension-producing (e.g., socialization and maturity demands and firmness in disciplinary matters) were associated in the young child both with self-assertion and social responsibility. Techniques which fostered self-reliance whether by placing demands upon the child for self-control and high level performance, or by encouraging independent action and decision-making, were associated in the child with responsible and inde-

pendent behavior. Firm discipline in the home did not produce conforming or dependent behavior in the nursery school. For boys, especially, the opposite was true. Firm, demanding behavior on the part of the parent was not correlated with punitiveness or lack of warmth. The most demanding parents were, in fact, the warmest.

These conclusions concerning the effects of disciplinary practices are consistent with the findings of a second study we conducted (Baumrind, 1967). In that study, a group of nursery school children who were both responsible and independent were identified. These children were self-controlled and friendly on the one hand, and self-reliant, explorative, and self-assertive on the other hand. They were realistic, competent, and content by comparison with the other two groups of children studied. In the home setting, parents of these children were consistent, loving, and demanding. They respected the child's independent decisions, but were very firm about sustaining a position once they took a stand. They accompanied a directive with a reason. Despite vigorous and at times conflictual interactions, their homes were not marked by discord or dissensions. *These parents balanced much warmth with high control, and high demands with clear communication about what was required of the child.* By comparison with parents of children who were relatively immature, parents of these highly mature children had firmer control over the actions of their children, engaged in more independence training, and did not reward dependency. Their households were better coordinated and the policy of regulations clearer and more effectively enforced. The child was more satisfied by his interactions with his parents. By comparison with parents of children who were relatively unhappy and unfriendly, parents of the mature children were less authoritarian, although quite as firm and even more loving.

A POSITION ON CHILD REARING

I would like now to move from a report of research findings into a presentation of some of my conclusions about child rearing. I want to make clear that experts in the field disagree just as parents do. The meaning I derive from my research findings is affected by my personal values and life experience, and is not necessarily the meaning another investigator would derive.

I have been quoted as opposing permissiveness, and to a certain extent that is true. I would like to describe my position on permissiveness in more detail. I think of the permissive parent as one who attempts to behave in a nonevaluative, acceptant, and affirmative manner toward the child's impulses, desires, and actions. She consults with him about policy decisions and gives explanations for family rules. She makes few demands of household responsibility and orderly behavior. She presents herself to the child as a resource for him to use as he wishes, not as an ideal for him to emulate, nor as an active agent responsible for shaping or altering his ongoing or future behavior. She allows the child to regulate his own activities as much as possible, avoids the exercise of control, and does not insist that he obey externally defined standards. She attempts to use reason and manipulation, but not overt power, to accomplish her ends.

The alternative to adult control, according to Neill, the best known advocate of permissiveness, is to permit the child to be self-regulated, free of restraint, and unconcerned about expression of impulse, or the effects of his carelessness. I am quoting from *Summerhill* now:

> *Self-regulation means the right of a baby to live freely, without outside authority in things psychic and somatic.* It means that the baby feeds when it is hungry; that it becomes clean in habits only when it wants to; that it is never stormed at nor spanked; that it is always loved and protected.
>
> *I believe that to impose anything by authority is wrong. The child should not do anything until he comes to the opinion—his own opinion—that it should be done.*
>
> Every child has the right to wear clothes of such a kind that it does not matter a brass farthing if they get messy or not.
>
> Furniture to a child is practically nonexistent. So at Summerhill we buy old car seats and old bus seats. And in a month or two they look like wrecks. Every now and again at mealtime, some youngster waiting for his second helping will while away the time by twisting his fork almost into knots.
>
> Really, any man or woman who tried to give children freedom should be a millionaire, for it is not fair that the natural carelessness of children should always be in conflict with the economic factor.[1]

Permissiveness as a doctrine arose as a reaction against the authoritarian methods of a previous era in which the parent felt that her purpose in training her child was to forward not her own desire, but the Divine Will. The parent felt that since the obstacle to worldly and eternal happiness was self-will, that the subduing of the will of the child led to his salvation. The authoritarian parent of a previous era was preparing his child for a hard life in which success depended upon achievement, and in which strength of purpose and ability to conform were necessary for success. With the advent of Freudian psychology and the loosening of the hold of organized religion, educated middle class parents were taught by psychologists and educators to question the assumptions of their own authoritarian parents. Spock's 1946 edition of *Baby and Child Care* advocated the psychoanalytic view that full gratification of infantile sucking and excretory and sexual impulses was essential for secure and healthful adult personalities. The ideal educated, well-to-do family in the late 1940's and 1950's was organized around unlimited acceptance of the child's impulses, and around maximum freedom of choice and self-expression for the child.

However by 1957 Spock himself changed his emphasis. He said, in the 1957 edition of his famous book, "A great change in attitude has occurred and nowadays there seems to be more chance of conscientious parents getting into trouble with permissiveness than with strictness."

I would like now to examine certain of the assumptions which have been made in support of permissiveness, most of which, when examined in a research setting, have not been supported.

1. One assumption previously made was that scheduled feeding and firm toilet training procedures have as their inevitable consequences adult neuroses. This apparently is not so. Unless the demands put upon the infant are unrealistic—as might be the demand for bowel training at five months—or the parent punishes the infant cruelly

---

[1] A. S. Neill, *Summerhill: A Radical Approach to Child Rearing* (New York: Hart, 1964), pp. 105; 114; 115; 138; 139.

for failure to live up to her demands—scheduled feeding and firm toilet training do not appear to be harmful to the child.

2. A second assumption, that punishment, especially spanking, is harmful to the child, or not effective in controlling behavior, is also not supported by recent research findings. On the contrary, properly administered punishment has been shown by the behavior therapists to be an effective means of controlling the behavior of children. This hardly comes as a surprise to most parents. Brutal punishment *is* harmful to the child. Threats of punishment not carried out are harmful to the child. A parent who threatens to punish must be prepared to deal with escalation from the child by prompt administration of punishment. She cannot appease. Otherwise the threat of punishment will actually *increase* the incidence of undesirable behavior, since it is just that undesirable behavior which will cause the parent to cancel the punishment, in an attempt to appease the child.

While *prompt* punishment is usually most effective, it is important for the parent to be certain that the child knows exactly why he is being punished, and what kind of behavior the parent would prefer and why. While extremely rapid punishment following a transgression works best in training a rat or a dog, a human child is a conscious being and should be approached as one. It should not be enough for a parent, except perhaps in critical matters of safety, to *condition* a child to avoid certain kinds of behavior by prompt punishment. The parent's aim is to help the child control his own behavior, and that end requires the use of reason and the bringing to bear of moral principles to define what is right and what is wrong conduct.

Properly administered punishment, then, provides the child with important information. The child learns what it is his parent wants, and he learns about the consequences of not conforming to an authority's wishes.

3. A third assumption that advocates of permissiveness have made is that unconditional love is beneficial to the child, and that love which is conditional upon the behavior of the child is harmful to the child. I think that the notion of unconditional love has deterred many parents from fulfilling certain important parental functions. They fail to train their children for future life and make them afraid to move towards independence. Indulgent love is passive in respect to the child—not requiring of the child that he become good, or competent, or disciplined. It is content with providing nourishment and understanding. It caters to the child and overlooks petulance and obnoxious behavior—at least it tries to. The effect on the child of such love is often not good. Once the child enters the larger community, the parents are forced to restrict or deprive. Accustomed as the child is to immediate gratification, he suffers greater deprivation at such times than he would if he were accustomed to associating discipline with love. He does not accept nor can he tolerate unpleasant consequences when he acts against authority figures. Such a child, even when he is older, expects to receive, and is not prepared to give or to compromise. The rule of reciprocity, of payment for value received, is a law of life that applies to us all. The child must be prepared in the home by his parents to give according to his ability so that he can get according to his needs.

The parent who expresses love unconditionally is encouraging the child to be selfish and demanding while she herself is not. Thus she reinforces exactly the behavior which she does not approve of —greedy, demanding, inconsiderate behavior. For his part, the child is likely to feel morally inferior for what he is, and to experience conflict about what he should become. I believe that a parent expresses her love most fully when she demands of the child that he become his best, and in the early years helps him to act in accordance with *her* image of the noble, the beautiful, and the best, as an initial model upon which he can create (in the adolescent years) his own ideal.

On the other hand, I do believe that to the extent that it is possible, a parent's *commitment* to the child should be unconditional. That is, the parent should stay contained *in* the experience with the child, no matter what the child does. Parental love properly expressed comes closest in my mind to the Christian notion of *Agape*. The parent continues to care for the child because it is her child and not because of the child's merits. Since she is human, the quality of her feeling for him depends upon the child's actions, but her interest in his welfare does not depend upon his actions and is abiding. This abiding interest is expressed not in gratifying the child's whims, nor in being gentle and kind with him, nor in approval of his actions, nor even in approving of what he is as a person. Unconditional *commitment* means that the child's interests are perceived as among the parent's most important interests, and that (no matter what the child does) the parent does not desert the child. But the love of a parent for a child must be demanding—not demanding of the unconditional commitment it offers—but rather demanding of the reciprocal of what it offers. The parent has the right—indeed, the duty—to expect obedience and growth towards mature behavior, in order that she can discharge her responsibilities to the child, and continue to feel unconditional commitment to his welfare. (Only parents are required, as an expression of love, to give up the object of that love, to prepare the object of love to become totally free of the lover.)

AUTHORITATIVE VERSUS AUTHORITARIAN PARENTAL CONTROL

Now that I have discussed the concept of permissiveness in child rearing, I would like to explain the distinction which I make between *authoritarian* and *authoritative* parental control.

I think of an *authority* as a person whose expertness befits him to tell another what to do, when the behavioral alternatives are known to both. An authority does not have to *exercise* his control, but it is recognized by both that by virtue of his expertness and his responsibility for the actions of the other, he is fit to exercise authority in a given area.

By *authoritative parental control* I mean that, in relation to her child, the parent should be an authority in the sense just defined.

1. *In order to be an authority, the parent must be expert.* It seems to me that many parents and teachers have come to the conclusion that they are not expert on matters which pertain to the young people placed in their charge. Therefore, since they are not expert, they abandon their role as authorities. I think instead that they should become more expert. Parents often do need more information

about children of all ages than they have, in order to be expert. But much of what a parent needs to know she can learn from observing her child and listening to him. A parent must permit her child to be a socialization agent for her, as well as the other way, if the parent is to acquire the information about the child and his peer group that she needs in order to make authoritative decisions about matters which affect the child's life. Unlike the authoritarian parent, the authoritative parent modifies her role in response to the child's coaching. She responds to suggestions and complaints from the child and then transmits her own more flexible norms to her child. In this way, by becoming more expert, the parent legitimates her authority and increases her effectiveness as a socializing agent.

2. *In order to be authoritative, the parent must be willing and able to behave rationally, and to explain the rationale for her values and norms to the child.* The parent does not have to explain her actions all the time to the child, especially if she knows that the child knows the reason but is engaging in harassment. But a parent does need to be sure that she herself knows the basis for her demands, and that the child also knows, within the limits of his understanding, the reasons behind her demands.

In authoritarian families the parent interacts with the child on the basis of formal role and status. Since the parent has superior power, she tells the child what to do and does not permit herself to be affected by what he says or does. Where parents do not consult with children on decisions affecting the children, authority can only rest on power. As the child gets older and the relative powers of parent and child shift, the basis for parental authority is undermined. Even the young child has the perfect answer to a parent who says, "you must do what I say because I am your mother," and that answer is, "I never asked to be born." The adolescent can add, "Make me," and many say just that when parents are unwise enough to clash directly with an adolescent on an issue on which the adolescent has staked his integrity or autonomy.

3. *In order to be authoritative, the parent must value self-assertion and willfulness in the child.* Her aim should be to prepare the child to become independent of her control and to leave her domain. Her methods of discipline, while firm, must therefore be respectful of the child's actual abilities and capacities. As these increase, she must share her responsibilities and prerogatives with the child, and increase her expectations for competence, achievement, and independent action.

I believe that the imposition of authority even against the child's will is useful to the child during the first six years. Indeed, power serves to legitimate authority in the mind of the child, to assure the child that his parent has the power to protect him and provide for him.

The major way in which parents exercise power in the early years is by manipulating the reinforcing and punishing stimuli which affect the child. What makes a parent a successful reinforcing agent or an attractive model for a child to imitate is his effective power to give the child what he needs—i.e., the parent's control over resources which the child desires, and his willingness and ability to provide the child with these resources in such a manner and at such a time that the child will be gratified and the family group benefitted. Thus, practically as well as morally, gratification of the child's needs within the realistic economy of the family, is a precondition for the effective imposition of parental authority. An exploited child cannot be controlled effectively over a long period of time. The parent's ability to gratify the child and to withhold gratification legitimates his authority. The child, unlike the adolescent, has not yet reached the level of cognitive development where he can legitimate authority, or object to its imposition, on a principled basis.

By early adolescence, however, power based on physical strength and control of resources cannot and should not be used to legitimate authority. The young person is now capable of formal operational thought. He can formulate principles of choice by which to judge his own actions and the actions of others. He has the conceptual ability to be critical even though he may lack the wisdom to moderate his criticism. He can see clearly many alternatives to parental directives; and the parent must be prepared to defend rationally, as she would to an adult, a directive with which the adolescent disagrees. Moreover, the asymmetry of power which characterizes childhood no longer exists at adolescence. The adolescent cannot be forced physically to obey over any period of time.

When an adolescent refuses to do as his parent wishes, it is more congruent with his construction of reality for the parent simply to ask him, "why not?" Through the dialogue which ensues, the parent may learn that his directive was unjust; or the adolescent may learn that his parent's directive could be legitimated. In any case, a head-on confrontation is avoided. While head-on confrontation won by the parent serves to strengthen parental authority in the first six years, it produces conflict about adult authority during adolescence.

Although a young person need feel no commitment to the social ethic of his parents' generation, he does have, while he is dependent upon his parents, a moral responsibility to obey rational authority, i.e. authority based on explicitly, mutually agreed-upon principles. The just restrictions on his freedom provide the adolescent with the major impetus to become self-supporting and responsible to himself rather than to his parents.

THE RELATIONSHIP OF INDIVIDUAL FREEDOM TO CONTROL

To an articulate exponent of permissiveness in child rearing, such as Neill, freedom for the child means that he has the liberty to do as he pleases without interference from adult guardians and, indeed, with their protection. Hegel, by contrast, defines freedom as the appreciation of necessity. By this he means that the man frees himself of the objective world by understanding its nature and controlling his reactions to its attributes. His definition equates the concept of freedom with power to act, rather than with absence of external control. To Hegel, the infant is enslaved by virtue of his ignorance, his dependence upon others for sustenance, and his lack of self-control. The experience of infantile omnipotence, if such he has, is based on ignorance and illusion. His is the freedom to be irresponsible, a very limited freedom, and one appropriate only for the incompetent.

For a person to behave autonomously, he must accept responsibility for his own behavior, which in turn requires that he believe the world is orderly and susceptible to rational mastery and that he has or can develop the requisite skills to manage his own affairs.

When compliance with parental standards is achieved by use of reason, power, and external reinforcement, it may be possible to obtain obedience and self-correction without stimulating guilt reactions. To some extent the parent's aggressiveness with the child stimulates counteraggressiveness and anger from the child, thus reducing the experience of guilt and of early internalizations of standards whose moral bases cannot yet be grasped. When the child accepts physical punishment or deprivation of privileges as the price paid for acts of disobedience, he may derive from the interaction greater power to withstand suffering and deprivation in the service of another need or an ideal and, thus, increased freedom to choose among expanded alternatives in the future.

Authoritarian control and permissive non-control both shield the child from the opportunity to engage in vigorous interaction with people. Demands which cannot be met or no demands, suppression of conflict or sidestepping of conflict, refusal to help or too much help, unrealistically high or low standards, all may curb or understimulate the child so that he fails to achieve the knowledge and experience which could realistically reduce his dependence upon the outside world. The authoritarian and the permissive parent may both create, in different ways, a climate in which the child is not desensitized to the anxiety associated with nonconformity, nor willing to accept punishment for transgressions. Both models minimize dissent, the former by suppression and the latter by diversion or indulgence. To learn how to dissent, the child may need a strongly held position from which to diverge and then be allowed under some circumstances to pay the price for nonconformity by being punished. Spirited give and take within the home, if accompanied by respect and warmth, may teach the child how to express aggression in self-serving and prosocial causes and to accept the partially unpleasant consequences of such actions.

The body of findings on effects of disciplinary practices give provisional support to the position that authoritative control can achieve responsible conformity with group standards without loss of individual autonomy or self-assertiveness.

38

My Parents Are My Friends

Joyce Maynard

EDITOR'S NOTE • *If you have read the preceding two articles, you have realized that having a family and raising children is a complex, demanding process. I have included this reading because it is a sensitive, poignant statement about what it is like to be a part of a close family unit in which people care for each other and show their caring. Ms. Maynard was not without guidance or direction or firmness when it was needed. Nor was she without warmth and love, which are always needed. This is an important selection. It is a first-hand, first-person glimpse at an emotionally healthy family. You will soon see why Joyce Maynard is not hesitant to call her parents her friends. How do you feel about your parents?*

On the bus to the airport, just after leaving my parents for a summer away from home, something quite sad happened, and I haven't been able to get it out of my head. The bus stopped in some small town, and a girl about my age got on—clearly, like me, going away for the summer. Her mother was at the bus stop with her

Joyce Maynard, "My Parents Are My Friends," *McCall's*, October 1972, p. 79. Copyright © 1972 by Joyce Maynard. Reprinted by permission of Curtis Brown, Ltd.

—a woman about my mother's age but very tired-looking, with her hair tied back and an apron on. The mother helped the girl with her luggage—a couple of shopping bags, cardboard boxes tied with string and a very fancy overnight case—then hugged her goodbye, and the girl stood on the steps of the bus with her arms at her sides. Then, she took her seat by a window, and the mother moved so that she was standing right next to the window, with just glass between them. She was crying by this time but trying to smile, and waving. And the girl sat stiff in her seat, looking straight ahead. Finally the bus pulled out, and the mother turned around and left. She was wearing that furry kind of bedroom slippers.

First I just felt so angry at the girl I wanted to shake her, and terribly, terribly sorry for the mother. I tried to imagine what the mother could have done to deserve that, and what the daughter felt like, and how that girl would be with her own kids—which brought me to parents and children generally, and what it was that mine did that worked so well. I missed them, but not in an unhealthy, dependent way; I just like being at home—enough, I think, so that it was important for me to get away last summer, as I did. I'm happy away from home, and not homesick, just as I know they're happy when I'm there and happy when I'm not, and their lives don't begin and end with the children (which, when one's children are 18 and 22, is a pretty dangerous place to have them begin and end).

We've got a pretty good thing going, our family. But we are hardly typical. What worked for us can't be taken as general rules. So—not presuming to suggest that this is how things should be done, but just that this is how we did things—here is a portrait of one good and loving parent-child relationship: my parents' and my own.

First, though, some kind of explanation, because there's a danger that I'll come out of this sounding like an apple polisher—the kind I always hated when I was little. (Pollyanna, I suspected, was too dull to get in trouble. As for Shirley Temple at her sunniest—well I always rooted for Jane Withers.) I feel dangerously close to becoming Pollyannified myself now. At an age when I should be rebelling, I'm without a cause. I think that's because my parents' standards are

so reasonable; it's hard to protest principles that make sense, principles based not on tradition or prejudice or an arbitrary laying down of laws for their own sake. There is a wholeness to our way of life: What we admire in human conduct is of a piece with what we admire in poems and flower gardens. In other words, what my parents passed on to us is not a bunch of unrelated fragments but a coherent set of values, all of which speak for reason, order, symmetry. Our lives are filled with family rituals, family phrases, family tastes.

Family. We didn't have religion, we didn't have a large circle of friends close by or a cozy network of relations. But we had a family style, a distinctive way of doing things. When my sister married, the first thing she asked for was a large schefflera tree. In our family *we have scheffleras*. In our family we dislike coloring books and painting by numbers; we admire Mexican crafts, we love Mozart operas and shortbread cookies... I could fill in all the blanks. Some kids don't even know what, if anything, their family represents.

We could be called opinionated. Certainly we are a hypercritical family—we don't lavish superlatives on things and places and people. I was raised to look closely, not to accept easily. My father and I took long walks together, examining mushrooms and leaves, stopping in midsentence and midstep sometimes to catch a birdcall. We went to museums together and talked about paintings, or sat side by side on the floor listening to music he conducted with a pencil in the air. My mother's training came evenings, after dinner, when she sat on the livingroom couch marking papers and I sat next to her, reading her corrections. Not just marked-in commas and circled misspellings, but paragraph-long notes on how a story might be improved. We talked about the scripts of TV commercials and the designs of cereal boxes and the arrangements of people's flower beds—the opinions never let up. I couldn't suspend judgment even when I wanted to; it was as if I went through life with X-ray glasses on, seeing through not just the things I wanted to see through but the things I'd just as soon have believed in, too. I longed to wallow in a sentimental movie with my friends, to join them in the delicious Friday night tears that followed every movie we'd see—*To Sir, With Love, The Sound of Music*—but I'd always end up munching popcorn while they wept, and commenting to my-self on the stiffness of an actor's speech or the corniness of the sound track.

I was old before my time, a junior sophisticate who could analyze the appeal of Barbi dolls compared to baby dolls long before I stopped playing with either. My sister and I weren't prodigies by any means; we were just raised in a household whose chief sport was conversation. While other families played basketball, we volleyed words and ideas. My parents never said "Don't talk back" (though rudeness was out), because we learned from argument. From Perry Mason and from my father, I learned how to find a loophole in a thought; from my mother, I learned how to present my case persuasively.

The criticism we applied to everything we encountered we applied to ourselves as well. Never "You are bad," but "You could do better." I like to see a job done really well, and if that means ripping out a seam and starting over, or spending all day in the library doing research for a term paper, I'll do it. My parents never let me feel satisfied with an encyclopedia-copied oral report or a hem held up with safety pins. My parents' greatest compliment to us was their high expectations. Not everything we did was wonderful to them just because we did it. They never implied that we were the most wonderful children in the whole world, but they certainly made us feel unique. So why would we want to copy other people instead of showing what *we* saw and felt?

My father taught me to appreciate the morning. Sometimes, when I've stayed up till three a.m. and the alarm inside my head, conditioned by my father's predawn rising, wakes me at seven, I wish ours had been the kind of household where everybody slept till ten and lounged in pajamas all afternoon. My father wouldn't have kept us from sleeping in, of course, but it would have saddened him. We would have missed the birds in full song and the angle of the sun before it's high and scorching and the feel of grass when it's still damp. Getting up early may sound like an unimportant thing, but it's central to everything my family cares about. Discipline, energy, activity, distaste for wastefulness, love of sunshine, and a pretty good balance, I think between order and freedom. There might be piles of clothes on the chairs in my bed-

room sometimes—four outfits tried on and discarded—but I always felt compelled to make my bed. We had something of the same balance in relation to meals. Breakfast, comfortable and free: bathrobes, Ann Landers, *TV GUIDE*, but dinner at a set time (*always* at six), sit-down, really quite formal, with no reading at the table and considerable thought to the way things looked.

I have friends whose families never eat a meal together. They drift in and out of the kitchen from five to seven, cooking hot dogs and munching potato chips standing up, or sitting down in front of the TV with a bowl of salad, gulped down in the space of a commercial. I've never been much of an eater myself (though my mother is a fine, creative cook), but meals have always meant a lot to me. Even if all I'm eating is an apple, I want to eat it at the table with my family, with places set and the good silver laid out. (Why should guests get silverware while children eat with stainless steel?)

And we never eat in silence, we never need to make polite conversation. Sometimes my mother will tell about a person she met on the street— what he wore, how he walked; she doesn't simply give the facts, she tells a story. My father is a dreamier observer who will tell us that he heard something interesting today, but forgot it, or that someone we know just gave birth to triplets, but he can't remember her name. He doesn't have the knack for minute detail my mother has but, like her, he understands the way people operate, why they do things. Our dinner conversation makes the food taste better. My parents are never boring.

We serve wine with dinner. We all know it's just about the cheapest kind you can buy, but my mother keeps it in a vintage bottle from years back and serves it in chilled crystal, not just for grown-ups. I've always preferred milk, but being offered wine (and having the luxury of refusing it) made me feel trusted. It has to do with the humiliation of childhood and the dignity that every child deserves to feel. (The liberal-minded parents in *Sunday, Bloody Sunday* who offer marijuana to their children were up to something entirely different. My mother gave us wine because it was part of a pleasant ritual, not to experience drunkenness.)

I remember my first high-school drinking parties—the line outside the bathroom of people looking sick and the limp bodies sprawled in heaps along the floor. For them liquor was booze, gulped down in closets and bathrooms at school or late at night in cars. Scotch tasted good because it was forbidden. It never was forbidden to me—and to me, it never tasted very good.

I cannot think of a single rule my parents ever told us to obey. What they gave us were principles —a concern for property, a desire to please them. Somehow, we just *knew*. I wouldn't have wanted to toss my mother's white linen sofa cushions on the floor (and I still remember how it pained me when a friend did once) because I was proud of our house and aware (as I told my friend, in what must have seemed like a hopelessly goody-goody tone) that my mother spent a lot of time making those pillows. Good behavior comes down to a good imagination—being able to see how things will look to another person, being able to tell if something you do will hurt him, being able to predict the consequences. Not that empty phrase, "Put yourself in someone else's shoes," but my favorite childhood game—fun, not Sunday school morality: putting myself in someone else's head.

In our town, the usual punishment for high school kids is grounding, keeping the villain at home for a few weeks and sometimes even locking him in his room. That accomplishes little except to make him more careful not to get caught next time. What it does is to humiliate. There's no dignity in being locked up or sent to bed at 6:30 or told: "You're my child. As long as you live in my house, you'll do as I say." I've never felt as though I were my parents' possession, and no child should. A child who does will realize that the only way to hurt his parents (and that's what he'll want) is to hurt himself, to break their favorite toy.

I've never felt that my fate was totally out of my hands, that no matter what I did, I could change nothing. (Parents say that so often: "I don't care what you say, I'm not changing my mind.") I always had a fairly early bedtime, but a flexible one. (Households with no bedtimes, where weary children are allowed to drag around until they finally collapse, have always saddened me. They're hard on the parents and, most of all, hard on the kids.) If I really wanted to stay up late to finish a book or watch TV, I could. I made sure I'd get that permission by not asking for it too often.

There's a distinction that has to be made be-tween treating children with the respect adults get and treating children like adults. My parents talked to us in a grown-up way, never baby talk. They let us see fairly grown-up books and movies (censorship, like locks on the liquor cabinet, only make the forbidden thing seem more exciting), and they exposed us to grown-up ideas. But they never made the mistake of turning us into little adults; we were never dragged out to join their cocktail parties or freed from the disciplines (not rules, but structures) of our lives. What my parents did was, quite simply, to treat us as politely as they'd treat an adult. I'm always embarrassed for my friends when their parents scold them in front of me, a guest. It's humiliating to them and, most of all, it's rude. My parents allowed us the dignity that so many children lose when their parents force them to wear clothes they dislike or eat foods they hate. Parents who do that, robbing their children of the adult right to choose, aren't just treating their children like children, they're treating them like babies. A child who announces that he doesn't like green sweaters or fried chicken is asserting himself for the first time. How can he ever have opinions on books and people and politics if he doesn't first have opinions on spinach?

I think it was my parents' own good manners in their relationship with me that have given me the good manners I now have in relation to other people. Simple good manners, especially among people of my generation, are so rare. Mine come quite naturally (I am the kind that everybody's grandmother loves) not because my mother ever drilled me on please and thank you, but because, even when she was angry, she was never impolite.

I remember a first-grade friend of mine who didn't know what her parents' first names were. In fact, she didn't know her parents *had* first names. What seems sad is that my friend never really thought of her parents as human beings. Except when they got mad at her, they never showed their feelings, never admitted their weak-nesses, as though saying "I'm sorry" or "I'm sad" would have made them harder to respect.

My parents never presented themselves to me as perfect and infallible, so I never had that awful moment so many children face when they suddenly discover their parents can be wrong—that Super-man is really just Clark Kent. The stories they told about their own childhoods weren't simply illustrations of how good they'd been, how hard the times were, and how grateful my sister and I should feel for having shoes with soles on them and schoolrooms with radiators; they were stories about the times my father played hooky and the day my mother cut off the lace from my grandmother's wedding gown.

I knew what my father's job was (so many children know a meaningless title and nothing else). I knew not only that my father was an English professor, but what his office looked like and what books he taught from, and sometimes I'd visit his class. Whenever my mother wrote a magazine article we'd all gather in the living room to hear her read the first draft and discuss the changes she should make. And even when I was very young, she consulted me ("What kinds of games do they play at recess?" "What's the name of a TV show with policemen in it?"). My parents never bought a piece of furniture that any one of us disliked. We didn't command the household, my sister and I, but we had a say in what went on. How can you have a comfortable relationship between parents and children if all the knowledge is on one side? They knew about us; it was only fair that we should know about them.

My father is a liberated man. He doesn't boss our household, nor is he bossed. My parents have no formal contract of dividing up the chores because they really don't need one—my father helps before my mother needs to ask him. Until I left home and encountered men making jokes about "never trusting a woman," and men who laughed at women drivers, I never understood what male chauvinism meant. It was a shock, discovering that not all men were like my father. (Most men with two daughters and no son would be disappointed.) But being insulated in that one area gave me something terribly valuable: complete confidence in myself. I never wished I were a boy or felt that, since I wasn't one, I would have any fewer options in my life.

Long before "recycling" was made an everyday word, we were doing it. A burned-out flashcube was a dollhouse aquarium; an old umbrella frame, trimmed and stuck on a base, became a comically ugly kitchen Christmas tree. My mother and I can't walk down the street on trash-collection day without finding some discarded treasure to bring home. We go to rummage sales for ten-cent dresses that we transform into evening gowns; we save popsicle sticks and plastic straws and aspirin bottles. We do not like to waste.

My mother's junk collecting has given me a well-trained eye that can look at a cork or a thimble and see the half dozen other things they might become. Her frugality is sometimes extreme, but it has taught me to take no amount of money lightly. I don't ever shop for the simple pleasure of spending money. My pleasure comes from saving it, and from getting something just as nice with a pot of batik dye and fabric or with a needle and thread.

Some people have nightmares about car accidents and forests full of wild animals and escaped convicts and falling from the top of a high building. My recurring nightmare is that our house burns down. I wake up, uncertain for a moment whether it happened or not, and terribly upset, not just because a house is worth a lot of money, and losing it means great expense, but because our house is so much a part of our family, so full of objects we're attached to. We never had a lot of money, but we always lived in style. Every piece of furniture we put in the house, every pillow, every bowl, is something we really care about. It's a house you can feel comfortable in—no slipcovers —but not a tumble-down house. Something happens to a family, I think, when they live in too much decorator-perfection or too much untidiness. There may be dust under the rug at our house, but the surfaces are neat, and when they begin to get messy and disorganized, so do I.

I think of one fine, earnest, committed family whose diningroom table is always cluttered with posters for the latest grape boycott or political campaign. The walls are covered with peace signs and taped-on newspaper clippings no one ever bothered to take down. Our kind of insulated comfort, our "gracious living," would probably seem irresponsible to them. My feeling is that not until you make a reassuring, comfortable base for security can you go beyond and deal with the discomforts of the outside world. My mother never needed to put a slipcover on the sofa or tell us not to bounce or we'd break the springs—we just knew. Our house is filled with plants and paintings and Mexican pottery and comfortable big pillows and straw baskets of fruit, and plenty of light. To lose it (and this is why the nightmare comes) would be to lose not just my roof but my foundation.

My parents made some bad mistakes, of course. Their way of doing things was so strong and definite that sometimes it was hard to keep in mind that other ways existed. Just because *we* didn't like gladiolas and store-bought birthday cards and Jell-O; just because *we* poured our milk in the cereal bowl before adding the cereal—that didn't mean that plenty of good people didn't have a perfect right to like things done their way. *We:* I use that word too much. My family is too close, perhaps, too much of a club; the delineations—*us* and *them*—are too clear. The critical faculties my parents gave me have made me more demanding than I should be, given me standards that the real, flawed world can't live up to. There are things my parents did and shouldn't have done and things they should have done and didn't. There was at times a feeling that our house was a factory of the arts, with every moment spent in what the experts call "creative play"—constant painting and writing and acting and dancing. My parents never really pushed, but they raised me to push myself too hard, to be impatient with myself when I wasn't doing something worthwhile.

I wish I'd been sent to church when I was little (if only to have had a religion to rebel against later; as is, I have nothing, plus an ignorance of the Bible that catches me up every time I read a book, almost, or go to a museum). The image of my mother playing any outdoor game besides croquet is impossible to picture. My father was more athletic, but never a player of baseball or a skier and, as a result, neither was I. I grew up dreading gym periods at school, spending more energy thinking up excuses than I would have spent out on the playing field, where teammates knew enough to keep the ball away from me. Only recently have I learned that I'm not so unco-ordinated after all, but I'm years behind now, and filled with willy, irrational fears (Will I hit my head? Will I fall? Will it hurt?) that I'm only beginning to overcome.

But I can't imagine feeling bitter toward my parents, as the girl on the bus to the airport with me must have felt not even to have blinked while her mother waved good-bye. I have friends who are embarrassed to be seen with their parents. Very occasionally I've been tempted to pretend I

didn't know mine, too (when my frugal mother returns a single bruised banana to the supermarket; when my father swims with me—in a bathing cap). Mostly I'm proud of them, and sure enough of myself not to worry about what people will think. I look at their faults and their strangeness with amusement and affection—not as odd, but as unique. I could no more hide my family and my upbringing than a friend of mine who's black could hide her blackness. And I want not just to recognize my family—to hold my father's hand when we cross the street and to sit with my mother at the movies—but to tell about it, too, because I can't help boasting—I've come out pretty happy. Saturday mornings, when I'm home, I like to go grocery shopping with my father. He's supposed to carry the shopping list my mother made up, but usually he loses it, so we drift through the aisles exclaiming on the price of lettuce, examining avocados and stocking up on boysenberry yogurt. I gave up drinking whole milk four years ago and haven't touched peanut-butter sandwiches since the days when I carried a lunch box, but he still asks me, every Saturday, "Do you need any milk? How are we fixed for peanut butter?" We look at the magazines together, he picks up some new brand of vitamins he thinks I need. We finish with soup, my father pacing in front of the Campbell's wall muttering, "What fine thing shall we have for lunch today?" and arriving, each time, at the chicken noodle as if it were a new discovery. We drive home at 20 miles an hour as high school kids, friends of mine, whiz past, honking. Sometimes I'm impatient, but my father hardly notices. He steers the car like a Viking, his back straight, both hands tight on the wheel, slowing down to ten when he spots an interesting bird. Halfway home he'll re-member—*mushrooms*, the one thing my mother specially asked for, and we'll turn back. They know us well at the checkout counter.

My mother and I cook together, side by side, my gestures just like hers, only less practiced. I've learned to scoop an egg out with my thumb to get every drop of the white, and then to beat it in the center of the bowl with the dough, already mixed, forming a well around my pool of frothy liquid. We rake leaves—she makes the piles, I jump in them, and we shop, not at big department stores (our town doesn't have any) but at funny, junky little shops we descend upon like hunters in search of treasure. Sometimes we go to an auction and come back with a boxful of handmade lace scraps whose possibilities—cuffs, collars, pockets, bodices—nobody else noticed, or an ancient mimeograph machine neither of us has any use for.

We don't spend all our time together. All three of us (and my older sister, who's married now) lead fairly independent lives. Saying that we love each other doesn't tell all that much—the most hostile children and the most frustrated parents can feel love. More than that, my parents are my friends.

Part Four · toward understanding maladaptive behavior and developing positive classroom management

Whether it be for good or evil, the education of the child
is principally derived from its own observation of the
actions, words, voice, and looks of those with whom it lives.
John Jebb (1775–1833)

The chapters and readings in this section are included to help expand the scope of your understanding of some of the problems, issues, and unanswered questions frequently associated with maladaptive behavior and classroom management.

Chapter Eleven, which explores the dynamics of alienation and maladaptive behavior, begins with Urie Bronfenbrenner's probing examination of the roots of alienation among youth. What causes alienated behavior? How does our society react to such behavior? What can we do about it? Bronfenbrenner offers us some interesting ideas. Delinquent behavior is typically a very expressive form of acting out angry feelings. Did it ever occur to you that some delinquents behave as they do because they perceive that they are expected to behave this way by those whom they take seriously? Morris Haimowitz suggests this startling possibility in reading 40. Delinquent behavior, of course, must be dealt with, an issue looked at by Fritz Redl in selection 41. We must be careful, warns Redl, to discern the difference among types of defiance, in order to know what is maladaptive and what is perfectly normal. In selection 42, Bruno Bettelheim talks about a form of maladjustment so subtle that it frequently goes unnoticed: the decision that some students make to fail. Why do some students want to fail? What are the underlying dynamics? This article will help you understand this phenomenon.

Maladaptive behavior and disciplinary problems are very much related to classroom management strategies. What are the issues? One issue involves the place and purpose of corporal punishment. Is it a good idea? Does it help to control a classroom? Do students respond with better behavior when corporal punishment is employed? These and many other important questions are addressed by Robert Ebel, who presents a strong case for corporal punishment in selection 43, and by Harvey Clarizio, who presents an equally strong case against its use in selection 44. William Morse in reading 45 offers some practical suggestions for handling classroom problems. Recently the use of drugs as a means to control classroom behavior has become a controversial issue. Should drugs be used? What are the implications of using drugs? Joseph Murray examines this problem in selection 46. Read it carefully. It will help you to make intelligent decisions if you are called upon to recommend in favor or against the use of drugs to modify behavior.

There is much more to understanding maladaptive behavior and classroom management strategies than can be covered in two chapters, but this section will give you a substantive overview of some of the problems and dynamics involved.

Chapter Eleven · origins and expressions of alienation and maladaptive behavior

39

The Roots of Alienation

Urie Bronfenbrenner

EDITOR'S NOTE · What causes alienated behavior? How is alienation related to idealism among youth? Are there fundamental differences in values between the generations? What do you suppose has been the effect of decreasing interaction between parents and children over the past 25 years? Dr. Bronfenbrenner addresses these and many other important questions that may help you to understand the roots of youthful alienation. He also expresses a very simple truth: Children need people in order to become human. Unfortunately, we do not seem to be doing such a good job of providing children with people. This is not an irreversible trend, but it is a trend. You will understand its implications more fully as you read. What can we do to decrease alienated behavior in individual families?

I. ALIENATION VS. IDEALISM

American college students in the 1970's are clearly a different breed from their predecessors of pre-

vious decades, but the distinctive characteristics of the new breed are both complex and paradoxical. Perhaps the most salient difference appears with respect to the attitudes of young people toward their own society. As is documented in the recent survey conducted by Daniel Yankelovich (1972) for the John D. Rockefeller, 3rd Fund, there is widespread disillusionment among youth with what they call "the system"—the major political, economic, and social institutions of the country. This rejection is not limited to the raucous, radical left; it is shared by the great majority of the nation's college students. "They believe that the country's major institutions—the political parties, the military, the penal system, and business—stand in need of drastic reform." (*New York Times* editorial on Yankelovich report, April 17, 1972.)

But those who would infer from this rejection of the system a clash in fundamental values between the generations, and who are thereby quickened to the fear—or hope—of social revolution, are probably misled. In the light of the evidence, the present generation of college students, in the absence of constructive moves from the rest of the society, are not likely as a group to achieve major social changes either through revolution or reform. Yet, the prospect offers no ground for complacency to those of conservative persuasion. For what we can anticipate from the coming generations of college students, so long as the rest of us continue to tolerate things as they are, is pervasive disaffection, erupting from time to time in pointless disruption, destruction, and tragic violence. It will not be a climate conducive to higher learning, or to the development of responsible leadership for our society.

The immediate and pressing reasons for this pervasive discontent lie, of course, in the genuine ills of contemporary society—notably poverty, racism, violence, and war. But the alienation of youth has deeper roots as well, that derive from psychological characteristics acquired through the curiously dissonant course of development through which these young people have passed.

To begin with, contrary to popular impression, the present generation of students—the same ones who are so critical of contemporary American institutions—hold personal, social, and political values that are almost indistinguishable from those of their parents. In the Yankelovich survey, youthful respondents answered in much the same way as their elders to questions concerned with what they deemed to be morally right or personally desirable. In the political realm, the profile of youth was strikingly similar to that for the nation as a whole: 70 percent of the students held what were referred to as "mainstream" views, and, among the rest, conservatives outnumbered radicals two-to-one. Where youth parted company with their elders was in their sharply negative evaluation of contemporary society and its institutions. But the values in the name of which these institutions were found wanting were precisely those which the young people shared with their elders. The paradox is nicely summarized in the aforementioned editorial from *The New York Times*: "The overwhelming majority of youth's moderate center are [sic] losing hope in the workability of the system to which they seem so eager to remain loyal." They are losing hope because the system did not respond.

Unfortunately, even this more balanced and sobering formulation is probably too optimistic, for it suggests, or at least permits the interpretation, that it is only the system which is at fault, that basically the students themselves are fine; they are "eager to remain loyal"; just make the system "workable," and they will respond.

Regrettably, the reality is not quite so reassuring. First of all, there are some students who are not so "eager to remain loyal." Although they represent but a small minority, the damage and destruction to human institutions and human lives that they can ultimately precipitate are incalculable.

But, from the point of view both of the fundamental responsibilities of the university and the welfare of the society, even more significant and disturbing than the destructive action of the minority of students is the social and political apathy of the majority. While perceiving gross injustice in the major institutions of their society, most stu-

dents are apparently not motivated to do very much about it. Unlike their predecessors in the 1960's, who actively sought to bring about social and political changes within the system, the present generation of college students, as revealed in recent surveys and special studies, feels powerless and already defeated.

What accounts for this change over less than a decade? From the perspective of human development, the roots of the process lie farther back in the history both of the society and of the individual. They relate to the general breakdown, since World War II, of the major institutions that carry responsibility for the development of the young—namely, the family, school, neighborhood, and the community.

II. THE ROOTS OF ALIENATION

To consider first what has been happening to the family: in the words of a report prepared for the White House Conference on Children (*Report to the President*):

> America's families and their children are in trouble, trouble so deep and pervasive as to threaten the future of the nation. The source of the trouble is nothing less than a national neglect of children and those primarily engaged in their care—America's parents (p. 252).

...it is not only children from disadvantaged families who show signs of progressive neglect. For example, an analysis carried out a few years ago (Bronfenbrenner, 1958) of data on child rearing practices in the United States over a twenty-five year period reveals a decrease in all spheres of interaction between parents and children. A similar conclusion is indicated by results of cross-cultural studies comparing American parents with those from Western and Eastern Europe (Bronfenbrenner, 1970; Devereux, Bronfenbrenner & Rodgers, 1969; Rodgers, 1971). Moreover, as parents and other adults have moved out of the lives of children, the vacuum has been filled by the age-segregated peer group. Recently, two of my colleagues (Condry & Siman, in press) have completed a study showing that, at every age and grade level, children today show a greater dependency on their peers than they did a decade ago. A parallel study (Condry & Siman, in press) indicates that such susceptibility to group influence is higher among children from homes in which one or both parents are frequently absent. In addition, "peer oriented" youngsters describe their parents as less affectionate and less firm in discipline. Attachment to age-mates appears to be influenced more by a lack of attention and concern at home than by any positive attraction of the peer group itself. In fact, these children have a rather negative view of their friends and of themselves as well. They are pessimistic about the future, rate lower in responsibility and leadership, and are more likely to engage in such antisocial behavior as lying, teasing other children, "playing hooky," or "doing something illegal."

. . . The family is changing not only in its function, but also in its structure. For example, in 1971, 43 percent of the nation's mothers worked outside the home; in 1948, the figure was only 18 percent. In 1971, 10 percent of all mothers of children under six were single parents bringing up children without a husband; half of these mothers also held down a job. Among families classified as living under poverty, 45 percent of all children under six are living in female-headed households. Fifty years ago, in the state of Massachusetts, half of all families had at least one other adult besides the parents living in the household; that figure today is less than 2.5 percent. (Bronfenbrenner and Bruner, 1972).

And even when the parent is at home, a compelling force cuts off communication and response among family members. To quote again from the White House Report (Report to the President, 1970):

> Although television could, if used creatively, enrich the activities of children and families, it now only undermines them. . . . The primary danger of the television screen lies not so much in the behavior it produces as the behavior it prevents—the talks, the games, the family festivities and arguments through which much of the child's learning takes place and his character is formed. Turning on the television set can turn off the process that transforms children into people.

In our modern way of life, children are deprived not only of parents but of people in general. A host of factors conspire to isolate children from the rest of society. The fragmentation of the extended family, the separation of residential and business areas, the disappearance of neighborhoods, zoning ordinances, occupational mobility, child labor laws, the abolishment of the apprentice system, consolidated schools, television, separate patterns of social life for different age groups, the working mother, the delegation of child care to specialists—all these manifestations of progress operate to decrease opportunity and incentive for meaningful contact between children and persons older, or younger, than themselves.

And here we confront a fundamental and disturbing fact: *Children need people in order to become human.* The fact is fundamental because it is firmly grounded both in scientific research and in human experience. It is disturbing because the isolation of children from adults simultaneously threatens the growth of the individual and the survival of the society. Child rearing is not something children can do for themselves. It is primarily through observing, playing, and working with others older and younger than himself that a child discovers both what he can do and who he can become—that he develops both his ability and his identity. It is primarily through exposure and interaction with adults and children of different ages that a child acquires new interests and skills and learns the meaning of tolerance, cooperation, and compassion. Hence to relegate children to a world of their own is to deprive them of their humanity, and ourselves as well.

Yet, this is what is happening in America today. *We are experiencing a breakdown in the process of making human beings human.* By isolating our children from the rest of society, we abandon them to a world devoid of adults and ruled by the destructive impulses and compelling pressures both of the age-segregated peer group and the aggressive and exploitive television screen, we leave our children bereft of standards and support and our own lives impoverished and corrupted.

This reversal of priorities, which amounts to a betrayal of our children, underlies the growing disillusionment and alienation among young people in all segments of American society. Those who grew up in settings where children, families, still counted are able to react to their frustration in positive ways—through constructive protest, participation, and public service. Those who come from circumstances in which the family could not function, be it in slum or suburb, can only strike out against an environment they have experienced as indifferent, callous, cruel, and unresponsive. This report . . . points to the roots of a process which, if not reversed, . . . can have only one result: the far more rapid and pervasive growth of alienation, apathy, drugs, delinquency, and violence among the young, and not so young, in all segments of our national life. We face the prospect of a society which resents its own children and fears its youth. . . . What is needed is a change in our patterns of living which will once again bring people back into the lives of children and children back into the lives of people (*Report to the President*, pp. 241–243).

. . . To be sure, these early humanistic values are often invoked later on by teachers and books in school, but again this occurs only at the verbal level. Moreover, especially in recent years, when presented in the classroom, these values have been recognized more in the breach than in the observance. In counter-reaction against the myths perpetuated in the teaching and texts of earlier generations, social science courses in today's schools emphasize the yawning gulf between American ideals and American reality. In foreign and domestic policy, in economic policy, in economic practice and social mores, the young person is repeatedly shown how the presumed values of the society are violated to insure the maintenance and aggrandizement of those already in power.

Thus, as he emerges from adolescence, the young person in America finds himself in a profound and crippling moral dilemma. By and large, he identifies with the ideals and values of his society, but he has been taught to recognize the widespread betrayal of these ideals and values in every day life, and has been given only minimal exposure to the substantial, if only occasional, achievements of the ideal, and—even more critically—to the concrete courses of action through which the ideal might be pursued. Neither in school, nor in the university, is he given much information or, above all, experience in how to use the institutions of his society—both public and private—to remedy social and political ills. In terms of social action, all he knows is the simplistic, one-shot [demand or destroy] so characteristic of the context in which

he has spent so much of his time—the age-segregated peer group and the commercial television screen. For those coming from environments in which the family was still strong, the aggressive impulse is inhibited by early-internalized humanistic values, but there is little knowledge or experience with an alternative course of action for resolving human problems by institutionalized means.

. . . The crucial question becomes, can our social institutions be changed, can old ones be modified and new ones introduced in such a way as to rebuild and revitalize the social context which families and children require for their effective function and growth. . . .

REFERENCES

Bronfenbrenner, U. Socialization and social class through time and space. In E. E. Maccoby, T. M. Newcomb, and E. Hartley (Eds.), *Readings in Social Psychology*, 3rd edition. New York: Holt, 1958, 400–425.

Bronfenbrenner, U. and Bruner, J. The President and the children. *The New York Times*, January 31, 1972, p. 41.

Bronfenbrenner, U. *Two Worlds of Childhood: U.S. and U.S.S.R.* New York: Russell Sage Foundation, 1970.

Cloward, R. D. Studies in tutoring. *Journal of Experimental Education*, Fall 1967, 36, 14–25.

Condry, J. C. & Siman, M. A. Characteristics of peer- and adult-oriented children. Unpublished manuscript, Cornell University, 1968.

Condry, J. C. & Siman, M. A. An experimental study of adult versus peer orientation. Unpublished manuscript, Cornell University, 1968.

Devereux, E. C., Jr., Bronfenbrenner, U., & Rodgers, R. R. Child rearing in England and the United States: A cross-national comparison.

Journal of Marriage and the Family, May 1969, 31, 257–270.

Garbarino, J. A note on the effects of television. In Bronfenbrenner, U. (ed.), *Influences on human development.* Hinsdale, Illinois: The Dryden Press, 1972.

Jarus, A., Marcus, J., Oren, J., & Rapaport, Ch. *Children and Families in Israel.* New York: Gordon and Breach, 1970.

National Commission on Resources for Youth, Inc. *Youth tutoring youth—it worked.* A final report, January 31, 1969. 36 West 44th St., New York, N.Y. 10036.

Parke, B. K. Towards a new rationale for cross-age tutoring. Unpublished manuscript, Cornell University, November 1969.

Profiles of Children: White House Conference on Children. Washington, D.C.: U.S. Government Printing Office, 1970.

Report to the President: White House Conference on Children. Washington, D.C.: U.S. Government Printing Office, 1970. 240–255.

Rodgers, R. R. Changes in parental behavior reported by children in West Germany and the United States. *Human Development,* 1971, 14, 208–224.

Yankelovich, D. *The changing values on campus: Political and personal attitudes of today's college students.* New York: Washington Square Press, 1972.

40

Criminals Are Made, Not Born

Morris L. Haimowitz

EDITOR'S NOTE · *We often hear about how society or the environment helps to make a person "criminal," but seldom is this process discussed in detail. This paper describes some specific and critical experiences that can conceivably lead a young person into a criminal career. This is not to suggest that all criminals take up a life of crime because of the dynamics outlined in this article, but we can reasonably speculate that more than a few young people learn that being a delinquent "somebody" is better than being a nondelinquent "nobody." Some of the reasons why some youth become criminals are expertly discussed in this selection.*

I. INTRODUCTION

A number of theories attempt to explain how people become professional criminals: poverty causes crime; "bad" neighborhoods cause crime; movies, TV, comic books, or radio crime stories cause crime; criminal associates cause crime; broken homes cause crime; race, nationality, neuroses, or

Reprinted from *Human Development: Selected Readings,* 2nd ed., Morris L. Haimowitz and Natalie R. Haimowitz, eds. (New York: Thomas Y. Crowell Company, 1966), pp. 391–403. By permission of the author.

crowded housing cause crime. These theories do not explain why most poor people never become professional criminals. Nor do most people from bad neighborhoods, or most children of broken homes, or most members of any race or nationality, or most neurotics become criminals. If crowded housing caused crime, all Eskimos would be criminals; actually, very few are.

Some studies show these factors to be associated with criminality. But science aims at generalizations which account for *all* cases, and not one of these theories accounts for even a majority of cases. What they do indicate is some *associated* factors, not the *causes* of crime. Let us illustrate the difference. Suppose we didn't know how a child is conceived and were seeking an explanation. We might make a survey and find the following factors associated with having children: poverty, illiteracy, race, religion, marriage, wedding rings, rural dwellings. Could we therefore state that poverty, illiteracy, and so on, were the causes of conception? Such a conclusion would completely overlook the crucial role of the sperm and ovary. Marriage is an associated factor, but it is not the cause of conception. The theories that poverty or race cause crime are as untrue as the ones that poverty or a wedding ring cause conception.

II. HYPOTHESIS

This paper seeks to develop the hypothesis that the only way a person can become a professional criminal is by getting the idea that he is expected to be an outlaw by those whom he takes seriously: his parents, friends, neighbors, teachers, clergymen, police, social workers, or judges. He must form a mental picture of himself as different from others, different in a way requiring a different vocational career and requiring that he associate with persons ostracized as he is.

This hypothesis refers to professional criminals, not to occasional lawbreakers or alcoholics, or persons who murder or steal in a passionate outbreak. It applies to those persons who belong to professional criminal societies and whose trade or occupation is criminal, with "professional" standards or skills. It is not always easy to tell which criminal is the professional and which is the amateur because many criminals have conflicting self-conceptions. And it is not easy to study the professional because he rarely goes to jail. Our jails are filled by the amateurs or neurotics, who play cops and robbers, who get a kick out of tearing up a place or doing something to get caught.

We like to think that there are two classes of occupations, the legal and the illegal, but the actual situation is not so simple. There are many gradations between the strictly honest and the strictly criminal. Many activities of business or professional men, repairmen, or governmental workers fall into criminal categories. In addition, there are other activities, not definitely criminal, nor yet definitely honest, in the shady or unethical category. Moreover, there are perfectly legal activities which are of questionable value, such as manufacturing, advertising, or selling hydrogen bombs, white flour, candy, alcohol, tobacco, patent medicines, or firearms, and which may be declared illegal in the future. Finally there are ideas which may be considered dangerous or illegal because they are new or different.

Some parents teach their children methods of stealing, but the usual delinquent cannot be explained so easily. Usually, his mother is frightened and embarrassed by his notoriety, even though she also may be secretly proud of her little rascal. This seems to be especially true of the mother whose husband is dead, divorced, or absent. The lonely mother is titillated by the adventures of her two-, three-, ten-, or twenty-year-old boy, and subtly encourages them by her exciting laughter or other reactions. Some criminals put on a "tough-baby" mask with an exaggerated masculinity.[1]

It is popular to explain socially disapproved behavior by labeling it neurotic. Suppose a man steals or damages property and finds himself waiting, terrified and yet wanting to be caught. He may experience an anxiety, like the child playing hide-and-seek, with excitement reaching a climax when he is discovered. Such a person would be a neurotic criminal. However, one can not say all criminals are neurotic, especially the one who performs his acts because he, his family, and his associates consider them proper and desirable. Furthermore, criminal law changes from time to time and is differently enforced from place to place. Betting is illegal in Chicago; legal in the suburbs. George Washington was a hero in America; a criminal in England.

III. THE SETTING: SOME FACTORS ASSOCIATED WITH CRIME

When we study criminals we find certain factors statistically associated with crime.

Most delinquents are found in the slums, yet most slum children never become delinquents. Most delinquents come from broken homes, yet most children from broken homes never become delinquents. Most delinquents are of a different racial or ethnic stock than the majority, yet race or ethnic affiliation is no guarantee of law-abiding or criminal behavior. Most delinquents are probably neurotic, but so are most non-delinquents. Most delinquents, finally, come from low-income families, but most persons with low incomes are law-abiding. A recent study of 2,000 white teen-agers by Nye and Short showed that delinquency was not as closely related to income, religion, or to broken homes, as to the feeling, "My parents hate me."

Most people who steal are not professional criminals. The act of stealing something probably involves a conscious decision. But the act of becoming a professional criminal appears to involve a long series of experiences in which a pattern of behavior occurs, a drifting into an unplanned habit of life which could have only one ending. The criminal may never have made a conscious decision to enter on a career of crime.

The people living in the slums and rooming house areas of the city are different from others not only in being on the average less well educated, earning less money, having higher mortality and morbidity rates, in appearing to have a higher rate of criminality, but also in being of different ethnic, racial, or national stocks. They are the newcomers. The immigrants usually settle in the slums; they bring with them not only poverty but also opinions as to what's right and what's wrong which were appropriate in the environment from which they came. It is a crime for the newcomer in Chicago to throw his garbage out the window; but home in the South it was perfectly proper to so feed the chickens and hogs. Prohibition was incomprehensible to Europeans accustomed to wine with dinner.

The rapid growth of the factories and of the slums housing the factory workers, the high rate of immigration, and the rapid technological developments have made this country, as well as other countries of our time, an area of cultural ferment, with rapidly changing ideas of what is criminal and what is proper. What is legal today may be criminal tomorrow.

All children get into mischief. Technically, you could say they violate the law. A little boy two years old pulls down the curtains in the living room. When they fall they knock over a lamp, dust flies all over the room, and his mother, hearing the commotion, runs in from the kitchen and helps him out of difficulty. He has behaved in utter disregard for life and property and is thus a lawbreaker, but no one calls him a criminal. His mother is caring for him all the time, getting him out of the refrigerator, turning off the gas which he has turned on, rescuing his toy rabbit from the toilet bowl. Like adults, all little children err, but few become gangsters.

Not all children, especially slum children, have a mother at home caring for them. They live in the "zones of transition," called such because these areas are changing from big homes to rooming houses, from residential to business, from native citizens to immigrants, from white to Negro to Mexican and Puerto Rican. But in one way such a zone is not changing. It always has had the highest crime rate of any area in the city. When the father is sick, dead, in jail, or shut out of home because he is unable to find a job and bring home money, the mother has to work, and cannot be home supervising the children; or perhaps she is sick or doesn't like caring for children.

A very high proportion of professional criminals come from the slums. Occasionally they come from nicer neighborhoods, but here too we find the unsupervised child. The child who steals and is caught and is arrested is delinquent; if he steals and is not caught or not arrested, he is not delinquent. Of course, police act more courteously to accused children of middle class or wealthy families. The policeman here says "naughty, naughty." He neither wants to give the child a record nor be sued for false arrest.

There are many ways a child may react to the fears and loneliness resulting from parental neglect. He can become a dreamer; he can become sick or develop an inferiority complex; or he can become a fighter, and demand attention, stating in effect, "Love me or fear me." The self-conception he forms is determined by the way he perceives certain crucial experiences.

IV. THE CRUCIAL EXPERIENCES

WITH PARENTS

Let's see what happens. A boy is involved in an incident during which someone is hurt or property is damaged or stolen. The injured party usually talks to the boy or his parents, and they make an amicable settlement. But sometimes the injured party feels frightened, angry with himself and his neighbors, and unable to deal with the situation alone, and so he calls the police. The boys see the police, and they all run away. One who did not run away, or was too slow, or had nothing to do with it, or has a bad reputation is caught. The parents are called in and they protect or spank the boy and everyone is satisfied. Or for some reason parents and sons are brought in for questioning. What concerns us is how the child learns that people expect him to be untrustworthy.

There are many ways parents may tell their children they are not to be trusted. They may be direct and say, "You are becoming a little hoodlum." Or they may be subtle and say, "My boy is good," and the boy knows they mean, "He is bad."

Here is an example of this. A juvenile officer was told that a fifteen-year-old boy had been committing delinquencies with a girl of his age. The girl had admitted relations with him. So the boy, accompanied by his mother, was brought in for questioning.

POLICE OFFICER: Did you see Miss X on December 15?

MOTHER: No, he didn't.

POLICE OFFICER: Did you meet Miss X after school that day?

MOTHER: No, why don't you leave him alone?

POLICE OFFICER: Did you have relations with her?

MOTHER: Why do you keep picking on him? He's a good boy; he would never do such a thing!

POLICE OFFICER: Why don't you let him talk for himself. I've been asking him questions for thirty minutes and you haven't let him answer once.

Was this mother so convinced of her son's innocence? It is natural for a mother to defend her son. Her words said, "He is a good boy," but her manner said, "He can't be trusted to speak; he is either too stupid to say the right thing, or he is terribly guilty." Thus she became an accessory to the crime.

And how would the boy feel in a spot like this? "To die, to sink through the floor, where can I hide? It's even harder when she lies. Why don't the police mind their own business?"

When persons important to the child don't trust him, he may come to distrust himself. The conception of oneself as a law-violator, or just a hateful, worthless, public nuisance does not usually develop full-blown in a few minutes. We don't know precisely how it happens. Little children interact thousands of times with others, thereby learning what is expected of them. Little children of two, three, or four years like to help their mothers in the kitchen—wash the dishes, peel the potatoes, string the beans, crack the nuts, mop the floor. They like to help their father repair the clock, fix the furnace, paint the chairs, drive the car. Some mothers and fathers find this "help" more than they can bear. They tell the child, "Go away! You can't wash the dishes, you'll break them; you can't paint the furniture; you can't mop the floor, scram!"

We have observed eleven-year-old children who could not clear the table or wash a dish ("She might break them," the mother would say); and we have observed other children, five years old, who could clear the table and wash and dry the dishes. One mother expects the child to break the dishes; the other mother expects the child to do a good job. Both children do what is expected of them, and by doing so, each is developing a self-conception.

Parents are very worried when their children are destructive. One mother who asked us for help could not understand her child: "Come see for yourself; that little boy was impossible." We went to her home, and she was right. He was impossible. But he wasn't learning how to be impossible all by himself; he was getting lots of help from his mother, and from his older brothers. During the hour of the visit we heard them tell him forty times, "Don't break the wall down; don't tear up your clothes; don't scream so loud; don't sweep the floor; don't be a bad boy; don't run; don't carry the tray. For God's sake, don't be impossible!" The boy told us, "I just wanted to help, and every time I try to help they make me do it wrong." His family wanted him to be good, but they told him they expected him to be bad. It appears that some children are more likely to act as people *expect* them to act than as they want to act. How many times a day may a parent tell the child, "I expect you to be bad." One hundred? and how many times by the child's sixth birthday? One hundred thousand? Some parents are more patient and can even enjoy the child's attempts to be useful. When the child strings one bean, they say, "Thank you," because they consider the child's age when judging his craftsmanship.

What is important is not so much just what words the parents say to the child as the way they act and the way their acts are interpreted by the child. The parents may say, "You are bad," but act as though the child were the most precious object in the world. Both the words and the other feelings are communicated. So the child may feel, "I am capable, but my parents are sometimes impatient."

If neglect, cruelty, or constant criticism indicate to the child he is the least *precious* object in the world, he will learn to see himself as no good. It may happen because the child is often neglected, left uncared for, unfed. Or no one takes time for the child or every time the child wants to help wash dishes, they say, "Go away, dishes are not for you, you just make a mess." This may happen thousands of times between his second and sixth year. And one day his mother decides he is now old enough to help, and she calls him in—but now he has learned "Dishes are not for me." He refuses to help wash the dishes, or gets a headache, or has to go to the bathroom. More extreme situations, such as the parent's leaving the child alone for days at a time, or beating him frequently, convey to him a sense of his worthlessness or undesirability.

WITH POLICE

Sometimes the boy is unsupervised, out on the streets. His parents prefer earning money to staying home and taking care of him. Something happens. He borrows a friend's bicycle, rides to the grocery store, goes inside, and buys an ice cream bar. As he comes out some bigger boys, wanting to share the ice cream, are waiting for him; he runs away from them, leaving the bicycle.

Meanwhile, the owner of the bicycle starts screaming, "Someone stole my bike." Fred says, "Tommy took it. I saw him." They find Tommy. He says he left it at the grocery store, but it is no longer there. The police are called. They try to locate Tommy's parents, but they are not at home. Now it is up to the police.

Usually the policeman is friendly but firm; he has children of his own who might have done the same thing, and he wouldn't want anyone roughing them up. He tells the boy, "You're a good boy. I know it was an accident. Be more careful next time," and let him go. If he has the time and the desire, if he is well trained, if he has been assigned to that neighborhood long enough to know it well, if he is patient, the policeman will talk to the natural leaders of the boys to convert the leaders from delinquent to productive activities. The policeman knows that most leaders of boys' gangs will cooperate if they are given a chance to participate in the planning and that these leaders can influence their followers better than anyone else. Or the policeman may recognize the need for community aid for these boys and will talk to local adult leaders—the clergyman, teacher, school principal, businessman, YMCA, or Lions Club officials for the purpose of getting more supervised activities underway. A number of studies have shown that participation in supervised activities deters juvenile delinquency. Even when such facilities are available, however, some supervisors refuse to permit delinquents to participate.

Often the policeman can't do these things. He doesn't have the time or the training. Perhaps he is under strain because it has happened several times before, or the citizen wronged is very angry or influential, or the policeman was recently reprimanded for being lax, or another child hit him in the ear with a snowball ten minutes earlier. Or, most important of all, the lad is impertinent. Then our young citizen—five, ten, fifteen years old—may be taken in and detained. The policeman may feel less likely to get into trouble by such action. Or he may feel, "Today I am starting a boy off on the wrong road, but I can't help it.'

Until this time the boy is like all the other kids; full of energy, going through many different kinds of activities all day long, singing, jumping, screaming, playing cops and robbers, tearing clothes, crying, fighting—just like everyone else. But once arrested he becomes different. He is asked questions which imply a difference—name, father's name, religion, age, father's occupation, nationality, race. Ordinary things become extraordinary. He never thought about such things before. He was just like everyone else until now. He wonders about himself. He is frightened but also may be very impressed with the whole procedure and perhaps with his own importance. He wants his mother. He is taken to a social worker. She is expected to ask questions. Tell me about your home, your father and mother, the implication being something is wrong with them. She might even go home and find out for herself. He is taken to a psychologist or sociologist. His intelligence is measured. His emotions are wondered at. He is taken to a judge: he hears lawyers talking about him. He is getting an education that his brothers and sisters and neighbors never dreamed about. Being in a detention home or jail can terrify a child. Everyone is saying, "Something's wrong with you."

He may be interrogated. Did you ever hear a policeman interrogating a teenager alleged to be guilty of a crime? The policeman acts and speaks as though the prisoner is guilty. It's his duty to clear up the crime. He is usually courteous, but sometimes he is filthy with insults, especially if the boy is a member of an ethnic group the policeman doesn't trust:

POLICE: What were you doing at that house?

BOY: I went there to collect $5.00 a man owed me.

POLICE: Don t you know they're a pack of thieves?

BOY: I didn't know that.

POLICE: If you sleep in a stable, you will smell like—.

BOY: I just went to collect my $5.00.

POLICE: Who did you lend it to?

BOY: Fred Johnson.

POLICE: Fred Johnson! He's an old-timer. Been in jail a dozen times. Why did you lend him $5.00?

BOY: He asked me for it. He lent me money when we were in school together.

SECOND POLICE: Oh boy! what a tale! [Sarcastically] They were planning another A&P job.

BOY: I never had anything to do with any A&P. I go to Brundy School.

POLICE: Who went through the transom, you or Fred?

POLICE: [All laugh] You're a damned liar! [Boy cries.][2]

Some policemen treat him like a son. Others, like a step-son. The policeman has a tough job. It sounds easy, "Just enforce law and order." But what does he do when John Doe, age eight, is caught for the third time stealing a bike? Scold him, let him go, arrest him? There must be an answer.

Why should a poorly paid, often semi-trained policeman be permitted to bear the burden of such a major decision? Many people are involved; many should help decide—maybe a community council, including teenagers as well as adults. One thing the police could do to give the boy some idea of the problems of policemen would be to invite delinquents to patrol the city a few hours a week in a police squad car. Most cities have enough squad cars to keep many delinquents occupied several hours a week. It might work, properly supervised so that the officers are instructed to try to be friendly, courteous, to explain their jobs, to listen to the problems of the boys as a sort of get-acquainted, how-do-you-do gesture, or as a long-term intensive activity.

IN COURT

The boy may be taken to court. What happens in the court room? The state's attorney may appear if enough publicity is involved, and he makes a speech, such as: "[Crime] by teen-agers must be stopped. The energetic measures taken by police to deal with these future hoodlums will be backed to the limit by the state's attorney's office.' (In this particular case, the judge in Boy's Court ordered bond increases from $100 to $4,000 for each of the six young men arrested.) The state's attorney continued his speech. "Either those boys will have a chance to reflect in jail while they are waiting trial, or their parents, through the expense of getting them out on bond, will realize that *parental irresponsibility doesn't pay.*"[3] His speech was longer. The boys might remember part of it, but we are sure they would like to forget that such a prominent man considered them "future hoodlums" and publicly proclaimed that not only they, but their parents as well, are tainted. Could the boys think: "He's important; he says we'll be criminals. He ought to know. I never thought I'd be a criminal; but he's a very important man." The public doesn't expect the state's attorney to furnish adequate homes, parents, playgrounds, and psychologists for these boys. But the public doesn't expect him to teach these boys that they are permanent public enemies either.

The judge at the Boy's Court has many problems. Among some boys who had been arrested for participating in a riot, two were dismissed. Here's what the newspapers said about these two: "John _____, 21, of Chicago, a laborer, and his brother, 19, of Chicago, unemployed, were dismissed. They said they merely stopped nearby to see what the trouble was and were arrested. Judge _____ told the defendants: 'We're going to give you a break. We operate on the theory that every dog is entitled to one bite.' "[4] Here were two bystanders arrested, taken to jail, and then instead of getting an apology for being inconvenienced, the judge says he will invoke a canine justice. But this is no dog's court. These boys, like the judge, are human. What can the judge do? The police say, "They are guilty—we saw them rioting." The boys say, "We broke no law." Citizens, relatives, and neighbors testify, orate, hiss, and applaud both sides. The judge doesn't know who is right or what to do. The boys are our concern here. They may get the impression: "We are not like other human beings. We are bad."

What can the judge do? The voters are angry because there was a riot; the police are angry because the boys were not convicted; the boys, because they were arrested and scolded; the judge, because he too is on public trial in a difficult situation. Because of this many judges try to protect themselves and the public by utilizing medical, sociological, psychological, or other professional advice. Sometimes, though, they lose their tempers.

The writer has no quarrel with these officials. Thousands of such items appear in the papers every year. The point is that the police, state's attorney,

and judges may not lead the defendants to expect honest, law-abiding behavior of themselves. If this were the end of it, probably the defendants would go back home and be upright citizens. The suggestions from the officials that they are disreputable might not be taken seriously. But this may not be the end.

Why should a solitary judge with fifty to one hundred cases in one day be permitted to make such vital decisions? Crime hurts everyone. These decisions are too important for any one person to make.

BACK HOME

The boy goes back home. Whether or not he was found guilty, he is not quite like his friends any more, but is an object of curiosity: "What did they do to you?" "My lawyers defended me," he says. "I saw the judge." An object of adoration: his picture was in the paper; he has had his IQ measured; he has talked to lots of policemen. An object of scorn—he was arrested, put in jail with crooks—he is vicious. For some of his friends he is a hero; for others he must never be played with again. If he should see them, they turn away: "My mother says not to play with you. The state's attorney says you're a hoodlum."

Little boys soon forget. They play together as usual, except for those whose mothers are constantly reminding them, protecting them from the "criminal," the bad apple in the neighborhood. Then something happens again. The newspapers have a heyday. Who did it? The citizens are upset and impatient. They put pressure on the police. The police have to do something. Well, everyone knows who did it. Didn't someone just leave the detention home? Wasn't his name in the paper? It makes no difference that he was at school or visiting in another city when it happened. He is apprehended because he is convenient. He is found not guilty, but everyone suspects him just the same. He is getting a reputation, and a self-conception.

Lots of boys find their home life uncomfortable. Pick a child up off the stret some night —say, at midnight. Take him home and you will see why he doesn't want to be home. His home may be physically repulsive; or it may be a lovely house but a miserable home. To say that it's the parent's fault misses the point. Most parents of delinquents are helpless, sorely in need of psychological, medical, religious, or economic aid. Responsibility lies not with irresponsible parents but with the community.

We assume that parents mean well but many just do not have the energy and skills necessary to win the confidence of their children and to make plans together. Parents expect their children to mature gradually and become independent. That this can be done gracefully is proved by many happy parents who help their children settle on their own. Even in the better neighborhoods a barrier often develops between the parents and children. Most children on the street go home after a while and play inside, but some can't go home. In many instances help for the parents would prevent a child from going to the street.

ON THE STREET

Our young citizen may find friends on the street where things are more pleasant, where he can be a hero. We assume everyone wants to be liked; everyone wants a word of praise, and if it is not available at home and is available on the street, then one goes to the street. A little boy knows where he is afraid to breathe and where he is a regular guy like all the rest.

The boys he plays with on the street may like to play volleyball. They have a volleyball and play all the time. They don't get into trouble. Or they may not have a volleyball. Slum children have less equipment than other children. What can you do on the street?

Everyone needs someone to idealize, someone to be like, someone to dream he is like. These street children could idealize their parents, but it is not likely since they don't enjoy their parents. Their hero could be a policeman who saves a man's life; but not if the policeman hurts them or depreciates them. We don't know enough about whom the street boys idealize. Maybe it's a famous boxer who can beat anyone in the whole world; or a cowboy movie star. These boys can't be cowboys; but they can fight, they can be brave, not afraid of their parents, not afraid of the police. They can learn to be tough.

If the street boy could get along with his mother, he might be home with her, learning to keep his room straight: "Freddie, hang up your clothes. Freddie, wash your hands; Freddie, shine your shoes this minute. Freddie, here's some new crayons. That's a sweet boy." His mother cannot be at ease until she knows he is responding to her attempts at socialization.

The boys on the street are learning a different moral code: Who can throw the stone the straightest. Who can run faster. Who is a sissy. Who can do things and not get caught. Hundreds of times a day a boy is learning the code of the street: Be loyal to friends—never betray a comrade. Find out who you can trust. Avoid the police.

Street boys go to school. The teacher knows they have been in trouble and if anything out of the ordinary occurs in the classroom, she knows who is to blame. Even if they are not really to blame, she can guess who were the agitators. Because the street boys have more than average trouble at home, they may be more restless than the average pupils and not perform well in school. You can't want to please a teacher if this makes you a sissy, especially if this teacher is always picking on you or your friends. The teacher is not going to be his ideal or model. She could if she had a class of fifteen children instead of thirty to sixty and if her salary made it unnecessary to hold down an extra job or two, and if teachers had high morale, and if she had time to consult with parents, social workers, religious workers, a physician, a psychologist, a reading specialist, to discuss the boy's problems, and if she had professional training and attitudes. Sometimes she can do it without all these. But aren't we foolish to expect miracles of semi-trained overworked teachers?

It takes most people years to settle down to one ego ideal. Little boys play at being policemen or cowboys or gangsters. When they are growing up they decide to be truck drivers or ambulance drivers or doctors. In school they want to be teachers or janitors or a principal or the coach. In college they want to be lawyers or scientists or philosophers or businessmen. After they leave college, they are deciding one day this, one day that. Who do I want to be like? What am I going to do? It takes years for the average citizen to decide.

Lots of people are helping the street boy to decide on his career. His mother and father and his home life are unbearable to him, so he joins the street boys. His friends on the street give him fellowship and praise for doing a good job. His teacher tells him he is too jumpy. The police suggest that he is a liar. The social worker suggests his family is tainted. The psychologist tells him he is not like other boys. The judge says, "Every dog deserves one bite." The state's attorney says, "You are the future hoodlums." Can one's career be that of a hoodlum?

REFORM SCHOOL

One day he is arrested, found guilty and goes to reform school. He is frightened and angry. He wishes he were home. He wants out: "Who are my friends and who are enemies?" He learns that some of the inmates are regular guys; others snitch on you. The guards, the hired hands around the place, can't be trusted; they are against you. "What are you here for?" a friend asks. "I grabbed a pocketbook and ran." "Is that all? Boy! I robbed five filling stations! You know that kid with the glasses, the tall blond one? He killed a policeman! When he says something, you'd better jump."

How do you rob a filling station? What do you do with the tires? Which lawyers will help you if you get caught? Which is the easiest way to rob the A&P? How do you steal a car? Where can you sell it? Who buys the parts? How can you be successful? This sounds like an exciting career. He never realized so many people are in this business. The reform school teaches much about crime, but little about reform.

The guards are afraid the boys will run away, hurt each other or hurt the guards. The superintendent has his job to do. He has to keep the boys clean, working, in school, has to buy the groceries, get a new psychologist to replace the one leaving for a better job, get three new attendants, make out dozens of reports, read what the wardens at other schools are doing, go to meetings, see visitors from the Rotary Club, decide what to do about a boy who is always fighting. If he is strict, the boys hate him more. If he is less strict, the place gets dirty and citizens complain; newspapers take pictures. There is never enough money. The superintendent does what he can. The boys are learning a career. They can't help it, and he can't help it.

And the respectable citizens back home are not aware of the fact that they are paying $500 to $5,000 per year to train each child to become a more professional criminal. Foster homes may be a better risk, especially if foster parents get special training in ways to handle these children; however it's hard to find parents who will take disturbed children.

AFTER REFORM SCHOOL

When the boy leaves the reform school, he goes home. He has been a disgrace to the family, and his welcome is thin: "Your mother is ashamed to walk down the street!" "We hope they reformed you." He is now perhaps nine, twelve, or fifteen years old. His sister says, "You have ruined my life." He wonders who his friends are. Maybe a brother is friendly to him. Maybe his mother. She gives him a new necktie. But can she give him what will save him from the electric chair or from a life sentence? If she can give him the trust and patience and ability to be responsible, and skill in holding a job—what every boy needs much and he needs immensely—she can save him. Usually she cannot, any more than she could before reform school. If he is to be helped, it will be by foster parents or officials of the institutional kingdoms, school, church, scouts, PTA, settlement house, working as an integrated unit. Today these kingdoms often work in competition and at odds with one another.

It is easy in the neighborhood to tell who can be trusted. Plenty of guys make nasty remarks. They go to school; they go to Sunday school; they brush their teeth and say, "Good afternoon," to the corner policeman. When their mothers see the returned "criminal" in the drug store, they say: "Look who's out! If I see my boy playing with you I'll call the police. Stay away." You can understand that such mothers are trying to protect their own boys. But they are helping another boy to become a criminal. If good boys won't play with him, who will? Underworld characters?

Other mothers don't know much about him. They are working or sick or preoccupied. Their sons are the street boys. The boys want to know about reform school. Did they beat you? Let me show you what I learned. Let's pull a job tonight.

I'll show you how to do it. I can chin with one hand.

He has to go to school. That's the law. The principal talks to him, the teacher talks to him, some kids talk to him, and what they say adds up to one thing: They are not his friends. They expect him to start something. It doesn't have to be that way. They could invite him to join the Scouts, or write on the school paper, or sing in the choir, or play on the team. If they did, it might save him.

His mother wants him to go to church. She has talked to the clergyman, who says he needs religion. He may not be as clean, as well dressed as the next boy—or he may be cleaner. The boy out of reform school wonders how his new clothes look. They feel strange. The people in Sunday school may not feel hostile toward him, but they are strangers. One looks at him in a friendly way; another says, "He just got out of reform school."

There is still a chance he won't go back to reform school or graduate into prison, but the chance is slim. Let a window be broken, a store burglarized, a car stolen, and the neighbors will know who to blame. A nice neighborhood finds it easy to blame someone for its troubles, not only because the accused may be guilty, but because he is the one expected to perform such acts in this community. If he does not expect of himself what they expect of him, he will go straight, perhaps leaving the community, perhaps even changing the community, but that is unlikely.

Even after he comes to expect vicious or criminal behavior of himself, he may still act like a good citizen most of the time. But it appears that the self-concept, the picture of himself inside, is more powerful than anything else in determining his behavior. Here is part of an interview between a prisoner and a prison counselor to illustrate this:

PRISONER: Why do I keep getting in trouble? I want to go straight, but I'll go out and before you know it I'm with the same crowd. I know it's wrong and yet there I am.

COUNSELOR: Maybe you are forced back to the old crowd.[5] Have you ever been treated like an ex-con?

PRISONER: I was going with a girl and couldn't get the nerve to tell her I'd been in the pen. I knew she'd find out sooner or later. I finally did in a way. I took to drinking.

COUNSELOR: You had to. It's too much to bear. You knew she wouldn't understand.

PRISONER: I began to hate her. She kept asking what was wrong and all that. In fact I don't think I minded it too much when I had to leave her, knowing what she would think of me.

COUNSELOR: It's hard to love a person when you expect her to hate you.

PRISONER: You know, she still comes to see me, so I was wrong about how she would feel.

The prisoner could not bring himself to tell his girl friend that he had been in jail for fear that she would hate him. Since it was not true that she hated him, we must conclude that the hatred was in himself, that he hated himself because he felt he was a criminal or because he expected her to hate him because he was a criminal. Of course, it is difficult for one who has been arrested many times to feel, "I'm an honest and respected man." He wanted to go straight but felt he was not honest. In not telling the girl, he was in fact dishonest. If he had felt he was an honest man, it would have been much easier for him to say, "I was convicted of a crime and spent some time in jail, but now I am honest." But his self-conception must have been: "I'm a criminal. She would hate criminals like everyone else hates them, perhaps even as I myself do. So I can't tell her." With such a self-conception, he could not be comfortable around law-abiding citizens.

Gradually, over the years, if he comes to expect of himself what his neighbors expect of him, he becomes a professional criminal. But if along the way he can find satisfactions and social approval from legitimate activities, he will obey the law. When he has learned over and over again that he can find no satisfaction this way, he welcomes the greetings of his professional associates in the underworld. As a professional criminal, he has standards of performance to live up to, friends who will help him when in trouble, visit him in prison, send him presents at Christmas, give him a home when he is sick, tell him where the police are lax and where strict—hideouts, fences, and lawyers. At twelve, fourteen, sixteen, or eighteen he has come to a conclusion about his career that ordinary boys may not make until they are twenty or even forty. And he could not have drifted into this career without the help of his family and neighbors who sought a scapegoat and unwittingly suggested to him that he become an outlaw.

V. IMPLICATIONS

When a crime is committed in a community, it is, in a sense, caused by everyone. No one grows up and lives alone; the criminal grows up with people. He is affected by his social experiences. If he wants to murder, people have made him want to murder; if he wants to break school windows, his environment has taught him how and given him a reason. And if he is punished by the community, it is because the community feels guilty for his crime, for failing to provide positive experiences in schools, for not protecting him from severe cruelty, neglect, starvation, and rejection. Those in the community who most demand his punishment are usually those who feel most guilty for their own failures, real or imaginary. They punish the criminal as they have been punished themselves. If they could forgive themselves, accept themselves, they could forgive the delinquent, accept and teach him, and, in so doing, convert him before he becomes a hardened unconvertible criminal. This conversion process is usually too big a job for any one school, teacher, policeman, judge, psychologist or social worker. It takes many people to make an ordinary little boy into a hardened criminal. It will take a lot of people to make a criminal into a good citizen. Every little boy or girl in trouble should be examined by a physician, a psychologist, a reading specialist, a social worker, and his home and neighborhood should be studied. Intelligent steps can then be taken by this team of people working with the community council, with the cooperation of the boy and taking into consideration his preferences, to give this boy what everybody needs: security, affection, adventure, a chance to get recognition, to learn, and to give to others the best that he has to give.

Every city and hamlet has some special programs for handling delinquents Every program in every city is different from the next. Naturally, some are more effective than others. Study and systematic evaluation of these programs are required to find out what works and what does not.

Statistics show considerable increase in juvenile crime, just as they show increase in divorce rate. This is not clear evidence of increase in juvenile crime or in broken marriages. The first could be a result of more accurate reporting or because there are more policemen; the second, of greater resort to legal processes because there is more money for divorce lawyers. In a rural community or village where everyone is known, the community is aware when a child takes another child's bicycle and tries private means to have it returned. No police are notified. In the secular, impersonal, anonymous city, a bicycle theft is more likely to be reported to the police. As our society becomes more secular, the official agencies are used more often. Two hundred years ago, divorce was rare: When a couple could not get along they either separated, the husband left, the wife ran away, they lived together but did not speak to one another, or they took lovers. The rise in the divorce rate does not necessarily mean a rise in unsuccessful marriages. In a friendly neighborhood, when children at play break a window, the parents may talk it over and decide who pays; but in an anonymous neighborhood, they may call the police. The two misdeeds are the same, but the "crime rate" is higher in one place than another.

PUNISHMENT

Sometimes a youth commits a crime which so angers the community that letting him go without "punishment" is impossible. Punishment in our society is either a fine, imprisonment, or the death penalty. There are no other punishments within our legal system. When I ask some of my legal advisers why we might not try out some other forms of punishment, they ask me to name one. I name several: for the youth who breaks windows and street lights, let him pick up glass and other debris from the streets for a few days. For the youth who breaks someone's jaw, let him take care of patients who have been injured. For those bigots who have been involved in racial demonstrations, let them meet with bigots on the other side. The attorney said about picking up debris, "That would be involuntary servitude, which would be illegal." I asked about the prisoners in jails who work for 15 cents a day. "They are not forced to work. If they don't work they don't get the 15 cents a day they need for cigarettes and candy." How about asking the tough to pick up debris or work in a hospital? My lawyer said "No."

The problem is that what punishment is to one may be reward to another. Sending a person to jail may be just what he has been hoping for, an opportunity to get away from his mother or wife or gang, relax, and get three square meals a day.

A good deal of evidence is accumulating to show that the majority of juvenile delinquents and criminals have been neglected or otherwise punished as infants and children. What will reduce crime, therefore, will be prevention of such punishment of these infants and small children, for it seems that by the age of four or five a child may believe "I am no good; people are no good; it is a dog-eat-dog world, and I'll take what I can get. The only mistake is getting caught." Those of us who assume that delinquency is an act of free will might contemplate this: We know a great deal about how persons become delinquent, and how delinquents may be converted into law-abiding citizens.[6] We know that if someone accepts the delinquent and is sufficiently persuasive in attempts to redirect him, the delinquent may discover a new self and a new model to follow. We know that if the delinquent is educated and trained in salable skills, and if opportunities for dignified work at acceptable wages are available, he will go to work.

If we know how to turn a delinquent into a law-abiding citizen—by voting more money for schools and for mental health research, by helping the Boy Scouts and the Girl Scouts, by providing parks and playgrounds supervised by professionally trained personnel, by volunteering our services as tutor or referee or big brother, by helping the parents of the potentially delinquent find suitable training and jobs—if we know this and refuse to act, arguments about free will fall on deaf ears. If we are free to cure the delinquent and do not, how ghastly incredible is our crime. Only determinism theory exonerates us: We are not free to change the delinquent even though we know how, just as he is not free to change himself unless we help him.

REFERENCES

1. See M. K. Bacon, Irvin L. Child, and Herbert Barry III, "A Cross-Cultural Study of Correlates of Crime," *Journal of Abnormal and Social Psychology*, LXVI (1963), 291–300.

2. This dialogue is quoted verbatim. Only names and obscenity are changed. The writer is grateful to many policemen in Chicago and prison officials in New York whose cooperation helped to formulate the ideas here.

3. Chicago Sunday *Tribune*, August 23, 1953, part 1, p. 25.

4. Chicago *Daily News*, August 17, 1953, p. 3.

5. In trying to be sympathetic, the counselor may be destructive. He suggests that the prisoner is not responsible for his behavior. A more constructive response would be, "Let's outline activities you can do when you leave the prison," although this would not be successful until the prisoner and counselor are involved with one another.

6. *See* William Glasser, *Reality Therapy* (New York: Harper and Row, 1965) for a description of highly skilled teams that convert the most delinquent girls and 20-year veterans of psychoses into responsible citizens.

41

Our Troubles with Defiant Youth

Fritz Redl

EDITOR'S NOTE · In this reading, Dr. Redl discusses the fallacy of the "delinquent" stereotype presented in the previous readings. He says there is a diversity of motivation and causes behind four kinds of defiant behavior. Too often we believe that defiant behavior is symbolic of exploding aggression when, in fact, it may be a symptom of passive submission. Once we understand that not all defiant behavior means the same thing, we may be in a better position to handle such behavior constructively. This reading will help you to do that.

The term "delinquency" is used these days generally in vague and confusing ways. Clinically the behavior referred to as "delinquent" may cover a wide range of entirely different afflictions. Sometimes the word is as loosely applied as the popular term "bellyache" which may cover anything from temporary upset after eating too much ice cream to stomach ulcers or acute appendicitis. Nobody in the medical field today would attempt to answer the question "what should be done about it" before finding out concretely just which of the afflictions gave rise to the "bellyache." Unfortunately, however, in the field of human behavior and mental health, the public has not yet reached as wise an acceptance of the variety of ills which may result in excessive aggression or as much respect for the need for specific diagnosis.

The concept of "defiant youth" does *not* coincide with the delinquency problem. Some "defiance" is part and parcel of the normal growth process. It may even be a desirable though an uncomfortable forerunner of a character trait commonly referred to as "integrity" or "spine." Other forms of defiance, however, do overlap with the kind of trouble usually referred to as "delinquency" and constitute a great strain on our communities. On the other hand, not all delinquents show overt defiant behavior. In fact some of the hardest to reach cases exhibit a very "slick" surface conformity as a safe cover for the cultivation of a totally immoral outlook on life or a safe buildup for a long-prepared criminal "splurge."

These facts leave persons concerned with the behavior of today's youth facing two important questions:

1. In what areas are confused public opinion and juvenile delinquency most seriously blocking clinical progress and preventive planning?
2. What types of youthful defiance need to be differentiated in order to begin wise preventive and therapeutic planning?

AREAS OF CONFUSION

There are three main areas of confusion.

1. The Individual and the Symbol. Most of us have been annoyed at one time or another by the fact that children go through a phase where they suddenly consider us, their parents and teachers, as just a general symbol of "the adult." They seem suddenly to have emptied us of all personal relationships with them. We stop being Mary's dad or Johnny's older friend and represent simply "those adults," the power group from whose grip they are trying to emancipate themselves.

However, we adults don't usually recognize that we begin to do the same thing to our children as soon as they enter the development phases of

Reprinted from *Children* 2 (January–February 1955): 5–9, Office of Human Development, Children's Bureau, U.S. Department of Health, Education, and Welfare.

preadolescence and adolescence. In these periods Daddy does have moments of reacting to his son not so much as a person, but as though he represented the "world of adults" pitched against "youth" which is getting out of hand. Dad's little boy suddenly becomes not his son whom he knows and loves so well, but just an "example" of the way postwar young people act when you don't "keep them in line."

This peculiar phenomenon, natural and harmless within limits, often becomes a real block to wise handling of youthful behavior. It is responsible for much avoidable antagonism between the generations. The more we feel threatened by what youngsters do, the more we fall into this form of stereotyping. As a result many situations grow into sham battles over a "cause," when the immediate problem could have been easily solved if the two adversaries had remained what they were to begin with: two *people* having it out.

2. Some of My Best Friends are Teenagers. There seems to be a tendency in the adult world toward hostility to youth as such which is in striking contrast to the fact that we all "like kids," especially our own or those entrusted to our care. Something seems to happen to the most child-acceptant of us when we suddenly switch from personal involvement with a child to a collective view of the youth problem. This shift in focus tends especially to occur when a youngster becomes involved in some rather atrocious crime—although the act has so obviously grown out of extreme disorganization within the world surrounding him, such a long and involved chain of disturbing events that nobody could logically regard the outcome as "typical" youthful behavior.

A 14-year-old boy tries to defend his mother against the onslaughts of his drunken father and hits him a bit too hard with the piece of pipe he grabs in despair. Why are our newspapers so ready to call this a "teenage crime"? By doing so aren't they implying that this boy is "typical" of the youth of our time, or at least that something about being a "teenager" has brought about the unfortunate event which so obviously stemmed from the pathology of the adults in the boy's life? On the other hand, do the papers write up as a typical teenage deed the heroism of Bobby, an Eagle Scout, who rescued a little girl from drowning? On the

contrary Bobby Smith, aged 15, remains Bobby Smith, not a representative of his age, and the heroism is credited to himself. In other words, teenagers are regarded as a breed suspect until proven innocent. Their bad deeds redound on the whole age group. Their good deeds point only to the exceptions that prove the rule.

When public attitudes incline toward stereotyping of this sort there is cause for deep concern. Collective suspicion and negativism of one group toward another always backfire by engendering conscious or unconscious collective counter-aggression and distrust from the other side. To increase intergroup tensions between the "world of grown-ups" and the "youth of our time" is the last thing we should do at this point in history. Since we have paid such prices in the past for collective prejudices in the areas of race, religion, class, and caste we should know something about the high cost of group psychological pathology.

3. An Optical Illusion. Adult disgust with "youth" is easily aroused when the young people gather in mobs. Their boisterous and rather inconsiderate behavior gets on our nerves and reinforces our suspicious stereotypes. Thus, unfortunately, we are taken in by a kind of "optical illusion," for loud and thoughtless behavior is often more typical of the group situation individuals are in than of the individuals themselves. If you doubt this, just remember the last large convention held in your town. Many riotous teenagers would have trouble living up to what otherwise dignified adults can do to hotel-room towels, ashtrays, and doorknobs when they are convening in somebody else's city.

While much remains to be learned about the impact of group psychological excitement on the behavior of the human individual, age, or "teenage," as such is not the main factor involved. The problem of how to predict which person's self-control and value system will melt under a certain amount of group psychological heat and how to help individuals keep sense and control intact under free-floating contagion is one of the most urgent research issues before us. Instead of allowing ourselves to become irritated at an "age range," we should take steps to investigate thoroughly this larger problem of group pathology.

In summary, it seems as important for the fields of mental hygiene and preventive psychiatry to tackle the collective confusions about youthful behavior in which the present adult generation indulges as to cope with the problems of youth itself. We have made wonderful strides with analogous problems in the field of physical medicine and health. Through the astounding successes of public-health education on a variety of levels, present public opinion is enlightened about the nature of invisible germs, accepts even unpleasant facts about the nutritive values of certain foods, and no longer quarrels with the wisdom of certain "first aid" directives even where these contradict deeply ingrained popular myths or personal feelings. But in the field of human behavior the major task of "deconfusing the public" lies ahead.

WHAT ABOUT "DEFIANCE"?

Without attempting anything as ambitious as an outline of symptomology and etiology of the "defiant child," we can differentiate a few of the outstanding problems that usually sail under this heading. Here too conceptual confusion, while not the core of the difficulty, is a dangerous roadblock on the way to progress.

1. Developmental Defiance. In spite of all the talk about "adjustment," we would not really want children to "adjust" to everything all the time. If they did we would think they lacked "spine." Healthy development on the part of a child is fostered by strengthening not only his ability to adjust to outside demands, but also his ability to defend his own integrity against wrong demands made by others. We want Johnny to be respectful to his teacher but we don't want him to run after the first designing bum that offers him candy just because the man is an adult and looks like a mixture of Abe Lincoln and Santa Claus. On the contrary, we want our children to retain the capacity for *intelligent rebellion*—courage to stick to what they believe in even against strong-armed pressure and the fear of becoming unpopular with the mob.

All traits that we want eventually to see in our children must grow through a range of developmental phases. "Intelligent rebellion," too, needs leeway to be learned and practiced. Of course, while being practiced it often looks any-

thing but intelligent and can be very annoying to the adult who has to live with it. We know from our studies of child development that certain age ranges seem to be especially cut out for the practice of "emancipation acrobatics." The negativism of the child between 3 and 5 as well as the strong "emancipation" efforts of the young adolescent are normal phases in child development. While uncomfortable for educator and parent, these rebellious phases are important as preparation for independence. We also know that defiance which is part of this developmental process is *not habit forming*. It tones down by itself as soon as the character trait of integrity, for the sake of which it was displayed, is sufficiently secured.

Although we have many books that tell us how to cultivate "intelligent rebellion" in the well-adjusted child in relation to the child's dependence on individuals, we have little information on how to help him keep his integrity when confronted with gang and mob pressure. One of the Nation's greatest problems at this time is to find out how to help our young people stick to what they believe in, even in defiance of whatever opinion or action might be popular at the moment with the rest of the youthful crowd. Actually a lot of behavior usually termed "defiance" is exactly the opposite. The 16-year-old who participates in an incident of vandalism because he is afraid of being called a sissy is not a *defiant* child. He is a coward, an overconformist, a spineless lickspittle for public acclaim. The fact that he is overdependent on the wrong opinions does not change the fact that submission rather than defiance is the real problem at hand.

Clinically speaking, then, we have to look a few inches below the surface before we can know what the problems in any specific "defiant act" really are. Where behavior falls into the category of "developmental defiance," it presents us with an educational challenge, but we must not be fooled into regarding it as "delinquency."

2. Reactive Defiance. Some youthful defiant behavior may be compared to the process of regurgitation. If you pour poison or stuff pins down somebody's throat, his organism will probably rebel by choking reactions to ward off the hurtful intrusion. Vomiting under such conditions is not symptomatic of illness. On the contrary, it is the defense of a healthy organism against hurt from the outside.

A lot of youthful "defiant" behavior falls into the same category. It is *not* the outcropping of a corrupt or morbid personality, but the defense of a healthy one against the kind of treatment that shouldn't happen to a dog, but often does happen to children. At close inspection even many of the rather frightening and disgusting outbursts of youthful defiance are of this type. In a group of normal schoolchildren bored beyond limit by stupid teaching methods, the intelligent ones will be the first to become "hard to handle." Their misbehavior is a defense against the demoralizing impact of excessive boredom. If a child with deep-seated anxieties is put into solitary confinement under frightening circumstances, the resulting temper tantrum will not be his "warped personality" coming to the fore but his desperate defense against total breakdown into mental disease. His frantic muscle spasms and aggressive mauling of the surrounding outside world are the expression of his inward terror.

Such "reactive defiance" calls for consideration not only of what's wrong with the child but also of what is wrong with what we are doing to him. Every case of really pathological and dangerous defiance which I have had a chance to study closely has had its origin at some time in "reactive" defiance. Many people had to do the wrong things consistently for a long time to the children involved to produce such a severe degree of disturbance. This means that one of our greatest preventive opportunities lies in developing and applying greater knowledge about the most advantageous setting for growing youngsters and in helping adults toward a maximum of wisdom in their reaction to youthful behavior.

3. Defiance as a Wrapping. Some defiant behavior is quite clearly "unprovoked," or at least seems so at first sight. Why should Billy, a well-loved and well-cared-for child, one day suddenly act up, hanging on to furniture and kicking and biting when you try to make him go to school? His unwarranted behavior toward you looks dangerously like the "rebellious child" in the making. It looks and feels like that, until you learn that Billy has deep-seated fears of any "crowd" situation—fears that are irrational but extremely intense. The panic aroused in Billy's mind is in itself a "sickness," an anxiety neurosis. This is the affliction, not the "disrespectful disobedience" which he displays when confronted with it.

Other "defiant acts" by youthful offenders may be the secondary accompaniment of any of a variety of mental diseases. I once knew a child who when compulsively hit by sudden intense spurts of fantasy images would get up during class and wander around, impervious to threats of punishment. He *seemed* to do all this "just in order to spite authority." Yet nothing was further from the truth. At these moments, he did not even *perceive* the teacher's presence nor any of the world around him. He had no thought of being "spiteful." It would have been easier to help him if he had, for this child was out of contact with reality far beyond the normal degree of childish daydreaming. This sickness is worse than the usual "defiance." But the important point is that it is *different* and calls for entirely different treatment and preventive measures.

Defiance which comes as a "wrapping" around some other disease is especially frustrating. Because in such cases the techniques so often found helpful in dealing with other defiant children are totally ineffectual, the adult's wrath at the defiant behavior is apt to be increased by his fury at his helplessness. The result is a loud cry for some form of physical punishment. Unfortunately, in these cases physical punishment is the most futile and most damaging technique we could use. Where defiance is a "wrapping" no matter how smell-proof or loose, the only thing to do is to tackle the disease behind the wrapping. All other efforts are useless.

THE DEFIANT EGO

By a "defiant ego" I mean the ego that has thrown itself on the side of the child's impulsivity, defending it against reason and the voice of his "better self" with enormous skill and strength.

This, unfortunately, is the most neglected although the most serious form of defiance. While from the outside it looks very much like other types of defiant behavior, at closer range it reveals itself as a most pernicious and serious affliction which educator and psychiatrist so far are completely helpless to change.

Children with "defiant egos" act destructively any time they so desire because they enjoy it. If they want their "fun" they are going to have it. Either they have not developed that "voice from within" that would make them feel bad about "fun" that is unjustly had at somebody else's expense; or they have developed very skillful tricks of putting that "voice" out of commission should it tend to interfere. Diagnosis, however, is not easy. The size of the offense or the intensity of the defiance gives no clue as to what type of defiance is involved. It is not true that rowdyism marks a child as sickest or worst, while milder or even "cute" forms of rebellion can be passed by as harmless. Nuisance value to others, or intensity and degree of defiance are only a few of the criteria for sizing things up for what they really are.

I know of actions close to murder, which have had little to do with real defiance, but are reactive or psychoneurotic in origin. I also know of cases where as mild a symptom as polite withdrawal from arts and crafts activities—but always exactly when whim dictated and always accompanied by total disinterest and bland imperviousness to the persuasiveness of others—proved to be the forerunner of very severe character disorders which later blossomed into openly recognizable symptom displays.

A detailed description of the "defiant ego" is not possible in the space available. However, this is the type of affliction which may justifiably be classified as "delinquency," even if the defiance displayed does not seem to have any "legal" implications. The early recognition of such afflictions and the determination of conditions for preventive and therapeutic work with them constitute the main themes of the present project at the Psychiatric Children's Unit at the National Institute of Mental Health.[1] [See "Child Study in a New Setting," *Children*, Vol. 1, No. 1.]

IN SUMMARY

The problem of "defiant youth" is complicated by the fact that the adult generation generally lacks conceptual clarity in discussing the issues involved.

Furthermore, "defiant" behavior by children seems to bring out the worst in adults, provoking them to react with their own feelings rather than with deliberate thought. The collective "suspicious antagonism" which communities often display against the "teenagers" as a "caste and class" is likely to foster or increase a collective spirit of defiance among youth itself.

The actual phenomenon of "defiance" has many degrees ranging from "light" to "severe and dangerous," from "cute" to "morbidly obnoxious." Unfortunately, the degree does not indicate in any given case what lies behind the behavior. No matter which specific form of behavior defiance may take, it may derive from any one, or a mixture of, at least four types of afflictions. . . .

The answer to the problem of defiant youth must be sought in the direction of more practice-geared research, greater concerted effort toward the education of the public to the causes of defiance, and more courage to think straight even under the impact of panic and wrath.

---

[1] Redl, F. & D. Wineman, *The Aggressive Child*, The Free Press, 1957.

42

The Decision to Fail

Bruno Bettleheim

EDITOR'S NOTE · Maladjustment can be ex-pressed in many different ways, and one dra-matic way, certainly, is maladjustment in learning. When a student does poorly in school or in a particular subject, it may be because he lacks sufficient maturation or the natural ability to cope with the task at hand. Sometimes, how-ever, a student does poorly because he decides to, which is the whole point of this reading. The motives for failing are many, and the author notes that they are not all necessarily negative in nature. In fact, Dr. Bettleheim observes that sometimes a child fails because of a "desire for inner honesty and truth." Sound strange? Read on to see how it can happen.

. . . A child's determination not to learn can often spring from wishes as positive, and at least as strong (though different), as those that motivate the good learner. Both learner and non-learner, often with equally strong desires, seek the same goal: success. Only what constitutes suc-cess in their eyes may lie at opposite ends of the continuum stretching from total failure to unusual achievement.

Reprinted from Bruno Bettleheim, "The Decision to Fail," *School Review* 69 (1961): 398–412, by permission of the University of Chicago Press. Copyright © The University of Chicago Press.

Sometimes this determination grows out of the parents' attitudes or social position. The child does not wish to do better than his parents because he does not want to make them seem inferior. Typical for this source of learning difficulties is the wish of most children to look up to their par-ents. Out of the need to rely on them, they anxiously protect the image of their parents as the best of all parents. Because our dominant creed is that every new generation will do better than the last, it often overshadows the fact that many children have reason to wish the opposite. This emotional block to learning has a very strong, positive motivation.

It is not as simple as if these parents might resent superiority in their children. On the con-trary, most of them tell the child he must acquire a better education than they themselves were able to. Nevertheless the parent who, with the very best of intentions, tries to encourage his child in this way may still make him feel guilty about his better opportunities. In order to avoid feeling guilty, he may quit learning at exactly the point where the education of one of his parents stopped. I have observed dropouts, or the sudden appearance of severe learning blocks, in many high school and college students, terminating a young person's edu-cation at exactly the point where that of a parent once ended.

A teacher does not need to express openly critical attitudes about the child's parents or their way of life to make him feel he must side with his parents against teacher and school. Sometimes the teacher, wishing the child to achieve middle-class standards, asks him to adopt principles of behavior that are above those of one or both of his parents. Such a child may, unbeknown to parent and teacher, express his deep loyalty to the parent by rejecting all that school (and with it, learning) stands for, because it seems to belittle his parents or their way of life or both.

Often severe blocks to learning are due to efforts at taking one parent's side against the other or a parent's side against the school. This happens, typically, when two parents have differing levels of education and one disparages the other. But here, as when the child protects both parents against the school, the block can be readily over-come once the underlying cause is recognized. What is needed is for both parents, or parents and school, to truly agree about what is desirable, and to make this clear to the child.

Two further steps are usually necessary to erase these learning inhibitions. First, we must show our appreciation of the child's wish to protest the pride of one or both parents by not doing better than they were able to; and second, we must convince him that he can do much more for his parents, and at the same time for himself, by satisfying their justified wish to be proud of his achievements.

The wish, by not learning, to protect a parent's pride or the validity of the parents' living conditions, does not begin to cover the variety of positive reasons for unconscious, though deliberate, failures in class. Realizing that these failures are due to laudable motives is the most important step in removing them. For this reason, and also because adults do not usually see anything positive in a child's determination not to learn, I should like to add a few more illustrations.

Some children are poor learners because they do not wish to compete, feeling that competition is wrong. Such thoughts in a school child are easy to understand if we consider how often they have been admonished not to take advantage of a brother or sister, to let others take a turn first, to be considerate of others' feelings, and so on. Other children feel so guilty or worthless that they do not dare to add to their faults by getting ahead of children they think are much worthier. In order to protect the other child (a positive desire) and not to add to their guilt, they stop learning so that others will more readily succeed. While the particular reasons may vary, the feeling that a child has no "right" to succeed is by no means rare.

Probably the commonest positive reason for not achieving academically is the wish to retain closeness to the beloved mother. To learn means to grow up. Therefore many children see it as giving up the mother, or certainly mothering, and this they are unwilling to do.

Equally positive, as an underlying motive for failure, is the desire we all have to be special, different, unique. If the need for status and self-respect is accepted as a positive motivation, then we must count the wish to be first among the lowly, rather than second among the best, with the group of learning inhibitions based on positive wishes.

The good learner who believes he can go to the top of the class is spurred by this conviction to work harder. As long as a child can believe that if he tries he will do well, he usually applies himself to gain status and self-respect. Even if his best efforts land him only in the mediocre group, he may still settle for that, as many children do, but only if he can be satisfied with being one of the gang.

If this moderate station is not enough for his self-respect, if he cannot give up the need to be special, or is frustrated in wanting to be one of the gang because the others reject him, then the wish to be unique is reinforced powerfully. He may then arrive at the conviction that he can gain status only by being the worst. In this way he attracts attention to himself; true, in a negative way, but attention nevertheless.

The learner who does poorly, on the other hand, is convinced he can never make the grade. He is impelled to stop learning by his wish to maintain his self-respect. Believing that he will fail even if he makes his best efforts, he protects himself by deciding not to learn. Then he will be able to tell himself that his failure is not due to inability, but to a deliberate act of will. Hence it is not rare for such a child to feel he can gain more status or self-respect through not learning than through diligent application.

When we wish to help such children, we must begin by realizing that almost never can a child recognize on his own that he chose failure because he was afraid he could never do best, or average, or was unacceptable to the gang. He may be only a little readier to accept the idea that he chose to be a huge failure rather than risk being a small failure or an insignificant success. The reason is that any such acknowledgment would destroy his chance of achieving self-respect through not learning. Instead, a child in such a predicament usually tells himself and others that he could do very well, could be tops if he wished. Only with such claims can he gain the attention accorded those who are genuinely different and still tell himself that his uniqueness is not a matter of inability, about which he thinks he can do nothing, but the result of a freely made decision. Only in this way can he protect the image of himself as an adequate person, the image he sought by defying schoolwork in the first place.

A child's need to protect his self-respect in this way is among the most dangerous blocks to learning. Once he has fallen into such a pattern, he honestly believes that his greatest desire is not to be special but to defy school and adults by deliberately not learning.

For other reasons, too, this is an insidious process. Because the further he falls behind, the more pretense of adequacy is threatened and the more drastic the steps he must take to protect it. That is why a fourth-grader can be satisfied that he is a big shot when he defies the teacher by not learning, while the seventh-grader must, in addition, defy police and society by delinquent acts. The fourth-grader who acts "dumb" is the easily admired clown. A few years later the same behavior makes him look stupid, and instead of being admired he is despised. By then it is usually too late to regain status by academic success, so the child tries to get it by delinquency.

When a child fails for such reasons, it is of little avail to encourage him to try harder so that he can string along within the middle group, because the decision not to learn was made to quiet the fear that his work would never get him much higher than that group of low achievers. A much better approach is to boost the child's self-esteem, since the lack of it drove him to find it by defiance. This can be done, for example, by showing him how ingenious he was in protecting himself and by giving him credit for his determination, without agreeing that its goals are desirable. Only much later, after he is convinced that we recognize his competence, can he be helped to see that he behaved like the fox with the sour grapes. At the same time we must help him to truly achieve in academic skills. Through many such efforts on our part he may eventually recognize that defiance of learning is not the only way to gain personal distinction.

To summarize, we must never forget that many learning inhibitions can come from a child's desire for inner honesty and truth, and from his trying to succeed in terms of his own life experience and of clear-cut desires and values.

As a matter of fact, given similar natural endowment, and with the whole pressure of school, parents, educational system, and society at large favoring success in learning, it often takes a great deal more determination on the part of the nonlearner to fail than for the good learner to do well in school. This is so because all the breaks, all the encouragement and rewards, are in favor of the learner. If, despite this powerful system of rewards, a child fails, then we must assume that his motives for not learning, as likely as not, are stronger than are those of the child who is successful in class.

After devoting so much space to those learning inhibitions that have positive motives, I come now to those caused by negativism. Some children may be set against the school, not because they wish to protect a parent's pride or be loyal to his way of life, but simply because they do not wish to acquire a different set of values.

Others do not learn because learning was not made attractive enough or because the teacher has hurt their feelings and they want to hurt hers in retaliation. A child may also be so tired, physically or emotionally, that to exert himself intellectually seems expecting too much of him, and he will not even do the little he could. All this is so well known that I mention it here only in passing.

Behind other learning inhibitions may lie the wish or the need to defy adults, to punish a parent, or to do both at the same time. A child often opposes his parent with "my teacher said so." This tempts us to overlook the fact that quite often the same child cannot accept what the freely quoted teacher says or stands for. Because he needs to defy authority and cannot do it without adult support, he claims the teacher's backing when he speaks up against his parent. The wise parent will not object, because to be able to use the teacher against the parent makes the teacher, school, and learning very attractive to the child. But if a child cannot so use the teacher to achieve some independence from his parents, he will have to defy the teacher instead, to gain independence from at least some adult.

Some children are quite overwhelmed at home, less frequently today by being pushed around or beaten down and more often by being nagged to desperation or driven to achieve beyond their ability. Their need to defy is so great that they will defy adult authority whenever they see a chance to do so without fatal hazards. Because our teachers are much more lenient than their nagging or driving parents, the child who does not dare to oppose an over-powering parent, defies the teacher instead by not learning. This is usually reinforced by a secondary gain; by not learning he can effectively punish the parents to whom he is otherwise subservient. Not learning in class has become the commonest whip that the middle-class child can hold over a parent whose pride is deeply hurt by the child's academic failure.

Similarly, intellectual superiority was, and sometimes still is, the whip that many a lower-class child, or the child of new immigrants, holds over his parents. Since this is an emotional motive for higher achievement, and often a powerful one, it does not concern us here. But as a negative motivation for academic success, it may round out our discussion of the negative motivations for academic failure.

So far I have spoken of learning inhibitions that extend, more or less, over the totality: school. Equally frequent are emotional blocks to learning that spring from the avoidance of a specific learning task or a specific subject matter, for a particular reason.

Contrary to widespread belief, a child with intelligence that is average or better will more often have trouble because he understands the content of a subject matter all too well than because he is inattentive or finds the task beyond his mental capacity. Mere inability to comprehend what is taught may lead to indifference to a subject matter. It is only if we do understand what the subject matter is about, but resist it out of moral scruples or because it scares us, that we actively reject it. Then a child cannot understand because he does not wish to understand.

Usually he has one of two reasons. Either the essential principles underlying a learning task would throw him into inner turmoil when applied to himself, or the particular content reminds him of experiences much too painful or threatening to think about. To ward off such pain, he convinces himself as well as others that he cannot understand how to apply what he dreads to apply to a personal problem; that he cannot grasp what (if he did grasp it) would remind him of an unbearably unpleasant experience.

Children whose own history is forbidden territory, or who cannot make sense of it, or only painfully so, protect themselves from finding any meaning in their personal history. One solution is to be totally uninterested in all history. Or else they deny there is any sense to the historical sequence of events. To insist that they should understand and accept as meaningful any sequence of events in the history of men or of nations means acquiring perceptions that would cause unmanageable anxiety if applied to themselves. They may therefore prefer not to understand the meaning of history. Otherwise they might have to realize, for example, that certain bad experiences of their past or present which, for emotional reasons, they wish to chalk up as random chance, really sprang out of basic and permanent attitudes in themselves or their parents.

That one's deep suffering was and is due to chance one can accept and still continue to live and to strive. Eventually the wheel of fortune turns, and what was due to bad luck may suddenly change for the better. But if we must accept our misfortunes as the result of consistent and irreversible attitudes, or the design of our parents, we can no longer hold on to the hope that things will change for the better very soon or at some time in the future.

Because the study of history normally means learning to make sense of a sequence of events, it is an enriching experience; merely recognizing this fact makes learning history possible and rewarding. (This is not true, of course, if for one reason or another a child cannot study the subject without direct application to himself.) But if the cost of this advantage is having to realize that one's own life is devoid of inner meaning, then the pain of the realization seems too high a price to pay. Thus in the case of history it is not an inability to comprehend, but rather a true understanding of its essence, that may block a student from learning.

To illustrate, though with a different subject matter, one adopted girl had severe difficulties at home though she maintained herself fairly adequately in her classes until high school, where she had to take a general science course. In this class she created continual disturbances and was in such severe conflict with her science teacher that most of the time she was sent from the room and spent her time in the office of the dean of students. The criticism at home and at school was so severe that within a few months her difficulties extended to other subjects as well. What had started as a resistance to attending only the science class became a head-on clash with all of school.

The reason this girl had to protect herself from attending the science class was that general biology and heredity were part of the subject matter. She did not want to learn about the beginning of life, since it reminded her too painfully of how badly her own had begun: her real mother had given her up, and her adoptive parents had no use for her. Up to then she had maintained herself by making herself believe that these were her true parents, despite their rejection. Now, even the teacher became her enemy, since she expected the child to remember how life really begins, which only increased her violent anger against her home. To this was added the reminder that the beginning of her life had been so different from that of her schoolmates; and with the study of heredity came the realization that she did not even share a common heredity with her adoptive parents. Since she was too intelligent not to understand what all this meant to her personally, her only way out was to misbehave. Then she would be sent from the class and not have to hear about matters that only created a dangerous rage in her. Had all this been recognized in time, the rejection of one subject matter might not have extended to the rejection of school in general.

In this example, all of school learning became unacceptable because of a single subject matter. But it happened rather late in the girl's educational career. Things are even more serious when this occurs early and around such basic subject matter as reading or arithmetic.

For example, one boy committed a crime at an early age, probably not quite knowing what he did. His parents impressed him with how severely he would have been punished had he not been an ignorant child. Realizing his inner destructive wishes, the only protection he knew of was not learning to read. If he could read (he thought), he could no longer claim ignorance of the law. But the pretended inability to read soon extended to all learning.

When we taught him that ignorance is no excuse before the law, he was able to recognize the protection and advantages of reading: if he could read, he could find out which actions are punishable and which are not.

It is well known that many children develop learning inhibitions because of the parental command not to know. Sometimes a child extends a parent's order not to explore his own body or what goes on in the parental bedroom, to mean that all curiosity is wrong. But without curiosity one cannot learn. Teachers can get a child to repeat what he is told, but without the child's own spontaneous wish to know, it is not learning but parroting. And a child can remain fixated at this level if he thinks it is bad to be curious or to wish to learn secrets.

Other children develop the notion that, while it is all right to look, they are not supposed to understand the meaning of what they see. This happens typically when a child observes his parents behaving in a way they either disapprove of (as in marital discord) or where they do not wish the child to understand their actions or motives. If such experiences are repeated, the child may get the idea that while his parents do not object to his observing details correctly, they severely disapprove his understanding what it all means. Such children may learn to recognize letters and words but, in obedience to what they consider a parental command, remain unable to understand sentences or the meaning of paragraphs. But reading without understanding is frustrating, not rewarding; if they are further criticized by their teachers for not understanding sentence meaning, they may give up learning altogether.

Nor is it always the parents who inhibit the child's ability to see and comprehend. The child himself may do so for what he considers valid reasons. One child claimed he could not see the words in his book clearly, and his behavior was such that there was reason to believe his vision was actually defective. Seeing the letters only vaguely, he could not read.

Eventually this boy was able to remember the first time his vision suddenly blurred; it was when he first saw his mother attending to his newborn brother. Seeing another child getting the attention he wanted was more than he could stand. So to blot out the experience, he became unable to see what went on.

The wish not to see what is painful to see is a relatively simple defense. Sometimes a more complex mechanism is at work, such as the one called *undoing*. An obvious and well-known form of undoing is what is technically called a *washing compulsion*. Lady Macbeth, deeply perturbed by the blood that once stained her hands, continued to clean them with such intensity that little time or energy was left for anything else in her life.

The need to undo, to reverse a too painful situation, may also find expression in reversal. This is an exchanging of letters in reading which can so distort the meaning that no progress in learning takes place. Often the deeper purpose of such behavior can be overlooked or explained away by pointing to the similarity in the appearance of the letters. But such simple explanations may only deprive the child of the help he needs, which alone will clear up his learning problem.

Other reversals may affect not letters, but words. One child who witnessed a terrifying scene early in life was so preoccupied with what he had seen that everything else that had happened in the past reminded him only of what he once saw. Thus he read the word *was* as *saw*.

Another child wished so intensely to be a boy that for time periods she delusionally believed she was one. She also resented her brothers' luck in belonging to the envied sex. So she went about correcting it. Whenever she encountered the words *boy* or *man* in her reading, she read *girl* and *lady*; if the printed page read *girl* or *woman*, she read it *boy* or *man*. Similarly, she read all *he's* for *she's* and the other way around.

While some reversals can be traced back to specific events, wishes, or anxieties, sometimes any reversal will do, if the child wishes to undo, or reverse, not a specific event, but the totality of his life situation. The shattering event in one boy's life was his mother's sudden desertion. Without any warning she took off with her lover and was never heard from again. The wish to undo this event was so overwhelmingly important to this boy that he reversed letters in every word he tried to read.

All learning is based on the manipulation of symbols and concerns itself with abstractions. Learning is a process of intellectualization, a process in which thought is freed of its personal emotional content and achieves a higher "objective" meaning for the symbols used in verbal or thought exchange. To the infant, the peculiar smell of his baby blanket, its color, texture, the strange way it was worn down by him, make it unique, entirely different from all other blankets produced in the same factory. His chair is unique to the infant, although it is identical with all other chairs in the dining room. The family's kitchen table is entirely different from all other tables that look like it and serve the same purpose.

As long as the child has not acquired sufficient identity in himself, he is interested only in the unique, not the general, aspects of objects. Not any blanket, but only his blanket, can give him security, though all blankets may make him feel warm. As long as he cannot afford to be covered by any other than his own blanket, he is not yet able to abstract from the unique meaning objects have for him, and he is not really ready to learn to deal with general, abstract concepts and their symbolic representations, such as words and numbers.

Some psychologists differentiate, therefore, between a perception of the world that is autocentric and one that is allocentric: "In the autocentric mode there is little or no objectification; the emphasis is on how and what the person feels; there is a close relation, amounting to fusion, between sensory quality and pleasure or unpleasure feelings, and the perceiver reacts primarily to something impinging on him. In the allocentric mode there is objectification; the emphasis is on what the object is like; there is either no relation or a less pronounced or less direct relation between perceived sensory qualities and pleasure-unpleasure feelings." When for the child "my blanket" changes into "the blanket I used to need to be able to fall asleep," he has made (in respect to blankets) the crucial step from an autocentric to an allocentric perception of the world.

Many steps are necessary in this development. Another important one is acquiring the conviction that objects remain the same; because if they did not, no generalization would be possible about them. (Thus the central problem of early Greek philosophy: how can we have secure knowledge about an ever changing world?) That is why the small child wishes to hear the same story over and over again, engages in the same game over and over again. Or as Schachtel puts it: "A change in the story is about as upsetting to the child as it might be to an adult to discover that overnight the table in the living room had changed its shape. The idea that one can make a story, hence also change it, dawns much later on the child than the earlier implicit conviction that a story is a piece of reality on which we can rely, so that any change interferes drastically with the important task of getting thoroughly acquainted with this particular piece of reality."

Or to put it differently: the story must first be recognized as a piece of reality and hence remain unchanging. Only then can it be comprehended as a symbol that merely represents a reality and hence is changeable, since at different times it represents different aspects of reality. For the greater part of man's history, and in nonliterate societies, the same stories were repeated over and over again. In this way one did not "tell a story"; it remained a significant part of reality, as the Scriptures were when read over and over without variation.

Learning to manipulate abstract symbols such as printed words or numbers thus presupposes at least a three-step development. First, the object has only a unique meaning, is little else but part and parcel of the perceiving person, receives its meaning only from the meaning it has for this person. Second, the object acquires an independent reality of its own. To do so it has to be perceived as unchanging, always one and the same. And finally, once it is fully grasped, its unchanging and independent existence becomes less important, while its generic qualities acquire ever greater importance. Only then can a symbol represent different examples of the same object.

Obviously, learning in school can take place only when the mental development of the child has by and large reached this third stage. Our reading readiness tests, for example, measure this when they require the child to connect a unique object as drawn, with its symbolic representation by a printed word.

Unfortunately, the child does not reach this third level all at once. For some experiences he may remain fixated on the first or second level, but for other experiences he may have reached the third level. If this is the case, serious learning difficulties may result when the child is expected to understand and manipulate the symbolic process but is still fixated on one of the two earlier levels. The learning difficulty will be most serious when he has not yet freed himself of the autocentric way of experiencing reality.

Such inability to abstract and go beyond the personal and emotional meaning is behind many reading difficulties, though it need not always interfere with learning to read altogether. Because if everything goes well, the child who learns to read can invest words with his unique meaning and it need not interfere with his ability to read. The dog, the cat, the table, the book about which the child reads in his primer can be the unique dog, cat, table, or book to which he is closely attached. He may insist, and rightly so, that one dog is entirely different from all other dogs; and, if the teacher agrees, she permits him to learn to read and spell *dog* without having to give up the deep personal meaning his dog has for him.

The symbol of the printed word refers to a particular object, such as a home; and, while the letters *h-o-m-e* must stand for all homes, in learning to read the child is not forced to accept this, if he does not wish to. He may think of this or that particular home. He may think that what he learns through reading about a home need not apply to his home. Thus despite the general nature of the printed word, nothing prevents the reader from giving it only a particular meaning in his mind.

Now it should be easy to see how to some children, one or another word in their readers is emotionally unacceptable. Sometimes a child will spontaneously find his own remedy. The pressure of his emotions will force him, in his reading, to express not the thoughts presented in the book, but those predominant in his mind.

Fortunately such "misreadings"—or one should say correct readings in terms of the child's interests and emotional needs, but incorrect in terms of the printed letters—are usually restricted to one word or a few emotionally loaded words. While bothersome, they need not interfere with the child's learning to read or his overall academic progress, provided the particular obnoxious words are not too crucial for getting the meaning of what he reads. But in order to remain narrowly circumscribed, it is often necessary that an understanding teacher (or, given the reality of our school situation, probably a careless one) does not focus her criticism on the child's few errors. If too much is made of them, the emotions connected with them may force the child to protect himself from recognizing what bothers him. This he may do by extending his misreadings to many other words, so that nobody, including himself, can guess what lay behind them in the first place.

One such child was the daughter of an albino. The mother's pale blond hair was less of an emotional problem to her daughter than the near blindness. That put the girl under a tremendous burden and also made her afraid she might have inherited her mother's disabilities. Whenever she saw the word *blond* in her reading, she misread it *blind*. These two words meant the same thing to the girl: "my mother's disabilities." For this emotional reason they were identical to her, and she reacted to what she saw as their common essential meaning: "blindness."

In this case the teacher was aware of the mother's condition and ignored the misreading. The result was that it remained restricted to these rather insignificant words, with no other effect on the girl's academic progress. Here, a deliberate and selective inattention to the reading difficulty was the best course of action. But inattentiveness is by no means suggested as the wisest procedure in all cases.

For example, one boy who spent his first years in an institution and was then in many foster homes, consistently read *house* for *home*. Never having known a home, he admitted he had at least lived in houses. When the teacher insisted that he read *home*, he changed his reading from *house* to *hole*. The teacher showed him that she could not view a house as an acceptable substitute for a home, though he had been forced to be satisfied with it. So he retired even further, into a hole, where he buried himself emotionally. For similar reasons he was unable to read or spell *love*, for which he regularly substituted *life*. Never having known love, he tried to comfort himself with the life that still lay ahead of him.

Up to then his difficulties were restricted to a simple substitution for a few offensive words; the new words were relatively appropriate, started with the same letter, and had as many syllables as the rejected word. But his second substitution, of *life* for *love*, was again not accepted by the teacher. Soon he misread all words, not just the few unacceptable ones that started with *h* (*home*), *l* (*love*), *m* (*mother*), and so on. Misreading so many words, he was constantly being corrected and criticized,

until eventually he gave up reading altogether. It took years of hard work and deliberate encouragement for him to again substitute words starting with the same letter for unacceptable words, and more years before the boy could again learn to read easily and well.

Another child, a girl with a very low opinion of herself, refused to capitalize her own name or *I*. To do either would have run counter to her inner honesty, because she felt that nothing about her was, or deserved to be, big. Though she felt very competitive toward her classmates, her feelings of worthlessness kept her from openly competing. The only way she knew of not to fall further behind was to keep the others from progressing. She was most ingenious in pursuing her goal, diverting the children's attention, occupying the teacher's time. Only after she was given ample recognition for her ingenuity was she able to relent, since the recognition reduced her inferiority feelings considerably.

Although most of my examples are from the area of reading and spelling, the same psychological problems may lead to learning inhibitions in any or all subject matter. I have concentrated on reading because it is basic to all other learning experiences. Without the ability to learn arithmetic a child can still progress up to a certain level in class, while without the ability to read, he cannot. Still, it may be of interest to note briefly how arithmetic lends itself better than reading to express certain crippling emotional preoccupations.

I have said that while in reading the symbol of the printed word *home* must stand for all homes, the child may have a particular home in mind and still learn to read. Not so in mathematics. There the very essence is that the printed number symbolizes not unique or vaguely incomparable situations. On the contrary, what holds true for one mathematical operation must hold equally true for all others. If seven minus two leaves five, this is true not only for apples, or any other unique set of objects or events, but equally true for when two people are subtracted from seven so that only five are left.

This may be one of the reasons why numbers have had a magical meaning from the earliest days of mankind. Whatever the reason, we do not have to understand it to understand some of the difficulties of learning arithmetic. Arithmetic is based on the principle that units are like each other, otherwise they could not be added. Children to whom numbers have retained their autocentric meaning—so that *one* stands for the father, *two* for the mother, and *three* for the child—may meet insurmountable difficulties when we ask them to add up to four or five.

One such child was adopted before the parents had a child of their own. He could readily add up to three but not beyond that, because, as he put it, to count to four was not the same as to count to three. In his life experience it was indeed not the same. The fourth addition to the family entailed an entirely different emotional experience than the condition of Three before a fourth member was added. Contrary to what the teacher wanted him to learn (that four is more than three), he knew he had had much more when there were only three and that four was much less than three. Moreover, four, to him, was not one added to three, but rather that Three (himself) was pushed out by Four, since the arrival of the fourth member meant there was no longer any place for him in the life of his parents.

Or again, a family of five children lost both their parents under very traumatic circumstances. The oldest boy was particularly hard hit by the loss and the changes it entailed in his position within the family. He had a hard time with all arithmetic operations where the number *five* (the number of the children) was involved, with one exception: he had no difficulty in adding two to five, since that seemed to restore the original family constellation. But when asked to subtract two from seven, it threw him into a panic that extended for a considerable time during which he was unable to function at all. He was fascinated by the number *eight* (his age when the deaths occurred) and introduced it in all kinds of anxious contexts. Whenever anything went wrong, he was convinced it was connected with eight. If somebody was late, he was eight minutes late; it would rain in eight minutes, and so on. Any arithmetic operation that involved numbers beyond eight was beyond his ken. All things had stopped for him with eight.

Other children find fractions extremely hard because in their homes it is not true that a pie is divided into six equal parts. In their emotional experience, and often in reality, the six pieces into which pies are divided in their families are never alike. Therefore they cannot accept as true and correct what the teacher tries to teach: that one sixth is exactly like the other five sixths.

Another child who could not master fractions suffered from the fact that he formed only an insignificant part of the whole family; he could bear neither the thought that a whole could be split, nor the thought that something could be only a fraction. Both ideas ran counter to his all-pervasive wish to be an integral part of a well-integrated whole.

As long as the child is not able to separate certain numbers from the emotional meaning they have for him, he cannot master mathematical processes involving them. The same is true not only for specific numbers but also for entire processes. Therefore many children find subtraction much more difficult than addition. This is so not only because it is the reverse of the process just learned, but also because most children are emotionally more in favor of adding something to their lives, but cannot afford to see anything subtracted from it. For similar reasons multiplication usually presents fewer emotional problems than division.

Conversely, there are children who have less trouble learning the more complicated processes such as division than the simpler process of multiplying. Multiplication involves a fast increase in numbers. But this they may fear more than anything else if they are afraid, for example, of the arrival of new siblings in the same sense that the Scriptures speak of multiplying. For similar reasons some children can learn to subtract but have great difficulties with addition.

One child, for example, had no difficulties with any multiplication tables except the table of fours. There were four in his family, and he feared nothing more than a fast increase in their number. Fast increases in the numbers *three, five,* or *seven* he did not fear and therefore mastered quite easily.

There are, of course, innumerable ways in which children can express one and the same emotional problem that perturbs them. Sibling rivalry, and the wish to do away with a hated newcomer, can therefore be expressed in a variety of ways. One bright youngster could perform rather difficult mathematical problems in addition, subtraction, multiplication, and division, but only if one allowance was made: the answer was always incorrect by one. She always deducted the one who she felt was one too many in her family: her younger sister.

As if to show that this was not a case of poor learning, she occasionally found another way to do away with one. Sometimes when several rows of problems were given to her, she would solve the top row of problems perfectly well; after all, she was the first to arrive in her family, and her arrival was perfectly correct. But the second row, representing her younger sister, was full of errors; it was all wrong just as the sister's arrival in this world was "all wrong."

Thus the common emotional difficulties that find expression in the failure to learn arithmetic remain those that relate to simple numbers and their relations. Much as the most serious emotional problems originate in the very simple experiences of childhood and only much later grow more intricate, so too, contrary to what one might expect, it is not the advanced and very complex mathematical processes that often stymie the child, but the very simplest steps in addition or subtraction. Trigonometry, or complex algebraic problems or formulas, may present difficulties of an intellectual nature, but they rarely lead to learning inhibitions. The reason is that they are too far removed from the direct and tangible nature of those life experiences that arouse emotions deep enough to block the child's ability to learn them.

It does not come naturally to the child to express the family constellations that upset him in such elusive formulations as algebraic equations. But simple addition or plane geometry can present insurmountable difficulties, as they do, for example, to the child who cannot understand the properties of triangles because he cannot understand the triangular relations within his family. Here it is only rarely the love triangle that is so baffling to the child, though this is sometimes the case. Much more often it is the fact that the two parents and the child form a triangle of such complex emotional relations that the child cannot understand the first thing about its form or inherent characteristics.

The unsolvable emotional problems that a triangle may present to the only child may be expressed by another child through a quadrangle or by his inability to grasp the relation of these two geometric forms to each other. This may be the case if he cannot accept the fact that what was once a family consisting of three elements suddenly changed, to his bewilderment, into a unit consisting of four elements.

At the same time, what may make one subject matter particularly difficult for one child, may, for other reasons, make it very attractive for others. The very abstract nature of mathematics can make it serve opposite emotions. A child who feels desperately unlike the other children in his home may throw himself into arithmetic because it teaches that all numbers are basically equal in their meaning. He may make his own, as if with a vengeance, that one fourth is like all other fourths, just to deny that he, one of the fourths of his family, is treated so differently from the other three fourths.

Thus if one wants to understand what may be emotionally implied in the learning of arithmetic, one has to start with the realization that each child is unique. To some, arithmetic is very difficult because they cannot separate the abstract processes of mathematical reasoning from their emotional involvement with numbers and their manipulation. By the same token mathematics is eminently attractive to those who can use it defensively to separate themselves from all related emotions. Basically both groups are equally unready to study mathematics, though the first may do very poorly, the second very well. Only those who have gained enough distance or control of their emotions not to let them interfere positively or negatively are really ready for the study of mathematics. . . .

Chapter Twelve · disciplinary issues and classroom management strategies

43

A Case for the Use of Corporal Punishment by Teachers

Robert L. Ebel

EDITOR'S NOTE · It used to be that a birch rod or its equivalent was as much a part of a teacher's standard equipment as are textbooks, blackboards, and curriculum guides. Not so any more. However, the controversy over whether to allow physical punishment rages on. Schools have different policies on this issue, and teachers have different points of view about it. Dr. Ebel is the father of three children, a former high school teacher and principal, and now a college professor with over thirty years experience with youth of different ages. How about it? Should teachers use corporal punishment? Dr. Ebel says they should. Be sure to read the selection immediately following for the other side of the coin.

As I began to write this paper, it occurred to me that perhaps I should rent a costume to wear in presenting it—a red costume with horns

This paper was presented at the American Educational Research Association's annual meeting, Washington, D.C., April 1975. Used by permission of the author.

and a tail with pitchfork and a satanic countenance. But then it also occurred to me that some of you would not need the help of a costume to recognize me for what I surely must be—an aggressive, vengeful, authoritarian beast; vicious, brutal, sadistic, inhuman. For to some, there is no possibility of proper or effective use of corporal punishment, no matter in what circumstances, no matter for what purpose, no matter with what discretion or restraint it might be applied. In the eyes of these people, the only justifiable policy is absolute prohibition of corporal punishment of any kind, now and forever more, as a means of correction or reproof.

I do not stand before you as an advocate of frequent infliction of severe physical pain on growing children. There are families, few I hope, in which young children are slapped or spanked daily; families in which a father may give one of his children "a good whipping" once or twice a week. I join in condemnation of such practices. I agree that there is something seriously wrong in homes where these things occur. But, I know, too, that there are homes and schoolrooms in which acts of serious and dangerous disobedience are never effectively corrected because the adults in charge have voluntarily disavowed, or have been prohibited from using corporal punishment. In these situations, adult responsibility for child control has been abandoned. A young child who has not been taught to obey the directives of his parents or his teachers is liable to suffer serious consequences in a sometimes hostile environment. In one specific instance I know of, the consequences to the child were fatal. In other cases, the persistently disobedient child simply becomes a socially obnoxious brat.

In my elementary school days, there were persistent rumors in the school yard that the principal of Emerson School had, and might occasionally use, a rubber tube to administer corporal punishment. We speculated as to how much the rubber tube might hurt—probably a great deal more than an ordinary hand spanking with which some of us were better acquainted. We guessed that it probably would hurt more than a wooden paddle, or even a leather strap. None of us that I knew of ever fell victim to the rubber tube. But all of us were aware of its availability as the ultimate punishment for gross misbehavior. The possibility that it might be used made a difference, a generally desirable difference I believe, in our behavior.

Total prohibition of corporal punishment in any form, for any purpose, under any circumstances seems to be part of a movement in education whose objective has been to promote student freedom, to safeguard student rights, and to guard against the abuse of the authority by teachers in their control of student behavior. It seems reasonably clear that the consequences of this movement have been a deterioration of environments for learning in some schools, and a corresponding decline in school achievement that is being widely reported. I am not suggesting that restoration of corporal punishment would cure the ills of contemporary schools. But the attitude toward student behavior that includes outrage at the suggestion of corporal punishment is the same attitude that has made the role of the teacher increasingly difficult and frustrating. As a consequence, teacher organizations tend to support retention, or reinstitution, of the possibility of using corporal punishment as one means of correction or control.

Note that it is the *possibility* of corporal punishment that is being supported here, not its frequent use, or its severity. Corporal punishment is a means of last resort when all else has failed. Some will say, "Better to fail than to use this means." That is a view which is being challenged in this paper.

Now education clearly is and ought to be much more concerned with developmental progress than with repressive restraint. Teachers properly emphasize the positive aspects of social and intellectual growth. They properly minimize the negative aspects of repressive punishment. But experience suggests very strongly that when the so-called negative controls on behavior are totally eliminated, progress in educational development will suffer, and sometimes quite seriously.

It is sometimes suggested that competent teachers can engage the interest of their pupils so completely, and motivate them so strongly, that behavior problems will never develop. It is said that any differences between pupil and teacher can be sidestepped by appropriate psychological finesse, and turned into a creative learning experience. There is much merit in both of these suggestions, if all that is implied is that these things can *often* be done. But here again, experience suggests that they cannot *always* be done. An otherwise capable teacher should not be disqualified for lack of special talent in these areas.

Further, and perhaps more importantly, high levels of concern for these aspects of teaching may actually inhibit good teaching. A teacher who is required, or elects to devote most of his creative energy to interesting and motivating pupils and most of his attention to finessing potential conflicts, may neglect the equally important, perhaps more important, job of instruction. To judge a teacher by his skill in avoiding behavior problems is to ignore the teacher's more basic responsibility for directing pupil learning.

The teacher who has least need for even occasional punishment is not necessarily the most effective educator. Situations which can sometimes be occasions of misbehavior can also contribute to useful learning. Responsibility for success in learning does not rest solely on the teacher. A teacher who successfully avoids all circumstances which might cause problems also avoids helping pupils to learn how to deal with those problems. The world punishes misbehavior. Should not the school help pupils to learn this very important fact?

Ultimately, the case for or against corporal punishment must rest on the effect it has on pupil achievement of whatever goals society has set for its schools.

At first glance, this may seem to be a question for research to answer. A closer look, and some sober reflections on past experience with similar research problems, suggests that research is unlikely to provide any very definite answers.

There is first of all the problem of what accomplishments the school can be reasonably expected to foster. Is it limited to measurable outcomes in the usual subjects of study? Or does it encompass also subtle, intangible, or slow-to-mature attitudes, values, etc.?

Then there is the problem of experimental manipulation of human beings in the school environment. Dare we permit physical punishment in an experimental group and prohibit it in a control group for no better reason than to find out how it works? And if we do, can our findings from an artificial experimental situation be expected to generalize to different natural situations? Finally, and most seriously, can the effect of this variable (i.e., physical punishment) be isolated from other variables which also affect accomplishment? Even if it can, will the effect be strong enough, in a short-run experiment, to yield statistically or practically significant findings?

A possible alternative to prospective experimental studies of the effects on learning of corporal punishment might be a retrospective survey of differences in pupil achievement between schools which tolerate and those which forbid corporal punishment. But here, too, the variable of interest is not easy to isolate from other influential variables. Schools which tolerate corporal punishment may enroll pupils and employ teachers who differ systematically from those in schools that forbid such punishment.

The inherent difficulty of sound experimental or survey research on the effects of corporal punishment suggests that one should view with considerable skepticism firm conclusions for or against its use that are allegedly based on research findings. Seldom does the scope of any particular research study justify a sweeping generalization that corporal punishment is or is not effective. Yet over and over in discussions of corporal punishment, data from a limited study of some particular aspect in some unique setting are used to support very general conclusions. Nor are these limited studies themselves usually free from defects of design or interpretation. The "weight of the evidence" from such studies may not be very heavy.

In discussions of corporal punishment, emotionally charged words and unsupported assertions are sometimes used in lieu of evidence or rational inference. A spanking is referred to as a "beating" or a "brutal assault." The motivation for correction is seen as simple "retaliation," made possible by the greater size and strength of the parent or teacher but not justified by any higher standards of conduct, or any sense of moral obligation. Evidence is seldom presented to support claims that children "learn aggression" from being punished, or that means of correction "far more effective" that corporal punishment are available.

Perhaps in the end we will have to rely on much more general, if much less rigorous, bases for inference. Several weeks ago an article in the *New York Times Sunday Magazine* contrasted the educational effects of free versus controlled school environments as seen by a perceptive and articulate parent. She found that the controlled environment was not only more productive educationally but also more satisfying to the pupil involved, her daughter. In this school, rather extensive use was made of rewards and punishments as instruments of control.

Most young people need control and know that they need it. Most prefer firm, consistent authoritative guidance to indecisive, uncertain vascillations in requirements, and unpredictable parent or teacher reactions. Most recognize the justice of punishment for some of the things they have done. Some, given the choice, prefer corporal punishment whose pain is quickly done with, to psychological punishment with its slower, more lingering psychic pain.

Assuming, for the sake of discussion, that punishment is occasionally necessary in guiding the development of young people (and in controlling the behavior of adults), can we say that psychological punishment (i.e., reproof, loss of privileges, isolation, time-out, etc.) is always preferable to physical punishment? I think not. Nor can we say that physical punishment is always preferable. The case I have been trying to make is that the possibility of carefully considered, carefully supervised, occasional use of moderate physical punishment should not be prohibited.

Let me conclude this presentation by setting forth thirteen propositions which may serve to summarize, supplement, and possibly rationalize the case for punishment as I see it. Note the significance of the number thirteen, a number much favored by devils, witches, and warlocks.

1. To punish is to impose a penalty for a fault, offense, or violation.

2. Socially sanctioned controls on individual behavior are necessary to group living, and punishment is one effective means of social control.

3. The need for punishment cannot be avoided by the use of rewards since withholding of a reward becomes automatically a form of punishment.

4. When punishment is administered by one with the authority and power to do so, it is almost always in response to an offense by the one punished. Seldom is it an expression of the punisher's "need to punish."

5. Punishment is intended more often and more directly to serve the needs of the group than to serve the needs of the individual.

6. The use of punishment is necessary to develop the child's sense of personal responsibility.

7. Habits of behavior established under threat of punishment may disappear once the threat is removed, unless as is usually the case, other good reasons for maintaining the behavior assume the behavior control function.

8. Punishment, judiciously applied, can strengthen the bonds of respect and affection between child and adult.

9. There are no good reasons to believe that psychological stress is less harmful or more lasting in its effects than physical pain.

10. Any form of punishment can be used wisely or abused.

11. As the child grows older, the effectiveness of physical punishment is likely to diminish, and the effectiveness of psychological punishment is likely to increase.

12. There are no good reasons to believe that unwise adults are more likely to misuse physical than psychological punishment.

13. The focus of an experimental research study on the effects of punishment is likely to be so narrow, so unique, so artificial, that the generalizability of the finding will be severely limited.

44

A Case against the Use of Corporal Punishment by Teachers and Some Myths about Its Use

Harvey Clarizio

EDITOR'S NOTE • Dr. Clarizio's views about the use of corporal punishment are quite different than those Dr. Ebel expressed in the preceding reading. Dr. Clarizio's exposure to youth ranges from being a playground director to working for six years as a school psychologist to being the father of four children. His feelings about corporal punishment are not the result of armchair theorizing. According to Dr. Clarizio, both teachers and students survive well in schools that prohibit the use of corporal punishment. What has your experience been? Is corporal punishment a wise idea?

This paper will explore four of the most common myths surrounding the use of corporal punishment in the schools. It will also attempt to provide alternatives to the use of corporal punishment as well as provide a model law prohibiting the use of physical punishment in the schools.

This paper was presented at the American Educational Research Association's annual meeting, Washington, D.C., April 1975. Used by permission of the author.

Myth 1. Physical punishment is a "tried and true" method. It is good for students. It helps them develop a sense of personal responsibility, learn self-discipline and develop moral character.

Studies of child-rearing practices, while admittedly not free from ambiguity and methodological problems, have consistently yielded a similar finding. As a general rule, the degree of physical punishment used by the parent is positively correlated with various forms of psychopathology, particularly delinquency and acting-out behavior (Feshbach and Feshbach, 1973). The very high recidivism rate of delinquents also indicates that punishment does little if anything to improve one's sense of personal responsibility. More recent work, in fact, indicates a near perfect correlation between the amount and severity of physical punishment suffered by a child from 2 to 12 and the amount and severity of antisocial aggressiveness that he displays during adolescence (Buttons, 1973; Welsh, 1974). There is surprisingly little evidence of inhibitory effects even when the punishment has been specifically directed toward aggressive infractions (Feshbach, 1973).

Another consistent finding is that physical punishment is negatively related to strength of conscience, whereas love-oriented techniques (praise, warmth, and reasoning) are positively related to conscience development (Hoffman, 1970; Sears, et al., 1957). The consistency of these two findings is especially impressive in light of the diversity of procedures, measures, and population used by different investigators.

That moral development is related to the use of physical punishment is not surprising in that physical punishment often represents or is perceived as representing a form of retaliation—a low level form of moral development (comparable to what would be regarded in Kohlberg's system as Stage One, whereby might is right and one behaves out of fear). The harsh tone of the teacher's voice along with other available cues at the time belies any gesture of good will on the educator's part or any genuine regret that he has over the occurrence of the incident. The teacher's anger and willingness to retaliate readily convey an eye for an eye and a tooth-for-a-tooth philosophy. Because physical punishment is usually based as much or more on the teacher's needs than on the child's needs, it appears to be used more for purposes of

retaliation than for education. Even on those occasions where the educator has the child's best interests at heart, the child is apt to see the physical punishment as arbitrary since it usually does not relate to the misbehavior (for example, being hit for coming in late from recess). If reasoning is to be used as a means of facilitating conscience development, then the child must be able to see a relationship between the physical punishment and his own behavior. To physically punish without a cognitive rationale not only offends the child's sense of justice, but leads to inappropriate generalization and the absence of guidelines for novel and ambiguous situations (Feshbach and Feshbach, 1973). Yet it is very difficult for people to respond to physical punishment in a cool, analytic, rational manner. For physical punishment often results in an upsurge of anger which precludes a rational distinction between the real causes of his predicament and the outcomes of his predicament. It is extremely difficult for a child (particularly for the behaviorally disordered child) to be logical in the heat of the moment. Psychologic—not logic—dictates the child's reactions.

One explanation as to why physical punishment increases aggressiveness but fails to promote good internal controls has to do with modeling. By punishing the child, the educator unwittingly provides a clear-cut model of the very kind of behavior from which he wants the student to refrain. What the child learns from the educator's example is that it is permissible to aggress toward those of lesser power, status and prestige. The combined findings of laboratory experiments, controlled field studies, and correlational studies provide substantial testimony that observing violence tends to foster aggressiveness (Bandura, 1973). In essence, we are telling the child that physical force is an acceptable way of resolving conflict—that it is all right to physically attack others when angry. Aggression begets aggression.

In brief, it seems clear that corporal punishment does not promote self-discipline. Once the authoritarian controls are gone, the child can once again do as he pleases.

Myth 2. Occasional paddling contributes substantially to the child's socialization.

While the dangers associated with the use of physical punishment over extended periods of time may be readily apparent, some educators maintain that the infrequent or what might sometimes be referred to as the judicious use of corporal punishment is beneficial to the child. At first blush, this suggestion seems to have merit. Upon closer inspection, however, it becomes evident that the occasional use of physical punishment, whether "judicious" or not, actually works to the child's and to the teacher's disadvantage. While resulting in immediate decrements in the undesired behavior, occasional punishment does not produce lasting changes. To be effective in suppressing behavior, punishment, unless traumatic in nature, must be applied consistently, particularly in the case of aggressors with few social skills. Yet in applied settings, the behavior to be eliminated is rarely punished each time it occurs because constant surveillance is prohibitive. This state of affairs leads to a situation in which the undesired behavior is intermittently reinforced. And, as you know, intermittent reinforcement results in increased response persistence. Thus, instead of weakening the undesired behavior, occasional punishment actually strengthens the behavior by allowing it to be reinforced on an intermittent schedule.

Myth 3. Corporal punishment is the only recourse in maintaining order. It is the only thing some kids understand. Alternatives to physical punishment are neither available nor realistic.

To say that corporal punishment is the only thing that some kids understand means only that some kids have not been exposed to other, more constructive forms of discipline (NEA, 1972). We must offer then another kind of example to follow other than corporal punishment. Exposing such children to more of the same kind of (corporal) punishment will certainly do nothing constructive relative to teaching them new ways of behaving. Sadly, just as physical punishment may be the only thing that some kids understand, it appears that physical punishment may be the only thing that some teachers understand.

In school systems that prohibit the use of corporal punishment, both teachers and students survive nicely without it. It is unfortunate that many educators are apparently unaware that effective and more humane alternatives do exist and are already in use to some degree. This lack of awareness is partly attributable to a simple lack of information regarding the availability of effective, humane approaches such as contracting and self-management. In part, however, the use of physical punishment discourages the educator from seeking the use of more constructive forms of school discipline. The teacher becomes accustomed to living with short-lived restraints, accompanied perhaps by a release of his own pent-up frustrations, instead of searching for ways to encourage acceptable behavior. Because physical punishment will often serve as a temporary inhibitor, the teacher is tricked into believing that he has struck upon an effective technique. Once they are convinced that punishment "works," there is a danger that what is considered "a last resort" will become the first method applied in future conflicts with students when one is angry. Discovering positive approaches requires more thought and ingenuity than a spanking requires, and overworked educators are understandably tempted, particularly when they are angry, to follow the path of least resistance.

The following list of techniques for maintaining discipline without inflicting physical pain on students was prepared by the NEA Task Force on Corporal Punishment (NEA, 1972).

Short-Range Solutions

1. Quiet places (corners, small rooms, retreats)
2. Student-teacher agreement on immediate alternatives
3. Teaming of adults—teachers, administrators, aides, volunteers (parents and others)—to take students aside when they are disruptive and listen to them, talk to them, and counsel them until periods of instability subside
4. Similar services for educators whose stamina is exhausted
5. Social workers, psychologists, and psychiatrists to work on a one-to-one basis with disruptive students or distraught teachers
6. Provision of alternate experiences for students who are bored, turned off, or otherwise unreceptive to particular educational experiences:
   a. independent projects
   b. listening and viewing experiences with technological learning devices
   c. library research
   d. work-study experience
7. In-service programs to help teachers and other

school staff learn a variety of techniques for building better interpersonal relations between themselves and students and among students:

    a. Class meetings (Glasser technique)
    b. Role playing
    c. Case study—what would you do?
    d. Student-teacher human relations retreats and outings
    e. Teacher (or other staff)—student-parent conferences

8. Class discussion—of natural consequences of good and bad behavior (not threats or promises); of what behavior is right; of which behavior achieves desired results; of causes of a "bad day" for the class

9. Privileges to bestow or withdraw

10. Approval or disapproval

11. Other staff members to work with a class whose teacher needs a break.

Intermediate-Range Solutions

1. Staff-student jointly developed discipline policy and procedures

2. Staff-student committee to implement discipline policy

3. Parent education programs in interpersonal relations

4. Staff in-service program on interpersonal relations, on understanding emotions, and on dealing with children when they are disruptive

5. Student human relations councils and grievance procedures

6. Training for students and teachers in crisis intervention

7. Training for students in student advocacy

8. Training for teachers in dealing with fear of physical violence

9. Regular opportunities for principals to experience classroom situation.

Long-Range Solutions in Schools

1. Full involvement of students in the decision-making process in the school

2. Curriculum content revision and expansion by students and staff to motivate student interest

3. Teacher in-service programs on new teaching strategies to maintain student interest

4. Alternate programs for students

5. Work-study programs

6. Drop-out—drop-back-in programs

7. Alternative schools within the public school system

8. Early entrance to college

9. Alternatives to formal program during last two years of high school

10. Few enough students per staff member that staff can really get to know students

11. Adequate professional specialists—psychiatrists, psychologists, social workers

12. Aides and technicians to carry out paraprofessional, clerical, and technical duties so that professional staff are free to work directly with students more of the time

13. A wide variety of learning materials and technological devices.

Long-Range Solutions With Other Agencies

1. Staff help from local and regional mental health and human relations agencies

2. More consultant staff to work with individual problem students

3. Long-range intensive in-service programs to prepare all staff to become counselors

4. Mass media presentations directed to both the public and the profession on the place of children in contemporary American society

5. Some educational experiences relocated in business, industry, and social agencies

6. Increased human relations training in preservice teacher education and specific preparation in constructive disciplinary procedures.

Myth 4. Those involved with schools favor the use of corporal punishment.

Although there has been only a limited amount of research on how popular physical punishment is, it appears that approximately 55–65% of school officials see it as effective and favor its use (Patterson, 1974). Only a third of parents feel that it is an effective technique. Students, like parents, also do not view physical punishment as an effective way to make students behave in school with opposition to corporal punishment being particularly noticeable among senior high students. Thus, school officials who permit the use of physical punishment should be aware that this strategy is not a popular one among either students or parents.

The small segment of students who do accept or favor corporal punishment as a means of correcting behavior may do so for a number of reasons, none of which are healthy. Some may simply accept it as a desirable way to handle conflict situations. Others may see it as an easy way out of trouble in that it does not take much of their time nor does it require them to change their behavior. For others, it is a good way to demonstrate their masculinity, toughness and endurance. For those motivated by excessive or neurotic guilt, it offers a quick sense of relief, thereby reducing the motivation to modify one's behavior. For the manipulative student, it becomes a way to expose the evils of authority, to polarize students and to justify their own behavior. Supporting the cause of any of the above purposes is educationally indefensible.

As for those parents who instruct schools to use physical force to bring about desired behavior in their children, we must remember this: that the physical type of discipline used at home has already produced a child who misbehaves at school. Can anyone seriously believe that following in the footsteps of an unsuccessful parent is a suitable model for professional educators? Rather than following the faulty example provided by unsuccessful parents, educators should provide an acceptable example for misguided parents to follow.

Allow me to close this address on a constructive note by quoting the law proposed by the NEA Task Force which outlaws the use of corporal punishment in the schools:

> No person employed or engaged by any educational system within this state, whether public or private, shall inflict or cause to be inflicted corporal punishment or bodily pain upon a pupil attending any school or institution within such education system; provided, however, that any such person may, within the scope of his employment, use and apply such amounts of physical restraint as may be reasonable and necessary:
>
> 1. To protect himself, the pupil or others from physical injury
>
> 2. To obtain possession of a weapon or other dangerous object upon the person or within the control of a pupil
>
> 3. To protect property from serious harm

and such physical restraint shall not be construed to constitute corporal punishment or bodily pain within the meaning and intendment of this section. Every resolution, bylaw, rule, ordinance, or other act or authority permitting or authorizing corporal punishment or bodily pain to be inflicted upon a pupil attending a school or educational institution should be void (NEA, 1972).

REFERENCES

Bandura, A. *Aggression: A Social Learning Analysis.* Englewood Cliffs, N.J.: Prentice-Hall, 1973.

Buttons, A. Some antecedents of felonious and delinquent behavior. *Journal of Clinical Child Psychology,* 1973, 2, 35–37.

Feshbach, N. The Effects of Violence In Childhood. *Journal of Clinical Child Psychology,* Fall 1973, 2, 28–31.

Feshbach, S. & Feshbach, N. Alternatives to Corporal Punishment. *Journal of Clinical Child Psychology,* Fall 1973, 2, 46–49.

Hoffman, M. Moral Development. In P. Mussen (Ed.) *Carmichael's Manual of Child Psychology.* New York: John Wiley & Sons, 1970, 261–360.

National Education Association. *Report of the Task Force on Corporal Punishment.* Washington, D.C., 1972.

Patterson, J. How Popular Is the Paddle. *Phi Delta Kappan,* 1974, LVI, 707.

Sears, R. et al. *Patterns of Child Rearing.* Evanston, Ill.: Row Peterson, 1957.

Welsh, R. Severe Parental Punishment and Delinquency. *Jr. Clinical Child Psychology,* 1974, 3.

45

Life-Space Interviewing: A Technique for Working with the Here-and-Now Problems of Youth

William C. Morse

EDITOR'S NOTE · All teachers at all levels must cope with classroom management problems of one sort or other. In this excellent article, Dr. Morse offers some very practical suggestions for coping with classroom disruptions as they occur. The strategy outlined here is particularly useful in resolving the inevitable altercations that come up time and again in the hectic pace of everyday classroom life.

A major problem for teachers is how to talk or counsel effectively with pupils and groups of pupils, whether it be for the purpose of exploring a general attitude, a motivational complex, or a control and management problem with mild or severe implications.

These conditions are apparent: (1) teachers cannot adopt a counselor's role, be it psychoanalytic

From *Conflict in the Classroom: The Education of Children With Problems,* 2nd edition, edited by Nicholas J. Long, William C. Morse, and Ruth G. Newman © 1971 by Wadsworth Publishing Co., Inc., Belmont, California 94002. Reprinted by permission of the publisher.

or non-directive; (2) it is not possible to refer all "working through of problems" to persons outside the classroom; (3) it is not adequate to continue to use an outmoded moralistic approach or some equally unsophisticated and undynamic method.

Any model worthy of teaching as a profession must embody the deepest understanding of individual and group dynamics. But it must be focused on practice suited to the "firing line" operation of teaching rather than the consultation room. There is considerable disagreement about the role of a teacher, but no one will argue that the profession is sorely in need of new methods for assisting in the socialization processes and for dealing with the increasingly complex and frustrating behavior that pupils bring to the school. Whatever we do should be based on the generic nature of the educative process and the legitimate responsibility of the school. The concept of LSI is geared to these propositions.

Several theoretical developments have produced the present theoretical stance.

1. The concept of milieu as developed by Lewin and Redl. The application to the school implies an awareness of the total psycho-social system of a school.

2. The concept of Life Space Interviewing by Redl is designed to work with behavior "in situ."

3. The concept of crisis intervention by Caplan and others makes it clear that active intervention in times of stress is a most productive teaching opportunity.

4. The concept of differential diagnosis and strategic planning emphasizes going beyond the symptom and applying a variety of stratagems.

5. The concept of coping skills gives a rationale to the newer methodology as a means for teaching the pupil-needed ego skills. There is no belief that this alone will always be sufficient, but it is implied that without such new skills, much traditional therapy pays a low dividend.

6. The empathic relationship which the teacher generates underlies any "technique," and is more imposing in its impact than is method per se.

The following steps are not meant as a formal series, for there will be a great deal of flexibility in the development of any situation. Teachers seldom can conduct an extensive sequence at one interview, but the process can still be seen in its entire scope.

It should be noted that the goals differ significantly. In depth work, the expectation is for long-term gradual emergence of a more healthy personality, with possible regression followed by integration and eventual independence. In LSI, the hope is for a degree of behavioral compliance accompanied by life space relief, fostering adjustment. Marginal behavior then, may be all one expects. Traditionally, teachers act as if they expect to induce an immediate character change by exterior verbal exchange.

I. INSTIGATING CONDITION

Goal. In LSI, a specific incident (or series) calling for interference starts off the interview, but not as a moral issue, which is the traditional approach. The choice of proper timing and selection of an incident is critical. Many times it is preferable to allow certain incidents to pass by until one worthy of exploration occurs. There is usually a need for some "on the spot" managerial involvement. In LSI, direct use is made of milieu reality events. Choice of time and place of handling is selected to enforce or mitigate.

Process. One first works to obtain the individual (or group) perception of the state of affairs. While this is partly a matter of permitting catharsis and ventilation, it is basically the mode of establishing relationship by emphasizing your real interest in the child's perceptions rather than in your opinions. It is a matter of psychological truth rather than legal truth to which the adult is sensitive. To listen is to accept: it requires empathic feeling. Frequently the interviewer will be faced with resistance that demands tact and skill to penetrate. You end up with his perceptions, and you have already begun to size up the dynamics of the situation.

II. TESTING FOR DEPTH AND SPREAD

Goal. Some events are, to the child, isolated in-

cidents. Others stand for something more extensive: "I always get caught," or "I can never do anything." To what is this event attached as the child sees it? One drops many issues that seem to have no significant attachments since to the child these have little meaning. On the other hand, if what happened is a symbol of life for the child, it deserves minute attention.

Process. What is the basic central issue involved? Is this symptomatic of general life experience? Is it attached to some deep personality aspect? ("Do teachers always pick on you?" "Are all the others leaving you out?" "You always get caught, others don't?") What is the psychological factor underlying the behavioral episode and the reason for the depth of reaction?

III. CONTENT CLARIFICATION

Goal. It should be noted that here the content focus is very different from the traditional approach where there is an emphasis on standardized morality and surface compliance. Nor is the concern with the fantasy, conscious and unconscious content through dreams, early conflicts, and so on as would take place in depth counseling. Nor is the emphasis only on feeling, as in the less directive efforts. It is on what happened in sequence, descriptive at this level and without implied judgment.

Process. The teacher explores what went on: the reality is reconstructed with attached feelings and impulses recognized. It is accepted in a non-valuative way, although pupils already know we have values in ourselves. We are interested in the world as the pupil perceives it—not in the "reality" world as we would see it at this juncture.

IV. ENHANCING A FEELING OF ACCEPTANCE

Goal. In truth, the way we conduct the interview is the only way we can cultivate a feeling of acceptance in the relationship with a child. Some have limited capacity to respond, but many find a really concerned, listening adult a new experience. We do not aim for a deep transference as in therapy. We aim to be seen as an understanding, helpful teacher–counselor, a role most pupils already anticipate for us.

In classical therapeutic work, significant transference is anticipated. In traditional teaching, the adult–teacher role is one of authority, paternalistic or autocratic. In LSI it is emphatic, with a deep involvement in understanding. This consists of non-interpretive utilization of basic conscious or unconscious motivations. It requires a non-defensive assured, reasonableness. It is permissive in the sense of recognizing "the right to be heard," not in condoning behavior unsuited to the setting, such as hitting or destroying. The adult accepts that behavior is caused, that change is slow and hard, that motivations must be understood—but on the ego level. Any portion of positive potential is nurtured in contrast to exclusive attention to the pathology.

Process. Obviously this is not only what is done, but the basic tone established, the acceptance, the ability one has with the pupil without losing the adult role. This is a most complex condition but one many teachers can accomplish. It requires essentially non-interpretive responding to deeper feelings, which sometimes the pupil does not consciously recognize in himself. The significant aspect is to deal with the feeling behind the defense, not counterattack the defense itself.

V. AVOIDING EARLY IMPOSITION OF VALUE JUDGMENTS

Goal. We aim to put understanding before judgment. Traditionally, teachers appeal to value a system, use threats, admonition, exhortations, and denial of impulses.

In the depth process, transference, resistance, interpretations, insight, identification, acceptance of impulses (interpretations of UnC. material), high verbal permissiveness, acting out are interpreted. Play therapy and projective devices may be employed in the quest of the "diseased" and deepest level of difficulty. Obviously these methods are suited to the traditional therapeutic settings and not to the classroom.

Process. In LSI, the perception of the pupil is accepted as a perception, but other perceptions are explored, too. The implications of his view are realistically contemplated in a non-punitive manner. The emphasis is on behavior and methods of coping with his problem in a more satisfactory way. Ego level interpretations may be given only on the basis of the overt data and, ideally, are acknowledged by the pupil in the life setting. Impulse control is studied, support planned, hurdle help provided, and coping skills "taught." Implications of the present behavior are faced in actuality, not as a threat. Arguments over "right" and "wrong" behavior imply the pupil does not know right from wrong, which is usually not the case, and a challenge often sets off a secondary adult–child contention. If no real (rather than abstract) violation of the rights of others has taken place, it may be impossible to find an appeal to the child anyway.

VI. EXPLORING THE INTERNAL MECHANICS FOR "CHANGE" POSSIBILITIES

Goal. The goal here is to find what superego values or fragments are relevant in the pupil's perception of events. It is a matter of presence of guilt and anxiety *vs.* just being caught. The pupil must be free to express antisocial values. Group-related guilt reduction must be explored.

The ending of this phase moves toward "What should be done about it?" Many issues resolve themselves at this point: on the other hand there may be extensive resistance which has to be handled over a long series of contacts.

Process. Essentially we ask, what will help the pupil with this problem as he sees it? How can I help, or who can help? Here we get important diagnostic cues regarding his self-concept and goals as well as rationalizations. We see something of his hope or despair, his belief in "instant change." Frequently there is again resistance and denial. The worker can clarify the reality of assumptions which the pupil makes, without judgmental overtones, always looking for evidence to consider.

VII. THE TWO RESOLUTION PHASES

Goal. In the traditional work of teachers, surface compliance is usually demanded for whatever it is worth. In depth work, the anticipation is for eventual transfer to life situations with the expectation that sometimes things get worse in the action arena for a time. In LSI, one cannot expect great changes or even any improvement at times. The whole environment of life milieu is utilized for any relief or alterations it may have to offer. This may mean mitigation of given critical conditions, or planning and building in some support in the milieu. The limited outcome may be evidence that something more intensive in the way of help may eventually be needed—deep therapy, institutional treatment, or whatever the condition reveals. There is no supposition that, in all cases, even a tolerable situation will result. While LSI has the long view, it has to operate in the immediate, so in a sense it requires a bifocal view of events. What can we do to prevent a repetition of this behavior?

Process: Presenting the "Adult" View. If the problem has not worked itself out to some reasonable next step, the adult at this stage begins to inject reality factors in an objective way: implications of behavior, standards, expectations. Reality limits are explained in a non-moralistic way. Why some attention must be given to the behavior is covered, but not vindictively. It may be a matter of basic social behavior or the nature of school and its inherent demands or the implications of nonconformity. Considerable skill is needed here to avoid the typical moralistic stance. At the same time adult responsibility must be acknowledged, and the nature of the real world frankly examined.

Process: Working through to a Solution—Strategic Planning. The reality demands are clarified and some reasonable first-step plan is developed. What is going to happen or will happen the next time? Here is where the sanctions, freedom restrictions, need for more intensive help, the special assistance, and behavior contingencies are discussed. It is essential that the plan be one which can be carried out, whether it be removal, a talk with parents, or a discussion with a third party. Thus, we are led again back to the milieu and its potentials. A pupil

should be left with a feeling of milieu solidarity and support for him in his dilemma, rather than permissiveness or escapism. Vague and severe threats have no place whatsoever. Discussion of extensive and obviously not-to-happen consequences of continued limit breaking serve only to confuse the issue. On the other hand, there should be no hiding or reluctance to examine what may actually have to take place. We have to help him feel we are non-hostile and that we have hopes of really helping him cope with the difficulty. Since many pupils feel they must test any stated plan, no non-workable program should be risked. That is, no plan is envisioned which will not be possible to conduct if the pupil needs to test it out. Here needed specialists are worked into the design and all of the school's resources are reviewed for potential help. It well may be that LSI and other methods will work in unison when the problem is a very complex one.

REFERENCES

Bandura, Albert. Social Reinforcement and Behavior Change—Symposium, 1962. *Am. Jo. Ortho.*, 33:4, July 1963.

Caldwell, Bettye M., Leonard Hersher, Earle Lipton, and others. Mother-Infant Interaction in Monomatric and Polymatric Families. *Am. Jo. Ortho.*, 33:4, July 1963.

Caplan, G. Mental Health Consultation in Schools. Milbank Memorial Fund Proceedings, 1955 Annual Conference.

Caplan, G. (ed) *Prevention of Mental Disorders in Children.* New York: Basic Books, 1961.

Dean, S. J. Treatment of the Reluctant Client, *Am. Psych.*, 13:11, November 1959, pp. 627–630.

Dittman, A. T. and H. L. Kitchener, L.S.I. and Individual Play Therapy, *Am. Jo. Ortho.*, 29:1, January 1959, pp. 19–26.

Kitchener, Howard L. The Life Space Interview in the Differentiation of School in Residential Treatment. *Am. Jo. Ortho.*, 33:4, July 1963.

Krasner, Leonard. Reinforcement, Verbal Behavior, and Psychotherapy. *Am. Jo. Ortho.*, 33:4, July 1963.

Worksheet on Conceptual Variations in Interview Designs with Children

PSYCHOANALYTIC	LIFE SPACE OR REALITY	TRADITIONAL
1. INSTIGATING CONDITION General personality problem, long-term, not responding to supportive and growth correctional effort	Specific incident (or series) of behavior usually calling for "on the spot" managerial interference	Both implied but interpreted as moral issue
2. GOAL Long term expectations of gradual emergence of more healthy personality, possible regression followed by integration and eventual independence	Degree of behavioral compliance accompanied by life space relief fostering adjustment	Induce an immediate character change, exterior change
3. SETTING Office isolation away from immediate life pressures, formal setting, sequence timed	Direct use of milieu reality aspects; choice of time, place to enforce or mitigate as needed	Isolated, integrated, frequent use of group or setting for pressure
4. RELATIONSHIP Classical transference, resistance inter-personal relationship	Emphatic, child identified role by adult	Adult role of authority; paternalistic, autocratic
5. CONTENT C. and UnC., fantasy, early conflicts, projection, focus on feeling, impulse exploration	What went on, reality exploration, reconstruction with attached feelings, impulses, recognized, accepted	Emphasis on the standard morality interpretation of event
6. PROCESSES Transference, resistance, interpretations, insight, identification, acceptance of impulses (interpretations of UnC. material), high verbal permissiveness, acting out interpreted	Causal behavior "accepted," clinical exploitation of L. S. events, ego-level interpretation, impulse-control balance critical, support given, explanations fostered, ego support, hurdle help, "skills" depicted, behavior implications faced	Appeal to value system, threats, admonition, exhortations, denial of impulses
7. RESOLUTION Eventual transfer to life situations	Support and milieu planning to mitigate critical conditions	Surface compliance or rejection

Lindsley, Ogden R. Experimental Analysis of Social Reinforcement: Terms and Methods. *Am. Jo. Ortho.*, 33:4, July 1963.

Long, Nicholas J. Some Problems in Teaching Life Space Interviewing Techniques to Graduate Students in Education in a Large Class at Indiana University. *Am. Jo. Ortho.*, 33:4, July 1963.

Morse, William C. Working Paper: Training Teachers in Life Space Interviewing. *Am. Jo. Ortho.*, 33:4, July 1963.

Morse, W. C. and E. R. Small. Group Life Space Interviewing in a Therapeutic Camp. *Am. Jo. Ortho.*, 29:1, January 1959, pp. 27–44.

Murphey, Elizabeth B., Earle Silber, George Coehlho, and others. Development of Autonomy and Parent-Child Interaction in Case Adolescence. *Am. Jo. Ortho.*, 33:4, July 1963.

Newman, Ruth G. The School-Centered Life Space Interview as Illustrated by Extreme Threat of School Issues. *Am. Jo. Ortho.*, 33:4, July 1963.

Redl, Fritz. Strategy and Techniques of the Life

Space Interview, *Am. Jo. Ortho.*, 29:1, January 1959, pp. 1–18.

Redl, Fritz. The School Centered Life Space Interview. Washington, D.C.: School Research Program, Washington School of Psychiatry, 1963.

Redl, Fritz. The Concept of Therapeutic Milieu. *Am. Jo. Ortho.*, 29:4, October 1959, pp. 721–727.

Redl, Fritz. The Life Space Interview in the School Setting—Workshop, 1961. *Am. Jo. Ortho.*, 33:4, July 1963.

Silver, Albert W. Delinquents in Group Therapy. *Am. Jo. Ortho.*, 33:4, July 1963.

Wineman, D. The Life Space Interview, *Social Work*, January 1959, pp. 3–17.

Zigler, Edward. Social Reinforcement, Environmental Conditions, and the Child. *Am. Jo. Ortho.*, 33:4, July 1963.

46

Questions about the Use of Drugs to Control Classroom Behavior

Joseph N. Murray

EDITOR'S NOTE • *It would be difficult to conclude a chapter on disciplinary issues and classroom management strategies without a discussion about the use of drugs to control classroom behavior. By no means is there universal agreement among educators, parents, or psychologists about whether or not drug therapy is a good idea. Ritalin and dexedrine are among the most widely used drugs, both of which are used, with varying degrees of success, to control hyperactive (hyperkinetic) youngsters. This is a fine overview article that will give you some of the important and basic information necessary for understanding the effects of drugs on behavior and the probable consequences of its use. How about it—would you encourage the use of drugs for your students or your children?*

In late June of 1970, the *Washington Post* reported that doctors in Omaha, Nebraska, were giving hundreds of school children

Joseph N. Murray, "Drugs to Control Classroom Behavior," *Educational Leadership* 31: 21–25 (October 1973). Reprinted with permission of the Association for Supervision and Curriculum Development and Joseph N. Murray. Copyright © 1973 by the Association for Supervision and Curriculum Development.

so-called behavior modification drugs to make them "behave" better. Five days later Huntley-Brinkley featured a news story about the Omaha situation on their national newscast. These, as well as other news media, posed some very real concerns about possible misuse of various drugs designed to modify the behavior of overactive children.

One of the major thoughts coming out of this issue questioned the right of educators, parents, school administrators, physicians, and others to suggest that a child be given medication to modify his behavior. As many began debating and discussing this issue, one thing became clear: there is throughout the United States a gross misunderstanding and consequent misuse of the psychopharmacologic process as it is used in attempting to modify the behavior of overactive youngsters.

QUESTIONS ABOUT DRUG USAGE

Educators, now and in the future, must make themselves more knowledgeable about the overactive child syndrome and the various methods for dealing with this type of problem youngster. The purpose of this article is to focus on many of the concepts related to the overactive child who is medicated with drugs such as Ritalin and Dexedrine in an effort to modify his overactive behavior. Many of the observations in this article were drawn from an 18-month study (1969–70) of Franklin County youngsters in and around Columbus, Ohio. During the course of the study it was possible to make observations of several recurring commonalities associated with the administration of Dexedrine or Ritalin to modify behavior.

As the study progressed, it became apparent that many questions beset educators and other professional people who are involved in some way with using medication in an attempt to control overactive behavior in youngsters. The following represent some of the more frequently asked questions.

WHY ARE SOME YOUNGSTERS MEDICATED WHILE OTHERS ARE NOT?

1. What is felt to be overactive behavior by one teacher is simply not over-active to another. Therefore, some youngsters who are recom-

mended for medication would not be if they had a different teacher.

2. Some teachers are capable, through various skills such as behavior modification techniques, to control overactive behavior effectively, while other less skilled or ambitious teachers will feel the need to recommend medication to control behavior.

3. Some teachers seem to be captured by a mystique surrounding the use of pills as a "cure-all." Apparently, many teachers equate the power of penicillin and other wonder drugs to the behavior modification drugs and, in so doing, hope for dramatic results.

4. Recommending medication to a parent seems to suggest a degree of professionalism and knowledgeability to some teachers. It provides a way of dealing with a problem with which few parents are familiar.

5. In some instances, teachers have tried virtually all ways to control a child's behavior, and almost out of desperation they resort to recommending medication to parents, hoping that this will solve the problem.

While these comments are critical of teachers, they do represent possible answers to the question, "Why are some youngsters medicated for overactive behavior while others are not?" It would be unfair to suggest that these reasons are representative of the majority of teachers recommending medication, but it would be equally unfair not to mention that a number of teachers operate with these rationales.

WHO SHOULD RECEIVE MEDICATION?

Burks (1964) refers to *hyperkinesis* as a type of overactive behavior. Hyperkinesis he defines as "the physiological expression or accompaniment of tension in an individual. Hyperkinetic behavior depicts the processes which are *not subject to conscious innervation*, but are primarily *energized by the autonomic nervous system*." His definition of hyperkinesis suggests that because of organic involvement, the youngster is physically unable to control his behavior.

On the other hand, the child who is used to a loosely structured or nonstructured environment, or who has certain personality needs which dictate acting out behavior, will manifest many of the same behaviors as the hyperkinetic. The causes, however, will often be environmental rather than organic. The environmentally based overactive is often referred to as the *hyperactive;* the organically based overactive as the *hyperkinetic.*

Sainz (1966) explained the results of a clinical test which he suggests is an effective way to determine whether a child is hyperactive or hyperkinetic. He placed hyperkinetic children (age range seven years through eleven years) in a playroom and administered 20 mg. of Ritalin to them. He suggested that if a child is hyperkinetic, the hyperkinesia will completely disappear in 15 minutes to one hour. On the other hand, if the child is hyperactive, his behavior remains the same or gets worse in that same time period. There is thus a need to determine as nearly as possible whether a child is hyperkinetic or hyperactive before considering him for referral to a physician for possible medication.

The classroom teacher does not have the clinical facilities that Sainz had. What clues can he look for to help substantiate the suspicion that a youngster is hyperkinetic rather than hyperactive? Knobel (1962) suggests that it might be possible to differentiate the hyperkinetic from the hyperactive by close observation of his behavior.

> The organic is erratic, without direction or objective. His behavior is almost ceaseless and without change in home, school, or any other social situation, and is generally accompanied by some slight choreoathetosic movement. (Choreoathetosic refers to slight, irregular, jerking movements caused by involuntary muscular contractions.) The aggressivity and impulsivity are without goal and apparently senseless. The child's inability to postpone gratification is endless and urgent whether he is at home, in school, or wherever he may be.

The hyperactive, on the other hand,

> . . . shows some direction and intentionality in his aggressivity and impulsivity. In this child it is possible to obtain certain structure and coordination in various aspects of his behavior which certainly might be different according to where the child finds himself or with whom he relates himself.

Closely observing a youngster's behavior by applying the criteria which Knobel suggests and comparing the behavior of the youngster to that of his peers will do much to help answer the question, "Who should receive medication?" In essence, every effort should be made to determine whether the child in question is hyperkinetic or hyperactive.

Closer observation of a youngster's behavior in a variety of settings will do much to prevent hyperactive youngsters from being unnecessarily medicated.

WHAT ARE SOME POSSIBLE CAUSES OF HYPERKINESIS?

Martin (1967) postulates, as do others, that hyperkinesis results from "minimal brain dysfunction" which may be a result of genetic, developmental, metabolic, toxic, or infectious processes. He also raises the question of fetal milieu with all of the pre-, para-, and post-natal possibilities for brain damage. Laufer and Denhoff (1957) hypothesize that "stimuli coming from the sensor and visceral receptors pass through the diencephalon on their way to cortical areas." The diencephalon, they theorize, may "serve to pattern, route, and give valence to these stimuli." In that case, any injury to, or malfunction of, the diencephalon would "alter resistance at the synapses and would thus allow incoming impulses to spread out on the usual pathways and irradiate large cortical areas." It should be mentioned that if this theory suggesting that an aberrated diencephalon may be responsible for hyperkinetic behavior has merit, the electroencephalograms used so often as a diagnostic tool in determining etiology would be of little value.

Millichap and Fowler (1967) suggest that the following factors are most often organic causes of hyperkinesia: brain injury or anoxia (oxygen debt) during pregnancy or birth, encephalitis, and meningitis. These, in turn, create brain lesions and other damage which can cause delayed maturation of that portion of the brain responsible for hyperkinetic behavior.

The delayed maturation concept is considered important by many, since it suggests that a youngster can actually "outgrow" his hyperkinetic problem during adolescence. If this theory has validity, this should indicate to educators the importance of controlling hyperkinesis with medication during the critical learning years. Failure to do so could result in the youngster's missing the basics of learning, thus developing a possible attitudinal problem and consequently entering into the adolescent period with educational and social skills considerably more deficient than they would be without a hyperkinetic disorder.

WHAT DRUGS ARE MOST FREQUENTLY USED TO CONTROL HYPERKINESIS?

Millichap and Fowler (1967) reviewed the published reports on drugs used to treat hyperkinetics. Based on calculations of the mean incidence of improvement and toxicity in these published reports, these researchers rated the drugs according to efficiency. This study, as well as others, suggests that Ritalin and Dexedrine are the two drugs used most frequently by physicians in treating hyperkinetic behavior disorders.

Of the two drugs, Ritalin is the newer. The first controlled study published on Ritalin was apparently conducted in 1958 by Knobel (1962). Dexedrine, on the other hand, has been used since at least 1937, when Bradley first published the results of his studies using amphetamines (Dexedrine) on hyperkinetic children (1941).

Ritalin, as described by CIBA Pharmaceutical Company, is "a mild stimulant and antidepressant which brightens mood and improves performance." Dexedrine, as described by Smith, Kline, and French Laboratories, is "a mild stimulant which can be used to restore optimism and mental alertness and to induce a feeling of energy and well-being." Both Ritalin and Dexedrine are *mild stimulants* and should not be confused with tranquilizers, as they are so frequently.

Nobody apparently knows for sure how Ritalin and Dexedrine work to control hyperkinesis. Knobel (1962) notes that Ritalin apparently makes its basic contribution as a "stimulator of the cerebral cortex, thereby allowing for true integration of behavior." Burks (1964) feels that Ritalin and Dexedrine probably act on lower brain centers and that the drug alters the function of the diencephalon in such a way that it once more can keep the cortex from being flooded by streams of unmodulated impulses coming in from sensory receptors.

Despite considerable doubt regarding the precise way in which Ritalin and Dexedrine work to modify behavior, a number of studies have illustrated their effectiveness.

Knobel (1962) studied the effects of Ritalin on 150 patients with the typical symptomatology of hyperkinesis. Results in this study were recorded through teachers' and parents' reports and direct clinical observation. The ages of the children ranged from seven through fifteen, with an average of 9.6 years. The sample included 110 boys (mean age 10.9) and 40 girls (mean age 8.22), all of whom had reported IQ's in excess of 90.

Knobel's study was conducted over a period of eight months. Dosages of Ritalin ranged from 20 to 40 mg. and were administered twice daily, one after breakfast and one after lunch. He reported that hyperactivity and aggressivity diminished in all children, with marked improvement in 40 percent of the patients. He classified his results as: (a) good improvement, (b) moderate improvement, and (c) no improvement. Sixty children (40 percent) demonstrated a good improvement, 75 (50 percent) showed moderate improvement, and 15 (10 percent) showed no improvement.

POSSIBLE SIDE EFFECTS

The producers of Dexedrine list the following possible side effects from taking Dexedrine: overstimulation, restlessness, insomnia, gastrointestinal disturbances, diarrhea, palpitation, elevation of blood pressure, tremor, sweating, and headache. While adverse reactions resulting from the use of Ritalin and Dexedrine have generally been few, individuals reportedly can differ markedly in their reaction to these drugs.

SUBJECTIVE FINDINGS

During the course of the 18-month study in Franklin County, a number of subjective observations were made regarding the use of medication on overactive youngsters. These observations did not lend themselves to objective assessment, but were felt to be an important and integral part of the findings of this study.

Many doctors prescribe Ritalin or Dexedrine to be taken during school hours, and frequently teachers give the medication to the child, especially to the younger child. In one instance, a child's medication had been changed without the teacher's knowledge, and the parents were giving the child a much stronger medicine at home while the teacher continued to add to the child's medicinal intake at school. Parents have also been known to give medication indiscriminately by issuing to a child more dosage than prescribed. The teacher, by giving medicine at school, could then increase even more the amount of medicine the child takes.

While most schools have policies regarding the issuance of medicine of any type to children, this policy seems to be violated when it comes to giving medication for overactivity. Ideally it would appear logical for teachers not to involve themselves with giving medication. Certainly if a teacher finds himself in a position in which he is asked to "remind" a child to take his medicine, he should have something in writing giving him permission to do so, and this should be signed by both parents. This would help protect the teacher from any consequences which might arise from his involvement with medicating the overactive child.

Both parents and teachers have a tendency to look upon medication as a cure-all for the child's problems resulting from overactivity. This creates high expectancy levels and consequently disappointment in many cases when these levels are not met by the child. The emphasis placed on medication to help modify overactivity appears to cause both teachers and parents to abandon other approaches to modifying behavior. Also, successful medical intervention with an overactive child causes a "snowballing" effect: in schools where success has been realized through medical intervention, many more teachers seem prone to refer youngsters for possible medication. When parents see success, they often inform their neighbors. It has been observed that many of these neighbors request that their child receive medical help for his overactivity, hoping to see similar improvement in their child.

The administration as well as the faculty of a given school seemingly has much effect on the number of children being medicated for overactivity within that school. Some schools in Franklin County have far more youngsters on medication than other schools that have comparable numbers of students, and it is suspected that the philosophy of those schools regarding medication for overactivity is largely responsible for this.

Of the 32 children involved in this study, 31 were boys. This seems to parallel the widely accepted idea held by many experts involved with exceptional children that in virtually all areas of exceptionality, boys outnumber girls. The basic reason for this is given as sex-linked, with a rather detailed explanation involving chromosomal combinations being offered as the cause. Some consideration should probably be given to the idea that our society traditionally recognizes boys as being more aggressive and outgoing, and thus possibly fosters more activity on the part of boys than girls.

A final subjective observation: most physicians who treated youngsters in this study prescribed medications at the parents' request after questioning the parents orally regarding their child's behavior. A few asked for a written description of the child's classroom behavior from the teacher. In nearly every case, the physician wanted to see the child in two weeks after the initial medication or earlier if complications arose from taking the medicine. In general, physicians were found to follow up closely on youngsters treated medically for overactivity.

DISCUSSION

It is difficult to say whether overactive youngsters should receive medication for their condition. In every instance, parents should make a decision after an accurate observation of the child's behavior has been made in a variety of settings, school and home, and after these findings have been reviewed by the family physician. Professionals should be consulted to help determine whether the cause of the overactive behavior is organically or environmentally based. Whenever possible, alternatives to medication for overactive behavior should be tried, with the use of medication coming after other alternatives have been exhausted.

It does appear that in specific cases where the child's behavior is organically based, medication can produce remarkably good results. There is, however, evidence which strongly suggests the unnecessary medication of youngsters who, in many cases, are simply products of unstructured and undisciplined environments. Only proper diagnosis of individual cases will help to ensure that medication is being properly employed, and even then the answer may not be apparent.

REFERENCES

C. Bradley and M. Bowen. "Amphetamine (Benzedrine) Therapy of Children's Behavior Disorders." *American Journal of Orthopsychiatry* 11: 92–97; January 1941.

Harold F. Burks. "Effects of Amphetamine Therapy on Hyperkinetic Children." *Archives of General Psychiatry* 11: 604–609; December 1964.

Mauricio Knobel, M.D. "Psychopharmacology for the Hyperkinetic Child." *Archives of General Psychiatry* 10: 198–203, September 1962. © 1962, the American Medical Association.

M. W. Laufer and E. Denhoff: "Hyperkinetic Behavior Syndrome in Children." *Journal of Pediatrics* 50: 463–68; June 1957.

Daniel M. Martin. "Hyperkinetic Behavior Disorders in Children." *Journal of Pediatrics* 40: 96–98; July 1967.

J. Millichap and Glenn Fowler. "Treatment of 'Minimal Brain Dysfunction' Syndromes." *Pediatric Clinics of North America* 14: 767–76; November 1967.

Anthony Sainz. "Hyperkinetic Disease of Children: Diagnosis and Therapy." *Diseases of the Nervous System* 27: 48–50; July 1966.

Part Five · toward understanding what happens within oneself

*"Know thyself" is indeed a weighty admonition. But in
this, as in any science, the difficulties are discovered only
by those who set their hands to it. We must push against a
door to find out whether it is bolted or not.*

Montaigne (1533–1595)

There are three basic questions that each of us must attempt to answer if we are to become more successful in being more open to our experiences and more capable of developing our potential: Who am I? What do I stand for? And why? Each of these questions deals with our sense of self—who we think we are, where we think we are headed, and how we plan to get there.

It is an interesting, if lamentable, fact of our educational system that we study almost everything else before we study ourselves. In an effort to encourage a bit of self-examination, the chapters and readings in this section are designed to probe the questions: What do I mean to myself? and How can I come to know myself better?

The selections in Chapter Thirteen were chosen to help you understand what it means to move in the direction of developing a healthy personality and to suggest some means for doing this. Abraham Maslow spent over thirty years researching and developing a psychology of health; in reading 47, he raises some penetrating questions related to popular ideas of adjustment, psychological health and emotional sickness, and personality problems. How can you know yourself better? What can you do to know others better? Sidney Jourard has developed a psychology of self-disclosure, which, though risky, is an exciting route to better self-other understanding (see reading 48). The psychological construct of the ego has come a long way since Freud's time. Reading 49 introduces you to a more contemporary discussion of how the ego can be divided into three different "ego-states." What does it mean to be a "fully-functioning person"? What can you do to move in that direction? Earl Kelley explores these and many related questions in his very sensitive offering in reading 50.

Chapter Fourteen, "Toward Understanding Oneself," is a logical conclusion to this section of the book—in fact, to this entire volume. What does it mean to be that self which one truly is? Carl Rogers may open new doors to your understanding of this question in reading 51. What factors influence how we present ourselves to others? Kenneth Gergen offers some interesting insights in selection 52. How do people rationalize their behavior? In his revealing analysis, in reading 53, Elliot Aronson may surprise you with his suggestions of the extremes of rationalization that we are capable of indulging in. What are the expressions and outcomes of an inferiority complex? What are signs of self-worth? What can we do to develop a healthier, more positive self-image? I hope my ideas in selection 54 will be helpful in answering these and related questions.

Chapter Thirteen · personality dynamics and personal growth

47

Toward a Psychology of Health

Abraham H. Maslow

EDITOR'S NOTE · *Dr. Maslow spent the better part of his professional life trying to understand what makes healthy people healthy, what brings out the best in people, and what enables some people to transcend the everyday, the ordinary, and the mundane in an effort to achieve their potential. Dr. Maslow had the deep conviction that the study of self-fulfilling people could teach us much about how to live healthier, more self-actualized lives. His book,* Motivation and Personality, *marks the shift away from studying maladjusted behavior to studying healthy behavior, as a means to make our lives more meaningful. What kind of a society do we need for healthy people to grow in? What is the difference between a healthy person and an unhealthy one? How would you assess your own mental health? This selection will help you to develop answers to these questions.*

There is now emerging over the horizon a new conception of human sickness and of human health, a psychology that I find so thrilling and so full of wonderful possibilities that I yield to the temptation to present it publicly even before it is checked and confirmed, and before it can be called reliable scientific knowledge.

The basic assumptions of this point of view are:

1. We have, each of us, an essential biologically based inner nature, which is to some degree "natural," intrinsic, given, and, in a certain limited sense, unchangeable, or, at least, unchanging.

2. Each person's inner nature is in part unique to himself and in part species-wide.

3. It is possible to study this inner nature scientifically and to discover what it is like (not invent—discover).

4. This inner nature, as much as we know of it so far, seems not to be intrinsically or primarily or necessarily evil. The basic needs (for life, for safety and security, for belongingness and affection, for respect and self-respect, and for self-actualization), the basic human emotions and the basic human capacities are on their face either neutral, pre-moral or positively "good." Destructiveness, sadism, cruelty, malice, etc., seem so far to be not intrinsic but rather they seem to be violent reactions *against* frustration of our intrinsic needs, emotions and capacities. Anger is *in itself* not evil, nor is fear, laziness, or even ignorance. Of course, these can and do lead to evil behavior, but they needn't. This result is not intrinsically necessary. Human nature is not nearly as bad as it has been thought to be. In fact it can be said that the possibilities of human nature have customarily been sold short.

5. Since this inner nature is good or neutral

rather than bad, it is best to bring it out and to encourage it rather than to suppress it. If it is permitted to guide our life, we grow healthy, fruitful, and happy.

6. If this essential core of the person is denied or suppressed, he gets sick sometimes in obvious ways, sometimes in subtle ways, sometimes immediately, sometimes later.

7. This inner nature is not strong and overpowering and unmistakable like the instincts of animals. It is weak and delicate and subtle and easily overcome by habit, cultural pressure, and wrong attitudes toward it.

8. Even though weak, it rarely disappears in the normal person—perhaps not even in the sick person. Even though denied, it persists underground forever pressing for actualization.

9. Somehow, these conclusions must all be articulated with the necessity of discipline, deprivation, frustration, pain, and tragedy. To the extent that these experiences reveal and foster and fulfill our inner nature, to that extent they are desirable experiences. It is increasingly clear that these experiences have something to do with a sense of achievement and ego strength and therefore with the sense of healthy self-esteem and self-confidence. The person who hasn't conquered, withstood and overcome continues to feel doubtful that he *could*. This is true not only for external dangers; it holds also for the ability to control and to delay one's own impulses, and therefore to be unafraid of them.

Observe that if these assumptions are proven true, they promise a scientific ethics, a natural value system, a court of ultimate appeal for the determination of good and bad, of right and wrong. The more we learn about man's natural tendencies, the easier it will be to tell him how to be good, how to be happy, how to be fruitful, how to respect himself, how to love, how to fulfill his highest potentialities. This amounts to automatic solution of many of the personality problems of the future. The thing to do seems to be to find out what one is *really* like inside, deep down, as a member of the human species and as a particular individual.

The study of such self-fulfilling people can teach us much about our own mistakes, our shortcomings, the proper directions in which to grow.

Every age but ours has had its model, its ideal. All of these have been given up by our culture; the saint, the hero, the gentleman, the knight, the mystic. About all we have left is the well-adjusted man without problems, a very pale and doubtful substitute. Perhaps we shall soon be able to use as our guide and model the fully growing and self-fulfilling human being, the one in whom all his potentialities are coming to full development, the one whose inner nature expresses itself freely, rather than being warped, suppressed, or denied.

The serious thing for each person to recognize vividly and poignantly, each for himself, is that every falling away from species-virtue, every crime against one's own nature, every evil act, *every one without exception records itself* in our unconscious and makes us despise ourselves. Karen Horney had a good word to describe this unconscious perceiving and remembering; she said it "registers." If we do something we are ashamed of, it "registers" to our discredit, and if we do something honest or fine or good, it "registers" to our credit. The net results ultimately are either one or the other—either we respect and accept ourselves or we despise ourselves and feel contemptible, worthless, and unlovable. Theologians used to use the word *"accidie"* to describe the sin of failing to do with one's life all that one knows one could do.

This point of view in no way denies the usual Freudian picture. But it does add to it and supplement it. To oversimplify the matter somewhat, it is as if Freud supplied to us the sick half of psychology and we must now fill it out with the healthy half. Perhaps this health psychology will give us more possibility for controlling and improving our lives and for making ourselves better people. Perhaps this will be more fruitful than asking "how to get *unsick*."

How can we encourage free development? What are the best educational conditions for it? Sexual? Economic? Political? What kind of world do we need for such people to grow in? What kind of world will such people create? Sick people are made by a sick culture; healthy people are made possible by a healthy culture. But it is just as true that sick individuals make their culture more sick and that healthy individuals make their culture more healthy. Improving individual health is one approach to making a better world. To express it in another way, encouragement of personal growth is a real possibility; cure of actual neurotic symptoms is far less possible without outside help. It is relatively easy to try deliberately to make oneself a more honest man; it is very difficult to try to cure one's own compulsions or obsessions.

The classical approach to personality problems considers them to be problems in an undesirable sense. Struggle, conflict, guilt, bad conscience, anxiety, depression, frustration, tension, shame, self-punishment, feeling of inferiority or unworthiness—they all cause psychic pain, they disturb efficiency of performance, and they are uncontrollable. They are therefore automatically regarded as sick and undesirable and they get "cured" away as soon as possible.

But all of these symptoms are found also in healthy people, or in people who are growing toward health. Supposing you *should* feel guilty and don't? Supposing you have attained a nice stabilization of forces and you *are* adjusted? Perhaps adjustment and stabilization, while good because it cuts your pain, is also bad because development toward a higher ideal ceases?

Erich Fromm, in a very important book[1], attacked the classical Freudian notion of a superego because this concept was entirely authoritarian and relativistic. That is to say, your superego or your conscience was supposed by Freud to be primarily the internalization of the wishes, demands, and ideals of the father and mother, whoever they happen to be. But supposing they are criminals? Then what kind of conscience do you have? Or supposing you have a rigid moralizing father who hates fun? Or a psychopath? This conscience exists—Freud was right. We do get our ideals largely from such early figures and not from Sunday School books read later in life. But there is also another element in conscience, or, if you like, another kind of conscience, which we all have either weakly or strongly. And this is the "intrinsic conscience." This is based upon the unconscious and preconscious perception of our own nature, of our own destiny, or our own capacities, of our own "call" in life. It insists that we be true to our inner nature and that we do not deny it out of weakness or for advantage or for any other reason. He who belies his talent, the born painter who sells

stockings instead, the intelligent man who lives a stupid life, the man who sees the truth and keeps his mouth shut, the coward who gives up his manliness, all these people perceive in a deep way that they have done wrong to themselves and despise themselves for it. Out of this self-punishment may come only neurosis, but there may equally well come renewed courage, righteous indignation, increased self-respect, because of thereafter doing the right thing; in a word, growth and improvement can come through pain and conflict.

In essence I am deliberately rejecting our present easy distinction between sickness and health, at least as far as surface symptoms are concerned. Does sickness mean having symptoms? I maintain now that sickness might consist of not having symptoms when you should. Does health mean being symptom-free? I deny it. Which of the Nazis at Auschwitz or Dachau were healthy? Those with stricken conscience or those with a nice, clear, happy conscience? Was it possible for a profoundly human person not to feel conflict, suffering, depression, rage, etc.?

In a word if you tell me you have a personality problem I am not certain until I know you better whether to say "Good!" or "I'm sorry." It depends on the reasons. And these, it seems, may be bad reasons, or they may be good reasons.

An example is the changing attitude of psychologists toward popularity, toward adjustment, even toward delinquency. Popular with whom? Perhaps it is better for a youngster to be *unpopular* with the neighboring snobs or with the local country club set. Adjusted to what? To a bad culture? To a dominating parent? What shall we think of a well-adjusted slave? A well-adjusted prisoner? Even the behavior problem boy is being looked upon with new tolerance. *Why* is he delinquent? Most often it is for sick reasons. But occasionally it is for good reasons and the boy is simply resisting exploitation, domination, neglect, contempt, and trampling upon.

Clearly what will be called personality problems depends on who is doing the calling. The slave owner? The dictator? The patriarchal father? The husband who wants his wife to remain a child? It seems quite clear that personality problems may sometimes be loud protests against the crushing of one's psychological bones, of one's true inner nature. What is sick then is *not* to protest

---

[1] Erich Fromm, *Escape from Freedom* (New York: Farrar, Straus, and Giroux, 1941).

while this crime is being committed. And I am sorry to report my impression that most people do not protest under such treatment. They take it and pay years later, in neurotic and psychosomatic symptoms of various kinds, or perhaps in some cases never become aware that they are sick, that they have missed true happiness, true fulfillment of promise, and rich emotional life, and a serene, fruitful old age, that they have never known how wonderful it is to be creative, to react aesthetically, to find life thrilling.

The question of desirable grief and pain or the necessity for it must also be faced. Is growth and self-fulfillment possible at all without pain and grief and sorrow and turmoil? If these are to some extent necessary and unavoidable, then to what extent? If grief and pain are sometimes necessary for growth of the person, then we must learn not to protect people from them automatically as if they were always bad. Sometimes they may be good and desirable in view of the ultimate good consequences. Not allowing people to go through their pain, and protecting them from it, may turn out to be a kind of overprotection, which in turn implies a certain lack of respect for the integrity and the intrinsic nature and the future development of the individual.

48

How Self-Disclosure Can Help You Develop a Healthy Personality

Sidney Jourard

EDITOR'S NOTE • Developing into an emotionally healthy, self-actualizing person does not miraculously happen to a select few. Rather, it can happen to any person who remains open to his or her feelings and experiences and is able to disclose his or her self to others. In order for people to move closer to understanding and accepting themselves, they must allow themselves to be known—really known—by at least one person. Which is the whole point of this selection. Dr. Jourard builds a substantial case to support his thesis that "every maladjusted person is a person who has not made himself known to another human being and in consequence does not know himself." How does self-disclosure work? Why does it work the way it does? What can you do to be a more self-disclosing person? If you are interested in being more open and honest in expressing the "real" you and also in being able to help others express their "real" selves to you, this selection will be a great assistance.

For a long time, health and well-being have been taken for granted as "givens," and disease has been viewed as the problem for man to solve. Today, however, increasing numbers of scientists have begun to adopt a reverse point of view; disease and trouble are the givens, and specification of positive health and its conditions are viewed as the important goal. Physical, mental, and social health are values representing restrictions on the total variance of being. The scientific problem here consists in defining health, determining its relevant dimensions, and identifying the independent variables of which these are a function.[1,2]

Scientists, however, are supposed to be hardboiled, and they insist that phenomena in order to be counted "real" must be public. Hence, many behavioral scientists ignore man's "self"—his experience of his situation—since it is essentially a private phenomenon. Others, however, are not so quick to allocate man's self to the limbo of the unimportant, and they insist that we cannot understand man and his lot until we take his experience into account.

I fall into the camp of those investigators who want to explore health as a positive problem in its own right and who, further, take man's self seriously—as a reality to be explained and as a variable which produces consequences for weal or woe. In this chapter, I would like more fully to explore the connection between positive health and the disclosure of self. First, some sociological truisms.

Social systems require their members to take certain roles. Unless the roles are adequately fulfilled, the social systems will not produce the results for which they have been organized. This applies to systems as simple as one developed by an engaged couple and to those as complex as a total nation among nations.

Societies have socialization "factories" and "mills"—families and schools—which serve the function of training people to take on the age, sex, and occupational roles which they shall be obliged to fulfill throughout their life in the social system.[3] Broadly speaking, if a person carries out his roles suitably, he can be regarded as a "normal" personality. *Normal personalities, however, are not necessarily healthy personalities.*[4]

Man has more to do with his energies than use them merely to produce popularity, approval, or mediocre anonymity in the mass. Yet many people seek these outcomes to action as ends in themselves, as the *summum bonum* to which all other considerations are subordinated. The curious thing is that, if a man places normality at the pinnacle of importance, many other values are in fact jeopardized. It is a matter of indifference to the social system whether such conformity is achieved at the price of idiosyncratic need gratifications, a sense of identity and selfhood, creativity, or even physical health. Such official indifference to all a man's being save his role conformity has longer-run deleterious effects on the social system. It costs the system progress and innovation. It makes for a "closed" and stagnant society rather than one which is "open."[5]

It is a truth that normality (role conformity) in some social systems produces physical illness of gradual onset; and if too many real idiosyncratic needs are stifled in the pursuit and maintenance of normality, then boredom, neurosis, or psychosis will be regular, predictable outcomes.

The "sociology of illness" tabulates incidents of assorted diseases in various age, sex, socioeconomic, and subcultural groupings—incidences which exceed those found in the population at large. For example, peptic ulcer occurs more commonly among men than among women, and schizophrenia occurs more commonly among lower-class people than among upper-middle-class folk. These correlations should not come as any surprise, for the illnesses arise for one reason, and one reason only: *the people who live the ways of life typical to their social position become ill because they behave in ways exquisitely calculated to produce just those outcomes.* They sicken because they behave in sickening ways.

TRANSPARENCY TO ONESELF

It should be true that healthy behavior feels "right," and it should produce growth and integrity of the system, "man." By "integrity" I mean resistance to illness, disintegration, or disorganization. Doubtless, when a person is behaving in ways that do violence to his integrity, warning signals are emitted. If only man could recognize these, diagnose them himself, and institute corrective action! Then he would live a hundred years. The potential of warning signals is capitalized upon by designers of machines; they build indicators which flash lights when output exceeds tolerances or when intakes are outside a specified range. Fuses blow, governors go into action, and power is shut off. "Normal" self-alienated man, however, often ignores his "tilt" signals—anxiety, guilt, fatigue, boredom, pain, or frustration—and continues actions aimed at wealth, power, or normality until his body "shrieks" loudly enough to be heard. The meaning of sickness is *protest*; it is the protest of a system which has sent warning signals to the "communication center" only to have these ignored. If ignored long enough, the system will no longer mediate even normal behavior, much less optimum behavior. Sickness saves the remnant of the system from total destruction by preventing further operation, until "needs"—inputs—are taken care of. In fact, "being sick"—going to bed—is a behavior undertaken to restore integrity. It is often the only behavior a person has available in our culture to secure some kinds of satisfactions which his "normal" mode of action fails to produce, e.g., passivity or authenticity. What a tragedy that in our society the only authentic "being" we are permitted by others and which we permit ourselves is being sick, and sometimes being drunk!

SELF-DISCLOSURE AND HEALTHY PERSONALITY

Healthy personalities play their roles satisfactorily and derive personal satisfaction from role enactment; more, they keep growing and they maintain high-level wellness.[6] It is probably enough, speaking from the standpoint of a stable social system, for people to be normal personalities. But it is possible to be a normal personality and be absolutely miserable. We would count such a normal personality unhealthy. In fact, normality in some social systems—successful acculturation to them—reliably produces ulcers, piles, paranoia, or compulsiveness. We also have to regard as unhealthy those people who have never been able to enact the roles that legitimately can be expected from them.

Counselors, guidance workers, and psychotherapists are obliged to treat both patterns of un-

healthy personality—those people who have been unable to learn their roles and those who play their roles quite well, but suffer agonies of boredom, anxiety, or stultification. If our clients are to be helped, they must change in *valued* directions. A change in a valued direction may be called growth. We who are professionally concerned with the happiness and growth of our clients may be regarded as professional lovers, not unlike the Cyprian sisterhood. It would be fascinating to pursue this parallel further, but for the moment let us ask instead what this has to do with self-disclosure.

To answer this question, let's tune in on an imaginary interview between a client and his counselor. The client says, "I have never told this to a soul, doctor, but I can't stand my wife, my mother is a nag, my father is a bore, and my boss is an absolutely hateful and despicable tyrant. I have been carrying on an affair for the past ten years with the lady next door, and at the same time I am a deacon in the church." The counselor says, showing great understanding and empathy, "Mm-humm!"

If we listened long enough we would find the client talks and talks about himself to this highly sympathetic and empathic listener. Later, the client may say, "Gosh, you have helped me a lot. I see what I must do and I will go ahead and do it."

Self-disclosure is a factor in effective counseling or psychotherapy. Would it be too arbitrary to assume people come to need help *because they have not disclosed themselves in some optimum degree to the people in their lives?*

An historical digression: Toward the end of the 19th century, Joseph Breuer discovered (probably accidentally) that when his hysterical patients talked about themselves, disclosing not only the verbal content of their memories, but also the feelings that they had suppressed at the time of assorted "traumatic" experiences, their hysterical symptoms disappeared. Somewhere along the line, Breuer withdrew from a situation which would have made him Freud's peer in history's hall of fame. When Breuer permitted his patients "to be," it scared him, one gathers, because some of his female patients disclosed themselves to be quite sexy, and what was probably worse, they felt sexy toward him. Freud did not flinch. He made the momentous discovery that neurotic people of his time were struggling like mad to avoid "being," to avoid being known, and to avoid "becoming."[7] He learned that his patients, when they were given the opportunity to "be" (which free association on a couch is nicely designed to do), would disclose that they had all manner of horrendous thoughts and feelings which they did not even dare disclose to themselves, much less express in the presence of another person. Freud[8] learned to permit his patients to be, through permitting them to disclose themselves utterly to another human. He evidently did not trust anyone enough to be willing to disclose himself vis-à-vis, so he disclosed himself to himself on paper and learned the extent to which he was himself self-alienated. Roles for people in Victorian days were even more restrictive than today, and Freud discovered that when people struggled to avoid being and knowing themselves, they got sick. They could only become well and stay relatively well when they came to know themselves through self-disclosure to another person.

SICKENING ROLES

Let me distinguish here between role relationships and interpersonal relationships—a distinction often overlooked in the spate of literature that deals with human relations. Roles are inescapable. They must be played or else the social system will not work. A role is a repertoire of behavior patterns which must be rattled off in appropriate contexts, and all behavior irrelevant to the role must be suppressed. But what we often forget is the fact that it is a *person* who is playing the role. This person has a self, or I should say he *is* a self. All too often the roles that a person plays do not do justice to all of his self. In fact, there may be nowhere that he may just *be* himself. Even more, the person may not *know* his self. He may be self-alienated. His real self becomes a feared and distrusted stranger. Estrangement, alienation from one's real self, is at the root of the "neurotic personality of our time" so eloquently described by Horney.[9,10] Fromm[11] referred to the same phenomenon as a "socially patterned defect." Self-alienation is a sickness so widely shared that no one recognizes it. We may take it for granted that all the clients whom we encounter are self-alienated to a greater or lesser extent. If you ask anyone to answer the question, "Who are you?" the answer will generally be "I am a psychologist," "a businessman," "a teacher," or what have you. The respondent will probably tell you the name of the *role* with which he feels most closely identified. As a matter of fact, the respondent spends a great part of his life trying to discover who he is, and once he has made some such discovery, he spends the rest of his life trying to play the part. Of course, some of the roles—age, sex, family, or occupational roles—may be so restrictive that they fit a person in a manner not too different from the girdle of a 200-pound lady who is struggling to look like Brigitte Bardot. There is Faustian drama all about us in this world of role playing. Everywhere we see people who have sold their souls (or their real selves) for roles: psychologist, businessman, nurse, physician, this or that.

It is possible to be involved in a social group such as a family or a work setting for years and years, playing one's roles nicely with the other members—and never getting to know the *persons* who are playing the other roles. Roles can be played personally and impersonally, as we are beginning to discover. A husband can be married to his wife for fifteen years and never come to know her. He knows her as "the wife." This is the loneliness which people try to counter with "togetherness."[12] But much of today's "togetherness" is like the "parallel play" of two-year-old children, or like the professors in Stringfellow Barr's[13] novel who lecture *past* one another alternately and sometimes simultaneously. There is no real self-to-self or person-to-person meeting in such transactions.

There is probably no experience more terrifying than disclosing oneself to "significant others" whose probable reactions are assumed, but not known. Hence the phenomenon of "resistance." This is what makes psychotherapy so difficult to take, and so difficult to administer. If there is any skill to be learned in the art of counseling and psychotherapy, it is the art of coping with the terrors which attend self-disclosure and the art of decoding the language, verbal and nonverbal, in which a person speaks about his inner experience.

Self-disclosure is a symptom of personality health *and* a means of ultimately achieving healthy personality. When I say that self-disclosure is a symptom of personality health, I mean a person who displays many of the other characteristics that betoken healthy personality *will also display* the ability to make himself fully known to at least one other significant human being. When I say that self-disclosure is a means by which one achieves personality health, I mean it is not until I *am* my real self and I act my real self that my real self is in a position to grow. One's self grows from the *consequence of being.* People's selves stop growing when they repress them. This growth-arrest in the self is what helps to account for the surprising paradox of finding an infant inside the skin of someone who is playing the role of an adult. Jurgen Ruesch[14] describes assorted neurotics, psychotics, and psychosomatic patients as persons with selective atrophy and overspecialization in various aspects of the process of communication. This culminates in a foul-up of the processes of knowing others and of becoming known to others. Neurotic and psychotic symptoms might be viewed as smoke screens interposed between the patient's real self and the gaze of the onlooker. We might call symptoms "devices to avoid becoming known."[15,16]

Alienation from one's real self not only arrests personal growth; it tends to make a farce out of one's relationships with people. The crucial "break" in schizophrenia is with *sincerity,* not reality.[17]

NONDISCLOSURE, STRESS, AND SICKNESS

Selye[18] proposed the hypothesis that illness as we know it arises in consequence of stress. Now I think unhealthy *personality* has a similar root cause, one which is related to Selye's concept of stress. Every maladjusted person is a person who has not made himself known to another human being and in consequence does not know himself. Nor can he be himself. More than that, he *struggles actively to avoid becoming known by another human being.* He works at it ceaselessly, twenty-four hours daily, and it is work![19,20] In the effort to avoid becoming known, a person provides for himself a cancerous kind of stress which is subtle and unrecognized, but none the less effective in producing not only the assorted patterns of unhealthy personality which psychiatry talks about, but also the wide array of physical ills that have come to be recognized as the province of psychosomatic medicine.[21]

REFERENCES

1. Jourard, S. M., *Personal Adjustment. An Approach through the Study of Healthy Personality.* New York: Macmillan, 1958 (2nd ed., 1963).

2. Maslow, A. H., *Toward a Psychology of Being.* Princeton: Van Nostrand, 1961.

3. Parsons, T., and Bales, R. F., *Family, Socialization, and Interaction Process.* Glencoe: Free Press, 1955.

4. Jourard, S. M., *Personal Adjustment. An Approach through the Study of Healthy Personality.* New York: Macmillan, 1958 (2nd ed., 1963).

5. Popper, K. R., *The Open Society and Its Enemies.* Princeton: Princeton University Press, 1950.

6. Dunn, H. L., "High-level Wellness for Man and Society," *Amer. J. Pub. Health,* 1959 (b), 49, 786–792.

7. Allport, G., *Becoming.* New Haven: Yale Univ. Press, 1955.

8. Freud, S., *The Interpretation of Dreams.* New York: Basic Books, 1955.

9. Horney, K., *Neurosis and Human Growth.* New York: Norton, 1950.

10. Horney, K., *The Neurotic Personality of Our Time.* New York: Norton, 1936.

11. Fromm, E., *The Sane Society.* New York: Rinehart, 1955.

12. Riesman, D., *The Lonely Crowd.* New Haven: Yale Univ. Press, 1950.

13. Barr, S., *Purely Academic.* New York: Simon & Schuster, 1958.

14. Ruesch, J., *Disturbed Communication.* New York: Norton, 1957.

15. Cameron, N. and Magaret, Ann, *Behavior Pathology.* Boston: Houghton Mifflin, 1951.

16. Mowrer, O. H., *The Crisis in Psychiatry and Religion.* Princeton: Van Nostrand, 1961.

17. Anonymous, "A New Theory of Schizophrenia," *J. Abn. Soc. Psychol.,* 1958, 57, 226–236.

18. Selye, H., *The Physiology and Pathology of Exposure to Stress.* Montreal: Acta, 1950.

19. Davis, F. H., and Malmo, R. B., "Electro-myographic Recording During Interview," Amer. J. Psychiat., 1951, 107, 908–916.

20. Dittes, J. E., "Extinction During Psychotherapy of GSR Accompanying 'Embarrassing' Statements,'" J. Abn. Soc. Psychol., 1957, 54, 187–191.

21. Alexander, F., Psychosomatic Medicine. New York: Norton, 1950.

49

Development and Expressions of Parent, Adult, and Child Ego States

Thomas A. Harris

EDITOR'S NOTE · *The psychological construct of the ego was first suggested by Sigmund Freud in the late nineteenth century. Since then, the concept has served as a somewhat ambiguous referent to a person's personality strength or "self." In the 1950s and 1960s, Dr. Eric Berne differentiated the ego construct into subcategories he called the child-ego, parent-ego, and adult-ego. And finally the idea of the ego began to make sense, particularly as it became possible to see the differential expressions of these three ego-states in actual behavior. How do we know when we are in our*

"child" ego-state? What behaviors are associated with the "parent" ego-state? How do we behave when we are in our "adult" ego-state? Dr. Harris discusses the basic dynamics associated with each of these three ego-states. This is an important reading that may help you to understand what happens within yourself.

Early in his work in the development of Transactional Analysis, Berne observed that as you watch and listen to people you can see them change before your eyes. It is a total kind of change. There are simultaneous changes in facial expression, vocabulary, gestures, posture, and body functions, which may cause the face to flush, the heart to pound, or the breathing to become rapid.

We can observe these abrupt changes in everyone: the little boy who bursts into tears when he can't make a toy work, the teen-age girl whose woeful face floods with excitement when the phone finally rings, the man who grows pale and trembles when he gets the news of a business failure, the father whose face "turns to stone" when his son disagrees with him. The individual who changes in these ways is still the same person in terms of bone structure, skin, and clothes. So what changes inside him? He changes *from* what *to* what?

This was the question which fascinated Berne in the early development of Transactional Analysis. A thirty-five-year-old lawyer, whom he was treating, said, "I'm not really a lawyer, I'm just a little boy." Away from the psychiatrist's office he was, in fact, a successful lawyer, but in treatment he felt and acted like a little boy. Sometimes during the hour he would ask, "Are you talking to the lawyer or to the little boy?" Both Berne and his patient became intrigued at the existence and appearance of these two real people, or states of being, and began talking about them as "the adult" and "the child." Treatment centered around separating the two. Later another state began to become apparent as a state distinct from "adult" and "child." This was "the parent" and was identified by behavior which was a reproduction of what the patient saw and heard his parents do when he was a little boy.

Changes from one state to another are apparent in manner, appearance, words, and gestures.

A thirty-four-year-old woman came to me for help with a problem of sleeplessness, constant worry over "what I am doing to my children," and increasing nervousness. In the course of the first hour she suddenly began to weep and said, "You make me feel like I'm three years old." Her voice and manner were that of a small child. I asked her, "What happened to make you feel like a child?" "I don't know," she responded, and then added, "I suddenly felt like a failure." I said, "Well, let's talk about children, about the family. Maybe we can discover something inside of you that produces these feelings of failure and despair." At another point in the hour her voice and manner again changed suddenly. She became critical and dogmatic: "After all, parents have rights, too. Children need to be shown their place." During one hour this mother changed to three different and distinct personalities: one of a small child dominated by feelings, one of a self-righteous parent, and one of a reasoning, logical, grown-up woman and mother of three children.

Continual observation has supported the assumption that these three states exist in all people. It is as if in each person there is the same little person he was when he was three years old. There are also within him his own parents. These are recordings in the brain of actual experiences of internal and external events, the most significant of which happened during the first five years of life. There is a third state, different from these two. The first two are called Parent and Child, and the third, Adult. (See Figure 1.)

These states of being are not roles but psychological realities. Berne says that "Parent, Adult, and Child are not concepts like Superego, Ego, and Id . . . but phenomenological realities."[1] The state is produced by the playback of recorded data of events in the past, involving real people, real times, real places, real decisions, and real feelings.

THE PARENT

The Parent is a huge collection of recordings in the brain of unquestioned or imposed external events perceived by a person in his early years, a

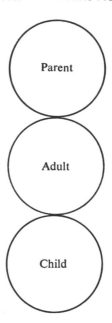

FIGURE 1.   The Personality

period which we have designated roughly as the first five years of life. This is the period before the social birth of the individual, before he leaves home in response to the demands of society and enters school. (See Figure 2.) The name Parent is most descriptive of this data inasmuch as the most significant "tapes" are those provided by the example and pronouncements of his own real parents or parent substitutes. Everything the child saw his parents do and everything he heard them say is recorded in the Parent. Everyone has a Parent in that everyone experienced external stimuli in the first five years of life. Parent is specific for every person, being the recording of that set of early experiences unique to him.

The data in the Parent was taken in and recorded "straight" without editing. The situation of the little child, his dependency, and his inability to construct meanings with words made it impossible for him to modify, correct, or explain. Therefore, if the parents were hostile and constantly battling each other, a fight was recorded with the terror produced by seeing the two persons on whom the child depended for survival about to destroy each other. There was no way of including in this recording the fact that the father was inebriated because his business had just gone down

---

[1] E. Berne, *Transactional Analysis in Psychotherapy* (New York: Grove Press, 1961), p. 24.

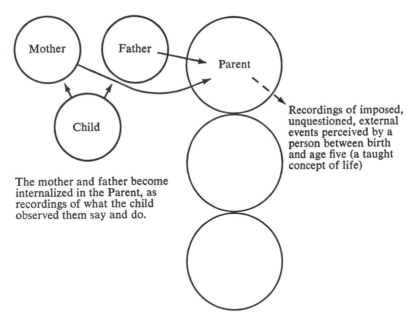

The mother and father become internalized in the Parent, as recordings of what the child observed them say and do.

Recordings of imposed, unquestioned, external events perceived by a person between birth and age five (a taught concept of life)

FIGURE 2.   The Parent

the drain or that the mother was at her wits' end because she had just found she was pregnant again.

In the Parent are recorded all the admonitions and rules and laws that the child heard from his parents and saw in their living. They range all the way from the earliest parental communications, interpreted nonverbally through tone of voice, facial expression, cuddling, or noncuddling, to the more elaborate verbal rules and regulations espoused by the parents as the little person became able to understand words. In this set of recordings are the thousands of "no's" directed at the toddler, the repeated "don'ts" that bombarded him, the looks of pain and horror in mother's face when his clumsiness brought shame on the family in the form of Aunt Ethel's broken antique vase.

Likewise are recorded the coos of pleasure of a happy mother and the looks of delight of a proud father. When we consider that the recorder is on all the time we begin to comprehend the immense amount of data in the Parent. Later come the more complicated pronouncements: Remember, Son, wherever you go in the world you will always find the best people are Methodists; never tell a lie; pay your bills; you are judged by the company you keep; you are a good boy if you clean your

plate; waste is the original sin; you can never trust a man; you can never trust a woman; you're damned if you do and damned if you don't; you can never trust a cop; busy hands are happy hands; don't walk under ladders; do unto others as you would have them do unto you; do others in that they don't do you in.

The significant point is that whether these rules are good or bad in the light of a reasonable ethic, they are recorded as *truth* from the source of all security, the people who are "six feet tall" at a time when it is important to the two-foot-tall child that he please and obey them. It is a permanent recording. A person cannot erase it. It is available for replay throughout life.

This replay is a powerful influence throughout life. These examples—coercing, forcing, sometimes permissive but more often restrictive—are rigidly internalized as a voluminous set of data essential to the individual's survival in the setting of a group, beginning with the family and extending throughout life in a succession of groups necessary to life. Without a physical parent the child would die. The internal Parent also is lifesaving, guarding against many dangers which, perceived experientially, could cause death. In the Parent is the recording, "Don't touch that knife!" It is a thunderous directive. The threat to the little person, as he sees it, is that his mother will spank him or otherwise show disapproval. The greater threat is that he can cut himself and bleed to death. He cannot perceive this. He does not have adequate data. The recording of parental dictates, then, is an indispensable aid to survival, in both the physical and the social sense.

Another characteristic of the Parent is the fidelity of the recordings of inconsistency. Parents say one thing and do another. Parents say, "Don't lie," but tell lies. They tell children that smoking is bad for their health but smoke themselves. They proclaim adherence to a religious ethic but do not live by it. It is not safe for the little child to question this inconsistency, and so he is confused. Because this data causes confusion and fear, he defends himself by turning off the recording.

We think of the Parent predominantly as the recordings of the transactions between the child's two parents. It may be helpful to consider the recordings of Parent data as somewhat like the recording of stereophonic sound. There are two sound tracks that, if harmonious, produce a beautiful effect when played together. If they are not harmonious, the effect is unpleasant and the recording is put aside and played very little, if at all. This is what happens when the Parent contains discordant material. The Parent is repressed or, in the extreme, blocked out altogether. Mother may have been a "good" mother and father may have been "bad," or vice versa. There is much useful data which is stored as a result of the transmission of good material from one parent; but since the Parent does contain material from the other parent that is contradictory and productive of anxiety, the Parent as a whole is weakened or fragmented. Parent data that is discordant is not allowed to come on "audibly" as a strong influence in the person's life.

Another way to describe this phenomenon is to compare it with the algebraic equation: a plus times a minus equals a minus. It does not matter how big the plus was, or how little the minus was. The result is always a minus—a weakened, disintegrated Parent. The effect in later life may be ambivalence, discord, and despair—for the person, that is, who is not free to examine the Parent.

Much Parent data appears in current living in the "how-to" category: how to hit a nail, how to make a bed, how to eat soup, how to blow your nose, how to thank the hostess, how to shake hands, how to pretend no one's at home, how to fold the bath towels, or how to dress the Christmas tree. The *how to* comprises a vast body of data acquired by watching the parents. It is largely useful data which makes it possible for the little person to learn to get along by himself. Later (as his Adult becomes more skillful and free to examine Parent data) these early ways of doing things may be updated and replaced by better ways that are more suited to a changed reality. A person whose early instructions were accompanied by stern intensity may find it more difficult to examine the old ways and may hang onto them long after they are useful, having developed a compulsion to do it "this way and no other."

The mother of a teen-ager related the following parental edict, which had long governed her housekeeping procedures. Her mother had told her, "You *never* put a hat on a table or a coat on a bed." So she went through life never putting a hat on a table or a coat on a bed. Should she occasionally forget, or should one of her youngsters break this old rule, there was an overreaction that seemed inappropriate to the mere violation of the rules of simple neatness. Finally, after several decades of living with this unexamined law, mother asked grandmother (by then in her eighties), "Mother, *why* do you never put a hat on a table or a coat on a bed?"

Grandmother replied that when she was little there had been some neighbor children who were "infested," and her mother had warned her that it was important they never put the neighbor children's hats on the table or their coats on the bed. Reasonable enough. The urgency of the early admonition was understandable. In terms of Penfield's findings it was also understandable why the recording came on with the original urgency. Many of the rules we live by are like this.

Some influences are more subtle. One modern housewife with every up-to-date convenience in her home found she simply did not have any interest in buying a garbage-disposal unit. Her husband encouraged her to get one, pointing out all the reasons this would simplify her kitchen procedures. She recognized this but found one excuse after another to postpone going to the appliance store to select one. Her husband finally confronted her with his belief that she was *deliberately* not getting a garbage disposal. He insisted she tell him why.

A bit of reflection caused her to recognize an early impression she had about garbage. Her childhood years were the Depression years of the 1930's. In her home, garbage was carefully saved and fed to the pig, which was butchered at Christmas and provided an important source of food. The dishes were even washed without soap so that the dishwater, with its meager offering of nutrients, could be included in the slops. As a little girl she perceived that garbage was important, and as a grown woman she found it difficult to rush headlong into purchasing a new-fangled gadget to dispose of it. (She bought the disposal unit and lived happily ever after.)

When we realize that thousands of these simple rules of living are recorded in the brain of every person, we begin to appreciate what a comprehensive, vast store of data the Parent includes. Many of these edicts are fortified with such additional imperatives as "never" and "always" and "never forget that" and, we may assume, pre-empt certain primary neurone pathways that supply ready data for today's transactions. These rules are the origins of compulsions and quirks and eccentricities that appear in later behavior. Whether Parent data is a burden or a boon depends on how appropriate to the present, on whether or not it has been updated by the Adult, the function of which we shall discuss in this chapter.

There are sources of Parent data other than the physical parents. A three-year-old who sits before a television set many hours a day is recording what he sees. The programs he watches are a "taught" concept of life. If he watches programs of violence, I believe he records violence in his Parent. That's how it is. That is life! This conclusion is certain if his parents do not express opposition by switching the channel. If they enjoy violent programs the youngster gets a double sanction—the set and the folks—and he assumes permission to be violent provided he collects the required amount of injustices. The little person collects his own reasons to shoot up the place, just as the sheriff does; three nights of cattle rustlers, a stage holdup, and a stranger foolin' with Miss Kitty can be easily matched in the life of the little person. Much of what is experienced at the hands of older siblings

or other authority figures also is recorded in the Parent. Any external situation in which the little person feels himself to be dependent to the extent that he is not free to question or to explore produces data which is stored in the Parent. (There is another type of external experience of the very small child which is not recorded in the Parent, and which we shall examine when we describe the Adult.)

THE CHILD

While external events are being recorded as that body of data we call the Parent, there is another recording being made simultaneously. This is the recording of *internal* events, the responses of the little person to what he sees and hears. (Figure 3.) In this connection it is important to recall Penfield's observation that "the subject feels again the emotion which the situation originally produced in him, and he is aware of the same interpretations, true or false, which he himself gave to the experience in the first place. Thus, evoked recollection is not the exact photographic or phonographic reproduction of past scenes or events. It is reproduction of what the patient *saw and heard and felt and understood*."[2] [Italics added.]

It is this "seeing and hearing and feeling and understanding" body of data which we define as the Child. Since the little person has no vocabulary during the most critical of his early experiences, most of his reactions are *feelings*. We must keep in mind his situation in these early years. He is small, he is dependent, he is inept, he is clumsy, he has no words with which to construct meanings. Emerson said we "must know how to estimate a sour look." The child does not know how to do this. A sour look turned in his direction can only produce feelings that add to his reservoir of negative data about himself. *It's my fault. Again. Always is. Ever will be. World without end.*

During this time of helplessness there are an infinite number of total and uncompromising demands on the child. On the one hand, he

---

[2] W. Penfield, "Memory Mechanisms," *A.M.A. Archives of Neurology and Psychiatry*, 67 (1952): 178–198, with discussion by L. S. Kubie et al.

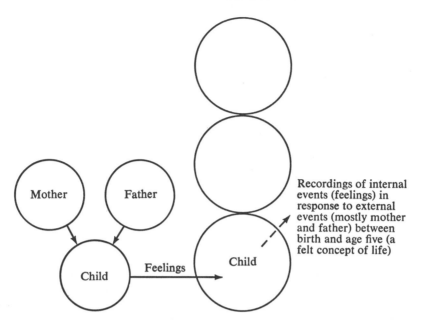

Recordings of internal events (feelings) in response to external events (mostly mother and father) between birth and age five (a felt concept of life)

FIGURE 3. The Child

has the urges (genetic recordings) to empty his bowels ad lib., to explore, to know, to crush and to bang, to express feelings, and to experience all of the pleasant sensations associated with movement and discovery. On the other hand, there is the constant demand from the environment, essentially the parents, that he give up these basic satisfactions for the reward of parental approval. This approval, which can disappear as fast as it appears, is an unfathomable mystery to the child, who has not yet made any certain connection between cause and effect.

The predominant by-product of the frustrating, civilizing process is negative feelings. On the basis of these feelings the little person early concludes, "I'm not OK." We call this comprehensive self-estimate the NOT OK, or the NOT OK Child. This conclusion and the continual experiencing of the unhappy feelings which led to it and confirm it are recorded permanently in the brain and cannot be erased. This permanent recording is the residue of having been a child. Any child. Even the child of kind, loving, well-meaning parents. It is the *situation of childhood* and *not* the intention of the parents which produces the problem. An example of the dilemma of childhood was a

statement made by my seven-year-old daughter, Heidi, who one morning at breakfast said, "Daddy, when I have an OK Daddy and an OK Mama, how come *I'm* not OK?"

When the children of "good" parents carry the NOT OK burden, one can begin to appreciate the load carried by children whose parents are guilty of gross neglect, abuse, and cruelty.

As in the case of the Parent, the Child is a state into which a person may be transferred at almost any time in his current transactions. There are many things that can happen to us today which recreate the situation of childhood and bring on the same feelings we felt then. Frequently we may find ourselves in situations where we are faced with impossible alternatives, where we find ourselves in a corner, either actually, or in the way we see it. These "hook the Child," as we say, and cause a replay of the original feelings of frustration, rejection, or abandonment, and we relive a latter-day version of the small child's primary depression. Therefore, when a person is in the grip of feelings, we say his Child has taken over. When his anger dominates his reason, we say his Child is in command.

There is a bright side, too! In the Child is

also a vast store of positive data. In the Child reside creativity, curiosity, the desire to explore and know, the urges to touch and feel and experience, and the recordings of the glorious, pristine feelings of first discoveries. In the Child are recorded the countless, grand *a-ha* experiences, the firsts in the life of the small person, the first drinking from the garden hose, the first stroking of the soft kitten, the first sure hold on mother's nipple, the first time the lights go on in response to his flicking the switch, the first submarine chase of the bar of soap, the repetitious going back to do these glorious things again and again. The feelings of these delights are recorded, too. With all the NOT OK recordings, there is a counterpoint, the rhythmic OK of mother's rocking, the sentient softness of the favorite blanket, a continuing good response to favorable external events (if this is indeed a favored child), which also is available for replay in today's transactions. This is the flip side, the happy child, the carefree, butterfly-chasing little boy, the little girl with chocolate on her face. This comes on in today's transactions, too. However, our observations both of small children and of ourselves as grownups convince us that the NOT OK feelings far outweigh the good. This is why we believe it is a fair estimate to say that everyone has a NOT OK Child.

Frequently I am asked, When do the Parent and Child stop recording? Do the Parent and Child contain only experiences in the first five years of life? I believe that by the time the child leaves the home for his first independent social experience—school—he has been exposed to nearly every possible attitude and admonition of his parents, and thenceforth further parental communications are essentially a reinforcement of what has already been recorded. The fact that he now begins to "use his Parent" on others also has a reinforcing quality in line with the Aristotelian idea that that which is expressed is impressed. As to further recordings in the Child, it is hard to imagine that any emotion exists which has not already been felt in its most intense form by the time the youngster is five years old. This is consistent with most psychoanalytic theory, and, in my own observation, is true.

If, then, we emerge from childhood with a set of experiences which are recorded in an inerasable Parent and Child, what is our hope for change? How can we get off the hook of the past?

THE ADULT

At about ten months of age a remarkable thing begins to happen to the child. Until that time his life has consisted mainly of helpless or unthinking responses to the demands and stimulations by those around him. He has a Parent and a Child. What he has not had is the ability either to choose his responses or to manipulate his surroundings. He has had no self-direction, no ability to move out to meet life. He has simply taken what has come his way.

At ten months, however, he begins to experience the power of locomotion. He can manipulate objects and begins to move out, freeing himself from the prison of immobility. It is true that earlier, as at eight months, the infant may frequently cry and need help in getting out of some awkward position, but he is unable to get out of it by himself. At ten months he concentrates on inspection and exploitation of toys. According to the studies conducted by Gesell and Ilg, the ten-month-old child

> . . . enjoys playing with a cup and pretends to drink. He brings objects to his mouth and chews them. He enjoys gross motor activity: sitting and playing after he has been set up, leaning far forward, and re-erecting himself. He secures a toy, kicks, goes from sitting to creeping, pulls himself up, and may lower himself. He is beginning to cruise. Social activities which he enjoys are peek-a-boo and lip play, walking with both hands held, being put prone on the floor, or being placed in a rocking toy. Girls show their first signs of coyness by putting their heads to one side as they smile.[3]

The ten-month-old has found he is able to do something which grows from his own awareness and original thought. This self-actualization is the beginning of the Adult. (Figure 4.) Adult data accumulates as a result of the child's ability to find out for himself what is different about life from the "taught concept" of life in his Parent and the "felt concept" of life in his Child. The Adult develops a "thought concept" of life based on data gathering and data processing.

The motility which gives birth to the Adult

---

[3] Arnold Gesell and Frances L. Ilg, *Infant and Child in the Culture of Today* (New York: Harper, 1943), pp. 116–22.

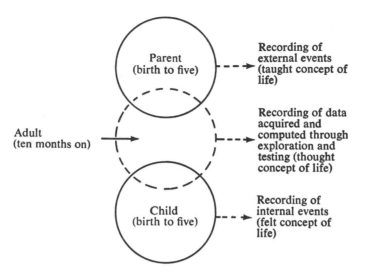

FIGURE 4. Gradual Emergence of the Adult, Beginning at Ten Months

becomes reassuring in later life when a person is in distress. He goes for a walk to "clear his mind." Pacing is seen similarly as a relief from anxiety. There is a recording that movement is good, that it has a separating quality, that it helps him see more clearly what his problem is.

The Adult, during these early years, is fragile and tentative. It is easily "knocked out" by commands from the Parent and fear in the Child. Mother says about the crystal goblet, "No, no! Don't touch that!" The Child may pull back and cry, but at the first opportunity he will touch it anyway to see what it is all about. In most persons the Adult, despite all the obstacles thrown in its way, survives and continues to function more and more effectively as the maturation process goes on.

The Adult is "principally concerned with transforming stimuli into pieces of information, and processing and filing that information on the basis of previous experience."[4] It is different from the Parent, which is "judgmental in an imitative way and seeks to enforce sets of borrowed standards, and from the Child, which tends to react more abruptly on the basis of prelogical thinking and poorly differentiated or distorted perceptions." Through the Adult the little person can begin to tell the difference between life as it was taught and demonstrated to him (Parent), life as he felt it or

wished it or fantasied it (Child), and life as he figures it out by himself (Adult).

The Adult is a data-processing computer, which grinds out decisions after computing the information from three sources: the Parent, the Child, and the data which the Adult has gathered and is gathering (Figure 5). One of the important functions of the Adult is to examine the data in the Parent, to see whether or not it is true and still applicable today, and then to accept it or reject it; and to examine the Child to see whether or not the feelings there are appropriate to the present or are archaic and in response to archaic Parent data. The goal is not to do away with the Parent and Child but to be free to examine these bodies of data. The Adult, in the words of Emerson, "must not be hindered by the name of goodness, but must examine if it be goodness"; or badness, for that matter, as in the early decision, "I'm not OK."

The Adult testing of Parent data may begin at an early age. A secure youngster is one who finds that most Parent data is reliable: "They told me the truth!"

"It really *is* true that cars in the street are dangerous," concludes the little boy who has seen his pet dog hurt by a car in the street. "It really *is* true that things go better when I share my toys with Bobby," thinks the little boy who has been given a prized possession by Bobby. "It really *does* feel better when my pants aren't wet," concludes

---

[4] Berne, *Transactional Analysis in Psychotherapy.*

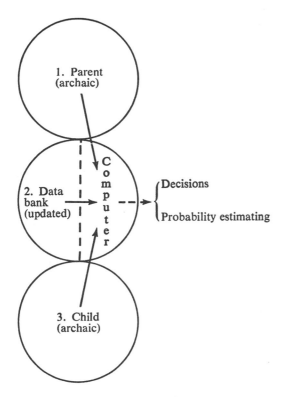

FIGURE 5.   The Adult Gets Data from Three Sources

childhood produced so many NOT OK recordings of this type can free us of their continual replay in the present. *We cannot erase the recording, but we can choose to turn it off!*

In the same way that the Adult updates Parent data to determine what is valid and what is not, it updates Child data to determine which feelings may be expressed safely. In our society it is considered appropriate for a woman to cry at a wedding, but it is not considered appropriate for that woman to scream at her husband afterward at the reception. Yet both crying and screaming are emotions in the Child. The Adult keeps emotional expression appropriate. The Adult's function in updating the Parent and Child is diagramed in Figure 6. The Adult within the Adult in this figure refers to updated reality data. (The evidence once told me space travel was only fantasy; now I know it is reality.)

Another of the Adult's functions is *probability estimating*. This function is slow in developing in

the little girl who has learned to go to the bathroom by herself. If parental directives are grounded in reality, the child, through his own Adult, will come to realize integrity, or a sense of wholeness. What he tests holds up under testing. The data which he collects in his experimentation and examination begin to constitute some "constants" that he can trust. His findings are supported by what he was taught in the first place.

It is important to emphasize that the verification of Parent data does not erase the NOT OK recordings in the Child, which were produced by the early imposition of this data. Mother believes that the only way to keep three-year-old Johnny out of the street is to spank him. He does not understand the danger. His response is fear, anger, and frustration with no appreciation of the fact that his mother loves him and is protecting his life. The fear, anger, and frustration are recorded. These feelings are not erased by the later understanding that she was right to do what she did, but the understanding of how the original situation of

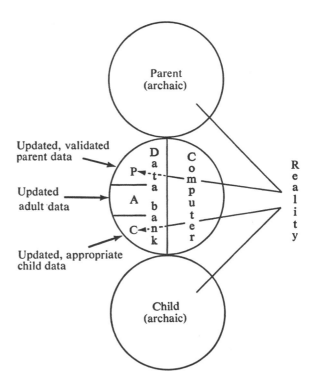

FIGURE 6.   The Updating Function of the Adult through Reality Testing

the small child and, apparently, for most of us, has a hard time catching up throughout life. The little person is constantly confronted with unpleasant alternatives (either you eat your spinach or you go without ice cream), offering little incentive for examining probabilities. Unexamined probabilities can cause more Adult "decay," or delay, than expected ones. There are similarities here to the stock ticker in investment concerns, which may run many hours behind on very active trading days. We sometimes refer to this delay as "computer lag," a remedy for which is the old, familiar practice of "counting to ten."

The capacity for probability estimating can be increased by conscious effort. Like a muscle in the body, the Adult grows and increases in efficiency through training and use. If the Adult is alert to the possibility of trouble, through probability estimating, it can also devise solutions to meet the trouble if and when it comes.

Under sufficient stress, however, the Adult can be impaired to the point where emotions take over inappropriately. The boundaries between Parent, Adult, and Child are fragile, sometimes indistinct, and vulnerable to those incoming signals which tend to recreate situations we experienced in the helpless, dependent days of childhood. The Adult sometimes is flooded by signals of the "bad news" variety so overwhelming that the Adult is reduced to an "onlooker" in the transaction. An individual in this situation might say, "I knew what I was doing was wrong, but I couldn't help myself."

Unrealistic, irrational, non-Adult responses are seen in a condition referred to as traumatic neurosis. The danger, or "bad news" signal, hits the Parent and the Child at the same time it hits the Adult. The Child responds in the way it originally did, with a feeling of NOT OK. This may produce all kinds of regressive phenomena. The individual may again feel himself to be a tiny, helpless, dependent child. One of the most primitive of these phenomena is thought blocking. One place this can be seen is in psychiatric hospitals that have a locked-door policy. When the door is locked on a new patient, his retreat is rapid and pronounced. This is why I am opposed to treating patients in a setting where the emphasis is on parental care. Catering to the helpless Child in the individual delays the reconstructive process of restoring the Adult to the executive function.

An ideal hospital would be a comfortable motel with "play area" for the Child, surrounding a clinic building devoted to activities designed for achieving autonomy of the Adult. The nurses would not wear uniforms or serve as parents to the patients. Instead, nurses in street clothing would apply their skills and training to help each individual learn the identity of his Parent, Adult, and Child.

In our treatment groups we use certain colloquial catch phrases such as, "Why don't you stay in your Adult?" when a member finds his feelings are taking over. Another of these is, "What was the original transaction?" This is asked as a means of "turning on the Adult" to analyze the similarity between the present incoming signal producing the present distress and the original transaction, in which the small child experienced distress.

The ongoing work of the Adult consists, then, of checking out old data, validating or invalidating it, and refiling it for future use. If this business goes on smoothly and there is a relative absence of conflict between what has been taught and what is real, the computer is free for important new business, *creativity*. Creativity is born from curiosity in the Child, as is the Adult. The Child provides the "want to" and the Adult provides the "how to." The essential requirement for creativity is computer time. If the computer is cluttered with old business there is little time for new business. Once checked out, many Parent directives become automatic and thus free the computer for creativity. Many of our decisions in day-to-day transactions are automatic. For instance, when we see an arrow pointing down a one-way street, we automatically refrain from going the opposite way. We do not involve our computer in lengthy data processing about highway engineering, the traffic death toll, or how signs are painted. Were we to start from scratch in every decision or operate entirely without the data that was supplied by our parents, our computer would rarely have time for the creative process.

Some people contend that the undisciplined child, unhampered by limits, is more creative than the child whose parents set limits. I do not believe this is true. A youngster has more time to be creative—to explore, invent, take apart, and put together—if he is not wasting time in futile decision making for which he has inadequate data. A little boy has more time to build a snowman if he is not allowed to engage Mother in a long hassle about whether or not to wear overshoes. If a child is allowed to be creative by painting the front room walls with shoe polish, he is unprepared for the painful consequences when he does so at the neighbor's house. Painful outcomes do not produce OK feelings. There are other consequences that take time, such as mending in the hospital after a trial-and-error encounter with a car in the street. There is just so much computer time. Conflict uses a great deal. An extremely time-consuming conflict is produced when what parents say is true does not seem to be true to the Adult. The most creative individual is the one who discovers that a large part of the content of the Parent squares with reality. He can then file away this validated information in the Adult, trust it, forget about it, and get on with other things—like how to make a kite fly, how to build a sand castle, or how to do differential calculus.

However, many youngsters are preoccupied much of the time with the conflict between Parent data and what they see as reality. Their most troubling problem is that they do not understand why the Parent has such a hold on them. When Truth comes to knock at the Parent's door, the Parent says, "Come, let us reason together." The little child whose father is in jail and whose mother steals to support him may have a loud recording in his Parent, "You never trust a cop!" So he meets a friendly one. His Adult computes all the data about this nice guy, how he gets the ball game started in the sand lot, how he treats the gang to popcorn, how he is friendly, and how he speaks in a quiet voice. For this youngster there is conflict. What he sees as reality is different from what he has been taught. The Parent tells him one thing and the Adult another. During the period of his actual dependency upon his parents for security, however tenuous this security may be, it is likely he will accept the parents' verdict that cops are bad. This is how prejudice is transmitted. *For a little child, it may be safer to believe a lie than to believe his own eyes and ears.* The Parent so threatens the Child (in a continuing internal dialogue) that the Adult gives up and stops trying to inquire into areas of conflict. Therefore, "cops are bad" comes through as truth. This is called *contamination* of the Adult.

50

The Fully Functioning Self

Earl C. Kelley

EDITOR'S NOTE · *Becoming a "fully functioning self" is not some lofty ideal attained only by giants among humankind. It is, rather, a goal any one of us is capable of attaining. In the preceding three selections, Maslow, Jourard, and Harris gave us some ideas about what a healthy personality is, how to encourage its growth, and how to understand its parts. In this fine selection, Dr. Kelley speculates about how people, such as you and I, become the way we are and how we can continue to develop (or, maybe, to begin to develop) a growing, expanding, creative self, which can function at its fullest potential. What does it mean to be a "total person"? This reading may help you to answer that question.*

In a discussion of the self, it will perhaps be helpful to attempt to say as well as we can what it is we are trying to discuss. This is done at the risk of using the conversation stopper, "Let's define it." Many a fine discussion has ended at this point.

The self consists, in part at least, of the accumulated experiential background, or backlog, of the individual. It is what has been built, since his life began, through unique experience and unique purpose, on the individual's unique biological structure. The self is therefore unique to the individual.

This self is built almost entirely, if not entirely, in relationship to others. While the newborn babe has the equipment for the development of the self, there is ample evidence to show that nothing resembling a self can be built in the absence of others. Having a cortex is not enough; there must be continuous interchange between the individual and others. Language, for example, would not be possible without social relationships. Thus, it is seen that man is necessarily a social being.

The self has to be achieved; it is not given. All that is given is the equipment and at least the minimal (mother and child) social environment. Since the self is achieved through social contact, it has to be understood in terms of others. "Self and other" is not a duality, because they go so together that separation is quite impossible.

The self consists of an organization of accumulated experience over a whole lifetime. It is easy to see, therefore, that a great deal of the self has been relegated to the unconscious, or has been "forgotten." This does not mean that these early experiences have been lost. It merely means that they cannot readily be brought into consciousness. We must recognize the fact that the unconscious part of the self functions, for weal or woe, depending on the quality of the experiences.

It is intended here, however, to deal with the conscious self. The unconscious self (not a separation but a continuum) is difficult to deal with for the very reason that it is below the level of consciousness. We want here to look especially at how the individual sees himself. This is indeed the critical point, because it is what the person *sees* that is enabling or disabling. The crucial matter is not so much what you are, but what you think you are. And all of this is always in relationship to others.

The fully functioning personality (self) needs to have certain characteristics. Here, perhaps, is as good a place as any to discuss word trouble. We live in a moving, changing, becoming-but-never-arriving world, yet our language was built by people who believed this to be a static world. I have often spoken of the adequate self, but "adequate" will not do, because it is static. In fact, "inadequate" is a more useful word than "adequate." If there were a word that combines "aspiring-becoming," it would come close to our needs. I have chosen "fully functioning," which I think I learned from Carl Rogers, as the best I can do. This expression at least implies movement.

In order for a person to be fully functioning, when he looks at his self, as he must, he must see that it is enough—enough to perform the task at hand. He must see in his experiential background some history of success. He needs to see process, the building and becoming nature of himself. This being so, he will see that today has no meaning in the absence of yesterdays and tomorrows. In fact, there could be no today except for both yesterday and tomorrow. He must like what he sees, at least well enough for it to be operational.

MANY PEOPLE DO NOT LIKE THEIR SELVES

Unfortunately, many people in the world today suffer from inadequate concepts of self, which naturally lead to mistaken notions of others. Perhaps everybody is afflicted thus to some degree. There may be some rare spirits who are not, but they are few indeed.

We see evidence of this all around us. We see people ridden by unreasonable fears. The fearful person looks at his self and sees that it is not sufficient to meet what he fears. Middle-aged graduate students are afraid to stick their necks out. They are afraid to write; they suffer from stage fright. The question uppermost in their minds is, "What will people think?" Their selves are veritable skeletons in their closets, and if one has a skeleton in his closet, it is best not to do anything except to keep quiet. Any move may reveal it. So they try to sit tight so that they may not be revealed to others. This is a great loss to others—to mankind—for new paths are forbidding and exploration is fraught with terrors.

THIS IS CRIPPLING

An inadequate concept of self, so common in our culture, is crippling to the individual. Our psychological selves may become crippled in much the same way as our physical selves may be crippled by disease or by an accident. They are the same, in effect, because each limits what we can do. When we see ourselves as inadequate, we lose our "canness." There becomes less and less that we can do.

Perhaps it is unfortunate that we cannot see the psychological self in the same way that we see the physical self. Our hearts go out to the physical cripple—we do not enter him in a foot race—but we expect the psychological cripple to step lively and meet all of the vicissitudes of life as though he were whole. Both kinds of cripples need therapy, though of different sorts. Many benefit by therapy, though all do not.

HOW DO WE GET THAT WAY?

Now we come to the question, "How do we get this way?" We get that way in the same way that a physical cripple does—by the lives we lead. Of course there are some cases of congenital defect, but if these were the only cripples we had, we would be fortunate indeed.

The newborn babe has enormous potential for health, but this health has to be built out of his experience with others. It has to be achieved, and it has to be achieved in relationship to others. The health potential then lies strictly in the quality of the people around him, since the infant, for many years to come, has, himself, no control over whom he will associate with.

Damage to the self, so disabling to so many of us, comes from the fact that we grow up in an authoritarian culture. While it is true that this is a democracy in governmental form, we have not achieved democracy in the home, the school or the church. The fact that we have a democratically chosen president or governor has no effect upon the developing child. He is built by the people close to him, and he does not elect them. The people close to him, having themselves been crippled, know no better than to continue the process.

The evils of authoritarianism are more extensive than is ordinarily understood. It is easy to see on a grand scale, as when a Hitler gains power. We all abhor a Hitler, but we seem to think that tyranny in small doses or on a smale scale is somehow good. All in all, it appears that small tyrants do more harm than grand ones. The small

tyrant operates on the growing edge of the personality of the young.

The trouble with the tyrant is basically that he does not have any faith in anyone except himself. He gets that way by living with people who never had any faith in him. Of course he does not really have any faith in himself either, but he has longed for and striven for a position of power over others weaker than himself. Getting his concept of others from his concept of himself, he believes that nothing worthwhile will happen unless he forces it to happen.

Lack of faith in others—the feeling that one has to see to it that others, who are perverse by nature, do what they should—starts a chain reaction of evils, one piled upon another. The burden one bears when he feels that he must watch others and coerce them must be unbearable. And so it turns out to be, for the tyrant deprives himself of others, and grows in the direction of more loneliness and hostility.

From this we can see what happens to the newborn babe as he faces the tyrant. Of course, the tyrant loves his baby in such manner as he is able to love. But he still regards the infant as a "thing," naturally in need of correction. One might think that the very young would not know the difference. But there are ample data to show that even in the first few days after birth, the child knows the difference between being loved and being viewed as in need of coercion. He knows whether the parent is doing things *with* him or *to* him. And the personality at that stage must be tender.

After five or six years of the authoritarian home, the child goes to school. The school is a place inhabited by adults, and too often these adults hold adult concepts of what a child ought to be. These concepts are unverified by the study of children. Here he meets preconceived standards, grade levels, and all of the other paraphernalia of the adult-centered school. If he does not measure up to these standards, then obviously he is perverse and in need of coercion. The fact that these standards are not derived from the child, that there is nothing about them in the Bible, that they arise and reside only in the minds of adults, bothers the adults not at all. Thus, coercion and criticism become the daily fare, while the deviations in behavior brought about by the uniqueness of the personality are stopped. Conformity is the way to the good life, and the best way to conform is to withdraw. One cannot be unique and extend himself and still conform. His uniqueness will show. Shells look a great deal alike, and so if one crawls into his shell, his differences will not be so apparent.

In our authoritarian culture, many forces converge upon the young individual which have the effect of making him think less of himself. The church is one of these forces. The concept of guilt, with its imaginary burden of sin, cannot help one to think well of himself. Of course one can acquire these damaging concepts without getting them at church. But those who have salvation to dispense hold a powerful weapon. When one is made to feel unworthy, he is crippled in some degree, because he cannot do what he otherwise might.

There is a distinction here between the effects of religion and the effects of the church as often administered. It is not religion per se which makes one think ill of himself. It is the representatives of religion who use authoritarian methods to gain their ends. Likewise schooling or education can be expanding in their nature. It is that the representatives of the school—teachers and administrators—often have their own ends to be served, not those of their learners. They act from their own fears, which cause them to dampen and delimit the expanding personalities of their young, thus defeating the very purpose for their being.

Nor is it intended here to deny the need for standards. A fully functioning personality cannot operate without standards. Such standards are the basis for aspiration, the basis for the hope for tomorrow. But it is doubtful that extrinsic, materialistic standards can be successfully applied. Standards have to be the product of values held, and of the life that has been led. The better the quality of the life that has been experienced, the better the values held and the standards which result from these values. Standards will be unique— not the same for everyone—even as the experience from which they are derived has been unique. They will be in terms of other human beings.

BASIS FOR HEALTHY GROWTH

The dynamic which changes a speck of protoplasm into a fully functioning human being is growth. The questions, then, are: What does he grow on?

What are the environmental conditions which feed him?

We need to consider that in growing up one is developing both his physical structure and his psychological structure. We are most familiar with the physical structure and are apt to think of that as growth. We know what the body needs to develop and that lack of development will result in physical crippling. We can identify the diseases of malnutrition and know that a man will not become truly a man in the best sense without an adequate supply of the required stuff of physical growth.

All of the time that the physical body is being developed, so also is the psychological self. The physical body fortunately stops growing after about 20 years. The psychological self, however, continues to grow throughout life. As the physical body has its own unique food requirements, so does the psychological self. This is a different kind of stuff, however, with a different point of intake. We feed the psychological self through the perceptive process. This is what comes into consciousness when stimuli from the environment impinge on the organism. It is the stuff of growth for the personality, and it builds attitudes, habits and knowledge. The perceptive stuff of growth provides the experiential background from which we operate. This controls what we do with the body. The quality of the perceptive stuff of growth therefore determines the quality of the behavior of the individual.

It is necessary here to make clear the fact that the physical body and the psychological self do not constitute a duality, even though it is necessary to speak of them one at a time. The organism is unitary in its operation. There is no body apart from personality, no psychological self without a body to inhabit. What affects one affects all. But that does not prevent speaking of a part. Although we know that hand and foot, attitude, emotion and habit are all one, we still can talk of the hand as having certain characteristics while the foot has others. Speaking of parts does not deny the unitary nature of the individual.

WE SELECT WHAT WE WILL PERCEIVE

Since in this paper we are primarily concerned with the development of the fully functioning self, we will discuss what feeds the self and how it is fed. As we have noted, perception is the stuff of growth for the psychological self. The perceptive process is the only avenue by which the self can be fed. Recent understandings as to the nature of this process have enabled us to see more clearly than before how the self is built.

One of the most revealing facts about perception is that it is *selective*. We do not see everything in our surroundings. There are thousands of coincidences in the situation in which we find ourselves at any point of time. To perceive them all would cause pandemonium. We therefore *choose* that which the self feeds upon. The direction of the growth of the self depends upon those choices.

The choices seem to be on the basis of experience and unique purpose. We all have a background of experience upon which perception is in part based. We cannot see that which we have no experience to see. But experience is not enough to account for what happens, for there are many objects in our surroundings with which we have had experience, but which we do not perceive.

The additional element which appears to determine perceptive intake is purpose. There is ample evidence now to show that all living tissue is purposive, and, of course, in man this purpose is partly, but only partly, on the conscious level. In perception, purpose operates automatically most of the time. And so, just as we do not eat everything, our psychological selves are particular as to what they feed on. What they take in has to suit their purposes, and has to fit onto their past experiences.

ENHANCEMENT AND DEFENSE

The self "looks out" upon the surrounding scene largely in terms of its own enhancement or defense. It tends to extend in the direction of that which promises to make it better off. It withdraws from that which seems likely to endanger it. This is largely true throughout life and entirely true in the early stages when the self is being established—when "self" and "other" first come into being. Altruism is a highly sophisticated concept, and, if it is achieved at all, it comes late. It is the result of great understanding of the self-other interdependency.

THE SELF NEEDS BOUNDARIES

If the self is going to reach out toward facilitating factors and withdraw from endangering ones, it has to have something to reach out from, something to hide behind. It helps to understand this if we assume that the self has to have boundaries in much the same sense that the physical self has to have a skin. The self has certain things that it will let in, others that it will keep out. The boundaries are not, of course, physical—to be seen—but neither is the self. A physical concept, however, helps us to comprehend it. So if we can imagine a physical shell, or armor, necessary for the confinement of the self, we then can imagine how it functions.

Some kind of boundary—a selective screen— is therefore essential to the maintenance of the self. We could not manage the affairs of living without something of this kind. It follows that the nature of the environment, whether it is seen to be facilitating or endangering, will determine the permeability of this screen. That is, the more facilitating the environment, the less need for protection. The more endangering the environment, the greater need for protection. Thus, under adverse conditions, the screen develops into a shell, so that very little is admitted. When this process is continued over a long period of time, that which enabled us to be selective in our perception becomes almost impermeable.

Boundaries then become barriers. Protection becomes isolation. The self becomes a prisoner in its own fort. We have all seen persons off whom words or ideas seemed to bounce. They have built their barriers against other people so strong that they have become inaccessible. Since fear feeds on itself, especially when a person is in isolation, it has a tendency to extend itself beyond the people who are endangering, to include all people.

When the fearful person withdraws within his psychological shell, communication is shut off. It is just as difficult for such a person to give as it is for him to receive. The self then is denied that which it feeds on. The psychological self feeds on ideas, which come from other people. Without the stuff of growth, the self becomes less adequate, and the whole person loses its ability to do, to venture, to create. The individual comes to see himself as impoverished, but he is not able to do much about it by himself.

THE LIFE GOOD TO LIVE

Such a person, however, by having enhancing relationships with others, can break down some of the barriers which separate him from others. By good experiences, he can become less fearful and more open. This process, too, feeds on itself, and can be built by the quality of his experience with others. Confidence opens the barriers so that the perceptive stuff of growth can again be received. He has to learn not to see others as threats, but as assets. Of course, this will not happen unless others cease to act toward him as threats. The parent or teacher who depends upon threats or other techniques of fear will not be able to open the self of one who is in his power.

Fortunate indeed, and not too common in this authoritarian culture, is the person who has had the opportunity to grow up with people whom he can see as facilitating. Most of us have to build our shell against others, and if we are to have fully functioning selves, we have to have experiences which will open these shells.

For the development of a fully functioning self, a person needs to have opportunity to live the life good to live. This life, or his world, needs to be populated by people whom he can view as facilitating. It is almost entirely a matter of people, not things. Facilitating people can be poor in material things. In fact, some of the happiest and most open people are found in poor material circumstances. The most closed and fearful people, the most authoritarian people, may be surfeited by the material goods of the earth. While this is no plea for poverty and privation, it seems that the very possession of great quantities of material goods is apt by its very nature to make the holder fearful that he will lose his goods to others. Vague fear always causes the personality to close up and to become less accessible.

The life good to live does not depend upon the material status of the person. It depends upon the quality of the people around him. He needs people who are open, so that he can feel their quality. He needs people who respect him as a person from the very beginning. It is paradoxical that many parents love their young, but do not respect them. Parents and teachers often say that the child is, of course, too young to be able to make any decisions for himself. It is true that the newborn infant cannot make decisions. But the babe can feel the difference between being held in respect and being regarded as though he had no personality. Respect for the budding self brings it out. Disrespect starts the process of closing up, which in some of our older children and adults is often so complete.

The life good to live is a cooperative one. No child is too young to sense whether or not he lives in a cooperative relation with the people around him. The reason that cooperation is so important is that the cooperative atmosphere is one of involvement. The growing self must feel that it is involved, that it is really part of what is going on, that in some degree it is helping shape its own destiny, together with the destiny of all. Perhaps there is no one quality more important for the developing self than this feeling of involvement in what is taking place. This is what gives a person a "reason to be." The lack of consultation and involvement is the cause of the continuing war between parents and their children, between teachers and learners, between teachers and administrators, employers and employees, ad infinitum. When the person is a part of something, then he becomes responsible.

Whenever the cooperative life is proposed, the authoritarians say, "Oh yes, you want children (or workers or teachers) to do just as they please!" This is a gross misunderstanding of the cooperative way of life, and the shell on such people is so thick that we are baffled in our efforts to reach them. The fact is that in the cooperative life there is much less freedom "to do just as they please" than there is under the surveillance of the autocrat. For the obligation is owed, and the responsibility is felt, to ourselves and to those who facilitate us. The obligation is with us 24 hours a day, rather than just when the autocrat is looking. We do not neglect or sabotage our own projects. This happens to the other's project, particularly if he has met us with threat or fear.

The cooperative life, where everyone from his beginning receives the respect due to a person, and, as he is able, becomes involved in and responsible for what goes on, is not an easy life. The obligation is continuous and pressing. But the difficulties of such a life are inherent in the living, and they cause the self to extend and stretch and grow. These difficulties have quite the opposite effect from those thought up by and inflicted on us by someone else. The latter, not having meaning to the person, cause him to withdraw and begin to calculate how he can protect himself.

THE FULLY FUNCTIONING PERSON

What is a person with a fully functioning self like? This can be answered only in terms of his behavior. Conclusions can be drawn from this behavior. The temptation here is to vest this person, like Rose Aylmer, with "every virtue, every grace." Rather than simply listing virtues, there are some characteristics not necessarily cherished in our culture, which such a person would logically have. From what has been stated here, it might be inferred that nobody has escaped with a fully functioning self. And it seems to be likely that very few survive home, church, and school without damage to the self.

Yet there are a good many people who, through contact with facilitating persons, have been reopened and whose selves function well. To argue otherwise would be to deny the potential for change and improvement on which life itself depends. In fact, it can be considered that no one can experience elation who has never known despair; no one can be courageous without having known fear. So the human personality is not doomed to endure its present state, but can be brought into flower by enhancing experiences. As Karen Horney has said, "My own belief is that man has the capacity as well as the desire to develop his potentialities and become a decent human being, and that these deteriorate if his relationship to others and hence to himself is, and continues to be, disturbed. I believe that man can change and keep on changing as long as he lives."[1]

The fully functioning personality thinks well of himself. He looks at himself and likes what he sees well enough so that he can accept it. This is essential to doing, to "can-ness." He does not see himself as able to do anything and everything, but he sees himself as able in terms of his experience. He feels he can do what is reasonable to expect on the basis of his experience.

Those who do not like what they see when they look at themselves are the fearful ones—not just afraid of present danger, but taking a fearful view of everything in general. Fear renders them helpless, and this leads to alienation from others and hostility towards others, thus shutting themselves off from the stuff they feed upon. The harmful ramifications of not accepting self are endless, because one attitude leads to another.

He thinks well of others. This comes about automatically because of the one-ness of the self-other relationship. It is doubtful that there can be a self except in relation to others, and to accept one implies the acceptance of the other. The acceptance of others opens a whole world with which to relate. It is the opposite of the hostility which results from non-acceptance of self.

He therefore sees his stake in others. He sees that other people are the stuff out of which he is built. He has a selfish interest then in the quality of those around him and has responsibility in some degree for that quality. The whole matter of selfishness and altruism disappears when he realizes that self and other are interdependent—that we are indeed our brother's keeper, and he is ours. Coming into the awareness of mutual need modifies human behavior. He comes to see other people as opportunities, not for exploitation, but for the building of self. He becomes a loving person, so that he can get closer to the real source of his power.

He sees himself as a part of a world in movement—in process of becoming. This follows from the whole notion of self and others and the acceptance that they can feed off each other and hence can improve. When one looks outward rather than inward, the idea of change—in self, in others, in things—becomes apparent. The acceptance of change as a universal phenomenon brings about modifications of personality. The person who accepts change and expects it behaves differently from the person who seeks to get everything organized so that it will be fixed from now on. He will not search for the firm foundation on which he can stand for the rest of his life. He will realize that the only thing he knows for sure about the future is that tomorrow will be different from today and that he can anticipate this difference with hopeful expectation.

Optimism is the natural outcome of an accepting view of self and hence of others. Such a person is a doer, a mobile person, one who relates himself

---

[1] Karen Horney, *Our Inner Conflicts* (New York: W. W. Norton & Co., 1945), p. 19.

in an active way with others. Such activity would be meaningless unless the person had hopes for improvement. As has been stated, today has no meaning except in relation to an expected tomorrow. This is the basis for hope, without which no one can thrive. Improvement is that which enhances and enriches self and others. Neither can be enhanced by itself.

The fully functioning personality, having accepted the ongoing nature of life and the dynamic of change, *sees the value of mistakes.* He knows he will be treading new paths at all times, and that, therefore, he cannot always be right. Rigid personalities suffer much from their need to be always right. The fully functioning personality will not only see that mistakes are inevitable in constantly breaking new ground, but will come to realize that these unprofitable paths show the way to better ones. Thus, a mistake, which no one would make if he could foresee it, can be profitable. In fact, much of what we know that is workable comes from trying that which is not. In our culture, it seems that most of our moral code is based on the values of rigid people who cannot bear to be wrong, and so, making a mistake is almost sinful. The effective person cannot afford to have his spirit of adventure thus hampered. He knows that the only way to find out is to go forward and to profit from experience —to make experience an asset.

The fully functioning self, seeing the importance of people, *develops and holds human values.* There is no one, of course, who does not come to hold values. Values come about through the life one lives, which determines what one comes to care about. The better the life, the better the values accumulated. The one who sees human beings as essential to his own enhancement develops values related to the welfare of people. Holding these values in a world which most people consider to be static, he encounters problems in meeting static mores. He is, therefore, on the creative edge of the generally accepted mores or morals. Values in terms of what is good for all people are continuously in conflict with materialistic values held by the majority.

He knows no other way to live except in keeping with his values. He has no need continuously to shift behavior, depending upon the kind of people nearest him. He has no need for subterfuge or deceit, because he is motivated by the value of facilitating self and others. While treading new paths is fraught with risk, he does not have to engage in a continuous guessing game to make his behavior match new people and also be consistent with what he has done before. A fully functioning person, holding human values, does not have to ask himself constantly what it was he said last week.

We are tempted to call this courage and integrity. This is another way of saying that one has what it takes to live as life really exists and to do it all in one piece. Can we call it courage when there is no alternative?

Since life is ever-moving and ever-becoming, *the fully functioning person is cast in a creative role.* But more than simply accepting this role, he sees creation going on all around him. He sees that creation is not something which occurred long ago and is finished, but that it is now going on and that he is part of it. He sees the evil of the static personality because it seeks to stop the process of creation to which we owe our world and our being. He exults in being a part of this great process and in having an opportunity to facilitate it. Life to him means discovery and adventure, flourishing because it is in tune with the universe.

51

To Be That Self Which One Truly Is: A Therapist's View of Personal Goals

Carl R. Rogers

EDITOR'S NOTE · Although we are not always certain what it means, each of us in our own way seeks to "find himself." In this selection, Dr. Rogers sensitively delves into his experience as a teacher, therapist, and counselor to describe the directions he has seen people take when they move closer to understanding and accepting themselves as individuals. As teachers, we need to comprehend as fully as possible the processes that free and release students to reach their potentials. As individuals, we need to know as much about how to be truly ourselves as we can if we are to reach our own potentials and thus perhaps become more effective teachers. In Rogers' words, each person must learn to "listen sensitively to himself." This reading may enhance that possibility.

THE QUESTIONS

"What is my goal in life?" "What am I striving for?" "What is my purpose?" These are questions

which every individual asks himself at one time or another, sometimes calmly and meditatively, sometimes in agonizing uncertainty or despair. They are old, old questions which have been asked and answered in every century of history. Yet they are also questions which every individual must ask and answer for himself, in his own way. They are questions which I, as a counselor, hear expressed in many differing ways as men and women in personal distress try to learn, or understand, or choose, the directions which their lives are taking.

In one sense there is nothing new which can be said about these questions. Indeed the opening phrase in the title I have chosen for this paper is taken from the writings of a man who wrestled with these questions more than a century ago. Simply to express another personal opinion about this whole issue of goals and purposes would seem presumptuous. But as I have worked for many years with troubled and maladjusted individuals I believe that I can discern a pattern, a trend, a commonality, an orderliness, in the tentative answers to these questions which they have found for themselves. And so I would like to share with you my perception of what human beings appear to be striving for, when they are free to choose.

SOME ANSWERS

Before trying to take you into this world of my own experience with my clients, I would like to remind you that the questions I have mentioned are not pseudo-questions, nor have men in the past or at the present time agreed on the answers. When men in the past have asked themselves the purpose of life, some have answered, in the words of the catechism, that "the chief end of man is to glorify God." Others have thought of life's purpose as being the preparation of oneself for immortality. Others have settled on a much more earthy goal—to enjoy and release and satisfy every purpose of life as being to achieve—to gain material possessions, status, knowledge, power. Some have made it their goal to give themselves completely and devotedly to a cause outside of themselves such as Christianity, or Communism. A Hitler has seen his goal as that of becoming the leader of a master race which would exercise power over all. In sharp contrast, many an Oriental has striven to eliminate all personal desires, to exercise the utmost of control over himself. I mention these widely ranging choices to indicate some of the very different aims men have lived for, to suggest that there are indeed many goals possible.

In a recent important study Charles Morris investigated objectively the pathways of life which were preferred by students in six different countries —India, China, Japan, the United States, Canada, and Norway (5). As one might expect, he found decided differences in goals between these national groups. He also endeavored, through a factor analysis of his data, to determine the underlying dimensions of value which seemed to operate in the thousands of specific individual preferences. Without going into the details of his analysis, we might look at the five dimensions which emerged, and which, combined in various positive and negative ways, appeared to be responsible for the individual choices.

The first such value dimension involves a preference for a responsible, moral, self-restrained participation in life, appreciating and conserving what man has attained.

The second places stress upon delight in vigorous action for the overcoming of obstacles. It involves a confident initiation of change, either in resolving personal and social problems, or in overcoming obstacles in the natural world.

The third dimension stresses the value of a self-sufficient inner life with a rich and heightened self-awareness. Control over persons and things is rejected in favor of a deep and sympathetic insight into self and others.

The fourth underlying dimension values a receptivity to persons and to nature. Inspiration is seen as coming from a source outside the self, and the person lives and develops in devoted responsiveness to this source.

The fifth and final dimension stresses sensuous enjoyment, self-enjoyment. The simple pleasures of life, an abandonment to the moment, a relaxed openness to life, are valued.

This is a significant study, one of the first to measure objectively the answers given in different cultures to the question, what is the purpose of my life? It has added to our knowledge of the answers given. It has also helped to define some of the basic dimensions in terms of which the choice is made. As Morris says, speaking of these dimensions, "it is as if persons in various cultures have in common five major tones in the musical scales on which they compose different melodies." (5, p. 185)

ANOTHER VIEW

I find myself, however, vaguely dissatisfied with this study. None of the "Ways to Live" which Morris put before the students as possible choices, and none of the factor dimensions, seems to contain satisfactorily the goal of life which emerges in my experience with my clients. As I watch person after person struggle in his therapy hours to find a way of life for himself, there seems to be a general pattern emerging, which is not quite captured by any of Morris' descriptions.

The best way I can state this aim of life, as I see it coming to light in my relationship with my clients, is to use the words of Søren Kierkegaard— "to be that self which one truly is." (3, p. 29) I am quite aware that this may sound so simple as to be absurd. To be what one is seems like a statement of obvious fact rather than a goal. What does it mean? What does it imply? I want to devote the remainder of my remarks to those issues. I will simply say at the outset that it seems to mean and imply some strange things. Out of my experience with my clients, and out of my own self-searching, I find myself arriving at views which would have been very foreign to me ten or fifteen years ago. So I trust you will look at these views with critical scepticism, and accept them only in so far as they ring true in your own experience.

DIRECTIONS TAKEN BY CLIENTS

Let me see if I can draw out and clarify some of the trends and tendencies which I see as I work with clients. In my relationship with these individuals my aim has been to provide a climate which contains as much of safety, of warmth, of empathic understanding, as I can genuinely find in myself to give. I have not found it satisfying or helpful to intervene in the client's experience with diagnostic or interpretative explanations, nor with suggestions and guidance. Hence the trends which I see appear to me to come from the client himself, rather than emanating from me.[1]

AWAY FROM FACADES

I observe first that characteristically the client shows a tendency to move away, hesitantly and fearfully, from a self that he is *not*. In other words even though there may be no recognition of what he might be moving toward, he is moving away from something. And of course in so doing he is beginning to define, however negatively, what he *is*.

At first this may be expressed simply as a fear of exposing what he is. Thus one eighteen-year-old boy says, in an early interview: "I know I'm not so hot, and I'm afraid they'll find it out. That's why I do these things. . . . They're going to find out some day that I'm not so hot. I'm just trying to put that day off as long as possible. . . . If you know me as I know myself—. (*Pause*) I'm not going to tell you the person I really think I am. There's only one place I won't cooperate and that's it. . . . It wouldn't help your opinion of me to know what I think of myself."

It will be clear that the very expression of this fear is a part of becoming what he is. Instead of simply *being* a façade, as if it were himself, he is coming closer to being *himself*, namely a frightened person hiding behind a façade because he regards himself as too awful to be seen.

AWAY FROM "OUGHTS"

Another tendency of this sort seems evident in the client's moving away from the compelling image

of what he "ought to be." Some individuals have absorbed so deeply from their parents the concept "I ought to be good," or "I have to be good," that it is only with the greatest of inward struggle that they find themselves moving away from this goal. Thus one young woman, describing her unsatisfactory relationship with her father, tells first how much she wanted his love. "I think in all this feeling I've had about my father, that *really* I *did* very much want a good relationship with him. . . . I wanted so much to have him care for me, and yet didn't seem to get what I really wanted." She always felt she had to meet all of his demands and expectations and it was "just too much. Because once I meet one there's another and another and another, and I never really meet them. It's sort of an endless demand." She feels she has been like her mother, submissive and compliant, trying continually to meet his demands. "And really *not* wanting to be that kind of person. I find it's not a good way to be, but yet I think I've had a sort of belief that that's the way you *have* to be if you intend to be thought a lot of and loved. And yet who would *want* to love somebody who was that sort of wishy washy person?" The counselor responded, "Who really would love a door mat?" She went on, "At least I wouldn't want to be loved by the kind of person who'd love a door mat!"

Thus, though these words convey nothing of the self she might be moving toward, the weariness and disdain in both her voice and her statement make it clear that she is moving away from a self which *has* to be good, which *has* to be submissive.

Curiously enough a number of individuals find that they have felt compelled to regard themselves as bad, and it is this concept of themselves that they find they are moving away from. One young man shows very clearly such a movement. He says: "I don't know how I got this impression that being ashamed of myself was such an *appropriate* way to feel. . . . Being ashamed of me was the way I just *had* to be. . . . There was a world where being ashamed of myself was the best way to feel. . . . If you are something which is disapproved of very much, then I guess the only way you can have any kind of self-respect is to be ashamed of that part of you which isn't approved of. . . .

"But now I'm adamantly refusing to do things from the old viewpoint. . . . It's as if I'm convinced that someone said, 'The way you will *have* to be is

---

[1] I cannot close my mind, however, to the possibility that someone might be able to demonstrate that the trends I am about to describe might in some subtle fashion, or to some degree, have been initiated by me. I am describing them as occurring in the client in this safe relationship, because that seems the most likely explanation.

to be *ashamed* of yourself—so *be* that way!' And now I'm standing up against that somebody, saying, 'I don't care *what* you say. I'm *not* going to feel ashamed of myself!'" Obviously he is abandoning the concept of himself as shameful and bad.

AWAY FROM MEETING EXPECTATIONS

Other clients find themselves moving away from what the culture expects them to be. In our current industrial culture, for example, as Whyte has forcefully pointed out in his recent book (7), there are enormous pressures to become the characteristics which are expected of the "organization man." Thus one should be fully a member of the group, should subordinate his individuality to fit into the group needs, should become "the well-rounded man who can handle well-rounded men."

In a newly completed study of student values in this country Jacob summarizes his findings by saying, "The main overall effect of higher education upon student values is to bring about general acceptance of a body of standards and attitudes characteristic of collegebred men and women in the American community. . . . The impact of the college experience is . . . to *socialize* the individual, to refine, polish, or 'shape up' his values so that he can fit comfortably into the ranks of American college alumni." (1, p. 6).

Over against these pressures for conformity, I find that when clients are free to be any way they wish, they tend to resent and to question the tendency of the organization, the college or the culture to mould them to any given form. One of my clients says with considerable heat: "I've been so long trying to live according to what was meaningful to other people, and what made no sense at *all* to me, really. I somehow felt so much *more* than that, at some level." So he, like others, tends to move away from being what is expected.

AWAY FROM PLEASING OTHERS

I find that many individuals have formed themselves by trying to please others, but again, when they are free, they move away from being this

person. So one professional man, looking back at some of the process he has been through, writes, toward the end of therapy: "I finally felt that I simply *had* to begin doing what *I wanted* to do, not what I thought I *should* do, and regardless of what other people feel I *should* do. This is a complete reversal of my whole life. I've always felt I *had* to do things because they were expected of me, or more important, to make people like me. The hell with it! I think from now on I'm going to just be me—rich or poor, good or bad, rational or irrational, logical or illogical, famous or infamous. So thanks for your part in helping me to rediscover Shakespeare's—'To thine own *self* be true.'"

So one may say that in a somewhat negative way, clients define their goal, their purpose, by discovering, in the freedom and safety of an understanding relationship, some of the directions they do *not* wish to move. They prefer not to hide themselves and their feelings from themselves, or even from some significant others. They do not wish to be what they "ought" to be, whether that imperative is set by parents, or by the culture, whether it is defined positively or negatively. They do not wish to mould themselves and their behavior into a form which would be merely pleasing to others. They do not, in other words, choose to be anything which is artificial, anything which is imposed, anything which is defined from without. They realize that they do not value such purposes or goals, even though they may have lived by them all their lives up to this point.

TOWARD SELF-DIRECTION

But what is involved positively in the experience of these clients? I shall try to describe a number of the facets I see in the directions in which they move.

First of all, the client moves toward being autonomous. By this I mean that gradually he chooses the goals toward which *he* wants to move. He becomes responsible for himself. He decides what activities and ways of behaving have meaning for him, and what do not. I think this tendency toward self-direction is amply illustrated in the examples I have given.

I would not want to give the impression that my clients move blithely or confidently in this direction. No indeed. Freedom to be oneself is a frighteningly responsible freedom, and an individual moves toward it cautiously, fearfully, and with almost no confidence at first.

Nor would I want to give the impression that he always makes sound choices. To be responsibly self-directing means that one chooses—and then learns from the consequences. So clients find this a sobering but exciting kind of experience. As one client says—"I feel frightened, and vulnerable, and cut loose from support, but I also feel a sort of surging up or force or strength in me." This is a common kind of reaction as the client takes over the self-direction of his own life and behavior.

TOWARD BEING PROCESS

The second observation is difficult to make, because we do not have good words for it. Clients seem to move toward more openly being a process, a fluidity, a changing. They are not disturbed to find that they are not the same from day to day, that they do not always hold the same feelings toward a given experience or person, that they are not always consistent. They are in flux, and seem more content to continue in this flowing current. The striving for conclusions and end states seems to diminish.

One client says, "Things are sure changing, boy, when I can't even predict my own behavior in here anymore. It was something I was able to do before. Now I don't know what I'll say next. Man, it's quite a feeling. . . . I'm just surprised I even said these things. . . . I see something new every time. It's an adventure, that's what it is— into the unknown. . . . I'm beginning to enjoy this now, I'm joyful about it, even about all these old negative things." He is beginning to appreciate himself as a fluid process, at first in the therapy hour, but later he will find this true in his life. I cannot help but be reminded of Kierkegaard's description of the individual who really exists. "An existing individual is constantly in process of becoming, . . . and translates all his thinking into terms of process. It is with (him) . . . as it is with a writer and his style; for he only has a style who never has anything finished, but 'moves the waters of the language' every time he begins, so that the most common expression comes into being for him

with the freshness of a new birth." (2, p. 79) I find this catches excellently the direction in which clients move, toward being a process of potentialities being born, rather than being or becoming some fixed goal.

TOWARD BEING COMPLEXITY

It also involves being a complexity of process. Perhaps an illustration will help here. One of our counselors, who has himself been much helped by psychotherapy, recently came to me to discuss his relationship with a very difficult and disturbed client. It interested me that he did not wish to discuss the client, except in the briefest terms. Mostly he wanted to be sure that he was clearly aware of the complexity of his own feelings in the relationship—his warm feelings toward the client, his occasional frustration and annoyance, his sympathetic regard for the client's welfare, a degree of fear that the client might become psychotic, his concern as to what others would think if the case did not turn out well. I realized that his overall attitude was that if he could *be*, quite openly and transparently, all of his complex and changing and sometimes contradictory feelings in the relationship, all would go well. If, however, he was only part of his feelings, and partly façade or defense, he was sure the relationship would not be good. I find that this desire to be *all* of oneself in each moment—all the richness and complexity, with nothing hidden from oneself, and nothing feared in oneself—this is a common desire in those who have seemed to show much movement in therapy. I do not need to say that this is a difficult, and in its absolute sense an impossible goal. Yet one of the most evident trends in clients is to move toward becoming all of the complexity of one's changing self in each significant moment.

TOWARD OPENNESS TO EXPERIENCE

"To be that self which one truly is" involves still other components. One which has perhaps been implied already is that the individual moves toward living in an open, friendly, close relationship to his own experience. This does not occur easily. Often as the client senses some new facet of himself, he initially rejects it. Only as he experiences such a hitherto denied aspect of himself in an acceptant climate can he tentatively accept it as a part of himself. As one client says with some shock after experiencing the dependent, small boy aspect of himself, "That's an emotion I've never felt clearly —one that I've never been!" He cannot tolerate the experience of his childish feelings. But gradually he comes to accept and embrace them as a part of himself, to live close to them and in them when they occur.

Another young man, with a very serious stuttering problem, lets himself be open to some of his buried feelings toward the end of his therapy. He says, "Boy, it was a terrible fight. I never realized it. I guess it was too painful to reach that height. I mean I'm just beginning to feel it now. Oh, the *terrible* pain. . . . It was *terrible* to talk. I mean I wanted to talk and then I didn't want to. . . . I'm feeling—I think I know—it's just plain strain—terrible strain—*stress*, that's the word, just so much *stress* I've been feeling. I'm just beginning to *feel* it now after all these years of it. . . . it's terrible. I can hardly get my breath now too, I'm just all choked up inside, all *tight* inside. . . . I just feel like I'm *crushed. (He begins to cry.)* I never realized that, I never knew that." (6) Here he is opening himself to internal feelings which are clearly not new to him, but which up to this time, he has never been able fully to experience. Now that he can permit himself to experience them, he will find them less terrible, and he will be able to live closer to his own experiencing.

Gradually clients learn that experiencing is a friendly resource, not a frightening enemy. Thus I think of one client who, toward the close of therapy, when puzzled about an issue, would put his head in his hands and say, "Now what *is* it I'm feeling? I want to get next to it. I want to learn what it is." Then he would wait, quietly and patiently, until he could discern the exact flavor of the feelings occurring in him. Often I sense that the client is trying to listen to himself, is trying to hear the messages and meanings which are being communicated by his own physiological reactions. No longer is he so fearful of what he may find. He comes to realize that his own inner reactions and experiences, the messages of his senses and his viscera, are friendly. He comes to want to be

close to his inner sources of information rather than closing them off.

Maslow, in his study of what he calls self-actualizing people, has noted this same characteristic. Speaking of these people, he says, "Their ease of penetration to reality, their closer approach to an animal-like or child-like acceptance and spontaneity imply a superior awareness of their own impulses, their own desires, opinions, and subjective reactions in general." (4, p. 210)

This greater openness to what goes on within is associated with a similar openness to experiences of external reality. Maslow might be speaking of clients I have known when he says, "self-actualized people have a wonderful capacity to appreciate again and again, freshly and naively, the basic goods of life with awe, pleasure, wonder, and even ecstasy, however stale these experiences may be for the other people." (4, p. 214)

TOWARD ACCEPTANCE OF OTHERS

Closely related to this openness to inner and outer experience in general is an openness to and an acceptance of other individuals. As a client moves toward being able to accept his own experience, he also moves toward the acceptance of the experience of others. He values and appreciates both his own experience and that of others for what it *is*. To quote Maslow again regarding his self-actualizing individuals: "One does not complain about water because it is wet, nor about rocks because they are hard. . . . As the child looks out upon the world with wide, uncritical and innocent eyes, simply noting and observing what is the case, without either arguing the matter or demanding that it be otherwise, so does the self-actualizing person look upon human nature both in himself and in others." (4, p. 207) This acceptant attitude toward that which exists, I find developing in clients in therapy.

TOWARD TRUST OF SELF

Still another way of describing this pattern which I see in each client is to say that increasingly he trusts and values the process which is himself. Watching my clients, I have come to a much better understanding of creative people. El Greco, for example, must have realized as he looked at some of his early work, that "good artists do not paint like that." But somehow he trusted his own experiencing of life, the process of himself, sufficiently that he could go on expressing his own unique perceptions. It was as though he could say, "Good artists do not paint like this, but *I* paint like this." Or to move to another field, Ernest Hemingway was surely aware that "good writers do not write like this." But fortunately he moved toward being Hemingway, being himself, rather than toward someone else's conception of a good writer. Einstein seems to have been unusually oblivious to the fact that good physicists did not think his kind of thoughts. Rather than drawing back because of his inadequate academic preparation in physics, he simply moved toward being Einstein, toward thinking his own thoughts, toward being as truly and deeply himself as he could. This is not a phenomenon which occurs only in the artist or the genius. Time and again in my clients, I have seen simple people become significant and creative in their own spheres, as they have developed more trust of the processes going on within themselves, and have dared to feel their own feelings, live by values which they discover within, and express themselves in their own unique ways.

THE GENERAL DIRECTION

Let me see if I can state more concisely what is involved in this pattern of movement which I see in clients, the elements of which I have been trying to describe. It seems to mean that the individual moves toward *being*, knowingly and acceptingly, the process which he inwardly and actually *is*. He moves away from being what he is not, from being a façade. He is not trying to be more than he is, with the attendant feelings of insecurity or bombastic defensiveness. He is not trying to be less than he is, with the attendant feelings of guilt or self-depreciation. He is increasingly listening to the deepest recesses of his physiological and emotional being, and finds himself increasingly willing to be, with greater accuracy and depth, that self which he most truly is. One client, as he begins to sense the direction he is taking, asks himself wonderingly and with incredulity in one interview, "You

mean if I'd really be what I feel like being, that that would be all right?" His own further experience, and that of many another client, tends toward an affirmative answer. To be what he truly is, this is the path of life which he appears to value most highly, when he is free to move in any direction. It is not simply an intellectual value choice, but seems to be the best description of the groping, tentative, uncertain behaviors by which he moves exploringly toward what he wants to be.

SOME MISAPPREHENSIONS

To many people, the path of life I have been endeavoring to describe seems like a most unsatisfactory path indeed. To the degree that this involves a real difference in values, I simply respect it as a difference. But I have found that sometimes such an attitude is due to certain misapprehensions. In so far as I can I would like to clear these away.

DOES IT IMPLY FIXITY?

To some it appears that to be what one is, is to remain static. They see such a purpose or value as synonymous with being fixed or unchanging. Nothing could be further from the truth. To be what one is, is to enter fully into being a process. Change is facilitated, probably maximized, when one is willing to be what he truly is. Indeed it is the person who is denying his feelings and his reactions who is the person who tends to come for therapy. He has, often for years, been trying to change, but finds himself fixed in these behaviors which he dislikes. It is only as he can become more of himself, can be more of what he has denied in himself, that there is any prospect of change.

DOES IT IMPLY BEING EVIL?

An even more common reaction to the path of life I have been describing is that to be what one truly is would mean to be bad, evil, uncontrolled, destructive. It would mean to unleash some kind of a monster on the world. This is a view which is very well known to me, since I meet it in almost every client. "If I dare to let the feelings flow which are dammed up within me, if by some chance I should live in those feelings, then this would be catastrophe." This is the attitude, spoken or unspoken, of nearly every client as he moves into the experiencing of the unknown aspects of himself. But the whole course of his experience in therapy contradicts these fears. He finds that gradually he can be his anger, when anger is his real reaction, but that such accepted or transparent anger is not destructive. He finds that he can be his fear, but that knowingly to be his fear does not dissolve him. He finds that he can be self-pitying, and it is not "bad." He can feel and be his sexual feelings, or his "lazy" feelings, or his hostile feelings, and the roof of the world does not fall in. The reason seems to be that the more he is able to permit these feelings to flow and to be in him, the more they take their appropriate place in a total harmony of his feelings. He discovers that he has other feelings with which these mingle and find a balance. He feels loving and tender and considerate and cooperative, as well as hostile or lustful or angry. He feels interest and zest and curiosity, as well as laziness or apathy. He feels courageous and venturesome, as well as fearful. His feelings, when he lives closely and acceptingly with their complexity, operate in a constructive harmony rather than sweeping him into some uncontrollably evil path.

Sometimes people express this concern by saying that if an individual were to be what he truly is, he would be releasing the beast in himself. I feel somewhat amused by this, because I think we might take a closer look at the beasts. The lion is often a symbol of the "ravening beast." But what about him? Unless he has been very much warped by contact with humans, he has a number of the qualities I have been describing. To be sure, he kills when he is hungry, but he does not go on a wild rampage of killing, nor does he overfeed himself. He keeps his handsome figure better than some of us. He is helpless and dependent in his puppyhood, but he moves from that to independence. He does not cling to dependence. He is selfish and self-centered in infancy, but in adulthood he shows a reasonable degree of cooperativeness, and feeds, cares for, and protects his young. He satisfies his sexual desires, but this does not mean that he goes on wild and lustful orgies. His various tendencies and urges have a harmony within him. He is, in some basic sense, a constructive and trustworthy member of the species *felis leo*. And what I am trying to suggest is that when one is truly and deeply a unique member of the human species, this is not something which should excite horror. It means instead that one lives fully and openly the complex process of being one of the most widely sensitive, responsive, and creative creatures on this planet. Fully to be one's own uniqueness as a human being, is not, in my experience, a process which would be labeled bad. More appropriate words might be that it is a positive, or a constructive, or a realistic, or a trustworthy process.

SOCIAL IMPLICATIONS

Let me turn for a moment to some of the social implications of the path of life I have attempted to describe. I have presented it as a direction which seems to have great meaning for individuals. Does it have, could it have, any meaning of significance for groups or organizations? Would it be a direction which might usefully be chosen by a labor union, a church group, an industrial corporation, a university, a nation? To me it seems that this might be possible. Let us take a look, for example, at the conduct of our own country in its foreign affairs. By and large we find, if we listen to the statements of our leaders during the past several years, and read their documents, that our diplomacy is always based upon high moral purposes; that it is always consistent with the policies we have followed previously; that it involves no selfish desires; and that it has never been mistaken in its judgments and choices. I think perhaps you will agree with me that if we heard an individual speaking in these terms we would recognize at once that this must be a façade, that such statements could not possibly represent the real process going on within himself.

Suppose we speculate for a moment as to how we, as a nation, might present ourselves in our foreign diplomacy if we were openly, knowingly, and acceptingly being what we truly are. I do not know precisely what we are, but I suspect that if we were trying to express ourselves as we are, then our communications with foreign countries would contain elements of this sort.

We as a nation are slowly realizing our enormous strength, and the power and responsibility which go with that strength.

We are moving, somewhat ignorantly and clumsily, toward accepting a position of responsible world leadership.

We make many mistakes. We are often inconsistent.

We are far from perfect.

We are deeply frightened by the strength of Communism, a view of life different from our own.

We feel extremely competitive toward Communism, and we are angry and humiliated when the Russians surpass us in any field.

We have some very selfish foreign interests, such as in the oil in the Middle East.

On the other hand, we have no desire to hold dominion over peoples.

We have complex and contradictory feelings toward the freedom and independence and self-determination of individuals and countries: we desire these and are proud of the past support we have given to such tendencies, and yet we are often frightened by what they may mean.

We tend to value and respect the dignity and worth of each individual, yet when we are frightened, we move away from this direction.

Suppose we presented ourselves in some such fashion, openly and transparently, in our foreign relations. We would be attempting to be the nation which we truly are, in all our complexity and even contradictoriness. What would be the results? To me the results would be similar to the experiences of a client when he is more truly that which he is. Let us look at some of the probable outcomes.

We would be much more comfortable, because we would have nothing to hide.

We could focus on the problem at hand, rather than spending our energies to prove that we are moral or consistent.

We could use all of our creative imagination in solving the problem, rather than in defending ourselves.

We could openly advance both our selfish interests, and our sympathetic concern for others, and let these conflicting desires find the balance which is acceptable to us as a people.

We could freely change and grow in our leadership position, because we would not be bound by rigid concepts of what we have been, must be, ought to be.

We would find that we were much less feared, because others would be less inclined to suspect what lies behind the façade.

We would, by our own openness, tend to bring forth openness and realism on the part of others.

We would tend to work out the solutions to world problems on the basis of the real issues involved, rather than in terms of the façades being worn by the negotiating parties.

In short what I am suggesting by this fantasied example is that nations and organizations might discover, as have individuals, that it is a richly rewarding experience to be what one deeply is. I am suggesting that this view contains the seeds of a philosophical approach to all of life, that it is more than a trend observed in the experience of clients.

SUMMARY

I began this talk with the question each individual asks of himself—what is the goal, the purpose, of my life? I have tried to tell you what I have learned from my clients, who in the therapeutic relationship, with its freedom from threat and freedom of choice, exemplify in their lives a commonality of direction and goal.

I have pointed out that they tend to move away from self-concealment, away from being the expectations of others. The characteristic movement, I have said, is for the client to permit himself freely to be the changing, fluid, process which he is. He moves also toward a friendly openness to what is going on within him—learning to listen sensitively to himself. This means that he is increasingly a harmony of complex sensings and reactions, rather than being the clarity and simplicity of rigidity. It means that as he moves toward acceptance of the "is-ness" of himself, he accepts others increasingly in the same listening, understanding way. He trusts and values the complex inner processes of himself, as they emerge toward expression. He is creatively realistic, and realistically creative. He finds that to be this process in himself is to maximize the rate of change and growth in himself. He is continually engaged in discovering that to be all of himself in this fluid sense is not synonymous with being evil or uncontrolled. It is instead to feel a growing pride in being a sensitive, open, realistic, inner-directed member of the human species, adapting with courage and imagination to the complexities of the changing situation. It means taking continual steps toward being, in awareness and in expression, that which is congruent with one's total organismic reactions. To use Kierkegaard's more aesthetically satisfying terms, it means "to be that self which one truly is." I trust I have made it evident that this is not an easy direction to move, nor one which is ever completed. It is a continuing way of life.

In trying to explore the limits of such a concept, I have suggested that this direction is not a way which is necessarily limited to clients in therapy, nor to individuals seeking to find a purpose in life. It would seem to make the same kind of sense for a group, an organization, or a nation, and would seem to have the same kind of rewarding concomitants.

I recognize quite clearly that this pathway of life which I have outlined is a value choice which is decidedly at variance with the goals usually chosen or behaviorally followed. Yet because it springs from individuals who have more than the usual freedom to choose, and because it seems to express a unified trend in these individuals, I offer it to you for your consideration.

REFERENCES

1. Jacob, P. E. *Changing Values in College* (New Haven: Hazen Foundation, 1956).

2. Kierkegaard, S. *Concluding Unscientific Postscript* (Princeton University Press, 1941).

3. Kierkegaard, S. *The Sickness Unto Death* (Princeton University Press, 1941).

4. Maslow, A. H. *Motivation and Personality* (Harper and Bros., 1954).

5. Morris, C. W. *Varieties of Human Value* (University of Chicago Press, 1956).

6. Seeman, Julius. *The Case of Jim* (Nashville: Educational Testing Bureau, 1957).

7. Whyte, W. H., Jr. *The Organization Man* (Simon and Schuster, 1956).

52

Three Factors Influencing How the Self Is Presented

Kenneth J. Gergen

EDITOR'S NOTE · Each of us has his or her own way for presenting the self. This is an important act because until we present ourselves in some identifiable way, others find it difficult to know how to behave toward us. How the self is presented is influenced by at least three factors, which Dr. Gergen identifies as the other, the interaction environment, and personal motivation. How does "the other" influence what and how the self is presented? In what ways do interaction environments determine how we behave and act? What motives influence how the self is presented? Why do you present your "self" the way you do under differing conditions? You may find some answers here.

We are indebted to Erving Goffman for directing attention to the following account of Preedy, an Englishman who is making his

From *The Concept of Self* by Kenneth J. Gergen. Copyright © 1971 by Holt, Rinehart and Winston, Inc. Reprinted by permission of Holt, Rinehart and Winston.

first appearance on the beach at a summer vacation spot:

> But in any case he took care to avoid catching anyone's eye. First of all, he had to make it clear to those potential companions of his holiday that they were of no concern to him whatsoever. He stared through them, round them, over them—eyes lost in space. The beach might have been empty. If by chance a ball was thrown his way, he looked surprised; then let a smile of amusement lighten his face (Kindly Preedy), looked around dazed to see that there *were* people on the beach, tossed it back with a smile to himself and not a smile at the people, and then resumed carelessly his nonchalant survey of space.
>
> But it was time to institute a little parade, the parade of the Ideal Preedy. By devious handlings he gave any who wanted a chance to see the title of his book—a Spanish translation of Homer, classic thus, but not daring, cosmopolitan too—and then gathered together his beach-wrap and bag into a neat sand-resistant pile (Methodical and Sensible Preedy), rose slowly to stretch his huge frame (Big-Cat Preedy), and tossed aside his sandals (Carefree Preedy, after all) [Sansom, 1956, pp. 230–231].

Undoubtedly, all of us can recognize a bit of Preedy in ourselves, as distasteful as the image may be. But we are all faced with the important task of providing others with an idea of who we are, for until others can identify us they cannot know how to behave toward us. To be a "foreigner" or "mentally ill," for instance, is of crucial significance for others in determining their actions. By the same token, the definition we present to others influences our level of reward or punishment in the relationship. To present oneself as "gruff" and "ill-tempered" is usually to reduce the pleasure we receive at the hands of others. Finally, by defining ourselves to others we can better predict their behavior. We know that to be perceived as "rich" yields certain responses; to be seen as "poor" yields different ones. Through self-presentation, the environment moves from a random state to one of order.

Self-conception has obvious implications for the way we publicly present ourselves to others. It would be very handy, of course, if there were a one-to-one relationship between people's private and public definitions of self. We could then be sure of the other's behavior and where we stood with respect to him. Indeed, Western culture generally condemns those whose public face differs from their private conception of self. We find this view reflected in Shakespeare's "To thine own self be true" as well as the contemporary country and western refrain:

> I'm just a country boy
> But there's one thing sure as shootin'
> I can't stand those folks who think
> They're so dad-burn high fallutin'
> I'd be the same in Hollywood
> As right in my own kitchen
> I believe in fussin' when you're mad
> And scratchin' when you're itchin'.

However, it is probable that this felicitous state does not commonly exist. A wide number of factors cause the person to shift his public identity as an actor in ancient times might have changed masks from one scene to the next.

What are the primary factors that produce such chameleon-like activity? Essentially, the major sources of influence fall into three main categories: the *other*, the *interaction environment*, and *motivation*. We shall briefly discuss each in turn.

THE OTHER

The identity of the other person and his behavior toward us can be central in determining the self-image that we present. If you have ever moved rapidly from one group to another or from one friend to another, you have undoubtedly noticed this fact in yourself. You may be energetic and happy-go-lucky with friends but appear serious and conscientious when conferring with a banker, and the "ideal" characteristics of self you present in a romantic relationship may jar with your identity as viewed by a brother or sister. As William James has said, a man has "as many different social selves as there are distinct groups of persons about whose opinion he cares" (1892).

Those around us may affect our "social selves" in three ways, two of which are familiar to us. First, others are continuously teaching us who we are. Others have varying images of us and depending on these images they treat us as a particular kind of person. Weinstein (1967) has called this process *altercasting*. We are cast into specific roles or identities by those around us. At the same time we are being cast into a particular identity, each of us harbors a multitude of self-concepts in various stages of development. Thus, the cues that others give to us about ourselves serve to reinforce certain of these concepts and reduce the salience of others. Continuous learning about self thus takes place.

A second reason that we shift public identities is related to the first. As pointed out earlier, we develop over time certain ways of viewing ourselves in the presence of particular people. With Fred we may have learned to see ourselves as "intense" and "philosophical," whereas Susan has always made us realize that we are "superficially frivolous." According to principles of association learning, the sheer presence of these persons should thereafter serve to elicit these differential views of self. We react with the "self" learned in the presence of the other. To spot Susan on the street may cause our face to blossom in smile, while our reaction to Fred's appearance may be an anguished grimace and eyes turned upwards toward the heavens.

Of course, both of these processes are "honest" ones; that is, the person may be fully convinced of the accuracy of his overt presentation at the moment. A third process, however, borders on a more selfish side of everyday relations. We are all interested in maximizing our benefits in social relations. We seek rewards and do our best to avoid punishment. The characteristics of others and their behavior toward us serve as cues for effective maximization. They aid us in performing optimally, often without regard to our sincerity.

While Goffman (1959, 1961) has discussed numerous ways in which this maximization takes place, an experiment by Gergen and Wishnov (1965) presents empirical evidence. The special interest of the study was in people's reactions to others who differ in self-esteem—from the flamboyant egotist to the diffident "poor mouth." It was reasoned that people who are extreme in their self-praise or their self-condemnation raise particular tactical problems for those who interact with them.

The egotist creates a power problem. By ac-

centuating his virtues he implies that others are not equal to him. His manner bespeaks his assumption that he deserves status, a greater share of whatever rewards are available, and the right to lead in decision making. Skillful self-presentation may be helpful in dealing with this kind of person; in particular, we might well react in kind, accentuating our assets and hiding our shortcomings. The self-derogator presents a far different type of problem. We may wish to nurture or aid him out of commiseration and at the same time wish to avoid further dealings with him because he seems so weak and dependent. Thus, we might be inclined to admit that we have shortcomings but not wish to identify ourselves as being on the same level as the other.

As a means of observing such strategies in action, undergraduate females were asked during a class period to rate themselves on a series of positive and negative characteristics (for example, "I am generally attractive to others," "I am often nervous and anxious"). Approximately one month later they participated in an experiment in which they were to exchange a set of written communications with another coed whose identity was unknown to them. These communications would "allow them to get acquainted" more rapidly. During this exchange, each subject received a set of self-ratings supposedly filled out by her partner. By design, one group received a set of ratings in which the partner described herself in most glowing terms. She enjoyed her work, her dating life, her home and saw herself as having no faults, but many virtues (egotism condition). A second experimental group received a self-description from the supposed partner that was quite opposite in character. She felt distinct lacks in all aspects of her life and saw numerous faults in herself with no redeeming virtues (humility condition). It was then the subject's turn to respond, and in part this response took the form of self-ratings of the same variety she had made a month earlier. The major interest of the study was to see the way she would change these ratings in reaction to the partner's rating.

Self-rating on both positive and negative characteristics is found in Figure 1. Both egotism and humility have strikingly different effects on the way subjects identify themselves. The egotist causes them to become much more positive about

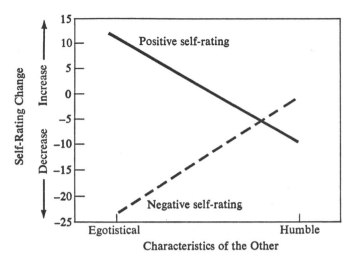

FIGURE 1. Self-Rating Change Produced by an Egotistical versus a Humble Other.

themselves—boosting their positive characteristics and de-emphasizing their negative ones—in an apparent attempt to offset the power balance. Humility, in contrast, causes subjects to portray themselves as being much more fault-ridden in terms of their characterization on negative traits. However, they are not willing to give up their claim to positive qualities. When faced with another's humiliation, the reaction seems to be one of commiserating by showing faults but retaining independence through the maintenance of positive characteristics.

THE INTERACTION ENVIRONMENT

In determining the self that we present, the environment in which the encounter takes place is as important as others' identities. We are not likely to identify ourselves in the same way at a formal dance as we do in a pool hall, regardless of who is present. Situations bring about shifts in identity primarily because they offer cues for maximization of reward. For example, we know from past experience what patterns of behavior are expected in varying circumstances. We know that we are expected to be polite and reserved in a religious setting, and, therefore, to avoid censure we may create the impression (however mistaken) of being

a "perfect gentleman." Likewise, immediate situations themselves have ways of creating exigent behaviors. In team sports, cooperation is the keynote, in debating, rationality and rhetoric are necessary to achieve success. As Goffman (1961) has shown, even patients entering a mental institution must learn how to behave as "proper" psychotics.

Environmental cues are demonstrated in a study by Gergen and Taylor (1969). Junior and senior ROTC students were to work together in pairs on one of two types of tasks. Half the subject pairs were to work on a task that demanded great productivity—maneuvering a mock submarine out of danger in a complex situation. The other half of the subjects were given a task for which social compatibility was most important—being understanding and tolerant in working out a set of ship maneuvers. Before work began each subject was to describe himself to his partner (who was either higher or lower than himself in ROTC rank) in order that they could be "better acquainted." The results showed that regardless of rank subjects in the productivity setting became more positive about themselves. They represented themselves as having many more positive qualities than they had professed a month earlier on a similar measure. Exactly the reverse took place when compatibility was at stake. In an apparent attempt to make themselves seem more "human" and less defensive, subjects de-emphasized their virtues and were more willing to admit shortcomings. On the job, people seem bent on displaying virtues; in social settings they are more likely to underestimate themselves.

PERSONAL MOTIVATION

The individual's presentation of self may be determined also by his motives in a relationship. If a person wishes to be treated with deference, his demeanor may be marked by superiority; if he wishes to be trusted, he may insure that his behavior is always consistent. Research on the effects of motivation on self-presentation has primarily concentrated on approval seeking. How do people manage their public identity in order to acquire the liking and acceptance of others? Unsurprisingly, the results of such studies (see Jones, Gergen, & Davis, 1962) show that in order to gain approval people typically emphasize their positive characteristics and withhold their personal failings from public view.

One exception to the general rule has been found (Jones, Gergen, & Jones, 1963). In this study it was discovered that in order to gain favor among their subordinates senior members of an organization presented themselves less positively on characteristics that were not relevant to their position of command. As Blau (1964) has reasoned, the senior person is seen by his juniors as remote, aloof, and threatening. By suggesting that he, too, has shortcomings, the senior member makes himself more accessible. Of course, he does it in such a way as not to undermine his position of seniority —the boss may admit he is a terrible golfer to facilitate interaction, but he is much less likely to admit that he sometimes makes poor professional decisions.

This discussion of self-presentation has emphasized the fact that people will often forego their true conceptions of self for purposes of social gain. However, before responding indignantly to the charade that surrounds us, we must take note of people's experience as they play the game. In a number of studies just discussed, subjects have been asked about their experiences—how honest did they feel they could be, how sincere did they feel, to what extent did the other person or situation make a difference to their behavior, and so

forth. Responses to such questions typically reveal that people do *not* generally feel insincere when they alter their social identity. They may describe themselves in one way at one moment and the reverse the next, and feel equally honest and sincere at both times. This finding is quite consistent with our earlier discussions of self-concept learning and role playing. As we pointed out, a person may harbor a variety of concepts of himself which differ in salience from moment to moment. When a particular role is used in a particular situation, the salience of certain concepts may increase and others may be lost from awareness. Thus, self-presentation may convince a person for the moment that he is indeed what he says he is. To be sure, not all presentation is accompanied by feelings of "true self." Highly learned concepts of self may be continuously salient and nag one when he violates them. However, there is a strong tendency in social relations for the person to become the mask.

REFERENCES

Blau, P. M. *Exchange and Power in Social Life.* New York: Wiley, 1964.

Gergen, K. J., & Taylor, M. G. Social expectancy and self-presentation in a status hierarchy. *Journal of Experimental Social Psychology,* 1969, 5, 79–92.

Gergen, K. J., & Wishnov, B. Others' self evaluations and interaction anticipation as determinants of self presentation. *Journal of Personality and Social Psychology,* 1965, 2, 348–358.

Goffman, E. *The Presentation of self in everyday life.* New York: Doubleday, 1959.

Goffman, E. *Asylums.* New York: Doubleday, 1961.

James, W. *Principles of psychology.* New York: Holt, 1892.

Jones, E. E., Gergen, K. J., & Davis, K. Some reactions to being approved or disapproved as a person. *Psychological Monographs,* 1962, 76, (whole No. 521)

Jones, E. E., Gergen, K. J., & Jones, R. G. Tactics

of ingratiation among leaders and subordinates in a status hierarchy. *Psychological Monographs*, 1963, 77 (Whole No. 566)

Sansom, E. *The Perfect Gentleman*. London: Heath, 1956.

Weinstein, A. *Altercasting and Interpersonal Relations*. In P. Secord & C. Backman (Eds.), *Readings in Social Psychology*. New York: Prentice-Hall, 1967.

53

The Rationalizing Animal

Elliot Aronson

EDITOR'S NOTE · One of the ways by which we can understand ourselves better is to try to understand the defenses we use, particularly the one discussed in this very interesting reading—rationalization. This is a defense we frequently use to explain away something that we said would happen, but did not or to do something we want to do, but need to justify. As Dr. Aronson points out, it is possible to rationalize behaviors that range from stupidity, to immorality, to cruelty. How does rationalization work? What steps are people willing to take to reduce what Dr. Leon Festinger has called "cognitive dissonance"? This article is a revealing look at what people are capable of doing when they must justify their actions.

Elliot Aronson, "The Rationalizing Animal," *Psychology Today* (May 1973): 46. Copyright © Ziff-Davis Publishing Company. Reprinted by permission of *Psychology Today Magazine*.

Man likes to think of himself as a rational animal. However, it is more true that man is a *rationalizing* animal, that he attempts to appear reasonable to himself and to others. Albert Camus even said that man is a creature who spends his entire life in an attempt to convince himself that he is not absurd.

Some years ago a woman reported that she was receiving messages from outer space. Word came to her from the planet Clarion that her city would be destroyed by a great flood on December 21. Soon a considerable number of believers shared her deep commitment to the prophecy. Some of them quit their jobs and spent their savings freely in anticipation of the end.

On the evening of December 20, the prophet and her followers met to prepare for the event. They believed that flying saucers would pick them up, thereby sparing them from disaster. Midnight arrived, but no flying saucers. December 21 dawned, but no flood.

What happens when prophecy fails? Social psychologists Leon Festinger, Henry Riecken, and Stanley Schachter infiltrated the little band of believers to see how they would react. They predicted that persons who had expected the disaster, but awaited it alone in their homes, would simply lose faith in the prophecy. But those who awaited the outcome in a group, who had thus admitted their belief publicly, would come to believe even more strongly in the prophecy and turn into active proselytizers.

This is exactly what happened. At first the faithful felt despair and shame because all their predictions had been for nought. Then, after waiting nearly five hours for the saucers, the prophet had a new vision. The city had been spared, she said, because of the trust and faith of her devoted group. This revelation was elegant in its simplicity, and the believers accepted it enthusiastically. They now sought the press that they had previously avoided. They turned from believers into zealots.

LIVING ON THE FAULT

In 1957 Leon Festinger proposed his theory of *cognitive dissonance*, which describes and predicts man's rationalizing behavior. Dissonance occurs whenever a person simultaneously holds two inconsistent cognitions (ideas, beliefs, opinions). For example, the belief that the world will end on a certain day is dissonant with the awareness, when the day breaks, that the world has not ended. Festinger maintained that this state of inconsistency is so uncomfortable that people strive to reduce the conflict in the easiest way possible. They will change one or both cognitions so that they will "fit together" better.

Consider what happens when a smoker is confronted with evidence that smoking causes cancer. He will become motivated to change either his attitudes about smoking or his behavior. And as anyone who has tried to quit knows, the former alternative is easier.

The smoker may decide that the studies are lousy. He may point to friends ("If Sam, Jack and Harry smoke, cigarettes can't be all that dangerous"). He may conclude that filters trap all the cancer-producing materials. Or he may argue that he would rather live a short and happy life with cigarettes than a long and miserable life without them.

The more a person is committed to a course of action, the more resistant he will be to information that threatens that course. Psychologists have reported that the people who are least likely to believe the dangers of smoking are those who tried to quit—and failed. They have become more committed to smoking. Similarly, a person who builds a $100,000 house astride the San Andreas Fault will be less receptive to arguments about imminent earthquakes than would a person who is renting the house for a few months. The new homeowner is committed; he doesn't want to believe that he did an absurd thing.

When a person reduces his dissonance, he defends his ego, and keeps a positive self-image. But self-justification can reach startling extremes; people will ignore danger in order to avoid dissonance, even when that ignorance can cause their deaths. I mean that literally.

Suppose you are Jewish in a country occupied by Hitler's forces. What should you do? You could try to leave the country; you could try to pass as "Aryan"; you could do nothing and hope for the best. The first two choices are dangerous; if you are caught you will be executed. If you decide to sit tight, you will try to convince yourself that you made the best decision. You may reason that while Jews are indeed being treated unfairly, they are not being killed unless they break the law.

Now suppose that a respected man from your town announces that he has seen Jews being butchered mercilessly, including everyone who had recently been deported from your village. If you believe him, you might have a chance to escape. If you don't believe him, you and your family will be slaughtered.

Dissonance theory would predict that you will not listen to the witness, because to do so would be to admit that your judgment and decisions were wrong. You will dismiss his information as untrue, and decide that he was lying or hallucinating. Indeed, Elie Wiesel reported that this happened to the Jews in Sighet, a small town in Hungary, in 1944. Thus people are not passive receptacles for the deposit of information. The manner in which they view and distort the objective world in order to avoid and reduce dissonance is entirely predictable. But one cannot divide the world into rational people on one side and dissonance reducers on the other. While people vary in their ability to tolerate dissonance, we are all capable of rational or irrational behavior, depending on the circumstances—some of which follow.

DISSONANCE BECAUSE OF EFFORT

Judson Mills and I found that if people go through a lot of trouble to gain admission to a group, and the group turns out to be dull and dreary, they will experience dissonance. It is a rare person who will accept this situation with an "Oh, pshaw. I worked hard for nothing. Too bad." One way to resolve the dissonance is to decide that the group is worth the effort it took to get admitted.

We told a number of college women that they would have to undergo an initiation to join a group that would discuss the psychology of sex. One third of them had severe initiation: they had to recite a list of obscene words and read some lurid sexual passages from novels in the presence of a male experimenter (in 1959, this really was a "severe" and embarrassing task). One third went through a mild initiation in which they read words that were sexual but not obscene (such as "virgin" and "petting"); and the last third had no initiation at all. Then all of the women listened to an extremely boring taped discussion of the group they had presumably joined. The women in the severe initiation group rated the discussion and its drab participants much more favorably than those in the other groups.

I am not asserting that people enjoy painful experiences, or that they enjoy things that are associated with painful experiences. If you got hit on the head by a brick on the way to a fraternity initiation, you would not like that group any better. But if you volunteered to get hit with a brick *in order to join* the fraternity, you definitely would like the group more than if you had been admitted without fuss.

After a decision—especially a difficult one that involves much time, money, or effort—people almost always experience dissonance. Awareness of defects in the preferred object is dissonant with having chosen it; awareness of positive aspects of the unchosen object is dissonant with having rejected it.

Accordingly, researchers have found that *before* making a decision, people seek as much information as possible about the alternatives. Afterwards, however, they seek reassurance that they did the right thing, and do so by seeking information in support of their choice or by simply changing the information that is already in their heads. In one of the earliest experiments on dissonance theory, Jack Brehm gave a group of women their choice between two appliances, such as a toaster or a blender, that they had previously rated for desirability. When the subjects reevaluated the appliances after choosing one of them, they increased their liking for the one they had chosen and downgraded their evaluation of the rejected appliance. Similarly, Danuta Ehrlich and her associates found that a person about to buy a new car does so carefully, reading all ads and accepting facts openly on various makes and models. But after he buys his Volvo, for instance, he will read advertisements more selectively, and he will tend to avoid ads for Volkswagens, Chevrolets, and so on.

THE DECISION TO BEHAVE IMMORALLY

Your conscience, let us suppose, tells you that it is wrong to cheat, lie, steal, seduce your neighbor's husband or wife, or whatever. Let us suppose further that you are in a situation in which you are sorely tempted to ignore your conscience. If you give in to temptation, the cognition "I am a decent, moral person" will be dissonant with the cognition "I have committed an immoral act." If you resist, the cognition "I want to get a good grade (have that money, seduce that person)" is dissonant with the cognition "I could have acted so as to get that grade, but I chose not to."

The easiest way to reduce dissonance in either case is to minimize the negative aspects of the action one has chosen, and to change one's attitude about its immorality. If Mr. C. decides to cheat, he will probably decide that cheating isn't really so bad. It hurts no one; everyone does it; it's part of human nature. If Mr. D. decides not to cheat, he will no doubt come to believe that cheating is a sin, and deserves severe punishment.

The point here is that the initial attitude of these men is virtually the same. Moreover, their decisions could be a hair's breadth apart. But once the action is taken, their attitudes diverge sharply.

Judson Mills confirmed these speculations in an experiment with sixth-grade children. First he measured their attitudes toward cheating, and then put them in a competitive situation. He arranged the test so that it was impossible to win without cheating, and so it was easy for the children to cheat, thinking they would be unwatched. The next day, he asked the children again how they felt about cheating. Those who had cheated on the test had become more lenient in their attitudes; those who had resisted the temptation adopted harsher attitudes.

These data are provocative. They suggest that the most zealous crusaders are not those who are removed from the problem they oppose. I would hazard to say that the people who are most angry about "the sexual promiscuity of the young" are *not* those who have never dreamed of being promiscuous. On the contrary, they would be persons who had been seriously tempted by illicit sex, who came very close to giving in to their desires, but who finally resisted. People who almost live in glass houses are the ones who are most likely to throw stones.

INSUFFICIENT JUSTIFICATION

If I offer George $20 to do a boring task, and offer Richard $1 to do the same thing, which one will decide that the assignment was mildly interesting?

If I threaten one child with harsh punishment if he does something forbidden, and threaten another child with mild punishment, which one will transgress?

Dissonance theory predicts that when people find themselves doing something and they have neither been rewarded adequately for doing it nor threatened with dire consequences for not doing it, they will find *internal* reasons for their behavior.

Suppose you dislike Woodrow Wilson and I want you to make a speech in his favor. The most efficient thing I can do is to pay you a lot of money for making the speech, or threaten to kill you if you don't. In either case, you will probably comply with my wish, but you won't change your attitude toward Wilson. If that were my goal, I would have to give you a *minimal* reward or threat. Then, in order not to appear absurd, you would have to seek additional reasons for your speech—this could lead you to find good things about Wilson and hence, to conclude that you really do like Wilson after all. Lying produces great attitude change only when the liar is undercompensated.

Festinger and J. Merrill Carlsmith asked college students to work on boring and repetitive tasks. Then the experimenters persuaded the students to lie about the work, to tell a fellow student that the task would be interesting and enjoyable. They offered half of their subjects $20 for telling the lie, and they offered the others only $1. Later they asked all subjects how much they had really liked the tasks.

The students who earned $20 for their lies rated the work as deadly dull, which it was. They experienced no dissonance: they lied, but they were well paid for that behavior. By contrast, students who got $1 decided that the tasks were rather enjoyable. The dollar was apparently enough to get them to tell the lie, but not enough to keep them from feeling that lying for so paltry a sum was foolish. To reduce dissonance, they decided that they hadn't lied after all; the task was fun.

Similarly, Carlsmith and I found that mild threats are more effective than harsh threats in changing a child's attitude about a forbidden object, in this case a delightful toy. In the severe-threat condition, children refrained from playing with the toys and had a good reason for refraining —the very severity of the threat provided ample justification for not playing with the toy. In the mild-threat condition, however, the children refrained from playing with the toy but when they asked themselves, "How come I'm not playing with the toy?" they did not have a superabundant justification (because the threat was not terribly severe). Accordingly, they provided additional justification in the form of convincing themselves that the attractive toy was really not very attractive and that they didn't really want to play with it very much in the first place. Jonathan Freedman extended our findings, and showed that severe threats do not have a lasting effect on a child's behavior. Mild threats, by contrast, can change behavior for many months.

Perhaps the most extraordinary example of insufficient justification occurred in India, where Jamuna Prasad analyzed the rumors that were circulated after a terrible earthquake in 1950. Prasad found that people in towns that were *not* in immediate danger were spreading rumors of impending doom from floods, cyclones, or unforeseeable calamities. Certainly the rumors could not help people feel more secure; why then perpetrate them? I believe that dissonance helps explain this phenomenon. The people were terribly frightened —after all, the neighboring villages had been destroyed—but they did not have ample excuse for their fear, since the earthquake had missed them. So they invented their own excuse; if a cyclone is on the way, it is reasonable to be afraid. Later, Durganand Sinha studied rumors in a town that had actually been destroyed. The people were scared, but they had good reason to be; they didn't need to seek additional justification for their terror. And their rumors showed no prediction of impending disaster and no serious exaggerations.

THE DECISION TO BE CRUEL

The need for people to believe that they are kind and decent can lead them to say and do unkind and indecent things. After the National Guard killed four students at Kent State, several rumors quickly spread: the slain girls were pregnant, so their deaths spared their families from shame; the students were filthy and had lice on them. These rumors were totally untrue, but the townspeople were eager to believe them. Why? The local people were conservative, and infuriated at the radical behavior of some of the students. Many had hoped that the students would get their comeuppance. But death is an awfully severe penalty. The severity of this penalty outweighs and is dissonant with the "crimes" of the students. In these circumstances, any information that put the victims in a bad light reduces dissonance by implying, in effect, that it was good that the young people died. One high-school teacher even avowed that anyone with "long hair, dirty clothes, or [who goes] barefooted deserves to be shot."

Keith Davis and Edward Jones demonstrated the need to justify cruelty. They persuaded students to help them with an experiment, in the course of which the volunteers had to tell another student that he was a shallow, untrustworthy, and dull person. Volunteers managed to convince themselves that they didn't like the victim of their cruel analysis. They found him less attractive than they did before they had to criticize him.

Similarly, David Glass persuaded a group of subjects to deliver electric shocks to others. The subjects, again, decided that the victim must deserve the cruelty; they rated him as stupid, mean, etc. Then Glass went a step further. He found that a subject with high self-esteem was most likely to derogate the victim. This led Glass to conclude, ironically, that it is precisely because a person thinks he is nice that he decides that the person he has hurt is a rat. "Since nice guys like me don't go around hurting innocent people," Glass's subjects seemed to say, "you must have deserved it." But individuals who have *low* self-esteem do not feel the need to justify their behavior and derogate their victims; it is *consonant* for such persons to believe they have behaved badly. "Worthless people like me do unkind things."

Ellen Berscheid and her colleagues found another factor that limits the need to derogate one's victim: the victim's capacity to retaliate. If the person doing harm feels that the situation is balanced, that his victim will pay him back in coin, he has no need to justify his behavior. In Berscheid's experiment, which involved electric shocks, college students did not derogate or dislike the persons they shocked if they believed the victims could retaliate. Students who were led to believe that the victims would not be able to retaliate *did* derogate them. Her work suggests that soldiers may have a greater need to disparage civilian victims (because they can't retaliate) than military victims. Lt. William L. Calley, who considered the "gooks" at My Lai to be something less than human, would be a case in point.

DISSONANCE AND THE SELF-CONCEPT

On the basis of recent experiments, I have reformulated Festinger's original theory in terms of the self-concept. That is, dissonance is most powerful when self-esteem is threatened. Thus the important aspect of dissonance is not "I said one thing and I believe another," but "I have misled people—and I am a truthful, nice person." Conversely, the cognitions, "I believe the task is dull," and "I told someone the task was interesting," are not dissonant for a psychopathic liar.

David Mettee and I predicted in a recent experiment that persons who had low opinions of themselves would be more likely to cheat than persons with high self-esteem. We assumed that if an average person gets a temporary blow to his self-esteem (by being jilted, say, or not getting a promotion), he will temporarily feel stupid and worthless, and hence do any number of stupid and worthless things—cheat at cards, bungle an assignment, break a valuable vase.

Mettee and I temporarily changed 45 female students' self-esteem. We gave one third of them positive feedback about a personality test they had taken (we said that they were interesting, mature, deep, etc.); we gave one third negative feedback (we said that they were relatively immature, shallow, etc.); and one third of the students got no information at all. Then all the students went on to participate in what they thought was an unrelated experiment, in which they gambled in a competitive game of cards. We arranged the situation so that the students could cheat and thereby win a considerable sum of money, or not cheat, in which case they were sure to lose.

The results showed that the students who had received blows to their self-esteem cheated far more than those who had gotten positive feedback about themselves. It may well be that low self-esteem is a critical antecedent of criminal or cruel behavior.

The theory of cognitive dissonance has proved

useful in generating research; it has uncovered a wide range of data. In formal terms, however, it is a very sloppy theory. Its very simplicity provides both its greatest strength and its most serious weakness. That is, while the theory has generated a great deal of data, it has not been easy to define the limits of the theoretical statement, to determine the specific predictions that can be made. All too often researchers have had to resort to the very unscientific rule of thumb, "If you want to be sure, ask Leon."

LOGIC AND PSYCHOLOGIC

Part of the problem is that the theory does not deal with *logical* inconsistency, but *psychological* inconsistency. Festinger maintains that two cognitions are inconsistent if the opposite of one follows from the other. Strictly speaking, the information that smoking causes cancer does not make it illogical to smoke. But these cognitions produce dissonance because they do not make sense psychologically, assuming that the smoker does not want cancer.

One cannot always predict dissonance with accuracy. A man may admire Franklin Roosevelt enormously and discover that throughout his marriage FDR carried out a clandestine affair. If he places a high value on fidelity and he believes that great men are not exempt from this value, then he will experience dissonance. Then I can predict that he will either change his attitudes about Roosevelt or soften his attitudes about fidelity. But, he may believe that marital infidelity and political greatness are totally unrelated; if this were the case, he might simply shrug off these data without modifying his opinions either about Roosevelt or about fidelity.

Because of the sloppiness in the theory, several commentators have criticized a great many of the findings first uncovered by dissonance theory. These criticisms have served a useful purpose. Often, they have goaded us to perform more precise research, which in turn has led to a clarification of some of the findings which, ironically enough, has eliminated the alternative explanations proposed by the critics themselves.

For example, Alphonse and Natalia Chapanis argued that the "severe initiation" experiment could have completely different causes. It might be that the young women were not embarrassed at having to read sexual words, but rather were aroused, and their arousal in turn led them to rate the dull discussion group as interesting. Or, to the contrary, the women in the severe-initiation condition could have felt much sexual anxiety, followed by relief that the discussion was so banal. They associated relief with the group, and so rated it favorably.

So Harold Gerard and Grover Mathewson replicated our experiment, using electric shocks in the initiation procedure. Our original findings were supported—subjects who underwent severe shocks in order to join a discussion group rated that group more favorably than subjects who had undergone mild shocks. Moreover, Gerard and Mathewson went on to show that merely linking an electric shock with the group discussion (as in a simple conditioning experiment) did not produce greater liking for the group. The increase in liking for the group occurred only when subjects volunteered for the shock *in order* to gain membership in the group —just as dissonance theory would predict.

ROUTES TO CONSONANCE

In the real world there is usually more than one way to squirm out of inconsistency. Laboratory experiments carefully control a person's alternatives, and the conclusions drawn may be misleading if applied to everyday situations. For example, suppose a prestigious university rejects a young Ph.D. for its one available teaching position. If she feels that she is a good scholar, she will experience dissonance. She can then decide that members of that department are narrow-minded and senile, sexist, and wouldn't recognize talent if it sat on their laps. Or she could decide that if they could reject someone as fine and intelligent as she, they must be extraordinarily brilliant. Both techniques will reduce dissonance, but note that they leave this woman with totally opposite opinions about professors at the university.

This is a serious conceptual problem. One solution is to specify the conditions under which a person will take one route to consonance over another. For example, if a person struggles to reach a goal and fails, he may decide that the goal wasn't worth it (as Aesop's fox did) or that the effort was justified anyway (the fox got a lot of exercise in jumping for the grapes). My own research suggests that a person will take the first means when he has expended relatively little effort. But when he has put in a great deal of effort, dissonance will take the form of justifying the energy.

This line of work is encouraging. I do not think that it is very fruitful to demand to know what *the* mode of dissonance reduction is; it is more instructive to isolate the various modes that occur, and determine the optimum conditions for each.

IGNORANCE OF ABSURDITY

No dissonance theorist takes issue with the fact that people frequently work to get rewards. In our experiments, however, small rewards tend to be associated with greater attraction and greater attitude change. Is the reverse ever true?

Jonathan Freedman told college students to work on a dull task after first telling them (a) their results would be of no use to him, since his experiment was basically over, or (b) their results would be of great value to him. Subjects in the first condition were in a state of dissonance, for they had unknowingly agreed to work on a boring chore that apparently had no purpose. They reduced their dissonance by deciding that the task was enjoyable.

Then Freedman ran the same experiment with one change. He waited until the subjects finished the task to tell them whether their work would be important. In this study he found incentive effects: students told that the task was valuable enjoyed it more than those who were told that their work was useless. In short, dissonance theory does not apply when an individual performs an action in good faith without having any way of knowing it was absurd. When we agree to participate in an experiment we naturally assume that it is for a purpose. If we are informed afterward that it *had* no purpose, how were we to have known? In this instance we like the task better if it had an important purpose. But if we agreed to perform it *knowing* that it had no purpose, we try to convince ourselves that it is an attractive task in order to avoid looking absurd.

MAN CANNOT LIVE BY CONSONANCE ALONE

Dissonance reduction is only one of several motives, and other powerful drives can counteract it. If human beings had a pervasive, all-encompassing need to reduce all forms of dissonance, we would not grow, mature, or admit to our mistakes. We would sweep mistakes under the rug or, worse, turn the mistakes into virtues; in neither case would we profit from error.

But obviously people do learn from experience. They often do tolerate dissonance because the dissonant information has great utility. A person cannot ignore forever a leaky roof, even if that flaw is inconsistent with having spent a fortune on the house. As utility increases, individuals will come to prefer dissonance-arousing but useful information. But as dissonance increases, or when commitment is high, future utility and information tend to be ignored.

It is clear that people will go to extraordinary lengths to justify their actions. They will lie, cheat, live on the San Andreas Fault, accuse innocent bystanders of being vicious provocateurs, ignore information that might save their lives, and generally engage in all manner of absurd postures. Before we write off such behavior as bizarre, crazy, or evil, we would be wise to examine the situations that set up the need to reduce dissonance. Perhaps our awareness of the mechanism that makes us so often irrational will help turn Camus' observation on absurdity into a philosophic curiosity.

54

Toward Developing a Healthy Self-Image

Don E. Hamachek

EDITOR'S NOTE · *A more complete, well-rounded, and healthy self-image can be developed by any person. It usually requires some investment in searching, wondering, and being open to change, but the interest earned in terms of feeling better about oneself is well worth the price. What are some ways to move toward a healthy self-image? A few ideas about what it means and how to go about achieving it, which I hope will be helpful to you, are presented in the following selection.*

The voluminous literature related to the idea of the self and self-concept leaves little doubt but that mental health and personal adjustment depend deeply on each individual's basic feelings of personal adequacy. Just as each of us must maintain a healthy orientation to objective reality, so, too, must we learn to think of ourselves in healthy ways. Feelings of personal inadequacy, helplessness, inferiority, insecurity, or worthlessness tend to erode and weaken, sometimes to the point of collapse, the main pillars of one's self-structure. The growth of an adequate self-concept, free of neurotic pride, unrealistic fears, and the

tyranny of irrational demands of conscience, is a critically important first step toward developing a healthy self-image. In the daily struggle to cope with the requirements of self and of reality and to deal firmly with threats, frustrations, and conflicts, we must have a firm grip on our own identity. Indeed, the admonition to "Know thyself" has been passed down through the ages as the criterion of wisdom and peace of mind until our present day where it has emerged from a religious-philosophical notion into a slogan for better mental health.

Attaining a healthy self-image with its concomitant feelings of adequacy, ableness, personal worth, and confidence is not some lofty goal beyond mortal reach, standing as a kind of poetic ideal. It is an attitude or cluster of attitudes which are learned and acquired, which means that sometimes "bad" (negative, destructive, self-defeating) attitudes must be replaced by healthier attitudes. Most people seem to want to move forward toward higher levels of physical and psychological health, although we would have to admit that there are those odd personalities who seem to get a perverse pleasure out of *un*health and suffering because it is the chief way of knowing they're alive. Sometimes a person says he would like to change his neurotic ways and have healthier attitudes about himself and others, but then says he can't change because, after all, his unfortunate childhood experiences made him the way he is. So busy is he contriving new defenses, inventing new excuses, and enjoying his own self-pity that he seldom has any energy left over for considering more constructive avenues for living. Along these lines, Maslow has suggested that:

> From Freud we learned that the past exists *now* in the person. Now we must learn, from growth theory and self-actualization theory, that the future also *now* exists in the person in the form of ideals, hopes, goals, unrealized potentials, mission, fate, destiny, etc. One for whom no future exists is reduced to the concrete, to helplessness, to emptiness. For him, time must be endlessly "filled." Striving, the usual organizer of most activity, when lost, leaves the person unorganized and unintegrated.[1]

There is little doubt but that past experiences can have a vast influence on current behavior.

However, even though we cannot change what happened yesterday, we can change how we feel about it today. We cannot change past experiences, but we can change our feelings *about* those experiences, which is one step in moving toward a healthy self-image.

SELF–OTHER UNDERSTANDING AS A GOAL

Sometimes it is assumed that one gets to know himself by learning about man in the abstract, i.e., man as a psychological, social, biological, economic, and religious being. Necessarily, then, the "knowledgeable person" winds up knowing about a fictional man fabricated from theories, research, and other people's experiences, not the man who lives and breathes, nor the one to whom the personal pronouns "I" and "me" apply. Indeed, it is possible to major in psychology and to end up knowing a very great deal about psychology, but very little about one's self. For instance, a man may have no idea whatsoever that his fear, let's say, of getting too "involved" with a woman is related to a basically bad relationship with his mother, even though he may be very well versed in the field of psychology and able to discuss at length other men's problems and hangups with women. Clearly, such information is not wisdom, nor does it bring peace of mind, nor does positive mental health commence and prevail because of it. Self–other understanding appears to be specific knowledge about how one's unique individuality grows in an interpersonal social context. How can one arrive at a deeper understanding of himself and others as unique individuals?

A maxim of Goethe may help here. "If you want to know yourself, observe what your neighbors are doing," he said. "If you want to understand others, probe within yourself." Most of us are inclined to do exactly the opposite. We observe the other person in order to understand him, and we probe within ourselves in order to understand ourselves better. Seems obvious enough, but it doesn't often work quite that simply. Why? Normally we look at the other person objectively, but look at ourselves subjectively. We see others with the 20–20 vision of sanity and realism—no myopia here—we behold their flaws, weaknesses, self-deceptions, and even recognize their prejudices masquerading as principles.

However, when we probe within ourselves, we are not inclined to see the same personal distortions. Indeed, most of us "see" only our good intentions, our fondest dreams and hopes, our secret fears and deepest needs, and our unremitting calls for love and recognition. If we persist in distorting our self-perceptions, then we can never change anything about us which may, in the interests of a healthier, more accurate self-image, need correcting. There are, however, ways to see ourselves more accurately and to know ourselves, as Goethe suggests, through "observing what our neighbors are doing."

SOCIAL FEELING AS AN AID

Adler's[2] concept of social feeling provides us with a useful conceptual tool for developing a healthy self-image. What does social feeling mean? Basically, it is a notion which refers to a person's ability to empathize with another; to see, hear, and feel with him. The usefulness of this concept lies in the fact that it combines the idea of social, which is an objective reference to common experiences, with the idea of feeling, which is a subjective reference to private experiences. The synthesis of the objective "social" with the subjective "feeling" is one way of bridging the gap between "you" and "me."

Self–other understanding involves, strangely enough, self-transcendence, which calls for one to go beyond his own private motives and thoughts in order to better understand and share another person's needs and goals. Social feeling is an attempt to understand one's self through the understanding of others. It is becoming less involved with one's own hopes, fears, shame, and doubt in order to become more in tune to how the other person thinks and feels. Erich Fromm,[3] for example, has observed: "I discover that I am everybody, and that I discover myself in discovering my fellow man, and vice versa." Self–other understanding through the process of social feeling means to see one's self (insight) by participating and sharing mutual concerns with another, or more succinctly, being an "I" for a "thou" as Buber[4] would say.

How can one practice social feeling and thereby understand himself and others better? Let's look at some ways.

HONESTY AS A WAY OF FACILITATING SELF–OTHER UNDERSTANDING

This does not mean being brutally and indiscriminately frank, but it does mean showing some of yourself to another person, exhibiting some of your own feelings and attitudes. This isn't particularly easy because from early childhood most people learn to play roles which mask their feelings, as if being honest about them would only hurt others and destroy relationships. Actually, the inevitable consequence of exposing and sharing feelings is usually greater interpersonal closeness. If I am honest with you, this encourages you to be more honest with me. If you are honest with me, I am freer to be more honest with you. And so the cycle goes. Consider an example.

Suppose a teacher has put in a relatively sleepless night and goes to class irritable, cranky, and short-tempered. He has two alternatives for handling his feelings. One, he can say nothing to the class and end up snapping at innocent students all day as if they were the cause of his sleepless night. Or, two, he could frankly admit to his irritable feelings, why they exist, and thereby give his students a chance to respond to his honesty. Once they know that his lack of patience and irritability are for a reason, then they will have less need to be defensive and irritable themselves. Furthermore, once the students learn that their teacher has *feelings*, not all of which are pleasant or good, then they are more apt to face up to and *admit feelings within themselves* which might otherwise have remained buried. If a teacher is honest with his students, shares with them some of his own personal self, he can be much more assured of his students giving him honest feedback about the conduct of the course, its content, and him as a teacher. Carl Rogers, discussing his way of facilitating or "teaching" a class, puts it this way:

> For me, trust is *the* important ingredient which the facilitator provides.... He will, I

hope, participate with his own feelings (owned as *his* feelings, not projected on another person). He may risk himself in expressing his problems and weaknesses.... The trust is something which cannot be faked. It is not a technique...if it is real and complete, even in a narrow area, it will have a facilitating effect upon the process of the group.[5]

In sum, honesty is one way of facilitating social feeling and healthy self–other understanding because it encourages greater freedom and openness of interpersonal exchange, the medium in which self-knowledge begins.

EMPATHIC LISTENING AS A WAY OF FACILITATING SELF–OTHER UNDERSTANDING

Another response which may be useful in developing a healthy self–other attitude is to listen. This doesn't merely mean to wait for a person to finish talking (and to spend our listening time preparing what we are going to say), but to try to see how the world is viewed by this person and to communicate this understanding to him. The sort of "total" listening we're talking about here is the kind that responds to the person's *feelings* as well as his *words*. It implies no evaluation, no judgment, no agreement (or disagreement). It simply conveys an effort to understand what the person is feeling and trying to communicate. It is an effort to communicate to the other person that we can accept the notion that his feelings and ideas are valid for *him*, if not for us.

One reason behind being a poor listener lies in the fact that it is difficult to do. We can test this out. For example, try establishing in any group discussion the ground rule that no person may present his own view until he has first satisfied the one who has just spoken that he fully comprehends what this person meant to communicate. That is, he must rephrase in his own words the total meaning of the other person's message and obtain this person's agreement that that was indeed what he said. In doing this we may find out that: (1) it is extremely difficult to get agreement between what was said and what was heard ("listened" to); (2) we frequently are remiss in our good intentions to listen; (3) when we do listen carefully, we have a hard time remembering what it was that we were going to say, and when we do remember, we find that it is a little off the subject; (4) much argument and irrational emotionality are absent from such a discussion because we spend less time responding to what we *thought* we heard or *wanted* to hear and more time responding to what was actually said, particularly when our misconceptions, if any, are cleared away.

Poor listeners are typically so preoccupied with their own sense of self-importance that they leave little room for expanding the range of their self–other knowledge. A person, whether a parent, a teacher, or a friend who talks a lot *could* have much that was meaningful to say, or he could be protecting himself from running the risk of having to change if he listened too carefully to another person's point of view.

Self-understanding is enhanced through understanding others. Understanding others is a function of one's capacity for social feeling. This capacity is both developed and encouraged by honest communication and good listening. Indeed, most of us know from personal experience that some of our most significant self–other discoveries have resulted from being in the company of persons characterized not only by their total honesty, but also by their lack of preconceptions about how they expect us to behave.

Self–other understanding, then, can be one step toward developing a healthy and accurate self-picture.

SELF-ACCEPTANCE: OUTCOMES AND CONSEQUENCES

While no single definition of self-acceptance is likely to be accepted by all who use the term, it generally has reference to the extent to which a person's self-concept is congruent with his description of his "ideal" self. Many self-concept studies, for example, in addition to asking subjects for *self-perceptions* also ask the subjects to go through the same set of items again and indicate how they would like to be *ideally*. Since most of us would like to be "better" than we are, the *ideal* self is usually judged to be at least as good as and almost

always better than the perceived or "actual" self. The differences between the scores for the perceived self and ideal self is the *discrepancy* score, which is obtained by subtracting the score of the perceived self from the score representing the ideal self. The larger this discrepancy score the more dissatisfied with himself and less accepting the person is presumed to be.

McCandless reviewed twelve studies designed to investigate the psychological consequences of discrepancies between the perceived self and the ideal self and concluded with the following:

> In summary, most research evidence indicates that people who are highly self-critical— that is, who show a large discrepancy between the way they actually see themselves and the way they would ideally like to be— are less well-adjusted than those who are at least moderately satisfied with themselves. Evidence indicates that highly self-critical children and adults are more anxious, more insecure, and possibly more cynical and depressed than self-accepting people. They *may* be more ambitious and driving, however. At least some evidence indicates that people experience conflict about the traits on which they have the greatest self-ideal discrepancy, and that this conflict is sharp enough to interfere with learning involving such areas.... There is some question whether the topic of self-ideal discrepancy is really different from the topic of positive and negative self-concepts.[6]

As you can see, research suggests that self-accepting persons are likely to have smaller self-ideal discrepancies than less self-accepting persons.

SELF-ACCEPTANCE AND ACCEPTANCE OF OTHERS

The notion that people who are self-accepting are accepting of others has considerable practical importance, particularly in light of the evidence suggesting that personal adjustment or maladjustment is socially learned. The self-rejecting person, if he also rejects others, is likely to be rejected by them in turn, with the inevitable consequence of reinforcing the original maladjustment. If, in counseling or psychotherapy, the self-concept can be improved and if this improvement results in increased acceptance of and by other people, then personal improvement is likely to occur. Raimy,[7] for example, has demonstrated that successful cases in psychotherapy enabled patients to acquire a more favorable view of themselves, whereas unsuccessful cases did not.

The overwhelming evidence from Wylie's[8] monumental review of the literature related to the self suggested that self-acceptance was related to adjustment. Generally, a high regard for one's self is reflected in a high level of personal adjustment. Moreover, there is evidence to show that people who are *self-accepting are more accepting of others.*[9, 10, 11] This means that if an individual thinks well of himself he is likely to think well of others, and that if he disapproves of himself he is likely to disapprove of others. Rogers[12] has noted that "when the individual perceives and accepts into one consistent and integrated system all his sensory and visceral experiences, then he is necessarily more understanding of others and is more accepting of others as separate individuals." A person who carries around a store of suppressed anger is more likely to feel hostile toward other people whose behavior, in his eyes, represents his own suppressed feelings than a person who is more open to his anger and willing to admit that his anger does exist. Or as another example, sometimes a person who feels threatened by his sexual impulses may be the first to criticize and moralize others whom he perceives as behaving in sexual ways. On the other hand, if he accepts his *own* sexual feelings he is usually more tolerant of sexual expressions by others. . . .

THE INFERIORITY COMPLEX: EXPRESSIONS AND OUTCOMES

Allport[13] has defined an inferiority complex as a "strong and persistent tension arising from a somewhat morbid emotional attitude toward one's felt deficiency in his personal equipment." What this refers to is an attitude which a person may have about feeling less able than others. Closely allied to, but not to be confused with, inferiority, is the feeling or conviction of inadequacy. However, where inferiority, whether conscious or unconscious, implies unfavorable comparison with others, inadequacy suggests personal inability to meet the demands of the situation.

The feeling of inferiority is no stranger to most people. For example, one study found that less than 12 percent of a group of college students report that they do *not* know what it is to suffer from gnawing feelings of inferiority.[14] Consider the data presented in Table One.

As you can see, there seem to be four main types. On the whole, women appear to be worse off than men. However, when we consider that women in our culture, from the time they are little girls, are taught to be more socially sensitive than men, this is not surprising. That is, the more sensitive one is about himself in relation to the world around him, the more likely he is to spot qualities in himself which are less well developed or executed than what he may see in other people.

TABLE 1. College Men and Women Reporting Inferiority Feelings

TYPE OF INFERIORITY FEELING	PERCENTAGE REPORTING PERSISTENT INFERIORITY FEELINGS	
	MEN	WOMEN
Physical	39	50
Social	52	57
Intellectual	29	61
Moral	16	15
None at all	12	10

Feelings of inferiority cannot be taken as an index of actual inferiority. A feeling of inferiority is a purely subjective affect related to the self, and is measured by the ratio between one's *success* and *aspirations* in a given direction. Objective facts seem to make little difference in determining whether a person feels inferior or not. The highest ranking student, or the funniest comedian, or the beauty contest winner may each suffer from a deep-seated sense of inferiority. On the other hand, the lowest student, the "unfunniest" man, or the plainest girl may not feel inferior at all. What one does or has or how one looks is far less important than how he feels about those things and what he aspires to be. For example, if a pretty girl aspires to be an excellent student, but falls short of that goal, being pretty is not likely to compensate for feeling academically inferior.

Important for us to understand is the fact that a sense of *inferiority is developmental or learned, rather than organic or innate.* This means that inferiority is in no sense necessary, and with insight into its causes and consequences, it can be handled, coped with, and in many instances, dispelled. Inferiority feelings are the result of too many failure experiences and frustrations; they are learned reactions that, if not corrected early, may eventually lead to the growth of deeply rooted attitudes of inferiority. Attitudes of this sort can dominate and condition a person to the point where he is left with a general feeling of not being able to do anything very well.

SYMPTOMS OF INFERIORITY

There are at least seven symptoms of inferiority feelings which we can be sensitive to in spotting its existence in others, or, for that matter in ourselves.

1. Sensitivity to Criticism. An inferiority-ridden person does not like his weaknesses pointed out to him. Criticism, as viewed by him, is further proof of his inferiority and serves only to accentuate the pain associated with it.

2. Overresponse to Flattery. The inferior-feeling person grabs at straws, particularly those constructed from praise and flattery because they help him stand more secure against his feelings of uncertainty and insecurity. The other response to flattery or praise, of course, is to stand in red-skinned embarrassment wondering, "How could anyone say anything good about me? Me, of all people!"

3. Hypercritical Attitude. This is a frequent defense and serves the purpose of re-directing attention away from one's own limitations. Whereas overresponse to flattery is defensive in character, hypercriticism takes the offensive and is used as a way of actively warding off the implications of inferiority. For example, if I feel inferior about the quality of something I've done in relation to yours and aggressively criticize your effort, you may become so busy defending what you've done that you won't notice the flaws in *my*

effort. In other words, hypercriticalness creates the illusion of superiority and relies on this illusion to belie inferiority.

4. Tendency toward Blaming. Whenever personal weaknesses and failures are projected onto others, it is relatively easy to find in them the cause of one's own failures, leading directly to the response of blaming. Indeed, some persons operate a kind of psychological "pulley system" in the sense of being able to feel normal or adequate only if they are pulling other people *down* and themselves *up* in the process. Unless others are made to appear inferior, some persons cannot feel even normal.

5. Feeling of Persecution. It is only a short step away from blaming others for one's personal misfortune to the position that they are actively seeking his downfall. For example, if you fail me in a course and I can believe that you failed me because you don't like me or are against me, then I am spared the pain of having to consider that I alone am responsible. In this way, not only do I blame you for my failure but I assign you a motive for doing it—you're out to get me.

6. Negative Feelings about Competition. An inferiority-ridden person is as anxious to win in competition as anyone else, but far less optimistic about winning. He is inclined to react to competition as would a person who knows that he lacks the skills or knowledge for successful competition. The psychologically inferior person is usually among the first to complain about the breaks, his opponents' good luck, or favoritism. In some instances, the attitude toward competition is so extreme that he refuses to participate in any competitive situation and tends to shy away in a fearful and hesitant manner.

7. Tendency toward Seclusiveness, Shyness and Timidity. Inferiority feelings are usually accompanied by a certain degree of fear, particularly in situations involving other people. Inferior-feeling persons prefer the cloak of anonymity, feeling that if they are neither seen nor heard their shortcomings (real or imagined) will less likely be seen. Not infrequently, students who feel less able than their peers sit near the back of the classroom because of the protection this offers. (If I'm not so easily seen, perhaps I will not so easily be called upon.)[15]

These are not mutually exclusive symptoms, but overlapping in expression and character. For example, timidity leads to avoidance of competition and also to greater sensitivity to criticism. At the same time, sensitivity to criticism can lead to blaming others or overresponding to flattery. All of these symptoms spring from a basic sense of inferiority and any one of them can serve as the catalytic agent, triggering a chain-reaction of defensive and generally self-destructive behavior.

There is still another, albeit distorted, expression of a sense of inferiority worth our consideration.

SELF-CONTEMPT AS A SUBSTITUTE FOR SELF-WORTH

A person who has almost, but not quite, lost his feeling of personal worth sometimes feels a strong need to condemn himself. ("I'm no good." "I can't do anything." "Others are better than me." "Look how stupid I am, etc.") Rollo May,[16] a practicing psychoanalyst, has noted that self-condemnation may not be so much an expression of self-punishment as it is a technique to get a quick substitute for a sense of worth. It is as though the person were saying to himself, "I must be important that I am so worth condemning," or "Look how good I am—I have such high ideals that I am ashamed of myself for falling so short of them." Allport has observed:

> The very nature of the neurotic disorder is tied to pride. If the sufferer is hypersensitive, resentful, captious, he may be indicating a fear that he will not appear to advantage in competitive situations where he wants to show his worth. . . . If he is over-scrupulous and self-critical, he may be endeavoring to show how praiseworthy he really is.[17]

Self-condemnation is not so much an honest statement of one's shortcomings as it is a cloak for arrogance. This mechanism of self-condemnation can be observed in various states of psychological depression. The student, for example, who does poorly on a test can always say, generally to himself, "If I had studied more, if I had really wanted

to do well on this test, I could have." Or the child who feels he is not loved by his parents can always say to himself something like, "If I were different, if I were not bad, they would love me." In the case of both the student and the child, self-condemnation is a means of avoiding a head-on confrontation with the possibility that he is not intellectually capable, in the first instance, and not loved in the other. The dynamics of self-condemnation works in such a way as to protect a person from the pain of feeling worthless. For he can always say, "If it were not for such and such a defeat, or bad habit, or lack of motivation, I would be as good as anyone else." The student who says, "I could've passed that test if I had studied harder," is really saying, "I'm really not that inadequate and furthermore it hurts to consider the possibility that I might be." An observation by Rollo May may help us understand better the hidden meaning behind self-condemnation:

> . . . the emphasis upon self-condemnation is like whipping a dead horse: it achieves a temporary life, but it hastens the eventual collapse of the dignity of a person. The self-condemning substitute for self-worth provides the individual with a method of avoiding an open and honest confronting of his problems of isolation and worthlessness, and makes for a pseudo-humility rather than the honest humility of one who seeks to face his situation realistically and do what he can constructively. Furthermore, the self-condemning substitute provides the individual with a rationalization for his self-hate, and thus reinforces the tendencies toward hating himself. And, inasmuch as one's attitude toward other selves generally parallels one's attitude toward one's self, one's covert tendency to hate others is also rationalized and reinforced. The steps are not big from the feeling of worthlessness of one's self to self-hatred to hatred for others.[18]

SIGNS OF A HEALTHY, POSITIVE SELF-IMAGE

Since this chapter is devoted to a discussion of ways and means for moving toward a healthy self-image, it seems altogether appropriate that we end it on a positive note.

Increasing literature and research devoted to the problem of self-concept leave little doubt but that mental health depends deeply on the quality of a person's feelings about himself. Just as an individual must maintain a healthy view of the world around him, so must he learn to perceive himself in positive ways. A person who has a strong, self-accepting attitude presents a behavioral picture very much the opposite of one who feels inadequate and inferior. Although there are certainly variations from one individual to another and for the same individual between situations, generally speaking, a person who has a healthy self-image can be characterized in the following ways:

1. He has certain values and principles he believes in strongly and is willing to defend them even in the face of strong group opinion; however, he feels personally secure enough to modify them if new experience and evidence suggest he is in error. (An insecure person finds it difficult to change his position for fear that it may be interpreted as weakness, or lack of ability, or competency. "You may be right, but I'm not wrong.")

2. He is capable of acting on his own best judgment without feeling excessively guilty or regretting his actions if others disapprove of what he's done. When he does feel guilty, he is not overwhelmed by the guilt. He can say, "I made a mistake—I'll have to improve," rather than "I made a mistake—how terrible I am."

3. He does not spend undue time worrying about what is coming tomorrow, or being upset by today's experience, or fussing over yesterday's mistakes. I remember a little poem which used to hang on the wall in my grandparents' living room. It goes like this:

It's easy enough to be pleasant
When Life flows along like a song,
But the man worth while
Is the man who can smile
When everything goes dead wrong.

4. He retains confidence in his ability to deal with problems, even in the face of failures and setbacks. He does not conclude, "Because I failed I am a failure," but is more likely to say, "I failed. I'll have to work harder."

5. He feels equal to others *as a person*—not superior or inferior—irrespective of the differences in specific abilities, family backgrounds, or attitudes of others toward him. He is able to say, "You are more skilled than I, but I am as much a person as you," which is different from thinking, "You are more skilled than I, therefore you are a better person." He is able to see that another individual's skills or abilities neither devalues nor elevates his own status as a person.

6. He is able to take it more or less for granted that he is a person of interest and value to others—at least to those with whom he chooses to associate. Another way of saying this is that he is not paralyzed by self-consciousness when in the company of other people.

7. He can accept praise without the pretense of false modesty ("Well, gosh, *anyone* could have done it."), and compliments without feeling guilty ("Thanks, but I *really* don't deserve it.").

8. He is inclined to resist the efforts of others to dominate him, especially those who are his peers. The resistance, in effect, is a way of saying, "I am as good as you—therefore there is no reason why I should be dominated by you."

9. He is able to accept the idea (and admit to others) that he is capable of feeling a wide range of impulses and desires, ranging all the way from being very angry to being very loving, from being very sad to being very happy, from feeling deep resentment to feeling great acceptance. It does not follow, however, that he *acts* on all his feelings and desires.

10. He is able to genuinely enjoy himself in a wide variety of activities involving work, play, creative self-expression, companionship, or, of all things, just plain loafing. An unknown author—a very wise person, no doubt—has expressed this idea in the following manner:

A master in the art of living draws no sharp distinction between his work and his play, his labor and his leisure, his mind and his body, his education and his recreation. He hardly knows which is which. He simply pursues his vision of excellence through whatever he is doing and leaves others to determine whether he is working or playing. To himself he always seems to be doing both.

11. He is sensitive to the needs of others, to accepted social customs and particularly to the idea that he cannot, willy-nilly, go about "self-actualizing" himself at the expense of everyone around him.

Perhaps we would do well to keep in mind that these are not destinations that only a fortunate few have passage to, or end states arrived at by a select number, but, rather, possibilities which any person desiring to better himself can hold as goals within his reach. Usually, motivation is more effective, and happiness more attainable, if a person concentrates on improvement rather than perfection.

IN PERSPECTIVE

Healthy people, research shows, see themselves as liked, wanted, acceptable, able, and worthy. Not only do they feel that they are people of dignity and worth, but they *behave* as though they were. Indeed, it is in this factor of how a person sees himself that we are likely to find the most outstanding differences between high and low self-image people. It is not the people who feel that they are liked and wanted and acceptable and able who fill our prisons and mental hospitals. Rather, it is those who feel deeply inadequate, unliked, unwanted, unacceptable, and unable.

Self and self-other understanding are not mystical ideals standing someplace "out there" as unreachable goals. Social feeling, empathic listening, honesty, and an understanding of how we use our defense mechanisms are all ways to assist in the development of greater self-awareness and self-understanding.

A person's feelings about himself are *learned* responses. Sometimes bad feelings have to be unlearned and new feelings acquired. This is not always easy, but it is possible. Sometimes this means "taking stock" of oneself—a kind of personal inventory. Or it may mean baring one's self to another person—a friend or therapist—so that the possibility for honest evaluation and feedback is more probable. And for certain, it means changing those things which one can and accepting those which one cannot.

For most persons, a positive, healthy self-image is quite within reach if they are willing to accept the risks and responsibilities for mature living.

If, as parents or as professional persons, we have a basic understanding of how a healthy self is developed and the conditions and interpersonal relations which nurture it, then we are in a position to move actively in the direction of *creating* those conditions and interpersonal relationships most conducive to positive mental health.

Perhaps the best place to begin is with ourselves.

REFERENCES

1. A. H. Maslow, "Some Basic Propositions of a Growth and Self-Actualization Psychology," in A. W. Combs (Ed.), *Perceiving, Behaving, Becoming.* Association for Supervision and Curriculum Development Year Book. Washington, D.C.: National Education Association, 1962, p. 48.

2. A. Adler, *The Individual Psychology of Alfred Adler.* New York: Basic Books, Inc., 1956, pp. 135–136.

3. E. Fromm, *Beyond the Chains of Illusion.* New York: Pocket Books, 1962, p. 186.

4. M. Buber, *I and Thou,* New York: Charles Scribner's Sons, 1958.

5. Carl R. Rogers, *Freedom To Learn.* Columbus, Ohio: Charles E. Merrill Books, Inc., 1969, p. 75.

6. B. R. McCandless, *Children: Behavior and Development* (2nd ed.), New York: Holt, Rinehart and Winston, Inc., 1967, p. 280.

7. V. C. Raimy, "Self-Reference in Counseling Interviews," *Journal of Consulting Psychology,* 1948, 12: 153–163.

8. Ruth C. Wylie, *The Self Concept.* Lincoln, Neb.: University of Nebraska Press, 1961.

9. Ruth C. Wylie, "Some Relationships between Defensiveness and Self-Concept Discrepancies," *Journal of Personality.* 1957, 25: 600–616.

10. R. W. Levanway, "The Effect of Stress on Expressed Attitudes toward Self and Others,"

Journal of Abnormal and Social Psychology, 1955, 50: 225–226.

11. E. L. Phillips, "Attitudes toward Self and Others: A Brief Questionnaire Report," *Journal of Consulting Psychology.* 1951, 15: 79–81.

12. Carl R. Rogers, *Client-Centered Therapy: Its Current Practice, Implications, and Theory.* Boston: Houghton Mifflin Company, 1951, p. 520.

13. G. W. Allport, *Patterns and Growth in Personality.* New York: Holt, Rinehart and Winston, Inc., 1961, p. 130.

14. Allport, pp. 130–131.

15. A. A. Schneiders, *Personality Dynamics and Mental Health.* New York: Holt, Rinehart and Winston, Inc., 1965, pp. 227–228.

16. Rollo May, *Man's Search for Himself.* New York: W. W. Norton and Company, 1953, pp. 98–101.

17. G. W. Allport, *The Individual and His Religion.* New York: Crowell-Collier and Macmillan, Inc., 1950, p. 95.

18. May, p. 100.

Index

529

DATE DUE	
FEB 12 1995	
FEB 13 1995	

GAYLORD   PRINTED IN U.S.A.